Financial Accounting Information

An Introduction to Its Preparation and Use

Third Edition

A. Thompson Montgomery
Linda K. Whitten
Thomas C. White III

K|H

Kendall/Hunt
Publishing Company
Dubuque, Iowa

3 2280 00574 9452

*To **A. Thompson Montgomery** whose memory lives on in his family, his friends, and the users of this book.*

Contents

Financial accounting and financial statements; Financial accounting vs. bookkeeping; Accounting as a language; Common difficulties in learning accounting; Organization of this text; Footnotes; Preview and overview of financial accounting; Your suggestions.

Chapter preview; Society's needs; Financial accounting and financial statements; Various users of financial statements: owners and potential owners, existing and potential creditors, current and potential suppliers, employees and unions, current and potential customers, managers; Other accounting systems; The financial statements: the balance sheet, the income statement, the statement of cash flows, the statement of retained earnings; Framework for financial reporting; Generally accepted accounting principles; Audited statements and the CPA: the annual report; Authoritative bodies; Accounting Associations; Chapter overview.

New vocabulary and concepts; Review questions; Mini-cases and questions for discussion.

Chapter preview; The concept of new worth; Various ways to measure the value of items owned: unadjusted original cost, liquidation value, adjusted original cost, current costs, constant purchasing power dollars; Entity convention; The balance sheet; The balance sheet equality: Liabilities and owner's equity; Balance sheet items and terminology: statement heading, assets, liabilities and owner's equity; Review of balance sheet classifications and format: current vs. noncurrent, monetary vs. nonmonetary; Relating to your special company; Information content of a balance sheet: balance sheet limitations, executory items; Chapter overview.

New vocabulary and concepts; Review questions, Mini-cases and questions for discussion; Essential problems; Supplementary problems.

3 - Analyzing a Balance Sheet   62

Chapter preview; Extending credit to customers; Importance of solvency and liquidity: overlapping terminology; Measures of liquidity and solvency: net working capital, current ratio, quick ratio; Equities as sources of assets; Net working capital and capital structure: different meanings of the terms "capital" and "investment;" Measures of capital structure and financial flexibility: long-term debt ratio, asset composition ratio; Other balance sheet-related ratios; Lack of consensus; Standards for comparison; Consistency; Materiality; Affirmatively misleading detail; Chapter overview.

New vocabulary and concepts; Review questions; Mini-cases and questions for discussion; Essential problems; Supplementary problems.

4 - Balance Sheet Changes and Income   92

Chapter preview; Events which change a balance sheet: first week, second week, third week, fourth week, total month, month-end adjustments; Transactions; Adjustments; Reversing Entries; The bookkeeping system: income, revenue and gains, expenses and losses; The statement of owner's capital; Income measurement: The accrual basis, Cash basis; Chapter overview.

New vocabulary and concepts; Review questions; Mini-cases and questions for discussion; Essential problems; Supplementary problems.

5 - Bookkeeping, the Accounting Cycle, and Internal Control   134

Chapter preview; Need for standardization of procedures; The debit/credit coding system: the T-account, the journal entry; The debit/credit code: assets, contra-assets, equities— liabilities and owner's equity, contra-equities, income statement accounts—revenues and gains, income statement accounts—expenses and losses; The chart of accounts; The journal(s) and the audit trail; The ledger(s) and posting; Interim trial balances; The worksheet and the pre-adjusting trial balance; Adjustments and the adjusted trial balance on the worksheet; Preparing the financial statements; Adjusting and closing the books; the Accounting Cycle: error corrections, opening reversals; Special journals—subsidiary ledgers—and closing: cash receipts journal, sales journal, cash disbursements journal, purchases journal; Subsidiary ledgers; Accounting systems and internal control: devices and documents used, important policies and procedures, independent review; Using computers and other automated equipment; Relative emphasis on bookkeeping procedures; Chapter overview.

New vocabulary and concepts; Review questions; Preparer problems.

ized; Issued, and outstanding; Retained earnings; Changes in stockholders' equity accounts: cash dividends, liquidity dividends, stock dividends, deficits, stock splits; Treasury stock retire stock; Stock subscriptions; Stock options—rights and warrants; The statement of retained earnings; What is stock worth? book value per share, market value; Summary of changes in stockholders' equity accounts; Preparer procedures; Chapter overview.

New vocabulary and concepts; Review questions; Mini-cases and questions for discussion; Essential problems; Supplementary problems; Preparer problems.

Chapter preview; Asset valuation under GAAP: what are these items? Consolidated financial statements; Current marketable securites; Allowance for bad debt: aging accounts receivable method, percentage ending accounts receivable method; Investments in stock: lower of cost or market, equity method, consolidated method, effects on cash from operating activities; Present value; Notes receivable: amortization of discounts, notes receivable discounted; Bond investments: bond acquisition, bond amortizaiton, straight-line method, effective yield method; Bond sinking fund; Property held under capital lease; Intangibles and other: goodwill, deferred charges, organizational costs; Financial instrument disclosure; Review of asset changes; Preparer procedures; Chapter overview.

New vocabulary and concepts; Review questions; Mini-cases and questions for discussion; Essential problems; Supplementary problems; Preparer problems; Appendix Problems.

Chapter preview; Objectives of Liability Measurement and Reporting: how much does this firm really owe to others; Estimated and contingent liabilities: estimated liabilities, contingent liabilities; Purchase commitments; Warranty costs; Minority interest; Obligations under pension plans; Deferred tax liabilities; Bonds payable: initial bond valuation, bonds issued at a discount bonds issued at a premium; Amortization of bond discount and premium: straight-line method, effective yield method, cash from operating activities; Other contra-liability accounts; Fully amortized loans; Capital lease obligations; Maturing long-term debt; Early debt extinguishment: early debt retirement, refunding, debt conversion; Review of liability changes; preparer procedures; Chapter Overview.

New vocabulary and concepts; Review questions; Mini-cases and questions for discussion; Essential problems; Supplementary problems; Preparer problems.

13 - Analyzing Financial Statements   534

Chapter preview; What can financial statements tell me: three components of overall management, four differing analysts' viewpoints; Investment safety; Operating effectiveness and efficiency; Efficient use of resources: aset turnovers, return on investment (ROI); Efficient financial management; Measures of owner return; Should they buy Columbia's stock? Is my manager doing a good job: analyzing operating performance, possiblly interrelating factors; Income statement ratios (vertical analysis); Items bypassing the income statement; How good is this supplier's financial management: solvency, debt capacity, profitability, dividend policy, asset replacement/expansion, manintence of optimal capital structure, owners' commitment, potential for raising additional capital; Limitations of financial statement analysis; Chapter overview.

New vocabulary and concepts; Review questions; Mini-cases and questions for discussion; Essential problems; Supplementary problems.

14 - Business Combinations   580

Chapter preview; All in the family; Business combinations; Consolidated Statements for poolings: elimination of intercompany ownership in a pooling, elimination of intercompany debt, elimination of intercompany nonownership investment, elimination of intercompany profit in inventory, elimination of intercompany transactions and accruals; Consolidated statements for purchases: elimination of intercompany ownership in a purchase, other eliminations in a purchase; Essential differences between pooling and purchases: differences in reported income, differences in asset valuations, implications of purchase vs. pooling treatments, unresolved issues; Minority interest; Interpreting consolidated financial statements; Statutory mergers; Segment reporting: identifying segments, segment information reported, analysis of segment information; Footnote disclosure: auditor's report, choice of accounting methods, accounting changes, supplementary information; Contingencies and commitments; Interim reports: interpreting interim reports; Chapter overview.

New vocabulary and concepts; Review questions; Mini-cases and questions for discussion; Essential problems.

PREFACE

The text is designed for use in a single course or a two-course sequence devoted to financial accounting at the undergraduate or graduate foundation level.

This book's approach differs significantly from that found in other elementary financial accounting texts. Through more than six years of classroom testing prior to publication of the first edition, it proved more effective than traditional approaches. Ten years of enthusiastic response by users of the book provide further validation. The approach is distinctive in three major ways:

1. **Most basic accounting topics are introduced in the context of solving a simple practical business problem to which the student can first readily relate.** The "why" thus is precedes the "what" as a motivation for learning; and the student can perceive from the outset accounting information in its critically essential service role rather than as an end in itself.

   In contrast to many other basic texts, this book does not assume that the student is sufficiently interested in accounting to identify solely with the accountant's objectives. Such an assumption is valid at the intermediate level where a tentative career commitment has been made. Since most elementary students are still involved in the career-decision process, the reader in this text is only asked to assume a businessperson's viewpoint and thus to appreciate the accountant's contribution.

2. **The student is continually asked to focus upon the financial statement effect of each transaction and adjustment rather than just its effect on particular accounts.** This subtle but important difference provides a progressively integrated perspective on the importance and usefulness of the accounting system as a whole. The accountant's standards and objectives are set forth and emphasized as pragmatic, feasible, proven solutions to difficult measurement choices, while bookkeeping procedures *per se* are deemphasized as simply traditional means for achieving such ends. This perspective is reinforced by the segregation of bookkeeping practices and procedures in the chapters.

3. **Subjects are sequenced and introduced only as needed to:**

- Develop an overall understanding of the operation of the basic accounting system as rapidly as possible, and

- Thereafter develop a series of progressively more sophisticated layers of understanding.

Our own testing of alternative approaches to basic accounting instruction, and numerous studies covering other disciplines, has shown that subject matter grouping logical to the individual once all material has been mastered does **not** necessarily provide the most effective or efficient sequence for the first introduction of such material. For example, whereas receivables, collections, discounts, and bad debt allowances form a logical grouping to treat exhaustively at the intermediate level, the elementary student can experience confusion and overload unless these topics are picked up in several consecutive passes, separated by sufficient time to allow complete "digestion" of the previous exposure. Also, although exhaustive treatment of logically-related topic groups works well at the intermediate level, after an integrated overview has been established, it is **not** and efficient approach to creating and reinforcing such a perspective.

The advantage of this text's orientation has been obvious for graduate MBA students and for those undergraduates not intending to become accounting majors. Not so obvious is its **even greater** benefit for the future accountant. Tradition and past practice have readily led to the inference that the future accounting major should start with intensive training, as distinct from education, in bookkeeping procedures. Six years of controlled experimentation prior to initial publication and ten years of experience with the first and second editions indicate the opposite conclusion. Accounting majors having the integrated overview and perspective obtainable from this book's approach find that they have a framework into which they can fit intermediate and advanced detail. At the intermediate and advanced levels, they consistently outperform others without such an overall perspective. This fact has been acknowledged in the AICPA's recommendations for a minimum of procedure in the elementary course. With accounting now a dynamic, constantly changing system, perhaps the simple answer is that initial emphasis on the "why" and the "what" rather than the "how" provides a better framework for ready integration of change.

Topic Sequence

Consistent with the approach of developing progressively more sophisticated layers of overall understanding, the first seven chapters cover the entire operation of the accounting system for a proprietorship without the complications of bad debts, discounts and premiums, price changes, and accelerated methods of depreciation and amortization. The balance sheet is first introduced as the core of the system, even though not necessarily the most important statement. Returning to the classical balance sheet approach, as opposed to the income statement approach, has proved the key to subsequent ease of understanding cash flow and constant dollar/current cost adjustment.

Immediately following a description of the environment of accounting (Chapter 1) and the balance sheet (Chapter 2), elementary balance sheet analysis is presented in Chapter 3 to reinforce the interrelationships of the various parts of this statement. Chapter 3 also serves to lay the foundation for cash flow understanding sufficiently early so that there is adequate time for the underlying concepts to be thoroughly assimilated before the statement of cash flows is introduced in Chapter 7. Simple transactions and adjustments first appear in Chapter 4 to integrate balance sheet changes with income measurement. The income statement and income measurement are discussed in Chapter 6. More specialized aspects of alternative timing of revenue recognition are presented in an Appendix to Chapter 6.

After the essential aspects of all financial statements and the basic accounting system have been introduced, a second layer of sophistication is provided by Chapter 8 and 9. These chapters focus on those GAAP alternative methods having the greatest impact on income—inventory flow and assumptions and depreciation electives. Two topics often ignored in elementary texts are briefly and simply introduced in these chapters: dollar-value LIFO and capital leases. To leave the elementary student with the impression that all or even most firms electing LIFO maintain layered records for every product or part, or that all long-lived assets in use are owned by the firm, is simply false. In Chapters 8 and 9 reference to constant dollar and current cost reporting for inventories and plant assets is included the details of the computation of such data are deferred to Chapter 15.

Chapter 10 introduces accounting for partnerships and corporations. At this stage, such otherwise complex materials can be readily understood as minor variations having no effect on the basic accounting system previously introduced and understood. A beginning student, even at the graduate level, can more readily identify with a small proprietorship than with an abstract corporation. Delaying corporate accounting complexities until Chapter 10 facilitates their assimilation.

The collection of topics in Chapters 11 and 12 is a continuation of the progressive layering approach. Chapter 11 covers the remaining asset-related topics for a single firm, none of which are essential to the earlier development of a basic understanding of the accounting system's operation and usefulness. Chapter 12 serves the same function for liabilities. Students without preconceptions that certain topics logically belong together have no difficulty accepting each topic in these two chapters independently as simply a more sophisticated measuring and recording problem related to a unique situation. Each topic can be viewed as an accessory compatible with, but not essential to, the basic system.

Since present value can no longer be ignored in the valuation of assets and liabilities, it is introduced conceptually in Chapter 11 with the techniques of computation segregated in Appendix B. Several topics not covered in many other elementary texts are briefly introduced in Chapters 11 and 12. The include capital lease accounting, accounting for fully amortized loans, debt refunding and conversion, tax allocation, and pension accounting. The treatment of these topics is highly simplified and not included with any intention of preempting traditionally intermediate territory. In recent years these items have become so significant for many firms that to completely ignore their presence in a basic text would be tantamount to pretending that computers did not exist.

In Chapter 13, statement analysis is used to reinforce the statement content and usefulness introduced in the preceding 12 chapters.

Chapters 14 and 15 may be considered as providing optional coverage. Even if only as outside reading, you are urged to provide your students with some exposure to the subjects of consolidation and accounting for the effects of inflation, covered in the last two chapters. For future accounting majors it will complete their overview of the road ahead. For the majority of your students who will have no exposure to accounting beyond managerial, this will be their last and only opportunity to become familiar with these vitally important areas.

Special Features

This book has many special features in addition to those enumerated above:

- Students focus upon objectives throughout the text. They start with learning objectives (introduction); move to the social-economic objectives of financial accounting (Chapter 1); then to the objectives and usefulness of each financial statement; and finally to the accountant's objective in measuring and reporting economic events— how the statements should reflect the effect of each transaction.

- The book is written in an informal and conversational tone that is less severe and less intimidating than other texts. This informality also encourages student involvement.

- Two sets of complete financial statements are included in Appendix A to provide familiarity with the total financial statement package.

- Each chapter starts with a preview of the material to be covered and its relevance, and each concludes with a summary of behavioral skills that the student should have developed from the chapter.

- Important common business and financial accounting terms are bolded when first introduced and then listed for review at the end of each chapter. An extensive glossary of more than 600 terms is included in Appendix C for easy student reference and review. Since a significant portion of elementary accounting involves language learning, students find a combined glossary, in lieu of individual chapter glossaries, a distinct advantage.

- Chapter review questions cover all important concepts introduced in the chapter.

- Chapter problems are designated as essential and supplementary, the latter group having particular relevance to graduate MBA foundation and more rigorous undergraduate courses.

- Complete solutions to all odd-numbered chapter-end problems are included in Appendix D. The student therefore has available additional examples of applications in each topic area beyond the illustrations included in the text material. The student also has the opportunity to solve the odd-numbered problems and have immediate reinforcement in a manner similar to that in a programmed text.

- Chapters contain mini-cases and questions for class discussion. These materials are designed to highlight many unresolved accounting issues and to stimulate interest beyond material covered in the text.

- The core accounting chapters contain pairs of integrative problems (one with solutions as a model) for the same two firms covering 18 periods of operation. The problems successively incorporate new materials as introduced and may be used independently or in conjunction with available practice sets (see below). Although integrative in intent, each integrative problem is written so that it may be assigned sequentially or independently as you desire.

The final, and perhaps the most welcomed, feature is that of **flexibility**. This text is larger than most because it incorporates optional materials enabling you to tailor your course to your personal course objectives.

For courses with a bookkeeping emphasis, Chapter 5 should be assigned in sequence. Thereafter the Preparer Procedures and Preparer Problems in subsequent chapters should also be assigned in turn. You may also wish to use the available practice sets with such a course. Even without the use of the practice sets, you should find that Chapter 5 and subsequent chapter preparer procedures provide students with a firm and adequate grounding of bookkeeping essentials.

For different elementary courses with less emphasis on procedures, the preparer procedures in subsequent chapters may be omitted. Chapter 5 is written so that it may be assigned in sequence, at any subsequent point, or as collateral reading.

Supporting Materials

A complete set of supporting materials is available to adopters of this text including:

- **Instructors Manual:** In addition to solutions for review questions, problems, and cases, the instructor's manual contains:

  - Alternative recommended assignments for courses of different duration, level, and objective.

  - Masters (for local reproduction) of a brief 25-minute diagnostic test covering essential arithmetic skills. Weaknesses in such skills can prove an insurmountable barrier to the learning of accounting. You may wish to use the test in counseling or screening prospective course registrants.

  - Synopses for each chapter together with suggestions as to points requiring emphasis.

  - Separate listings of assignment problems and cases giving coverage, completion times, and level of difficulty.

  - Transparency masters of major text exhibits and illustrations for use with an overhead projector.

  - Masters (for local reproduction) of blank balance sheet diagrams and working papers.

  - Masters (for local reproduction) of key data sheets for even-numbered essential and supplementary material.

- **Test Bank:** Included in the computerized test bank are multiple choice questions, problems, and essay questions. The computerized program allows for creation of four test versions.

- **Case Book**: Cases for both financial and managerial accounting (also to be used with the accompanying managerial text). Cases are both structured and unstructured. Computerized solution approaches are encouraged. Cases are designed for M.B.A. foundation courses and more rigorous undergraduate curriculum.

- **CAAT**: A Computer assisted accounting tutorial (MS-DOS format) includes transactions and adjusting entries using both journal entries and the balance sheet diagram approach. Students may either used self-generated or default data. An integrative practice set (Auto Parts Store) is included for additional practice. A section on ratio analysis is also included.

- **Integrative Practice Sets:** A unique book of practice sets is available for use in conjunction with the text. Ten independently assignable practice sets may be used either with the second integrative problem series (see special features above) or with a third parallel problem series included with the sets. The first integrative problem series from the text is also included along with completed journals, ledgers, and worksheets to serve as a model. The practice sets are designed to require either full or partial completion. Masters (for local reproduction) of partial solutions, together with complete solutions for both problem series, are available in the accompanying Instructor's Manual.

Changes from the Second Edition

For instructors who wish to emphasize procedure, this edition includes more optional bookkeeping procedures and problems. We encourage use of the ten aforementioned sequential pairs of integrative problems for the same two firms in conjunction with the practice sets. The transactions and adjustments for these firms become increasingly more sophisticated over successive periods paralleling topics as they are introduced in the text. The additional preparer materials, problems, and practice sets should create exposure equivalent to the traditional "principles" texts.

The unique Balance Sheet Diagram has been extended to illustrate the income statement effect of new transactions and adjustments throughout most chapters. The resulting statement-effect focus facilitates student understanding of cash flow and inflation adjustment that can otherwise prove troublesome within the confines of the debit/credit model. Throughout all chapters, problems have been revised.

Most chapters have been substantially or completely rewritten to incorporate more illustrations, additional coverage, and the numerous suggestions received from users of the second edition. The concept of cash flow has been updated reflecting FASB Statement No. 95.

Present value coverage has been moved to Appendix B. Chapter 15 has been rewritten to incorporate the provisions of FASB Statement No. 89. The areas of coverage are listed in the detailed Table of Contents.

Finally, the flexibility of the book for adaptation to different course emphasis has been further enhanced.

Acknowledgments

Education is exciting because we are continually challenged to review and modify concepts and teaching techniques. Over 15,000 students at San Francisco State University alone have acted as catalysts for the changes in this edition. We are grateful for this interaction and special thanks must be made to Richard Dizon, Barbara Graves, John Pluth, and Judy Yamamoto.

We are grateful to Professors Steven Mintz (SFSU), Ross Arrington (SFSU), and Ricky Ambrose (College of San Mateo) for their helpful comments. We are especially endebted to B. Mack Tennyson (College of Charleston) for his extensive help in the revision of Chapters 1 through 4.

Special thanks are extended to Natalie Montgomery for her contribution in editing the first draft, Rod Whitten for manuscript preparation, and to Dean Arthur Cunningham for his unfailing support throughout the project.

Also we appreciate the support of our editor, Charles Borgquist, and Ruth Burlage, Director of Production Editorial at Kendall/Hunt.

Obviously none of the foregoing individuals is responsible for any errors that may be contained herein.

ATM Foundation
San Francisco, CA
May, 1988

Student
Introduction

Financial Accounting and Financial Statements

This text is designed for your use in an elementary financial accounting course. Financial accounting covers those activities related to the preparation of certain reports that are known as financial statements. These statements report the financial status of a firm at a particular time, the firm's activities and resulting profits or losses during the same period.

The primary objective of this text is to help you learn how to read and understand financial statements. You cannot become an expert financial statement analyst in one course, but you can develop a working understanding of the statements themselves, what information they contain, and what they do not contain.

Business people in any position of significant responsibility need to read and understand financial statements. They need to be able to interpret financial statement information as a basis for their business decisions. They also should know how their personal decisions and actions may affect their own firm and be reflected on its future financial statements.

To be able to understand financial statements, you will need to learn both the language of accounting and the basic elements of the system followed by accountants. Understanding the accounting system will enable you to know what information the accountants include and do not include in their reports, when and where the information is included, and how it is measured and reported. You will then be in a position to appreciate the vital role accountants serve within the firm and in society.

Financial Accounting vs. Bookkeeping

One way to view financial statements is as if they were reports, like newspaper reports, on the condition and performance of business. The statements are the final reports and the accountants are the reporters. A newsreporter's activities, in turn, can be divided into two categories. First, the newsperson decides what events are worth reporting, when they should be reported, and how they should be described or evaluated. Once these decisions have been reached, the new data can be recorded and the news report written.

In accounting, the reporting function can be similarly divided between accounting and bookkeeping. The accountant, following accounting standards, decides which business events should be reported in the financial statements, when they should be recognized, and how they should be measured or valued. Once these decisions are made, the bookkeeper does the accrual recordkeeping following the practices and procedures set forth by the accountant. These practices and procedures are often called the bookkeeping system, and are introduced in Chapter 5 and in subsequent chapters.

This book is written so that:

• Chapter 5 and the subsequent chapters covering preparer procedures may be covered in sequence for those courses in which the instructor wishes to emphasize bookkeeping, or

- Chapter 5 may be assigned at some later point with preparer procedures in other chapters omitted for those courses in which the instructor wishes to de-emphasize bookkeeping, or

- Chapter 5 and chapter preparer procedures may be assigned as collateral reading by instructors who wish to focus exclusively in accounting.

You should make sure that you clearly understand your instructor's plans for your particular course. Whether or not you become involved with bookkeeping or preparer procedures, it is important that you maintain in your mind the distinction between user ideas and preparer procedures. Too often, elementary accounting students let themselves focus almost entirely on bookkeeping details and thus fail to gain an overall understanding of accounting.

Accounting as a Language

The financial statements contain summary information covering all of the economic events affecting a business during a particular time period, usually a year. If accounting reports were prepared in narrative English (like a newspaper article), they would probably run for thousands of pages and be too long to read. Accountants have, therefore, developed a highly condensed and coded way to report, in a few pages, thousands of events and their effects.

Appendix A contains the actual financial statements for the Xerox Corporation and for the AT & T Company for the year 1987. When you first look at these statements, they may seem confusing. After you have successfully completed this course, you should be able to read them with confidence in your ability to understand these and similar statements.

Turn now to Appendix A and carefully look over the two companies' financial statements.

At first glance you can see that the statements contain many different items with dollar values. To intelligently read and interpret the information in these statements, you must first learn the accountant's language.

As is true with other languages, the language of accounting involves both vocabulary and grammar. Learning the vocabulary involves becoming familiar with both the exact definition of accounting words and how they are used. Both parts are essential. For example, imagine you were thinking of buying a friend's business, a record store. One of the major items you would be purchasing would be your friend's inventory on hand of records, disks, and tapes. Suppose you had before you an accountant's report showing that your friend had the following items in his business:

Cash	$ 500
Merchandise inventory	8,000
Supplies	300
Total Current Assets	$8,800

What would you be buying? The accountant's definition of "merchandise inventory" is merchandise on hand for sale to customers. The definition of "supplies" is materials for use in the business and not for sale. With these definitions you would be close to knowing what you would be buying. But does the $8,000 represent the retail selling price or does it represent the wholesale cost paid by your friend? Remember that accounting vocabulary involves knowing both the definition and how the term is used. In this case you would also need to know that accountants generally value inventory at the business firm's cost rather that at the intended selling price. With a complete understanding of the accounting term "merchandise inventory," you would know that you would be buying records, disks, and tapes which had a total cost to your friend's firm of $8,000 and, hopefully, could be sold for much more.

The grammar part of the accounting language is much simpler than other languages. Accounting "grammar" involves merely an agreed ordering of information. A telephone book also has an agreed ordering of information; subscribers are listed in alphabetic order. Suppose you were looking up the telephone number of someone named Hunter. Would you have to check every name in the phone book? Because of the known ordering, you could go right to the H's, and if you found Humble, Hunt, and Huntington you would know that Hunter was not listed. Similarly, the financial statements have a conventional ordering. If you are looking for a specific item, you can go directly to a particular report and find the portion of that report where the item should appear. You will either find the item, or else its absence will indicate either that the firm doesn't have it or that the amount is too insignificant to report separately.

To assist you in identifying the vocabulary with which you must become familiar, when a new accounting or business term is first introduced in this text it will be bolded. At the end of each chapter, you will find a list of the more important terms introduced in that chapter. Also included at the back of the book is a glossary of common business and accounting vocabulary. If a word or phrase is new to you and its exact meaning is not clear in the context of the chapter, be sure to use the glossary. Otherwise you could be unnecessarily confused or even worse, might misunderstand subsequent material or problems using the term.

Common Difficulties in Learning Accounting

Unfortunately, quite a number of students find elementary accounting a difficult course. You may avoid most difficulties if you are aware of the causes, properly diagnose the problem, and take corrective action. Experience has shown that the following items may be sources of difficulty in many courses and especially in elementary accounting:

1. You may not accept personal responsibility for learning. A text or an instructor cannot teach you accounting. They can help you learn accounting once you choose both to take responsibility to learn and also to put forth whatever effort is necessary for you.

2. You may not have adequate prerequisite knowledge and skills. To learn accounting effectively and efficiently, you need three skills. You should have the ability to read the English language carefully and precisely. You should have a general understanding of and ability to conceptualize common business language and problems. Finally, and most importantly, you must have the ability to deal with simple arithmetic and simple algebraic concepts. Deficiency in any of these areas, and especially with algebra, can make the learning of accounting unnecessarily difficult if not effectively impossible.

Financial accounting is not as mathematically oriented as, say, an elementary statistics course. Nevertheless it requires competence and speed with respect to computation of ratios and percentages, calculation of simple and compound interest, and solution of simple algebraic equations in the form of:

$$A + B - C = D$$

where you must find the value of any one item given the other three. Difficulty with prerequisite knowledge is probably the primary reason that, in many colleges, as many as 40 percent of those students enrolling in elementary accounting fail the course.

If you know you are deficient in any of the three skills mentioned, you should seriously consider delaying your attempt to master basic accounting until you have completed necessary remedial courses. There is no time available while you are studying accounting to also learn how to read carefully, to develop an understanding of common business practices and terminology, or to become proficient with ratios, percentages, and simple algebra.

If you are uncertain about the adequacy of your prerequisite skills, you should immediately seek the counsel of your instructor. He or she has available a brief diagnostic test covering essential arithmetic and algebraic skills that you may wish to use to help you make your decision.

3. You may not devote sufficient time and effort to learning. Most students find that successful learning of accounting requires an investment of at least six to eight hours of intensive outside preparation per week in the typical course. Some students find that they can read or skim over material and do minimum assigned problems in much less time. They fail to use the extra time for mastering vocabulary and concepts and for reinforcement (see items 4 and 5 below). Eventually, they discover, the hard way, that many more hours than those previously "saved" are required to catch up. A few find it impossible to catch up.

4. You may not thoroughly master new vocabulary and concepts with each chapter before proceeding to the next. Each chapter builds upon vocabulary and concepts introduced in previous chapters. To avoid great and unnecessary confusion and extra effort, you must master the material in each chapter as assigned and not let yourself fall behind. Chapters in this text contain checklists to test yourself before proceeding. These checklists will be described later in this introduction.

5. You may not adequately reinforce your new knowledge. Effective learning of new knowledge and skills requires reinforcement involving both repetition and application. This text contains numerous detailed examples illustrating the application of the ideas presented. If you fail to make the effort to understand the source and the meaning of each number in each illustration or exhibit before proceeding with the reading materials, you may miss the chance to pinpoint misunderstanding or lack of knowledge at a time when it could be immediately reviewed and clarified before it becomes a source of major confusion.

Also, as will be further explained below, each chapter contains numerous review questions and problems, with all odd-numbered problems having solutions in the back of the book. These provide you with additional opportunity to verify and to apply your new knowledge in those subject areas that you personally perceive to require additional reinforcement for you.

6. You may fail to seek assistance from others when required. Students may avoid asking questions of their fellow students or their instructor because they think they will appear stupid. Unless one is truly exceptional, it is very difficult to learn all introductory accounting without some assistance. If you share your confusion with your classmates and your instructor, they may help you.

7. You may not prepare properly for accounting examinations. Most elementary accounting examination questions require precise answers. Correct answers require knowledge of all the vocabulary and concepts related to the item being examined. A general, as distinct from a specific, understanding often will not suffice. Knowing almost all of the necessary parts is usually not enough. The missing or unclear part can be vital. Continual review and self-testing as you proceed through the course will pinpoint problem areas in sufficient time for corrective action before examinations.

8. You may merely memorize vocabulary, concepts, and example problem solutions. Some rote memorization of accounting vocabulary and concepts is necessary, but it is not sufficient to learn elementary accounting. To be of value, accounting knowledge must also be generalized so as to be readily applicable to new problem situations.

9. You may fail to identify the real source of your difficulty. It is important that you properly identify the source of a difficulty. Many students' problems in elementary accounting courses are caused by one or more of these nine items. If you are having trouble and the real source is one or more of these nine items, to decide merely that the problem is accounting will be counterproductive. Only when the real cause is identified can your difficulty be readily resolved. You should seek assistance from your instructor if you experience difficulty and cannot pinpoint the cause.

Organization of this Text

The presentation order of new material in this text differs from that in many other elementary accounting books. If you should have a friend in another class using a different text, do not fear that you are missing something. You will have covered all of the same important material by the end of the course. You will probably find the sequence in this book easier to grasp.

Research and probably your own past experience have shown that one learns most easily and rapidly when in a problem-solving situation. Learning is more efficient when one experiences a need to learn and an immediate benefit—when one sees the road ahead and is actively involved in the learning process. Each chapter will start with a preview of its coverage—what you can learn. Where practicable, you will then be presented with a user problem situation. The new material that will follow will relate to your understanding and solving of the problem. It will also provide additional tools for solving similar problems. The introductory user problem is designed to give you an objective or reason for learning all of the new material presented.

You can choose to be actively involved in the learning process as you proceed through this book. This choice will allow you to learn accounting most rapidly and efficiently. Alternatively, you can choose to rely on your instructor to induce your involvement. The latter choice will always prove less efficient, and often does not work. If you do not become actively involved, you will fail to learn accounting. If you do choose involvement, you will have a successful learning experience.

If you do assume responsibility for your learning and make a commitment to active involvement you will find special opportunities in many chapters. At points where your existing intuitive knowledge can be related to accounting, you will be asked a question before being provided with an explanation. At places where it is important for you to verify the adequacy of your understanding before proceeding, the text will give you a problem and suggest you pause and work out your own solutions before reading further. Appendix D at the back of the book contains solutions to all odd-numbered Essential and Supplementary Problems in each chapter. Appendix E contains illustrative solutions to the odd-numbered preparer (bookkeeping) problems. Chapters themselves contain exhibits and illustrations and should you require further examples of a particular application for better understanding, you can use the odd-numbered problems and solutions as additional clarifying exhibits.

Also, as you know, new knowledge must be further reinforced and tested before you can be certain that it is mastered. At the end of the chapters, you will find materials intended to provide opportunity for self-checking and reinforcement:

1. **Chapter Overview**. Section reviewing the major new materials in the chapter with which you should be familiar.

2. **New Vocabulary and Concepts**. List of the important new accounting terms and concepts introduced. Definitions of terms may be found in the glossary (Appendix C) at the back of the book. New concepts may be reviewed in the chapter itself.

3. **Review Questions.** Questions designed for you to test your understanding of new major ideas.

4. **Mini-cases and Questions for Discussion.** Brief cases and questions designed to clarify issues and to introduce others for consideration.

5. **Essential Problems.** Problems designed to provide opportunity for you to demonstrate proper application of the essential ideas already introduced in the text. Solutions to odd-numbered problems are provided in Appendix D at the back of the book.

6. **Supplementary Problems.** Additional problems provided for further reinforcement and for extension of concepts to new or ambiguous situations not specifically covered in the text. Solutions to odd-numbered problems are provided in Appendix D. Note that starting in Chapter 4, two integrative problems (one with solutions and the other without) are provided for two firms. These problems continue in most succeeding chapters, enabling you to integrate progressively your newly acquired knowledge with that previously learned.

7. **Preparer Problems.** Problems designed to provide students with an opportunity to reinforce preparer procedures by using problems and illustrations previously introduced in the chapter.

You can only be sure that you have mastered the essential material in each chapter when you are confident that you could, if asked:

- Accurately define new vocabulary listed.
- Accurately explain new concepts listed.
- Answer all review questions.
- Intelligently discuss issues raised in the mini-cases and questions and,
- Solve all essential problems.

Footnotes

You will probably notice more footnotes in this book than in other elementary texts with which you might compare it. Don't let yourself be intimidated by footnotes! You will find that, in certain topic areas, you are sufficiently interested to want more precise information. In this book many footnotes are used to provide such additional precision. This approach is used to separate the less important material from the main ideas.

Preview and Overview of Financial Accounting

Understanding financial accounting essentially involves your being able to read and understand the four financial statements and to know how they are prepared by accountants. Business activities and the reports about them are complex. This text will provide you with a means to understanding. Consider the following simplified example a preview of the road ahead.

Assume the following facts:

1. On January 1, 19X0, you started your own trucking business by investing $20,000 cash.

2. On January 2 you purchased a used truck costing $12,000. You are paying for the truck in three payments — $4,000 down, $4,000 plus 10 percent interest on the $8,000 balance on next January 1, and $4,000 plus 10 percent interest on January 1, 19X2.

3. During 19X0 you collected $24,000 cash from customers for trucking services you supplied.

4. During 19X0 you paid out $6,000 for fuel, oil, maintenance, license fees, and insurance.

At the end of the year, an accountant could prepare a report for your firm which would give you the following information.

STATEMENT OF YOUR FIRM'S POSITION AS OF 12/31/X0

Your firm's possessions:

Cash remaining	$ 34,000
Truck's cost	12,000
Less adjustment for truck wearing out (depreciation)	(2,000)
Total possessions	$ 44,000

Your firm owes others within a year:

Second truck payment due	$ 4,000
One year's interest owed on $8,000 outstanding truck loan	800
Total	$ 4,800

Your firm owes others more than a year from now:

Third truck payment	4,000
Total owed others	$ 8,800

Your share of the firm's possessions:

Your capital in the business	35,200
Total owed others plus your share	$ 44,000

STATEMENT OF YOUR FIRM'S PROFIT FOR THE YEAR 19X0

Earned from customers	$ 24,000
Less: Operating costs paid	6,000
Now owed as interest on outstanding truck loan	800
Current resources from business operations	$ 17,200
Less adjustment for truck wearing out (depreciation)	(2,000)
Profit for year	$ 15,200

Note in this example the increase in the cash is the same as "cash remaining" on the statement of your firm's financial position, because there were no beginning cash. this is a new firm.

Cash Remaining – Beginning Cash = Increase in Cash

STATEMENT OF CASH FLOWS FOR THE YEAR 19X0

Your firm's operations	
Operating profit for the year	$ 15,200
Add operating costs, which did not decrease cash:	
Depreciation — never involves cash	2,000
Interest on truck — not yet paid	800
Net cash generated through operations	$ 18,000
Your firm's investments	
less truck purchase	(12,000)
Your firm's financing	
Owner investment during 19X0	20,000
Loan on truck	8,000
Increase in cash for year	$ 34,000

Accountants have a special vocabulary to condense these descriptions. For example, accountants would call these reports the Balance Sheet, the Income Statement, and The Cash-Flow Statement. They also have abbreviated titles for each item appearing in the report. Nevertheless, these same types of reports are prepared for all businesses. Even the reports for a firm as large as General Motors will follow the same ideas demonstrated in the simplified example above.

As you proceed through this text, think back to this example. If you cannot see how new information is an expansion of the ideas incorporated in this example, then either:

1. You misunderstand the new idea and should obtain clarification, or
2. You are making an essentially simple system unnecessarily complicated—you are looking for complexity that just isn't there.

Your Suggestions

Obviously the effectiveness of this book for you will depend on factors such as your interest and effort and your classroom experience. It also will depend on how well this book is organized and written for you personally. If you like this text, be sure to tell your instructor. Also, as authors, we are very interested in obtaining your specific comments and suggestions to incorporate in future revised editions. You may send your ideas to the A. Thompson Montgomery Foundation, School of Business, San Francisco State University, 1600 Holloway Ave., San Francisco, CA 94132, or give them to your instructor for forwarding. Your ideas will be appreciated and considered.

1

Financial Accounting Information and Its Environment

Chapter Preview

The purpose of this chapter is to present a perspective of (1) the financial accounting system, (2) the individuals and groups involved, and (3) the role of accounting and accountants in society. In this chapter, you should be able to determine:

1. The importance of accounting information to its users and to society;

2. The identity of various types of users and their information needs;

3. The general information contained in the four major financial statements that will be the central focus of this book;

4. The system of reporting standards currently applied to financial statements in the United States;

5. The role of the independent CPA in verifying that generally accepted accounting standards have been followed;

6. The role of the various authoritative bodies involved in setting and changing such standards;

7. The modification proposed to make a firm's financial statements better reflect evolving business practices and changing economic conditions.

With an overview of the function of accounting and its environment, you will be in a better position to learn about the financial accounting system and the financial statements themselves. You will have the initial perspective which is essential to your understanding of the material in subsequent chapters and its rationale.

(If you have not already read the Introduction for Students, you should do so before proceeding with this chapter.)

Society's Needs

All societies must deal with the problem of rationing scarce resources. In particular, each society's economic system must direct new capital—additional wealth—to the most efficient producers who produce the goods and services society wants.

Whatever the economic system for achieving the allocation of resources—free markets, partially controlled markets, or government controlled directives—society and its managers need information on which to base the resource-allocation decisions. This includes information about (1) the amount of resources a particular producer or firm currently controls, (2) how efficiently the firm uses its resources, and (3) the way in which additional resources are allocated in the firm. In all societies the system for gathering and reporting this necessary information is known as the accounting system.

Consider an example of accounting information used as the basis for resource allocation. Imagine you are the benevolent dictator of a tiny island. Your local subjects' survival and prosperity depend on catching fish and selling them to nearby islands. All fishing is controlled by two families—Family A and Family B. In one sense you are the owner of two firms, each managed for you by one of the families.

Every year each family receives the cash proceeds from the fish it catches and sells. Sale proceeds are used to cover fishing costs—maintenance and replacement of fishing boats and fishing gear, supplies, and living expenses. At year end, any excess sales receipts over monies spent for fishing costs is considered cash profit. This cash is then turned over to you to use or distribute as you think best.

A year has just ended and you receive a total of $25,000 from the two families. You decide that you will need $14,000 to maintain the living style appropriate to your position. The rest you wish to apportion to the families for use in expanding fishing capacity—for additional boats and gear. So long as fish are available, it is assumed additional capacity means greater prosperity for everyone.

To produce the greatest benefit to the island as a whole, you wish to allocate the $11,000 ($25,000-$14,000) where it will be used most efficiently. You may define efficiency as the most profit earned per fishing boat. You may also assume that equipment costs will adequately maintain the fleet. Other factors you consider relate to the recent history of each family. Have they been expanding their capacity (investment in boats and gear) while still maintaining profitability? Have they been distributing all of their cash profits to you? Exhibit 1.1 summarizes the information available to you for your decision. How would you allocate the $11,000 and what is your reasoning?

Exhibit 1.1

DATA COVERING FAMILY A AND B FOR PREVIOUS YEAR

	Family A	Family B
Boats with gear currently controlled	8	4[*]
Efficiency of recent resource usage:		
Fish sale proceeds	$100,000	$35,000
Fishing costs (maintenance, supplies)	74,000	18,000
Equipment costs (replacement boats)	10,000	7,000
Cash Profit	$ 16,000	$10,000
Profit per boat	$ 2,000	$ 2,500
Recent resource changes:		
Sources of new resources:		
Cash from fishing activities	$ 26,000	$15,000
Cash from last dictator allocation	0	5,000
Total	$ 26,000	$20,000
How the new resources were used:		
Used for new boats and gear	$ 10,000	$10,000
Distributed to dictator	15,000	10,000
Retained in family	1,000	0
Total	$ 26,000	$20,000

* Family B began the year with 3 boats

As explained in the introduction for students, you are now at one of those points where you would benefit greatly if you would pause and attempt to answer the allocation question raised before proceeding to the next paragraph. Regardless of whether you arrive at the "answer" given, your effort to reach a reasonable decision will direct your attention to the issues involved and will make the following solution and explanation easier for you to understand.

Given your objective to maximize efficiency, you should allocate all $11,000 to Family B. Family B is earning $2,500 cash profit per boat, as compared to $2,000 per boat for A. Also note that, with twice as many boats, A is catching and selling more than three times as many fish as B but not earning even twice as much cash profit! Family B should also be favored because last year it expanded its fleet by one boat with gear and still maintained profitability. Also, Family B is distributing all of its profits to you. A is holding back $1,000.

The importance of this fishing example is to demonstrate the need for accounting information in economic decision-making, and also provide a highly simplified model of several basic types of financial information. The financial information includes:

- The resources controlled by the firm and where they came from;

- The efficiency or profitability of the firm in using existing resources to generate new resources (sales);

- The sources of additional resources coming under the firm's control and where they are used.

Financial Accounting and Financial Statements

The system that provides financial information is known as **financial accounting**. Financial accounting is concerned with the measurement and reporting of resources—goods, services and property—and their flows. Available resources, claims against these resources, and flows in and out are measured and reported in monetary terms. In the U.S. the monetary unit for recording and reporting is the dollar.

Financial accounting is the process of recording accounting information and the preparation of the **financial statements** of a firm or business. The statements summarize the financial status of a firm at a particular time and they report the firm's activities and resultant profits or losses,[1] they also report the flows of resources, and the distribution or retention of profits.

The four financial statements are (1) a Balance Sheet, (2) an Income Statement, (3) a Statement of Cash Flows, and (4) a Statement of Retained Earnings, together with supporting footnotes and other data.

The **Balance Sheet** shows a picture, at a specific date, of the firm's financial position. This shows what resources the firm has, what it owes to others, and what is left for the owners. The **Income Statement** shows the results of the firm's activities that are directly related to earning a profit during the year. The **Statement of Cash Flows**

---

[1] In the preceding simplified fishing illustration, profits were measured on a cash basis (cash received less cash disbursed). In later chapters you will find that, in financial accounting, other items such as amount not yet collected from customers on charge sales, amounts not yet paid to employees and suppliers for goods and services already received, and the using up of resources acquired in previous years, are also included in the measurement of profit or loss.

shows major resource changes during the year. It indicates how or from where cash was obtained and how it was used. The **Statement of Retained Earnings** shows the changes in retained Earnings during the period.

Various Users of Financial Statements

In the U.S., resource allocation decisions are made by individuals, firms, and governments. All of these groups may use financial statements as a basis for decisions. Individuals or firms who invest resources in businesses are known as **investors**. Investors are the primary users of financial statements.

There are several different categories of investors who are interested in the financial accounting information concerning a firm. The following descriptions of people with problems are designed to help you see the need for financial statements by different groups of people.

Owners and Potential Owners

Archie owns a record shop. He took a salaried position with a company in another state. He hired Betty to manage his store for him. Archie receives a check each month representing business profits. How can he know whether Betty is doing a good job? Is the profit he is getting all that he can reasonably expect? Should he consider selling his business and investing his money elsewhere

Betty is considering buying the business from Archie and becoming its owner rather than just the salaried manager. She thinks she is doing a good job but would like to compare the firm's performance with other similar firms. To pay for the value of a going business, she knows she will probably have to offer Archie more than he has invested. Also, she needs to know current profits to estimate whether her possible investment would be a good choice compared to other alternatives.

As investors, the current owner(s) of a firm are interested in knowing how well the firm is doing. Potential owners of the firm need information to evaluate the desirability of making an ownership investment.

Existing and Potential Creditors

Charles lent $5,000 to the business owned by his friend, Dave. The loan isn't scheduled to be repaid for another few months, but Charles has heard rumors that Dave's business isn't doing well. Charles wants to know how safe his loan is.

Frances has been asked to lend $3,000 a year to a business owned by an acquaintance. She wants to know how well the business is doing and if it's safe for her to make the loan.

Existing and potential **creditors**–those who lend resources to a firm–need information to evaluate the desirability of their investment.

Current and Potential Suppliers

Harriet owns a dressmaking firm. She has been supplying dresses to a shop owned by Judy. Judy is very slow paying her bills for dresses she purchases from Harriet. Judy always has plausible excuses and promises to do better next month. Harriet is trying to decide whether to go along with Judy, or insist that the past-due bills be paid before any more dresses will be sold on account.

Larry manufactures water skis. Nate's company wishes to purchase $500 worth of skis on account. That is, he wants to open an account with Larry's firm and pay for the skis within 30 days after delivery. Larry needs to decide whether to extend credit to Nate, or request cash at the time of purchase.

Suppliers of goods and services on account to customers are investing in the customer's firm. When items are supplied on account or credit, the supplier becomes a creditor and is making a short-term loan to the customer. As in the case of creditors lending money, suppliers need information in order to evaluate the safety and desirability of their investment.

Employees and Unions

Pauline is thinking of going to work for the ACE Company. The starting pay sounds good, but Pauline wants to join a rapidly growing firm with opportunities for advancement. She wants to know how big ACE is in comparison to its competitors and how rapidly it is growing.

Sanchez is the bargaining agent for the ACE Company employees' union. He wants to know how profitable the company is and how much profit its owners are taking home. He intends to use this information to support the wage demands he is making in the contract negotiations.

Employees and their unions are vitally interested in the firm's survival and possible growth, as well as its ability to pay its wages when due.

Current and Potential Customers

Ursula is the purchasing agent for a large manufacturer. She is buying a certain machine part exclusively from the Weinberg firm. Price, quality, and delivery are satisfactory. However, Ursula is concerned whether the Weinberg Company is doing well as a business. If not, having only one established supplier for the needed part might be a problem.

Yolanda is a buyer for a large department store. She is thinking of placing an order with a new source or supplier. The supplier is not accustomed to handling large orders. It would have to borrow funds for additional materials and equipment in order to fill the order. Yolanda is concerned whether this source is in a good enough financial position to borrow the money to fill this order.

Current and potential customers of the firm depend on it to supply a product or service. This dependency makes customers interested in the firm's economic health.

Managers

A firm's managers are vitally interested in their firm's financial statements, but their interest is different from that of other users. Managers, as insiders, already have access to more detailed data than appears in the statements. In fact, a firm's management is responsible for the initial preparation of the financial statements. Financial statements essentially report to outsiders on the success or failure of managements' performance. Just as your grades measure your academic performance, the firm's financial statements measure managerial performance.

The focus of this text is how various events and activities affect financial statements. As a future manager you will need to know how accountants will measure and report the events under your control.

Each of the people discussed above is faced with a decision. Each need financial accounting information from the financial statements.

Owners, creditors, suppliers, employees, unions, and customers have a relationship with the firm or are considering one. They are users of the firm's financial statements. In addition, financial statements are useful to: business managers; trade associations; financial analysts; government agencies that regulate and encourage business activity; and researchers with diverse interests.

Other Accounting Systems

As mentioned above, a firm's managers have ready access to separate sets of accounting reports with extensive details. These reports are prepared exclusively for use by those working for the firm. Two subsystems are involved in the managerial accounting system. One acts as the data base for both internal (managerial reports) and external (financial statements) reporting and is called the **cost accounting system**. The other includes budgets, performance reports and special analysis relating to particular management decisions. Managerial accounting is not covered in this text.[2]

Managerial accounting is just one of several other types of accounting. Organizations established for making a profit have certain common objectives. Financial

----

[2]   See the companion volume to this text, Managerial Accounting Information.

accounting provides reports on the status and activities of these organizations. Governments and "not-for-profit" institutions have different objectives and are subject to different legal requirements. A different accounting system, with quite different reports, exists for these organizations. It is called **fund accounting**.

Another separate type of accounting is **tax accounting**. Individuals and businesses are taxed with the dual objectives of obtaining money and of accomplishing certain social goals. Tax objectives and tax regulations can be unrelated to the firm's economic objectives. So accounting for tax purposes is separate and distinct from financial accounting. The Internal Revenue Code governs the preparation of tax returns while, accounting principles and standards guide the preparation of financial statements. These two sets of regulations or standards differ significantly. You should be careful not to assume that any tax rules apply to financial accounting.

Tax management involves planning, tax return preparation, and compliance with tax regulations. Good tax management enables a firm to legally minimize its taxes. Accountants are usually involved with tax accounting, so a brief introduction to income taxation is provided later in this text.

The Financial Statements

Financial statements are prepared for investors and others for use in making investment and credit decisions. The statements provide information useful in predicting future cash flows as well as measuring the efficiency of resource allocation. There are four different types of desired information, and each is supplied by a different financial statement.

Appendix A contains the actual financial statements for the Xerox Corporation for the year 1987. Study these while you read the description of each financial statement. Much of the terminology will be new. However, each statement will have some meaning for you. See how each statement tells you something different about the company. At first do not expect to understand everything in these statements. The major objective of the material in this book is to provide you with the ability to read and fully understand financial statements.

The Balance Sheet

The Balance Sheet, which is also called a Statement of Financial Position, supplies information on what resources the firm currently controls. It shows what they are and who has claims against them. Among other things, the balance sheet provides you with information which will help you answer the following questions:

1. How large is the firm in terms of the total resources that it controls?

2. What kind of resources are in the firm? Are most of the resources committed to present activities, or can they move rapidly into new business opportunities?

3. How much cash does the firm have? How much cash can it obtain quickly? How much cash is owed to it, and how much cash does it owe to others?

4. How heavily in debt is the firm? Will it be able to borrow more cash if it needs to? Is it able to meet its obligations when they are due?

5. How much do the owners currently have invested in the firm? What proportion of the owners' investment is firmly committed? What proportion represents past profits currently held in the firm as additional owner investment?

The Income Statement

The Income Statement measures the current profit of the firm. Profitability is a measure of the efficiency of resource usage. Among other things, the income statement provides you with answers to the following questions:

1. How large is the firm in terms of its total volume of sales activity?

2. How profitable is the firm? Is it making more or less profit than similar firms?

3. Are the profits going up or down? Are profits remaining proportionate to changes in sales?

4. Does the firm appear to be charging lower prices than similar firms? Are its costs of doing business proportionally the same as other similar firm?

5. Profitability is one indication of debt-paying ability. Does the firm appear to be in a good position to pay its bills? Are profits adequate to cover current interest costs on debt?

The Statement of Cash Flows

The Statement of Cash Flows provides information concerning how much cash was generated by the firm during the preceding year and how this cash was used. This statement can provide answers to the following questions:

1. How much in new cash resources did the firm generate or obtain during the past year?

2. Where did this cash come from? Was cash obtained from creditors? From owners? From profits retained in the business? Is the firm changing the extent of its indebtedness?

3. What has management been doing with this new cash? Are resources being committed to the replacement or expansion of the firm's buildings or equipment? What portion is being used to retire debt? How much is being distributed to owners?

The Statement of Retained Earnings

The statement of Retained Earnings shows the changes in retained earnings for the year. This statement provides answers to the following questions:

1. How much income was earned during the past year?

2. Were there any dividends declared during the past year?

3. Were there any prior period adjustments made for prior years?

After you develop an understanding of the various items on each statement, you can acquire the tools of analysis that will enable you to answer these questions. For the moment, it is sufficient to have a general idea of what each statement can tell you.

Framework for Financial Reporting

It should be obvious that unless financial statements are reasonably accurate, resource-allocation decisions may be poorly made. Investors may make bad investments and creditors may make bad loans. This is a problem because it is virtually impossible for a firm's financial statements to be completely accurate. Much of the data included in financial statements must be estimated. Estimated data cannot be completely accurate.

Financial statements must include estimates because all of the facts are not known at the time the statements are prepared. Some items are being sold or used, other items are being purchased. There is always unfinished business. Only when the firm goes out of business will everything be known. But users of financial information cannot wait until then; they desire data at least once a year and often more frequently. Financial statements are, therefore, like progress reports.

Consider the following example to clarify the concept of progress reporting. Mike, a business major, just purchased a calculator. How long does Mike plan to own and use his calculator? In other words, what is the useful life of the calculator for him? Mike's type of calculator should last five years under normal usage. If he will graduate in three years and plans on selling the calculator at that time, the useful life of the calculator is three years for him. However, Mike may decide after he graduates to keep the calculator to use on the job, or on the other hand, a new type of more useful calculator may become available next year which will make his calculator obsolete. Thus the three year useful life is an estimate.

Financial statements need to be as accurate as possible to be useful and not mislead users. Accuracy implies that the information in the statements should be complete and all significant or material data must be disclosed. The accounting methods used should be appropriately selected and used consistently from year to year. This will allow users to compare the firm's performance with other similar firms and evaluate the firm's performance over time.

Relevance and reliability are the primary qualities which make accounting information useful for decision-making.[3] **Relevance** requires that the information make a difference in the decision process due to predictive value, feedback value and timeliness. Information must be useful in predicting future outcomes and provide the user with feedback about the accuracy of past predictions. Both require that the information be provided in time for decision making. Financial information should also be reliable. **Reliability** relates to verifiability, neutrality, and representational faithfulness. Information must be neutral—free from bias—and verifiable by others. Representational faithfulness relates to how well the statements measure the real position of the firm.

In the interest of fairness and objectivity accountants follow the assumption of **conservatism**. In the cases of estimates, accountants prefer understatement of the income and/or assets to overstatement. Losses are recognized and reported as soon as they can be estimated. Gains, on the other hand, are never recognized until they actually occur.

Generally Accepted Accounting Principles

Reasonably uniform methods of measurement and reporting are necessary to achieve relevance, reliability, and comparability as discussed above. In the United States, the accounting profession uses the existing body of theory and practice as a guide for the preparation of financial information. These practices are called Generally Accepted Accounting Principles (**GAAP**).[4]

You will need to become familiar with GAAP to intelligently use financial statements. This familiarity will help you to understand the highly summarized and condensed data appearing in the various financial statements. A knowledge of GAAP allows you to understand how and when certain events are recognized and reported, and how the financial effects of these events are measured or estimated.

GAAP has evolved over many years and is continually modified to reflect changes in society. GAAP is not completely logical and consistent. Like our system of law, some requirements have outlived their usefulness. Changes take place slowly, because GAAP is tied to society's framework of slow-changing conventions, expectations, regulations, and legal contracts.

GAAP currently is composed of two segments: a significant amount of custom and procedure that are institutionalized into practice, and numerous decisions by authoritative accounting groups. Cumulative summaries of latest official designs and pronounce-

---

[3] Qualitative Characteristics of Accounting Information, "Statements of Financial Accounting Concepts No. 2 " (Stamford, Conn: FASB May 1980)

[4] Currently there is an attempt to replace the term GAAP with the term "financial accounting standards." However, GAAP remains the most commonly used term.

ments are revised annually.[5] New standards as they become official throughout the year are published in the monthly Journal of Accountancy.[6]

Exhibit 1.2

Independent Auditor's Report

To the Stockholders and Board of Directors of the XYZ Company:

We have audited the accompanying balance sheets of the XYZ Company as of December 31, 19X2 and 19X1 and the related statements of income, Retained Earnings and Cash Flows for the years then ended. These financial statements are the responsibility of the Company's management. Our responsibility is to express an opinion on these financial statements based on our audits.

We conducted our audits in accordance with generally accepted auditing standards. Those standards require that we plan and perform the audit to obtain reasonable assurance about whether the financial statements are free of material misstatement. An audit includes examining, on a test basis, evidence supporting the amounts and disclosures in the financial statements. An audit also includes assessing the accounting principles used and significant estimates made by management, as well as evaluating the overall financial statement presentation. We believe that our audits provide a reasonable basis for our opinion.

In our opinion, the financial statements referred to above present fairly, in all material respects, the financial position of XYZ Company as of December 31, 19X2 and 19X1, and the results of its operations and its cash flows for the years then ended in conformity with generally accepted accounting principles.

A, B, and C
Certified Public Accountants
Chicago   March 1, 19X3

A current example of the need to modify GAAP, and of the accountant's caution in making radical changes concerns GAAP standards for valuing resources that a firm owns. In the next chapter, you can learn that traditionally, accountants initially value resources at their historical cost and never increase their reported value. If the value should decrease, then value of the assets will be reduced at the time the decrease in value is determined. With high inflation, this conservative valuation approach can result in potentially misleading reports. Rather than changing the valuation to the current value, GAAP now encourages larger firms to provide supplementary data reflecting adjustments for general price level changes and for current costs. Thus, investor expectations and contractual arrangements based on historical cost reporting are satisfied, while more current (and possibly more relevant) data are provided. This vital topic of valuation will be covered more thoroughly later in the text.

Within the U.S. financial accounting system, statements are first prepared for the firm by its own accountants. Statements at this stage are known as **unaudited financial**

---

[5] Two good summaries are the latest editions of: Accounting Standards, Financial Accounting Standards Board, McGraw-Hill, Inc., New York, N.Y.; and Miller's Comprehensive GAAP Guide, by Martin A. Miller, Harcourt Brace Jovanovich, Inc., New York, N.Y.

[6] Published by the American Institute of Certified Public Accountants, New York, N.Y.

statements.[7] Although these unaudited statements are supposedly prepared following GAAP standards, there is no legal requirement that unaudited financial statements actually conform to GAAP or that they fairly and objectively provide all relevant informantion.

As a potential user you must recognize unaudited financial statements are of limited use. Even if management believes the statements to be completely fair and has no intent to deceive you, there is still a question of errors and objectivity.

Audited Statements and the CPA

In an attempt to resolve the questions of fairness, objectivity, and conformance with GAAP, the financial statements and their supporting records are subjected to an independent verification or audit by a Certified Public Accountant or **CPA**. The CPA examines the statements, together with the records, procedures, and controls used by the firm. The objective of the examination is to attest to the overall fairness of the statements and conformance with GAAP. Upon completion of the audit, the CPA prepares a report stating a professional opinion on the fairness of the statements. If the audit discloses a failure to follow GAAP it will be noted in the opinion which accompanies the audited financial statements. Exhibit 1.2 is an example of an **auditor's opinion**.

Note that this is a "clean" opinion. It reports that the statements conform with GAAP. It also discloses that the statements are relevant and reliable and that the accounting principles have been consistently applied. It also gives the auditor's opinion that the statements present the information fairly.

You should not make the mistake of viewing the auditor's activities as merely examining the financial statements themselves. The auditor must make a detailed examination of the firm's procedures, internal control systems, and supporting data. The independent CPA will also search for evidence of fraud or theft in the firm;[8] the auditor will attest that the statement disclosures of the firm's activities meets additional legal requirements not specified by GAAP.[9] The auditor looks for ways the company's internal system might be improved to better conform to both GAAP and management policy. When the audit is completed the CPA will submit an audit to management with detail findings and recommendations. The Auditor's opinion will be included in the Company's Annual Report along with the Financial Statements.

The primary role of the CPA is to audit financial statements and to lend credibility to statements prepared by the company's management. Should a user suffer damages as a

---

[7] Unaudited statements are those which have not been independently verified. See next section, covering Audited Statements and the CPA.

[8] Often the general public perceives the auditor's secondary role of potential theft investigation as the primary or even the only purpose for an audit.

[9] Examples of such legal requirements are contained in the Foreign Corrupt Practices Act that resulted from the "Watergate" revelations. Despite its name, this law requires detailed disclosure of payments made to foreign officials as well as domestic political contributions. It prohibits such payments being buried under captions like "miscellaneous expenses."

result of significant departures from GAAP or lack of fair presentation and these short-comings were not noted in the auditor's opinion, then the CPA may then be personally liable. This potential exposure to lawsuits reinforces professionalism and tends to make the CPA careful and thorough. The CPA's careful and thorough verification makes **audited financial statements** credible and, therefore, valuable.

A CPA may also be retained by a client firm to maintain accounting records and prepare the financial statements. CPA's also provide services to clients in the areas of tax-return preparation and management consulting. Professional standards require that when a CPA provides those services, a separate CPA will be engaged for the independent audit and opinion.

The Annual Report

You can find the auditor's opinion, together with the financial statements, in the firm's published **Annual Report**. Annual reports are referred to as "published" because they are printed and distributed annually to shareholders and others by the company. In addition, annual reports usually include:

1. The president's letter reviewing the highlights of the recent year's activities and earnings and sometimes setting forth future plans;

2. Abstracts of significant comparative data;

3. Listing of directors and officers;

4. Descriptions and pictures of company activities and products; and

5. Other information considered beneficial to readers.

The auditor's opinion covers only the financial statements and accompanying footnotes. It specifically does not attest to the fairness and completeness of other information, especially of forecasts, included in the annual report.

Authorative Bodies

A very important organization is the Financial Accounting Standards Board (**FASB**). Founded in 1973, the FASB is the private sector standard-setting body. The FASB develops and issues rules on accounting practice called Statements of Financial Accounting Standards.

The Government Accounting Standards Board (GASB), founded in 1984, establishes financial accounting standards for state and local government units.

Two U.S. government agencies also have significant and growing influence over financial accounting: the Securities Exchange Commission (SEC) and the Internal Revenue Service (IRS). The SEC is empowered by Congress to ensure the adequacy of information disclosed in the financial statements of publicly traded firms. Until recently, the SEC has generally restricted its activities to enforcing the GAAP and supporting the GAAP standards set forth by the FASB. It has, however, been progressively more active in "pushing" the AICPA and the FASB to modify auditing standards and the GAAP. In a few celebrated cases, the financial reporting system has failed to adequately identify poor management or outright fraud leading to the bankruptcy of very large corporations. The accounting system, the accounting profession, and the SEC currently are the objects of severe criticism. The result may be a far more active role for the government and, in particular, the SEC in the establishment and enforcing of accounting standards.

The other government agency which influences financial accounting is the IRS. The IRS determines the reporting standards for income-tax purposes. Although there is no intended similarity between taxable income and accounting income; tax requirements often are incorporated into the GAAP. Since the objectives of tax rules and the GAAP are different, many companies must maintain a dual set of accounting records.

One additional organization, the Financial Executives Institute (FEI), although neither governmental nor made up of accountants, has significant influence over GAAP. The FEI is comprised of preparers of financial statements. Its Committee on Corporate Reporting regularly makes recommendations to the FASB and the SEC for improving the content and usefulness of financial statements.

Accounting Associations

Certified Public Accountants, or CPA's, generally are members of a society in the state in which they are licensed to practice. These states societies arrange for conferences, seminars, and other instruction for the continuing education of CPAs. The largest state societies also publish periodicals containing articles and information of interest and value to members.

In addition to the state CPA societies, many CPAs are members of the national association known as the American Institute of Certified Public Accountants (**AICPA**). The AICPA performs a multitude of services. Twice a year, it prepares and administers the national uniform three-day CPA examination. It publishes the *Journal of Accountancy*, which contains articles and information of immediate practical interest to members, including summaries of new FASB standards and various pertinent changes in government regulations The AICPA also conducts conferences and seminars for continuing member education, markets self-study materials, and represents the CPA profession before Congress, the courts, and various rule-making bodies.

Managerial accountants—those that are employed by firms issuing financial statements—have a professional association known as the National Association of Accountants (NAA). The NAA conducts conferences and seminars. It has instituted a professional examination with the intention of motivating professionalization and training of managerial accountants. Persons passing this NAA examination are identified as having a Certificate in Management Accounting, (CMA). The NAA monthly periodical, is called *Management Accounting*, which contains articles of practical interest to members.

The American Accounting Association, or AAA, is an association of instructors of accounting. It conducts conferences and seminars and publishes the *Accounting Horizons, Issues in Accounting Education*, and *The Accounting Review*. These journals contain both articles and information related to accounting education and also articles of a theoretical nature.

As a potential user of financial statements, you need not be as concerned as the accountant with all of these associations, agencies, and publications. However, financial accounting is a dynamic and changing system. A particular disclosure will have one meaning today because it is measured a certain way. In the future, as the GAAP changes, it may be prepared differently and therefore mean something different. There will be changes made between the time this text is written and the time you use it.

There also will be changes while you are taking this course. As a user, you must keep yourself advised of major changes in GAAP so as to fully understand the financial statements.

Chapter Overview

Based upon the material introduced in this chapter, you should be able to explain:

- The need for and usefulness of financial information in our economy;

- The essential information contained in the four major financial statements—the Balance Sheet, the Income Statement, the Statement of Cash Flows, and the Statement of Retained Earnings;

- How owners, creditors, suppliers, employees, and/or unions,customers and managers may all be viewed as users of financial accounting information, and the interest each has in financial statements;

- The essential difference in purpose among the various accounting systems—financial accounting, managerial accounting, fund accounting, and tax accounting;

- The relationship among financial statements prepared by a firm's management, GAAP, the CPA, and the system which enables the user to rely on their fairness and completeness;

- The roles of the FASB, the SEC, the FEI, the AICPA, the NAA, and the AAA in establishing GAAP.

New Vocabulary and Concepts

AICPA	Fund accounting
Annual report	GAAP
Auditor's financial statements	Income Statement
Auditor's Opinion	Investors
Balance Sheet	Managerial accounting
Conservatism	Relevance
Cost accounting system	Reliability
CPA	SEC
Creditors	Statement of Cash Flows
FASB	Statement of Retained Earnings
Financial accounting	Tax accounting
Financial statements	Unaudited financial statements

- The distinction among financial accounting, managerial accounting, fund accounting, and tax accounting;

- The objectives of GAAP;

- The objective of independent verification and the role of the CPA;

- The roles of the FASB, GASB, SEC, IRS, AICPA, NAA, and FEI.

Review Questions

1. What is financial accounting? How does it differ from managerial accounting? Fund accounting? Tax accounting?

2. What four separate accounting reports are usually known collectively as the Financial Statements?

3. What type of accounting information is provided on each of the four reports making up the Financial Statements?

4. Identify six major groups of individuals who are interested in the firm's financial statements and briefly discuss why each is interested.

5. Why must financial statements contain estimates? Explain with an example.

6. What is the accounting principle of conservatism? What is its purpose?

7. a) What are GAAP? b) Why must GAAP continually change? c) Why are changes in GAAP usually made slowly and carefully? d) Who establishes or modifies GAAP?

8. a) What is a CPA? b) What is the primary role of the CPA?

9. In addition to having GAAP, what system is practiced in the U.S. with the objective of ensuring fairness and objectivity in financial statements?

10. What is the purpose of the auditor's opinion and where can it be found?

11. a) What information is always included in the annual report? b) What additional information may also be included? c) Of all the information that may be included in an annual report, which is covered by the auditor's opinion? Which is not?

12. a) How does government in the U.S. influence GAAP? b) What agencies are involved, and how does each influence GAAP?

Mini-Cases and Questions for Discussion

MC **1.1** The chief negotiator for Gigantic Corporation was meeting with the bargaining agent of the union which represented Gigantic's employees. Gigantic's representative says "I have here a preliminary set of unaudited financial statements for last year which clearly show that the corporation cannot afford any wage increases." The union bargaining agent responds, "Don't try that again; our accountant has prepared statements which show that Gigantic can clearly afford a 15 percent increase across the board." Can either of these sets of figures be considered as clearly objective or unbiased? If the two negotiators wish to start from the same set of objective or neutral data, what would you suggest they do?

MC **1.2** Mr. John Smith owns and operates a small janitorial service. For years he has employed Mr. Fred Smart, a CPA, to keep all of his accounting records and also to prepare unaudited financial statements and his tax returns for him. Mr. Smith wants to sell his business and retire. He has found a potential buyer, who wishes to see a set of audited financial statements. Mr. Smith calls his CPA and says, "Fred, I need a set of certified financial statements. After all these years, it shouldn't be too much trouble. How soon can you get them to me?" Mr. Smart replies, "Sorry, John, but I can't give an opinion on your statements. If you have to give your buyer certified statements, you will have to get a different CPA. If it meets with your approval, you might suggest offering your buyer access to your last five years' tax returns as a possible alternative." Why won't Smart give an opinion on Smith's financial statements? Aren't tax returns identical with financial statements? Explain.

MC **1.3** Give an example of why each of the following investors might be interested in the financial statements of the ABC Company. Explain what they would be looking for, where they might find it, and why they might be more or less interested in certain information than other types of investors.

   a) Al Bernstein, an owner looking for high profits, even if a little risk is involved.

   b) Charlotte Drake, a retired widow looking for an ownership investment providing steady income.

   c) Ernie Fong, a bank loan officer reviewing a loan application.

   d) Mike Hamilton, a credit manager asked to approve an account for a new customer.

   e) Ida Jung, a union bargaining agent preparing for wage negotiations.

   f) Karen Lovejoy, a jewelry buyer in a department store seeking a new supplier.

MC **1.4** What criteria, other than profit compared to resources employed, might a potential investor wish to consider?

MC **1.5** Can, a CPA who is retained/paid by the firm being audited really be an objective/neutral judge of the firm's financial statements? Explain.

MC **1.6** What would be the advantages and disadvantages of having GAAP set by government regulation, i.e., similar to tax code and regulations?

2

Reading and Understanding the Balance Sheet

Chapter Preview

The objective of this chapter is to introduce the Balance Sheet—its information, its usefulness, and its limitations. You can learn:

1. How the balance sheet is like a photograph of a firm's financial condition at one point in time;

2. The various items which are included in the balance sheet "picture" and some specific items which are not included;

3. How balance sheet items are conventionally classified and the meaning of the different classifications;

4. The accountant's basis for valuing balance sheet items, and why this basis has been selected;

5. Why balance sheet items naturally fall into two major groups assets and equities and why totals of these groups equal each other — why the balance sheet balances;

In subsequent chapters, you will learn that the balance sheet forms the core of the financial accounting system. A clear understanding of this "core statement" gained in this chapter will provide you with the basic foundation on which you can build all of your accounting knowledge.

The Concept of Net Worth

To help you understand this chapter, you will be asked to assume different roles. First suppose you are a close friend of Mr. John Jones. John Jones has his own mobile food service business known as Jones' Canteen Company. He owns a special food vending truck and sells coffee, soft drinks, and food items.

John Jones is applying for a personal loan at his local bank. The loan officer, Barbara Kane, asks him for a statement of personal **net worth** as part of his loan application. Ms. Kane explains that personal net worth means what he owns less what he owes to others.

John Jones comes to you for help in preparing the net worth statement. He tells you that, as of today, 12/31/X2, he has the following possessions and debts:

- Clothing and other personal effects: original costs, $2,000; estimated value if sold, $100; estimated original usefulness remaining, 50 percent; estimated replacement cost of used items in similar condition, $600.

- TV and stereo: original cost, $1,100; estimated value if sold today, $150; estimated original usefulness remaining, 80 percent; estimated replacement cost of used items in similar condition, $300.

- Balance in personal checking and savings accounts, $5,000.

- Amount owed and payable currently on personal charge accounts, $400.

- Balance in business checking account, $600.

- Balance of business cash on hand, $50.

- Money owed by good customers who were short of cash, $30.

- Inventory on hand of food and supplies recently purchased: original cost and replacement cost of food, $175, and of supplies, $25; estimated recovery if sold today $75.

- Vending truck: original cost two years ago, $15,000; estimated used sale value today, $10,000; estimated remaining usefulness, four more years; estimated used sale value four years from now, $3,000; estimated replacement cost of used truck in similar condition today, $11,500.

- Amount owed on business charge accounts, $225.

- Amount owed on business loan (for truck purchase), $9,000 - $3,000 over the next year and the rest payable more than a year from now.

For guidance, John Jones has also given you a copy of the bank's sample personal net worth statement which he had received from Ms. Kane. (See Exhibit 2.1)

Exhibit 2.1

SAMPLE PERSONAL NET WORTH STATEMENT

Items Owned:	Value
Personal bank accounts	$2,000
Other personal items	6,000
Business bank accounts	5,000
Business receivables	10,000
Business inventory and supplies	15,000
Business equipment	20,000
Total	$58,000
Less Amounts Owed:	
Personal charge account	900
Personal loans	4,000
Business charge accounts	7,000
Business loans	11,000
Total	22,900
Equals Personal Net Worth	$35,100

Attempt to prepare Jones' personal net worth statement from the information given. You will learn accounting more rapidly if you will try to do this before looking ahead for the "correct" answer.

Various Ways to Measure the Value of Items Owned

If you determined Jones' personal net worth to be some amount between $6,380 and $14,355, you are correct. You understand the basic idea behind personal net worth — what John owns minus what he owes to others. Different possible "correct" answers result from a lack of precise agreement on how to measure the value of what John owns.

Now, change roles and assume that you are the bank officer. John Jones has presented you with Exhibit 2.2. Note that there are five different columns. One column for each of five different valuation assumptions. Mr. Jones has explained that he wasn't sure what you wanted, so to be safe, he gave you all five.

As the bank's loan officer, you are interested in Mr. Jones' personal net worth for several different reasons. First, you want to see whether he already has too much debt in comparison to his possessions. Second, you want to know whether he has any valuable items that he could pledge as collateral for his loan.[1] Notice those items where the

---

[1] As a loan officer, you would also be very much interested in information concerning John Jones' income or business earnings. However, this information is not included on a personal net worth statement, and is not relevant to this example.

amount has to do with cash: cash on hand, cash to be received, or cash to be paid. For these items, the same amounts appear in all five columns. These are known as monetary items. **Monetary items** involve cash, a right to receive a specific amount of cash on a given date, or an obligation to pay a specific amount of cash at a specific date. Cash can be counted and cash that is to be received or paid by existing agreement can be determined with certainty.[2] Therefore, there is no immediate problem in valuing monetary items. The difficult valuation problems involve the nonmonetary items, such as clothing and effects, TV and stereo, food and supplies, and the truck.

Unadjusted Original Cost

Remembering you are the loan officer, study Exhibit 2.2. The first column indicates Jones' possessions at their unadjusted **original cost**. Do you think this column gives the best picture of Jones' personal net worth now? Remember from Chapter 1, that some of the goals of business financial statements are that they be objective, reliable, and relevant. Is unadjusted original cost objective, reliable, and relevant? It certainly is reliable, there are no estimates, and it can be easily verified.

What about relevance? As the loan officer, you would probably conclude that using unadjusted original cost — to value Jones' clothing now at $2,000, or his two-year old truck at $15,000 — is not relevant to the decision you must make as a loan officer. Since it reflects no adjustment or allowance for wear, it is not a fair measurement of today's value. It is not relevant in estimating Jones' current net worth. For exactly this reason, accountants do not use unadjusted original cost to value assets on financial statements.

Liquidation Value

Now look at column 2 of Exhibit 2.2. In this column Jones' possessions are measured at the amount of cash that could be realized from their quick sale or **liquidation value**. Do you think this column gives you the best picture of Jones' current net worth? You probably find the answer to this question more difficult. First, the net worth is based solely on an estimate. People often tend to over-estimate the value of their things. Therefore the amounts are not very reliable. In this extreme case they are not very relevant. If Jones were to default on his loan and the bank had to sell his possessions to repay the loan, then these estimates could be helpful. However, as a loan officer you wouldn't be inclined to make the loan if you believed Jones' possessions would need to be liquidated to pay off the loan. You want Jones to stay in business and repay his loan. After all, as a

---

[2] More complex issues involving the measurement of certain monetary items will be discussed in Chapters 11 and 12. Where payments are scheduled years in the future, discounted present value may be relevant. Monetary items held over time during periods of inflation may also result in holding gains or losses.

Exhibit 2.2

PERSONAL NET WORTH STATEMENTS FOR JOHN JONES AS OF 12/31/X2

	Col 1 Unadjusted original cost	Col 2 Liquidation values	Col 3 Adjusted original cost	Col 4 Constant Purchasing power	Col 5 Current costs
What Jones Has:					
Personal Items					
Clothing and effects	$ 2,000	$ 100	$ 1,000[a]	$ 1,200[b]	$ 600[c]
TV and Stereo	1,100	150	880[a]	1,150[b]	300[c]
Checking and savings	5,000	5,000	5,000	5,000	5,000
Business Items					
Checking and cash	650	650	650	650	650
Owed from customers	30	30	30	30	30
Food and supplies	200	75	200	200	200[c]
Truck	15,000	10,000	11,000[a]	12,000[b]	11,500[c]
Total	$23,980	$16,005	$18,760	$20,230	$18,280
What Jones Owes:					
Personal accounts	400	400	400	400	400
Business accounts	225	225	225	225	225
Business truck loan	9,000	9,000	9,000	9,000	9,000
Total	$ 9,625	$ 9,625	$ 9,625	$ 9,625	$ 9,625
Jones' Net Worth	$14,355	$ 6,380	$ 9,135	$10,605	$ 8,655

a Expiration of usefulness (depreciation).
b Reflects expiration of usefulness and loss of purchasing power of dollar since acquisition.
c Reflects current replacement costs of items in similar condition.

banker you are in the business of lending or renting money, and you would like Jones as a repeat customer. Therefore, you probably reject a liquidation measurement as not very reliable nor relevant.

Accountants do not choose liquidation measurement in preparing the financial statements. Financial statements are prepared with the assumption that the firm is going to stay in business. This is known as the "**Going-concern Assumption.**"

Adjusted Original Cost

Column 3 of Exhibit 2.2 is headed: **Adjusted original cost**. The measurements in this column are in accordance with current Generally Accepted Accounting Principles.

Jones' personal and business possessions are valued at their original cost less an allowance for wear and tear or expiration of usefulness. The clothing and effects reflect a 60 percent loss of usefulness, and the TV and stereo a 20 percent drop. Food and supplies original cost is not adjusted,because these items were recently purchased and there is no expiration of usefulness to the firm. The truck valuation has been reduced to reflect depreciation. The method of calculation will be explained a little later in this chapter.

The accounting profession has settled on adjusted original cost as the best balance between reliability and relevance. Adjusted original cost is reliable because it is associated with an identifiable transaction.

Adjusting the amounts for wear and tear, obsolescence, etc. makes the reported assets more relevant to the needs of users. However, statements prepared on an adjusted original cost basis do not reflect recognition of inflationary effects on resources held by the firm. The result of inflation is generally only recognized and reported at the time when an item is sold.

Current Costs

The values for nonmonetary items shown in column 5 reflect the **current costs** of similar items. This measurement basis may seem most reasonable to you. Many people would probably agree that it is both fair and relevant. The problem with current cost as a reporting basis is that, for many items, it can be very difficult and costly to obtain a reliable figure. Current costs would have to be estimated in many cases, and different estimators would probably not agree on the same figure. How accurately could you estimate the current cost of a 25-year-old factory built from materials no longer available? For these two reasons — expense and reliability — accountants in the United States do not use current-cost measurements for financial statements.

Constant Purchasing Power Dollars

Column 4 is simply the costs from column 3 increased to reflect the effects of inflation. The adjusted original costs are restated in **constant purchasing power dollars**. The resulting inflation-adjusted costs do not reflect actual price changes of the specific items. Monetary items are not increased since dollars do not increase with inflation. Also note that items such as food and supplies are not adjusted. These items have been so recently acquired that inflation has had little effect.

Adjusting the original cost figures for the impact of inflation may present more relevant information about the company. Comparisons between years would be more meaningful. The feedback value of the financial statements would be improved.

This increase in relevance can be obtained with surrendering only a small decline in reliability.

The original cost figure is simply multiplied by an inflation factor. This will be reliable if the inflation factor correctly shows the change in prices for the item being adjusted. Accountants generally use indicators of inflation such as the consumer price index. Some firms provide original cost data adjusted for inflation as a supplement to their regular financial statements.[3]

Entity Convention

The John Jones example properly includes Jones' personal possessions and debts as part of his personal net worth statement. However, your objective is to learn about business balance sheets. Accounting balance sheets are prepared for business firms or economic entities. They are similar to net worth statements but include information concerning only the business and its activities. Financial Statements do not provide information about the firm's owners or investors, except for the amount invested.

In Jones' case, since his business is not incorporated it is a **proprietorship**. The bank, and the government consider both Jones' business and personal items collectively. However, so that John and others may evaluate the condition of his business by itself, accountants prepare financial statements for his canteen firm as a distinct entity separate from his personal life and separate from any other businesses which he may own. If John also owned a sporting goods store accountants could prepare two sets of financial statements, one for the canteen **business entity** and one for the sporting goods store business entity. On the balance sheet for Jones' business, his personal assets and personal liabilities would be excluded since they are not part of his business or economic entity.

The Balance Sheet

One of the three basic types of financial statements shows the resources a firm controls and who has claims against these resources. This information is provided in a balance

---

[3] General-price-level inflation adjustment is objective and does not reflect changes in the general purchasing power of the dollar. However, the results can be confusing and difficult to understand, especially when reported values of an inventory of hand calculators are adjusted upward for general inflation, even though the price of the calculator may be declining. Current cost reporting may initially be appealing and appear most relevant. However, should current costs be market value (selling price) or replacement costs? How can one objectively determine the market value of a special purpose factory or piece of equipment that has no ready market? Also can one objectively determine the replacement cost of something that is still useful but no longer available or that is not intended to be replaced after it wears out? The measurement of estimating of current costs can be so costly and the process so subjective (and therefore open to manipulation, since not objectively verifiable) that accountants have traditionally rejected using current costs in the regular statements. This subject is discussed more thoroughly in this text.

sheet. The balance sheet is a report of things owned by a business and the amounts owed to others. Exhibit 2.3 shows a balance sheet prepared for Jones' business for the same date as his personal net worth statement. Study Exhibit 2.3 carefully. It introduces some very important accounting concepts and vocabulary.

Notice that the title specifies the name of the business entity involved — Jones' Canteen Company. This particular report is called a balance sheet and is "as of" a particular date. A balance sheet is sometimes called a statement of financial position. Its purpose is to report the firm's financial position as of the close of business on the statement date. A balance sheet is like a photograph. It gives information only at one point in time.

Look at the left half of the balance sheet. It shows the resources in the business. **Assets** are economic resources owned by the business which have future value to the business. Assets may be tangible properties such as inventory or buildings. They may also be intangible items such as patents or copyrights. In the United States, assets are listed first on the balance sheet.

Note in Exhibit 2.3 that assets are divided into two groups: current assets and long-

Exhibit 2.3

JONES' CANTEEN COMPANY BALANCE SHEET
AS OF 12/31/X2

Assets			Liabilities and Owner's Equity	
Current Assets:			**Current Liabilities:**	
Cash	$	650	Note Payable	$ 3,000
Accounts receivable		30	Accounts Payable	225
Inventory		175	Total Current Liabilities	$ 3,225
Supplies		25		
Total Current Assets	$	880	**Long-term Debt:**	
			Noncurrent Note Payable	6,000
Long-lived Assets:			Total Liabilities	$ 9,225
Equipment-truck	15,000			
Less accumulated				
depreciation	(4,000)	11,000	Owner's Equity	2,655*
Total Assets		$11,880	Total Equities	$11,880

* Determined by subtracting total liabilities from total assets ($11,880 - 9,225).

lived assets. **Current assets** will be used up or converted into cash within one year or the operating cycle whichever is longer.

In the normal **operating cycle**, some cash is used to purchase inventory (See Illustration 2.1). The inventory is then sold to customers for cash or on account. If the inventory is sold on account, the receivable is later collected, the customers pay their bills with cash, and the cycle is complete. Since inventory and accounts receivable are part of the operating cycle they are generally current. Supplies and prepaid expenses are also current assets. These will be discussed later in this chapter.

Look at the current assets in Exhibit 2.3. John has cash, accounts receivable, inventory, and supplies. On a balance sheet, the amount shown for **cash** includes both cash on hand and in banks. **Accounts receivable** indicates the amount of cash due from customers for charge sales. The customer has purchased the goods or services offered by the firm but has not yet paid cash for them. Such events are known as **credit sales** or sales on account. The term **"inventory"** refers to the merchandise Jones has on hand for sale to customers. His inventory might include coffee, soft drinks, and other saleable food. **Supplies** are those items on hand that will be used up, rather than sold, in the operation of his business. For example, Jones' supplies might include cups and napkins.

Within the set of noncurrent or long-lived assets, Jones has only one type— **property and equipment**. These assets represent tangible or physical assets owned by the business and intended for use in the business. Tangible assets with expected usefulness of more than a year are identified as property and equipment and classified as long-lived assets. Property and equipment provide the physical means to do business and are often informally referred to as capacity assets. If Jones did not own his truck and merely rented one on a month-to-month basis, it would not be shown as an asset.[4] And a firm

Illustration 2.1

The Operating Cycle

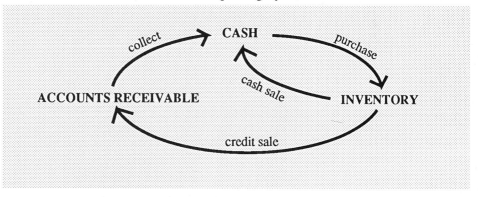

that sells trucks classifies trucks intended for sale to customers as inventory, rather than as property and equipment.

Note in Exhibit 2.3, that Jones' truck is first shown at its original cost, $15,000. Immediately below it is subtracted an adjustment in the amount of $4,000. This adjustment is called **accumulated depreciation**. Accumulated depreciation represents an estimate of the amount of the cost that has been used as a result of wear and obsolescence. The undepreciated net carrying value (**book value**) of the truck is shown as $11,000.

---

[4] There are some leased assets that are exceptions. A lease that can't be cancelled and that extends over most of the asset's useful life may qualify as a Capital Lease (to be discussed in Chapter 11). Assets held under capital lease are shown in the balance sheet as if they were owned.

To understand book value review what you know about Jones' truck. Two years ago it cost $15,000. Four years from now John expects to sell it for $3,000. The truck may still be useful to someone after John sells it, but its planned useful life to Jones is only six years. Over the six years the unrecoverable cost to him is $12,000. This is in addition to the cost of gas, oil, and repairs. Each year some of the $12,000 cost is used. A simple way to show the **cost expiration**, would be to depreciate it by $2,000 each year. This method of allocating cost expiration evenly over the life is known as straight-line depreciation and is one of the methods acceptable under GAAP.

Under **straight-line depreciation** the total amount to be depreciated over the asset's useful life to the firm is first determined by subtracting the expected salvage value recovery from the original cost ($15,000 – 3,000 = $12,000). The total cost to be allocated is then divided by the years of useful life to determine the amount of each year's depreciation:

$$\frac{\textbf{Cost} - \textbf{Salvage Value}}{\textbf{Estimated Useful Life}} = \textbf{Depreciation per period}$$

$$\frac{\$15,000 - \$3,000}{6 \text{ Years}} = \$2,000 \text{ depreciation per year}$$

Note that the original cost and the amount of accumulated depreciation are shown separately. The original cost shown is not directly reduced $2,000 per year. Also, accumulated depreciation is an adjustment or valuation item. It does not indicate the amount set aside for a new truck. If John were also setting aside money, this money would be shown as a separate asset.

At the bottom of the balance sheet is the total of the adjusted original costs of all assets in the Jones firm at the balance sheet date. The amount of $11,880 is shown as total assets.

Items on the right side of a balance sheet are called **equities**. Equities are claims against the firm's total assets. By law, creditors — those to whom the firm owes money — have first claim on the firm's total assets for the amount owed to them. These claims are called **liabilities**. The owner's claim is secondary, or residual. John Jones' owner's equity — identified as **owner's capital** — represents the net worth. This is the difference between total assets and total creditor claims. This is Jones share of the canteen business as distinct from his total personal net worth discussed earlier.

The Balance Sheet Equality

Since creditors and investors claims are against the total assets, the total equities always equals total assets. It's just that simple. This is the reason balance sheets are called "Balance Sheets."

The total equities can be no more and no less than the total assets to be claimed. If total assets increase, the amount available to be claimed has gone up. If there are no additional creditor claims, then the owners' residual claim increase to balance. If total assets decrease, then total claims must decrease. This balance is always maintained and is the foundation for understanding the entire accounting system.[5]

Illustration 2.2

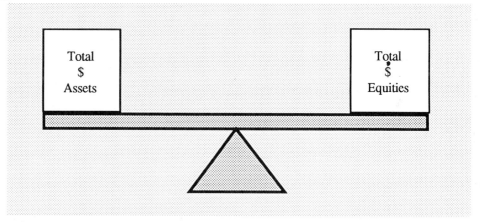

Total Assets = Total Liabilities + Owner's Equity

Liabilities and Owner's Equity

Liabilities are the amounts owed by the firm to creditors as of the balance sheet date. Liabilities are divided into two groups: **current liabilities** and noncurrent liabilities. Current liabilities are those liabilities payable within one year of the balance sheet date and will be paid for out of current assets. **Long-term debt** or noncurrent liabilities generally include those liabilities due more than one year after the balance sheet date.

Under current liabilities, Jones' balance sheet shows two items: notes payable and accounts payable. The **note payable** represents the $3,000 due the bank on the truck within one year. When John purchased his truck, he signed a promissory note, promising to pay specific amounts on specific dates. Liabilities covered by promissory notes are classified separately on the balance sheet as notes payable.

Accounts payable is the amount John owes his suppliers for goods and services purchased on account but not yet paid. When John buys something on account, the amount owed is shown on the balance sheet under accounts payable.

The $6,000 in notes payable on the truck is classified as a long-term debt. The $6,000 balance is not due within one year. Total liabilities as of the balance sheet date amount to $9,225 ($3,225 current liabilities + $6,000 long-term debt).

---

[5] It is, of course, possible that a firm's total liabilities could end up being more than its total assets. In such a situation it would be insolvent, not a going concern, and conventional financial statements would not be prepared.

Exhibit 2.4

TYPICAL ITEMS FOUND ON MANY BALANCE SHEETS

XYZ Company (entity name)
Balance Sheet (name of statement)
As of X/X/XX (date of statement)

Assets	Equities
Current Assets:	**Current Liabilities:**
Cash	Current notes payable
Marketable securities	Accounts payable
Notes receivable	Wages and salaries payable
Accounts receivable	Interest payable
Less allowance for doubtful accounts	Taxes payable
Inventory	Current capital lease obligations
Supplies	Unearned revenue
Prepaid items	
Total Current Assets	Total Current Liabilities
Long-lived Assets:	**Long-Term Debt:**
Investments	Noncurrent notes payable
Property, plant and equipment	Bonds payable
Land	Bond discount or premium
Buildings	Noncurrent capital lease obligations
Less accumulated depreciation	Deferred income taxes
Equipment	Total Liabilities
Less accumulated depreciation	
Office furniture and fixtures	
Less accumulated depreciation	
Properties held under capital lease	**Owner's Equity:***
Less accumulated depreciation	Owner's capital
Intangible and other assets:	
Leasehold improvement	
Franchises, patents, copyrights,	
trademarks	
Deferred charges	
Goodwill	
Total Assets	Total Equities

* See Chapter 10 for further details on owner's equity for partnerships and corporations.

Since total assets for Jones' company were $11,880 the balance of the total assets not claimed by creditors amounted to $2,655. This residual amount is called owners equity.

Total Assets – Total Liabilities = Owner's Equity

Another term used for this residual amount is **net assets**. Net worth, or net assets refers to the worth of the business to John as the owner. It would not refer to Jones' overall personal net worth, which would also include other personal assets and liabilities. It is not the business' net worth to a potential buyer.[6] Net assets or owner's equity is simply the difference between total assets as measured by accountants and total liabilities.

The **balance sheet equality** (total assets equal total equities) can be restated as: total assets equal total liabilities plus **owner's equity** (TA = TL + OE). In this form the two distinct types of claims — creditors' and owner's — are emphasized. This equality always exists regardless of the size and complexity of the business.

Balance Sheet Items and Terminology

Moving from the John Jones example to balance sheets in general, Exhibit 2.4 lists items that appear on many balance sheets for firms larger than Jones'. As you study it, pay attention to the sequence in which items are listed. Look for the distinction between assets and liabilities and between current and noncurrent items. Use your intuition to guess the meaning of unfamiliar items before verifying their definitions listed below. Different business firms often use differing terminology for the same thing. However, you can determine the meaning by the placement of accounts on the statement.

Statement heading

Exhibit 2.4 shows that a financial statement will indicate the name of the entity, the type of report, and the date of the report. Otherwise, the user would be unable to identify what is being reported, or for whom, or as of what date. Since a balance sheet is like a photograph of the firm's position at one point in time, a balance sheet will be prepared "as of" a specific date.

Assets

Recall that assets are resources owned by the entity which have future usefulness or benefit to the entity, and which can be measured in monetary terms. Assets may be tangible

---

[6] Accounts do not measure and report all assets. An example wold be the value of human resources to the firm. In addition, current values are not reflected on the balance sheet, which may understate the firm's net worth.

(physical) or intangible (a legal claim or right). Nonmonetary assets are initially valued at their **fair market value at the time of acquisition**. In most cases, the acquisition or historical cost is acceptable evidence of the fair market value. Assets are listed in the order of **liquidity** or ability to convert the asset to cash.

CURRENT ASSETS include cash and any other assets that are expected to be converted into cash or consumed within a year or within the firm's normal operating cycle if the operating cycle is longer than a one year.

• **Cash** is the total of all currency on hand and on deposit in banks, that is available for immediate withdrawal. Any significant amount of cash not readily available for immediate use should be classified as noncurrent.[7]

• **Marketable securities** are short-term investments including treasury bills and notes, bank certificates, and similiar items. These investments are temporary uses of excess cash and are expected to convert to cash whenever case is needed. Marketable securities are conventionally valued at cost or current sale value, whichever is lower.

• **Current notes receivable** include promissory notes committing borrower or customer to pay the company a specific amount of cash on a specific date within one year.

• **Accounts receivable** are claims against customers for cash resulting from completed sales on account. These claims are not evidenced by promissory notes.

• **Allowance for doubtful accounts.** Not all customers pay their bills. An estimate is made of the proportion of accounts receivable that experience indicates will probably not be collected. This estimate is shown as a "valuation allowance" or a contra asset. It is subtracted from accounts receivable so that net accounts receivable indicates the amount of cash that will probably be collected. Allowance for doubtful accounts is sometimes called "allowance for uncollectibles."

• **Inventory** is merchandise or finished products on hand for sale to customers. For manufactures, inventory also includes raw materials used in production and partially-completed products on hand.

• **Supplies** are materials on hand for use rather than sale.

• **Prepaid items** include services paid for in advance and normally used within one year. Prepaid items are rights to receive goods and services in contrast to receivables that are rights to receive cash. Examples of prepaid items would include rent paid in advance and the unexpired cost of future insurance premiums.

---

[7] In making commercial loans, banks may require the borrower to keep a compensating balance on deposit at all times. This compensating balance is effectively unavailable for use. The company may, also, be setting aside monies for a major expense that is anticipated for the future.

LONG-LIVED ASSETS include assets other than those classified as current. This classification may also be designated as "noncurrent assets" but the more positive and descriptive term **"long-lived assets"** is gaining acceptance. Remember that long-lived can mean any asset not intended to be consumed or collected within one year (or accounting period). It does not necessarily imply a life of many years into the future. There are generally three groupings of assets in this category: Investments; Property, Plant and Equipment; and Intangibles.

INVESTMENTS include noncurrent receivables, securities held for purposes other than short-term investments of idle cash, and any other assets that the firm has acquired as an investment. Also included is savings segregated for a specific future purpose. None of these assets are expected to be liquidated — converted to cash — within one year of the balance sheet date.

PROPERTY, PLANT AND EQUIPMENT normally includes all tangible assets owned by the firm other than current inventory and supplies. The asset must be used in the operations of the company before it is included in this category. This category of long-lived assets is also sometimes called plant assets, fixed assets, or capacity assets.

• **Land** includes the cost of land owned by the firm for use in operations. The cost includes the purchase price and the cost of any permanent alterations to the land such as clearing, grading, and landscaping. Firms that regularly sell land to customers treat land for sale as inventory. Land purchased purely as an investment or for future use is classified in the investments account. The accountant assumes that costs assigned to land do not lose value, wear out, or become obsolete. Therefore, land is not normally adjusted for depreciation.

• **Buildings, equipment, office furniture and fixtures, and any other owned tangible assets** include the items which were acquired and are being used by the firm. They are reported at their original cost before adjustment for accumulated depreciation.

• **Accumulated depreciation** is a valuation item or contra asset used to reduce the book value of tangible property and equipment to reflect use and obsolescence. Accumulated depreciation is also called allowance for depreciation. The amount represents merely a valuation subtraction or a contra asset.

• **Properties held under capital lease** include only special types of long-term leases. They are included here when the firm effectively owns and controls the leased asset. Properties under ordinary leases, called **operating leases**, are not shown as assets on the balance sheet. Accounting for capital leases will be covered in Chapter 11.

INTANGIBLES is the third major subdivision of long-lived assets. **Intangible assets** are privileges or rights acquired via an identifiable expenditure for an item which has no physical properties. Intangibles are initially valued at original cost. These assets are often undervalued since accountants place the cost of purchasing the assets rather than the cost of developing (research and development) the assets. As the usefulness expires, the cost is allocated and the value is reduced. Intangible assets include such things as leasehold improvements, franchises, patents, copyrights, trademarks, and goodwill.

• **Leasehold improvements** indicate the unexpired costs of improvements which have been physically attached by the firm to property that it does not own. These improvements have to be abandoned when the firm gives up the property at the end of the lease term. If such improvements are made to owned properties, or are not physically attached, they are included in the property and equipment category.

• **Deferred charges** represents prepayments stretching significantly beyond one year, and therefore not classified as "prepaid items." Deferred charges will be discussed in Chapter 11.

• **Goodwill** appears only when a firm has purchased another firm. It represents the amount paid for the other firm in excess of the fair market value of the net assets acquired. Goodwill will be discussed in Chapter 14.

Liabilities and Owner's Equity

As previously described, equities are claims against total assets. There are two general classifications of equities: creditor equities (liabilities) and owner's equity. Liabilities are existing obligations to make a future payment of cash or to supply products or services. They represent claims against the firm's total assets for goods or services already supplied by the creditors to the firm. Future interest (not yet owned) or future rent would not be shown as a liability. Owner's equity represents the residual share (after creditor claims have been satisfied) of the owner in the firm's assets.

CURRENT LIABILITIES include those obligations for goods delivered or services already performed that will require current assets for settlement. Most current liability categories are self-explanatory. It is common to separate current liabilities by type of creditor: "**current notes payable**" to creditors who have been given promissory notes; "accounts payable" to suppliers of goods and services who have not been given promissory notes; "**wages payable**" to employees; "**interest payable**" to creditors who loaned funds; "**taxes payable**" to governments; "**current capital lease obligations**" to lessors under capital leases; "unearned revenue" (described below); "estimated warranty costs" (described below); and so forth.

• **Unearned revenue** is an obligation to deliver goods or services to customers who pay in advance. Unearned revenue may also be identified as "revenue collected in advance" or as "unearned income." Prepaid subscriptions are an example of unearned revenue.

LONG-TERM DEBT includes all liabilities that are not current as of the balance sheet date. It includes all obligations for goods and services already provided to the firm where the payment date is more than one year in the future or will not use current assets for payment. You may find this classification identified as "noncurrent liabilities." As in the case of long-lived assets, the long-term debt should be understood as including any obligations maturing beyond one year from the balance sheet date. It does not necessarily imply maturity of many years into the future.

• **Noncurrent notes payable** are promissory notes and mortgages maturing in excess of the firm's time definition for current, which is generally one year in the future.

• **Bonds payable** are long-term debt instruments used by corporations. They are securities exchanged for money loaned to the company on a long-term basis. Bonds payable indicates the amount that must be paid at the maturity date of the bonds.

• **Bond discounts and bond premiums** are valuation items related to bonds payable and will be discussed in Chapter 12.

• **Noncurrent capital lease obligations** disclose the remaining noncurrent liability under lease contracts which are determined to be capital leases.

• **Deferred income tax** discloses income taxes that are postponed because of timing differences between reporting profit for accounting purposes and profit for tax purposes. This will be discussed in Chapter 8 and 12.

OWNER'S EQUITY This category represents the residual claim against total assets after subtracting all creditor claims. It does not attempt to indicate market value, liquidation value, or any other form of value. For a proprietorship, owner's equity often includes only a single item identified with the proprietor's name as "John Doe, Capital" or "Mary Smith, Capital." For partnerships and corporations discussed in Chapter 10, owner's equity includes more subdivisions.

Review of Balance Sheet Classifications and Format

The various classifications or categories of balance sheet information already introduced can be confusing. You might wish to review them.

Current vs Noncurrent

Assets shown in a balance sheet are classified as either current (cycling to cash or consumable within a year) or long-lived (all others). Similarly, liabilities are classified as either current (payable or providable within a year) or as long-term debt (payable beyond one year from the balance sheet date). These classifications are important when evaluating the firm's ability to pay its bills when due. It will be helpful to thoroughly familiarize yourself with the ordering, description, and classification of the more common assets appearing in Exhibit 2.3. The asset ordering roughly corresponds to the ease of conversion into cash of each asset.

Monetary vs Nonmonetary

Although not classified as such on the conventional balance sheet, both assets and liabilities may be grouped as either monetary (cash or commitment for a specific cash amount at a specified time) or nonmonetary (all other). Measurement standards differ between monetary and nonmonetary assets. Valuation of nonmonetary assets usually involves more estimating and more assumptions.

Monetary assets include cash, some marketable securities, all current and noncurrent receivables, and some noncurrent investments. All other assets are nonmonetary. Monetary liabilities include most liabilities. Nonmonetary liabilities include unearned revenue and estimated warranty costs.

Relating to Your Special Company

One of the most effective ways you can grasp new accounting concepts and terminology is to relate them to a business that you already understand. At this point, you should pick a firm to serve as "your company." It can be any business you might like to own, real or imaginary. The important thing is that your business be small enough and real enough to you so you can visualize all of its activities easily.

Prepare a balance sheet for your hypothetical company as of the end of last year. Be sure to include all the assets you think would be in your firm and all of the liabilities reasonable for your type of business. Fill in dollar amounts which seem appropriate. Make your balance sheet balance.

When you complete your balance sheet, you should have a much clearer understanding of balance sheets. If there is anything about your firm that doesn't clearly fit, or anything in Exhibit 2.4 you can't relate to your company, now is the time to find out. Review the explanations in this chapter or in the glossary, ask a fellow student or your instructor for help. Don't go to the next chapter until the ideas of a balance sheet and your company are clear and comfortable.

Information Content of a Balance Sheet

What does a balance sheet tell you about a firm? Of equal importance, what does it not tell you about the firm?

The balance sheet provides a picture of the company's financial position at one date. By comparing it with the firm's previous balance sheets, you can get a sense of the direction in which the firm is moving. Is it growing? Is the composition of its assets changing? Are there more or less current versus long-lived assets, more or less merchandise inventory, receivables, plant and equipment, and so forth? How heavily is the company in debt?

You can also gain valuable information about a firm by comparing its balance sheet with those of other companies in the same industry. The same questions would be relevant. The next chapter will provide several tools and different perspectives to assist you with balance sheet analysis.

Exhibit 2.5

EXAMPLE COMPANY BALANCE SHEET

Entity Name
BALANCE SHEET
As of X/X/XX

ASSETS		EQUITIES	
Current Assets:		**Current Liabilities:**	
Cash	$ 50	Current Notes payable	$ 25
Marketable securities	200	Accounts payable	300
Current notes receivable	20	Wages & salaries payable	40
Accounts receivable	500	Interest payable	275
Allowance for doubtful accounts	(5)	Taxes payable	85
Inventory	800	Current capital lease	
Supplies	35	obligations	30
Prepaid Items	100	Unearned revenue	45
Total Current Assets	$1,700	Total Current Liabilities	$800
Long-lived Assets:		**Long-Term Debt:**	
Long-term investments	300	Noncurrent notes payable	75
Property and equipment:		Bonds payable	400
Land	150	Noncurrent capital lease	
Buildings	900	obligations	225
Accum. depr. buildings	(250)	Total Liabilities	$1,500
Equipment	700		
Accum. depr. equip	(350)		
Properties held under			
capital lease	400		
Accum. depr. capital lease	(100)		
Intangible and other assets:			
Leasehold improvement	60		
Patents	90	Owner's Capital:	2,100
Total Assets	$3,600	Total Equities	$3,600

Balance Sheet Limitations

Nonmonetary assets are shown at adjusted original cost and not in terms of current value. Adjustments involve estimates. The estimates may be the best available; they may objectively made, fair, and relevant; and they may be verified as conforming with GAAP by a CPA's audit. But they are still estimates.

The balance sheet is an incomplete picture. There may be intangible items that have been acquired at considerable cost, and may have great future value, but accountants do not report them on the balance sheet as assets. These important intangibles are currently not reported because there is no generally agreed way to measure them fairly and objectively. One example would be the value of human capital in the firm, the team of trained employees and managers, who have learned to work together. Another example would be customer goodwill in response to past satisfactory experience or advertising. Such "non-reported assets" will be discussed more fully in Chapter 11.

Executory Items

Another example of something that may appear to be an unreported asset involves future sales to customers or future interest to be earned. When two individuals or firms have an agreement or contract and , with respect to some portion, neither party has performed, that portion is said to be executory. For example, assume your firm had received an order from a customer for 200 widgets at $10 each, 100 widgets for immediate delivery and 100 for delivery next year. Further assume that, because of a temporary stockout this week, you had delivered 40 widgets and only billed your customer for $400. In this situation, the balance of the order (160 widgets or $1600) to be delivered (performed) in the future would be executory. Your firm's balance sheet would show neither your future claim for $1,600 nor your future obligation to deliver 160 widgets—60 as soon as possible and 100 next year—since this portion of your contract would still be executory.[8]

Other examples of executory items that will not appear as assets on a balance sheet include future interest on notes receivable or other investments and future rental payments from tenants under ordinary operating leases.[9] Similarly, other examples of executory items that will not be included as liabilities are future interest on notes payable or other obligations and future rental payments to landlords under ordinary leases.

In addition to executory items, you should not expect to find items reflecting social benefits and social costs. These are some of the reasons:

- Society has not explicitly assigned the responsibility for such items to the particular firms.

- Financial accounting's role is to report the measurable economic events actually affecting the entity, not what might affect it.

- Even known benefits or obligations which cannot readily be quantified in financial terms are excluded from the statements. For example, the future benefits from advertising, employee training, and research-and-development activities are too subjective

---

[8] In a different situation, where your customer had paid in full inadvance, your accountant would include the $2,000 received in your cash balance and your obligation to complete matchingyour customer's performance as a $1,600 current liability (revenue collected in advance). In this case, no portion of the order would be executory. Under GAAP, executory claims against others are not considered to be assets since the claims are not enforceable until your firm performs.

[9] Capital leases are a partial exception and will be discussed further in Chapters 11 and 12.

to measure with any degree of reliability. Therefore, how could even more nebulous social benefits and costs be fairly quantified?

For the present, the balance sheet reveals all of the readily available resources owned or effectively controlled by the firm and all of its legally recognized existing liabilities. The resources you can expect to find on a balance sheet as assets will:

* Be in the form of properties, rights, or enforceable claims;

* Have been acquired through exchange transactions with others;

* Be capable of objective measurement in units of currency;

* Represent expected future benefits to the firm.

To reinforce your new knowledge of balance sheets, turn to the Statements of Financial Position for the Xerox Corporation and for the American Telephone and Telegraph Company reproduced in Appendix A. You have not yet been given an explanation for all the items shown, but you still should be able to recognize the similarity to Jones' balance sheet.

Chapter Overview

Based upon the material presented in this chapter, you should have a basic understanding of the balance sheet as prepared for proprietorships. You should be able to explain:

* The concepts of assets and equities;

* How equities include liabilities and owner's equity;

* The various alternatives for asset measurement and which alternatives accountants follow in financial statements prepared in accordance with GAAP.

* The various common specific asset and liability items which may appear on a balance sheet, what is included under each item, and generally how it is measured;

* The two valuation items or contra assets — allowance for doubtful accounts and accumulated depreciation, and the function or purpose of each;

* The classifications of assets and liabilities, their meaning, and their significance;

* Items that might be considered as assets and liabilities but which are not included as such on the balance sheet; and the reasons why they are excluded.

New Vocabulary and Concepts

Accounts payable
Accounts receivable
Accumulated depreciation
Adjusted original cost
Allowance for doubtful accounts
Assets
Balance sheet equality
Bond discount
Bond premium
Bonds payable
Book value
Business entities
Cash
Constant purchasing power dollars
Cost expiration
Credit sales
Current assets
Current capital lease obligations
Current costs
Current liabilities
Current notes payable
Current notes receivables
Deferred charges
Deferred income tax
Depreciation
Equities
Executory
Fair market value (at time of acquisition)
Going-concern assumption
Goodwill
Intangible and other assets
Interest payable

Inventory
Land
Leasehold improvements
Liabilities
Liquidity
Liquidation value
Long-lived assets
Long-term debt
Long-term investments
Marketable securities
Monetary items
Net assets
Net worth
Noncurrent capital lease obligations
Noncurrent notes payable
Notes payable
Operating cycle
Operating leases
Original cost
Owner's capital
Owner's equity
Prepaid items
Properties under capital lease
Property and equipment
Proprietorship
Straight-line depreciation
Supplies
Taxes payable
Unearned revenue
Wages payable

- The business entity and the going concern as defining the scope of a balance sheet;

- Reported assets as distinct from all things of value;

- Equities and the balance sheet equality;

- Categories of assets and equities;

- Basis for initial asset valuation;

- Adjusted cost and depreciation as basis for continuing asset valuation;

- Current vs. noncurrent classifications;

- Monetary vs. nonmonetary items

Review Questions

1. Why don't accountants use unadjusted original cost or liquidation prices as the fundamental basis for asset measurement?

2. a) What is the going-concern assumption? b) How does it affect asset measurement?

3. a) What is the entity convention? b) How does it affect the contents of financial statements?

4. a) What is the status of current costs or replacement costs as a basis for accounting asset measurement? b) Why haven't they been used in the regular financial statements?

5. How is general inflation and the consequent loss of purchasing power reflected in financial reports?

6. What is the difference between monetary and nonmonetary assets?

7. Why are nonmonetary items more difficult to value than monetary ones?

8. a) What is meant by depreciation? b) How is it shown on the balance sheet? c) What effect does it have on assets?

9. Why does the balance sheet balance?

10. Why is owner's equity referred to as a residual claim?

11. Describe the normal operating cycle.

12. What is the difference between current and noncurrent assets? Liabilities?

13. What two items properly classified as current assets will not be normally converted into cash within one year of the balance sheet date?

14. What is an example of an item properly classified as an asset, which is not legally owned by the firm?

15. Current liabilities are normally broken down into separate categories on what basis?

16. a) What are executory items? b) Are they included in financial statements? c) If not, why are executory items excluded?

17. What is the information content of a balance sheet? What are some things it can tell you?

Mini-Cases and Questions for Discussion

MC 2.1   Jack Silver is an elementary accounting student who, having understood the balance sheet equation to be assets = equities, maintains that it is impossible for total equities to ever be greater than total assets. Betty Hart disagrees. She says, "For a going concern, total liabilities will be less than total assets. Since owner's equity represents just the residual balance, total equities can and will equal total assets. However, many things can happen to a firm which will result in total liabilities exceeding total assets. If that happens, even with owner's equity down to zero, total equities could be greater than total assets."

"What could ever make total liabilities greater than total assets?" replied Jack. "After all, every time a firm borrows money, they have both a new asset and a new liability. How can liabilities ever become greater than assets?"

Who is correct? Could total assets ever become less than the amount of total liabilities, or, alternatively, could total liabilities be incurred in excess of total assets? If so, how? Would a balance sheet normally be prepared in such circumstances? Discuss.

MC 2.2   Mary Diamond, also an elementary accounting student, is enrolled in the course only because it is required. "I'm going to be a personnel major, and I can't see why or when I'll ever have to use a balance sheet after I complete this course," she says.

Prepare an explanation for Mary of how she will use balance sheets as a personnel officer and also in other required business courses. If you don't know, find out from other students or your instructor. Also you should be able to give at least one specific example of how understanding and using balance sheets will be valuable to Mary and each student in your class, once you know their intended careers. Try it.

MC 2.3   Are the following items properly included on the balance sheet as assets? Explain. If yes, at what amount should they be initially recorded and how should they be classified?
   a) The firm is leasing its current office. The lease has four more years to run. Under the lease terms, the firm has given the landlord, as a security deposit, $15,000 representing the last 90 days rent.
   b) A drug manufacturer has a special-purpose machine for manufacturing Zlotz. The machine is two years old, originally had an expected life of nine years, and originally cost $145,000. The firm believes it could recover $20,000 if the machine were sold for parts and scrap. The firm to date has accumulate $30,000 of depreciation related to this machine. Zlotz has just been declared unsafe by the Food and Drug Administration. No more can be manufactured and sold.
   c) The firm's president has just purchased a $10 "show" ticket on a particular horse in the sixth race at a local track. The race has not yet started. If the horse wins the race, he estimates the ticket will pay $50. If the horse "places," the ticket will pay $40. If the horse "shows," it will pay $25.
   d) The ABC Corporation has just hired a new president for a salary of $20,000 per month. The executive recruiter who located the new president and persuaded him to consider the firm receives the equivalent of one month's presidential salary as a fee.
   e) The firm has just purchased brochures costing $15,000, which it plans to distribute free as part of a major advertising campaign in two months.
   f) New building has just been purchased for $200,000. The amount of $20,000 cash and a 10-year promissory note for $180,000, plus normal interest, has been given to the seller. The note is secured by a mortgage agreement which provides that title does not pass to the buyer until the note is paid in full.
   g) A milk distributor receives, from a deceased widow's estate, a painting valued at $20,000. The widow's will provided the bequest in gratitude for the firm's milk which the widow's cats had enjoyed for many years. The painting is to be hung in the company's president's office.
   h) As an incentive to locate in the community and provide jobs, the firm has been given title to an acre of land on which it is constructing a factory building. The land is appraised at $120,000. It would normally be assessed for property tax purposes at $40,000, and property taxes would normally be $3,000 per year, at current rates. However, part of the incentive "package" provided a forgiveness of property taxes for the first ten years.

MC 2.4   Is each of the following items monetary or nonmonetary? Explain.

a) $500 deposited with the lessee as a cleaning deposit on a one- year lease.

b) $1,000 deposit with a lessee as security deposit, representing the last two months' rent on a three-year lease.

c) A share of common stock in the General Motors Corporation costing $60 and with a current market value of $70.

d) A $400 gift certificate good for one year at a local clothing store.

Essential Problems

EP 2.1   Mr. Smith is applying for a bank loan and must prepare a statement of personal net worth following the format given Exhibit 2.1. His possessions and debts as of 12/31/X9 are:

Personal possessions: Adjusted cost,	$ 500
Balance in personal bank account,	1,500
Amount owed on personal bills,	300
Balance of cash on hand in business,	100
Business accounts receivables,	200
Personal automobile: Original cost,	4,000
Estimated depreciation on the automobile,	2,000
Amount owed by business to suppliers,	400
Cost of merchandise on hand for sale,	800

Prepare a personal net worth statement as of 12/31/X9 for Mr. Smith to give his bank using adjusted cost valuation.

EP 2.2   Referring to the data in Problem 1 above, prepare a balance sheet in proper form for Mr. Smith's business. Remember the economic entity concept.

EP 2.3   Given the following data as of 12/31/X8 for the Jones Company, determine the amount of owner's capital in the business as of that date:

Total current assets	$400	Total current liabilities	$200
Total long-lived assets	$500	Total long-term debt,	$300

EP 2.4   For each of the following items, indicate by letter code whether it is:

(CA)   A current asset;
(LLA)   A long-lived asset item;
(C/A)   A Contra-Asset item which subtracts from assets;
(CL)   A current liability;
(LTD)   A long-term debt item.

Accounts payable	Cash
Account receivable	Copyrights
Accumulated depreciation	Equipment
Allowance for bad debts	Franchises
Bonds payable	Interest payable
Buildings	Inventory
Investments and fixtures	Office furniture and fixtures
Land	Patents
Leasehold improvements	Prepaid items
Marketable securities	Properties under capital lease
Notes payable (due within one year)	Supplies
Notes payable (due beyond one year)	Taxes payable
Notes receivable (due within one year)	Wages and salaries payable

EP 2.5   What are the six items commonly classified as current assets on most balance sheets?

EP 2.6   Assume you are comparing balance sheets of firms A and B and know that they are in the same business and that both use straight- line depreciation for long-lived assets. You see, for firm A: long-lived assets $300,000, accumulated depreciation $250,000, book value $50,000; and for firm B: long-lived assets $70,000, accumulated depreciation $20,000, book value $50,000. Assuming no inflation, which probably is the larger firm, the firm with greater capacity? Which firm probably has the newest equipment?

EP 2.7   Given that a particular firm had on its balance sheet current assets consisting of cash, accounts receivable, inventory, and prepaid items; and the balances of these items were cash $100, accounts receivable $400, inventory $600, and prepaid items $200; and that total current assets equaled $1,250; how much was the amount provided as an allowance for bad debts?

EP 2.8   Given the following accounts and their balances for the Johnson Company as of 12/31/X2, prepare the current assets portion of the firm's balance sheet in the proper order giving the subtotal for current assets.

Accounts receivable	$12,000	Inventory	$15,000
Allowance for bad debts	500	Marketable securities	5,000
Cash	3,000	Prepaid items	1,200
Current notes receivable	2,000	Supplies	800

EP 2.9   Given the following accounts and their balances for the Johnson Company as of 12/31/X2, prepare the current liability portion of the firm's balance sheet giving the subtotal for current liabilities.

Accounts payable	$ 7,000	Interest payable	$ 1,200
Current capital lease		Unearned revenue	2,400
obligations	1,500	Taxes payable	800
Current notes payable	600	Wages and salaries payable	1,600

EP 2.10   The following data (in thousands of dollars) are taken from the Whitney Company's balance sheet as of 12/31/X8. Complete the balance sheet in good form determining the missing amounts in the process.

Accounts payable	$ 250	Other current liabilities	?
Accounts receivable	420	Owners' capital	?
Accumulated depreciation	?	Supplies	$ 25
Building & equipment	400	Total assets	1,225
Cash	?	Total current assets	955
Inventory	475	Total current liabilities	?
Land	50	Total equities	?
Long-term debt	100	Total liabilities	400
		Total Property, Plant & Equip.	?

EP 2.11   Given the following information, prepare in good form a balance sheet for the Smith Company for the end of calendar year 19X5. Determine and include the correct amounts for prepaid items, accumulated depreciation on buildings, wages payable, owner's capital, and total equities.

Accounts payable	$ 125	Land	$ 250
Accounts receivable	340	Marketable securities	200
Accumulated depreciation		Note payable (due beyond	
on building	?	one year)	400
Accumulated depreciation		Owner's capital	?
on equipment	120	Prepaid items	?
Allowance for doubtful accts	40	Supplies	25
Buildings	425	Taxes payable	165
Cash	100	Total assets	2,350
Equipment	570	Total current assets	1,100
Intangibles	50	Total current liabilities	500
Interest payable	35	Total equities	?
Inventory	400	Total liabilities	900
Investments	150	Wages payable	?

EP 2.12   Given the following information as of 12/31/X5 (in thousands of dollars), prepare in good form a balance sheet for the Jones Company. Include correct amounts for accounts receivable, bonds payable, buildings, long-term investments, owner's capital, total assets, total current liabilities, total equities, and total liabilities.

Accounts payable	$ 28	Long-term investments	$?
Accounts receivable	?	Marketable securities	20
Accumulated depreciation		Noncurrent notes payable	5
on building	95	Owner's capital	300
Accumulated depreciation		Prepaid items	7
on equipment	105	Unearned revenue	11
Allowance for uncollectibles	4	Supplies	8
Bonds payable	?	Taxes payable	30
Buildings	?	Total assets	?
Cash	10	Total current assets	190
Current notes payable	14	Total current liabilities	?
Current notes receivables	6	Total equities	?
Deferred charges	25	Total liabilities	?
Equipment	210	Total long-term debt	105
Interest payable	9	Total property and	
Inventory	58	equipment	205
Land	15	Wages and salaries	
Leasehold improvements	16	payable	3

Supplementary Problems

SP   2.13   Mary Chin prepared this unaudited balance sheet data for her bookstore as of 12/31/X4:

Cash	$ 3,000	Accounts payable	$ 4,000
Receivables	6,000	Notes payable	6,000
Inventory	12,000		
Prepaid rent	1,200		
Equipment	5,000	Owner's equity	17,200
Total Assets	$27,200	Total Equities	$27,200

Mary also provided you with the following additional information:

- The $3,000 cash balance was taken from her firm's bank statement. On 12/31/X4, three checks totaling $270 had not yet cleared the bank, and currency amounting to $105 was in the firm's cash register.

- Receivables included a $2,000 personal loan that Mary had made to her brother. Previous experience had shown that two percent of year-end customer receivables eventually proved to be uncollectible.

- Inventory includes books that Mary had taken home for personal use, or had given to friends, that had a selling price of $300. Their costs had been $180.

- The prepaid rent was a security deposit made with the landlord representing the final month's rent under Mary's lease. Her lease ran through 19X6.

- The equipment represented the cost of bookstands and of the used cash register acquired on 1/1/X1. These items were expected to be no longer usable and to have a sale value of $200 at the time of the lease expiration.

- The $4,000 of accounts payable included a personal account of Mary's at a local clothing store for $210. She had not included the December utilities cost estimated at $115, as the bill had not been received by year-end.

- Notes payable included a $1,000 current bank loan to the firm, a $3,000 loan due on 3/1/X6 that Mary had used to purchase the store's equipment, and a $2,000 loan against Mary's personal car.

Prepare a balance sheet in good form for Mary's bookstore following GAAP.

SP   2.14   George Gonzales Record Shop's unaudited balance sheet assets as of 12/31/X6 were given as:

Cash	$ 7,000	Receivables	$ 9,000
Inventory	20,000	Supplies	2,000
Prepaid items	3,000	Leasehold improvement	6,000

As part of the audit, it is determined that:

- The cash balance includes in George's personal checking account of $1,240.

- The accounts receivable supporting detail indicated four accounts totaling $125 for which the most recent invoices had been returned marked "moved, left no forwarding address" by the post office.

- Inventory had been determined by taking beginning inventory of $15,000 (as of 1/1/X6), adding total purchases of records of $45,000, and then subtracting the cost of records actually sold to customers during the year — $40,000. A physical inventory revealed records on hand and unsold that had cost of $18,700.

- The $2,000 shown for supplies is the cost of all supplies purchased during the year. Supplies costing $400 were unused as 12/31/X6. The $3,000 prepaid item was the cost of a comprehensive insurance policy providing one year's coverage and acquired on 1/1/X6.

- The leasehold improvement represented $6,000 George had spent renovating his store just before opening for business on 1/1/X4. George's lease will terminate on 12/31/X9, and he does not anticipate that it will be renewed.

Required:

a) Following GAAP, what changes (if any) should be made in the amounts to be reported on George's 12/31/X6 balance sheet? Explain any changes that you feel appropriate.

b) What amount should be reported as total current assets?

c) If the firm's total liabilities as 12/31/X6 were $5,235, what was George's owner's equity?

d) What was the cost of the records apparently shoplifted by customers during the year?

3

Analyzing the
Balance Sheet

Chapter Preview

The objective of this chapter is to increase your understanding of the balance sheet and its usefulness for analyzing a firm's financial position. In this chapter, you can:

1. Determine the importance of solvency and liquidity to a firm;

2. Learn several balance sheet ratios that show the firm's relative liquidity;

3. Become familiar with the concepts of capital structure, net working capital, net working capital as funds, and the various sources of funds available to a firm.

4. Acquire several tools of balance sheet analysis that provide information concerning a firm's debt capacity and financial flexibility;

5. Become alert to the lack of uniformity in accounting and financial-analysis terminology, concepts, and practices;

6 Learn various methods of comparison useful in evaluating a company's financial position;

7. Understand the importance of two more accounting standards — consistency and materiality — to financial analysis.

The material in this chapter should reinforce the basic knowledge of balance sheet structure that you began building in Chapter 2.

Extending Credit to Customers

Put yourself in the role of Jack Sargent, sales and credit manager for the Acme Wholesale Supply Company. One of your salespeople has just come back into town with two very large orders, one from the Dilemma Company and one from the Rosy Company. Neither firm has ever purchased from you before. Each could be a valued customer. Both wish to purchase on account and you must decide whether to extend credit privileges to these firms. Along with other information, you obtain recent comparative balance sheets for both companies, which are reproduced in Exhibits 3.1 and 3.2. Assume that all other information is inconclusive, neither good nor bad. Based on their balance sheets, would you extend credit to these firms on their large initial orders? Can you get some idea from the balance sheets about how well these firms are managed? Do both appear to be able to pay future bills on time?

Before reading ahead for the answer, take the time to study Exhibits 3.1 and 3.2. You may assume, in this example, that Dilemma's order totals $40,000, Rosy's $30,000, and that both firms are in the same business and have approximately the same volume of sales. For each company, write down your decision on a piece of paper, along with notes as to your reasons. Be sure to note all of your reasons, pro and con. You will probably be pleasantly surprised how much you already understand! Before proceeding with your analysis, you should notice two things. First, the balance sheets are presented vertically, with equities below assets. This method of presentation is known as report or statement form. Second, you have balance sheet data for two years for each company. This will allow you to draw some tentative conclusions about directions in which each firm may be moving. Comparing data for the same firm for successive years is known as **trend analysis**. Comparing data between two different firms or between a firm and industry average data or norms is known as **comparative analysis**. You should also note in Exhibit 3.2 that data for the most recent year are in the first column, followed by the older data. This is common in financial reporting. You can make major errors if you don't check captions and assume that information runs left to right. Make your analysis before reading any further.

Exhibit 3.1

DILEMMA COMPANY

Comparative Balance Sheets
As of 12/31/X4 and 12/31/X3

Assets	19X4	19X3
Cash	$ 5,000	$ 20,000
Accounts receivable (net)	70,000	80,000
Inventory	35,000	95,000
Supplies	10,000	5,000
Total Current Assets	$ 120,000	$ 200,000
Property and equipment	830,000	830,000
Accum. depr. — prop. and equip.	(340,000)	(300,000)
Total Assets	$ 610,000	$ 730,000

Equities

	19X4	19X3
Current notes payable	$ 280,000*	$ 25,000
Accounts payable	15,000	160,000
Other current liabilities	5,000	10,000
Total Current Liabilities	$ 300,000	$ 195,000
Long-term debt	200,000	100,000
Total Liabilities	$ 500,000	$ 295,000
Owner's capital	110,000	435,000
Total Equities	$ 610,000	$ 730,000

* All to suppliers and all due within 60 days.

Exhibit 3.2

ROSY COMPANY

Comparative Balance Sheets
As of 12/31/X4 and 12/31/X3

Assets	19X4	19X3
Cash	$ 30,000	$ 25,000
Marketable securities	80,000	60,000
Accounts receivable (net)	60,000	50,000
Inventory	55,000	60,000
Supplies	3,000	2,800
Prepaid items	2,000	2,200
Total Current Assets	$ 230,000	$ 200,000
Land	35,000	35,000
Property and equipment	70,000	70,000
Accum. depr. — prop. and equip.	(35,000)	(30,000)
Total Assets	$ 300,000	$ 275,000
Equities		
Accounts payable	$ 40,000	$ 75,000
Other current liabilities	10,000	25,000
Total Current Liabilities	$ 50,000	$ 100,000
Long-term debt	0	75,000
Total Liabilities	$ 50,000	$ 175,000
Owner's capital	250,000	100,000
Total Equities	$ 300,000	$ 275,000

What did you decide about granting credit to the Rosy Company? Since all other information was neutral, most credit managers would find the Rosy Company picture almost too good to be true. How many of these good points did you find?

1. Even if Rosy were destroyed by fire January 1, 19X5 and lost all long-lived assets, inventory and receivable records; Rosy could still meet all of its obligations from cash and marketable securities. This would still be true if your $30,000 claim is included. At the end of 19X4, Rosy was certainly in an excellent position to pay bills. Trend analysis reveals that at the end of 19X3 Rosy was solvent. On 12/31/X4 Rosy's picture was even better. Unfortunately, few real companies are as "rosy."

2. Rosy could probably undertake more long-term debt. Proportionately, it has very little total debt. Only about 17 percent of total assets have been financed by creditors. There is no long-term debt at this time. Equities can be viewed as the claims on the firm's total assets. If the business should fail, a new creditor would have very little competition from other creditors in claiming Rosy's assets. Rosy would appear to be a good risk if it wanted a long-term loan.

3. Rosy also has a relatively small proportion of its assets tied up in noncurrent items. It could move very quickly into a different line of business if it were necessary to do so. It is in a favorable position to adapt to a changing world.

4. Finally, comparative analysis with Dilemma, reveals that Rosy is currently doing about the same volume of business with less that 1/10 of the investment in property and equipment.

The "dilemma" with the Dilemma Company is not yours or Jack Sargent's. It appears to be simply a question of how the firm can survive more than 60 days. Dilemma is a terrible credit risk. Admittedly, Dilemma's balance sheet is made extreme, to highlight the issues.

1. Without obtaining a large amount of new assets quickly, Dilemma will be unable to pay its existing debt. 19X3 is bad, and 19X4 is ridiculous!

2. Dilemma's prospect of borrowing money is terrible. The company is heavily in debt, with over 80 percent of its assets supplied by creditors. It is doubtful, in an actual business situation, that existing creditors would have ever allowed things to get so bad. It appears that other suppliers haven't been paid on time and have demanded interest-bearing promissory notes. There's a good chance that Dilemma is favoring you with a big order because no one else will take it. Trend analysis reveals that the extreme debt situation in 19X4 is even worse than in the previous year.

3. Dilemma appears heavily committed to its present type of business. Eighty percent of its capital is in long-lived assets. This fact is not necessarily undesirable; but it may make a firm less able to respond rapidly to changing market conditions.

4. It appears that Dilemma has substantial excess capacity. Compare Dilemma's investment in long-lived assets to Rosy's. Since both firms are doing about the same volume of business, something is wrong. Why does Dilemma have seven times as much tied up in capacity assets?

5. Another signal is the difference in inventory levels. The two firms are in the same business and doing about the same volume. However, Dilemma's inventory is $35,000 and Rosy's inventory is $55,000. There is an optimum amount of merchandise to have on hand for a given level of sales. Too much inventory 1) requires more storage space, 2) may result in spoilage, 3) runs the risk that some items may go out of style, and, 4) ties up money in unneeded merchandise. If you have too little inventory, you will lose sales because you are out of stock. If Rosy's inventory is about right, then Dilemma's stock is dangerously low. If Dilemma's inventory is

satisfactory, then Rosy has too much. Note the drastic difference in Dilemma's inventories for both years. Remember that balance sheets cannot provide you with all the answers, but they can often raise important questions. From your own analysis and the one above, you should have a feeling of satisfaction and perhaps amazement at the amount of information contained in the Dilemma's and Rosy's balance sheets. If so, this example served its purpose. Now you may continue with some of the important concepts and tools for analysis of balance sheets.

Importance of Solvency and Liquidity

Have you assumed that the first objective of a business is to make a profit? Some firms in the United States pursue this goal exclusively. It is possible for firms to fail even though growing and making a profit, if they cannot pay their bills. The ability to meet current obligations, when due, is known as **solvency**. The ability to get cash to avoid insolvency or for other purposes is **liquidity**.

Your primary objective is survival. Only if you survive can you graduate from college, contribute to society, make money, and do whatever you want to do with your life. Similarly, a company's primary objective is survival. Only if it survives can it earn profits. Survival in the short run for a business is liquidity. If it cannot meet its obligations with cash when due, its creditors can refuse to provide further support.

Simply stated: liquidity is the ability to write a check whenever necessary to meet your obligations. Cash and assets readily converted to cash and the ability to borrow additional funds relate to liquidity. Solvency relates to the ability to pay debts. An insolvent entity does not have cash to meet its financial commitments.

Suppose your firm's balance sheet revealed:

Assets		Equities	
Cash	$ 0	Wages payable	$ 10,000
Inventory	500,000	Other current liabilities	60,000
Land, buildings,		Long-term debt	0
and equipment	1,000,000		
Accumulated depreciation	(300,000)	Owner's Capital	1,130,000
Total Assets	$1,200,000	Total Equities	$1,200,000

You lack liquidity and are in trouble. Your firm has a sufficiently low proportion of debt to owners equity, so that you probably can raise the needed cash. But suppose you couldn't. Even if your creditors could wait until you sold some inventory, your employees cannot. If you are even temporarily insolvent and cannot meet the payroll, your employees will probably leave. Try to visualize how a growing, profitable firm can become insolvent. Suppose, in 19X5, your firm has a good volume of business and has the following balance sheet:

Assets			**Equities**	
Cash	$	10,000	Current liabilities	$ 95,000
Accounts receivable (net)		90,000	Long-term debt	105,000
Inventory		75,000		
Property and equipment (net)		125,000	Owner's Capital	100,000
Total Assets	$	300,000	Total Equities	$ 300,000

Customers enjoy using your products and you can double you business in the next six months. Try to project your balance sheet assets at twice the current volume of business:

- Cash $12,000 (*You would have a little more cash because of increased activity.*)

- Accounts receivable (net) $180,000 (*Twice the sales volume would mean at least twice the receivables.*)

- Inventory $125,000 (*You may not need to double your stock, but you would need more to facilitate doubling your sales volume.*)

- Property and equipment (net) $125,000 (*Note. This projection assumes you are presently operating with excess capacity. Otherwise you might have to add another $125,000 of property and equipment.*)

- Total Assets $442,000

To double your volume in this example, you would need $442,000 of assets in your business even if you wouldn't require more capacity assets.[1] You only have $300,000. Where are you going to get the other $142,000? Your suppliers will be providing a small portion of this by providing more goods and services on account. The remainder can only come from new long-term borrowing, from new investment supplied by you, or from profits retained in the business. If you are making enough profit each month and can leave it in the business, or otherwise raise $142,000 for the business, then doubling your volume can be accommodated.

If you cannot obtain all of the $142,000 and you still try to double your profitable volume, you will probably run out of cash and become insolvent. Potential creditors are not eager to make loans to firms that are insolvent or close to insolvency.

Subsequent chapters will cover the flows of assets and liabilities that bring about a cash shortage.

---

[1] Do **not** attempt to use the exact proportions of his projection as guides for any other situation. It is purely an example. In managerial accounting and financial management courses, you will learn forecasting techniques for necessary and effective cash management.

Overlapping Terminology

Before proceeding, several terms that overlap in meaning and are often misused require clarification. "Solvency" refers to the ability to pay (legal obligations) when due. An insolvent firm cannot pay these bills. When a court has declared a firm legally insolvent, it is "bankrupt."

"Liquidity" is a broader term also referring to the ability to make cash payments. Liquidity refers to the ability to get cash. A firm with very little liquidity might be solvent after selling off other assets. A firm with adequate liquidity would not only be solvent, but would have sufficient additional cash or ready cash sources to enable management to take advantage of profitable opportunities.

Not only is solvency a minimum of survival for a firm, but sufficient liquidity is essential to a continuing successful operation. The balance sheet analyst is therefore first interested in checking the firm's degree of liquidity. Should liquidity be insufficient to maintain solvency, all other financial statement analysis would probably be irrelevant.

Measures of Liquidity and Solvency

Concepts and ratios commonly used to evaluate liquidity and solvency include: **Net Working Capital**, **Current Ratio**, and **Quick Ratio**. Since there is overlap between the terms of liquidity and solvency only the term liquidity will be used.

Net Working Capital

Total current assets (CA) minus total current liabilities (CL) is known as Net Working Capital (NWC). It is viewed as one indicator of a firm's liquidity. However, when comparing different firms, the amount of working capital may prove difficult to interpret. Suppose you were comparing the relative liquidity of firms, P and Q, and wanted to know which firm is more liquid.

Net Working Capital = Total Current Assets – Total Current Liabilities

You have the following information:

	P	Q
Total Current Assets	$ 37,086	$ 377,186
less Total Current Liabilities	14,876	251,793
Net Working Capital	$ 22,210	$ 125,393

It is more revealing to convert these dollar amounts to simple ratios or proportions.

Current Ratio

A commonly used liquidity ratio that simply expresses working capital in relative terms is known as the current ratio.[2] It is calculated by dividing total current assets by total current liabilities:

$$\text{Current ratio} = \frac{\text{Total Current Assets}}{\text{Total Current Liabilities}}$$

$$\text{Current ratio for Firm P} = \frac{37,086}{14,876} = 2.49 \text{ to } 1$$

$$\text{Current ratio for Firm Q} = \frac{377,186}{251,793} = 1.50 \text{ to } 1$$

In calculating and using ratios, you are using a rough indicator rather than a precise instrument. It would serve no purpose to know that your body temperature was 101.276543 degrees. A thermometer which would give you such a reading would be rather expensive. Knowing you have a fever of about 101, is adequate. Likewise, balance sheet ratios are usually rounded.

What does the ratio reveal? What is a "normal" current ratio? If a current ratio is less than 1 to 1, the firm does not have enough current assets to cover its existing current obligations. A ratio of 1 to 1 or up to 1.60 to 1 is pretty risky, since not all current assets are usually in the form of cash, and it may take months for them to be turned into cash. A ratio of 2 to 1 is generally fairly safe. In this example, P is adequately solvent. Although Q has more than 5 times the net working capital as P, it is considerably less solvent.

Historically a good, safe level was often defined as at least 2 to 1. With today's better cash-management techniques, 1.70 or above may be satisfactory. However, any generalization cannot be accurate for all types of industries. Service industries with no significant inventories can operate with a much lower current ratio. The best standard for comparison purposes is the current ratio of other successful firms in the same industry and comparing this year's ratios with those of previous years.

---

[2] The current ratio is sometimes called the working capital ratio.

Quick Ratio

The current ratio is helpful, but is only a crude measure of liquidity.

Would you consider Company Z as being safe with the following current items?

*Cash	$ 1,000	Accounts payable	$ 8,000
*Marketable securities	0	Wages payable	40,000
*Receivables (net)	2,000	Other current liabilities	2,000
Inventory	70,000		
Supplies	10,000		
Prepaid items	17,000		
Total Current Assets	$ 100,000	Total Current Liabilities	$ 50,000

* Current Monetary assets

The current ratio of Company Z is an apparently safe 2 to 1. But the company appears to be in trouble. This example is deliberately extreme.

For fun, you can make it even worse. Imagine that the balance sheet is dated January 31, that Z is in the party decorations business, and that all of the inventory represents Halloween, Christmas, and New Year's items. Would you like to be one of Z's employees? To overcome this problem with the current ratio, another more rigorous ratio is used. This is the quick ratio or, the acid-test ratio. This ratio compares only the current monetary assets with current liabilities.

$$\text{Quick ratio} = \frac{\text{Current Monetary Assets}}{\text{Current Liabilities}}$$

$$\text{Quick ratio for Company Z} = \frac{3,000}{50,000} = 0.06 \text{ to } 1$$

Remember that **current monetary assets** include cash and definite commitments of specific amounts of cash to be received within one year. Normally, current monetary assets include cash, marketable securities, and current receivables.

A quick ratio of 1 to 1 or greater is generally safe. Below 1:1 may indicate problems. The Z Company's quick ratio would be 0.06 to 1, which clearly highlights its crisis.

Equities: Sources of Assets

To further analyze balance sheets, you will need to see how these statement provide information on the sources of the assets invested in a business. Study the balance sheet given below. Of the $390,000 of total assets in the business, how much was supplied by the owner? How much by long-term creditors? How much by short-term creditors?

Assets		Equities	
Total Current Assets	$150,000	Total Current Liabilities	$ 75,000
Total Long-lived		Total Long-term debt	125,000
Assets (net)	240,000	Owner's Capital	190,000
Total Assets	$390,000	Total Equities	$390,000

The equities represent the sources of total assets. Of the $390,000 of total invested in the business, $75,000 came from short-term creditors, $125,000 came from long-term creditors, and $190,000 represents the owner's investment. Total assets in a business can come from three sources.

First, short-term creditors commit goods, services, and occasionally cash to the firm for a very short period, usually 30 days. However, as accounts are being paid, new goods and services are being obtained on account. So, even though each individual investment is short-term, the revolving effect results in the total amount of current liabilities representing a fairly stable commitment.

Long-term creditors are a second possible source of capital. Long-term creditors commit cash or long-lived assets in exchange for interest-bearing obligations. The amount of total assets supplied through noncurrent liabilities is often fairly permanent because maturing long-term debt is often refinanced with new debt.

Owners provide the other two sources. An owner can invest additional amounts in the firm. Also, if the firm is profitable, the owner can increase the firm's assets by not withdrawing profits from the business. Profits and withdrawals and their effect on the balance sheet will be discussed in Chapter 4.

Net Working Capital and Capital Structure

You understand that equities are sources of the capital resources (assets) in the business and that short-term creditors (current liabilities) provide a portion of current assets required in the business. New working capital is simply the amount of net current assets in the firm, or the amount of total current assets not supplied by current creditors. A business that has $80,000 of total current assets and $35,000 of total current liabilities, therefore, is said to have $45,000 of net working capital.

The concept of net working capital has several uses. As cited earlier it is a measure of solvency in absolute terms — the current ratio expressed as a difference in amount rather than a ratio. As such, it can be incorporated in loan agreements, where the creditor is concerned that the firm will maintain adequate solvency to protect the creditor's investment. The loan agreement might simply require that, should net working capital fall below a specified dollar amount, the loan becomes immediately due and payable.

Net working capital is also a convenient resource grouping for predicting cash flows and the amount of the additional cash needed in the firm. Although you have seen that, in extreme cases, adequate net working capital may still not guarantee sufficient cash to meet immediate current liabilities, generally net working capital will either cycle into cash or else reduce the necessity of future cash outlays (for supplies and prepaid items) within the firm's normal operating cycle. as a long-term measure of adequate financing, the level of net working capital often proves a better indicator of future solvency than the amount of cash on hand at a particular point in time.[3]

Net working capital is so commonly used as the basis for long-term solvency management, that the terms **funds** is now generally used to mean net working capital rather than just cash. Be careful when you read "additional funds" to visualize additional net working capital and not just additional cash.

Referring back to the earlier example of the need for additional resources to finance a doubled level of volume, you were actually forecasting needs for additional funds. Remember you projected requirements for an additional $142,000 of current assets (cash, receivables and inventory in this illustration) and you anticipated that only a portion of these additional current assets would be supplied by increased current liabilities. The balance would represent additional requirements for funds or net working capital.

Diagram 3.1

TOTAL ASSETS	=	TOTAL EQUITIES

Current Assets:	Current Liabilities:
Long-Lived Assets:	Long-Term Debt:
	Owner's Equity:

[3] To insure solvency, most firms will separately plan or budget their cash flows on a day-to-day basis as part of internal financial management. this cash management activity is independent of the financial statements, and is usually covered in managerial accounting or financial management courses.

If a firm needs additional funds, what are its possible sources? A short-term loan (current liability) is not the answer. The result of a short-term loan would be increased cash and increased current liabilities — no change in net working capital and therefore no additional funds. To see the possible sources of funds available to a firm, first look at **Balance Sheet Diagram** 3.1.

Diagram 3.2

Smith Company Condensed Balance Sheet as of 12/31/XX

Current Assets:	$35,000	**Current Liabilities:**	$15,000
		Long-Term Debt:	18,000
Long-Lived Assets:	40,000	**Owner's Equity:**	42,000
Total Assets	$75,000	**Total Equities**	$75,000

Diagram 3.3

Smith Company Capital Structure as of 12/31/XX

Net Working Capital:	$20,000	**Long-Term Debt:**	$18,000
Long-Lived Assets:	40,000	**Owner's Equity:**	42,000
Long-Term Assets	$60,000	**Long-Term Equities**	$60,000

Balance Sheet Diagram 3.2 shows the balance sheet, in summary form, of the Smith Company as of 12/31/XX. Now compare Balance Sheet Diagram 3.3 with 3.2. What is the only difference? In Balance Sheet Diagram 3.3, the amount of Smith's resources (assets) supplied through short-term financing (by current creditors) has been eliminated along with the equivalent current liabilities. What remains, in summary form, is known as the **capital structure** of the firm. A firm's capital structure consists of its long-term investments — by long -term creditors and owners.[4]

Different Meanings of the Terms "Capital" and "Investment"

Before proceeding, you should pause and reflect on the many potentially confusing uses of the words "capital" and "investment". Historically, the term capital was restricted to owner's equity as in proprietor's capital. It used to refer only to that residual equity claim. Common usage of working capital or net working capital referring to an asset eliminated the owner's equity limitation. Also the term capital assets is often used synonymously with long-lived or noncurrent assets. Capital generally refers to all assets or resources invested in the business, although more commonly to the long-term assets invested — net working capital plus capital (long-lived) assets. Although the firm's capital structure consists of its long-term assets and their sources — long-term debt and owner's equity — the term primarily refers to the sources side.

    The term investment and the term equity originally referred only to owner's investment and owner's equity. With the realization that all assets are invested/committed to the firm by someone, investment (and investor) now covers both creditor investment and owner investment. Paralleling this expansion of meaning, the term equity now covers both creditor equities (liabilities) and owner's equities.

Measures of Capital Structure and Financial Flexibility

As you can see in Balance Sheet Diagram 3.3, if a firm needs additional funds immediately, the only two possible outside sources would be additional long-term debt, or additional owner investment. In any firm, these are the only two possible "outside" sources of funds. (Remember that funds are defined as net working capital and not as just cast.) Additional funds could also be obtained from "inside" the firm either through sale of long-lived assets or through owners reinvesting (or not withdrawing) funds earned in future operations of the business. If long-lived assets were sold for their value shown, they would disappear from the balance sheet and the current assets (normally cash) would increase without any increase in current liabilities. Net working capital or funds would thus be increased. Two measures of potential outside sources are **Long-term Debt Ratio** and **Asset Composition Ratio**.

---

[4] Since the capital structure of the firm implies, by common usage, a long-term commitment, the term "long-term capital structure" would be redundant.

Long-term Debt Ratio

As you have seen, maintaining adequate liquidity may require raising additional funds from both long-term creditors and owners. The availability of funds from long-term creditors is dependent upon the firm's **debt capacity**. A firm's debt capacity can be thought of as the proportion of its assets that could be financed by debt. This will vary for different firms in different industries, and upon the past performance of the firm's management.

Assume your firm obtained a short-term bank loan of $100,000.

	Before Loan	Loan		After Loan
Total Current Assets	$150,000	+ 100,000	=	$250,000
Total Current Liabilities	100,000	+ 100,000	=	200,000
Net Working Capital	$ 50,000			$ 50,000

A convenient measure of long-term debt capacity is the long-term debt ratio. It is determined by dividing long-term debt by the sum of long-term debt and owner's equity.[5]

$$\textbf{Long-term debt ratio} = \frac{\textbf{Total Long-term Debt}}{\textbf{Total Long-term Debt + Owner's Equity}}$$

or

$$\textbf{Long-term debt ratio} = \frac{\textbf{Total Liabilities} - \textbf{Total Current Liabilities}}{\textbf{Total Equities} - \textbf{Total Current Liabilities}}$$

This form of the debt ratio will always result in a number less than one expressing that proportion of assets currently financed by long-term creditors. For example, the Smith firm's long-term debt ratio would be 0.300:

$$\text{Long-term debt ratio} = \frac{\$18,000}{\$60,000} = 0.300 = 30\%$$

Indicating that the firm's capital structure currently involved 30 percent debt and 70 percent owner financing.

---

[5] Unfortunately, there is no agreement among analysts on the precise components of the debt ratio. Throughout this text, Total Long-Term Debt/Total Long-Term Debt + Owners' Equity will be used. Variations include: Total Liabilities/Total Equities, Total Liabilities/Owners' Equity, and Total Long - Term Debt/Owners' Equity. Any of these alternatives, consistently applied and interpreted can signal similar proportionate debt information.

A firm's theoretical capacity for additional long-term debt can be calculated. Suppose you wish to determine the amount of funds that Smith could obtain from additional long-term borrowing if the capacity for similar firms, expressed as a long-term debt ratio, was 40%.

At debt capacity for this firm, the new total amount of long-term debt ($18,000 + X) would equal 40 percent of the total of long-term debt and owner's equity ($42,000 + 18,000 + X). Expressed as an equation, this relationship would be:

$$\frac{\$18,000 + X}{\$60,000 + X} = .400$$

Solving for X would indicate that the firm could borrow $10,000 of additional funds and still be within its debt capacity.

There is no ideal long-term debt ratio for all firms, since different types of business involve different risks. There are, however, averages for particular industries. Also, the long-term debt ratio is interpreted differently than the current and quick ratios. The higher it is, the more risky the firm.

Asset Composition Ratio

In addition to funds from long-term creditors or owners, one internal source of funds for a firm could be from the sale of long-lived assets. However, a going concern could hardly afford to sell its fixed assets, and still remain in business. So, the relative proportions of a firm's investment in net working capital versus long-lived assets can be of considerable interest to existing and potential investors. For instance, if working capital is a high proportion of assets, it might provide more attractive security or collateral for a loan. If you were making a loan to a firm wouldn't you prefer readily collectible current receivables or readily saleable merchandise or supplies, instead of property and equipment which might not be easily convertible into cash?

The relative liquidity of the firm's assets is an indication of the firm's ability to change with the times. Over a period of years, consumer tastes and industry's products change. It has been estimated that over 75 percent of items on the market today did not exist twenty years ago. A firm with a high percentage of its resources in net working capital can "move" more readily into new products or new lines of business. A firm with a high percentage of its assets in long-lived assets is less flexible. Firms which are in capital intensive industries (high amounts of Property, Plant and Equipment) like railroads will have less flexibility than firms in services industries. There is no commonly recognized ratio for reflecting financial flexibility. The most logical ratio, and probably the one used intuitively by most analysts, would be the Asset Composition Ratio:

$$\text{Asset composition ratio} = \frac{\text{Net Working Capital}}{\text{Net Working Capital} + \text{Long-lived Assets}}$$

OR

$$\text{Asset composition ratio} = \frac{\text{Total Current Assets} - \text{Total Current Liabilities}}{\text{Total Assets} - \text{Total Current Liabilities}}$$

The higher this ratio, the more liquid would be the firm's assets. In the case of the Rosy Company for 19X4 (Exhibit 3.2) the asset composition ratio would be:

$$\frac{\$180,000}{\$250,000} = 0.720$$

Other Balance Sheet-Related Ratios

There are several other ratios that are also important in assessing liquidity and debt capacity as well as balance-sheet-related ratios and percentages that are important to the measurement of a firm's performance and efficiency. All of these additional tools incorporate data from other financial statements to which you have not yet been sufficiently exposed. Chapter 13 introduces these additional ratios after you become familiar with more detailed accounting information in other financial statements.

Lack of Consensus

Perhaps your most difficult problem in learning financial accounting, is the lack of consensus on terminology and concepts. As you learn accounting terminology, you will find that many different terms are used interchangeably for the same thing. You will also discover that GAAP allow alternative treatments by different firms for the same event.

This lack of standardization results from the fact that accounting statements were prepared and analyzed for centuries before any attempt at standardization. As GAAP evolve accountants dislike specifying one single term or reporting practice; especially when other terms have been standard in certain industries for many years. Therefore, you must be constantly alert to the varying interpretations of many terms. When you encounter specific terms such as working capital, capital, or equity, or when you are thinking of using ratios calculated by someone else, it is advisable to check the definition or formula used.

Standards for Comparison

In analyzing financial statements, you must determine the basis for what is desirable and undesirable. Available standards for comparison come from trend analysis and comparative analyses.

Trend analysis involves studying the same firm over a period of months or years. In trend analysis, one is usually limited to the conclusion that conditions are either better, unchanged, or worse. A particular item could be worse than the previous year and still be the best in the industry.

To have an adequate basis of evaluation, comparative analysis is desirable. Comparative analysis involves comparing data from one firm to that of similar firms or to industry averages. Common size statements, statements where the numbers have been converted to a percentage of Total Assets are useful for this analysis.

Each type of analysis has its limitations and dangers. To establish a trend, you need data for several years. But even if such data is readily available, firms change their activities over time, and data from five years ago could be irrelevant to today's world. Also, to make a valid comparison, you need other companies in the same industry. It is difficult to compare details of company D with company E if D's business includes making tractors, making hair shampoo, and producing TV movies, while E makes tractors, runs large produce farms, and owns a professional basketball team.[6] As you can see, statement analysis has characteristics of a highly specialized and intuitive art.

Consistency

It should be obvious that if certain assets are included on one year's balance sheet but omitted from the next, trend or comparative analysis could be limited. Similar difficulties could exist if particular items were measured one way one year and another way the next. In Chapters 7 and 8, you will discover that GAAP allow different approaches to measurement and reporting. This can result in significantly different amounts for similar assets. Inventory and fixed assets, which often represent more than half of a firm's assets, are subject to these varying measurements. If a firm could elect one measurement option one year and a different one in the following year, the results would be misleading.

Read again the auditor's opinions contained in Appendix A. Note the opinions specifically state that the "standards applied and accounting practices followed" are consistent with prior years statement preparation. If a change is desirable, GAAP require that the change be highlighted in the opinion to alert the user. Also the effect of the change — the difference in results as between the new way and the old way, must be disclosed in the footnotes. If there is a necessary departure from **consistency** and the effect distorts trend analysis, most firms will also provide data for the prior five or ten years, restated to the new basis.

---

[6] To reduce such difficulties, GAAP provide for disclosure of certain supplementary information on separate segments of diversified firms.

Materiality

While being introduced to basic constraints underlying all GAAP, you should be aware of another principle known as **materiality**. Accountants use the word "material" to mean "significant." Material or significant is used in the sense that amounts are said to differ materially if the result may cause a financial statement user to make a different business decision. The principle of materiality merely focuses accountants' activities and reporting standards on items which have a significant impact on the statement user's decisions and interpretations. It implies that details of trivial and inconsequential items should not clutter up the financial statements.

The application of materiality can be readily perceived with an example involving thumbtacks. Suppose your firm has a bulletin board and you purchase a box of thumbtacks for 75 cents. The thumbtacks clearly are owned and have future value; therefore they qualify as an asset. Except for occasional loss or bending, the thumbtacks take a long time to lose their usefulness. Therefore, they wouldn't be a current asset. When the thumbtacks costing 75 cents are acquired should a new long-lived asset — thumbtacks — be recorded and shown on the balance sheet?

Under GAAP, cash would be reduced by 75 cents, but the new "asset" would be ignored as not material. The 75 cents would be considered to have been used up, and owner's capital would be reduced.

Materiality can be easily understood. However, determination is more difficult in practice. A simple test for materiality is the "10% rule". For example, would a cash shortage of $500 at the end of the day be material for a retailer? If the total cash collected for the day was $350,000, then the answer is no (350,000 x .10 > 500). If total collections were $3,500, then it would be material (3,500 x .10 < 500).

As another example, suppose a particular small manufacturer had, in addition to land and a factory building, factory equipment costing $30,000 and office furniture and fixtures costing $25,000. Clearly, both groups are material to the small firm, valued at $150,000, and probably should be separately disclosed on the balance sheet. But what if the manufacturer were very large, with factory equipment costing $17,000,000 and only $25,000 of office assets? Most accountants would probably not disclose the $25,000 separately. Instead, equipment would be shown as $17,025,000. GAAP have no precise guidelines for materiality. Materiality is a matter of judgement and is determined by the firm's accountant.

Affirmatively Misleading Detail

Earlier, in the discussion of balance sheet ratios, it as pointed out that computation to many decimal places is often wasteful effort. Excessive detail may do something worse than waste time and effort; it may be affirmatively misleading. That is, it may imply to the user a false degree of accuracy. Think about depreciation. Assume that your firm purchased for $6,113 a truck with a five-year useful life and which you expect to sell for

$1,012 at the end of five years. You elect to depreciate the truck in approximately even amounts each year. At the end of the second year the truck is reported at:

Equipment	$ 6,113.00
Less accumulated depreciation	(2,040.40)[7]

This would be arithmetically accurate but misleading. Depreciation is only an estimate, and $2,040.40 implies nonexistent accuracy. To report depreciation rounded to $2,000 might be preferable.

Similarly, although accounting records are kept in precise numbers, for reporting data on financial statements, accountants always round cents to the nearest dollar. Large firms, round to the nearest thousand-dollar amount. This practice is indicated in the heading by "(000 omitted)." Rounding does not imply sloppiness or inability to calculate. Rounding reminds the user that the numbers are estimates. In this text, wherever practical, problems are designed to come out even in order to avoid such difficulty. If you are required to perform a specific calculation to demonstrate your competence in using a formula, carry it to two decimals. But if you are preparing a statement, beware of excessive detail on estimated items. Be sure to ascertain your instructor's standards for your examinations.

Chapter Overview

From the material covered in this chapter, you should be able to:

- Identify the various contributors of capital to the firm;
- Explain the meaning and importance of solvency, liquidity, and debt capacity to a business;
- Calculate and interpret balance sheet analysis tools, including the current, quick, and long-term debt ratios, and the asset composition ratio;
- Define net working capital and describe several of its uses;
- Explain what is meant by a firm's capital structure;
- Discuss, with examples, the difficulties inherent in the lack of uniformity in accounting and financial-analysis terminology, concepts and practices; and describe how these inconsistencies arose;
- Define and give examples of the significance and application of the GAAP principles of consistency and materiality.

---

[7] A $6,113 cost minus $1,012 estimated recovery equals $5,101 to be allocated over the five year useful life. A precise annual allocation would be $5101 divided by 5, or $1,020.20.

New Vocabulary and Concepts

Affirmatively misleading details	Funds
Asset composition	Liquidity
Asset composition ratio	Long-term debt ratio
Balance sheet diagram	Materiality
Capital structure	Monetary assets
Comparative analysis	Net working capital
Consistency	Quick ratio
Current ratio	Solvency
Debt capacity	Trend analysis

• Equities disclose both claims against and sources of assets;

• The significance of solvency, debt capacity, and liquidity to a firm;

• The reasons that the constraints of consistency and materiality are part of GAAP.

• Net Working Capital = Current Assets - Current Liabilities

• Current Ratio $= \dfrac{\text{Current Assets}}{\text{Current Liabilities}}$

• Quick Ratio $= \dfrac{\text{Current Monetary Assets}}{\text{Current Liabilities}}$

• Long-Term Debt Ratio $= \dfrac{\text{Long-term debt}}{\text{Long-term debt} + \text{Owner's Equity}}$

• Asset Composition Ratio $= \dfrac{\text{Net working capital}}{\text{Net working capital} + \text{Long-lived assets}}$

Review Questions

1. What is the significant difference between the "horizontal" and the "vertical" (report or statement format) presentation of balance sheets?

2. When accounting information for two successive years is shown on a financial statement, which year is usually shown first?

3. What is the first objective of a business organized with the intention of making a profit?

4. (a) Why is maintaining solvency so important to a business? (b) What are the risks of insolvency?

5. (a) What are the advantages of liquidity? (b) How does liquidity differ from solvency?

6. (a) What does the current ratio measure? (b) Is it a good indicator of liquidity? (c) of solvency? (d) How does it differ from the quick ratio?

7. Explain how a firm experiencing increasing profitable sales can involuntarily go out of business, i.e., can fail.

8. What is a reasonably safe quick ratio for the average company?

9. Explain how a current ratio can appear adequate even though a firm may be facing insolvency.

10. (a) What is net working capital and how is it determined? (b) What is its significance?

11. (a) What is a firm's capital structure? (b) How does the firm's capital structure reveal the only two outside sources of funds?

12. (a) What are the two "outside" sources of funds for a firm? (b) What are two "inside" sources of funds for a firm? (c) Why can't a new short-term loan be a source of funds?

13. (a) What is meant by a firm's debt capacity? (b) How can it be measured?

14. (a) What ratio is commonly used to measure liquidity? (b) Explain how this ratio provides a measure or indication of liquidity.

15. What is the difference between trend analysis and comparative analysis?

16. What is consistency?

17. How could consistency make your job of trend analysis easier, while at the same time providing no help to a possible real difficulty you may encounter in performing comparative analysis?

18. (a) What is materiality? (b) Explain how materiality may differ between two firms.

19. Give an example of something that might be affirmatively misleading.

20. Describe a reporting practice which accountants follow to avoid being affirmatively misleading.

Mini-Cases and Questions for Discussion

MC 3.1 The Sharp Company's fiscal year ended on March 31. The firm's current and quick ratios had been averaging 1.52 and 0.84 respectively. Its long-term debt ratio had been 0.421. Relevant industry "norms" were 1.81, 0.92, and 0.312 for these ratios. During March, the firm made a concerted effort to collect receivables, with the result that they were unusually low. The firm practically stopped all purchases of new merchandise during the month and, by month end, inventory was abnormally low. Sales to customers for the first week in April were included with March data. The firm explained that these sales would have been made in March if it hadn't been for bad weather. On April 4th some equipment costing $400,000 ($50,000 down and the balance covered by a five-year promissory note) was picked up at the suppliers. This equipment had been badly needed since the first of the year. It had been available for pickup since March 10.

    a)   What was the company trying to accomplish?

    b)   Why was it taking these actions?

    c)   As an investor, would you like the firm's auditor to report any of these occurrences as exception in the opinion? Which events and why?

MC 3.2 The Klute Company had Current Assets of $200,000 and Current Liabilities of $40,000. It also had an outstanding loan agreement which provided that "$100,000 of net working capital shall be Maintained." The firm considered purchasing some new equipment costing $80,000 for cash. Could it do this without violating the loan agreement? Discuss the issues.

MC 3.3 The following information is available:

Fairfax Company Balance Sheet
as of 12/31/X2

Assets			Equities		
Cash	$	100	Current notes payable	$	120
Marketable securities		50	Accounts payable		250
Current notes receivable		25	Unearned revenue		80
Accounts receivable (net)		200	Total Current Liabilities	$	450
Total Current Assets	$	375	Long-term debt		350
Total long-lived assets		2,025	Total Liabilities	$	800
			Owner's Capital		1600
Total Assets	$	2,400	Total Equities	$	2,400

a) Was the Fairfax Company's quick ratio a reasonably safe 1.07 or a potentially dangerous 0.83 ? Discuss the issue.

b) Four different analysts have determined Fairfax's long-term debt ratio to be as follows:

Analyst 1: 0.333   Analyst 2: 0.500
Analyst 3: 0.150   Analyst 4: 0.222

They each claim that they are correct. Is this possible? Discuss.

MC 3.4 The current and quick ratios for the Jinx Company as of 12/31/X2 were 2.40 and 1.22. Six
months later the firm was insolvent and went into receivership. How could this happen? If it
could happen, what is the value of ratio analysis? Discuss.

MC 3.5   Paul and Carol were studying two balance sheets from two different companies: Company F and Company G (see summary data below). Carol says, "Company F looks as if it may have trouble staying in business. Most of the assets have been borrowed from creditors and will have to be repaid. In fact, the equivalent of 85 percent of the existing assets will have to be repaid to creditors within a year, and only 25 percent of the existing assets are readily convertible to cash within a year."

Paul replies, "I don't see it that way at all. To me, it looks as though Company F is much safer than Company G. "After all, it has more than twice as many assets. Company F has $100,000 of assets which will more than cover the $85,000 of current liabilities. Also, to protect itself, I am sure Company F had arrangements long before the balance sheet date to refinance most of its current debt on a long-term basis just in case."

Balance Sheet Summary Data	Company F	Company G
Assets:		
Total Current Assets	$ 25,000	$ 30,000
Total Long-lived Assets	75,000	10,000
Total Assets	$ 100,000	$ 40,000
Equities:		
Total Current Liabilities	$ 85,000	$ 15,000
Total Long-term Debt	5,000	15,000
Total Liabilities	$ 90,000	$ 30,000
Total Owner's Equity	10,000	10,000
Total Equities	$ 100,000	$ 40,000

Which of these opposing views is more nearly correct? Can you identify and clarify the misconceptions held by the person who was incorrect? Discuss.

Essential Problems

EP 3.1   Given the following information for the Pamela Company and the Paul Company:

a) Which company was more solvent as of 19X3? Explain.

b) Did either firm have a solvency problem as of the end of 19X3? If so, which? Explain.

c) Which company had more apparent debt capacity and liquidity as of the end of 19X3? Explain.

	19X4	19X3
Pamela Company		
Current ratio	1.88	1.75
Quick ratio	1.24	1.19
Long-term debt ratio	0.133	0.360
Asset composition ratio	0.404	0.299
Paul Company		
Current ratio	2.61	1.22
Quick ratio	1.45	0.54
Long-term debt ratio	0.302	0.154
Asset composition ratio	0.204	0.295

EP 3.2 Using the data provided above for the Pamela Company and the Paul Company:

a) Which company was more solvent as of 19X4?

b) Which company most significantly improved its solvency position during 19X4?

c) Did either firm have a possible solvency problem as of the end of 19X4? If so, which?

d) Which company had more apparent debt capacity and liquidity as of the end of 19X4?

e) Which company improved its apparent debt capacity during 19X4?

EP 3.3 Data selected from the balance sheet for the Dowd Company are presented below. Using these data, calculate the following ratios and percentages for the year 19X4:

a) Current ratio.

b) Quick ratio.

c) Long-term debt ratio.

d) Asset composition ratio.

e) Assuming that, in Dowd's industry, a long-term debt ratio of 0.25 is acceptable, does Dowd have some available debt capacity as of the end of 19X4.

f) How much cash could Dowd probably borrow on a long-term basis without much difficulty at the end of 19X4 if all non-balance-sheet considerations were satisfactory to potential creditors?

DOWD COMPANY SELECTED BALANCE SHEET DATA

Assets:	19X5	19X4
Cash	$ 5,000	$ 15,000
Marketable securities	15,000	20,000
Receivables (net)	15,000	12,000
Inventory	20,000	15,000
Supplies	5,000	6,000
Prepaid items	3,000	2,000
Total Current Assets	$ 63,000	$ 70,000
Long-lived assets (net)	62,000	65,000
Total Assets	$ 125,000	$ 135,000
Equities		
Total Current Liabilities	$ 30,000	$ 40,000
Total Liabilities	$ 35,000	$ 50,000
Owner's Equity	90,000	85,000
Total Equities	$ 125,000	$ 135,000

EP 3.4   Using the data provided above for the Dowd Company, calculate the following ratios and percentages for the year 19X5:

   a) Current ratio.

   b) Quick ratio.

   c) Long-term debt ratio.

   d) Asset composition ratio.

   e) For each ratio, indicate whether 19X5 was better or worse than 19X4.

   f) Does Dowd appear to have a solvency problem at the end of 19X5?

   g) Assuming that, in Dowd's industry, a long-term ratio of 0.25 is acceptable, does Dowd have some available debt capacity as of the end of 19X5?

   h) How much cash could Dowd probably borrow on a long-term basis without much difficulty at the end of 19X5 if all non-balance-sheet considerations were satisfactory to potential creditors?

EP 3.5   Assume that you are the credit manager for the Ajax Supply Company, and you are asked for credit approval by two potential new customers, the Betty Company and the Mary Company. You have the balance sheet information given below and all other data are neutral, neither positive nor negative. Your firm follows a policy, which you recommended, and which states:

"No credit shall be given to customers without other exceptionally favorable information unless they maintain a current ratio of at least 1.70 and a quick ratio of at least 1.00"

Would you approve credit for either Betty or Mary or both? Explain.

	Betty Company	Mary Company
Cash	$ 22,100	$ 26,400
Receivables	29,600	2,400
Inventory	31,000	38,200
Other Current Assets	1,900	3,400
Total Current Liabilities	$ 47,000	$ 32,000

EP 3.6 Assume that you are a bank loan officer and the Zilch Company has applied for a six-month $50,000 loan. Your bank has the following policy:

"Where loan funds are available, loans shall be made to all applicants whose general credit information is good. However, in no case shall a loan be made to a firm whose ratios and percentages, immediately after the loan is made and when the proceeds are still in cash, depart from the following minimums: Current ratio at least 1.50, quick ratio at least 0.90, and long-term debt ratio no greater than 0.100"

Data that do not include the anticipated loan have been supplied by the Zilch Company and are given below. You may assume that all other credit information is favorable (good), and that you have adequate available funds to loan. Would you authorize the loan? Explain your actions.

Cash	$15,000	Total Current Liabilities	$100,000
Marketable securities	20,000	Total Liabilities	130,000
Receivables (net)	70,000	Owner's Equity	270,000
Inventory	40,000		
Supplies	10,000		
Prepaid items	5,000		

Supplementary Problems

SP 3.7 The following data are taken from the PBFF Company's balance sheets as of 12/31/X1 and 12/31/X0 (000 omitted):

	12/31/X1	12/31/X0
Accounts payable	80	70
Accounts receivable (net)	38	30
Cash	42	93
Current notes payable	15	20
Inventory	94	56
Marketable securities	0	27
Long-lived assets (net)	115	495
Noncurrent notes payable	25	177
Other current liabilities	15	25
Owner's equity	?	?
Prepaid items	12	12
Supplies	14	14

Assume that the firm had no other assets or liabilities than those shown. For 12/31/X0 determine: (a) Owner's equity. (b) Net working capital. (c) Current ratio. (d) Quick ratio. (e) Long-term debt ratio. (f) Asset composition ratio.

SP 3.8   Determine the following for the PBFF Company as of 12/31/X1 from data given with SP 3.7 above:

    a) Owner's equity.

    b) Net working capital.

    c) Current ratio.

    d) Quick ratio.

    e) Long-term debt ratio.

    f) Asset composition ratio.

    g) Was the company more solvent at the end of 19X1 than at the beginning? Explain.

    h) Did the company have more available debt capacity at the end of 19X1 than at the beginning? Explain.

SP 3.9   Using the balance sheets for 12/31/86 and 12/31/87 for the American Telephone & Telegraph (Appendix A at back of book), determine the following as of 12/31/86: (a) Net working capital. (b) Current ratio. (c) Quick ratio. (d) Long-term debt ratio. (e) Asset composition ratio.

SP 3.10 Referring to the American Telephone & Telegraph (see SP 3.9), determine the following as of 12/31/87: (a) Net working capital. (b) Current ratio. (c) Quick ratio. (d) Long-term debt ratio. (e) Asset composition ratio. (f) Was the company apparently more solvent than at the beginning of its fiscal year? Explain. (g) Did the company apparently have more available debt capacity than at the beginning of its fiscal year? Explain.

SP 3.11 Using the balance sheets for the Xerox Corporation for 12/31/86 and 12/31/87 (Appendix A at the back of book), determine, as of 12/31/86, the same ratios required in SP 3.9 above. Note that, for Xerox, you should consider all current assets except inventories and other current assets as being quick assets. Also, in calculating the long-term debt ratio, you should not include "Outside Shareholders' Interests in Equity of Subsidiaries" as a liability. This item is a form of ownership equity and is discussed in Chapter 14. It should be added to "Total Stockholders' Equity" to arrive at total owner's equity.

SP 3.12 Refer to SP 3.10 and SP 3.11 above. For the Xerox Corporation, as of 12/31/87, give the information required in SP 3.10 above, items (a) through (g)

4

Balance Sheet Changes
and Income

Chapter Preview

The objectives of this chapter are to introduce you to the events which change a firm's financial position, the double-entry accounting system for recording them, and the concept of income as measured by accountants. Based upon the material introduced in this chapter, you can learn to:

1. Distinguish between events which accountants report as changing the firm's financial position and those which do not affect balance sheet amounts;

2. Distinguish between transactions and adjustments;

3. Demonstrate (in terms of increases and decreases) the effect upon the balance sheet of most common transactions and adjustments;

4. Explain why every entry always maintains balance sheet equality;

5. Describe the information content of the income statement and how it relates to the income box on the balance sheet diagram.

6. Explain the interrelationships among balance sheets, statements of owners' capital, and income statements.

7. Explain the difference between accrual and cash-basis accounting.

With this fundamental knowledge, you can begin to understand how the entire financial accounting system is based on the balance sheet and balance sheet changes. You will see how you can go back to the balance sheet whenever you are unsure of any event's economic effect. And you will have an initial insight into the meaning of income to the firm and particularly to the firm's owners.

Events Which Change a Balance Sheet

Pat Ward is a business school graduate who is interested in plants. During her senior year, she inherited $50,000 from her grandfather. She decided to open a business specializing in the sale and care of indoor plants. She calls her firm the "Potted Planter."

Pat is concerned about the profitability of her new business. If the Potted Planter is not profitable and if she cannot withdraw some of its profits for personal use, she can not afford to have her own business. Pat's memory of elementary accounting, is unclear but she remembers the value of accounting information. She recalls the balance sheet diagram and remembers that for a going concern, the balance sheet always balances. She remembers that if her firm generates income, the result is reflected on the balance sheet by an increase in her owner's equity. She reasons that if her share in the Potted Planter's assets (net assets) increase in total dollars, the amount of such increase would show she was better off than before. She also knows the opposite is true. If her owner's equity drops in total dollars, the firm experienced a loss.

Pat's memory of the method accountants use to define and measure income is fuzzy. However, she is aware that some events that increase or decrease owner's equity do not involve income or loss. When she started the business with $20,000 from her inheritance, the firm's assets consisted of only $20,000 cash and, since there were no liabilities, her balancing owner's equity was $20,000. This increase in owner's equity from zero to $20,000 is not an increase in her wealth. She simply took $20,000 from her personal savings **account** and invested it in the business. Equally true, an owner withdrawal of assets is not a business loss, even though owner's equity is reduced by the amount of the withdrawal. Pat realizes that Potted Planter's income (profit or loss) is reflected by changes in her owner's equity, except for those coming from owner investments or withdrawals.

Pat drew a balance sheet diagram. She added a box in the owner's equity section which she labeled "income". Her intention was to place all changes affecting owner's equity, other than her personal investments and withdrawals, in the box. The net amount in the box would indicate the firm's income.[1] Pat's modified diagram is shown as Balance Sheet Diagram 4.1.

Pat makes a note of everything that happens to her business each day. One night a week she records the effect of the previous week's happenings on her balance sheet diagram.

---

[1]   The Income Statement will be introduced in Chapter 6. You will find that the Income Statement is simply a formal presentation of the financial data gathered in the "income box".

Diagram 4.1

ASSETS	EQUITIES
Current Assets:	Current Liabilities:
	Long-Term Debt:
Long-Lived Assets:	Owner's Equity:
	Pat Ward, Capital
	Income

First Week

During the first week, her diary contained the following events

1. Opened a special bank account on February 1, 19X0 in the business name and transferred $20,000 into it.

2. Signed a year's lease on a store.

3. Gave landlord $2,000 representing the first and last month's rent. (Rent is $1,000 per month)

4. Two used display counters and a cash register, together costing $12,500, are acquired. The sum of $10,500 cash is paid, and Pat signs a promissory note for the $2,000 balance. The note matures (that is, becomes due and payable) in two years. The note also provides for 12 percent interest to be paid annually.

5. Met a really nice guy who likes plants. He agreed to come to work for me when I can afford help.

At the end of the week she recorded the effects of these events as shown in Balance Sheet Diagram 4.2. Note that she numbers the effect of each event separately for her records.

Diagram 4.2   Balance Sheet Effect of First Week's Event

ASSETS		EQUITIES	
Current Assets:		**Current Liabilities:**	
Cash	+ $20,000 (1)		
	− 2,000 (3)		
	− 10,500 (4)	**Long Terrm Debt:**	
		Noncurrent Note Payable + $2,000 (4)	
Prepaid Rent	+ 2,000 (3)		
Long Lived Assets:		**Owner's Equity:**	
Equipment	+ 12,500 (4)	Pat Ward, Capital + $20,000 (1)	
		Income	
Total Assets	22,000	**Total Equities**	22,000

Effect of (1) Opening the bank account increases cash in the business by $20,000. No other asset or liability was affected. Therefore, to make the balance sheet balance, Pat's share (owner's capital) of total assets is increased by $20,000.

Event (2) Signing the lease has no affect upon Pat's statement. It did not change the financial position of her business. It is an **executory agreement**. Executory agreements are mutual promises to exchange money, goods, or services in the future where neither party to the agreement has yet performed. At the time of signing the lease, Pat is not obligated to the landlord. She does not owe the landlord rent until she uses the store.[2]

---

[2] Should one party cancel an executory agreement after performance has been started and before it has been completed by the other party, there may be damages for breach of contract. However, such damages cannot be determined until the matter is settled, and they would depend on the demonstrable costs incurred by the party having partially performed. at the time the executory agreement is made, there exists no obligation for past performance and no reason to anticipate possible future failure and damages.

Effect of (3) The payment on the lease decreases cash in the business by $2,000. Pat now has a receivable for services — the use of the store — from the landlord (prepaid rent). One asset (cash) has merely been exchanged for another (prepaid rent). Total assets did not change. No liabilities were involved. Therefore, there was no possible change in owner's equity as a result of this particular event.

Effect of (4): Purchasing the equipment increases Long-lived assets (equipment) by $12,500. Cash decreases $10,500. Long-term debt increases $2,000. These effects together maintain the overall balance, therefore there is no effect on owner's equity. Note that the future interest liability on the promissory note at the time of signing is executory, and is not recorded on the balance sheet. At the time of signing, no interest has as yet been earned by the investor holding the note, and no interest is owed by Pat.

Effect of (5) The agreement with the "real nice guy" is an executory agreement. Pat is not obligated to pay her new friend wages unless she asks him to come to work and he actually works.

Second Week

To save work, starting with the second week Pat recorded only those events that affected her firm's balance sheet diagram. The events recorded during the second week are listed:

6. Inventory of plants costing $3,000 are purchased on account from a wholesale supplier.

7. Supplies for use in the business costing $200 — pots, potting soil, etc. — are purchased for cash.

8. Spent $100 on cleaning and painting supplies. Used them all during the week, cleaning and fixing up the interior of store.

Draw the balance sheet diagram and attempt to properly record the effect of these three events. Then look on the next page for the solution.

Notice that Balance Sheet Diagram 4.3 shows the balance sheet effect of only the second week's events. The cumulative effect of all events will be illustrated later in this chapter. Each event is recorded independently of the others and in such a way that the overall balance sheet balance, or equality, is maintained.

Diagram 4.3   Balance Sheet Effect of Second Week's Events

ASSETS			EQUITIES		
Current Assets:			**Current Liabilities:**		
Cash	−	$200 (7)	Accounts Payable	+	$3,000 (6)
	−	100 (8)	**Long-Term Debt:**		
Inventory	+	3,000 (6)			
Supplies	+	200 (7)	**Owner's Equity:**		
Long-Lived Assets:					

Owner's Equity box:

Income		
−	100	(8)

Changes in Total Assets		2,900	**Changes in Total Equities**		2,900

Effect of (6): The purchase of the plant increases Assets (inventory) by $3,000. Liabilities (accounts payable) increases $3,000. There was no effect on owner's equity.

Effect of (7): Buying the supplies is an exchange of assets. Supplies increases $200 and cash decreases $200.

Effect of (8): Purchasing supplies decreased cash $100. Although future benefits or future cost savings would result from the cleaning and painting, there is no objectively measurable benefit beyond the current year since the lease only runs for one year. The future benefit is too uncertain to qualify for treatment as an asset. With cash decreased by $100, and no new asset resulting, total assets are therefore reduced by $100. Liabilities are unaffected; so, owner's equity must be reduced $100 to reflect the assets used and to maintain the balance. The change in owner's equity did not reflect an owner investment or withdrawal, so Pat has recorded it in her "income box". This is an **expense**.

Third Week

At the start of the third week, Pat opened her store for business. On the advice of other experienced business people, she adopted the following policies and practices:

a)   All sales of plants in the store will be for cash.

b)   When she delivers plants to a customer's home or provides services (e.g. watering, fertilizing, re-potting, pruning,), she will charge for her time and materials and send a bill to the customer.

c)   She will not attempt to record the outflow of plants (inventory) sold to customers on a weekly basis. Only the inflow of sales proceeds — cash and new accounts receivable based on invoices written — will be recorded.

The events recorded during the third week were as follows:

9.   Total sales (cash sales) to customers for the week were $960.

10. Total invoices for home sales and services (credit sales) for the week were $220.

11. Small packages of dirt, fertilizer, and chemicals costing $500 were purchased from the wholesaler on account. In response to customers requests, these items were acquired for display and sale.

You should attempt to record the effect of these events on a balance sheet diagram before proceeding.

Diagram 4.4   Balance Sheet Effect of Third Week's Events

ASSETS			EQUITIES		
Current Assets:			**Current Liabilities:**		
Cash	+	$960 (9)	Accounts Payable	+	$500 (11)
Accounts Receivable	+	220 (10)			
			Long-Term Debt:		
Inventory	+	500 (11)			
Long-Lived Assets:			**Owner's Equity:**		

	Income	
+	960	(9)
+	220	(10)

Changes in Total Assets	1,660	**Changes in Total Equities**	1,660

Effect of (9): Sales of $960 increases Assets (cash). There is no other effect on assets since it was decided to record outflow of merchandise later. Liabilities are not affected. The owner's equity increase is shown in the income box. This represents **revenue**.

Effect of (10): Invoicing her customers increases Assets (accounts receivable) by $220. Liabilities were unchanged; therefore, owner's equity must be increased by $220 in the income box, a revenue.

Effect of (11): Purchasing additional inventory for $500 increases assets. Liabilities (accounts payable) increase $500. The balance is maintained; therefore there is no effect on owner's equity.

Fourth Week

The business diary revealed the following financial events:

12. Cash sales for the week were $2,040.

13. Credit sales, or sales on account, for the week were $480.

14. Purchased additional plants on account, cost $800.

15. Some of the customers previously invoiced paid $150 on their accounts.

16. Paid the plant wholesaler $2,500 on account.

17. Pat withdrew $500 cash for personal use.

You can pause to determine how to record these events before you proceed.

Diagram 4.5

Balance Sheet Effect of Third Week's Events

ASSETS			EQUITIES		
Current Assets:			**Current Liabilities:**		
Cash	+	$2,040 (12)	Accounts Payable	+	$800 (14)
	+	150 (15)		–	2,500 (16)
	–	2,500 (16)			
	–	500 (17)	**Long-Term Debt:**		
Accounts Receivable	+	480 (13)	**Owner's Equity:**		
	–	150 (15)	Pat Ward, Capital	–	500 (17)
Inventory	+	800 (14)			
Long-Lived Assets:					

	Income	
+	2,040	(12)
+	480	(13)

Changes in Total Assets	320	**Changes in Total Equities**	320

Effects of Events (12), (13), and (14) are the same (with different dollar amounts) as Events (9), (10), and (11) previously described.

Effect of (15): Collecting receivables is a simple exchange of assets. Cash is increased and accounts receivable decreased by the amount collected.

Effect of (16): Paying a previously recorded liability reduces both cash and the liability by the amount paid. There is no effect upon owner's equity.

Effect of (17): The effect of an owner withdrawal of cash is the exact opposite of an owner investment. Cash is reduced and Pat's Capital is reduced $500. This $500 reduction of owner's equity is made directly to Pat's Capital. It is not included in the income box, since it reflects an owner withdrawal which is not part of income.

Diagram 4.6   Balance Sheet Effect of First Month's Events (Transactions)

ASSETS			EQUITIES		
Current Assets:			**Current Liabilities:**		
Cash	+ $20,000 (1)		Accounts Payable		
	− 2,000 (3)			+ $3,000 (6)	
	− 10,500 (4)			+ 500 (11)	
	− 200 (7)			+ 800 (14)	
	− 100 (8)			− 2,500 (16)	$1,800
	+ 960 (9)				
	+ 2,040 (12)		**Long-Term Debt:**		
	+ 150 (15)		Noncurrent Notes Payable +	2,000 (4)	
	− 2,500 (16)				
	− 500 (17)	$7,350	**Owner's Equity:**		
Accounts Receivable			Pat Ward, Capital		
	+ 220 (10)			+ 20,000 (1)	
	+ 480 (13)			− 500 (17)	
	− 150 (15)	550			
Inventory				Income	
	+ 3,000 (6)			− 100 (8)	
	+ 500 (11)			+ 960 (9)	
	+ 800 (14)	4,300		+ 220 (10)	
Supplies	+ 200 (7)			+ 2,040 (12)	
Prepaid Rent	+ 2,000 (3)			+ 480 (13)	
Long-Lived Assets:					
Equipment	+ 12,500 (4)				
Total Assets		26,900	**Total Equities**		26,900

Total Month

The balance sheet effect of each week's events has been shown separately to focus on the effect of each distinct item. The effect of all events is cumulative. Balance Sheet Diagram 4.6 shows the effect of events during the month that changed the firm's financial position. Remember that Event (2) and (5) are not shown, since they did not affect the firm's position at the time. Assume you are Pat Ward. As an owner-investor you are anxious to know where the business now stands and how well it is doing. From Balance Sheet Diagram 4.6, prepare a preliminary balance sheet as of the end on the month. Then check your result against Exhibit 4.1. Does Exhibit 4.1 fairly present the financial position of the Potted Planter as of the end of the month? What is incorrect? Do you need any more facts before you could complete the preparation of a proper month-end statement?

Exhibit 4.1

POTTED PLANTER PRELIMINARY BALANCE SHEET
As of 2/28/X0 (Unadjusted)

Assets		Equities	
Cash	$ 7,350	Accounts payable	$ 1,800
Accounts receivable	550	Total Current Liabilities	1,800
Inventory	4,300		
Supplies	200	Noncurrent notes payable	2,000
Prepaid rent	2,000	Total Liabilities	$ 3,800
Total Current Assets	$14,400		
Equipment	12,500	Pat Ward, Capital	23,100
Total Assets	$26,900	Total Equities	$26,900

Month-end Adjustments

If you have not already identified them, there are four improperly reported asset accounts: A) inventory, B) supplies, C) prepaid rent, and D) equipment.

A and B): The Inventory account and the Supplies account are presently overstated. These two accounts must be adjusted downward to show that inventory was sold and that supplies were used. Pat must take a physical count of the supplies and inventory remaining to determine the amount of the **adjustments**.[3] Assume that a physical count of

[3] In the usual situation, a physical count of inventory would be necessary only once a year for the annual financial statements. Techniques for estimating these amounts, in cases of more frequent "interim" reports will be discussed in Chapter 8.

inventory reveals an inventory of healthy plants and other merchandise costing $2,850 and unused supplies of $75.

C) The Prepaid rent account shows two months rent. One month has been used. So, $1000 must be adjusted downward to recognize that expense.

D) Finally an adjustment for one months depreciation must be reflected in the Equipment account. Pat estimates the useful life of the equipment to be ten years and that it can then be sold for $500.

In addition to adjustments to the assets, can you think of any liabilities that Pat has at the end of the month which have not been recorded? Utilities (E) and interest (F) need to be recorded.

E) Pat owes the local power and telephone companies for services consumed. Neither bill has arrived and therefore nothing was recorded. She estimates the total of both at $140 for the month. The utilities have supplied the service, they have earned the $140, therefore Pat owes it to them for services already performed.

F) Interest needs to be recorded for the noncurrent notes payable. Assume the equipment was purchased at the beginning of the month so one month's interest is owed.

For Pat's balance sheet to accurately reflect her firm's position as of the end of the month, the preliminary balances must be adjusted to reflect five (A-E) additional facts. From the information given, use a balance sheet diagram to show these balance sheet effects on a separate piece of paper before proceeding.

The five necessary adjustments, as shown on Balance Sheet Diagram 4.7 are:

Adjustment (A) Cost of Goods Sold: After counting her inventory Pat determined that Ending inventory has a cost of $2,850. Looking at Exhibit 4.1, the total inventory purchased is $4,300. Note there was no beginning inventory since this was a new business. the beginning inventory in March will be February's ending inventory, $2,850. Therefore, the difference of $1,450 has been sold to customers, discarded, or stolen. Inventory is therefore reduced by $1,450. No other asset or liability is involved in this adjustment. Therefore, Owner's Equity is reduced via the income box by $1,450 to reflect this usage of assets, **cost of goods sold.**

Total Available = Ending Inventory (still have) + Sold (gone)

Beginning Inventory (2/1/X0)	$ 0
Purchases	4,300
Goods Available for Sale	$ 4,300
less Ending Inventory (2/28/X0)	2,850
Cost of Goods Sold	$ 1,450

Adjustment (B) Supplies Used: There are $75 of supplies still on the shelf. The unadjusted balance sheet shows $200 in supplies. So $125 of supplies were used. Owner's Equity is reduced by $125 in the income box to reflect assets used.

Beginning Supplies (2/1/X0)	$ 0
Purchases	200
Supplies Available for Use	$ 200
less Ending Inventory (2/28/X0)	75
Supplies Used	$ 125

Adjustment (C) Prepaid Rent Expiration: $1,000 of prepaid rent representing the first month's rental payment has now been "used." It no longer represents a claim for services to be received. The service has been received. Prepaid rent is therefore reduced by $1,000. No other assets or liabilities are affected. Therefore Owner's Equity is reduced by $1,000 to reflect this **asset expiration**.

Adjustment (D) Equipment Depreciation: Some of the future usefulness of the equipment has expired. Over the ten years of its useful life, this equipment will cost Pat $12,000 (cost $12,500, minus resale value of $500). The $12,000 will be the result of the gradual wear and possible growing obsolescence or incapacity of the equipment. Do you think Pat should reduce this asset by the full $12,000 at the end of the first month? Or should she ignore the eventual "loss" and only record the $12,000 reduction when the equipment is sold?

Neither of these extremes results in a fair picture during the ten years that the equipment is used. The $12,000 cost expiration or "loss" is best spread over the ten years of useful life. The $1,200 per year is $100 per month. Accumulated depreciation immediately beneath equipment should be shown as $100. Accumulated depreciation is a negative or **contra-asset** valuation item. It subtracts from total assets. Increasing accumulated depreciation by $100 has the effect of reducing total assets by $100. Since no liabilities are affected, owner's equity is reduced by $100 in the income box to reflect this asset expiration.

$$\frac{\text{Cost - Salvage value}}{\text{\# of useful periods}} = \textbf{Depreciation per period}$$

$$\frac{\$12,500 - \$500}{10 \text{ Yrs x 12 Months/Yr}} = \$100 \text{ depreciation per month}$$

Diagram 4.7   Balance Sheet Effect of Month-End Adjustments

ASSETS			EQUITIES		
Current Assets:			**Current Liabilities:**		
Inventory	–	$1,450 (A)	Accounts Payable	+	$140 (E)
Supplies	–	125 (B)	Interest Payable	+	20 (F)
Prepaid Rent	–	1,000 (C)			
			Long-Term Debt:		
			Owner's Equity:		
Long-Lived Assets:					
Accum. Depr. on Equip.	–	100 (D)			

Owner's Equity Income box:

	Income	
–	1,450	(A)
–	125	(B)
–	1,000	(C)
–	100	(D)
–	140	(E)
–	20	(F)

Changes in			**Changes in**		
Total Assets	–	2,675	**Total Equities**	–	2,675

Adjustment (E) Utilities Liability: The firm has an additional liability of $140, and this must be added to Accounts Payable. The benefits of the power and phone service have already been used. So there is no new asset. Total assets are unchanged and liabilities are increased by $140; (Owner's Equity) is reduced in the income box by an equal amount to balance. This is an **accrued liability**.

Adjustment (F) Interest Liability: Pat needs to add the **accrual** of the month's interest on the noncurrent notes payable to interest payable, a current liability. The liability is current since interest is to be paid annually. There is no new asset, so total assets are unchanged and liabilities are increased by $20; (Owner's Equity) is reduced in the income box by an equal amount to balance.

Principal	**x**	**Interest Rate**	**x**	**Time**	**=**	**Interest Expense**
$2,000	x	.12	x	1/12	=	$20

Exhibit 4.2

POTTED PLANTER BALANCE SHEET
As of 2/28/X0 (Adjusted)

Assets		Equities	
Cash	$ 7,350	Accounts payable	$ 1,940
Accounts receivable	550	Interest Payable	20
Inventory	2,850	Total Current Liabilities	1,960
Supplies	75	Noncurrent notes payable	2,000
Prepaid rent	1,000		
Total Current Assets	$ 11,825	Total Liabilities	$ 3,960
Equipment	12,500		
Accumulated depreciation	(100)	Pat Ward, Capital	20,265
Total Assets	$ 24,225	Total Equities	$ 24,225

Exhibit 4.2 gives the adjusted balance sheet for Potted Planter for the end of the month. This statement gives Pat a reasonable estimate of her financial position after one month of operation. Study Exhibit 4.2 and compare it to Pat's position immediately following her investment of $20,000 in the firm.

Is Pat better off at the end of the first month of operation than at the beginning? Her share of the total assets in the business has gone from $20,000 to $20,265. This is true even after withdrawing $500 for personal use. She has an increase of $265 in her claim against the Potted Planter's total assets. So she is better off by $765. This is good, considering she has only been selling to customers for two weeks.

As of the end of the first month of operation, Pat Ward's firm had a profit or income of $765. Pat withdrew $500 of this profit leaving $265 as the addition to owner's equity in the business.

Transactions

Before going further into the concept of income and how it is measured and reported by accountants. It is important to understand how and when different events affecting a balance sheet are recorded. Exchanges take different forms. Cash is paid out for supplies, services, and to settle obligations. Goods and services are received in exchange for an obligation to pay cash. Cash and obligations to receive cash are received in exchange for goods and services. All of these exchanges were completed during the period, and specific information concerning these events was available to Pat before the end of the period. No estimating is necessary. **Transactions are completed economic events which involve exchanges with other entities, and where notification is received**

prior to the end of the period. The process of recording the effect of each separate transaction is known as a **transaction entry**. Each transaction has a dual effect on the Potted Planter balance sheet. Any change to a particular item requires changes to other items, in order to maintain the balance sheet equality. Thus the origin of the term *"double-entry system."*

Adjustments

Adjustments (A through F) are different from transactions.[4] Along with transactions, they record an economic change in the firm's position and are balanced (double-entry). However, they do not reflect a completed exchange with outsiders. Adjusting entries record asset expirations: inventory, supplies, prepaid rent, and equipment.[5]

The **adjusting entry** for the telephone and utility obligation involves an incomplete exchange, and notification has not been received. The amount owed is estimated. The process of recording the effect of each of these adjustments is known as making adjusting entries or accruing liabilities.

Transactions involve exchanges with others outside the firm and are recorded as they occur. However, it is generally too costly to record such transactions as inventory sold to customers or internal use of supplies on a day-to-day basis. Instead, the accountant updates the records to reflect such events. The accountant also adjusts the balance sheet by accruing receivables earned and payables owed for which notification has not been received. This part of the adjusting process will be discussed thoroughly later in this chapter.

It is helpful to think of all adjustments as one of two types: permanent and temporary. **Permanent adjustments** update the firm's records to reflect asset expirations and other systematic modifications of valuation accounts.[6] For these adjustments, there is no risk that the recording of a future transaction will result in double counting. Inventory and depreciation adjustments are examples of permanent adjustments.

---

[4] The trend of common use is to consider all events affecting financial statements as transactions. The distinction between transactions and adjustments has been found to be an effective learning aid.

[5] Inventory sold to customers represent an exchange with outsiders. However, Potted Planter (and many retailers) cannot afford to record the outflow of inventory as it occurs. Sale proceeds from the exchange are recorded, and the merchandise outflows are ignored until the end of the period. Periodic adjustment to reflect merchandise outflow, deterioration, and loss is then processed like an expiration not involving an exchange.

[6] In Chapter 11 you will be introduced to valuation accounts and adjustments other than accumulated depreciation. These valuation accounts and adjustments include potentially uncollectible receivables, executory interest on receivables and payables, and similar items.

Reversing Entries

Temporary adjustments, in contrast, all carry the risk of double counting because of future transactions. Adjustments of this type pick up portions of receivables or payables for which notification will be forthcoming. Adjustment E for the Potted Planter picks up a $140 estimate of a forthcoming monthly utility bills. When the total monthly utility bills arrive, if the transaction is recorded normally, the $140 will be double-counted. To avoid this problem, these types of adjustments are only recorded "temporarily." As soon as necessary statement data is complete, temporary adjustments are reversed or backed out of the records. They are not erased, but their effect is nullified by an opposite or reversing entry. Such reversals are purely procedural and have no ultimate effect on the statements. They will be illustrated along with detailed bookkeeping procedures in Chapter 5.

The Bookkeeping System

From the Potted Planter example, you can see how important it is for an accountant to record each transaction as it occurs. Otherwise, transactions might be forgotten, and the ending balances would be incorrect. The examples in this book involve relatively few transactions, and their effect can be recorded on a single page. Many firms have hundreds or even thousands of transactions every day, clearly too many for our little diagrams.

The financial-accounting bookkeeping system is designed to accommodate thousands of transactions. Essentially it involves two separate records; a **journal** and a general ledger. The journal is a "diary" in which each separate transaction is first recorded when it occurs. It shows the transactions effect upon different accounts.

An account is a file containing a specific type of information. In the Potted Planter example there would be accounts for Cash, Accounts Receivable, Inventory, Suppliers, Prepaid Rent, Equipment, Accumulated Depreciation, Accounts Payable, Noncurrent Notes Payable, and Pat Ward Capital, all appearing on the balance sheet. Note that there is no need to have accounts for Total Current Assets, Total Assets, Total Current Liabilities, Total Liabilities, and so forth. These classification totals and subtotals are found at the time the statements are prepared.

A transaction is first recorded in the journal. It shows how much to change the balances of each account affected by the transaction. Each recording is called a **journal entry**. An example of a journal entry would be the Potted Planter transaction (15), where $150 was collected from the credit customers. The journal entry could be written:

> *"Increase the cash balance by $150, and decrease the balance of accounts receivable by $150 to record the collection of receivables."*

Bookkeepers record journal entries in a special debit/credit language or code, to save writing long sentences each time. This code is explained in the next chapter.

The second major record in the financial accounting system is a collection of all the firm's accounts called the **general ledger**. The instructions from the journal are recorded in the appropriate account balances in the general ledger. This is known as **posting**. The ledger is organized by account name, or sometimes by account index number. Both the journal and the ledger then contain the same information. In the journal, changes to account balances are in chronological order. In the ledger, this information is posted and sorted by account order.

Each year or period, accountants follow a regular series of steps known as the **accounting cycle**. A simplified version of the accounting cycle:

1. Journalize transactions as events occur,

2. Post transactions from the journal to the ledger,

3. Prepare a trial balance to make sure no errors in posting or journalizing have destroyed the balance sheet equality,

4. Make adjustments on a separate worksheet,

5. Prepare financial statements from ending adjusted account balances appearing on the worksheet,

6. Journalize and post year-end adjusting entries,

7. Closing, i.e., transferring balances of any detail subaccounts into the main balance sheet accounts.

With the advent of computers, the pattern of the traditional accounting cycle is altered or bypassed for most transactions. Today, transaction data may be derived and recorded continuously as a by-product of other computerized activities, such as summary batches. Posting and trial balancing become automatic, simultaneous operations. In most cases, the individual journal entry for each distinct transaction occurs only in bookkeeping procedures which is illustrated in Chapter 5. You will be continuously asked to focus on the balance sheet effect of the accountant's application of GAAP to various transactions and adjustments in this text. These effects will always be the same, regardless of the degree and type of automation in a particular firm.

Income

Like all investors, Pat is concerned with how well the business is doing — whether it is making a profit and how much. In accounting terminology the terms **net income** and **earnings** are synonymous with profit. Negative income and negative earnings are synonymous with net loss.

Net income is the net change in owners equity as a result of operations. Net income is revenue minus expenses.

Revenue and Gains

Revenue is the inflow of net resources as a result of the firm's major or central operations. It is generally the total sales of goods and services rendered to customers during the period. Revenue and gains increase owners equity and are shown on the Balance Sheet Diagram as a plus in the income box. Non-customer revenues (gains) can arise from investments made by the firm and from the sale of assets other than inventory for more than their accounting book value.[7] Asset inflows loaned by creditors or invested by owners do not represent revenues or gains.

In the Potted Planter example, $3,000 of cash sales and $700 of credit sales represent revenues and are reflected by pluses in the income box. Pat Ward's investment of $20,000 and the portion of equipment provided in exchange for the $2,000 noncurrent promissory note are not revenues or gains.

Revenue is usually considered to be earned when a product is delivered to customers or when a service is rendered.

Expenses and Losses

An expense is defined as a reduction of owner's equity as a result of the firm's major or central operations. Note that the making of an investment, the purchase of an asset, or the payment of a previously recorded liability merely involve exchanges of assets and liabilities and, therefore, are not expenses. Expenses and losses are shown on the balance sheet diagram as a minus in the income box. Expenses are normally associated with the earning of revenues. Losses can result from decreased value of investments or losses on the sale of assets. Expenses and losses can result from:

1. Payments to suppliers either for goods and services already consumed or else for the use of resources (interest on loans and rent on property or equipment) where the expense and liability have not been previously recorded (8);

2. Expirations (use, deterioration, or loss) of assets (A), (B), (C), (D); and

3. Loss on the sale of assets other than inventory.

4. Recording new liabilities without the creation of new assets (E), (F).

For Potted Planter, expenses included:

(8)	Cleaning and painting supplies	$ 100
(A)	Merchandise delivered to customers	1,450
(B)	Supplies used	125
(C)	Prepaid rent expiration	1,000
(D)	Equipment depreciation	100
(E)	Utilities	140
(F)	Interest expense	20
	Total expenses	$2,935

[7] A reduction of liabilities not accompanied by a corresponding reduction in assets or increase in owner's equity can also represent revenue in rare cases.

With $2,935 of expenses during the first month and $3,700 of revenues earned, the Potted Planter net income for the period was $765.

Illustration 4.1

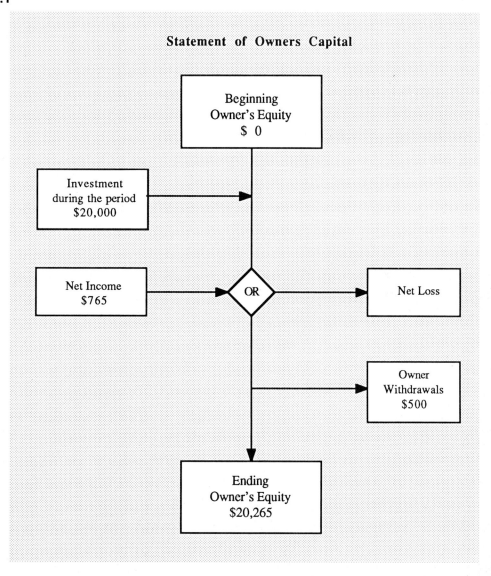

Statement of Owners Capital

Recall that $765 was the amount of increase in Pat's well-offness which was previously measured by taking the increase in her owner's equity of $265 and adding her withdrawals of $500. Since owner investments and owner withdrawals are excluded in the measurement of income the relationship between the owner's equity section in two successive balance sheets can be seen in Illustration 4.1 and in the formula:

Beginning Owner's Equity	+	Additional Owner Invest.	+	Net Income	−	Owner Withdrawals	=	Ending Owner's Equity
$0		$20,000		$765		$500		$20,265

The Statement of Owner's Capital

Exhibit 4.3 is an example of a schedule known as the **Statement of Owner's Capital**. It is often included with a set of financial statements.[8] Note that this statement merely shows the relationship previously cited. It explains the differences between the owner's equity sections on successive balance sheets. Balance Sheet Diagram 4.8 demonstrates the relationship or connection between the statement of owner's capital and two successive balance sheets. This illustration also reveals the connecting role between successive balance sheets of a firm's income statement. The income statement discloses the details of all revenues and expenses for the period. These were the pluses and minuses in the income box on the balance sheet diagram.

Exhibit 4.3

POTTED PLANTER
STATEMENT OF OWNER'S CAPITAL
for the month ending 2/28/X0

Pat Ward, Capital 2/1/X0	$ 0
Net income	765
Owner investment	20,000
Owner withdrawals	(500)
Pat Ward, Capital 2/28/X0	$ 20,265

---

[8] For corporations, a similar statement known as the Statement of Retained Earnings may be prepared. This statement will be discussed in Chapter 10.

Income Measurement

The second major financial statement, the income statement, is illustrated for the Potted Planter in Exhibit 4.4. The income statement merely identifies and classifies all revenues and expenses that are in the income box on the balance sheet diagram. The income statement itself will be discussed more thoroughly in Chapter 6. For now you should note that

Income				
–	100	(8)	– 1,450	(A)
+	960	(9)	– 125	(B)
+	220	(10)	– 1,000	(C)
+	2,040	(12)	– 100	(D)
+	480	(13)	– 140	(E)
			– 20	(F)

the sum of all the items in the income box equals $765, the amount of the firm's net income. All plus items in the box represent revenues and all minus items in this example represent expenses[9]. In the bookkeeping system accountants establish temporary accounts to accumulate revenue and expense information for each reporting period. At the end of the period, after adjustments, the balances in these temporary accounts provide the data for the income statement. These accounts are then closed or emptied. Their balances is transferred to owner's equity to complete the balance in the balance sheet.

Exhibit 4.4

THE POTTED PLANTER INCOME STATEMENT
for month ending 2/28/X0

Net sales		$ 3,700
Cost of goods sold		1,450
Gross profit		$ 2,250
Operating expenses:		
Rent	$ 1,000	
Supplies	125	
Utilities	140	
Maintenance	100	
Depreciation	100	
Interest	20	1,485
Net income		$ 765

---

[9] In Chapter 5, you will find that certain revenues that are not part of normal day-to-day operations may be called "gains"; and, similarly, certain expenses may be identified as "losses".

Diagram 4.8

Balance Sheet Effect Worksheet for The Potted Planter
(Effect of all transactions and adjustments during the first month)
(b) = beginning balance   (π) = net income

ASSETS			EQUITIES		
Cash	$ 0 (b)		Accounts Payable		
	+ $20,000 (1)			$ 0 (b)	
	– 2,000 (3)			+ $3,000 (6)	
	– 10,500 (4)			+ 500 (11)	
	– 200 (7)			+ 800 (14)	
	– 100 (8)			– 2,500 (16)	
	+ 960 (9)			+ 140 (E)	$1,940
	+ 2,040 (12)				
	+ 150 (15)		Noncurrent Notes Payable		
	– 2,500 (16)			0 (b)	
	– 500 (17)	$7,350		+ 2,000 (4)	2,000
Accounts Receivable					
	0 (b)		Pat Ward, Capital		
	+ 220 (10)			0 (b)	
	+ 480 (13)			+ 20,000 (1)	
	– 150 (15)	550		– 500 (17)	
Inventory	0 (b)			+ 765 (π)	20,265
	+ 3,000 (6)				
	+ 500 (11)				
	+ 800 (14)				
	– 1,450 (A)	2,850			
Supplies	0 (b)				
	+ 200 (7)				
	– 125 (B)	75			
Prepaid Rent	0 (b)				
	+ 2,000 (3)				
	– 1,000 (C)	1,000			
Equipment	0 (b)				
	+ 12,500 (4)				
Accum. Depr. Equipment					
	0 (b)				
	– 100 (D)	(100)			
Total Assets		**26,900**	**Total Equities**		**26,900**

Income

–	100	(8)
+	960	(9)
+	220	(10)
+	2,040	(12)
+	480	(13)
–	1,450	(A)
–	125	(B)
–	1,000	(C)
–	100	(D)
–	140	(E)
–	20	(F)
+	765	(π)

Balance Sheet Diagram 4.8 pictures the entire recording process for the Potted Planter's first month of operation. In this example, the basic balance sheet diagram has been expanded to show all balance sheet accounts, beginning balances, changes, and ending balances for the period.

Accrual Basis

Are you surprised that the credit sales are still included as revenue? Are you confused to find that February expenses include $140 for utilities not yet paid.

GAAP require that financial reporting follow the **accrual basis** rather than the cash basis. The accrual system is based on the premise that the cash flow's actual timing of is not relevant to when revenue is actually earned or when expense is actually incurred. Under GAAP, revenue is recognized and reported by accountants when it is earned rather than when the resulting cash is collected. Expenses are recognized when they are incurred. An expense is incurred whenever the firm uses goods or services, not necessarily when there is a payment of cash. The cash payment relating to an expense may have occurred in a previous period; it may occur in the current period; or in a future period.

If the payment is made in periods before the goods or services are used, the payment creates an asset. If the payment occurs in periods after the goods or services are used, then there is a liability.

On the accrual basis, Pat Ward's first month revenue was $3,700. The $3,700 included $3,000 of cash sales plus $150 of receivables collections plus $550 of monies earned, but not yet received. Her expenses, measured on the accrual basis, totaled $2,935 and included:

Cost of rent paid in advance that had expired	$ 1,000
Cost of maintenance items purchased and used	100
Cost of gardening supplies purchased and used	125
Portion of equipment cost that had expired	100
Cost of plants purchased and disposed of	1,450
Estimated cost of utilities consumed	140
Interest accrued on the notes payable	20
	$ 2,935

Cash Basis

Under **cash basis** accounting, instead of a $765 profit the firm would have reported a $12,150 loss for the month. Cash basis profit or loss is simply cash receipts from operations minus cash outflows from operations. On a cash basis, Pat would recognize and report only $3,150 of cash receipts, since only that amount had been collected from customers. Pat's cash payments for operations are $15,300:

paid to landlord	$ 2,000
paid for cleaning items and paint	100
paid for supplies	200
down payment on equipment	10,500
payment on accounts payable	2,500
	$15,300

Exhibit 4.5 compares Pat's expenses on a cash basis and on an accrual basis. Study this exhibit carefully. Can you discern the essential similarities and essential differences between accrual-basis expenses and those determined on a cash basis?

Exhibit 4.5

COMPARISON OF INCOME FOR THE POTTED PLANTER
DETERMINED ON A CASH BASIS AND ON AN ACCRUAL BASIS

Item	Cash Basis	Accrual Basis	Explanation of accrual basis
Revenue	$ 3,150	$ 3,700	Cash basis includes only revenue collected.
Less expenses:			
Rent	2,000	1,000	Only $1,000 of advance rental payments has been earned by landlord and used.
Cleaning and painting supplies	100	100	These maintenance items purchased with cash have been used.
Gardening supplies	200	125	Only $125 of gardening supplies purchased with cash have been used.
Equipment	10,500	100	Only $100 of the cost of the equipment has expired (depreciated).
Inventory	2,500	1,450	Plants costing only $1,450 have been used.
Utilities	0	140	Although no cash has been paid, $140 of utilities have been used.
Interest	0	20	Although no cash has been paid $20 of interest is owed on the note.
Total expenses	$15,300	$ 2,935	
Net Income	(12,150)	765	

There are three distinct patterns to observe in comparing accrual and cash-basis expenses. These patterns correspond to the three types of expenses described above:

- Cash outflows in the current period for goods or services consumed during the same period are expenses under both systems ($100 for cleaning and painting items).

- Commitments to pay cash in future periods for goods or services already consumed during the current period are expenses under the accrual system and are ignored under the cash basis system ($140 of utilities).

- Cash outflows for the acquisition of assets are treated as expenses under the cash basis. Under the accrual system only the portion of the asset which is deemed to have expired is treated as as expense. This is true regardless of when payment is made for the asset. For example, only $1,450 of the $2,500 of inventory acquired during the month is expensed. $1,050 is carried forward to future periods as an asset.

It is generally recognized that $3,700 of revenue earned is a better measure for estimating Pat's profit than the $3,150 of cash collected. Similarly, $2,935 of costs consumed is a fairer estimate of the expenses incurred. Information on cash flows is important and will be discussed further in Chapter 7. Cash-basis measurement may also be an attractive option where allowed for income tax purposes. However, cash-basis income is not considered an appropriate financial accounting measure of earnings. GAAP require that the accrual method be followed for most firms.

Chapter Overview

Based upon the material introduced in this chapter, you should now be able to explain:

- Why certain events have no effect on a firm's financial position;
- How other events affect specific items appearing on the balance sheet;
- Why all events that affect the firm's financial position will be reflected by changes to the balance sheet;
- Why the balance sheet effect of all changes is always dual or complementary, thus maintaining the balance sheet equality;
- Why events affecting a firm's position are either resource exchanges with other entities or economic changes in resources already held by the firm;
- What changes result in what accountants define as income;
- Financial position and income are measured on what is known as the "accrual" basis rather than the "cash" basis.

New Vocabulary and Concepts

Account	General Ledger
Accounting cycle	Goods available for sale
Accrual Basis	Income
Accrual	Journal
Accrued liability	Journal entry
Adjusting entry	Ledger
Adjustments	Net income/earnings
Asset expiration	Permanent adjustment
Balance sheet effect worksheet	Posting
Cash basis	Revenue
Cost of Goods Sold	Statement of Owner's Capital
Contra-asset	Temporary adjustment
Executory agreements	Transaction entry
Expense	Transactions

- The role of executory agreements in accounting measurement,
- The difference between transactions and adjustments,
- The necessity of double entry,
- Expirations of costs/assets,
- The function of an account, a journal entry, the journal, posting, and the ledger,
- Net Income = Total Revenue – Total Expenses,
- Ending Owner's Capital = Beginning Owner's Capital + Additional Owner Investment + Net Income (or – Net Loss) – Owner Withdrawals,
- Cash Basis Income = Cash Inflows
  (other than borrowings or owner investments) – Cash Outflows
  (other than loan principal repayments or owner withdrawals),
- The several steps in the accounting cycle and their purpose,
- Income as revenue minus expenses,
- Income as a change in owner's equity not resulting from donations or owner-involved transactions,
- Accrual-basis vs. cash-basis accounting.

Review Questions

1. Why do accountants record transactions continually throughout the year rather than once a year when statements are prepared?

2. Why do accountants make adjustments only when necessary for statement preparation instead of continually throughout the year?

3. a) What is an executory agreement? Explain with an example. b) What is the effect of an executory agreement on the balance sheet? Explain.

4. What is meant by the expiration or using up of costs or assets? There are four different types of assets which are used or expire in the Potted Planter example. What are they?

5. What is meant by the statement, "This transaction represents an exchange of assets"? Give numerical examples of such transactions and explain the effect of each on the balance sheet.

6. What is meant by the statement, "This transaction represents an investment of resources in the firm by a creditor or an owner"? Give numerical examples of such transactions and explain the effect of each on the balance sheet.

7. What is meant by the statement, "This transaction represents a payment of a liability," or the statement, "This transaction represents a withdrawal of assets by the owner"? Give numerical examples of such transactions and explain the effect of each on the balance sheet.

8. What is meant by the statement, "This transaction represents an inflow of resources from a customer and therefore represents revenue"? Give numerical examples of such transactions and explain the effect of each on the balance sheet.

9. What is meant by the statement, "This transaction or adjustment represents an expense"? Give numerical examples of such transactions demonstrating: a) asset expiration, b) a current cash outflow, c) a commitment for future cash outflow, and explain the effect of each on the balance sheet.

10. In the Potted Planter example, there were five end-of-period adjustments. Four represented adjusting the balance sheet for asset expirations, and one was a liability accrual. What is a liability accrual, and why was this done?

11. If, during a year, a firm had total sales all of which were made on account, totaling $100,000, revenues earned would be $100,000 even though perhaps only $80,000 of cash had been collected by year end. Why is revenue $100,000 and not just $80,000? Explain.

12. If total owner's equity is greater at the end of a period than it was at the beginning, there may have been income during the period. What could have occurred which would have resulted in increased owner's equity even if there had been no income?

13. Total owner's equity can be smaller at the end than at the beginning of a year and yet there could still be income earned during the year. Explain with an example. How this could be possible.

14. Explain the following items and their function or purpose in the accounting system: a) account, b) journal entry, c) journal, d) ledger, e) posting.

15. Estimates are necessary and may be significant in the preparation of financial statements. Give two examples of adjustments which required estimates in the Potted Planter case. What exactly is being estimated in each?

Mini-Cases and Questions for Discussion

MC 4.1   Florence doesn't see any sense in adjusting for asset expirations. She maintains, "I don't see why adjustments have to be made each year for asset expirations. Take a company with a truck costing $10,000, which they plan to use for four years and then sell for $2,000. Why should they take off $2,000 of additional accumulated depreciation each year? Why not have it on the balance sheet as $10,000 until they get rid of it? And even it they do want to reduce the net book value of the truck each year, why should this have any effect on owner's equity? Why don't accountants just leave owner's equity alone unless the owners put more cash in or take cash out? After all, long-term loans are not changed unless there is an additional loan or a repayment. Why treat owner's equity differently?"

Can you explain to Florence why it is desirable or necessary to record asset expirations each year? Clarify why asset expirations must have the effect of reducing owner's equity, even though the owners don't take any cash out of the business. Discuss.

MC 4.2   Trent Jones is the manager of a small restaurant. He is concerned with reported income, especially since the restaurant owner gives him a share of profits. The annual income statement has just been prepared, and Trent is arguing with the restaurant's accountant. He says, "Charlie, we made more money than this. This income figure of yours is crazy; it's way too low. I have no quarrel with your revenue figures. Our customers all pay cash, and I know that total is correct.

"But some of these expenses are downright ridiculous. You're including stuff for which we haven't even been billed, let alone haven't paid. there are amounts included in expense for telephone and electric power. We get billed and we pay for those next month. You also are including such things as wages our employees earned between the last payday and the end of the year. Charlie, you know the next payday is next month. That's when they get paid. Those wages should be part of next month/year's expenses. It's O.K. if you want to show these things as owed on the balance sheet. But that has nothing to do with income."

As Charlie, the accountant, what could you explain to Trent to justify your financial statements?

MC 4.3   Is it possible for a firm to report $10,000 of net income, and not have enough excess cash around for the owner to withdraw the $10,000 profit? If so, where is the $10,000? Discuss.

MC 4.4   If reported profit increases owner's equity, why doesn't the owner take his profits out of owner's equity and leave the firm's assets in the business? Discuss.

MC 4.5   Why does GAAP require accrual accounting? If accountants are looking for objectivity, why do they get involved in the estimates required under the accrual system? What could be more objective and verifiable that cash-basis accounting? Cash either comes in or it doesn't; and the same for cash outflows. If everybody uniformly followed cash-basis accounting, wouldn't there be adequate comparability among different firms? In fact, under accrual accounting one firm might estimate one way and another firm another. Wouldn't cash-basis accounting be even more comparable? Discuss these issues.

Essential Problems

EP 4.1   The Albertson Company was founded early in 19X1. For each of the following events occurring during 19X1 considered independently, indicate all the effects, if any, on the balance sheet, using the following codes:

IA	Increase in assets
DA	Decrease in assets
IL	Increase in liabilities
DL	Decrease in liabilities
IO	Increase owner's equity directly
DO	Decrease owner's equity directly
REV	Increase owner's equity via the income box — revenue
EXP	Decrease owner's equity via the income box — expense
NC	No change in the firm's balance sheet accounts

1. Owner decides to change the name of the business.

2. Owner invests $20,000 in the business.

3. An insurance policy providing one year's coverage is purchased for $900 cash.

4. Business borrows $10,000 from the bank on a current note.

5. Owner borrows $5,000 from a finance company for personal use.

6. Customers purchase goods and services (sales) for $2,000 cash.

7. Customers purchase goods and services (sales) totaling $3,000, on account.

8. Merchandise inventory costing $2,700 is purchased on account.

9. Supplies costing $600 are purchased on account.

10. Customers pay $2,500 on their accounts.

11. Leasehold improvements costing $6,000 are made with a $1,500 cash payment and the balance on a current note payable.

12. The $10,000 bank loan is repaid together with $700 of interest.

13. Equipment costing $20,000 is acquired for $12,000 cash and a noncurrent note payable due in five years for the balance.

14. $4,000 is loaned to a supplier on a six-month promissory note.

15. Customers purchase some merchandise paying $3,200 cash (assume inventory outflow recorded later as part of the adjusting process).

16. Utility bills totaling $300 have been received and paid.

17. $1,000 is paid on accounts payable.

18. Owner withdraws $500 from the business for personal use.

EP 4.2   The Barstow Company was formed at the beginning of 19X3, and the events occurring during 19X3 are given below. For each of these events considered independently, indicate all the balance sheet effects (if any) in terms of the letter codes given in EP 4.1.

1. Owner invests $50,000 in the firm.

2. Firm signs a two-year renewable lease on a store at a monthly rental of $1,000 payable in advance.

3. The landlord is given $2,000 covering the first month's rent and the last month's rent as a security deposit.

4. Equipment is purchased for the store costing $25,000 with a payment of $5,000 cash and a three-year promissory note for the balance.

5. Leasehold improvements are made to the store costing $20,000 and paid in cash.

6. Supplies costing $4,000 are acquired, for $1,000 cash and the balance on account.

7. Helen Barstow pays a personal clothing bill of $300 with cash from the business.

8. Merchandise costing $70,000 is acquired on account.

9. Customers purchase goods and services priced at $200,000, $25,000 for cash and the balance on account. (Assume that the outflow of inventory is recorded later as part of the adjusting process).

10. $155,000 is collected from customers on their accounts.

11. An insurance policy costing $2,800 and providing coverage for 19X3 and 19X4 is acquired on account.

12. Wages and salaries totaling $90,000 are paid to employees.

13. $11,000 is paid to the landlord covering rent through December, 19X3.

14. The utilities bill for $6,400 is received and recorded.

15. Interest on the $20,000 note of $1,500 is accrued as interest payable.

16. A spare room in the back of the store is sublet to a nearby store for storage use. Rent of $100 per month is to be received at year-end.

17. The $1,500 of accrued interest payable is paid.

18. $60,000 is paid on accounts payable.

19. The firm loaned $15,000 to a supplier. The note is to be repaid in six months.

20. Helen withdrew $20,000 for personal use.

EP 4.3   a) Create a balance sheet diagram with an income box (similar to Illustration 4.1) for the Albertson Company using the information given in EP 4.1. Identify each effect with its transaction number in parenthesis. Note that all numbered events do not necessarily represent accounting transactions, that each event is to be considered by itself (independently from all others). Year-end adjustments for Albertson are not part of this problem.

b) What was the amount of Albertson's 19X1 income before any adjustments?

c) Prepare, in good form, a balance sheet before adjustments for Albertson as of 12/31/X1. Indicate the owner's equity identified as "Mike Albertson, Capital" and give a single balance resulting from the effect of all transactions (affecting owner's equity) including those affecting the income box.

EP 4.4 a) Create a balance sheet diagram with an income box (similar to Illustration 4.1) for the Barstow Company using information given in EP 4.2. Identify each effect with its transaction number in parentheses. Note that all numbered events do not necessarily represent accounting transactions, that each event is to be considered by itself (independently from all others). Year-end adjustments for Barstow are not part of this problem.

b) What was the amount of Barstow's 19X3 income before any adjustments?

c) Prepare, in good form, a balance sheet before adjustments for Barstow as of 12/31/X3. Indicate the owner's equity identified as "Helen Barstow, Capital" and give a single balance resulting from the effect of all transactions (affecting owner's equity) including those affecting the income box.

EP 4.5 The following information is given for the Albertson Company at the end of 19X1. Determine which require a year-end adjustment, and using the letter codes given in EP 4.1, indicate the effects on the Balance Sheet. Note that all letter-coded items do not necessarily involve adjustments to the Albertson Company's financial statements, and that each is to be considered by itself (independently from all others).

A) Mr. Albertson got a parking ticket while on personal business. He estimates the fine will cost $20.

B) Interest earned but not yet received on the $4,000 loan to the supplier is $320.

C) The remaining accounts receivable were all expected to be collected early in 19X2.

D) A physical count revealed that merchandise inventory costing $850 was still on hand and unsold. An adjustment is required for the merchandise sold or otherwise missing.

E) A physical check revealed that supplies costing $150 were still on hand and unused. An adjustment is required for those supplies apparently used.

F) The insurance coverage acquired at the beginning of the year has expired, and an adjustment is required to reflect this cost expiration.

G) It is estimated that depreciation of $1,200 should be accumulated during 19X1 for the equipment.

H) $500 of the leasehold improvement is estimated to have expired and should be amortized.

I) Interest totaling $650 is owed at year-end and payable early in 19X2 on both the current and noncurrent notes.

J) The amount owed for utilities consumed by year-end but not yet billed is estimated at $35.

EP 4.6   The following information is given for the Barstow Company at the end of 19X3. Determine which require a year-end adjustment, and using the letter codes given in EP 4.1, indicate the effects on the Balance Sheet. Note that all letter-coded items do not necessarily involve adjustments to the Barstow Company's financial statements, and that each is to be considered by itself (independently from all others).

A) Interest earned, and not yet received, on the $15,000 supplier's note receivable amounted to $800.

B) Of the remaining accounts receivable at year-end, all were expected to prove collectible.

C) $300 of rent through December has been earned on the storage space sublease.

D) Ending inventory on hand and unsold as of 12/31/X3 had a cost of $27,000.

E) Supplies on hand and unused at year-end cost $1,100.

F) The only rental payment having future value as of 12/31/X3 was the $1,000 final-month security deposit.

G) One half of the insurance coverage had expired at year-end.

H) It is estimated that depreciation of $3,000 should be accumulated during 19X3 for the equipment.

I) Although the current lease expires at the end of 19X4, Helen has renewal options through 19X7 and expects to exercise these options. The leasehold improvements should therefore be amortized in equal amounts over the five-year period.

J) At year-end, $2,000 is owed by Helen Barstow on her home mortgage.

K) Interest totaling $650 has accrued on the $20,000 noncurrent note payable since the date of the last $1,500 payment.

L) Wages and salaries estimated at $1,600 have been earned by employees since the last payday.

M) Utilities costing an estimated $300 have been consumed but not yet billed to the firm.

EP 4.7   a) Create a balance sheet diagram with an income box (similar to Illustration 4.1) and indicate the balance sheet effects of all necessary adjustments for the Albertson Company from the information given in EP 4.5. Identify each effect with its adjustment identification letter following in parenthesis.

b) What is the combined net effect on Albertson's 19X1 income of all of the above adjustments?

EP 4.8   a) Create a balance sheet diagram with an income box (similar to Illustration 4.1) and indicate the balance sheet effects of all necessary adjustments for the Barstow Company from the information given in EP 4.6. Identify each effect with its adjustment letter in parenthesis.

b) What is the combined net effect on Barstow's 19X3 income of all of the above adjustments?

EP 4.9   a) Based on the information supplied in EP 4.1 and EP 4.5), prepare a complete balance sheet effect worksheet (similar to Balance Sheet Diagram 4.8) indicating the effects of all transactions and adjustments for the Albertson company for 19X1.

b) What was Albertson's 19X1 income (after adjustments)?

c) Prepare in good form a final balance sheet for the Albertson Company as of 12/31/X1. Indicate the final balance for Mike Albertson Capital as a single figure including both the effects of owner transactions and of income statement items.

EP 4.10   a) Based on the information supplied in EP 4.2 and EP 4.6, prepare a complete balance sheet effect worksheet (similar to Balance Sheet Diagram 4.8) indicating the effects of all transactions and adjustments for the Barstow Company for 19X3.

b) What was Barstow's 19X3 income (after adjustments)?

c) Prepare in good form a final balance sheet for the Barstow Company as of 12/31/X3. Indicate the final balance for Helen Barstow Capital as a single figure including both the effects of owner transactions and of income statement items.

EP 4.11   Data from Fox Company's Balance Sheet as of the end of the year are shown below. Since the day of the balance sheet, several events listed below have occurred. Considering each event separately, what would be the effect of each event on the firm's financial position? You need not prepare an entire new balance sheet for each event; just indicate the revised amounts for:

> Total Current Assets
> Total Assets
> Total Current Liabilities
> Total Liabilities
> Owner's Capital

BALANCE SHEET DATA AT END OF YEAR

Cash	$4,000
Notes receivable	2,000
Accounts receivable (net)	6,000
Inventory	3,000
Supplies	800
Prepaid Items	200
Investments	4,000
Land	1,500
Buildings and equipment	7,000
Less accumulated depreciation	(2,000)
Intangibles	500
Notes payable	3,500
Accounts payable	2,500
Taxes payable	1,600
Other current liabilities	1,400
Long-term note payable	4,500
Owner's capital	?

Events since the End of the Year:

a) The company was burglarized one evening. Merchandise costing $1,200 not covered by insurance was stolen.

b) Of the $6,000 accounts receivable net, $2,500 was owed by an old reliable customer. The customer was killed in an accident and it is discovered that he was broke and his estate cannot pay his bills.

c) The $4,000 in investments represents corporate bonds. The issuing corporation goes bankrupt and the most the Fox Company can anticipate recovering is $1,200.

d) An explosion does $4,000 worth of damage to the building and equipment. Only $3,000 of repair cost will be recovered from insurance.

e) A pending lawsuit against the company for $10,000 was settled out of court. The firm agreed to pay $3,000 in two installments. The first installment of $1,500 is due in 90 days, and the second in two years.

EP 4.12   The Daisy Company's Balance Sheet as of 12/31/X1 is given below.

a)   Prepare a new balance sheet reflecting the effect of all of the listed transactions.

b)   What, if anything, appears to be missing from this problem. Discuss

DAISY COMPANY BALANCE SHEET as of 12/31/X1			
Cash	$ 4,000	Accounts payable	$ 20,000
Accounts receivable	20,000	Other current liabilities	10,000
Inventory	30,000	Total Current Liabilities	30,000
Total Current Assets	$ 54,000		
Equipment (net)	70,000	Total Liabilities	30,000
		Owner's capital	94,000
Total Assets	$124,000	Total Equities	$124,000

January 19X2 Transactions:

1. Credit sales to customers were $35,000.
2. $15,000 was collected on accounts receivable.
3. Paid $12,000 on accounts payable
4. Borrowed $10,000 from the bank on a note payable due in two years.
A. The cost of the merchandise that was sold to customers was $20,000.

EP 4.13   Data from the George Company's balance sheet as of the end of the year are given below.

(a) What was the accounting measurement of the resources invested in the company as of the balance sheet date? Who are providing these resources to the firm?

(b) How much has been provided by short-term creditors?

(c) By long-term creditors?

(d) By the owners?

(e) If the owner had only actually put $160,000 into the company, how much profit has been accumulated in the company since its beginning which the owner has yet withdrawn for personal use?

Total Current Assets	$200,000
Total Assets	500,000
Total Current Liabilities	100,000
Total Liabilities	125,000

EP 4.14   Selected data from the year-end balance sheets for the years 19X2 and 19X1 for both the Able Company and the Baker Company are given below. You may assume that both firms are in the same type of business and that their capacity assets were all recently acquired.

a) Which form has the greater amount of resources invested as of the end of 19X2?

b) Which firm, as of the end of 19X2, has the greater proportion of its resources supplied by creditors, i.e., is more heavily in debt:

c) Which firm during 19X2 increased its size in terms of total resources invested?

d) Assuming no owner withdrawals or investment during 19X2, had either firm had a loss (negative profit) during the year? Explain.

Able Company	19X2	19X1
Total Current Assets	$300,000	$305,000
Total Assets	400,000	425,000
Total Current Liabilities	150,000	105,000
Total Liabilities	200,000	150,000

Baker Company		
Total Current Assets	$100,000	$ 90,000
Total Assets	300,000	250,000
Total Current Liabilities	75,000	80,000
Total Liabilities	200,000	50,000

Supplementary Problems

SP 4.15   The Wade Company's year-end balance sheet for 19X2 is given below. Prepare a 12/31/X3 Balance Sheet in good form from the following information:

1) Total sales to customers amounted to $600,000, $50,000 for cash and the balance on account.

2) $540,000 was collected on accounts receivable. There were no anticipated uncollectible accounts.

3) An additional $10,000 of marketable securities were purchased for cash.

4) The note receivable was collected together with $450 of interest.

5) Inventory costing $400,000 was purchased on account.

6) Supplies costing $5,000 were purchased for cash.

7) $3,000 of additional prepaid items were purchased on account.

8) All current liabilities at the beginning of the year were paid in full.

9) $350,000 was paid on accounts payable.

10) $75,000 of wages and salaries were earned and paid.

11) $20,000 of interest was paid on the noncurrent note.

12) $5,000 of maintenance and repairs expense were paid.

WADE COMPANY BALANCE SHEET
as of 12/31/X2

ASSETS		EQUITIES	
Cash	$ 10,000	Current Notes payable	$ 15,000
Marketable securities	25,000	Accounts payable	90,000
Current Notes receivable	5,000	Taxes payable	14,000
Accounts receivable (net)	75,000	Other current liabilities	6,000
Inventory	100,000		
Supplies	28,000	Total Current Liabilities	$125,000
Prepaid items	7,000	Noncurrent notes payable	175,000
Total Current Assets	$250,000	Total Liabilities	$300,000
Investments	110,000		
Land	60,000		
Equipment	510,000		
Less accumulated deprec.	(70,000)		
Leasehold Improvements	40,000	Owner's capital	600,000
Total Assets	$900,000	Total Equities	$900,000

A) Year-end merchandise inventory was $110,000.

B) Year-end supplies was $13,000.

C) Prepaid insurance of $5,000 was determined to have expired.

D) Equipment depreciated an additional $60,000.

E) Amortization of $12,000 on the leasehold improvement.

Year-end accrued liabilities, with no corresponding new assets were:

F) $2,000 for Utilities consumed.

G) $5,000 for wages and salaries earned.

H) $10,000 of property taxes accrued.

I) $3,000 of miscellaneous (other) liabilities were incurred.

SP 4.16 Refer to the Wade Company 19X2 balance sheet in SP 4.15. Assume that, instead of the events listed in SP 4.15, a different set of events occurred during 19X3. Prepare a Balance Sheet in good form for the Wade Company as of 12/31/X3.

1) Sales to customers were $500,000, all on account.

2) Collections on accounts receivable were $475,000 and there were no anticipated uncollectible accounts.

3) $15,000 of marketable securities were sold at their cost.

4) The note receivable was extended for another year. However, $600 in interest was collected.

5) Inventory at a cost of $300,000 was purchased on account.

6) Supplies at a cost of $2,000 were purchased on account.

7) All current liabilities at the beginning of the year, except the current note payable, were paid in full.

8) $1,200 interest was paid on the current note payable, and the note was refinanced with a new note in the same amount, due next year.

9) $200,000 was paid on accounts payable.

10) $30,000 of wages and salaries were earned and paid in cash during the year.

11) $20,000 of interest was paid on the Noncurrent Notes Payable.

12) The owner withdrew $39,400 in cash for personal use.

A) Year-end merchandise inventory amounted to $150,000.

B) Year-end supplies inventory amounted to $10,000.

C) The prepaid insurance was determined to have expired.

D) Equipment depreciated an additional $70,000.

E) Amortization was $10,000 on leasehold improvement.

Year-end accrued liabilities, with no corresponding new assets, were:

F) $ 3,000 Maintenance

G) $2,000 Utilities consumed

H) $12,000 Taxes payable accrued

I) $1,000 Miscellaneous (other)

SP 4.17 Integrative Problem.

Luigi Cavelli was the owner-manager of Luigi's Auto Parts, a retail store. Luigi's firm's balance sheet as of the end of Period 1 is given below:

LUIGI'S AUTO PARTS BALANCE SHEET AS OF END OF PERIOD 1

ASSETS		EQUITIES	
Cash	$ 3,450	Accounts payable	$13,000
Accounts receivable	40,000	Wages and salaries	600
Inventory	35,000		
Supplies	50	Total Current Liabilities	$13,600
		Noncurrent note payable	24,000
Total Current Assets	$78,500	Total Liabilities	$37,600
Leasehold improvement	2,850	Luigi Cavelli, Capital	43,750
Total Assets	$81,350	Total Equities	$81,350

During Period 2 (you can visualize one period in these integrative problems as being the equivalent of one year or one quarter), the following 18 summary transactions occurred:

1) An additional owner investment of $2,000 was made by Luigi.

2) Insurance was acquired on account costing $900.

3) Rent of $6,000 was paid to the landlord covering Period 2 and part of Period 3.

4) Supplies costing $50 were purchased for cash.

5) Inventory costing $25,000 was acquired on account. Inventory purchases were added directly to the inventory account.

6) $1,900 was spent on leasehold improvements.

7) Cash sales to customers totaled $11,000.

8) Sales to customers on account totaled $29,000.

9) Accounts receivable totaling $27,000 were collected. All remaining receivables were expected to be collected in the following period.

10) $3,000 was borrowed from the bank in exchange for a short-term promissory note payable.

11) $6,000 was acquired from a relative in exchange for a note payable in Period 5.

12) A cash register costing $1,200 was acquired with a $300 cash down payment and a note due in Period 6 for the balance.

13) The $3,000 short-term bank loan was repaid together with $120 of interest.

14) Interest of $240 was paid on the $6,000 note to a relative.

15) Wages and salaries paid to employees (covering prior period's obligations and current pay) totaled $7,850.

16) Invoices received for utilities and services consumed during the period totaled $260.

17) $25,200 was paid on accounts payable.

18) Luigi withdrew $1,500 in cash for personal use.

At the end of Period 2, nine adjustments were necessary:

A) The cost of goods sold to customers. A year-end physical count of inventory revealed merchandise costing $36,000 to be on hand and unsold.

B) Supplies unused at period-end had cost $10.

C) The unexpired insurance coverage cost $600.

D) The amount of rent representing an advance for the next period was $1,500.

E) Depreciation on equipment for Period 2 was estimated at $75.

F) Necessary amortization of leasehold improvement for the period was $250.

G) The costs of utilities and other services consumed but not yet billed at the end of the period was estimated as $40.

H) $720 of interest on the long-term note and $36 of interest on the cash-register note had accrued since the last payment.

I) Wages and salaries estimated at $750 were earned by employees since last the payday.

Required:

a) Complete a balance sheet effect worksheet (per Balance Sheet Diagram 4.8) for Luigi's store for Period 2. Identify beginning balances as "(b)" and the effect of transactions and adjustments with their numbers or letters. Also identify all revenue and expenses in an income box. Provide necessary space on your worksheet by entering account titles as follows:

Account	Line number	Account	Line number
Cash	1	Current Notes Payable	1
Accounts Receivable	17	Accounts Payable	5
Inventory	21	Wages and Salaries	12
Supplies	25	Interest Payable	16
Prepaid Items	29	Noncurrent Notes Payable	19
Equipment	35	Luigi Cavelli, Capital	24
Accum. Depr. Equip.	38		
Leasehold Improvement	41		

b) Determine the net income for Luigi's Auto Parts for Period 2.

c) Prepare in good form the statement of owner's capital for the firm for Period 2.

d) Prepare in good form the balance sheet for Luigi's Auto Parts as of the end of Period 2.

e) Determine for Luigi's Store as of the end of Period 2:

   1. The amount of net working capital in the business;

   2. The current ratio (to two decimals);

   3. The quick ratio (to two decimals);

   4. The long-term debt ratio (to three decimals); and

   5. The asset composition ratio (to three decimals).

SP 4.18   Integrative Problem

Irene Morton is the owner-manager of Irene's Sport Shop, a retailer of sports equipment and clothing. Irene's firm's balance sheet as of the end of Period 1 is given below:

IRENE'S SPORT SHOP BALANCE SHEET AS OF END OF PERIOD 1			
ASSETS		**EQUITIES**	
Cash	$ 4,000	Accounts payable	$ 30,000
Accounts receivable	81,000	Wages and salaries	1,500
Inventory	45,000		
Supplies	150	Total Current Liabilities	$ 31,500
		Noncurrent note payable	30,000
Total Current Assets	$130,150	Total Liabilities	$ 61,500
Leasehold improvement	11,250	Irene Morton, Capital	79,900
Total Assets	$141,400	Total Equities	$141,400

During Period 2 (you can visualize one period in these integrative problems as being the equivalent of one year or one quarter), the following 18 summary transactions occurred:

1) An additional owner investment of $2,500 was made by Irene.
2) Insurance was acquired on account costing $1,800.
3) Rent of $8,800 was paid to the landlord covering Period 2 and part of Period 3.
4) Supplies costing $600 were purchased for cash.
5) Inventory costing $52,000 was acquired on account. Inventory purchases were added directly to the inventory account.
6) $6,000 was spent on leasehold improvement.
7) Cash sales to customers on account totaled $40,000.
8) Sales to customers on account totaled $60,000.
9) Accounts receivable totaling $59,000 were collected. All remaining receivables were expected to be collected in the following period.
10) $10,000 borrowed from the bank in exchange for a short-term promissory note payable.
11) $5,000 was acquired from a relative in exchange for a note payable in Period 5.
12) Two cash registers costing a total of $2,400 were acquired with a $400 cash down payment and a note due in Period 6 for the balance.
13) The $10,000 short-term bank loan was repaid together with $300 of interest.
14) Interest of $200 was paid on the $5,000 note to a relative.
15) Wages and salaries paid to employees (covering prior period's obligations and current pay) totaled $26,500.
16) Invoices received for utilities and services consumed during the period totaled $600.
17) $59,400 was paid on accounts payable.
18) Irene withdrew $2,100 in cash for personal use.

At the end of Period 2, nine adjustments were necessary:

A) The cost of goods sold to customers. A year-end physical count of inventory revealed merchandise costing $47,000 to be on hand and unsold.

B) Supplies unused at period-end had cost $300.

C) The unexpired insurance coverage cost $900.

D) The amount of rent representing an advance for the next period was $2,200.

E) Depreciation on equipment for Period 2 was estimated at $150.

F) Necessary amortization of leasehold improvement for the period was $1,150.

G) The costs of utilities and other services consumed but not yet billed at the end of the period was estimated as $75.

H) $1,280 of interest on the long-term note and $80 of interest on the cash-register note had accrued since the last payment.

I) Wages and salaries estimated and $2,000 were earned by employees since the last payday.

Required:

a) Complete a balance sheet effect worksheet (per Balance Sheet Diagram 4.8) for Irene's store for Period 2. Identify beginning balances as "(b)" and the effect of transactions and adjustments with their numbers or letters. Also identify all revenue and expenses in an income box. Provide necessary space on your worksheet by entering account titles as follows:

Account	Line number	Account	Line number
Cash	1	Current Notes Payable	1
Accounts Receivable	17	Accounts Payable	5
Inventory	21	Wages and Salaries	12
Supplies	25	Interest Payable	16
Prepaid Items	29	Noncurrent Notes Payable	19
Equipment	35	Irene Morton, Capital	24
Accum. Depr. Equip.	38		
Leasehold Improvement	41		

b) Determine the net income for Irene's Sport Shop for Period 2.

c) Prepare in good form the statement of owner's capital for the firm for Period 2.

d) Prepare in good form the balance sheet for Irene's Sport Shop as of the end of Period 2.

e) Determine for Irene's Store as of the end of Period 2:

1. The amount of net working capital in the business;

2. The current ratio (to two decimals);

3. The quick ratio (to two decimals);

4. The long-term debt ratio (to three decimals); and

5. The asset composition ratio (to three decimals).

5

Bookkeeping, the Accounting Cycle and Internal Control

Chapter Preview

The objective of this chapter is introduce basic bookkeeping, the accounting cycle and internal control systems—the procedures used to classify, record, and summarize all data that becomes part of the financial statements. In this chapter, you can:

1. Learn the value of standardized accounting procedures;

2. Become familiar with the double entry debit/credit system and its advantages as an error-prevention and error-checking device;

3. Learn how transactions and adjustments are first recorded via a journal entry using the debit/credit code;

4. Review in more detail the basic accounting records involved and the accounting cycle, which were first introduced in Chapter 4;

5. Become familiar with certain accounting terminology, tools, and practices including journal entries, special journals, the audit trail, the worksheet, closing and reversing entries, and subsidiary accounts;

6. Learn the importance of internal control over accounting systems and the major concepts, objectives, and devices that may be involved.

With this information, you will be able to understand and converse with accountants in their professional language. Accountants have specific procedures which they use to accomplish the objectives discussed in this text. If you desire to learn these procedures, this chapter provides the foundation knowledge for you to understand and learn the preparer procedures. Additional preparer procedures will be introduced at the end of subsequent chapters.

Need for Standardization of Procedures

Imagine a typical firm with many thousands of transactions and adjustments necessary during the year. Can you visualize the chaos that would result if each one of the firm's accountants used his own individual system for processing data? If each firm had its own unique system for accounting, what would be necessary when a new accountant was hired, even temporarily? Extensive specialized and costly training in the firm's own unique system would be required. And in peak-load periods, or when an employee was temporarily absent, the firm could not take advantage of available temporary help. No one (except those who already knew the system) could be brought in on a short-term basis.

To minimize or eliminate this training problem, firms in the U.S. generally follow a uniform, conventional bookkeeping system. The underlying principle of the system is double-entry or dual-effect, which has been demonstrated in previous chapters. The conventional coding language employed is "debit/credit. When accounting records are maintained on computers, the traditional debit/credit instructions may be replaced by simple instructions to increase or decrease an account balance. Some accounting programs for microcomputers are programmed to maintain accounting records with inputs entirely on a plus or minus basis.The material in this chapter is provided so that you may comprehend accounting practices under either plus/minus or debit/credit coding.

The Debit/Credit Coding System

In Chapter 2 you learned that the foundation of the financial accounting system is the basic balance sheet equality (total assets equal total equities). In Chapter 4 you learned that transactions and adjustments affecting the balance sheet result in changes to the accounts necessary to both reflect the event and maintain the balance sheet equality. In the fifteenth century, a system was developed with the objective of maintaining this equality, even when thousands of changes (entries) need to be recorded.

The debit/credit coding system is very simple. Please do not make it difficult merely because you cannot accept its simplicity. "**Debit**" comes from the Latin word debere and stands for "left" as on the left side. "**Credit**," also from Latin, credere, stands for "right," as on the right side. Debit is usually abbreviated "Dr" (or "DR") and credit as "Cr" (or "CR"). One form of portraying a balance sheet is to show assets on the left side of the page and equities on the right. The debit/credit system assumes that all asset accounts will have left-side positive balances and all equity accounts will have right-side positive balances. Given this assumption, total debits, which mean only left-side balances, will always equal total credits, which mean only right-side balances.

The T-account

A common way of portraying this idea in textbooks is to show accounts in the form of a "T" or T-accounts. Each T-account then has space for left-side amounts (Debits) and right-side amounts (Credits). Note the similarity of a T-account to the balance sheet, which has left-side items (assets) and right-side items (equities). For example:

Asset Accounts

DR	CR
+	−
$ 100	$ 40
70	

Note that debit or left-side is abbreviated "DR," and the credit, or right-side, is abbreviated "CR.? Note also that the balance in the above account is "130 debit"; 170 debit offset by 40 credit equals 130 debit. Accounts can also have credit balances. For example:

Equity Accounts

DR	CR
−	+
$ 100	$ 200
	50

The above balance would be "150 credit." An example of the operation of this system will serve to show its simplicity. Suppose a new firm, the AJAX Company, had just been started, and its only transaction so far was the owner investing $70,000 in the business on January 1, 19X1: $50,000 cash, and merchandise costing $20,000. The balance sheet would show:

AJAX COMPANY BALANCE SHEET
as of 1/1/X1

ASSETS		EQUITIES	
Cash	$ 50,000	Liabilities	$ 0
Inventory	20,000	Owner's Equity	70,000
Total Assets	$ 70,000	Total Equities	$ 70,000

The three accounts in T-account form would show:

Cash

DR	CR
+	−
1/1 $ 50,000	

Inventory

DR	CR
+	−
1/1 $ 20,000	

Owner's Capital

DR	CR
−	+
	1/1 $ 70,000

Note that total debits—left-side balances—of $70,000 equal total credits—right-side balances—of $70,000.

The Journal Entry

Now follow the recording of a few transactions using the debit/credit convention in T-account form. Suppose AJAX purchased an additional $5,000 of merchandise on account (Accounts Payable) on January 3. To record the balance sheet effect, one would need to increase the inventory account by $5,000 and to increase accounts payable by the same amount. Following the debit/credit coding, the journal entry for recording this transaction would be:

Date	Explanation	PR	DR	CR
Jan 3	Inventory		5,000	
	Accounts Payable			5,000

Note that debit/credit positioning is similar to a programming language. This entry can be decoded as instructing: "Post $5,000 to the debit (left) side of the Inventory account" (increasing this asset by $5,000), and "post $5,000 to the credit (right) side of the Accounts Payable account" (increasing this liability by $5,000).

Remember from Chapter 4 that a journal entry is an instruction to change account balances to reflect the effect of one specific event. Since the account balances must, in turn, be kept in balance—total debits must equal total credits, the instruction to change account balances—the journal entry—must always maintain the balance sheet equality. Also remember that the recording process is incomplete until the instruction has been carried out—by posting the journal entry to the ledger or T-accounts.

Before proceeding, try setting up the four necessary T-accounts involved on a separate sheet of paper. Record the original owner investment as shown above. Now record the purchase on account of merchandise costing $5,000.

You are correct and are well along the road to understanding the debit/credit system if your T-accounts show:

Cash			Accounts Payable		
DR		**CR**	**DR**		**CR**
+		−	−		+
1/1 $ 50,000					1/3 $ 5,000

Inventory			Owner's Capital		
DR		**CR**	**DR**		**CR**
+		−	−		+
1/1 $ 20,000					1/1 $ 70,000
1/3 5,000					

Note that the entry itself is balanced: $5,000 in debits equal $5,000 in credits. And, after posting, the T-account balances still reflect the equality (Total Assets $75,000 = Total Liabilities $5,000 + Owner's Capital $70,000).

Suppose AJAX paid $2,000 to suppliers on its Accounts Payable on Jan 12. The effect would reduce Cash by $2,000 and reduce Accounts Payable by the same amount. What would be the journal entry to record this transaction? Write down the journal entry and follow its instructions by posting to your T-accounts before proceeding.

The journal entry would be:

Date	Explanation	PR	DR	CR
Jan 12	Accounts Payable		2,000	
	Cash			2,000

Immediately after posting, the accounts would show:

	Cash				Accounts Payable	
DR		**CR**		**DR**		**CR**
+		−		−		+
1/1 $ 50,000		1/12 $ 2,000		1/12 $ 2,000		1/3 $ 5,000

	Inventory				Owner's Capital	
DR		**CR**		**DR**		**CR**
+		−		−		+
1/1 $ 20,000						1/1 $ 70,000
1/3 5,000						

Note that the balance continues to be maintained in several forms. The entry itself is balanced. The total of the net balances in each of the accounts balances: $73,000 of net debits and credits. The total of all debits and credits in the system before netting each account still balances: $77,000 each of debits and credits.

The Debit/Credit Code

In all, there are six possible different types of accounts, four for the balance sheet and two for the income statement.

Balance Sheet Accounts

- Asset accounts
- Contra-asset accounts
- Equity accounts
- Contra-equity accounts

Income Statement Accounts

- Revenue and gain accounts
- Expense and loss accounts

These six different types of accounts are shown in relationship to each other on Balance Sheet Diagram 5.1.

Assets

Asset accounts normally have debit balances. To increase an asset account, you debit it, or post to the left side. To decrease an asset account, you credit it.

ASSET ACCOUNTS

DR	CR
+	−
debits increase account balance	credits decrease account balance

Contra-Assets

Contra-asset accounts, such as Accumulated Depreciation are used to accumulate certain asset reductions. They are included in the balance sheet along with assets, but each subtracts from its related asset.

Note that a contra-asset account does not represent an additional asset. It is merely a valuation account related to another asset account, and therefore is always properly identified to indicate the account to which it relates. "Accumulated Depreciation" is an inadequate and improper identification for such an account. "Accumulated Depreciation—Buildings" or "Accumulated Depreciation—Equipment" would be a more appropriate account title.

A minus effect to assets on the balance sheet diagram will always be a credit and this credit will either:

• Decrease asset account itself (where no contra-asset account is involved); or
• Increase contra-asset account.

Contra-asset accounts are contra, or opposite, to assets and normally have a credit balance. Remember that a positive balance in a contra-asset account will reduce total assets. To record additional accumulated depreciation of $100, for example, the minus $100 balance sheet effect is accomplished by increasing the balance in Accumulated Depreciation with an instruction to credit the account (post on the right side). To decrease a contra-asset account you would debit.

CONTRA-ASSET ACCOUNT

DR	CR
−	+
debits decrease account balance	credits increase account balance

Equities—Liabilities and Owner's Equity

Equity accounts normally have credit balances. How would you increase the balances in an equity account? How would you decrease it? Equity accounts are the opposite of asset accounts. They are increased by crediting and decreased by debiting or **charging**. "Charge" is often used synonymously for debit.

EQUITY ACCOUNTS

DR	CR
−	+
debits decrease account balance	credits increase account balance

Contra-Equities

Contra-equity accounts are shown on the balance sheet along with equities, but they subtract from their related equity accounts. They are therefore contra, or opposite to, equity accounts, and normally have a debit balance. Contra-equity accounts are increased by charging (debiting) and decreased by crediting.

CONTRA-EQUITY ACCOUNTS

DR	CR
+	−
debits increase account balance	credits decrease account balance

To review, asset accounts normally have debit balances and equity accounts credit balances. Contra accounts are opposites of their suffix designation.

Income Statement Accounts: Revenues and Gains

In Chapter 4, you learned that revenues and gains increase owner's equity, and that during the year accountants store revenue information in temporary revenue and gain accounts (shown as increases in the income box on the balance sheet diagram). Since revenues and gains eventually increase owner's equity, and since equity accounts normally have a credit balance, a positive balance in a revenue or gain account must also be a credit balance. Revenue or gain accounts are increased by crediting and decreased by debiting.

REVENUE AND GAIN ACCOUNTS

DR	CR
−	+
debits decrease account balance	credits increase account balance

Income Statement Accounts: Expenses and Losses

Expense and loss accounts are temporarily established each period to store reductions to owner's equity that have a minus effect in the income box. Refer to Balance Sheet Diagram 5.1 and note that expense accounts are just like contra-equity accounts. Expense accounts accumulate reductions to owner's equity. A positive balance in an expense account will therefore be a debit balance that will eventually reduce owner's equity. To accomplish a minus effect in the income box you would increase an expense or loss account balance by debiting or charging and decreased by crediting.

EXPENSE AND LOSS ACCOUNTS

DR	CR
+	–
debits increase account balance	credits decrease account balance

Expense accounts and contra accounts can be confusing unless you remember that they accumulate reductions. Where these accounts are involved, a minus effect on the balance sheet diagram is accomplished by increasing the balance in the expense or other contra account itself. For example, to record the year-end adjustment for an additional $100 of depreciation on equipment (which would have the balance sheet effect of a minus to total assets and a minus in the income box) the adjusting entry would be:

Date	Explanation	PR	DR	CR
Dec 31	Depreciation Expense		100	
	Accumulated Depreciation			100

An easy way to remember the debit/credit code is merely to think of the various T-accounts in terms of the balance sheet as shown on Balance Sheet Diagram 5.1. All you have to remember is:

1. Asset accounts are on the left side of the balance sheet and have left side (debit) normal or positive balances;

2. Equity accounts (liabilities and owner's equity) are on the right side of the balance sheet and have right side (credit) normal or positive balances.

3. An increase to owner's equity is a credit; therefore The Chart of Accounts revenue or gain, which increases owner's equity, must be a credit;

4. Contra-asset accounts accumulate asset reductions or offsets; therefore contra-asset accounts accumulate have a right side (credit) normal or positive balance.

5. Expense, loss, and contra-equity accounts accumulate reductions to equities; therefore expense, loss, and other contra-equity accounts have a left side (debit) normal or positive balance.

Diagram 5.1   Summary of the Debit/Credit Code or Programming Language

Asset Accounts			Liability Accounts	
DR	CR		DR	CR
+	−		−	+

Contra-Asset Accounts			Contra-Liability Accounts	
DR	CR		DR	CR
−	+		+	−

Owner's Capital	
DR	CR
−	+

Contra-Equity Accounts	
DR	CR
+	−

Income

Revenues		Expenses	
DR	CR	DR	CR
−	+	+	−

The Chart of Accounts

How does the accountant know which accounts are involved in a specific journal entry? the answer depends upon two things: The nature of a specific transaction or adjustment being recorded, and the firm's chart of accounts. An account is simply a file for the accumulation of data for a specific item or group of items. All proprietorships will normally have balance sheet accounts for Cash, Accounts Payable, and Owner's Capital. If a firm is involved in selling merchandise on account, using supplies, and has prepaid items (insurance, rent, interest, and so forth), it will also have accounts for Accounts Receivable, Inventory, Supplies, and Prepaid Items. The number and type of specific accounts that are maintained for an individual firm will depend both on the nature of its business and also upon the degree of detail believed necessary and desirable. For example, a small firm may find that a single balance sheet account for Equipment would be sufficient for all of its depreciable assets. A larger manufacturing firm might wish to have separate accounts for Factory Equipment, Office Furniture and Fixtures, Vehicles, and so forth.

You should understand that a firm's **chart of accounts** is uniquely determined by its financial reporting requirements, with additional detail as may be necessary or desirable for internal reports and income tax returns. Therefore one firm's chart may be quite different from another's even when they are both the same size and in the same line of business.

Working closely with the firm's auditor, the controller or chief accountant in each firm will determine which accounts are necessary both to conform to GAAP and also to provide the firm's managers and statement readers with desirable but not excessive detail. Each account will be given a specific title to be used uniformly in all journal entries affecting the account. Also each account will usually be given a unique number with the numbers assigned in groups (0 - 100 for current assets, 100 - 199 for long-lived assets, and so forth) to facilitate sequential filing by type for ease of location; and also to be used in lieu of the account title for machine or computer processing. Machine and computer processing systems can more readily locate, store, sequence, sort, batch, and summarize account information by a logically constructed numerical coding system than they can with only account titles.

All accounts designated for use in a specific firm will be listed in the firm's chart of accounts. Exhibit 5.1 is a chart of accounts covering those accounts necessary for the Potted Planter (Chapter 4) transactions and adjustments and for similar transactions and adjustments included in the preparer problems at the end of this chapter. Note that the chart includes temporary revenue and expense accounts that will be discussed more fully in Chapter 6. At this point you need only understand that revenue accounts accumulate increases in the balance sheet diagram income box as credits; and that expense accounts accumulate income box decreases as debits.

Exhibit 5.1   INTRODUCTORY CHART OF ACCOUNTS

ACCOUNT NUMBER	ACCOUNT TITLE
001-099	**Current Assets**
	Current Monetary Items
001	Cash
002	Current Marketable Securities
003	Current Notes Receivable
004	Accounts Receivable
005	Interest Receivable
006	Rent Receivable
	Inventories
010	Inventory
	Other Current Assets
020	Supplies
021	Prepaid items
100-199	**Long-Lived Assets**
	Property, Plant and Equipment
112	Equipment
	Intangible and Other
120	Leasehold Improvements
200-299	**Contra Assets**
213	Accumulated Depreciation, Equipment
300-399	**Current Liabilities**
	Current Monetary Liabilities
300	Current Notes Payable
301	Accounts Payable (trade)
302	Wages and Salaries Payable
303	Interest Payable
304	Taxes Payable
305	Rent Payable
308	Other Current Liabilities

400-499	**Long-term Debt**
400	Noncurrent Notes Payable
500-599	**Owner's/Partners'/Stockholders' Equity**
500	Proprietor's Capital
600-699	**Contra Equities**
700-799	**Revenues**
	Primary
700	Gross Sales
	Other
711	Interest Revenue
712	Rent Revenue
800-899	**Expenses**
	Operating
800	Cost of Goods Sold
801	Wages and Salaries
802	Rent
803	Interest
804	Taxes (other than income taxes)
805	Supplies
806	Insurance
808	Depreciation
809	Amortization
811	Maintenance and Repairs
812	Utilities
813	Miscellaneous
900-999	**Other Accounts**
910	Owner Withdrawal
950	Income Summary

Note in Exhibit 5.1 that a chart of accounts does not contain any accounts for balance sheet totals such as total current assets, total assets, total current liabilities, total liabilities, or total equities. It also provides no income statement totals for net sales, gross profit, earnings before taxes, income from operations, or even net income. All of these subtotals and totals are developed in the final statements themselves and not in the accounts.

The groupings within the chart of accounts are designed to be helpful in obtaining certain totals and subtotals. For example, from the chart given as Exhibit 5.1 the book-keeper knows that total current assets is the sum of the balances in all accounts from 001 through 099 less the balances in any current contra accounts in the 200 series. Similarly, total assets is the sum of the balances in all accounts from 000 through 299; and so forth. This feature can be especially helpful to the programmer in a computer system.

In succeeding chapters, as new types of accounts are introduced, this chart will be expanded. You may wish to turn to Appendix D at the back of the book before proceeding. There you will find a complete chart of accounts covering all accounts introduced in this text.

Exhibit 5.2

POTTED PLANTER
Transactions during first month of operation

(1) Owner deposits $20,000 cash in business.

(2) Signing lease not a transaction.

(3) Paid landlord $2,000 in advance rent.

(4) $100 expenditure for supplies consumed.

(5) Tentative employment agreement not a transaction.

(6) Purchased inventory costing $3,000 on account.

(7) Purchased supplies costing $200, paying cash.

(8) Purchased equipment costing $12,500, paying $10,500 cash and executing a noncurrent $2,000 note at 12 percent interest for the balance.

(9) First week cash sales were $960.

(10) First week credit sales were $220.

(11) Purchased inventory costing $500 on account.

(12) Second week cash sales were $2,040.

(13) Second week credit sales were $480.

(14) Purchased inventory on account costing $800.

(15) Collected $150 cash on Accounts Receivable.

(16) Paid $2,500 on Accounts Payable.

(17) Owner withdrew $500 cash for personal use.

The Journal(s) and the Audit Trail

Recall from Chapter 4 that the journal entry is the point of entry into the accounting system. All transactions and adjustments are first recorded or **journalized** as an instruction, advising which accounts are to be changed and by how much. This instruction, which is made for each separate event (transaction or adjustment), is known as a journal entry. The journal entry may be accompanied by a brief written explanation such as "purchase of inventory," "collection of receivable," and so forth.

It may be desirable to check back through the accounts to the original source at some later time. Therefore a journal entry is dated with the day of initial recording, and the source documents (sales slips, supplier invoices, and so forth) are filed by or identified with the same date. Where this proves impractical, the entry description will reference the information source. Thus an **audit trail** is established. If one wishes to check back (audit) to the source of a given entry, the journal will provide the necessary cross reference.

You will find in the following pages that the audit trail is also carried forward from the journals into the ledgers at the time of posting. Thus an important corrective control is maintained allowing a bookkeeper to track back and forward and correct any error that is discovered at any point in the process.

The journal or diary in which the journal entry is first recorded is known as the **General Journal**. Each page in the General Journal provides columns for: date of entry, account title and entry description; posting reference; and, finally, one column for debit (DR) amounts and one column for credit (CR) accounts. Exhibit 5.3 illustrates the general journal for all transaction entries for the first month for the Potted Planter described in Chapter 4.

Note that, in place of the date of the entry, the transaction number or adjustment letter (from Exhibit 5.2) is given. Also note that in the PR (posting reference) column the account number is shown indicating that the posting to that account in the ledger has been completed.

In addition to its General Journal, a firm may have special journals for specific types of transactions. Where a large number of transactions always affect one account the same way and usually also affect one of a few other accounts, a special journal can simplify the recording process. Special journals and their operation will be illustrated and discussed later in this chapter. Note that where special journals have been established, only those transactions and adjustments that do not fall within the scope of the special journals are recorded in the General Journal.

The Ledger(s) and Posting

For each account listed in the firm's chart of accounts, a separate page as illustrated in Exhibit 5.4 (or a machine posted card, segment on a magnetic card, disc or tape not illustrated) will be maintained to accumulate all debits and credits to that account. All open or active accounts are kept in a combined file known as the General Ledger.

Exhibit 5.3   General Journal for The Potted Planter

GENERAL JOURNAL				Page No.1
Date	Explanation	PR	DR	CR
(1)	Cash	001	20,000	
	Pat Ward, Capital	500		20,000
	To record owner investment			
(3)	Prepaid items	021	2,000	
	Cash	001		2,000
	To record payment of advance rent			
(4)	Maintenace and repairs	811	100	
	Cash	001		100
	To record supplies purchased and used			
(6)	Inventory	010	3,000	
	Accounts payable	301		3,000
	To record purchase of inventory on account			
(7)	Supplies	020	200	
	Cash	001		200
	To record purchase of supplies for cash			
(8)	Equipment	112	12,500	
	Cash	001		10,500
	Noncurrent note payable	400		2,000
	To record acquisition of equipment			
(9)	Cash	001	960	
	Gross sales	700		960
	To record cash sales			
(10)	Accounts receivable	004	220	
	Gross sales	700		220
	To record credit sales			
(11)	Inventory	010	500	
	Accounts payable	301		500
	To record purchase of inventory on account			

	GENERAL JOURNAL			Page No.2
Date	Explanation	PR	DR	CR
(12)	Cash	001	2,040	
	Gross sales	700		2,040
	To record cash sales			
(13)	Accounts receivable	004	480	
	Gross sales	700		480
	To record credit sales			
(14)	Inventory	010	800	
	Accounts payable	301		800
	To record purchase of inventory on account			
(15)	Cash	001	150	
	Accounts receivable	004		150
	To record collection of accounts receivable			
(16)	Accounts payable	301	2,500	
	Cash	001		2,500
	To record payment of accounts			
(17)	Pat Ward, Capital	500	500	
	Cash	001		500
	To record owner withdrawal			

Exhibit 5.4   The General Ledger

Cash						Account No. 001	
DATE		DESCRIPTION	POST REF.	Debit	Credit	BALANCE	
						Debit	Credit
19X0							
Feb	*1*	*Balance*	✔			*00*	
	1		*1*	*20,000*		*20,000*	
	3		*1*		*2,000*	*18,000*	
	4		*1*		*100*	*17,900*	
	7		*1*		*200*	*17,700*	
	8		*1*		*10,500*	*7,200*	
	9		*1*	*960*		*8,160*	
	12		*2*	*2,040*		*10,200*	
	15		*2*	*150*		*10,350*	
	16		*2*		*2,500*	*7,850*	
	17		*2*		*500*	*7,350*	

Journal entry instructions are periodically followed by posting to the individual accounts in the ledger. As posting is completed, the account number to which the debit or credit amount has been posted is recorded in the "Post. Ref." (Posting Reference) column of the journal to indicate that posting is completed and to provide cross reference. At the same time the source journal page number is recorded in the Post. Ref. column of the ledger to maintain the audit trail. For certain balance sheet accounts, it is often desirable to maintain detailed supporting individual accounts.

For example, a firm would want separate accounts with separate balances for each customer's accounts receivable and each supplier's accounts payable. In these cases, the detailed "sub accounts" are maintained in separate **subsidiary ledgers**. Posting is made to the detailed or subsidiary accounts within the subsidiary ledger. Periodically the master or **control account** in the general ledger is updated to reflect the current balance of all accounts in its subsidiary ledger. Accounts receivable and accounts payable subsidiary ledgers are illustrated and discussed later in this chapter.

Exhibit 5.5 illustrates a general ledger in **T-account** form. In the reference column to the left of the amount (on both the debit and credit sides of the account) is normally shown the journal page number from which the posting originated (the audit trail). In this exhibit the transaction numbers are shown instead for reference.

Note: The balances that remain in the above accounts are in agreement with the Adjusted Trial Balance amount in Exhibit 5.6.

Exhibit 5.5   T-Account Ledger after transactions posted

001			Cash		301			Accounts Payable
(1)	20,000	(3)	2,000		(16)	2,500	(6)	3,000
(9)	960	(4)	100				(11)	500
(12)	2,040	(7)	200				(14)	800
(15)	150	(8)	10,500					1,800
		(16)	2,500					
		(17)	500					
	7,350				400			Noncurrent Notes Payable
							(8)	2,000
004			Accounts Receivable					
(10)	220	(15)	150					
(13)	480				500			Pat Ward, Capital
	550				(17)	500	(1)	20,000
								19,500
010			Inventory					
(6)	3,000				700			Gross Sales
(11)	500						(9)	960
(14)	800						(10)	220
	4,300						(12)	2,040
							(13)	480
								3,700
020			Supplies					
(7)	200				811			Mainentance & Repairs
					(4)	100		
021			Prepaid Items					
(3)	2,000							
112			Equipment					
(8)	12,500							

Interim Trial Balances

Periodically throughout the period, a **trial balance** is taken of all the accounts in the ledger(s). A trial balance involves totaling all the debit and credit amounts separately to see whether the totals agree. Even if the ledger(s) is(are) in balance, there could still be errors such as an amount posted to the wrong account. But if the ledger is not in balance, an error must exist. The purpose of frequent trial balances is to minimize effort in case of error. If an out of balance condition is discovered, then only those entries and postings since the last trial balance need to be reviewed in order to locate the error. The first two columns of Exhibit 5.6 illustrates a trial balance.

The trial balance can be considered a control function, an action taken to prevent or identify an error. Other control functions previously mentioned were ensuring that each journal entry by itself was in balance and also maintaining the audit trail. Overall internal control will be discussed later in this chapter.

The Worksheet and the Preadjusting Trial Balance

At year or period end, management and outsiders want statements as soon as feasible. To temporarily bypass the time consuming process of journalizing and then posting necessary adjusting entries, in a manual accounting system the accountant first completes a 10 column end of cycle **worksheet**. The net balance before adjustment from each account in the General Ledger is first recorded in the first two (debit and credit) columns of the worksheet. Exhibit 5.6 illustrates a partially completed worksheet for the Potted Planter firm (introduced in Chapter 4) with the preadjusted end of month account balances recorded. These accounts are the same as shown in Exhibit 4.1 in Chapter 4 except that:

- Accounts are in the chart of accounts order,

- Items are classified as debits or credits according to the debit/credit code, and

Exhibit 5.6   Potted Planter Worksheet

Accounts	Before adjusting Debit	Before adjusting Credit	Adjustments Debit	Adjustments Credit	Adjusted Debit	Adjusted Credit	Income statement Debit	Income statement Credit	Balance sheet Debit	Balance sheet Credit
Cash	$ 7,350	$								
Accounts receivable	550									
Inventory	4,300									
Supplies	200									
Prepaid Items	2,000									
Equipment	12,500									
Accounts payable		1,800								
Noncurrent notes payable		2,000								
Owner's capital		19,500								
Gross sales		3,700								
Maintenance and repairs	100									
Total	$27,000	$27,000								

- The effects of revenue and expense transactions for the month are shown in temporary revenue and expense accounts and have not yet been combined (closed) with the $19,500 of owner's capital.[1]

- Other balance sheet accounts reflect the balance of all transactions recorded during the period.

Note in Exhibit 5.6 that the first two columns of the worksheet are trial balanced to make sure that all accounts are in balance before making any adjustments.

Adjustments and the Adjusted Trial Balance on the Worksheet

Continuing with the process of preparing the worksheet, the accountant then records year or period-end adjustments directly in the second two columns of the worksheet as shown in Exhibit 5.8. Recall from Chapter 4 that six period-end adjustments were necessary for the Potted Planter.

Exhibit 5.7   The Potted Planter adjustments

(A) Adjust for ending inventory, determined to be $2,850.

(B) Adjust for ending supplies, determined to be $75.

(C) Adjust for expiration of $1,000 of rent prepayment.

(D) Adjust for $100 of depreciation on equipment.

(E) Accrue $140 of utilities liabilities and related expense.

(F) Accrue $20 of interest on the noncurrent note payable.

These adjustments are recorded in the second two columns in the exhibit. The **adjusted trial balance** of all accounts are then determined and recorded in the third pair of columns as also shown in Exhibit 5.8 by adding the first two columns (Trial Balance) to the third and fourth columns (the adjustments).

Note that data are now available on the worksheet for use in preparing the income statement and the final balance sheet. Adjusting entries have not yet been journalized or posted to the accounts. The information flow follows the flowchart given as Diagram 5.2. As the information flows from left to right across the worksheet, this process is called "Extending the balances."

---

[1] In this illustration, the $500 owner withdrawal has been debited directly to owner's capital when it occurred. A more common treatment would be to create a separate account to accumulate withdrawals "Owner's Drawing" during the year. If the owner's drawing account is used it will appear separately on the worksheet (not illustrated) and then closed to owner's capital along with the revenue and expense accounts after adjustment.

Exhibit 5.8

Potted Planter Worksheet

Accounts	Before adjusting Debit	Credit	Adjustments Debit	Credit	Adjusted Debit	Credit	Income statement Debit	Credit	Balance sheet Debit	Credit
Cash	$ 7,350	$	$	$	$ 7,350					
Accounts receivable	550				550					
Inventory	4,300			(A) 1,450	2,850					
Supplies	200			(B) 125	75					
Prepaid Items	2,000			(C) 1,000	1,000					
Equipment	12,500				12,500					
Accounts payable		1,800		(E) 140		1,940				
Noncurrent notes payable		2,000				2,000				
Owner's capital		19,500				19,500				
Gross sales		3,700				3,700				
Maintenance and repairs	100				100					
Cost of goods sold			1,450 (A)		1,450					
Supplies expense			125 (B)		125					
Rent expense			1,000 (C)		1,000					
Accumulated depreciation				(D) 100		100				
Depreciation expense			100 (D)		100					
Utilities expense			140 (E)		140					
Interest payable				(F) 20		20				
Interest expense			20 (F)		20					
Net Income										
Total	$27,000	$27,000	$2,835	$2,835	$27,260	$27,260				

Preparing the Financial Statements

Recall from Chapter 4 that the income statement reports the firm's revenues and expenses for the period (illustrated on the Balance Sheet Diagram as pluses and minuses in the income box). Within the conventional bookkeeping system, temporary revenue and expense accounts are established each year to accumulate the pluses (credits) and minuses (debits). The adjusted balances in these accounts for the Potted Planter are shown starting with Gross Sales in the third pair of columns in the worksheet (Exhibit 5.8).

In Exhibit 5.9 you can see the balances of these temporary revenue and expense accounts are extended forward to the fourth pair of columns on the worksheet. They provide the necessary information for the Potted Planter's Income Statement first given as Exhibit 4.4 and repeated as Exhibit 5.10.

Also in Exhibit 5.9 the balances of the permanent or real balance sheet accounts are extended forward to the last pair of columns. They do not balance without the inclusion in owner's capital of the net income for the period (the algebraic sum of the items in the income box). With this amount included as shown, $765 in this example, data are now available to prepare the firm's end of period balance sheet first given as Exhibit 4.2 and repeated as Exhibit 5.11.

Exhibit 5.9   The Potted Planter Worksheet

Accounts	Before adjusting Debit	Before adjusting Credit	Adjustments Debit	Adjustments Credit	Adjusted Debit	Adjusted Credit	Income statement Debit	Income statement Credit	Balance sheet Debit	Balance sheet Credit
Cash	$ 7,350	$	$	$	$ 7,350		$	$	$ 7,350	$
Accounts receivable	550				550				550	
Inventory	4,300			1,450	2,850				2,850	
Supplies	200			125	75				75	
Prepaid Items	2,000			1,000	1,000				1,000	
Equipment	12,500				12,500				12,500	
Accounts payable		1,800		140		1,940				1,940
Noncurrent notes payable		2,000				2,000				2,000
Owner's capital		19,500				19,500				19,500
Gross sales		3,700				3,700		3,700		
Maintenance and repairs	100				100		100			
Cost of goods sold			1,450		1,450		1,450			
Supplies expense			125		125		125			
Rent expense			1,000		1,000		1,000			
Accumulated depreciation				100		100				100
Depreciation expense			100		100		100			
Utilities expense			140		140		140			
Interest payable				20		20				20
Interest expense			20		20		20			
Net Income							765			765
Total	$27,000	$27,000	$2,835	$2,835	$27,260	$27,260	$3,700	$3,700	$24,325	$24,325

In addition to providing a tool for preparation of year end financial statements, the worksheet is also used to prepare interim statements or reports. As previously mentioned, the costly and time consuming process of making complete adjusting and closing entries is only necessary once a year or period. Yet management and investors may desire more frequent reporting. As illustrated for the Potted Planter, by using the worksheet, statements can be prepared at the end of one month's operations without completing the adjusting and closing process. These interim adjusting entries appear only on the worksheet and are not posted in the accounting books. In practice, interim financials are usually prepared quarterly.

Adjusting and Closing the Books

After the end of year (period) worksheet has been completed and the financial statements have been prepared, adjusting journal entries are prepared and posted to the ledger. The adjusting journal entries for the potted planter are illustrated in Exhibit 5.12. The next step is to **close** all temporary accounts. Balance sheet accounts are permanent or **real accounts**. These balances carry forward from year to year. Last year's ending cash balance is this year's beginning cash balance, and so forth.

Exhibit 5.10

THE POTTED PLANTER INCOME STATEMENT
For month ending 2/28/X0

Net Sales		$ 3,700
Cost of Goods Sold		1,450
Gross Profit		$ 2,250
Operating Expenses:		
Rent	$ 1,000	
Supplies	125	
Utilities	140	
Maintenance	100	
Depreciation	100	
Interest	20	1,485
Net Income		$ 765

Exhibit 5.11

POTTED PLANTER BALANCE SHEET
As of 2/28/X0

Assets		Equities	
Cash	$ 7,350	Accounts payable	$ 1,940
Accounts receivable	550	Interest payable	20
Inventory	2,850	Total Current Liabilities	$ 1,960
Supplies	75		
Prepaid rent	1,000	Noncurrent notes payable	2,000
Total Current Assets	$11,825	Total Liabilities	$ 3,960
Equipment	12,500		
Accumulated depreciation	(100)	Pat Ward, Capital	20,265
Total Assets	$24,225	Total Equities	$24,225

All other nonbalance sheet accounts are temporary or **nominal accounts**. They are used temporarily to store specific information needed for certain reports and are "emptied" at year-end. The process of emptying these temporary accounts at year-end by transferring their balances to the appropriate permanent accounts is called closing. The most common accounts involved in closing are the revenue and expense accounts used to store income

Diagram 5.2   Flow of Accounting Information

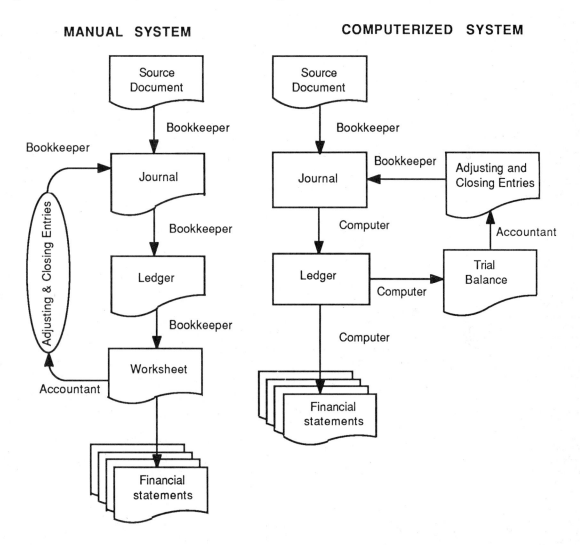

statement information. At year end via closing entries the balances of all revenue and expense accounts are transferred to the single account Income Summary. For a proprietorship, income summary (along with a proprietor's withdrawals account if such is maintained) is closed to owner's capital.[2]

---

2   Income summary may be allocated to different partner's capital accounts in a partnership or to retained earnings in a corporation (see Chapter 10).

Exhibit   5.12   The Potted Planter Adjusting Entries

GENERAL JOURNAL					Page No.3
Date	Explanation	PR	DR	CR	
(A)	Cost of goods sold	800	1,450		
	Inventory	010		1,450	
	To adjust for inventory				
(B)	Supplies expense	805	125		
	Supplies	020		125	
	To adjust for supplies used				
(C)	Rent expense	802	1,000		
	Prepaid items	021		1,000	
	To adjust for expiration of prepaid rent				
(D)	Depreciation expense	808	100		
	Accumulated depreciation - equipment	213		100	
	To adjust for depreciation				
(E)	Utilities expense	812	140		
	Accounts payable	301		140	
	To accrue liability for utilities				
(F)	Interest expense	803	20		
	Interest payable	303		20	
	To accrue interest on the note payable				

The closing process takes place after the worksheet is completed, the financial statements prepared, and all necessary year-end adjustments have been journalized and posted. The purpose of closing is to empty all nominal accounts by transferring their balances to the appropriate real or balance sheet accounts.

Nominal accounts requiring closing at year-end will include all revenue and expense accounts, and may involve certain other accounts depending upon the system used in the particular firm.[3] To illustrate the closing process, refer to the adjusted balances in the ledger accounts for the Potted Planter shown in the third pair of columns on the work-sheet (Exhibit 5.9). The closing entries for the Potted Planter are illustrated in Exhibit 5.13.

Exhibit 5.13   The Potted Planter Closing Journal Entries

GENERAL JOURNAL   Page No.3

Date	Explanation	PR	DR	CR
c-1	*Gross sales*	700	3,700	
	Maintenance and Repairs	811		100
	Cost of Goods Sold	800		1,450
	Supplies Expense	805		125
	Rent Expense	802		1,000
	Depreciation Expense	805		100
	Utilities Expense	812		140
	Interest Expense	803		20
	Income Summary	950		765
c-2	*Income Summary*	950	765	
	Pat Ward, Capital	500		765

Note that the net amount transferred to income summary of $765 equals the firm's net income for the period.

Since, in the Potted Planter example, owner withdrawals have already been debited directly to owner's capital, the final closing entry would simply close income summary to owner's capital.

This entry increases the balance in Pat's capital account to $20,265 which balances the other real accounts and which appears on the ending balance sheet (Exhibit 5.11).

The T-Account, General Ledger after posting, and Adjusting and Closing Entries are illustrated in Exhibit 5.14.

---

[3] Other common temporary accounts not representing revenue or expense that may be involved in the adjusting and closing process include owner withdrawals, gross purchases, purchase discounts, and other inventory related accounts to be introduced in Chapter 8. Owner withdrawals is closed to owner's capital. Until covered in Chapter 8, you may assume that gross purchases and purchase discounts are included inventory.

Exhibit 5.14 T Account Ledger after adjusting and closing

001			Cash
(1)	20,000	(3)	2,000
(9)	960	(4)	100
(12)	2,040	(7)	200
(15)	150	(8)	10,500
		(16)	2,500
		(17)	500
✔	7,350		

004			Accounts Receivable
(10)	220	(15)	150
(13)	480		
✔	550		

010			Inventory
(6)	3,000		
(11)	500		
(14)	800		
	4,300	(A)	1450
✔	2,850		

020			Supplies
(7)	200	(B)	125
✔	75		

021			Prepaid Items
(3)	2,000	(C)	1,000
✔	1,000		

112			Equipment
(8)	12,500		
✔	12,500		

213			Accumulated depreciation
		(D)	100
		✔	100

301			Accounts Payable
(16)	2,500	(6)	3,000
		(11)	500
		(14)	800
			1,800
		(E)	140
		✔	1,940

303			Interest Payable
		(F)	20
		✔	20

400			Noncurrent Notes Payable
		(8)	2,000
		✔	2,000

500			Pat Ward, Capital
(17)	500	(1)	20,000
			19,500
		c-2	765
		✔	20,265

700			Gross Sales
		(9)	960
		(10)	220
		(12)	2,040
		(13)	480
c-1	3,700		3,700

800			Cost of Goods Sold
(A)	1,450	c-1	1,450

802			Rent Expense
(C)	1,000	c-1	1,000

803			Interest Expense
(F)	20	c-1	20

805			Supplies Expense
(B)	125	c-1	125

808			Depreciation Expense
(D)	100	c-1	100

811			Mainentance & Repairs
(4)	100	c-1	100

812			Utilities Expense
(E)	140	c-1	140

950			Income Summary
c-2	765	c-1	765

The Accounting Cycle

Chapter 4 first introduced you to the accounting cycle. The term accounting cycle is used to describe the several steps or stages of the accountant's activities during the year as previously described. To review, the accounting cycle may be seen as having eight sequential steps or phases:

1. Possible opening reversals.

2. Journalizing and posting transactions throughout the year;

3. Interim trial balances;

4. Initial worksheet preparation, and the preadjusting trial balance;

5. Adjustments on the worksheet, and the adjusted trial balance;

6. Financial statement preparation;

7. Journalizing and posting adjusting and closing entries, and;

8. Post-closing trial balance.

Error Corrections

Because of the risk of additional errors, and of the possibility that someone might be able to manipulate the firm's accounting records, accountants are careful to preserve the audit trail even where an error has been made. When the error has been posted, two different approaches may be used. The simplest is to make an additional correcting entry identified as such to achieve the desired balances in the appropriate accounts.

The second approach involved making two entries: the first reversing or "backing out" the incorrect posting, and the second giving the desired result originally intended. This approach is generally used because it creates an audit trail which is easier to see.

Opening Reversals

In some accounting systems, reversing entries are used at the beginning of the year, to reverse the prior year's temporary year-end accrual adjustments. This is done to avoid the possibility of double counting when notification covering the item which had been accrued subsequently arrives and is recorded.

For example, in the case of the Potted Planter, $140 of utilities expense was accrued at month end and is shown as a liability.

Date	Explanation	PR	DR	CR
12/31	*Utilities Expense*		*140*	
	Accounts Payable			*140*
	To record year-end accrual			

The accrual was anticipating the invoice, which had not been received and journalized by the closing date. Assume that, in the following month, an invoice arrived totalling $300, $140 of which represented costs of the prior month's services. If the full $300 is normally recorded as a liability and as utilities expense, $140 will have been double counted.

To avoid double counting, the bookkeeper would have to check each incoming invoice to see whether some portion had already been accrued, and then pick up only the not yet accrued portion. Rather than check hundreds or thousands of incoming invoices to see if some portion had already been accrued by one of perhaps a dozen year-end adjusting entries, and rather than record only part of the new invoice, the accountant will reverse the previous temporary accruals at the start of the new accounting period.

Date	Explanation	PR	DR	CR
1/1	Accounts Payable		140	
	Utilities Expense			140
	To reverse year-end accrual			

In the previous example, after reversal, no liability for utilities service will be in the accounts, and utilities expense will start the period with a credit (negative) balance of $140.

Utilities Expense		Accounts Payable	
DR	**CR**	**DR**	**CR**
+	−	−	+
	140 (Reversing entry)	(Reversing 140 entry)	140 (Beginning balance)

The $300 incoming invoice can then be recorded routinely without having to be checked to see if a portion has already been recorded in a previous period:

Date	Explanation	PR	DR	CR
1/16	Utilities Expense		300	
	Accounts Payable			300
	To record utilities invoice			

Utilities Expense		Accounts Payable	
DR	**CR**	**DR**	**CR**
+	–	–	+
(Invoice) 300	140 (Reversing entry)	(Reversing 140 entry)	140 (Beginning balance) 300 (Invoice)

Without the reversing entry the following more complicated entry would be made to record the invoice:

Date	Explanation	PR	DR	CR
1/16	Utilities Expense		160	
	Accounts Payable			160
	Portion of invoice not previously accrued			

Utilities Expense		Accounts Payable	
DR	**CR**	**DR**	**CR**
+	–	–	+
(Partial 160 invoice)			140 (Beginning balance) 160 (Partial Invoice)

Note, regardless of the method used, utilities expense for the new period is $160. Reversing entries only simplify the recording process.

Special Journals, Subsidiary Ledgers and Closing

As mentioned in the chapter, firms will often use special journals to save time in recording volumes of similar transactions affecting a limited number of accounts. The most common special journals are:

1. The Cash Receipts Journal
2. The Sales Journal
3. The Cash Disbursements (or Payments) Journal
4. The Purchases Journal

Cash Receipts Journal

The Cash Receipts Journal is illustrated in Exhibit 5.15. Note that a single entry is completed on one line with the cash received recorded in the cash debit column. Where the entry is a cash sale (Lines 2 and 3), the other portion of the entry is recorded in the sales credit column and the account to be credited is identified as sales. Receivable collection without a discount (Lines 4 and 5) requires an entry in the accounts receivable credit column and the account must also be credited to the individual customer's accounts receivable in the subsidiary ledger. Where the receivable collection also involves a discount granted for prompt payment, the amount of the discount is recorded in the sales discount debit column to balance the entry.

The credit for cash receipts not involving cash sales or receivable collections is recorded in the sundry (all other) credits column and identified with the appropriate account to be credited.

As with the General Journal, the posting reference column is completed at the time of ledger posting. Note that only a single ledger posting is required, perhaps weekly or monthly, for the column totals for:

Exhibit 5.15   CASH RECEIPTS JOURNAL   Page No.1

Date		Account Creditied	Post Ref.	Other Accounts CR	Accounts Receivable CR	Sales CR	Sales Discounts DR	Cash DR
Feb	1	Pat Ward, Capital		20,000				20,000
	9	Gross sales				960		960
	12	Gross sales				2,040		2,040
	20	Mary Jones			80			80
	22	John Smith			70			70

Sales Journal

The sales journal is illustrated in Exhibit 5.16. This journal is used only for sales on account. Since all of these transactions involve an equal debit to accounts receivable and credit to gross sales, only a single column for the dollar amount is necessary. Note that an additional column is provided to cross reference the number of the invoice on which the customer was billed. In posting, the debits are recorded individually to the specific customer's accounts receivable (see discussion of subsidiary ledgers below) and the credit in total for the week or month to gross sales.

Exhibit 5.16   SALES JOURNAL   Page No.1

Date	Invoice No.	Account Debited	Post Ref	Accounts Rec. DR and Sales CR
Feb 14	1234	John H. Smith		80
15	1235	Mary F. Jones		70
15	1236	Arturo Gomez		70
24	1237	Susan Wong		90
27	1238	Acme Decorators, Inc.		390

Cash Disbursements Journal

The cash disbursements journal is shown as Exhibit 5.17. Note the provision for recording check number, and that the total cash disbursement is recorded in the cash credit column. Since most cash disbursements are against accounts payable, a separate column is provided for these debits. The debit portion of a payment of a payable without discount is recorded in the accounts payable debit column and identified with the name of the particular supplier's accounts payable (see discussion of subsidiary ledgers below). Where a discount is taken, the amount of the discount is recorded in the purchase discounts credit column to balance the entry. For cash disbursements not involving payment of accounts payable the balancing debit is recorded in the sundry (all other) accounts column and the account to be debited is identified.

Exhibit 5.17   CASH DISBURSEMENTS JOURNAL   Page No. 2

Date	Check No.	Account Debited	Post Ref.	Sundry Accounts DR	Accounts Payable DR	Purchase Discount CR	Cash CR
Feb 2	1287	Prepaid items		2,000			2,000
4	1288	Repairs and Maintenance		100			100
5	1289	Supplies		200			200
10	1290	Equipment		10,500			10,500
26	1291	Green Thumb Suppliers			2,500		2,500
28	1292	Pat Ward, Capital		500			

In posting from the cash disbursements journal to the ledgers, amounts from the sundry accounts column are debited to the specified accounts. Amounts from the accounts payable column are debited to the individual supplier's payables account (see discussion of subsidiary ledgers below). Total purchase discounts and total cash disbursements for the week or month are credited to these accounts respectively.

Purchases Journal

The last, and perhaps the most complex, of the four most common special journals is the purchases journal illustrated in Exhibit 5.18. Note that the purchases journal is used only for purchases on account. Cash purchases are recorded in the cash disbursements journal discussed earlier. Since only purchases on account are recorded in the purchases journal, the amount of each purchase is recorded as a credit to accounts payable. Since many firms record merchandise (inventory) purchases first to a separate purchases account rather than directly to inventory, a separate column is provided for the balancing debit. Similarly a separate column is provided for debits to supplies. Debits to other accounts are recorded along with the specific account involved in the sundry (all other) debits section. In posting from the purchases journal to the ledger, credits are posted individually to specific suppliers' payables accounts (see discussion of subsidiary ledgers below). Totals for the week or month are posted to the accounts for purchases and supplies respectively. Sundry account debits are posted to the account specified.

Exhibit 5.18   PURCHASES JOURNAL   Page No.1

Date	Account Credited	Post Ref.	Accounts Payable CR	Purchases DR	Supplies DR	Sundry Accounts DR		
						Account	Post Ref.	Account DR
Feb 11	Green Thumb Suppliers		3,000	3,000				
18	McCormick Nursery		500	500				
25	Green Thumb Suppliers		800	800				

Subsidiary Ledgers

As discussed in the chapter, a firm with more than a few customers to whom it extends credit, or more that a few suppliers from whom it purchases goods and services on account, must maintain individual receivable and payable accounts for each distinct customer and supplier. An individual customer's receivable account is shown in Exhibit 5.19. Such accounts are kept in a separate file (usually alphabetically) known as the Accounts Receivable (Subsidiary) Ledger. Where **subsidiary accounts** are maintained, the single account for accounts receivable in the general ledger is known as the control or controlling account. Periodically the balances of all the subsidiary accounts are proofed or reconciled with the total in the control account. Note in Exhibit 5.19 that a third column is provided for the latest current balance in the account (normally a debit balance). Should a credit balance occur (customer overpayment) this would be shown by indicating the balance in parentheses.

Subsidiary accounts for individual suppliers are maintained in the Accounts Payable (Subsidiary) Ledger with the general ledger account acting as the control account. An individual supplier's payable account is shown in Exhibit 5.20. The operation of the accounts payable subsidiary account is identical to that for receivables except for the fact that the normal account balance is a credit.

Exhibit 5.19   ACCOUNTS RECEIVABLE LEDGER

NAME: *Mary F. Jones*
ADDRESS: *145 Folger St., San Francisco, CA 94123*

Date		Item	Post Ref.	Debit	Credit	Balance DR/(CR)
Feb	*15*	*Plants and fertilizer*		*80*		*80*
	20	*Payment*			*80*	*0*

Exhibit 5.20   ACCOUNTS PAYABLE LEDGER

NAME: *Green Thumb Suppliers*
ADDRESS: *214 Dolmas St., Tiburon, CA 94920*

Date		Item	Post Ref.	Debit	Credit	Balance CR/(DR)
Feb	*11*	*Purchase*			*3,000*	*3,000*
	25	*Purchase*			*800*	*3,800*
	26	*Payment*		*2,500*		*1,300*

Accounting Systems and Internal Control

Charts of accounts, general and special journals, general and subsidiary ledgers, and worksheets are all the parts of the firm's accounting system. Other devices and procedures are also employed to assure internal control. The journal entry, the audit trail, and the trial balance are examples of internal control procedures already mentioned. The term "internal control" in the broad sense refers to all aspects of a firm's systems and procedures designed to implement top management's policies and directives. With reference to accounting systems, a firm's internal controls, or internal checks, refer to those systems and procedures designed and operated to yield accurate accounting data and to safeguard assets in conformance with management policies and GAAP requirements. A common misunderstanding of the necessity for internal controls is that asset security is the primary focus. Actually the primary focus is to assure accuracy of the financial statements, with asset security a secondary and necessary part of achieving statement accuracy. An underlying principle of internal control is that all information that ends up in the financial statements should be subject to substantial internal checks and verification. Although a definitive coverage of internal control is beyond the scope of this text, a few basic elements and techniques will be cited so that you may appreciate the importance of internal control and the concepts involved.

Devices and Documents Used

In addition to the accounting "books" and records previously cited, a firm will often require:

- *Use of Cash Registers*: By requiring use of cash registers or sales terminals to record all customer sales, a firm effectively involves its customers (who are accustomed to seeing a sale recorded and being offered a register receipt) in assuring that employees do not "pocket" cash proceeds from sales. Some firms go further in involving their customers in the process of ensuring that all sales are entered into the register. Approaches used include advising customers that they can only obtain refunds or credits if returned merchandise is accompanied by the register tape, offering discounts to customers who are not offered a register receipt at the time of sale, and coupon printing on the back of register tape with prizes or discounts offered to customers.

- *Documentary Evidence of Transactions*: All journal entries for transactions (as distinct from adjustments) may be required to be supported and cross referenced to source documents such as receiving records, shipping records, payroll sheets, timecards, or approved supplier invoices (or vouchers-see below).

- *Register or Logs of Assets*: A separate running listing (inventory) of all assets supposedly on hand (other than cash, accounts receivable, merchandise or product inventory, and supplies) may be required. The register will provide detailed descriptions, dates of acquisition and disposition, and location. Items such as marketable securities, insurance policies, notes receivable, and long-lived assets will be included in such registers; and the registers will periodically be verified by physical inspection of each item listed as being on hand.

- *Petty Cash Receipts*: All cash disbursements other than by check may be required to be accompanied by a written receipt identifying the purpose of the disbursement and bearing an authorized signature.

- *Vouchers*: A firm may require that all cash disbursements (checks drawn) be accompanied by a voucher authorizing same. A voucher is a form identifying the purpose of the disbursement and bearing an authorized signature; and vouchers, in turn, may be serially numbered and accounted for in a separate voucher register.

Important Policies and Procedures

Perhaps of even greater importance to adequate internal control are specific policies and procedures relating to personnel including:

- *Independence from Operations*: Management should make sure that its accountants remain exclusively "independent scorekeepers" and are not assigned business operation responsibilities. Otherwise they would be placed in a conflict of interest position reporting their own performance.

- *Defined Responsibilities*: Management should assign each accountant clearly defined, understood, and accepted responsibilities; and ensure such responsibilities neither overlap nor leave areas uncovered.

- *Adequate Competence*: Management should determine that each accountant employed is adequately qualified and skilled to accept the responsibilities assigned.

- *Segregated Responsibilities for Related Activities*: Management should make sure that all activities related to a particular transaction or event are not assigned or even available to one individual. For example, responsibilities for the authorization, preparation, signing, and recording of checks should be divided among several individuals all of whom would have to conspire if cash were to be taken without immediate recognition of the fact. Similarly, steps must be taken to ensure that computer programmers do not have unmonitored/unrecorded access to operating files, and that computer operators do not have unmonitored/unrecorded access to computer programs, and so forth.

- *Periodic Rotation of Employees*: Where possible, periodic rotation of employees among different jobs will serve several purposes. Employee skills will be upgraded, leading to potential advancement and the ability to cover absence in an emergency. Also the development of undesirable individual shortcuts will be discouraged, while simultaneously providing fresh perspectives that might both encourage the development of desirable system improvements and also enhance employee morale.

- *BONDING AND INSURANCE:* A firm may require that accountants in key positions be bonded and that the firm have insurance against employee misappropriation of assets. Bonding and insurance can have three benefits: Investigation by the bonding/insurance company may uncover an undesirable employee background, the firm will be insured against significant loss should it occur, and the process itself may tend to reinforce employee integrity.

Independent Review

Finally, an essential aspect of effective internal control is review by an independent auditor. Larger firms have qualified accountants with no direct responsibilities for performing day to day accounting responsibilities who are designated as **internal auditors**. It is the responsibility of the internal auditor both to assure that existing policies, procedures, and systems of **internal control** are operating as intended, and to recommend improvements. During a firm's annual audit, the outside auditor or CPA similarly makes a detailed study of the design and implementation of the firm's internal control system. A more detailed and more costly examination of the underlying data is required only where inadequacy or breakdown is uncovered. Therefore the motivation for good internal control includes a reduced annual audit fee.

Using Computers and Other Automated Equipment

The focus in this chapter, and in the preparer procedure and problem supplements to this and subsequent chapters, is on the manual accumulation, recording, classification, summarization, and reporting of financial accounting data. This emphasis is intended to increase your basic understanding of the various steps required, regardless of the methods actually employed.

Even some of the smallest firms today use computers or other computerized equipment to perform many tasks integral to the accounting system. Microcomputers are capable of storing ledgers and preparing financial statements for smaller firms today. Those firms that cannot afford to keep their own complete accounting records, or who choose not to, may find it economical to subcontract portions of their accounting.[4] The details of partially or fully automated accounting systems are beyond the scope of this text. Most colleges and universities offer special courses in accounting systems or information systems in which such automation is covered.

Although the details of automated systems are beyond the scope of this text, it is important that you perceive how the advent of the automated system significantly changes the role and the responsibility of the bookkeeper. Whereas formerly the bookkeeper performed and had control over the entire accounting cycle, now it is common for the bookkeeper to only initiate the original entry in a form acceptable to the computer. This reduction of overall activity places much greater responsibility for accuracy on the originator of the entry. The computer thereafter "blindly" follows whatever instruction it is given. Posting to the ledger, preparation and statements are processed by the computer. The one primary difference is the timing of adjusting entries. Adjusting entries must be

---

[4] For example, the complex calculations and record keeping involved in processing payroll often makes it economically desirable for firms with as few as a dozen employees to subcontract their payroll operation to a service bureau.

entered into the journal **before** the statements can be processed by the computer. Closing and reversing entries would be done the same way as in a manual system.

Today's accounting personnel are expected to be able to:

- Select the packaged system or service center package from those currently available;

- Operate an in house computer that performs the firm's accounting processes; and

- Instruct the computer programmer (or actually to program the computer) on how desired bookkeeping processes should be performed.

Finally, with the use of Electronic Data Processing (EDP), accounting operations are processed within the computer, creating special problems in verifying the accuracy of financial data. The traditional audit trail may be nonexistent, the accuracy of internal processing will be verified by inputting sample data and comparing the results with those generated by the computer with this verified output. Internal control and auditing where computers are involved require highly specialized technical knowledge that most users of such systems do not possess.

Relative Emphasis on Bookkeeping Procedure

This chapter has introduced the basic elements of bookkeeping and internal control systems employed by accountants. As previously described in the Student Introduction at the beginning of this book, this text is written so that you may:

- Either limit your bookkeeping exposure to the general concepts so far covered in this chapter, or

- Develop a more thorough knowledge by being exposed to additional information and problems involving the actual recording and classification of information following the debit/credit model.

If it is your intention, or that of your instructor, that you limit your bookkeeping exposure to the materials already covered, you should skip the Preparer Information and Preparer Problems in subsequent chapters. You will find that the most of each subsequent chapter is written without reference to the debit/credit code or to the recording process. The accountant's measuring, recording, and reporting activities are described in terms of their ultimate financial statement effect. Your attention will be focused on increases and decreases on the balance sheet diagram with which you are already familiar.

On the other hand, if it is your intention, or that of your instructor, that you gain additional exposure to the debit/credit system in operation, you should study the preparer materials in each chapter. You may also desire or be required to complete the Financial Accounting Information Integrative Practice Sets.[5]

A word of caution: many beginning accounting students become so involved with bookkeeping procedures that they lose sight of financial statement effects and fail to grasp the essential operation, logic, and usefulness of the accounting system as a whole and of the financial statements themselves. These students may end up as programmed bookkeepers or technicians with little or no understanding of accounting as a whole, its strengths, and its weaknesses. To help you avoid this pitfall and maintain perspective, bookkeeping procedures are carefully segregated in "preparer procedures" in subsequent chapters. You can therefore clearly maintain the distinction between the financial accounting, measuring, and reporting system itself and the bookkeeping or recording system that merely serves to implement financial accounting.

Chapter Overview

Based upon the material introduced in this chapter, you should now be able to:

- Explain the debit/credit coding system and describe which types of accounts normally have debit or credit balances;

- Describe a journal entry and its function, with examples;

- Describe posting, and explain trial balances and the audit trail;

- Explain the two distinct uses of reversing entries with examples;

- Describe the worksheet and its function;

- Describe the typical accounting cycle;

- Explain the meaning and importance of internal control as it applies to accounting systems, and describe several common devices and documents and several desirable policies and procedures designed to accomplish internal control;

- Describe the differences between manual and computerized accounting systems and;

- Define and describe the function of certain specific accounting practices including closing, subsidiary accounts, and control accounts.

---

[5] By A. Thompson Montgomery and Linda K. Whitten, Kendall/Hunt Publishing Company, Dubuque, Iowa, 1988.

New Vocabulary and Concepts

Adjusted Trial Balance	Internal Control
Audit trail	Journalize
Charging	Nominal accounts
Chart of accounts	Real accounts
Close/closing	Subsidiary accounts
Control account	Subsidiary ledgers
Credit	T-account
Debit	Trial balance
General Journal	Voucher
Internal auditor	Worksheet

Review Questions

1. Why is the standardization of accounting practices and procedures essential within one firm and among different firms?

2. Define the terms debit and credit.

3. (a) Which accounts normally have debit balances? (b) Which accounts normally have credit balances?

4. For the following types of accounts, how are they (a) increased and (b) decreased:

Asset accounts	Owner's Equity accounts
Contra-asset accounts	Contra-equity accounts
Liability accounts	Revenue and gain accounts
Contra liability accounts	Expense and loss accounts

5. Describe the audit trail and its purpose.

6. Describe a trial balance and its purpose.

7. (a) Describe the 10 column worksheet and its purpose. (b) Describe the sequential steps in the preparation and completion of such a worksheet.

8. What are two uses of reversing entries? Explain with examples.

9. Describe the eight steps of the accounting cycle.

10. (a) What is the difference between real and nominal accounts? (b) Why does the accountant use nominal accounts? (c) What is meant by closing?

11. (a) What is the difference between subsidiary and control accounts? (b) Why does the accountant use subsidiary accounts?

12. (a) What is a chart of accounts? (b) What is its purpose?

13. Identify and explain the use of at least ten different types of documents or records that may be part of a firm's accounting system.

14. (a) What is meant by internal control? (b) What are the objectives of internal control for accounting? (c) What device involves customers in the internal control process? (d) Identify and explain the purpose of at least six policies and procedures affecting accounting employees that are useful and/or necessary for effective internal control.

Preparer Problems

Normally the preparer problems throughout this book are tied in with the essential and supplementary problems in the same chapter. However, this chapter is essentially an extension of Chapter 4, integrating bookkeeping procedures into the material introduced in that chapter. In the following problems you are therefore asked to refer back to certain essential and supplementary problems in Chapter 4.

For working papers to use in preparer problem solutions, if not otherwise advised by your instructor, you will find that a pad of two column paper for journal entries, and several sheets of ten column paper for worksheets, will be a worthwhile time saver. These materials should be available at your campus bookstore. Lastly, in selecting the appropriate account title and number to use in the required entries, ledgers, and worksheets, refer to the Introductory Chart of Accounts given as Exhibit 5.1 in this chapter. You may also refer to the complete Illustrative Chart (containing all accounts introduced in the text) that may be found in Appendix D at the back of the book along with the solutions to the odd numbered preparer problems. Use whichever chart is most convenient.

PP 5.1 Prepare journal entries for each of the transactions given for the Albertson Company in EP 4.1 (Chapter 4) that do have an effect upon the firm's financial position. Identify your entries with the event number given in EP 4.1.

PP 5.2 Follow the same instructions given in PP 5.1 for data given for the Barstow Company in EP 4.2.

PP 5.3 Prepare journal entries for each of the end of period adjustments given for the Albertson Company in EP 4.5. Identify your entries with the adjustment letter code given in EP 4.5.

PP 5.4 Follow the same instructions given in PP 5.3 for the end of period adjustments given for the Barstow Company in EP 4.6.

PP 5.5 Refer to SP 4.15 for the Wade Company:
(a) Prepare journal entries for all transactions identifying each by transaction number rather than date. (b) Prepare necessary year end adjusting entries.

PP 5.6 Refer to the alternative data given for 19X3 for the Wade Company in SP 4.16. Complete requirements (a) and (b) as given in PP 5.5 using the alternative 19X3 data given.

PP 5.7   Refer to SP 4.17 for Period 2 for Luigi's Auto Parts:

(a) Preparer journal entries for all transactions identifying each by transaction number rather than by date.

(b) Prepare "T" accounts for all necessary ledger accounts and record the Period 1 ending balances as the beginning balances for Period 2.

(c) Post all transaction entries to the ledger "T" accounts referencing the posted entry with account numbers and the ledger accounts with transaction numbers in place of journal page number.

(d) Prepare a trial balance of all ledger accounts in the ten column worksheet. Label all worksheet columns in good form.

(e) Record the necessary Period 2 adjustments in the adjustment columns of the worksheet; and complete and balance the adjusted account balances in the appropriate columns.

(f) Record the revenue and expense account balances in the income statement columns of the worksheet.

(g) Record the balance sheet account balances in the appropriate columns and balance both income and balance sheet columns by recording the net income for the period.

(h) Prepare the Period 2 income statement, statement of owner's capital, and ending balance sheet in good form.

(i) Prepare and post year-end adjusting entries.

(j) Prepare and post year-end closing entries.

PP 5.8   Refer to the data given in SP 4.18 for Period 2 for Irene's Sport Shop. For Irene's firm complete requirements (a) through (j) as given in PP 5.7.

PP 5.9   Obtain or prepare both a cash receipts and a sales journal. To one or the other of these special journals, as appropriate, journalize the following transactions.

(1) Cash sales totalling $4,000.

(2) Sales on account to Leonard Schwarz of $2,000.

(3) Collection of $3,000 on accounts receivable from Mike Smith.

(4) Collection of note receivable of $5,000 plus interest of $400.

(5) Sales on account to Sally White of $2,500.

(6) Cash sales totalling $1,500.

(7) Collection of $1,000 on accounts receivable from Leonard Schwarz.

Note: Use the transaction number to identify the entry instead of the date.

PP 5.10 Obtain or prepare both a cash receipts and a sales journal. To one or the other of these special journals, as appropriate, journalize the following transactions:

(1) Collection of note receivable of $12,000 plus $1,200 interest.

(2) Sales on account to Jose Garcia of $500.

(3) Cash sales of $400.

(4) Collection of $2,000 on accounts receivable from Marilyn Wong.

(5) Sales on account to Sally Washington of $300.

(6) Collection of $200 on accounts receivable from Jose Garcia.

(7) Cash sales of $1,800.

Note: Use the transaction number to identify your entry instead of the date.

PP 5.11 Obtain or prepare both a cash disbursements and a purchases journal. To one or the other of these special journals, as appropriate, journalize the following transactions:

(1) Cash purchase of merchandise of $2,000 with check number 747.

(2) Purchase of merchandise costing $8,000 on account from the Jones Manufacturing Company.

(3) Purchase of equipment costing $6,000 with check number 748 as payment in full.

(4) Purchase supplies on account costing $450 from the Smith Supply Company.

(5) Pay $2,000 on accounts payable to the Jones Manufacturing Company with check number 749.

(6) Pay miscellaneous expenses totaling $440 with check number 750.

(7) Purchase equipment on account costing $7,000 from the Clark Company.

Note: Use the transaction number to identify the entry instead of the date.

PP 5.12 Obtain or prepare both a cash disbursements and a purchase journal. To one or the other of these special journals, as appropriate, journalize the following transactions:

(1) Purchase equipment on account costing $5,000 from the Acme Manufacturing Company.

(2) Pay utilities bill (not previously accrued) with check number 283 in the amount of $400.

(3) Pay $3,000 on accounts payable to the Gonzales Supply Company with check number 284.

(4) Purchase merchandise costing $13,000 on account from the Hamilton Wholesale Company.

(5) Purchase supplies costing $800 on account from the Zorn Stationery Company.

(6) Pay $1,000 on accounts payable to the Tong Corporation with check number 285.

(7) Purchase merchandise costing $6,000 with check number 286.

(8) Purchase supplies costing $100 with check number 287.

Note: Use the transaction number to identify the entry instead of the date.

6

Income Statements and Revenue Recognition

Chapter Preview

The chapter objective is to complete your introduction to the accounting of net income and how it is measured and reported by accountants. In this chapter you can:

1. Learn the usefulness of income detail;
2. Reinforce and expand your understanding of how income components are identified (introduced in Chapter 4);
3. Become familiar with the presentation format for income data;
4. Learn the principles of revenue recognition;
5. Understand how expenses are matched with revenue;
6. Learn tools of trend and comparative analysis.

You should have a clear understanding of the essential structure and operation of the entire financial accounting system after completing this chapter. Subsequent chapters will merely contain amplifications to this system

Need for Income Detail

The Potted Planter has grown significantly in size since it was organized. The firm is now profitable and has two stores, a complete nursery and a plant store. The previous year's balance sheet (as of 12/31/X2) is given in Exhibit 6.1. Note that the balance sheet is dated as of December 31. Pat's **fiscal year** is the same as the calender year. The fiscal years of many retailers' end in January. By the end of January, the Christmas season has been completed, merchandise exchanges and returns have been processed, and any excess inventory has been reduced through post Christmas sales. For most retailers, the end of January provides a much better time to consider the business year completed and another about to begin. Since Pat's business is plants, she would not be concerned with post-Christmas sales, and December 31 would be a good point to end her year.

Exhibit 6.1

POTTED PLANTER BALANCE SHEET AS OF 12/31/X2

Assets		Equities	
Cash	$ 9,000	Accounts Payable	$ 80,000
Accounts Receivable (1)	90,000	Wages and Salaries Payable	2,200
Inventory	135,000	Taxes Payable (4)	40,800
Supplies	2,000		
Prepaid Insurance	1,500	Total Current Liabilities	$123,000
		Noncurrent Notes Payable	130,000
Total Current Assets	$237,500	Total Liabilities	$253,000
Property and Equipment (2)			
Land	$ 30,000		
Building	150,000		
Accum. Depr.	(80,000)		
Equipment	90,000		
Accum. Depr.	(40,000) 150,000		
Other:			
Deferred Charges (3)	1,500	Pat Ward, Capital	136,000
Total Assets	$389,000	Total Equities	$389,000

Notes:

(1) For simplification, it is assumed that all customer receivables are expected to be collected and, therefore, no allowance for bad debts is necessary.

(2) Currently Pat owns one nursery and leases a second smaller store.

(3) Final month's rent on leased store, lease expires in nine years.

(4) Includes property taxes of $1,000 and income taxes of $39,800. Income taxes are for illustrative purposes only, since sole proprietorships do not pay income taxes.

For 19X3, Pat's business income was $159,150 before income taxes. Although she is pleased with the overall result, Pat wants to know the details of the various revenues and expenses to calculate her net income for the year. She wants these details so she can compare 19X3's with the previous year ending 12/31/X2, (Exhibit 6.2). She also wants to compare her performance to that of other nurseries.

Exhibit 6.2

POTTED PLANTER INCOME STATEMENT
for year ending 12/31/X2

Net Sales		$ 800,000
Cost of Goods Sold		480,000
Gross Profit		320,000
Less Operating Expenses		
Wages and salaries	$ 140,000	
Utilities	10,000	
Interest	15,600	
Rentals	18,000	
Depreciation	30,000	
Property taxes	2,400	
Supplies	3,000	
Insurance	1,500	220,500
Income before Income Taxes		$ 99,500
Provision for Income Taxes[a]		39,800
Net Income		$ 59,700

[a] This item normally only appears on corporate income statements and is included here for illustrative purposes only.

The following summary events occurred during 19X3 for the Potted Planter.[1] Those transactions with which you are already familiar are marked with an asterisk.

Events Involving Sales Revenue

*1. Cash sales to customers totaled $300,000.

*2. Sales to customers on account totaled $900,000.

---

[1] In actuality, many more individual transactions occurred. For simplification, they are summarized by transaction type.

3. Customers returned merchandise originally sold for $120,000. Of these sales, $36,000 were originally cash sales and a cash refund was given. The balances were originally sales on account or credit sales, and the related accounts receivables were reduced accordingly.

4. Customers ordered "special order" merchandise priced at $75,000, and they paid this amount in advance.

5. By year-end, special order merchandise priced at $60,000 had been obtained and delivered to some of the customers who had paid in advance.

Events Involving Acquisition of New Assets

*6. Pat invested an additional $20,000 cash in the business.

*7. Inventory costing $650,000 was acquired from suppliers on account.

*8. Various supplies costing $3,000 were acquired, $2,000 on account and the balance for cash.

*9. An insurance policy providing three years' coverage beginning on 1/1/X3 was acquired with a $4,500 cash payment.

*10. Additional display counters and cash registers costing $15,000 were acquired with a $4,000 down payment. A long-term interest bearing promissory note to be paid on 7/31/X5 was given to the supplier covering the balance.

11. $13,600 was spent on redecorating and rewiring the leased store.

12. $37,500 was advanced to suppliers for special order merchandise.

13. Special order merchandise costing $30,000 which had been paid in advance was received.

14. $15,000 was borrowed from the bank on a short-term loan.

Events Involving Exchanges of Assets

*15. Accounts receivable collected from customers were $766,000.

16. $30,000 of temporary excess cash was invested in short-term marketable securities.

17. Later, to obtain needed cash, short-term marketable securities costing $20,000 were sold for $25,000.

18. A current notes receivable for $40,000 plus interest was accepted from customers in settlement of overdue accounts receivable.

19. Current notes receivable for $35,000 plus $3,150 of interest was collected.

Events Involving Payments of Liabilities and Operating Costs

*20. Invoices for utilities and other services costing $20,000 were received.

*21. $662,000 was paid on accounts payable.

22. The short-term bank loan of $15,000 was repaid together with $700 of interest.

23. The $2,200 of wages and salaries owed as of 12/31/X2 and an additional $217,000 earned by employees during the current year through the last pay period were paid.[2]

24. $7,800 representing interest for the first six months on the noncurrent notes payable was paid.

25. Property taxes of $200 per month were payable on August 31. The $1,000 owed as of 12/31/X2 and the balance covering February through August was paid.[3]

26. The firm's income tax liability of $39,800 as of 12/31/X2 was paid.

27. Rental payments of $18,000 were made on the second store.

Other Events

28. Collected interest totalling $1,300 on marketable securities.

29. Pat withdrew $90,000 cash for personal use.

Balance Sheet Effect of Transactions

As mentioned above, the summary events/transactions identified with an asterisk are similar to those first introduced in Chapter 4. Their combined effect upon the firm's beginning balance sheet[4] is shown on Balance Sheet Diagram 6.1.

---

[2] For simplification, payroll withholding, payroll taxes, and other employee benefit deductions are ignored in this example and may be ignored in all problems in this text unless otherwise specified.

[3] In a real situation, The Potted Planter as a proprietorship would not be required to pay taxes. Pat as an individual would be liable for property and income taxes on all of her property and income including that of her business. Only corporations are subject to separate taxation. Property and income taxes are included in this example to better illustrate income statement classifications later in this chapter.

[4] Note that the prior fiscal year's or period's ending balance sheet is also, by definition, the current year's or period's beginning balance sheet.

Diagram 6.1   The Potted Planter–Balance Sheet Effect of Transactions
with an asterisk
(b) = beginning balances as of 1/1/X3,
(r) = remaining balances

Current Assets:				Current Liabilities:			
Cash	$ 9,000	(b)		Accounts Payable			
	+ 300,000	(1)			$ 80,000	(b)	
	+ 20,000	(6)			+ 650,000	(7)	
	− 1,000	(8)			+ 2,000	(8)	
	− 4,500	(9)			+ 20,000	(20)	
	− 4,000	(10)			− 662,000	(21)	$ 90,000 (r)
	+ 766,000	(15)		Wages and Salaries			
	− 662,000	(21)	$ 423,500 (r)		2,200	(b)	2,200 (r)
Accounts Receivable				Taxes Payable			
	90,000	(b)			40,800	(b)	40,800 (r)
	+ 900,000	(2)					
	− 766,000	(15)	224,000 (r)				
Inventory	135,000	(b)		**Long-term Debt:**			
	+ 650,000	(7)	785,000 (r)	Noncurrent Notes			
Supplies	2,000	(b)			130,000	(b)	
	+ 3,000	(8)	5,000 (r)		+ 11,000	(10)	141,000 (r)
Prepaid Insurance							
	1,500	(b)					
	+ 4,500	(9)	6,000 (r)	**Owner's Equity:**			
Long-lived Assets:							
Land	30,000	(b)	30,000 (r)	Pat's Capital			
Buildings	150,000	(b)	150,000 (r)		136,000	(b)	
Accum. Depr. Buildings					+ 20,000	(6)	
	(80,000)	(b)	(80,000) (r)				
Equipment	90,000	(b)					
	+ 15,000	(10)	105,000 (r)				
Accum. Depr. Equip.							
	(40,000)	(b)	(40,000) (r)				
Def Charges	1,500	(b)	1,500 (r)				
	TOTAL ASSETS		**$1,610,000**	**TOTAL EQUITIES**			**$1,610,000**

Income
+ 300,000   (1)
+ 900,000   (2)
− 20,000   (20)

You should verify and reinforce your understanding of the balance sheet effect of each of these transactions before proceeding to the new types of transactions.

Sales Returns

The independent effect of transaction (3), (4), and (5) is shown on Balance Sheet Diagram 6.2. For customer returns (transaction 3) the effect is the exact opposite or reversal of the original effect of cash and credit sale transactions (1) and (2). Cash or accounts receivable is reduced and the asset reduction is balanced by an equal reduction of equities via the income box. Note that the minus $120,000 in the box on Balance Sheet Diagram 6.2 can be viewed either as an expense (a certain portion of customer returns are an inevitable cost of doing business) or as a revenue reduction. Most firms, and the illustrations in this text, choose the latter view and subtract **sales returns and allowances** from gross sales to arrive at **net sales** for the period.

Diagram 6.2   Balance Sheet Effect of Events (3), (4), and (5)

Current Assets:			Current Liabilities:		
Cash	–	36,000 (3)	Unearned Revenue	+	75,000 (4)
	+	75,000 (4)		–	60,000 (5)
Accounts Receivable	–	84,000 (3)	Long-term Debt:		
Long Lived Assets:			**Owner's Equity:**		
			Income		
			– 120,000 (3)		
			+ 60,000 (5)		

Unearned Revenue and Recognition of Revenue

Where a customer orders goods or services but the firm has yet to make delivery, neither party has performed. These executory agreements are not reflected in the financial statements themselves. However, transaction (4) provides an example of a different situation. One party to the exchange transaction (the customer) has performed (paid cash), but the sale transaction has not been completed (the merchandise has not been delivered). Therefore, Pat now has a liability either to deliver merchandise priced at $75,000 or else to return an equivalent amount of cash. Such a liability for future delivery of goods or services is recorded as unearned revenue, or revenue collected in advance of being earned. Other examples of unearned revenue not illustrated include magazine subscriptions, season tickets, prepaid travel packages, and so forth.

When performance of the second party has occurred the sale is completed. The previously unearned revenue has now been earned and the corresponding amount $60,000 in the Potted Planter example is transferred from the liability classification to owner's equity via the income box.[5] Although inventory is sold to customers throughout the year, most retailers do not record inventory outflows at that time. Rather, the entire outflow of inventory occurring during the year is determined and recorded at year-end as a single adjustment. This common approach is known as the Periodic Inventory Method. In contrast, the Perpetual Inventory Method records inventory outflows daily or weekly. Both methods will be discussed further in Chapter 8.

Acquisition of New Assets

The independent effect of transactions (11), (12), (13), and (14) is shown on Balance Sheet Diagram 6.3. Transaction (11) results in the acquisition of an intangible asset. Leasehold improvement is the right to use the improvements that have been permanently attached to the landlord's property over the remaining life of the lease. Since the decorations and wiring cannot be removed, they are not classified as equipment. Because these items have future usefulness, they are not immediately expensed. Transaction (12), the deposit with suppliers, creates another prepaid item: the current right to receive merchandise.[6] Transaction (13) is a decrease to prepaids, because the prepaid inventory has arrived. Inventory is increased. Transaction (14) involves the simple acquisition of an asset (cash) in exchange for a promise to pay cash in the near future (current notes payable).

---

[5] Although not illustrated in this text, some firms record all revenue as earned during the year, and then make an adjustment reducing revenue and increasing unearned revenue for sales that are incomplete at year-end. This method requires an additional reversing entry at the beginning of the year. Either approach results in the same amounts shown in the financial statements. Also remember from Chapter 2 that a firm's year-end unearned revenue (liability) is matched by a prepaid item (asset) on its customer's balance sheet.

[6] In effect, this right could be thought of as "inventory receivable." However, since conventionally the term receivable is restricted to designating future receipts of cash, those deposits or advance payments that are made for future goods or services are designated as Prepaid Items.

Diagram 6.3   Balance Sheet Effect of Events (11), (12), (13), and (14))

Current Assets:		Current Liabilities:
Cash	− $136,000 (11)	
	− 37,500 (12)	Current Notes Payable + $15,000 (14)
	+ 15,000 (14)	
Inventory	+ 30,000 (13)	
Prepaid Items	+ 37,500 (12)	**Long-term Debt:**
	− 30,000 (13)	
Long Lived Assets:		**Owner's Equity:**
Leasehold Improvement +	13,600 (11)	

Exchange of Current Assets

The independent effects of transactions (16) through (19) are shown on Balance Sheet Diagram 6.4. These transactions involve the exchange of current assets. However, note only transactions (17) and (19) involve income. The $5,000 gain in liquidation of some of the marketable securities increases the firm's total assets with no corresponding increase in liabilities. Therefore, owner's equity is increased to balance via the income box. Similarly, the $3,150 of interest received increase total assets and is balanced by a plus in the income box. Transaction (17) results in a $5,000 gain on the sale of marketable securities. Marketable securities which had a book value of $20,000 were sold for $25,000.

Diagram 6.4   Balance Sheet Effect of Events (16), (17), (18), and (19)

Current Assets:		Current Liabilities:
Cash	− $30,000 (16)	
	+ 25,000 (17)	
	+ 38,150 (19)	
Marketable Securities		**Long-term Debt:**
	+ 30,000 (16)	
	− 20,000 (17)	
Current Notes Receivable		**Owner's Equity:**
	+ 40,000 (18)	
	− 35,000 (19)	Income
Accounts Receivable	− 40,000 (18)	+ 5,000 (17)
		+ 3,150 (19)

Payments of Liabilities and Operating Costs

The independent effects of transactions (22) through (27) are shown on Balance Sheet Diagram 6.5. The direct payment of a previously recorded liability, transaction (26), has no effect on the income box. However, in cases where the payment exceeds the recorded liability and no new asset is acquired, the difference must be expensed by including a minus or decrease to the income box. The interest obligations had not been previously recorded as liabilities and associated expenses; and therefore the payments resulted in a minus $700 and a minus $7,800 in the box transactions (22) and (24). Similarly, the $1,400 portion of the current year's property tax obligation (through August) was previously unrecorded, and therefore necessitated a minus $1,400 in the box to balance transaction (25). The current year's portion of wage and salary payments ($217,000) and the rental payments of $18,000, were similarly expensed via the income box—transactions (23) and (27).[7]

Diagram 6.5   Balance Sheet Effect of Events (22) Through (29)

Current Assets:		Current Liabilities:	
Cash	− $15,700 (22)	Current Notes Payable − $15,000 (22)	
	− 219,200 (23)	Wages and Salaries − 2,200 (23)	
	− 7,800 (24)		
	− 2,400 (25)	Taxes Payable − 1,000 (25)	
	− 39,800 (26)	− 39,800 (26)	
	− 18,000 (27)		
	+ 1,300 (28)	**Long-term Debt:**	
	− 90,000 (29)		
Long Lived Assets:		**Owner's Equity:**	
		Pat's Capital − $90,000 (29)	

Income	
−	700 (22)
− 217,000	(23)
−	7,800 (24)
−	1,400 (25)
−	18,000 (27)
+	1,300 (28)

---

[7] As a matter of internal bookkeeping procedure, most firms first record payroll obligations as a liability (with a plus to the payable and a minus in the box), and then record payment of the previously recorded liability (no effect in the box). The ultimate statement effect is the same under this alternate procedure.

Other Revenue

The effect of transaction (28) is also shown on Balance Sheet Diagram 6.5. As the interest receivable had not been previously recorded, the interest represents revenue and is recorded as such in the income box.

Owner Withdrawals

The owner withdrawal, transaction (29), although reducing both assets and owner's equity, is an owner transaction and therefore is not reflected in the income box. Generally a separate owner's drawing account is set up and closed to owner's capital at the end of the period. The purpose for a separate drawing account is to create a summary of owner's withdrawals for the period. In this text, you may deduct owner's drawing directly from the capital account at the time of withdrawal since all illustrations are summary transactions.

Pat's year-end balance sheet before adjustments is illustrated in Exhibit 6.3. It reflects the effect of all 29 summary transactions previously given. Note that the sum of the income box items is shown as a distinct addition to Pat's capital account.

Exhibit 6.3

THE POTTED PLANTER BALANCE SHEET
as of 12/31/X3 before adjustments

Assets			Equities	
Cash		$67,950	Accounts Payable	$90,000
Marketable Securities		10,000	Unearned Revenue	15,000
Current Notes Receivable		5,000	Total Current Liabilities	105,000
Accounts Receivable		100,000	Noncurrent Notes Payable	141,000
Inventory		815,000		
Supplies		5,000	Total Liabilities	$246,000
Prepaid Items*		13,500		
Total Current Assets		$1,016,450		
Property and Equipment:				
Land	$ 30,000			
Building	150,000			
Accum. Depr	(80,000)			
Equipment	105,000			
Accum. Depr	(40,000)	165,000		
Other:				
Leasehold impr.	13,600		Pat Ward, Capital	66,000
Deferred charges	1,500	15,100	Income box items**	884,550
Total Assets		$1,196,550	Total Equities	$1,196,550

*Includes both prepaid insurance and deposit on special merchandise on order from supplier.
**Normally would be combined with $66,000 into single account.

Year-end Adjustments

As you learned in Chapter 4, net income cannot be determined until after the necessary year-end adjustments have been included. At 12/31/X3, the 12 adjustments given below were necessary for The Potted Planter. Adjustments similar to those with which you are already familiar are marked with an asterisk.

(A)* A physical count of inventory on 1/1/X3 revealed merchandise costing $140,000.

(B)* An inventory of supplies on hand at year-end revealed supplies costing $1,000.

(C)* The prepaid insurance of $1,500 on 1/1/X3 represented the final year's coverage of a previous policy. The coverage had expired by 12/31/X3.

(D)* Depreciation on buildings and equipment for the year totalled $32,000, with $20,000 applicable to the building and the balance to equipment.

(E)* Utilities and other services consumed by year-end but not yet billed by the supplier were estimated to cost $800.

(F) Wages and salaries earned by employees between the last payday and year-end were estimated to amount to $3,000.

(G) Interest owed for the second six months on long-term debt and as yet unpaid amounted to $8,500.

(H) Property taxes applicable to the past five months and payable in April of 19X4 totalled $1,000.

(I) Income tax liability for the year was estimated at $63,660.[8]
(J) Interest earned, but not yet received at year-end, on marketable securities and notes receivable was $2,100.

(K) Since the lease on the plant store had eight remaining years, it was decided to amortize the $13,600 leasehold improvement by $1,700 each year.

(L) Of the $141,000 of noncurrent notes payable, one note for $20,000 will be due and payable in cash on 9/15/X4. The balance of the notes are not due until after 1/1/X5.

---

[8] As illustrated in Exhibit 6.2, even though The Potted Planter is not incorporated it will be assumed that it is subject to income taxes to illustrate tax reporting. Actually a proprietorship is not taxed as an entity separate from the owner.

Balance Sheet Effect of Adjustments

The balance sheet effect of adjustments (A) through (L) is shown on Balance Sheet Diagram 6.6. The most important adjustment is generally for cost of goods sold (A).

Diagram 6.6   Balance Sheet Effect of Adjustments

Current Assets:				Current Liabilities:			
Interest Receivable	+	$ 2,100	(I)	Current Note Payable	+	$20,000	(L)
Inventory	–	675,000	(A)*	Accounts Payable	+	800	(E)*
Supplies	–	4,000	(B)*	Wages and Salaries	+	3,000	(F)
Prepaid Items	–	1,500	(C)*	Interest Payable	+	8,500	(G)
				Taxes Payable	+	1,000	(H)
					+	63,660	(I)
				Long-term Debt:			
				Noncurr. Note Pay.	–	20,000	(L)
Long-Lived Assets:				**Owner's Equity:**			
Accum. Depr. Bldg	–	20,000	(D)*				
Accum. Depr. Equip.	–	12,000	(D)*				
Leasehold Improvement	–	1,700	(K)				

Owner's Equity:

Income		
– 675,000	(A)*
– 4,000	(B)*
– 1,500	(C)*
– 32,000	(D)*
– 800	(E)*
– 3,000	(F)
– 8,500	(G)
– 1,000	(H)
– 63,660	(I)
+ 2,100	(J)
– 1,700	(K)

* indicates adjustments previously illustrated in Chapter 4.

Recall from the discussion of The Potted Planter's inventory in Chapter 4 that most retailers cannot afford to keep daily records of the cost of merchandise transferred to customers. Instead, they accumulate data on purchases of merchandise throughout the year. At the end of the year beginning inventory and net purchases are added together to create goods available for sale. Ending Inventory, based on an actual year-end physical count, is subtracted from goods available for sale to determine **cost of goods sold**. Cost of goods sold represents the cost of items sold, spoiled, discarded as damaged, or shoplifted.

For many firms, cost of goods sold is one of the largest annual expenses. To highlight its importance and to clarify its calculation for the statement reader, many financial statements include a separate schedule of cost of goods sold, even though such a schedule is not required by GAAP. Exhibit 6.4 provides a schedule of cost of goods sold.

Exhibit 6.4

SCHEDULE OF COST OF GOODS SOLD FOR THE POTTED PLANTER
for the year ending 12/31/X3

Beginning merchandise inventory (as of 1/1/X3)	$ 135,000
Net purchases during year	680,000
Cost of goods available for sale	$ 815,000
Less ending merchandise inventory (as of 12/31/X3)	(140,000)
Cost of Goods Sold	$ 675,000

This exhibit illustrates the method of determining cost of goods sold for firms using the periodic inventory method.

Adjustments for supplies used (B), expiration of prepaid insurance (C), depreciation (D), and for the accrual of the utilities liability (E) all result in expenses in the income box as described in Chapter 4. Similarly the accrual of liabilities for wages and salaries (F), interest (G), property taxes (H), and income taxes (I), all reduce owner's equity via the income box, since they are not involved with the acquisition of assets.

Amortization of the leasehold improvement (K) is similar to the calculation for depreciation. The difference between depreciation and amortization is there is no salvage value for amortization nor is an accumulated amortization account created. Instead the account amortized is simply reduced.

Cost ÷ number of useful periods = Amortization per period

$13,600 ÷ 8 years = $1,700 amortization per year

The accrual of interest revenue (J) is recorded with a plus amount in the income box and the creation of a new asset, interest receivable. Finally, since $20,000 of notes previously classified as noncurrent will require settlement in cash within one year, an adjustment to reclassify the liability to show as current is made (L).

In Chapter 4 you learned that the sum of the items in a firm's income box equalled that firm's net income. Exhibit 6.5 indicates the income effects of all summary transactions and adjustments for the current year. Note that the effects of transactions (6) and (29) are specifically excluded from the income box. These two transactions involve owner investments and withdrawals, affect the owner's capital account directly, and are not part of the measurement of income.[9] Adjustment (L) involves a simple liability reclassification and has no income effect.

For ease of understanding, revenues and gains can be visualized as "any plus in the income box"; and expenses or losses as "any minus in the income box", exceptions are sales returns and allowances and sales discounts. These accounts will be discussed later.

To prepare an income statement, the various revenues and expenses must be identified and grouped by type. Exhibit 6.5 lists all of the items in the income box for the most recent year together with their transaction numbers and adjustment letters. Opposite each

Exhibit 6.5

ITEMS INCLUDED IN THE POTTED PLANTER INCOME
for the year ending 12/31/X3

Transactions:

+	300,000	(1)	Sales completed
+	900,000	(2)	Sales completed
−	120,000	(3)	Sales return
+	60,000	(5)	Sales completed
+	5,000	(17)	Gain on securities sale
+	3,150	(19)	Interest collected
−	20,000	(20)	Utilities services consumed
−	700	(22)	Interest paid
−	217,000	(23)	Wages and salaries paid
−	7,800	(24)	Interest paid
−	1,400	(25)	Property taxes paid
−	18,000	(27)	Rent payments
+	1,300	(28)	Interest collected

Adjustments:

−	675,000	(A)	Cost of goods sold
−	4,000	(B)	Supplies used
−	1,500	(C)	Insurance expiration
−	32,000	(D)	Building & Equipment Depreciation
−	800	(E)	Utilities consumed
−	3,000	(F)	Wages and salaries owed
−	8,500	(G)	Interest owed
−	1,000	(H)	Property taxes owed
−	63,660	(I)	Income taxes owed
+	2,100	(J)	Interest earned
−	1,700	(K)	Leasehold improvement amortization
+	95,490		Net income

[9] Gifts received by the firm and prior period adjustments would also be excluded from income.

amount is shown the type of revenue or expense involved. These revenue and expense items are then combined by similar type and shown in a the income statement.

The Income Statement

The algebraic sum of items in the income box equals the firm's net income. As first discussed in Chapter 4, accountants keep separate accounts during the year for the revenue and expense items illustrated in the "income box". The accounts in the box then provide the data base from which the income statement is prepared. At year-end, these accounts are closed (the balances are transferred) to Owner's Capital.

Note on the income statement that $120,000 of sales returns have been subtracted from $1,260,000 of total or **gross sales** to arrive at the $1,140,000 of reported net sales. Most of the various revenues and expenses are given descriptive terms identifying their type. Minor exceptions would be the expenses related to inventory and income taxes. Instead of "inventory expense" and "income tax expense," cost of goods sold and **provision for income taxes** are commonly used.

Exhibit 6.6

THE POTTED PLANTER INCOME STATEMENT
for the year ending 12/31/X3
(multiple-step format)

Net Sales		$1,140,000
Cost of goods sold		675,000
Gross profit		$ 465,000
Less operating expenses		
Wages and salaries	$ 220,000	
Utilities	20,800	
Interest (expense)*	17,000	
Rent (expense)*	18,000	
Depreciation	32,000	
Property taxes	2,400	
Supplies	4,000	
Insurance	1,500	
Amortization of leasehold improvement	1,700	317,400
Income from Operations		$ 147,600
Other Revenue and Expenses		
Gain on sale of securities	$ 5,000	
Interest (revenue)*	6,550	11,550
Income before income taxes		$ 159,150
Provision for income taxes		63,660
Net Income		$ 95,490

* It is important not to confuse rent and interest expense with rent and interest revenues.

There are two GAAP approved Formats for the income statement. Usage among publicly traded firms in the United States is about equal. The two formats are the multiple-step and the single-step.

Multiple-Step Format

Exhibit 6.6 is an income statement prepared following the multiple-step format. Under this format, the subtotal gross profit discloses the difference between net sales and cost of goods sold. Gross profit may also be identified as gross margin or as trading profit. Following gross profit, all other normal operating expenses of the firm are shown. Revenues other than sales, and sometimes certain expenses considered as nonoperating, are separately grouped and shown below operating expenses. There is no GAAP requirement as to the ordering, degree of detail, or captioning of operating expenses.

In the multiple-step format, operating expenses are followed by other revenues and gains that are not part of the normal operations of the business. Although not illustrated, other expenses and losses that are not part of normal operations could similarly be segregated.[10]

The multiple-step format provides the reader with more information than the single-step format (discussed below) because it segregates incidental revenues and expenses, and provides a subtotal for gross or trading profit from the principle operations of the business. As will be amplified in Chapter 13 covering statement analysis, a firm's gross profit (especially when calculated as a percentage of sales) can provide the statement reader meaningful indicators of the firm's pricing and procurement policies in comparison to competitors.

Single-Step Format

Exhibit 6.7 shows the same data as contained in Exhibit 6.6 for The Potted Planter, but following the single-step format. All revenues and gains are shown first and then followed by all expenses and losses. A gross profit subtotal is not shown. The single-step format is most commonly used by service firms that do not sell products and firms which operate and sell in many industries. Both the single-step and multiple-step formats are acceptable under GAAP.

---

[10] Examples of other revenues and gains would include revenue from secondary activities rent revenue from tenants using excess capacity, gains on the disposal of long-lived assets, and earnings on marketable securities and investments. Examples of other expenses and losses would include costs of secondary operations, losses on asset dispositions, and "write-downs" of assets to reflect unusual cost/value expiration.

Exhibit 6.7

THE POTTED PLANTER INCOME STATEMENT
for the year ending 12/31/X3
(Single-step format)

Net sales		$1,140,000
Gain on sale of securities		5,000
Interest revenue		6,550
Total revenue and gains		$1,151,550
Less expenses and losses:		
Cost of goods sold	$ 675,000	
Wages and salaries	220,000	
Utilities	20,800	
Interest (expense)	17,000	
Rent (expense)	18,000	
Depreciation	32,000	
Property taxes	2,400	
Supplies	4,000	
Insurance	1,500	
Amortization of leasehold improvement	1,700	992,400
Income before income taxes		$ 159,150
Less provision for income taxes		63,660
Net Income		$ 95,490

Net Sales

Note that under either format, it is customary to start with net sales rather than disclosing gross sales less sales returns and allowances and sales discounts.[11] Gross sales are originally recorded net of any trade and volume discounts. Volume or trade discounts from posted or "sticker" prices, which are given at the time of sale are not recorded. Sales discounts are offered in some industries to encourage faster payment on accounts. The payment terms must be clearly understood and stated on the sales invoice at the time of the sale. An example of payment terms on a sales invoice is *2/10, n/30*. This means that the buyer is expected to pay by the 30th day after the invoice, but if payment is made by the 10th day, then a 2 percent discount can be deducted. If a company sells $100,000 of merchandise and payment is made within the discount period (10 days), then the company would accept $98,000 as full payment. However, if the payment is not made within this discount period (10 days), then the company would expect a payment of $100,000 within 30 days of the invoice.

---

[11] Where sales returns and allowance are a regular part of a business and are material in amount, GAAP require than an estimate of anticipated returns and allowances also be incorporated in the financial statements.

Revenue Recognition

In the Potted Planter example, revenue was recognized or recorded at the time sales were completed or interest was earned. Even though collection on sales, interest, or rental payment receipt has not yet occurred under the accrual system required by GAAP, revenue earned is recorded as a receivable and recognized as revenue in the current period.

An increase in owner's equity reflecting an increase in assets or the reduction of a liability that does not result from an owner investment or a gift received by the firm is a revenue or gain.

Generally, revenue and gains result from the performance of a service (including granting the right to use money or other assets) or the transfer of title to goods or other assets held specifically for sale to customers, or realized gain on the sale of other assets. Revenue recognized or reported in the current period can be related to:

- Cash inflow in prior periods (Goods delivered and services performed in the current period, but paid for in prior periods).
- Cash inflow in the current period (Delivery of goods and services in the same period as payment).
- Cash inflow in future periods (Delivery of goods or services in exchange for a receivable).

Note that the foregoing definition of revenue does not pinpoint the timing of its recognition. For most firms, revenue is recognized at the time of sale or upon delivery of goods and services where all 1) costs associated with the sale have either been incurred and 2) legal title for the goods has passed to the buyer, and 3) where the collection of cash is reasonably assured. For some firms, these criteria may be met before the time of sale and for others not until the cash is actually in hand.

Where costs are known and both the sale and collection are assured prior to an actual sale or long-term contract, GAAP allow for earlier recognition of revenue. For certain precious metals (such as gold and silver) and agricultural products (such as corn and wheat) with ready markets, revenue is recognized upon completion of production. Inventory is therefore carried at selling price. On long-term construction projects, revenue may be recognized in portions, as the project is completed and partial payments are received. This is called the **percentage of completion method**. If the project will span over one accounting period, the single large scale is essentially divided into annual portions and treated as several smaller yearly "sales" with accompanying estimates of proportionate cost of goods sold.[12]

---

[12] A more thorough treatment alternate timing of revenue recognition is covered in the appendix to this chapter.

At the other extreme, where a sale is completed but collection cannot be reasonably estimated, recording of revenue is deferred and only recognized in proportion to the installments collected. Under the **installment basis** revenue is recognized only when collected.[13]

Expense Recognition

Of equal importance to the appropriate timing of revenue recognition is the timing of expense recognition, the **matching principle**. The objective of GAAP is that expenses be "matched" with those revenues they were intended to generate.

Any reduction of owner's equity reflecting the reduction of an asset or the increase of liability that does not result from owner withdrawals is an expense or loss.

As first described in Chapter 4, an expense recognized in a given period can be related to a cash outflow in a prior period (an asset expiration), to a cash outflow in the current period (payment for something currently consumed), or to a cash outflow in a future period (a payable for something already consumed).

Other Revenues and Expenses

Other revenues and expenses result from nonoperating activities. Examples of other revenues include rental or leasing of excess assets such as buildings, equipment, or services resulting from excess capacity. Investment and dividend revenues would also be included in this category. Other expenses include interest expense and other financing expenses.

Other revenues and expenses result from financing activities, both borrowing and investing, a non-operating business activity. These items are segregated since they are unique to the firm and are not as useful in comparing performance with other firms.

Ordinary Gains and Losses

Gains and losses included in the other revenue and expense section of the income statement are considered "ordinary". Ordinary gains and losses are all gains and losses which fail to meet the criteria of "extraordinary". **Extraordinary items** will be discussed later in the chapter. Exhibit 6.8 illustrates a typical ordinary loss. A gain or loss is the difference between book value and the sales amount of the asset. The equipment had a book value of $60,000 and it was sold for $45,000 resulting in a $15,000 loss. Gains and losses on disposal of assets are generally considered ordinary. Transaction (17) for The Potted Planter demonstrates an ordinary gain.

---

[13] The use of installment sales method to defer recognition of income although limited for financial reporting was widely used for income taxes prior to the Tax Reform of 1986.

Exhibit 6.8

DISPOSAL OF EQUIPMENT

Equipment Cost	$ 100,000
less Accumulated Depreciation	40,000
Book Value	$ 60,000
Price Equipment was Sold	45,000
Loss on Sale of Equipment	$ 15,000

Expenditures

An **expenditure** may be defined as either an outflow of cash (other than to owner's equity or in settlement of a previously recognized liability) or as the incurrence of a liability for property, goods, or services received or consumed. When an expenditure occurs, the accountant will either **capitalize** or **expense** the goods or services received. If the expenditure resulted in the acquisition of an item or right with future value, such item or right will be "capitalized" or set up as an asset. If the expenditure does not result in the acquisition of something with future value, it is expensed or "written off" as an immediate reduction of owner's equity (a minus in the income box).

Provision for Income Taxes

Also note that whereas property taxes are included as part of operating expense, the income tax expense called Provision for Income Taxes, is segregated at the bottom of the statement following a subtotal for income before (income) taxes. The final net amount affecting owner's equity is identified as net income, and it is commonly referred to as the **bottom line**. In Pat's case, since her firm is a proprietorship and not subject to the income taxes, which were included only for illustrative purposes, a proper income statement would end with $159,150 (and the corresponding income tax liability would also be omitted from the balance sheet). Since $159,150 would be the bottom line, it would then be identified as net income rather than as income before income taxes.

As will be discussed further in Chapters 10 when a business is incorporated, it becomes a legal entity distinct from its owners. As a separate legal entity, a corporation is subjected to income tax, and the necessary provision for this expense is shown as a deduction following income derived from all ordinary revenues and expenses gains and losses (as illustrated for The Potted Planter).

Segregating Nonrecurring Items

A firm may also have certain revenues, gains, expenses, or losses that are nonrecurring. These include extraordinary items, discontinued operations, and changes in accounting methods. GAAP require that nonrecurring items be segregated from potentially repeatable income, income from continuing operations. Nonrecurring items, therefore are shown below the subtotal income from continuing operations. Income from continuing operations represents income from all revenues, gains, expenses, and losses except extraordinary items, discontinued operations, and changes in accounting methods.

Discontinued Operations

Discontinued operations are segments of the business which have been sold or negotiations have been completed to sell or eliminate the operation before the financial statements are prepared. This can include a product line or a division of the business. GAAP require that all revenue and expenses from the discontinued operation and the gain or sale, if sold, be segregated on the income statement since the discontinued operation is nonrecurring and therefore will not predict future income. Both the income and any resultant gain or loss on disposal must be net of the appropriate income tax for that operation. Exhibit 6.9 illustrates the proper treatment for a discontinued operation. If The Potted Planter had discontinued a third operation during the year, and that operation had produced $50,000 in revenues and $60,000 in expenses the operation would have had a net loss. The company would use that loss to reduce overall income taxes. This amount is shown as the tax savings due to operations for the discontinued segment. If the operation was sold for $200,000 and the assets less liabilities for that operation (book value) was $150,000, then the sale resulted in a gain. The gain would increase income taxes which is shown reducing the gain on disposal.

Extraordinary Items

Extraordinary items must meet three criteria:

1. Material in amount;

2. Unusual or outside the scope of the firm's typical operations, and

3. Not expected to recur in the foreseeable future.

Because these items are not expected to happen again soon, they should be segregated and not be included in income from continuing operations. Examples of extraordinary items are natural disasters (such as floods, fires, earthquakes), theft, gains and losses from early retirement of long-term debt, and gains and losses from lawsuits. All gains and losses will be reported net of the appropriate income tax for the item. Assume that The Potted Planter had an extraordinary loss due to an earthquake of $80,000 in addition to the 41 transactions and adjusting entries given. Exhibit 6.9 illustrates the appropriate treatment for the extraordinary item. The loss of $80,000 (net of an insurance recovery) is reduced by an income tax savings of $32,000. If The Potted Planter had an extraordinary gain, then the extraordinary gain would also have been reduced due to an increase in taxes.

Exhibit 6.9

Nonrecurring Items on the Income Statement		
Income from continuing operations		$ 95,490
Discontinued Operations		
Loss from operations of discontinued		
segment. (Net of taxes, $4,000)	(6,000)	
Gain on disposal of segment		
(Net of taxes, $20,000)	30,000	24,000
Income before Extraordinary Items and		
Cumulative Effect of Accounting Change		$ 119,490
Extraordinary loss (Net of taxes, $32,000)		(48,000)
Cumulative Effect of Accounting Changes		
(Net of taxes, $2,000)		(5,000)
Net Income		$ 66,490

Changes in Accounting Methods

Changes in accounting methods will be discussed in Chapter 9. At this point you need only be aware that changes in accounting methods will be reported net of tax.

Prior Period Adjustments

In this and the preceding chapter, changes affecting owner's equity other than those reflecting owner transactions (owner investments and owner withdrawals) were identified as being either revenues or expenses of the current period and included in the income box; and therefore, by definition reported on the current period's income statement. One exception to this rule has previously been noted. The balancing effect of a gift or donation received by the firm is not considered to be revenue, is not included in the income box, and is not reported on the income statement. The balance sheet adjustment is made directly to owner's equity (or to additional paid in capital for a corporation).

GAAP allow one other type of item to bypass the income statement and affect owner's equity directly. This exception involves prior period adjustments. Prior period adjustments are narrowly defined to include only corrections of errors in financial statements from prior periods, and realization of certain tax benefits. Such adjustments must be noted on the financial statements to show the effect on prior financial statements. Prior period adjustments will not be further discussed in this text. You need to be aware that the only changes affecting owner's equity that are not included on the income statement are:

- owner transactions
- gifts received by the firm, and
- prior period adjustments

Identifying Income Statement Accounts

Since the primary emphasis of this chapter is on income, the discussion so far has focused on the preparation of the Potted Planter's Income Statement for the year ending 12/31/X3 (Exhibit 6.6). Balance Sheet Diagram 6.7 illustrates a comprehensive integrated model of the complete year's accounting activities. The 41 summary transactions and adjusting entries are added to the beginning account balances from the 12/31/X2 Balance Sheet (Exhibit 6.1) to create the Income Statement for 19X3 (Exhibit 6.6) and the 12/31/X3 Balance Sheet (Exhibit 6.10). The Statement of Owner's Capital (Exhibit 6.10) is a formal summary of the activity in Pat Ward's Capital Account for the year.

If you are given account balances for a given year after adjustments and after closing, you know that all of these accounts are balance sheet accounts. All non-balance sheet accounts are emptied and their balances transferred to owner's capital as part of the closing process. Suppose you are given account balances before closing. How can you positively identify which accounts are:

1. Balance sheet accounts?
2. Income statement accounts?
3. Other temporary accounts used to accumulate data during the year that will be closed to balance sheet or income statement accounts as part of the adjusting/closing process?

Balance sheet accounts can be recognized from memory of the typical accounts illustrated in this text together with reasoned observation of similar titles. For example, "merchandise on hand" can readily be understood as inventory. Also, liability account titles will usually include the word "payable."

For income statement accounts, revenue account captions will generally include one of these words: sales, fees, gain(s), revenue, or earned. Expense account titles, except for Cost of Goods Sold (or Cost of Sales) and Provision for Taxes, will generally include the word "expense" or the word "loss".

There are temporary accounts that do not appear on any statement, but are closed into income. They include gross sales, sales returns and allowances, sales discounts, gross purchases, freight-in, purchase returns and allowances, and purchase discounts. These accounts are components of net sales and net purchases. The components to net purchases is discussed in Chapter 8.

Owner's drawing and owner investment, if accumulated separately, are two temporary accounts closed to the Balance Sheet account, Owner's Capital.

Diagram 6.7   **Balance Sheet Effect Worksheet for The Potted Planter**
for the Year ending 12/31/X3

Cash	9,000	(b)	−	30,000	(16)		Current Notes Payable		+	15,000	(14)	
	+300,000	(1)	+	25,000	(17)				−	15,000	(22)	
	− 36,000	(3)	+	38,150	(19)				+	20,000	(L)	20,000
	+ 75,000	(4)	−	662,000	(21)							
	+ 20,000	(6)	−	15,700	(22)		Accounts Payable			80,000	(b)	
	− 1,000	(8)	−	219,200	(23)				+	650,000	(7)	
	− 4,500	(9)	−	7,800	(24)				+	2,000	(8)	
	− 4,000	(10)	−	2,400	(25)				+	20,000	(20)	
	− 13,600	(11)	−	39,800	(26)				−	662,000	(21)	
	− 37,500	(12)	−	18,000	(27)				+	800	(E)	90,800
	+ 15,000	(14)	+	1,300	(28)							
	+766,000	(15)	−	90,000	(29)	67,950	Wages and Salaries			2,200	(b)	
Marketable Securities		+	30,000	(16)					−	2,200	(23)	
		−	20,000	(17)	10,000				+	3,000	(E)	3,000
Current Notes Receivable		+	40,000	(18)			Interest Payable		+	8,500	(G)	8,500
		−	35,000	(19)	5,000							
Interest Receivable		+	2,100	(J)	2,100		Taxes Payable			40,800	(b)	
Accounts Receivable			90,000	(b)					−	1,000	(25)	
		+	900,000	(2)					−	39,800	(26)	
		−	766,000	(15)					+	1,000	(H)	
		−	84,000	(3)					+	63,660	(I)	64,660
		−	40,000	(18)	100,000		Unearned Revenue		+	75,000	(4)	
Inventory			135,000	(b)					−	60,000	(5)	15,000
		+	650,000	(7)								
		+	30,000	(13)			Noncurrent Notes Payable			130,000	(b)	
		−	675,000	(A)	140,000				+	11,000	(10)	
Supplies			2,000	(b)					−	20,000	(L)	121,000
		+	3,000	(8)								
		−	4,000	(B)	1,000		Pat Ward, Capital			136,000	(b)	
Prepaid Items			1,500	(b)					−	90,000	(29)	
		+	4,500	(9)					+	20,000	(6)	
		+	37,500	(12)					+	95,490	(π)	161,490
		−	30,000	(13)								
		−	1,500	(C)	12,000							
Land			30,000	(b)	30,000							
Building			150,000	(b)	150,000							

Income box:

+ 300,000	(1)	− 675,000	(A)
+ 900,000	(2)	− 4,000	(B)
− 120,000	(3)	− 1,500	(C)
+ 60,000	(5)	− 32,000	(D)
+ 5,000	(17)	− 800	(E)
+ 3,150	(19)	− 3,000	(F)
− 20,000	(20)	− 8,500	(G)
− 700	(22)	− 1,000	(H)
− 217,000	(23)	− 63,660	(I)
− 7,800	(24)	+ 2,100	(J)
− 1,400	(25)	− 1,700	(K)
− 18,000	(27)	+ 1,300	(28)

+ 95,490   π

Accumulated Depreciation	(80,000)	(b)	
	− 20,000	(D)	(100,000)
Equipment	90,000	(b)	
	+ 15,000	(10)	105,000
Accumulated Depreciation	(40,000)	(b)	
	− 12,000	(D)	(52,000)
Leasehold Improvement	+ 13,600	(11)	
	− 1,700	(K)	11,900
Deferred Charges	1,500	(b)	1,500
TOTAL ASSETS			**484,450**

| **TOTAL EQUITIES** | | | **484,450** |

Exhibit 6.10

THE POTTED PLANTER BALANCE SHEET
as of 12/31/X3

Assets			Equities	
Cash		$ 67,950	Current note payable	$ 20,000
Marketable securities		10,000	Accounts payable	90,800
Receivables:			Wages and salaries	3,000
Notes	$ 5,000		Interest payable	8,500
Interest	2,100		Taxes payable	64,660
Accounts	100,000	107,100	Unearned revenue	15,000
Inventory		140,000	Total Current Liabilities	$201,960
Supplies		1,000		
Prepaid items		12,000	Noncurrent Note Payable	121,000
Total Current Assets		$338,050	Total Liabilities	$322,960
Property, Plant, and Equipment				
Land	$ 30,000			
Building	150,000			
Accum. depr.	(100,000)			
Equipment	105,000			
Accum. depr.	(52,000)	133,000		
Intangibles				
Lsehold impr.	$ 11,900			
Deferred charges	1,500	13,400	Pat Ward, Capital	161,490
Total Assets		$484,450	Total Equities	$484,450

THE POTTED PLANTER STATEMENT OF OWNER'S CAPITAL
For the Year ending 12/31/X3

Pat Ward, Capital, 1/1/X3	$ 136,000
Additional Investment	20,000
Net Income	95,490
	$ 251,490
Withdrawals	90,000
Pat Ward, Capital, 12/31/X3	$ 161,490

Analysis of the Income Statement

The income statement discloses all material revenues and expenses. How useful is the data? Recall from the Potted Planter example that Pat wished to compare her firm's performance to prior years. She knows that her current year's net income (after taxes) of $95,490 represents an improvement over that of the previous year $59,700. However, she wishes to analyze the revenue and expense components to see why she has more income, so that she can improve or at least maintain this performance in the future.

Comparison to prior years performance is called trend analysis. In analyzing the two most recent income statements for the firm, comparing actual dollar amounts can be confusing and misleading. For instance, supplies expense has increased but so have sales. Is this good or bad? To facilitate comparison, two different approaches involving the translation of absolute dollars to percentages are often employed.

Vertical Analysis

One approach is known as **vertical analysis**. It involves translating all line item amounts on each statement to percentages of a common base, net sales. This is called a **common size statement**. Percentages are generally rounded to one decimal. Exhibit 6.11 illustrates Pat's two most recent income statements together with the percentages of net sales. Observe that the most recent data are often presented first to focus attention on the most recent year.

In Exhibit 6.11, you can see that Pat's total operating expenses increased slightly in proportion to sales, and that these increases were more than offset by increases in gross profit and other revenues. The overall result was a substantial increase in net income, not only in dollars but in proportion to sales. More sophisticated analysis will be covered in Chapter 13.

Exhibit 6.11   VERTICAL ANALYSIS OF INCOME DATA FOR POTTED PLANTER STORES
for the years ending 12/31/X3 and 12/31/X2

Item	12/31/X3		12/31/X2	
	$	%	$	%
Net sales	1,140,000	100.0	800,000	100.0
Cost of goods sold	675,000	59.2	480,000	60.0
Gross profit	465,000	40.8	320,000	40.0
Wages and salaries expense	220,000	19.3	140,000	17.5
Utilities expense	20,800	1.8	10,000	1.3
Interest expense	17,000	1.5	15,600	1.9
Rental expense	18,000	1.6	18,000	2.3
Depreciation expense	32,000	2.8	30,000	3.8
Property tax expense	2,400	0.2	2,400	0.3
Supplies expense	4,000	0.4	3,000	0.4
Insurance expense	1,500	0.1	1,500	0.2
Lse. impr. amort.	1,700	0.1	0	0.0
Total Operating Expenses	317,400	27.8	220,500	27.6
Gain on securities	5,000	0.4	0	0.0
Interest revenue	6,550	0.6	0	0.0
Total other revenue	11,550	1.0	0	0.0
Income before taxes	159,150	14.0	99,500	12.4
Provision for income taxes	63,660	5.6	39,800	5.0
Net Income	95,490	8.4	59,700	7.5

Note: If the dollar amounts were omitted from this exhibit, this would be an example of Common Size Income Statements.

Gross Profit Ratio

What causes the relationship between gross profit and sales to change? You are correct if you recognize that both sales and cost of goods sold may be involved. The sales price may have increased, the cost of goods decreased, or any combination resulting in a decrease in cost relative to the sales price. The ratio which illustrates this relationship is the gross profit ratio:

Gross Profit Ratio = Gross Profit ÷ Net Sales

$$19X3 \qquad \frac{\$465,000}{\$1,140,000} = 40.8\%$$

Horizontal Analysis

Another technique for comparing statements that is often used for trend analysis is commonly referred to as **horizontal analysis** and is illustrated in Exhibit 6.12. Horizontal analysis involves determining the percentage change of each line item over that of prior years. Horizontal analysis reveals a 42.5 percent sales increase accompanied by only a 40.6 percent increase in cost of goods sold. Total operating expenses are shown as increasing at a slightly greater rate than sales 43.9 percent. The overall result is net income increasing at an even greater rate than sales.

Exhibit 6.12   THE POTTED PLANTER-HORIZONTAL (TREND) ANALYSIS OF INCOME DATA
for the years ending 12/31/X3 and 12/31/X2

Item	12/31/X3	12/31/X2	Percent Change
Net sales	$1,140,000	$800,000	+ 42.5
Cost of goods sold	675,000	480,000	+ 40.6
Gross profit	465,000	320,000	+ 45.3
Wages and salaries expense	220,000	140,000	+ 57.1
Utilities expense	20,800	10,000	+ 108.0
Interest expense	17,000	15,600	+ 9.0
Rental expense	18,000	18,000	0.0
Depreciation expense	32,000	30,000	+ 6.7
Property tax expense	2,400	2,400	0.0
Supplies expense	4,000	3,000	+ 33.3
Insurance expense	1,500	1,500	0.0
Lse. impr. amort.	1,700	0	*
Total Operating Expenses	317,400	220,500	+ 43.9
Gain on securities	5,000	0	*
Interest revenue	6,550	0	*
Total other revenue	11,550	0	*
Income before taxes	159,150	99,550	+ 59.9
Provision for income taxes	63,660	39,800	+ 59.9
Net Income	95,490	59,700	+ 59.9

* undefined

Comparative Analysis

In addition to trend analysis of her own firm's performance compared to that of prior years, Pat also wants to compare her performance to that of other firms. She can do this by comparing her statements, using both vertical and horizontal analysis, with data obtained for competitors. In many industries, trade associations collect data from members and disseminate industry average information for comparative analysis. Comparative analysis compares the firm's performance to that of competitors or industry averages. It can be useful in highlighting areas of potential improvement, or at least in providing reassurance that others have the same problems. For instance, if Pat determined that other firms' cost of goods sold was significantly lower as a percentage of sales. She might wish to give more attention either to obtaining lower prices from suppliers or else raising prices to customers. If others were experiencing equal or greater wage and salary increases, she might be less concerned and more accepting of the possibility that these cost increases could not be readily passed on to customers in her industry. Comparative analysis will be further illustrated and discussed in Chapter 13.

Return on Investment

It should be obvious that income statements also provide the data for determining the firm's or owner's return on capital (assets) invested. ROI (return on investment) analysis involves more sophisticated ratios that will be deferred until Chapter 13. It is only important at this point that you appreciate the power and potential significance of the income statement and the detailed information it contains. Many businesspersons and financial analysts feel that the income statement is the most important of all the financial statements.

Accounting Income vs Taxable Income

In concluding this discussion of income a word of caution: in Chapter 1, you were warned not to confuse accounting income with taxable income. Taxable income results from tax laws and tax regulations that incorporate many public policy considerations not related to the measurement of accounting or economic income for a firm. Businesses generally have different taxable income than their reported income due to the timing differences of revenue and expenses between the tax code and GAAP. The determination of taxable income and tax liability is briefly discussed later in the text. This subject is mentioned once again, to make sure you do not confuse tax regulations with accounting principles.

Preparer Procedures

You will find all accounts necessary for the preparer problems in this chapter in Exhibit 6.13 and in Exhibit 5.1 in Chapter 5. Alternatively you may wish to use the complete chart of accounts covering all items introduced in this text, which you will find at the beginning of Appendix D in the back of the book.

Additions to Chart of Accounts

To accommodate transactions and adjustments introduced in this chapter, the partial chart of accounts first introduced in Chapter 5 as Exhibit 5.1 must be expanded to include accounts in Exhibit 6.13:

Exhibit 6.13   **Additions to Chart of Accounts**

Nonmonetary Current Liabilities
311   Unearned Revenue
312   Deferred Gross Profit on Installment Sales (current)

Other Noncurrent Liabilities
411   Deferred Gross Profit on Installment Sales (noncurrent)

Other Revenue
713   Gain on Current Marketable Securities
717   Miscellaneous Revenue

Extraordinary Revenue and Revenue Related to Discontinued Operations
720   Extraordinary Gain
721   Revenue Related to Discontinued Operations

Operating Expenses
804   Taxes (other than income taxes)
813   Miscellaneous

Other Expenses
824   Provisions for Income Taxes

Extraordinary Expenses and Expenses Related to Discontinues Operations
830   Extraordinary Loss
831   Expenses Related to Discontinued Operations

Other Accounts
900   Sales Returns and Allowances
910   Owner Withdrawals

New Transactions

Three types of transactions were introduced in this chapter: those involving merchandise returns, unearned revenue and the subsequent realization of such revenue, and the sale of marketable securities at a gain.

Merchandise returns, or the granting of an allowance (post-sale discount) to customers in lieu of actual returns, require an entry reducing receivables or cash and increasing the contra account for sales returns and allowances. Examples would be:

	DR	CR
Sales Returns and Allowances	*600*	
Accounts Receivable		*600*
To record the return of merchandise sold for $600 on account		
Sales Returns and Allowances	*50*	
Cash		*50*
To record refund of $50 on cash sale where merchandise returned		
Sales Return and Allowances	*100*	
Accounts Receivable		*100*
To record granting of an allowance/adjustment for defective		
merchandise not returned		

Unearned revenue or customer deposits for future delivery of goods or services are recorded as:

Cash	*75*	
Unearned Revenue		*75*
To record receipt of customer advance		

When the merchandise is delivered or the service performed, the revenue is realized/earned and the event is recognized by:

Unearned revenue	*75*	
Gross Sales		*75*
To record completion of sale on customer advance		

Where current marketable securities are sold for more than their book value, a gain is realized and a compound entry is involved:

Cash	*5,000*	
Current Marketable Securities		*4,750*
Gain on Current Marketable Securities		*250*
To record the sale of marketable securities		

New Adjustments

Two year-end adjustments were introduced in this chapter: the accrual of a tax liability and the reclassification of a liability from noncurrent to current. Accrual of tax liabilities are of two kinds: income taxes applicable to corporations and other taxes such as property taxes. Both accruals involve debiting the appropriate expense account and crediting taxes payable:

	DR	CR
Property Tax Expense	*500*	
Taxes Payable		*500*
To record accrual of property taxes		
Provision for Income Taxes	*6,000*	
Taxes Payable		*6,000*
To record accrual of income taxes		

Reclassification merely involves transferring an amount from one account to another:

Noncurrent Notes Payable	*10,000*	
Current Notes Payable		*10,000*
To reclassify currently maturing liability		

Chapter Overview

From the material in this chapter, you should be able to:

- Explain with examples how various transactions and adjustments affect owner's equity on the balance sheet, and which of these effects are included in the income box;

- Define the purpose of temporary revenue and expense accounts established by accountants, their relationship to the income box on the balance sheet diagram, and explain why such accounts are known as temporary;

- Explain the function of the income statement and the difference between the two common formats in use for presenting income statement information;

- Define the terms Provision for Income Taxes, Income from Continuing Operations, and Net Income, and describe those different situations where each is appropriately used;

- Describe in general terms the possible alternatives for the timing of revenue recognition;

- Describe the matching principle for expense recognition;

- Explain why nonrecurring items are segregated on the Income Statement;

- Explain with examples the difference between and purpose of trend analysis and comparative analysis, and the different approaches of vertical and horizontal analysis as applicable to income statements.

New Vocabulary and Concepts

Bottom line
Capitalize
Common size statement
Cost of goods sold
Discontinued operations
Expenditure
Expense (verb)
Extraordinary items
Fiscal year
Gross Sales

Horizontal analysis
Income from operations
Installment basis
Matching Principle
Net sales
Percentage of completion method
Provision for income taxes
Sales returns and allowances
Vertical analysis

• Timing of revenue and expense recognition
• Matching of expenses with revenues
• Extraordinary and discontinued items, repeatable income, and income from operations

Review Questions

1. What is a firm's fiscal year? Can it be different from the calendar year? Why would this be desirable? Explain and give examples.

2. What is the difference between the single-step and the multiple-step format for income statements? Are they both acceptable under GAAP?

3. How does sales revenue affect owner wealth?

4. Are sales returns and allowances expenses or revenue adjustments? Explain.

5. Do all firms report cost of goods sold? If not, why not?

6. (a) Explain with examples what is meant by Unearned Revenue. (b) Why is it reported as a liability? (c) How is this liability "paid" or extinguished, and what happens to it? (d) What is the relationship between a prepaid item (asset) and unearned revenue (liability)?

7. (a) What is gross profit? (b) Does it include "other" revenue? (c) Explain.

8. Is all revenue considered operating revenue? If not, what would be examples of other revenues? Explain.

9. Are all expenses and losses operating expenses? If not, what would be examples of nonoperating expenses and losses?

10. Why do accountants use temporary accounts during the year for revenue and expense items? Explain.

11. To what does "closing" refer, in relation to revenue and expense accounts? Explain.

12. Is the balance sheet equality maintained among all the balance sheet accounts themselves during the year? If not, how is this equality or balance restored at year-end?

13. What is income from operations? What does it mean and what is its usefulness?

14. Can income from continuing operations be the same as net income?

15. (a) Is the timing of revenue recognition always the point of sale? (b) If not, what other alternatives might be appropriate?

16. What are accruals and deferrals? Give examples of each.

17. What are examples of current asset expiration?

18. What is meant by the matching principle and how does it relate to the timing of expense recognition?

19. Both comparative analysis and trend analysis can be useful in analyzing operating performance. Explain their difference, what each involves, and the distinct usefulness of each approach.

20. Explain with examples the difference between vertical analysis and horizontal analysis as applied to income statements.

Mini-Cases and Questions for Discussion

MC 6.1 Ms. Prudence Struthers is an efficiency expert who has been examining your office procedures to locate areas of unnecessary activities and paperwork. She, unfortunately, knows nothing about accounting. "Have I found a really unnecessary make-work program in the accounting department!" she proclaims. "Do you know those featherbedders use a whole series of temporary holding records during the year, and then they transfer the information to where it was supposed to go anyway? They even have a fancy word for it called 'closing.' I think we should 'close down' their little make-work game."
Explain to Ms. Struthers why temporary accounts are desirable even if they are later closed.

MC 6.2 A professional sports team or club which sells season tickets defers revenue for the proportion of games remaining to be played. If season ticket sales increased dramatically this year, wouldn't the practice of deferring recognition of the revenues unfairly "hide" this good news from creditors and owners studying income statements? Discuss.

MC 6.3 Below are listed several instances (a) through (f) accounting errors. You may assume the errors are discovered only after the financial statements are published and therefore will be picked up in the subsequent year's financial statements. For each error, discuss the effect (understated, no effect, or overstated):

   i)   Quick ratio
  ii)   Current ratio
 iii)   Long-term debt ratio
 iv)   Current year's reported income
  v)   Subsequent year's reported income

Also discuss the possible effect upon or fairness for:

vi) Current owner, that may sell ownership interest on basis of the current incorrect statements.

vii) New owner, that might buy ownership interest on the basis of the current incorrect statements.

a) Inventory costing $50,000 was overlooked and therefore not included during the year-end physical inventory.

b) A year-end purchase of $10,000 of supplies on account was not recorded. The supplies themselves had been placed in the storeroom and were included in the year-end physical inventory.

c) $120,000 of credit sales to customers made during the week following the year end were included along with the previous month's business.

d) An insurance policy costing $9,000 covering the following year had been acquired from the firm's insurance provider just prior to year end. Neither the policy nor the broker's invoice were recorded.

e) On the last day of the year, the owner withdrew merchandise costing $4,000 for personal use. The withdrawal was not recorded.

f) At year end, $600 of interest was owed to the firm on its investments. The item had not been accrued.

MC 6.4 Mary Porter and Sally Greenbaum are arguing over the importance of different information appearing on an income statement. Mary says, "I don't see why accountants bother with a subtotal for income from continuing operations. The really important information is what actually happened to the firm last year--everything that happened. Net income gives the complete picture." Sally replies, "Sure, net income gives the complete picture, but a statement user can only do something in the future. Therefore, the really important piece of information is not net income but income from continuing operations. You can forecast on the basis of income from continuing operations. It can be dangerous to base a forecast on net income."

Who is right? Discuss.

MC 6.5 "Depreciation and amortization expenses are not adequate in today's world. There are many instances where total depreciation of a particular asset should far exceed 100 percent of its cost even if there was still some anticipated salvage value. Reported profits today are phony profits, because they can't be taken home."

Do you agree with this statement? Discuss.

MC 6.6 Why isn't profit recognized when the merchandise or product is ready to sell? After all, it's only a matter of timing. The item will be sold eventually. Discuss.

Essential Problems

EP 6.1   Given the following accounts and their adjusted balances (in thousands of dollars) for the Snow Company as of 12/31/X7, select those accounts that should appear on Snow's 19X7 income statement and prepare the statement in good form following the multiple-step format. Note that the firm is subject to both property and income taxes.

Accounts Payable	$25	John Snow, Capital*	142
Accounts receivable	50	Land	30
Accum. depr.--building	60	Net sales	400
Accum. depr.--equipment	45	Noncurrent notes payable	72
Building	140	Prepaid items	8
Cash	15	Provision for income taxes	18
Cost of goods sold	220	Rent revenue	2
Depreciation expense	20	Supplies	5
Equipment	90	Tax expense (property taxes)	6
Insurance expense	4	Wage and salaries expense	100
Interest expense	7	Wages and salaries	3
Inventory	36		

* As of 12/31/X6

EP 6.2   Given the following accounts and their adjusted balances (in thousands of dollars) for the Sargent Company as of 12/31/X5, select those accounts that should appear on Sargent's 19X5 income statement, and prepare the statement in good form following the multiple-step format. Note that the firm is subject to both property and income taxes.

Accounts payable	$ 27	Interest Payable	13
Accounts receivable	68	Interest revenue	2
Accum. depr.--buildings	90	Inventory	60
Accum. depr.--equipment	70	Land	40
Buildings	150	Loss on equipment disposition	16
Cash	14	Marketable securities	17
Chris Sargent, Capital*	89	Noncurrent notes payable	108
Cost of goods sold	250	Prepaid items	9
Current notes payable	25	Provision for income taxes	23
Current notes receivable	11	Unearned revenue	18
Deferred charges	12	Sales returns and allowances	20
Depreciation expense	15	Supplies	4
Equipment	100	Property tax expense	10
Gross sales	520	Taxes payable	6
Insurance expense	5	Wages and salaries expense	130
Interest expense	17	Wages and salaries payable	3

* As of 12/31/X4

EP **6.3**   From the data given in EP 6.1, prepare an income statement in good form for the Snow Company for 19X7 following the single-step format. Note that the firm is subject to both property and income taxes.

EP **6.4**   From the data given in EP 6.2, prepare an income statement in good form for the Sargent Company for 19X5 following the single-step format. Note that the firm is subject to both property and income taxes.

EP **6.5**   From the data given in EP 6.1, prepare a balance sheet in good form for the Snow Company as of 12/31/X7.

EP **6.6**   From the data given in EP 6.2, prepare a balance sheet in good form for the Sargent Company as of 12/31/X5.

EP **6.7**   From the following list of transactions and adjustments for the Know Company for January, 19X1, identify by the letter R or E those which involve revenue or expense. Indicate, for each item that represents revenue or expense, whether the eventual effect upon owner's equity is an increase or decrease.

1) Owner invests $100,000 cash in the business.

2) Merchandise costing $50,000 is purchased on account.

3) Current month's rent of $400 is paid in cash (liability not previously recorded).

4) Customers purchase merchandise paying $40,000 cash.

5) Customers purchase merchandise selling for $30,000 on account.

6) A utilities bill for $200 is received and recorded.

7) Wages totaling $20,000 are paid in cash (liability not previously recorded).

8) $25,000 is collected on accounts receivable.

9) $30,000 is paid on accounts payable.

10) $5,000 of supplies are purchased on account.

A) A physical count of inventory at the end of the month revealed merchandise costing $8,000.

B) $2,000 of supplies are determined to have been used up, and an adjustment is made for the expiration.

C) $300 of interest owed to the bank is accrued as a current liability.

EP **6.8**   Based upon data given in EP 6.7, prepare a schedule of cost of goods sold, an income statement in good form following the multiple-step format, and a balance sheet in good form. You may assume that the firm had just started in business this month.

EP 6.9 The following adjustments at year-end (12/31/X3) are necessary for the Chowchilla Company. For each adjustment indicate:

- i) The accounts affected;
- ii) Whether each account is a balance sheet (B/S), revenue (R), or expense (E), account;
- iii) Whether the account balance should be increased or decreased (remember that expense account balances are normally increased during the year, and that the amount of their ending balance then decreases owner's equity at closing).

- a) One of the firm's accounts receivable in the amount of $800 is determined to be uncollectible. It is removed from the books and the appropriate expense is called "bad debt expense."

- b) Supplies on hand at the beginning of the year were $1,000, and purchases of supplies were $5,000. A year-end inspection reveals that supplies with an estimated cost of $1,500 are still on hand. Adjustment is necessary for this asset expiration.

- c) It is determined that $750 of interest is owed to the firm on a note receivable which has not been received or recorded.

- d) $600 of rent revenue has accrued on the excess storage space lease.

- e) $1,700 of accrued wages and salaries are owed to employees.

- f) It is estimated that the next telephone bill will be for $500, $300 of which will be charges for the year just ended.

EP 6.10 The Chowchilla Company's accountant mistakenly prepared its income statement without including the necessary adjustments given in EP 6.9. Prepare a revised income statement including the necessary adjustments and following the single-step format. The statement before adjustments and in multiple-step format was as follows:

Sales		$200,000
Cost of goods sold		103,500
Gross profit		$ 96,500
Operating Expenses:		
Wages and salaries	$ 78,000	
Utilities	5,000	
Interest	1,500	84,500
Net income		$ 12,000

EP 6.11 The Springfield Company (a proprietorship) sells and services electronic control equipment. Data (in thousands of dollars) possibly relating to 19X8 revenues and expenses are given below. (a) Prepare a schedule of cost of goods sold for 19X8 in good form, (b) Prepare an income statement, balance sheet, and statement of owner's capital in good form at the end of 19X8. Use the multiple-step format for the income statement. The 12/31/X7 balance sheet contained the following balances:

Accounts payable	$122
Accounts Receivable	70
Cash	100
Owner's capital	125
Supplies	5
Wages and salaries payable	3

19X8 Events:

Asset Increases

1) $200 cash received from customers as deposits for merchandise to be delivered
2) $50 cash received from customers for merchandise delivered
3) $450 accounts receivable for merchandise delivered
4) $390 cash collected on accounts receivable
5) $305 inventory purchased on account
6) $15 supplies purchased on account
7) $5 supplies purchased for cash

Asset Decreases

4) $390 accounts receivable reduction for customer payments on their accounts
7) $5 cash paid for supplies purchased for cash
8) $350 cash paid on accounts payable
9) $103 cash paid to employees including $3 owed at end of previous year
10) $16 cash paid for rent not previously recorded as a liability
11) $10 cash paid for utilities including $2 owed at end of previous year
12) $12 cash withdrawn by owner for personal use
13) $40 accounts receivable reduction for returned merchandise
A) $80 represented the year-end inventory balance
B) $8 represented the year-end supplies balance

Liability Increases

1) $200 increase in unearned revenue, representing customer deposits received for merchandise to be delivered
5) $305 accounts payable increase for merchandise purchased on account
6) $15 accounts payable increase for supplies purchased on account
C) $4 accounts payable increase representing accrual for utilities owed at year-end
D) $2 accrual of wages and salaries owed at year-end
E) $6 accrual of rent owed at year-end

Liability Decreases

8) $350 accounts payable reduction representing payment
9) $3 wages and salaries payable reduction representing payment
14) $50 reduction fo unearned revenue representing delivery of merchandise

EP 6.12 The Remington Company (a proprietorship) sells and services earth moving equipment. Data (in thousands of dollars and with transaction/adjustment identification codes) possibly relating to 19X4 revenues and expenses are given below. (a) Prepare a schedule of cost of goods sold for 19X4 in good form. (b) Prepare an income statement, a balance sheet, and a statement of owner's capital at the end of 19X4 in good form. Use the multiple-step format for the income statement. The 12/31/X3 balance sheet contained the following balances:

Accounts payable	$123
Accounts receivable	161
Cash	85
Interest payable	10
Interest receivable	2
Noncurrent notes payable	240
Owner's capital	230
Prepaid items	4
Wages and salaries payable	4

Asset Increases

Cash
1) $12 representing cash sales
2) $11 representing interest received on notes receivable $2 of which had been accrued at the end of 19X3
3) $14 representing rent (at $1 per month) received covering 2/1/X4 through 3/31/X5 for unneeded warehouse space
4) $780 representing collections of accounts receivable
5) $300 representing deposits received from customers for equipment to be delivered

Interest receivable
G) $3 representing interest earned but not yet received on notes receivable as of 12/31/X4

Accounts receivable
6) $868 representing sales on account

Inventory
7) $620 representing purchases on account

Supplies
8) $9 representing purchases for cash
9) $20 representing purchases on account

Prepaid rent
10) $44 representing rental, at $4 per month, paid in advance.

Asset Decreases

Cash
8) $9 for cash purchases of supplies
10) $44 for rent including $8 covering January and February of 19X5
11) $400 representing payments made on accounts payable
12) $6 refunded to customers for merchandise returned

13) $158 paid to employees including current wages and salaries and the $4 that had been accrued at the end of 19X3
14) $12 for utilities including $2 that had been owed at the end of 19X3
15) $26 for interest on notes payable including $10 that had been owed at the end of 19X3

Interest receivable
2) $2 representing collection of interest accrued as of 12/31/X3

Accounts receivable
4) $780 representing receivables collections

Inventory
A) $382 represented the year-end inventory balance

Supplies
B) $8 represented the year-end supplies balance

Prepaid rent
C) $48 representing rent for 19X4 that had expired

Liability Increases

Accounts payable
7) $620 representing purchases of inventory on account
9) $20 representing purchases of supplies on account
D) $1 representing accrual of utilities consumed but unpaid as of 12/31/X4

Wages and salaries payable
E) $7 representing wages and salaries owed but unpaid as of 12/31/X4

Interest payable
F) $8 representing interest owed on notes payable and unpaid as of 12/31/X4

Unearned Revenue
3) $3 representing rent received for unused warehouse space for first three months of 19X5
5) $300 representing deposits from customers on equipment to be delivered

Liability Decreases

Accounts payable
11) $500 payment
14) $2 payment of utilities accrued as of 12/31/X3

Wages and salaries payable
13) $4 payment of amount owed as of 12/31/X3

Interest payable
15) $10 payment of amount owed as of 12/31/X3

Unearned revenue
17) $200 representing price of merchandise paid for in advance by customers and now delivered

EP 6.13 Convert the Bauer Company income statement given below into a common size income statement.

Bauer Company Income Statement
for the year ended 12/31/X6

Sales		$500,000
Less cost of goods sold		300,000
Gross Profit		$200,000
Less Operating Expenses:		
Wages and salaries	$112,000	
Rentals	20,000	
Utilities	4,000	
Insurance	6,000	
Supplies	9,000	
Depreciation on equipment	18,000	
Amortization of leasehold improvement	22,000	191,000
Income from Operations		$ 9,000
Less: extraordinary loss on long-lived asset	18,000	
extraordinary loss on inventory	27,000	45,000
Net loss		$(36,000)

EP 6.14 Convert the Mason Company income statement given below into a common size statement.

Mason Company Income Statement
for the year ended 12/31/X6

Sales		$750,000
Less cost of goods sold		412,500
Gross Profit		$337,500
Less operating expenses:		
Wages and salaries	$157,500	
Rentals	30,750	
Utilities	5,250	
Insurance	8,250	
Supplies	17,250	
Depreciation on equipment	27,000	
Amortization on leasehold improvement	33,000	279,000
Net Income		$ 58,500

EP 6.15 Calculate the cost of goods sold ratio for both the Bauer and Mason Companies for 19X6.

EP 6.16 Compare the performance of the Bauer Company to the Mason Company. Does Mason appear to be doing a better job at generating revenue and controlling costs than Bauer, or vice versa. Assume that a significant cost difference is one that exceeds 0.5 percent of sales.

SP 6.17 The balance sheet data for the Albert Company as of 12/31/X5 (000 omitted) are given below, together with summary transactions and adjustments for 19X6. (a) Prepare in good form a balance sheet as of 12/31/X6, an income statement, and a statement of owner's capital for the year ending 12/31/X6.

Cash	$80	Accounts payable	$75
Accounts receivable	132	Taxes payable	40
Inventory	110	Other current liabilities	27
Supplies	35	Noncurrent notes payable	120
Prepaid insurance	8	Owner's Equity	?
Land	40		
Buildings	200		
Accumulated depreciation, buildings	(131)		
Equipment	190		
Accumulated depreciation, equipment	(140)		
Patents	16		
Deferred charges	6		

1) Sales totaled $900,000, of which $100,000 were cash sales.
2) Receivables collections totaled $782,000.
3) Inventory costing $585,000 was purchased on account.
4) Wages and salaries of $120,000 were earned and paid.
5) Utilities costing $6,000 were consumed and paid.
6) All 12/31/X5 current liabilities were paid.
7) $500,000 was paid on accounts payable.
8) Inventory costing $20,000 was lost due to flood damage. Once every four or five years the firm experiences water damage.
9) One of the firm's patents, with a 12/31/X5 unamortized cost of $5,000, was determined to be worthless.
10) Owner withdrew $21,000 cash for personal use.
11) Equipment costing $15,000, with a book value of $5,000, was sold for $7,000 cash.
12) Earthquake damage to the building necessitated repairs costing $25,000, which had been paid.
13) $9,000 of interest was paid on the noncurrent note.
14) $20,000 of income taxes had been paid.
A) At year-end, saleable inventory costing $85,000 was still on hand.
B) At year-end, supplies costing $10,000 were unused.
C) The 12/31/X5 prepaid insurance was two years of coverage.
D) Additional depreciation of $9,000 on buildings and $15,000 on equipment was determined to be appropriate.
E) $2,000 of amortization on the remaining patents should be taken.
F) Of the $12,000 of interest earned on the noncurrent notes payable, $9,000 had been paid by year-end.
G) Wages of $8,000 were earned but unpaid at year-end.
H) Income taxes were estimated at $34,000; $20,000 had been paid.

SP 6.18 The balance sheet data for the Brandywine Company as of 12/31/X2 (000 omitted) are given below, together with summary transactions and adjustments for the year 19X3. (a) Prepare in good form a balance sheet as of 12/31/X3, an income statement, and a statement of owner's capital for the year ending 12/31/X3.

Cash	$ 65	Current note payable	$ 95
Accounts receivable	184	Accounts payable	112
Inventory	147	Accrued wages payable	14
Supplies	32	Taxes payable	30
Prepaid services	11	Other current liabilities	18
Land	60	Owner's Equity	?
Buildings and equipment	430		
Accumulation depreciation	(210)		
Franchise	20		

1) Net sales, all on account, totaled $800,000.
2) Receivable collections totaled $850,000.
3) Inventory costing $528,000 was purchased on account.
4) Wages and salaries of $130,000 were earned and paid.
5) Utilities costing $5,000 were consumed and paid.
6) All 12/31/X2 current liabilities except the current note payable were paid.
7) $450,000 was paid on accounts payable.
8) The $95,000 current note was paid, plus $8,000 interest.
9) $100,000 cash was borrowed on a five-year note.
10) Supplies costing $25,000 were purchased on account.
11) The new supplies were stolen the day after they arrived. Unfortunately, thefts occurred quite regularly in the firm's area. There was no insurance recovery.
12) The owner withdrew $15,000 of cash for personal use.
13) Equipment costing $10,000, with a net book value of $6,000, was sold for $3,000 cash.
14) Damages, payable within 120 days, of $40,000 were awarded to a customer injured by a flash fire in the firm's washroom. The damages have been paid.
A) Year-end physical inventory disclosed inventory costing $150,000.
B) Year-end supplies on hand and cost $4,000
C) All of the prepaid janitorial services were used.
D) Additional depreciation of $30,000 was determined to be appropriate.
E) The franchise was being amortized at a rate of $4,000 per year.
F) Interest of $6,000 on the new noncurrent note was owed and unpaid.
G) Wages of $9,000 were earned and unpaid.
H) Income taxes of $6,000 was accrued at year-end.

SP 6.19 Integrative Problem: The following events occurred during Period 3 for Luigi's Auto Parts:

1) Sales totaled $50,000, $12,000 for cash and the balance on account.
2) Receivables collections totaled $44,000.
3) Inventory costing $31,000 was purchased on account.
4) Wages and salaries totaling $10,000 were paid including the $750 of prior period's obligation.

5) Interest of $1,716 was paid including the prior period's obligation of $756.
6) Supplies costing $150 were purchased on account.
7) $3,000 of rent was paid in advance.
8) A bill for $180 for utilities and services consumed during Period 3 was received and paid.
9) $32,150 was paid on accounts payable.
10) Luigi withdrew $2,000 for personal use.

Adjustments were made for $36 of accrued interest owed on the equipment note (A); $4,500 expiration of prepaid rent (B); $300 expiration of prepaid insurance (C); $250 amortization of leasehold improvement (D); $30,000 of inventory delivered to customers (E); $110 of supplies used (F); $600 in wages and salaries owed but not yet paid (G); $75 in depreciation on equipment (H); and $30 for utilities and services consumed but not yet billed (I).

Luigi's firm's balance sheet as of the end of Period 3 is given below:

LUIGI'S AUTO PARTS BALANCE SHEET AS OF THE END OF PERIOD 3

ASSETS		EQUITIES	
Cash	$13,144	Accounts payable	$13,030
Accounts receivable	36,000	Wages and salaries	600
Inventory	37,000	Interest payable	36
Supplies	50	Total Current Liabilities	$13,666
Prepaid items	300	Noncurrent notes payable	30,900
Total Current Assets	$86,494	Total Liabilities	$44,566
Equipment	1,200		
Accum. depr. equip.	(150)		
Leasehold improvement	4,250	Luigi Cavelli, Capital	47,228
TOTAL ASSETS	$91,794	TOTAL EQUITIES	$91,794

During Period 4, the following events occurred affecting the financial position of Luigi's Auto Parts: (Note: Items marked with an asterisk have been illustrated in previous periods.)

*1) Regular sales total $65,000 of which $15,000 were for cash and the balance on account.

2) Customers returned merchandise prices at $3,000 and originally purchased on account.

3) Customers returned merchandise priced at $1,500 originally purchased for cash and were given a cash refund.

4) Some of the merchandise sold on account proved defective, and the customers were given a $500 allowance in lieu of returning the merchandise or replacing same.

5) Customers ordered special-order merchandise priced at $6,000 paying cash in advance.

*6) Merchandise, both regular and special-order costing $36,000, was purchased on account and received. Inventory purchased were added directly to the inventory account.

7) By the end of Period 4, special-order merchandise priced at $4,000 had been delivered to the customers.

*8)   Supplies costing $200 were purchased on account.

*9) $34,500 was collected from customers on receivables. All remaining receivables were believed to be collectible in full in the following period.

10)   A promissory note receivable with a face value of $2,000 and due early in Period 5 was accepted at the beginning of Period 4 in settlement of $2,000 of accounts receivable. The note provided for $100 of interest per period payable at maturity.

*11) The period's rent of $4,500 was paid in advance.

*12) Wages and salaries totaling $12,000 were paid to employees including the $600 unpaid at the end of the prior period.

*13) Interest of $1,032 was paid representing all the current period's interest and the $36 accrued at the end of the previous period.

14)   A bill for utilities and services consumed in the current period for $300 was received and recorded.

15)   Luigi sublet some spare storage space to a nearby store early in Period 4. Rental was agreed at $330 per period, and Luigi received $110 at the time of signing the sublet agreement.

*16) $35,580 was paid on accounts payable.

*17) Luigi withdrew $4,000 for personal use. A separate account had been established to accumulate withdrawals and be closed to proprietor's capital at period-end.

At the end of Period 4:

*A)   Merchandise costing $35,000 was determined to be still on hand and unsold.

*B)   Supplies costing $60 were determined to be on hand and unsold.

*C)   The remaining prepaid insurance coverage of $300 and the prepaid rent of $4,500 had expired.

*D) $900 in wages and salaries had been earned by employees and were unpaid at year-end.

*E) $50 of utilities and other services had been consumed but unbilled by the end of the period.

*F) $250 of leasehold improvement amortization was taken.

*G) $75 of depreciation on equipment was recorded.

H) $220 rent was receivable from the tenant subletting the spare storage space, and the $110 already received had been earned.

I) $100 of interest had been earned on the promissory note accepted from the customer.

J)   Luigi's store was liable for a newly passed inventory tax payable early in Period 5. The tax was estimated at $700.

K)   Of the $30,00 of noncurrent notes payable appearing on Luigi's balance sheet at the end of Period 3, notes with a face value of $30,000 will mature in Period 5 and must be reclassified.

L)   Near the end of the period, a customer obtained a court judgment for damages in the sum of $5,000 against Luigi's store for injuries allegedly resulting from failure of one of Luigi's products. The firm gave a thirty-day non-interest-bearing promissory note for $5,000 in settlement. The incident was clearly extraordinary in nature and not expected to recur.

Required:

a) Complete a balance sheet effect worksheet (per Balance Sheet Diagram 4.9) for Luigi's store for Period 4. Identify beginning balances as "(b)" and the effect of transactions and adjustments with their numbers or letters. Also identify all revenue and expense effects upon Luigi's capital in an income box. Provide necessary space on your worksheet by entering account titles as follows:

Account	Line number	Account	Line number
Cash	1	Current notes payable	1
Current notes receivable	12	Accounts payable	4
Accounts receivable	14	Wages and salaries	10
Interest receivable	20	Interest payable	13
Rent Receivable	22	Taxes payable	15
Inventory	24	Unearned revenue	17
Supplies	27	Noncurrent notes payable	22
Prepaid items	30	Luigi Cavelli, Capital	24
Equipment	33		
Accum. depr. equip.	34		
Leasehold improvement	36		

b) Prepare the income statement in good form following the multiple-step format for Luigi's Auto Parts for Period 4.

c) Prepare in good form the statement of owner's capital for the firm for Period 4.

d) Prepare in good form the balance sheet for the firm as of the end of Period 4.

e) Determine for Luigi's Store as of the end of Period 4:

   1. The amount of net working capital in the business;

   2. The current ratio (to two decimals);

   3. The quick ratio (to two decimals);

   4. The long-term debt ratio (to three decimals);

   5. The asset composition ratio (to three decimals).

   6. The gross profit ratio (to three decimals).

SP 6.20 Integrative Problem: The following events occurred during Period 3 for Irene's Sport Shop:

1) Sales totaled $105,000, $40,000 for cash and the balance on account.
2) Receivables collections totaled $64,000.
3) Inventory costing $56,000 was purchased on account.
4) Wages and salaries totaling $26,800 were paid including the $2,000 of prior period's obligation.
5) Interest of $3,140 was paid including the prior period's obligation of $1,360.
6) Supplies costing $550 were purchased on account.
7) $5,300 of rent was paid in advance.
8) A bill for $700 for utilities and services consumed during Period 3 was received and paid.
9) $58,625 was paid on accounts payable.
10) Irene withdrew $7,000 for personal use.

Adjustments were made for $80 of accrued interest owed on the equipment note (A); $6,600 expiration of prepaid rent (B); $900 expiration of prepaid insurance (C); $1,150 amortization of leasehold improvement (D); $54,000 of inventory delivered to customers (E); $500 of supplies used (F); $1,200 in wages and salaries owed but not yet paid (G); $150 in depreciation on equipment (H); and $50 for utilities and services consumed but not yet billed (I).

Irene's firm's balance sheet as of the end of Period 3 is given next.

IRENE'S SPORT SHOP BALANCE SHEET AS OF THE END OF PERIOD 3

ASSETS		EQUITIES	
Cash	$8,635	Accounts payable	$23,050
Accounts receivable	83,000	Wages and salaries payable	1,200
Inventory	49,000	Interest payable	80
Supplies	350	Total Current Liabilities	$24,330
Prepaid items	900		
		Noncurrent notes payable	37,000
Total Current Assets	$141,885	Total Liabilities	$61,330
Equipment	2,400		
Accum. depr. equip.	(300)		
Leasehold improvement	14,950	Irene Morton, Capital	97,605
Total Assets	$158,935	Total Equities	$158,935

During Period 4, the following events occurred affecting the financial position of Irene's Sport Shop: (Note: Items marked with an asterisk have been illustrated in previous periods.)

*1) Regular sales total $115,000 of which $45,000 were for cash and the balance on account.
2) Customers returned merchandise priced at $2,000 and originally purchased on account.

3) Customers returned merchandise priced at $750 originally purchased for cash and were given a cash refund.

4) Some of the merchandise sold on account proved defective, and the customers were given a $250 allowance in lieu of returning the merchandise or replacing same.

5) Customers ordered special order merchandise priced at $8,000 paying cash in advance.

*6) Merchandise, both regular and special order costing $62,000, was purchased on account and received. Inventory purchases were added directly to the inventory account.

7) By the end of Period 4, special order merchandise priced at $6,000 had been delivered to the customers.

*8) Supplies costing $350 were purchased on account.

*9) $65,000 was collected from customers on receivables. All remaining receivables were believed to be collectible in full in the following period.

10) A promissory note receivable with a face value of $1,000 and due early in Period 5 was accepted at the beginning of Period 4 in settlement of $1,000 of accounts receivable. The note provided for $25 of interest per period payable at maturity.

*11) The period's rent of $6,600 was paid in advance.

*12) Wages and salaries totaling $27,400 were paid to employees including the $1,200 unpaid at the end of the prior period.

*13) Interest of $1,940 was paid representing all the current period's interest and the $80 accrued at the end of the previous period.

14) A bill for utilities and services consumed in the current period for $700 was received and recorded.

15) Irene sublet some space storage space to a nearby store early in Period 4. Rental was agreed as $450 per period, and Irene received $150 at the time of signing the sublet agreement.

*16) $62,200 was paid on accounts payable.

*17) Irene withdrew $15,000 for personal use. A separate account had been established to accumulate withdrawals and be closed to proprietor's capital at period-end.

At the end of Period 4:

*A) Merchandise costing $50,000 was determined to be still on hand and unsold.

*B) Supplies costing $150 were determined to be on hand and unsold.

*C) The remaining prepaid insurance coverage of $900 and the prepaid rent of $6,600 had expired.

*D) $800 in wages and salaries had been earned by employees and were unpaid at year-end.

*E) $100 of utilities and other services had been consumed but unbilled by the end of the period.

*F) $1,150 of leasehold improvement amortization was taken.

*G) $150 of depreciation on equipment was recorded.

H) $300 rent was receivable from the tenant subletting the spare storage space, and the $150 already received had been earned.

I) $25 of interest had been earned on the promissory note accepted from the customer.

J) Irene's store was liable for a newly passed inventory tax payable early in Period 5. The tax was estimated at $1,200

K) Of the $37,000 of noncurrent notes payable appearing on Irene's balance sheet at the end of Period 3, notes with a face value of $35,000 will mature in Period 5 and must be reclassified.

L) Near the end of the period, a customer obtained a court judgment for damages in the sum of $10,000 against Irene's store for injuries allegedly resulting from failure of one of Irene's products. The firm gave a 30-day noninterest-bearing promissory note for $10,000 in settlement. The incident was clearly extraordinary in nature and not expected to recur.

Required:

a) Complete a balance sheet effect worksheet (per Balance Sheet Diagram 4.9) for Irene's store for Period 4. Identify beginning balances as "(b)" and the effect of transactions and adjustments with their numbers or letters. Also identify all revenue and expense effects upon Irene's capital in an income box. Provide necessary space on your worksheet by entering account titles as follows:

Account	Line number	Account	Line number
Cash	1	Current notes payable	1
Current notes receivable	12	Accounts payable	4
Accounts receivable	14	Wages and salaries	10
Interest receivable	20	Interest payable	13
Rent Receivable	22	Taxes payable	15
Inventory	24	Unearned revenue	17
Supplies	27	Noncurrent notes payable	22
Prepaid items	30	Irene Morton, Capital	24
Equipment	33		
Accum. depr. equip.	34		
Leasehold improvement	36		

b) Prepare the income statement in good form following the multiple-step format for Irene's Sport Shop for Period 4.

c) Prepare in good form the statement of owner's capital for the firm for Period 4.

d) Prepare in good form the balance sheet for the firm as of the end of Period 4.

e) Determine for Irene's Store as of the end of Period 4:

1. The amount of net working capital in the business;

2. The current ratio (to two decimals);

3. The quick ratio (to two decimals);

4. The long-term debt ratio (to three decimals);

5. The asset composition ratio (to three decimals).

6. The gross profit ratio (to three decimals).

Preparer Problems

PP 6.1   a) Prepare journal entries in good form for the 14 transactions for Albert Company for the year ending December 31, 19X5 in SP 6.21. Identify each transaction entry by number.

b) Prepare journal entries in good form for the 8 necessary year-end adjustments for the Albert Company. Identify each adjusting entry by number.

c) Set up T accounts for the balance sheet accounts for the Albert Company as of 12/31/X4 and post the year-end balances to these accounts.

d) Set up additional T accounts for revenues, expenses, and owner withdrawals as necessary; and post all 29 journal entries from part (a) above to these accounts.

e) Determine the ending balance in all accounts before adjustment and prepare a trial balance.

f) Obtain or prepare a ten-column worksheet and post the preadjusted account balances from (e) above.

g) Post the 8 year-end adjustments (from Part (b) above) to the worksheet, and prove the debit/credit equality.

h) On the worksheet complete (and prove the balance) the adjusted balances of all accounts.

i) Complete the worksheet for the income statement and balance sheet columns including the balancing net income entry.

j) Post all adjustments to the T accounts developed in parts (c) and (d) above.

k) Prepare the entries closing all revenue and expense accounts to Income Summary and Owner Withdrawals to owner's capital.

PP 6.2   Prepare journal entries for the 12 transactions and adjustments for the Brandywine Company for 19X3 as given in SP 6.22.

PP 6.3   Prepare journal entries for the 12 transactional adjustments given for the Knox Company in EP 6.7.

PP 6.4   Prepare journal entries for all transactions and adjustments given for the Remington Company in EP 6.12

PP 6.5   Prepare journal entries for all transactions and adjustments for Luigi's Auto Parts for Period 4 given in SP 6.25.

PP 6.6   Follow instructions (a) through (k) given in PP 6.1 for Irene's Sport Shop for Period 4 from information given in SP 6.26.

APPENDIX

Alternative Timing of Revenue Recognition

Revenue is assumed to be realized (and therefore should be recognized and reported) when two conditions have been met:

1. The costs or expenses related to the sale have all been incurred or can reasonably be measured, and
2. The sale has been completed or is assured; and either cash has been received or else its future collection is reasonably expected.

Depending upon particular circumstances, these two conditions may be met at various points during the production process, upon completion of he production process, at the point of sale, or subsequent to the sale when the cash is received. When these conditions are met prior to completion of production, the percentage of completion method of revenue recognition is appropriate. When met at the point that production is completed, the production basis is used. When not met until sale has occurred, the completed contract or point of sale basis is used. Finally, where intended collection of cash is deferred at the time of sale and where such collection cannot be reasonably assured, the installment method of recognition is required.

Long-term Construction Contracts

Revenue recognition on long-term construction contracts may be accounted for under two methods: the completed contract method or the percentage of completion method. Revenue, costs, and gross profit are recognized under the completed contract method only when the contract is completed. The advantage of this method is that no estimates are applied since all the expenses have occurred. The major disadvantage of this method is that it may distort earnings since costs and revenues are not allocated over the accounting periods during construction. GAAP recommend the use of this method only when it is not feasible to use the percentage of completion method.

The percentage of completion method allocates revenue, costs and gross profit over the life of the contract using estimates to determine the portion earned in each accounting period. This method treats the contract like a "continuous" sale creating better matching of the firm's revenues and expenses for each period. GAAP prefer that this method be used unless the following conditions are not met:

- A contract with enforceable rights for both the buyer and seller outlining all necessary conditions;

- The buyer makes periodic payments to the seller at specified points during the contract period and;

- Reasonable estimates can be made to estimate progress on the project, and estimate revenues and costs to complete the contract.

Percentage of Completion Method

At the end of each year or period, under the percentage of completion method, the year's increment or portion of the total contract completed in the current year is determined. The basis for such calculation is the ratio of costs incurred in the current year to a continuously updated estimate of the total project costs. The result in percentage is then applied to the total expected revenues and costs to determine the portion of revenue, costs, and gross profit to be recognized in the current year.[14]

Exhibit 6.14 illustrates a contract for $500,000 with estimated costs to be incurred of $400,000. In year 1, 19X1, the firm incurred $200,000 in project costs. The estimated costs to complete the project were an additional $200,000 so the original estimate of total costs of $400,000 remained the same. The project was 50 percent completed (costs to date divided by estimated total costs) therefore 50 percent of the revenue was recognized

---

[14] The cost-to-cost basis of estimating percentage of completion may be replaced by other measures deemed more appropriate. Also note that, in any given year where total costs estimates indicate an overall loss on the project, the entire anticipated los for portion not previously reported, must be recognized.

in 19X1. Since revenue less costs equals gross profit ($250,000 - 200,000) $50,000 of gross profit was recognized in the first year.

Exhibit 6.14

Percentage of Completion Method

	19X1	19X2	19X3
current construction costs	$200	$160	$ 90
prior construction costs	—	200	360
construction costs to date	$200	$360	$450
estimated costs to complete	200	90	—
estimated total construction costs	$400	$450	$450
percent completed	50%	80%	100%
Revenue recognized to date	$250	$400	$500
Revenue recognized current period	$250	$150	$100
less current construction costs	200	160	90
Gross profit/loss recognized current period	$ 50	$ (10)	$ 10

In the second year, 19X2, the estimated total contract costs increased to $450,000. The project was estimated to be 80 percent completed at that point ($360,000 costs to date divided by $450,000 estimated total costs). Revenue recognized in 19X2 can be calculated two ways. Since 50 percent was recognized in 19X1, and the project was 80 percent completed by the end of 19X2, then 30 percent (80-50) was recognized in 19X2 or $150,000. Revenue can also be calculated by subtracting last year's revenue to date from this year's revenue to date ($400,000 – 250,000 = $150,000). The gross profit recognized in 19X2 was negative (a loss) because costs exceeded revenue. This reduces the gross profit previously recognized so that gross profit recognized to date will reflect the contract's gross profit for the work completed.

Exhibit 6.15

Percentage of Completion Method

	Construction in Progress	Recognize Revenue	Partial Billings
19X1	$200,000 costs 50,000 gross profit	$250,000	$250,000
19X2	160,000 costs (10,000) loss	150,000	150,000
19X3	90,000 costs 10,000 gross profit	100,000	100,000
	$500,000		$500,000
Contract completed	(500,000)		(500,000)

Exhibit 6.15 illustrates how construction costs and gross profit/loss are accumulated over the project's life in a construction in progress account. When construction in progress is greater than partial billings, the difference is shown on the balance sheet as part of inventories. If partial billings exceeds construction in progress, then the difference is treated as a current liability. Note that neither situation exists in the illustration.

The current revenue, costs, and gross profit/loss are recognized on the current income statement. If the project's estimated total costs are projected to exceed total revenues, then the entire estimated loss should be recognized in the current period. The loss, and any previously recognized gross profit are added to current construction costs on the income statement.

Completed Contract Method

No revenues, costs, or gross profit is recognized under the completed contract method until the project is complete. Exhibit 6.16 illustrates the completed contract method using the data from the percentage of completion illustration.

Exhibit 6.15

Completed Contract Method			
	Construction in Progress	Recognize Revenue	Partial Billings
19X1	$200,000		$250,000
19X2	160,000		150,000
19X3	90,000		100,000
	$450,000		$500,000
Contract completed	(450,000)*	500,000	(500,000)

*The difference between construction in progress and Revenue is gross profit.

Construction in progress is increased each year for the construction costs incurred. Partial billings is increased according to the billing terms stated in the contract. The balance sheet treatment for construction in progress and partial billings is the same using either contract method. If construction in progress is greater than partial billings, the difference is listed as an asset under inventories, and if partial billings exceeds construction in progress, the difference is treated as a current liability. Upon completion of the project, partial billings and construction in progress are eliminated and revenue, costs, and gross profit are recognized on the income statement. The income statement is not affected by the contract during construction unless a loss on the total contract is estimated. If a loss is estimated, it is recognized immediately.

Revenue is assumed to be realized (and therefore should be recognized and reported) when two conditions have been met:

1. The costs or expenses related to the sale have all been incurred or can reasonably be measured, and
2. The sale has been completed or is assured; and either cash has been received or else its future collection is reasonably expected.

Depending upon particular circumstances, these two conditions may be met at various points during the production process, upon completion of the production process, at the point of sale, or subsequent to the sale when the cash is received. When these conditions are met prior to completion of production, the percentage of completion method of revenue recognition is appropriate. When met at the point that production is completed, the production basis is used. When not met until sale has occurred, the completed contract or point of sale basis is used. Finally, where intended collection of cash is deferred at the time of sale and where such collection cannot be reasonably assured, the installment method of recognition is required.

Installment Sales

As previously mentioned, when sales are made with contract terms of regular payments spreading over an extended period and collection is so uncertain that payment cannot be reasonably assured, the installment sales method may be used. Although the customer takes delivery at the time the contract is accepted, legal title remains with the seller until the final payment is made.

As credit rating methods have improved, the installment method has become less accepted. Both GAAP and the IRS limit the use of this method.[15]

If the collection on installment sales is material, both installment sales and cost of goods sold recognized must appear on the income statement to show the gross profit realized. Both interest revenue and operating expenses from installment sales will be recognized in the period incurred rather than matching with revenue recognition.

Bad debt provisions are estimated and booked only if a loss is expected on repossession of goods.

Diagram 6.8 illustrates the statement effect of an installment sale of $900. Note that deferred gross profit of $360 is a contra account to installment sales accounts receivable and is increased by the installment sales less cost of goods sold ($900 − 540). the gross profit recognized will be in proportion to the collections during the year. Gross profit recognized in 19X1 would be $90 since $225 was collected during the year ($360 deferred gross profit times 25 percent collected). The deferred gross profit would be recognized over the three year life of the contract as shown in Exhibit 6.17. Gross profit recognized in 19X2 would be 35 percent of the $360 gross profit, and 19X3 would be the remaining 40 percent.

---

[15] The 1986 Tax Act eleminated the use of the installment sales method for revolving charge accounts.

Diagram 6.8

Installment Sales
for the year 19X1

Cash	+	225
Installment Sales Accounts Receivable	+	900
	–	225
Deferred Gross Profit	–	360
	–	90
Inventory	–	540

Income
+ 90

If installment sales are material, the firm must disclose installment sales recognized ($225 collected) and the $135 of cost of goods sold ($540 x 0.25) separately on the income statement.

Exhibit 6.17

Installment Sales

Year	Cash Collected	Percent of Sales	Gross Profit Recognized
19X1	$225	25%	$ 90
19X2	315	35%	126
19X3	360	40%	144
	$900	100%	$360

Cost Recovery Method

The cost recovery method is used for installment sales when the firm sells a segment of division of the firm when the conditions of the sales price is dependent on the company's future profitability. In that case, since both the amount to be received and the timing cannot be estimated, no gross profit is recognized until all of the cost of goods sold has been collected.

Production Basis

In cases where established markets and market prices exist for a firm's product(s), there exists no questions as to the ability to sell the product or to collect cash once production has been completed. For certain precious metals (such as gold and silver) and agricultural products (such as corn and wheat), revenue can be recognized at the time production is completed, since the earnings process is considered virtually complete.

Finished inventory is "written up" to net realizable value (selling price less any additional costs to prepare the inventory for sale) and treated as a receivable with a corresponding recognition of gross profit.

Appendix Problems

AP6.21 The Jones Construction Company entered into a contract early in 19X4 to construct a new high-rise office building complex for the Smith Company. The contract was for $140,000,000 and Jones estimated its total costs at $112,000,000. On 12/31/X4, Jones estimated that the job was 20 percent completed and that its costs incurred to date amount to $25,000,000. Following the percentage-of-completion method, in its 19X4 income statement for this job, what was Jones' (a) Total revenue? (b) Total expenses? (c) Gross profit?

AP 6.22 Refer to the data given in SP 6.21. During 19X5 Jones incurred additional costs of $60,000,000. At the end of 19X5 Jones estimated that the project was 70 percent completed. The project was completed in late 19X6. Completion cost incurred during 19X6 were $32,000,000. Following the percentage-of-completion method, relating to this project and rounding to thousands of dollars what was (were) Jones' (a) 19X5 revenue? (b) 19X5 expenses? (c) 19X5 gross profit? (d)19X6 revenue? (e) 19X6 expenses? (f) 19X6 gross profit?

AP 6.23 The Smith Company sold parcels of undeveloped land by mail on the installment basis with terms of 10 percent down and 30 percent per year for each of the next three years. During 19X2 its new sales totaled $2,000,000 and it collected $200,000 in down payments. With respect to the 19X2 installment sales, collection of $500,000, $400,000, and $300,000 were received during 19X3, 19X4, and 19X5 respectively. The land in question cost Smith $1,200,000. Ignoring sales in subsequent years, and assuming Smith followed the installment method for recognizing gross profit on its income statement, what would Smith's gross profit be reported as: (a) For 19X2? (b) For 19X3? (c) For 19X4? (d) For 19X5?

AP 6.24 Refer to the Smith Company in SP 6.23. Assume 19X3 additional installment sales were $2,500,000 of land costing $1,650,000. Down payments collected during 19X3 totaled $250,000. Collections against 19X3 installment sales totaled $600,000, $800,000, and $850,000 during 19X4, 19X5, and 19X6 respectively. Ignoring sales made in prior and subsequent years, what would Smith's gross profit be reported as: (a) For 19X3? (b) For 19X4? (c) For 19X5? (d) For 19X6?

7

The Statement of Cash Flows

Chapter Preview

The objective of this chapter is to present the financial statement which summarizes the firm's significant activities—the Statement of Cash Flows. In this chapter you can:

1. Develop an appreciation of the usefulness of the information concerning cash transactions;

2. Become familiar with the Statement of Cash Flows;

3. Learn how the firm's operating, investing and financing activities for the period are summarized on the Statement of Cash Flows;

4. Learn how to derive cash from operating activities from income and balance sheet data reported under the accrual basis;

5. Learn about the investing and financing activities which do not involve cash flow;

6. Develop an understanding of how the Statement of Cash Flows explains the essential differences between two successive balance sheets and how it ties in with the income statement and statement of owner's capital.

With an understanding of the Statement of Cash Flows, you will have completed the introduction of the content and function of the four financial statements required by GAAP.

Need for Cash Flow Information

Investors and creditors need information to be able to predict and assess a firm's liquidity, and more precisely the ability of the firm to its pay bills. To fill this information need, The Statement of Financial Position was added as the fourth financial statement in 1971.[1] GAAP allowed the statement to reflect the changes in the company's position based on changes in net working capital, or on a cash basis. Recall that the limitations of information based on changes in net working capital was presented in Chapter 3. Net working capital includes assets which may not be very liquid. You can't meet the payroll with inventory.

The classic example of the failure of net working capital to predict liquidity was the bankruptcy of the W. T. Grant Company. The company continued to report positive income and working capital from operations, while cash flow was negative. The company's

Illustration 7.1   W.T. Grant Company, Net Income, Working Capital Provided by Operations, and Cash Provided by Operations for the Fiscal Years ending January 31, 1966 to 1975.

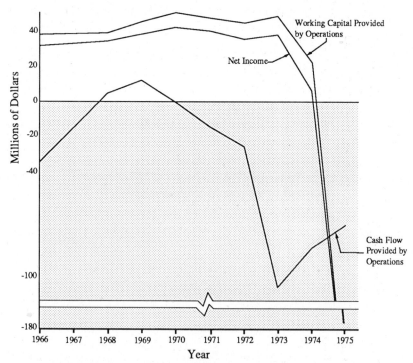

Source: James A Largay, III and Clyde P. Stickney, "Cash Flows, Ratio Analysis, and the W. T. Grant Company Bankruptcy." *Financial Analysts Journal*, July-August, 1980, p. 54.

---

[1] "Reporting Changes in Financial Position (amended)," FASB Statement No. 19, Financial Accounting Standards Board, Stamford, CT 06905, March, 1971.

decreasing cash flow was masked due to increases in receivables and inventory. Measurement of liquidity through cash flow instead of working capital, would have predicted the company's growing liquidity crisis almost a decade sooner.

GAAP was changed in 1987 to standardize the reported information on the statement of changes in financial position requiring cash reconciliation rather than allowing the net working capital approach.[2] The statement was redesigned to require classification of the firm's events by function and the name was changed to the "statement of cash flows." The three functions defined are operating, investing, and financing. Investing and financing activities which do not involve cash transactions were removed from the body of the statement of changes in financial position and placed in a separate schedule for the statement of cash flows. Finally, the new statement is required to reconcile beginning cash to ending cash.

Purpose of the Statement of Cash Flows

The primary purpose of the statement of cash flows is to provide information about cash receipts and payments during the period. The secondary purpose is to provide information divided into operating, investing and financing activities. The statement meets the basic objectives of financial accounting to present information which allows users to predict the amounts, timing and uncertainty of cash flows, and to disclose changes in economic resources and the claims to those resources.

The statement of cash flows discloses the firm's financial flexibility and future operating capability. Specifically the statement was created to assess the firm's ability to:

- Generate positive future cash flows;
- Meet obligations and pay a return to the owners;
- To obtain external financing;
- Assess the reasons for the difference between reported income and cash flow; and
- Assess noncash aspects of investing and financing transactions on the firm's flexibility and operating capacity.

Statement of Cash Flow Classifications

The firm's activities are divided into four classifications: operating, investing, financing, and noncash investing and financing activities. The statement must be prepared to reconcile beginning and ending cash balances. **Cash** may be defined as cash or cash and cash equivalents.

---

[2] "The Statement of Cash Flows," FASB Statement No. 95, Financial Accounting Standards Board, Stamford, CT 06905, November, 1987.

Illustration 7.2   Cash Flow

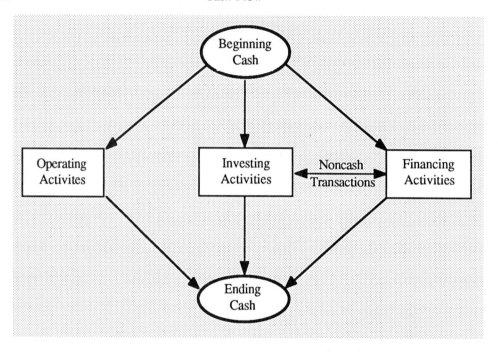

Cash and Cash Equivalents

GAAP recommend that the statement of cash flows include cash equivalents with cash in its reconciliation between beginning and ending cash. **Cash equivalents** include all highly liquid securities purchased within three months of their maturity date. You should note that when the statement of cash flows reconciles for "cash and cash equivalents," the balance sheet should also report "cash and cash equivalents" as one number. If cash equivalents are not included in cash, they should be classified as marketable securities.

Cash flows from Operating Activities

Operating activities focus on the cash flows derived from the income statement relating to operating income. There are two GAAP approved formats for reporting the firm's operating activities: the direct and indirect methods. The **direct method** requires recalculation of the firm's revenues and expenses from the accrual basis to cash basis. Although this is the recommended method, many analysts are concerned that preparation of income on the cash basis will confuse readers who are more familiar with accrual basis reported income. In addition, the preparation costs in converting income to this method may be more costly than benefits derived.

The **indirect method** is more familiar to financial statement readers because it continues the same approach that was used in the statement of financial position. This method reconciles reported income with noncash revenue and expenses and changes in certain current assets and current liabilities. Exhibit 7.1 presents the financial statements for The Potted Planter for the year-ended 12/31/X5. During 19X5 Pat Ward closed down her original downtown store and opened two suburban stores. As you proceed through The Potted Planter example, recall from Chapter 3 that an increase in a firm's level of operations necessitates an additional long-term commitment of resources.

Exhibit 7.1

The Potted Planter Comparative Balance Sheets
as of December 31, 19X4 and 19X5 ($ in thousands)

ASSETS:	12/31/X5	12/31/X4
Cash	$ 88	70
Marketable Securities	12	10
Current Notes Receivable	0	5
Accounts Receivable	200	110
Inventory	190	150
Supplies	2	4
Prepaid Items	8	6
Total Current Assets	$500	$355
Land	70	30
Buildings	280	150
Accumulated Depreciation, Bldg	(20)	(120)
Equipment	150	110
Accumulated Depreciation, Equip	(50)	(40)
Leasehold Improvements	58	15
Total Assets	$988	$500
EQUITIES:		
Current Notes Payable	$ 40	$ 25
Accounts Payable	135	100
Wages and Salaries Payable	2	3
Interest Payable	25	10
Taxes Payable	88	70
Total Current Liabilities	$290	$208
Noncurrent Notes Payable	255	121
Total Liabilities	$545	$329
Pat Ward, Capital	443	171
Total Equities	$988	$500

Exhibit 7.1
(continued)

The Potted Planter Income Statement
for the year ended 12/31/X5 ($ in thousands)

Net Sales		$ 2,000
Cost of Goods Sold		(1,200)
Gross Profit		$ 800
Less Operating Expenses		
Wages	$ 400	
Utilities	40	
Rent	45	
Depreciation	30	
Property Taxes	14	
Supplies	8	
Insurance	3	
Amortization	5	(545)
Income from Operations		$ 255
Other Gains and Expenses:		
Gain on Sale of Land & Bldg	300	
Interest expense	(30)	270
Income before provision for income taxes		$ 525
Provision for Income Taxes		(210)
Net Income		$ 315

The Potted Planter Statement of Owner's Capital
for the Year Ended 12/31/X5 ($ in thousands)

Pat Ward, Capital 1/1/X5	$ 171
Additional Owner Investment	27
19X5 income	315
Owner Withdrawal	(70)
Pat Ward, Capital 12/31/X5	$ 443

Additional Information about 19X5:

1. Marketable Securities were purchased and sold (at cost) throughout the year.

2. The current note receivable was collected on 1/1/X5.

3. The downtown store was sold for $360,000 in January. The original cost was $30,000 for land and $150,000 for building. The book value of the building at the time of disposal was $30,000.

4. Property was purchased for a new store for $350,000. The land was valued at $70,000 and the building at $280,000.

5. New equipment was purchased for $40,000 with a 3 year note.

6. Leasehold improvements were made on the newly rented store for $48,000 and were paid for in cash.

7. The current note payable as of 1/1/X5 was paid off and new current notes were acquired during the year.

8. $215,000 was borrowed on a 10 year note to finance the firm's expansion.

Direct Method

The first step in the preparation of the statement of cash flows is to determine the changes in account balances for the successive balance sheets. This was done for The Potted Planter for 19X5 in Exhibit 7.2. Consider the following example for calculating cash from operating activities under the direct method. Exhibit 7.1 presents the 12/31/X4 and 12/31/X5 balance sheets for The Potted Planter with the income statement and statement of owner's capital for the year-ended 12/31/X5. Reported net sales for The Potted Planter were $2 million in 19X5. To convert net sales to cash basis, you must calculate the amount collected from customers during the year:

Reported Net Sales – Increase A/R + Decrease A/R = Cash Collected on Sales

Increases in receivables indicate that collections on accounts were less than the year's cash and credit sales. Therefore you must subtract the increase in accounts receivable from reported net sales to calculate cash inflow from sales of $1,910,000 ($2,000,000 – 90,000).

Cost of goods sold would be converted to cash basis for cash outflow for inventory:

Cost of Goods Sold + Increase Inventory – Decrease Inventory = Cash Paid for Inventory

Increases in inventory indicate that cash was spent for inventory used, cost of goods sold, and for additional merchandise on hand at the end of the year. The increase in inventory must be added to cost of goods sold to calculate cash spent on inventory for the year of $1,240,000 ($1,200,000 + 40,000).

Operating expenses would be converted to cash expenditures by adding the decrease in current operating payables or subtracting for increases in operating payables:

Accounts Payable	increase	– $35,000
Wages Payable	decrease	+ 1,000
Interest Payable	increase	– 15,000
Taxes Payable	increase	– 18,000

When current liabilities increase, you can think of the amount of the increase as the portion of the current year's operating expenses not yet paid, and therefore not representing cash outflows. If payables decrease, the decrease represents payments exceeding the current expenses because if payables did not change, the cash payments would equal operating expenses except for noncash expenses such as depreciation and amortization.

Exhibit 7.2

The Potted Planter Comparative Balance Sheets
for December 31, 19X4 and 19X5 ($ in thousands)

ASSETS:	X4	X5	Change	
Cash	$ 70	$ 88	+ 18	Increase
Marketable Securities	10	12	+ 2	Increase
Current Notes Receivable	5	0	− 5	Decrease
Accounts Receivable	110	200	+ 90	Increase
Inventory	150	190	+ 40	Increase
Supplies	4	2	− 2	Decrease
Prepaid Items	6	8	+ 2	Increase
Total Current Assets	$355	$500		
Land	30	70	+ 40[1]	Increase
Buildings	150	280	+ 130[2]	Increase
Accumulated Depreciation, Bldg	(120)	(20)	+ 100	Decrease
Equipment	110	150	+ 40[3]	Increase
Accumulated Depreciation, Equip	(40)	(50)	− 10	Increase
Leasehold Improvements	15	58	+ 43	Increase
Total Assets	$500	$988		
EQUITIES				
Current Notes Payable	25	40	+ 15	Increase
Accounts Payable	100	135	+ 35	Increase
Wages and Salaries Payable	3	2	− 1	Decrease
Interest Payable	10	25	+ 15	Increase
Taxes Payable	70	88	+ 18	Increase
Total Current Liabilities	$208	$290		
Noncurrent Notes Payable	121	255	+ 134[4]	Increase
Total Liabilities	$329	$545		
Pat Ward, Capital	171	443	+ 272[5]	Increase
Total Equities	$500	$988		

1   Purchase for $70, Proceeds of Sale $30.
2   Purchase for $280, Proceeds of Sale $150.
3   New Equpment of $40 acquired with a noncurrent notes payable.
4   Proceeds new loan $215, Payment old loan $121, New loan of $40 for equipment.
5   Net income $315, additional owner investment $27, owner withdrawal $70.

Exhibit 7.3

Direct Method
Operating Activities

Cash inflows:
Collection on sale of goods or services to customers
Collection of interest and dividends
Collection on other revenues (e.g. rent)

Cash Outflows:
Payments for inventory
payments for other operating expenses
payments for interest (expense)
payments for taxes

Net cash provided (used) by operating activities

Cash outflows from operating activities include the cost of inventory plus cash outflows for other operating expenses plus cash payments for interest and taxes as illustrated in Exhibit 7.4.

Exhibit 7.4

Direct Method
The Potted Planter Operating Activities
for the year-ended 12/31X5 ($ in thousands)

Cash flows from operating activities:	
Cash received from customers	$ 1,910
Cash paid to suppliers for inventory	(1,240)
Cash paid for other operating expenses*	(462)
Interest payments	(15)
Taxes paid**	(206)
Net cash provided (used) by operating activities	$ (13)

* Wages expense + utilities expense + rent expense + supplies expense
+ insurance expense – increase in Accounts Payable + decrease in Wages Payable.

** Property taxes + income taxes – increase in taxes payable.

You should note that gains and losses on long-lived assets, whether extraordinary or not, are not included in cash provided by operating activities.

The advantage of using the direct method is that it is consistent with the cash data used by lending institutions to make credit decisions. Bankers are lobbying to make this method required. However, there does not appear to be support for this method beyond financial institutions. Opponents argue that some accounting systems would have to be altered to gather the information to prepare the statement and that the cost would outweigh the benefits. In addition, since a schedule disclosing cash from operating activities prepared under the indirect method must accompany the statement if the direct method is used, some analysts feel it is an additional amount of work which may actually confuse the reader. Critics are concerned that the direct method may actually promote the concept that cash income is a better predictor of performance than accrual income.

Indirect Method

The indirect method reconciles accrual basis to cash basis income through adjustments for noncash revenues and expenses, gains and losses on long-lived assets, extraordinary gains and losses, and changes in certain current assets and current liabilities. The following accounts will not be included: cash, marketable securities, current notes receivable, and current notes payable.[3] Cash is not included since the statement's purpose is to reconcile the change in cash. The other accounts will be excluded since they represent investing and financing activities. Exhibit 7.5 lists the changes from accrual basis to cash basis.

Exhibit 7.5

Changes from Reported Income to Net Cash Provided by Operating Activities Include:

NET INCOME

Add: Noncash expenses:
         Depreciation
         Amortization of intangibles

     Loss on Disposal of Assets

Decrease	Accounts Receivable (net)
Decrease	Interest Receivable
Decrease	Rent Receivable
Decrease	Inventory
Decrease	Supplies
Decrease	Prepaid Items
Increase	Accounts Payable
Increase	Wages and Salaries Payable
Increase	Interest Payable
Increase	Taxes Payable

Less: Gain on Disposal of Assets

Increase	Accounts Receivable (net)
Increase	Interest Receivable
Increase	Rent Receivable
Increase	Inventory
Increase	Supplies
Increase	Prepaid Items
Decrease	Accounts Payable
Decrease	Wages and Salaries Payable
Decrease	Interest Payable
Decrease	Taxes Payable

[3] Current notes receivable should be included in the reconciliation for cash from operating activities if the note was created in settlement of customer sales. Current Notes Payable should be included if the note resulted from settlement of operating expenses or purchase of current assets.

Exhibit 7.6 illustrates the format used in the indirect method for cash provided by operating activities. Note that regardless of the method used, direct or indirect, net cash provided by operating activities is the same. The indirect method converts net income to cash provided by operating activities rather than converting the entire statement to cash basis.

In The Potted Planter example, net income is adjusted by noncash expenses of depreciation and amortization; the gain on the sale of land and building; and the changes in the balances of accounts receivable, inventory, supplies, prepaid items, accounts payable, wages and salaries payable, interest payable, and taxes payable. The change in marketable securities, notes receivable and notes payable were omitted since they are not operating activities.

The advantage of using the indirect method is the statement creates a link between the balance sheet and the income statement. This method is expected to be used because it is familiar to readers. It is effectively the same format used for cash from operations on the former statement, the statement of changes in financial position.

Exhibit 7.6

Indirect Method
The Potted Planter Operating Activities
for the year-ended 12/31/X5 ($ in thousands)

Net Income		$ 315
Adjustments to reconcile net income:		
Depreciation	$ 30	
Amortization	5	
Gain on sale of land and building	(300)	
Increase in accounts receivable	(90)	
Increase in inventory	(40)	
Decrease in supplies	2	
Increase in prepaid items	(2)	
Increase in accounts payable	35	
Decrease in wages and salaries payable	(1)	
Increase in interest payable	15	
Increase in taxes payable	18	
Total adjustments		(328)
Net cash provided (used) by operating activities		$ (13)

Investing Activities

Cash purchases and proceeds from the sale of long-lived assets, marketable securities, and notes receivable (current and noncurrent) are included in **investing activities**. Recall that notes receivable resulting from the settlement of customer sales are considered part of operating activities.

Illustration 7.3

Investing Activities

Proceeds		Payments
sale of long-lived assets principal of notes receivable sale of marketable securities	→ Cash →	purchase long-lived assets purchase marketable securities issue notes receivable

In The Potted Planter example (Exhibit 7.7), cash inflows from investing activities include the $360,000 proceeds on the sale of land and building. Recall that the $300,000 gain on the sale was excluded from cash from operating activities so that the entire proceeds from the disposal could be reported as an investing activity. Collection of the current notes receivable of $5,000 is also included in the firm's cash inflow from investing activities. Recall that interest collected on notes is part of operating activities.

Exhibit 7.7

The Potted Planter Investing Activities
for the year-ended 12/31/X5 ($ in thousands)

Cash flows from investing activities:	
Payment for purchase of marketable securities	$ (2)
Collection on the current notes receivable	5
Proceeds from the sale of land and building	360
Payment for the purchase of land an building	(350)
Payment for leasehold improvement	(48)
Net Cash Used in Investing Activities	($35)

Cash outflows for investing activities include $2,000 in net payments for the purchase of marketable securities,[4] purchase of land and building for $350,000, and $48,000 spent on leasehold improvements.

Financing Activities

Financing activities report the changes in the capital structure. Sources of capital or cash inflows for financing activities include issuance of new current notes payable, long-term debt, and additional owner investment. Recall that notes payable resulting from settlement of operating expenses should be excluded from this category. Cash outflows include repayment of debt principal and owner withdrawals.

---

[4] GAAP allow both the gross and net methods for reporting purchases and sales of marketable securities. The gross method requires all purchases and sales to be reported while the net method reports only the net change in cash (e.g. $30,000 purchases less $28,000 sales). GAAP recommend the gross method be applied for securities maturing beyond 90 days of the purchase date.

Illustration 7.4

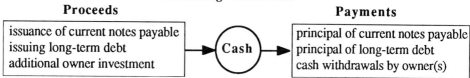

Financing Activities

In The Potted Planter example (Exhibit 7.8), cash inflows from financing activities include proceeds from issuing a new $15,000 current note payable, noncurrent notes payable of $215,000, and $27,000 additional cash owner investment. Cash was used to retire noncurrent notes payable of $121,000 and for owner withdrawals of $70,000.

Exhibit 7.8

The Potted Planter Financing Activities
for the year-ended 12/31/X5 ($ in thousands)

Cash flows from financing activities:	
Proceeds from new borrowing of current notes payable	$ 15
Proceeds on new borrowing of noncurrent notes payable	215
Payment of noncurrent notes payable	(121)
Additional owner investment	27
Owner withdrawals	(70)
Net cash provided by financing activities	$ 66

Noncash Investing and Financing Activities

Resource exchanges which are investing and/or financing activities which do not affect cash flow are not included in the body of the statement of cash flows. GAAP require these noncash activities to be placed in a supplemental schedule accompanying the statement of cash flows. Long-lived assets acquired by direct trade with an older asset "traded-in" would be an example of an investing activity not involving cash flow. Assets acquired by issuance of new debt or by an additional owner investment would also be a noncash investing and financing activity. These transactions do affect the capacity and capital structure of the firm and therefore need to be reported.

Also, in the case of corporations, as will be discussed in later chapters, sometimes long-term creditors are allowed to exchange their creditor claim for an ownership share. Such action may significantly alter the firm's capital structure, and is clearly a financing activity, but does not involve cash flow.

Exhibit 7.9

Investing and Financing Activities
not Involving Cash Flow

- All or a portion of marketable securities or a long-lived asset obtained in exchange for additional debt;
- New asset obtained in trade on the disposition of an old asset;
- New asset obtained as direct investment by owner(s);
- Extinguishment of debt in exchange for additional ownership claims;
- Extinguishment of long-term debt through payment of a long-lived asset sinking fund (see Chapters 11 and 12);
- Extinguishment of preferred stock in exchange for common stock (see Chapter 10); and
- Distribution of assets to owner(s).

Some transactions do not fit completely into one category. Consider a purchase of new equipment for $100,000 with a down payment of $10,000 and signing a five-year note for $90,000 plus interest for the balance. The $10,000 down payment is clearly an investing activity involving cash flow, but the $90,000 portion of the purchase would be a noncash investing and financing activity. Therefore, $10,000 would be reported as an investing activity, and the $90,000 would be reported as a noncash investing and financing activity.

Clearly all of the activities discussed in this category are important for the analysis of the firm, and therefore must be reported.

The Potted Planter would report noncash investing and financing activities as:

"Purchased equipment through the issue of a 3-year note payable of $40,000."

The completed statement of cash flows for The Potted Planter using the direct method is shown in Exhibit 7.10. Note that the direct method requires a reconciliation of the indirect method as well. Had the indirect method been used, no reconciliation for the direct method would be required.

Exhibit 7.10

Direct Method
The Potted Planter Statement of Cash Flows
for the year-ended 12/31/X5 ($ in thousands)

Cash flows from operating activities:

Cash received from customers	$ 1,910	
Cash paid to suppliers for inventory	(1,240)	
Cash paid for other operating expenses	(462)	
Interest payments	(15)	
Taxes paid	(206)	
Net cash used in operating activities		$ (13)

Cash flows from investing activities:

Proceeds from sale of land and building	360	
Collection on the current notes receivable	5	
Payment for purchase of marketable securities	(2)	
Payment for the purchase of land and building	(350)	
Payment for leasehold improvements	(48)	
Net cash used in investing activities		(35)

Cash flows from financing activities:

Proceeds from new borrowing of current notes payable	15	
Proceeds on new borrowing of noncurrent notes payable	215	
Principal payments on noncurrent notes payable	(121)	
Additional owner investments	27	
Cash owner withdrawals	(70)	
Net cash provided by financing activities		66
Net decrease in cash		$ 18
Cash at beginning of year		70
Cash at end of year		$ 88

Reconciliation of net income to net cash provided by operating activities:

Net income		$315
Adjustments to reconcile net income:		
Depreciation	$ 30	
Amortization	5	
Gain on sale of land and building	(300)	
Increase in accounts receivable	(90)	
Increase in inventory	(40)	
Decrease in supplies	(2)	
Increase in prepaid items	2	
Increase in accounts payable	35	
Decrease in wages and salaries payable	(1)	
Increase in interest payable	15	
Increase in taxes payable	18	
Total adjustments		(328)
Net cash used in operating activities		$ (13)

Noncash investing and financing activities:
Equipment purchased through the issue of a 3-year note payable for $40.

Review of Possible Sources of Cash

As first mentioned in the discussion of capital structure in Chapter 3, a firm has several internal and external sources of cash.

Illustration 7.5

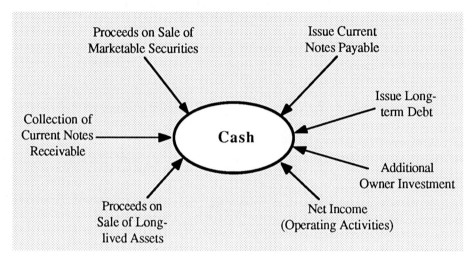

Internal Sources

Two **internal sources** of additional cash are sale of long-lived assets and cash from operating activities. During the year, Pat sold her old downtown location for $360,000 but cash used in operating activities was ($13,000). Therefore, her internal sources yielded a net source of cash of $347,000.

External Sources

Recall from the discussion of capital structure in Chapter 3 that a firm has only two possible **external sources** of cash, additional borrowing and additional owner investment. A balance must be maintained between the two categories and the long-term debt ratio should not exceed the industry standard. Excessive borrowing through short-term debt (current notes payable) will diminish net working capital and impair both the current and quick ratios possibly creating a solvency problem.

Various Components of Financial Management

The Potted Planter case demonstrates many of the aspects of financial management. The overall management of any firm can be viewed as made up of three distinct components: operating management, financial management, and tax management. **Operating management** is essentially involved in using the resources already in the firm to generate revenue and, hopefully, profits. The income statement reports on the activities of operating management.

Financial management involves planning the investment goals of the firm. The planning includes determining how much new capital (assets) is required in the firm and how new and existing capital should be allocated among various uses. Often investment planning is referred to as **capital budgeting**. Capital budgeting decisions would include determining:

- Whether or not to add or discontinue products, product lines, plant and equipment, and so forth;
- Whether new desired capacity should be leased or purchased;
- Which among several competing assets or groups of assets should be leased/ purchased;
- How much income should be distributed to owners and how much should be retained in the business; and
- How much cash is necessary to support planned levels of operations.

Capital budgeting is a financial management function and its aspects are dealt with in managerial accounting and financial management courses. Financial accounting is concerned with reporting the results of these activities.

Financial management also plans the acquisition or inflow of needed additional resources. Recall that investing activities involve reporting the proceeds from the sale of any surplus assets while financing activities report new capital (cash) raised from creditors and owners.

Financial management strives to maintain a desirable capital balance between debt and equity. Financing is a skilled activity involving extensive knowledge of the **capital markets**—the possible outside sources of additional capital. Financing is covered in financial management courses. Again, financial accounting is concerned with reporting the results of financing activities—where additional resources were obtained.

Uses of Cash Flow Information

Visualize how cash flow information often is a vital concern to anyone wishing to analyze and evaluate the performance of a particular firm. Cash flow information provides you, as a user, with a summary of the company's operating, investing, and financing activities during the most recent period. With cash flow information you have an indication of profitability: cash was either generated or lost in operating activities.[5] This will help you predict the firm's ability to continue to pay its bills and meet other obligations (e.g. dividends to stockholders will be discussed in Chapter 10). Also, you can determine whether the firm has been replacing or expanding its capacity, and whether it is expanding through financing activities or internally through operations. Or you can determine if the firm is in a "steady state," or is shrinking in size. You can also find out how the firm may be altering its proportion of long-term debt to owner's equity. And finally, you have information on cash withdrawn by the owners.

Cash flow statements, of course, can be useful to many people other than bank loan officers. Other interested users may include:

- Suppliers and other creditors concerned about payment on their existing and future accounts, bonds, or loans;
- Owners concerned about the availability of dividends; and
- Management attempting to schedule major acquisitions of new assets.

Remember that all these people need to base their decisions on a **pro forma** or projected statement of cash flows. The historical statement of cash flows presented in this chapter provides a basis for such a projection or forecast.

Cash flow information is essentially the basis for many business decisions. In courses in managerial accounting and financial management, you will find that cash flow data, and not financial accounting accruals, are the basis for particular decisions such as:

- Add new product/discontinue existing product;
- Make vs. buy;
- Lease vs. buy;
- Make new investments; and
- Continue operations/discontinue operations.

Although beyond the scope of this text, it is also important to recognize that more sophisticated investment or investor's decision models project cash flows in lieu of projecting earnings.

Statement Analysis

Assume that you are a competitor of The Potted Planter. Essential to the continued successful operation of your firm is "intelligence," or information, concerning the outside factors that could significantly affect your business. You need current information and forecasts concerning the overall economy; prices and changes in varieties of plants and other items in inventory; supply of labor and cost of wages; environmental regulations, taxation changes, and many other factors. It would also be important for you to know

---

[5] Remember that positive cash from operating activities does not always indicate profit.

what your competitors have done and are doing. Are they accelerating the replacement of equipment or just routinely replacing equipment as it wears out? Are they expanding their capacity assets; e.g. are they expanding the number of outlets? Is it possible that they are changing their patterns of capital financing, including changing their proportion of long-term debt to total equities?

You do not necessarily wish to just copy your competitors' actions, assuming that you could do so. At the same time you certainly want to take advantage of any new ideas discovered or developed by your competitors. You also want as much warning as possible of any potential new competitive threat, so that you can consider an appropriate response. For instance, a pattern of accelerated replacement of equipment could be a signal of new technology which you haven't heard about or considered seriously. Significant expansion of capacity could signal a potential invasion of your market. Note that The Potted Planter sold its old downtown location this year and opened two new stores, one purchased and the other leased in suburban shopping centers.

A major change in industry patterns of long-term debt proportion could indicate that, in contrast with the past, creditors are more or less willing to extend debt financing to your industry and to you. What happened to The Potted Planter's long-term debt ratio during the year?

This information may be obtained from the financial statements. Note that changes of capacity and financing are highlighted on the statement of cash flows. Ratio analysis can then be made using information on the other financial statements. Remember that often the statements do not provide many answers, but they can focus your attention on areas requiring further investigation through other sources, as in the situation of The Potted Planter's apparent shift to the suburban market.

Preparer Procedures

No new accounts were introduced in this chapter so there are no additions to the chart of accounts. This section will introduce preparation of the worksheet for the statement of cash flows.

The worksheet process is similar to the end-of-period worksheet learned in Chapter 5 to prepare the income statement and balance sheet. The cash flow worksheet reconciles the balance of each account for the successive balance sheets to the statement of cash flows. Note that the worksheet is prepared in chronological order working left to right (Exhibit 7.11) while a comparative balance sheet presents the most recent balance sheet on the left. (refer to Exhibit 7.1)

In setting up the worksheet first you must enter the balance sheet accounts according to their balance (DR/CR) and calculate the change in balance. Note that as with any worksheet, the totals must balance before you can continue.

Using the additional information given, you are now ready to justify the changes in account balances in the appropriate columns (DR/CR). Note that each change in balance appears in the statement of cash flows or the schedules which accompany it. Each entry will be coded with a letter as you identified adjusting entries on the worksheet in Chapter 5.

Exhibit 7.11 The Potted Planter Cash Flow Worksheet (Indirect Method)

Debits	12/31/X4	12/31/X5	Change	Debit		Credit	
Cash	70	88	18	(w)	18		
Marketable Securities	10	12	2	(m)	2		
Current Notes Receivable	5	0	(5)			(n)	5
Accounts Receivable	110	200	90	(e)	90		
Inventory	150	190	40	(f)	40		
Supplies	4	2	(2)			(g)	2
Prepaid Items	6	8	2	(h)	2		
Land	30	70	40	(o)	70	(d)	30
Buildings	150	280	130	(o)	280	(d)	150
Equipment	110	150	40	(v-1)	40		
Leasehold Improvements	15	58	43	(p)	48	(c)	5
Totals	660	1,058	398				
Credits							
Accumulated Depreciation, Bldg	120	20	(100)	(d)	120	(b)	20
Accumulated Depreciation, Equip	40	50	10			(b)	10
Current Notes Payable	25	40	15			(q)	15
Accounts Payable	100	135	35			(i)	35
Wages and Salaries Payable	3	2	(1)	(j)	1		
Interest Payable	10	25	15			(k)	15
Taxes Payable	70	88	18			(l)	18
Noncurrent Notes Payable	121	255	134			(v-2)	40
				(s)	121	(r)	215
Pat Ward, Capital	171	443	272	(u)	70	(a)	315
						(t)	27
Totals	660	1,058	398				
Cash Flow from Operating Activities:							
Net Income				(a)	315		
Depreciation				(b)	30		
Amortization				(c)	5		
Gain on Sale of Land and Building						(d)	300
Increase Accounts Receivable						(e)	90
Increase Inventory						(f)	40
Decrease Supplies				(g)	2		
Increase Prepaid Items						(h)	2
Increase Accounts Payable				(k)	35		
Decrease Wages and Salaries Payable						(j)	1
Increase Interest Payable				(k)	15		
Increase Taxes Payable				(l)	18		
Cash Flow for Investing Activities:							
Payment for purchase of Marketable Securities						(m)	2
Collection on Current Notes Receivable				(n)	5		
Proceeeds from Sale of Land and Building				(d)	360		
Payment for Purchases of Land and Building						(o)	350
Payment for Leasehold Improvement						(p)	48
Cash Flow from Financing Activities:							
Proceeds from New Current Notes Payable				(q)	15		
Proceeds on New Noncurrent Notes Payable				(r)	215		
Payment on Noncurrent Notes Payable						(s)	121
Additional Owner Investment				(t)	27		
Owner Withdrawals						(u)	70
Noncash Investing and Financing Activities							
Purchase of Equipment with New Debt						(v-1)	40
Issuance of New Noncurrent Note Payable for Equipment				(v-2)	40		
Net Increase in Cash						(w)	18
					1,984		1,984

When you have completed the process, the totals on the statement of cash flows will not balance until you enter the change in cash just as the statement columns on the worksheet in Chapter 5 did not balance until you entered "net income."

You can then verify your work by preparing journal entries for your adjustments. **Note that these journal entries are for checking purposes only and are not entered into the company's books** (remember they have already been entered into the books in the appropriate accounts as transactions or adjusting entries). The following presents several verifying entries for The Potted Planter. Note that the change in cash category substitutes for "cash", since all entries affect the determination of cash activity.

Net income results in an increase to owner's capital. It is also the starting number for determining cash from operating activities using the indirect approach.

	DR	CR
(a) *Operating Activities: Net Income*	*315,000*	
Pat Ward, Capital		*315,000*

Adjusting net income for noncash expenses requires adding back expenses which do not result in a cash outflow. Therefore "operating activities: Depreciation Expense" is debited to represent an increase in cash income over net income.

(b) *Operating Activities: Depreciation Expense*	*30,000*	
Accumulated Depreciation, Building		*20,000*
Accumulated Depreciation, Equipment		*10,000*

Disposal of assets require removal of any resulting gain or loss from income, removal of all asset and contra-asset accounts, and determining cash inflow from investing activities.

(d) *Investing Activities: Proceeds on Sale of Land & Bldg*	*360,000*	
Accumulated Depreciation, Bldg	*120,000*	
Land		*30,000*
Bldg		*150,000*
Operating Activities: Gain on Sale		*300,000*

An increase to Accounts Receivable represents credit sales not collected. Therefore, the increase in receivables results in a decrease or credit to cash revenue and ultimately income.

(e) *Accounts Receivable*	*90,000*	
Operating Activities: Increase in Accounts Receivable		*90,000*

The acquisition of marketable securities is an investing activity creating cash inflow. The decrease in cash outflow is credited to "Investing Activities: Purchase of Marketable Securities."

	DR	CR
(m) Marketable Securities	*2,000*	
Investing Activities: Purchase of Mkt Securities		*2,000*

The collection on the principal of notes receivable is an investing activity creating cash inflow. This cash inflow is reported as a debit to "Investing Activities: Collection of Notes Receivable" and a credit to current notes receivable reflecting removal of the account from the books.

(n) Investing Activities: Collection of Notes Receivable	*5,000*	
Current Note Receivable		*5,000*

Additional owner investment represents a credit to Owner's Capital and a debit to cash from "Financing Activities: Additional Owner Investment."

(t) Financing Activities: Additional Owner Investment	*27,000*	
Pat Ward, Capital		*27,000*

Owner withdrawals decrease cash and are represented by a credit to "Financing Activities: Owner Withdrawal."

(u) Pat Ward, Capital	*70,000*	
Financing Activities: Owner Withdrawal		*70,000*

Noncash investing and financing activities are the only entries which do no affect the cash balance. These transactions are included for analysis purposes since they do affect the firm's capacity and capital structure.

(v-1) Equipment	*40,000*	
Noncash Investing & Financing: Purchase of Equip		*40,000*
(v-2) Noncash Investing & Financing: Purchase of Equip	*40,000*	
Noncurrent Notes Payable		*40,000*

The last entry verifies the change in the cash balance and therefore is the only entry to the cash account.

(w) Cash	*18,000*	
Increase in Cash		*18,000*

Chapter Overview

From the material in this chapter you should be able to:

- Explain the concept of the statement of cash flows and how it creates a link between financial statements;

- Describe the differences between operating, investing, and financing activities involving cash;

- Describe how changes in some noncash current assets and current liabilities are used to determine cash from operating activities under the direct and indirect methods;

- Explain the differences between cash from operating activities using the direct and indirect methods giving the advantages of each;

- Prepare a statement of cash flows using both the direct and indirect methods for cash provided (used) by operating activities;

- Explain why noncash investing and financing activities need to be reported and give examples;

- Give examples of possible sources of cash, distinguishing between internal and external sources;

- Explain the functions of financial management and how they relate to cash flow; and

- Describe the usefulness of the statement of cash flows.

New Vocabulary and Concepts

Capital budgeting	Financing activities
Capital markets	Indirect method
Cash equivalents	Internal sources (cash)
Cash	Investing activities
Direct method	Operating activities
External sources (cash)	Operating management
Financial management	Pro forma statement

- Noncash investing and financing activities

- Possible internal and external sources of cash

- Possible needs for or uses of cash

- Statement of cash flows as a link between successive balance sheets

Review Questions

1. Why did the statement of cash flows replace the statement of changes in financial position?

2. What is the purpose of the statement of cash flows and what information does it provide?

3. What does "cash" generally include in the statement of cash flows?

4. What are the four classifications of activities on the statement of cash flows and give examples of each?

5. Why should a firm report noncash investing and financing activities?

6. Why is it necessary to convert the income statement to cash basis when preparing cash from operating activities?

7. What are the differences in approach between the direct and indirect method for determining cash from operating activities?

8. What are two possible "internal sources" of cash?

9. What are the two possible "external sources" of cash?

10. Why are gains and losses on the disposal of assets reported on the income statement excluded from cash from operating activities? Where are they reported?

11. What is the difference between operating and financial management?

12. Explain how the statement of cash flows articulates with the other financial statements.

Mini-Cases and Questions for Discussion

MC 7.1 Eslita Moreno has received job offers from two firms in the same business: the Sugar Company and the Tare Company. She is interested in staying for many years with the firm she chooses, and therefore wants a company whose owner is really interested in making the business a long-run success. She has heard rumors that the owner of one of the two firms is really "milking the business for all he can get now," but she isn't sure whether this is true or to which firm the rumor applies.

You have cash flow information for both firms for the past four years. Each year the pattern in each company essentially repeats. Below is information for each firm for a typical year. What could you tell Eslita about her concern?

	Sugar Company	Tare Company
Cash from operating activities:	$100,000	$200,000
Cash from investing activities:		
Sale of Long-lived Assets	10,000	
Purchase of Long-Lived Assets		(140,000)
Cash from financing activities:		
Proceeds new long-term debt	20,000	
Payment to retire long-term debt		(50,000)
Cash owner withdrawal	(130,000)	(10,000)
Increase in cash	0	$ 30,000

MC 7.2 Bob Tindel is attempting to evaluate the recent activities of the Lubbock Company. Its Statement of Cash Flows reports the following data in thousands of dollars:

Cash from operating activities:		$(75)
Cash from investing activities:		
Proceeds on sale of equipment		25
Cash from financing activities:		
Proceeds new long-term debt	$50	
Cash owner withdrawals	(20)	30
Decrease in cash		$(20)

What can Bob infer with respect to the most recent activities of the Lubbock Company? Is it profitable? Are the owners assisting during its difficulties? Is the firm replacing or expanding its capacity? Discuss the information content of the statement of cash flows.

MC 7.5 Caroline Morrison believes that any effort spent to separately disclose extraordinary items on the Statement of Cash Flows is misdirected. She reasons that:

a) The information refers to what has already happened, not what might happen in the future. It is, therefore, irrelevant to decision-making, which must be related to the future.

b) To report cash provided by operating activities as what it would have been without extraordinary items is contrary to historical fact.

Discuss Caroline's position.

MC 7.6 How can a cash flow statement prepared for the past year be useful for predicting cash flows in the current year? Don't decisions have to be based on future or anticipated cash flows? Discuss.

Essential Problems

EP 7.1 The Wellmat Company recorded the following transactions.during 19X5. Identify each event by category:

Operating Activity	inflow/outflow
Investing Activity	inflow/outflow
Financing Activity	inflow/outflow
Noncash Investing and Financing Activity	

a)	Net income	$70
b)	Depreciation Expense	5
c)	Payment on current note payable	11
d)	Payment for purchase of marketable securities	7
e)	Interest payment made	4
f)	Payment for purchase of land	42
g)	Cash owner withdrawal	5
h)	Sold investments for cash (Cost $10))	8
i)	Accounts payable decrease	6
j)	Received interest on noncurrent note receivable	2
k)	Accounts receivable increase	4

EP 7.2 Prepare a statement of cash flows using the indirect method for the Wellmat Company (see EP 7.1). Cash balances were:

Cash 1/1/X5	$34
Cash 12/31/X5	44

EP 7.3 The Molina Company Income Statement for the year-ended 12/31/X7 and changes in the current assets and liabilities for the year are given below. Prepare cash provided by operating activities using the direct method.

The Molina Company Income Statement
for the year-ended 12/31/X7

Sales		$150
Cost of Goods Sold		(90)
Gross Profit		$ 60
Operating expenses:		
Depreciation	$10	
Wages and Salaries	8	
Interest	2	(20)
Income before income tax		$ 40
Provision for income tax		(16)
Net Income		$ 24

	increase/(decrease)
Cash	$4
Accounts Receivable	5
Inventory	(10)
Accounts Payable	(6)
Wages Payable	3

EP 7.4 Using the data in EP 7.3 for the Molina Company, prepare a schedule of cash provided by operating activities using the indirect method.

EP 7.5   Prepare a Statement of Cash Flows in good form for the Wahoo Company for the year-ended 12/31/X1 from the data below. Use the direct method for cash provided by operating activities.

Wahoo Company Comparative Balance Sheets
as of December 31, 19X1 and 19X0

	12/31/X1	12/31/X0
Cash	$109	$ 40
Accounts Receivable	250	200
Inventory	40	20
Total Current Assets	$399	$260
Investments	92	90
Land	80	105
Buildings	200	200
Accum. Depr. Buildings	(140)	(120)
Equipment	160	150
Accum. Depr. Equipment	(70)	(50)
Leasehold Improvement	72	80
Total Assets	$793	$715
Accounts Payable	$100	$ 95
Wages and Salaries Payable	5	5
Taxes Payable	35	30
Total Current Liabilities	$140	$130
Noncurrent Note Payable	163	160
Total Liabilities	$303	$290
Owner's Capital	490	425
Total Equities	$793	$715

Wahoo Company Income Statement
for the year-ended 12/31/X1

Sales		$1,200
Operating Expenses:		
Wages and Salaries	$900	
Utilities and insurance	140	
Interest	7	
Depreciation on buildings	20	
Depreciation on equipment	25	
Leasehold amortization	15	
Loss on sale of equipment	5	1,112
Income before income tax		$ 88
Income Tax		20
Net Income		$ 68

Additional Information:
1. Equipment which cost $17 was sold for $7.
2. No additional owner investment was made during the year.

EP 7.6   Prepare a Statement of Cash Flows in good form for the Hogan Company for the year-ended 12/31/X1 from the data below. Use the direct method for cash provided by operating activities.

Hogan Company Comparative Balance Sheets
as of December 31, 19X1 and 19X0

	12/31/X1	12/31/X10
Cash	$ 135	$ 100
Accounts Receivable	220	200
Inventory	285	300
Total Current Assets	$ 640	$ 600
Investments	200	210
Equipment	420	350
Accum. depr. Equipment	(180)	(150)
Leasehold improvement	150	170
Total Assets	$1,230	$1,180
Accounts Payable	$ 210	$ 200
Wages and Salaries Payable	30	30
Interest Payable	35	25
Taxes Payable	15	20
Total Current Liabilities	$ 290	$ 275
Noncurrent Notes Payable	400	350
Total Liabilities	$ 690	$ 625
Owner's Capital	540	555
Total Equities	$1,230	$1,180

Hogan Company Income Statement
for the year-ended 12/31/X1

Sales		$2,500
Cost of Goods Sold		(1,500)
Gross Profit		$1,000
Operating Expenses:		
Wages and salaries	$780	
Depreciation on equipment	30	
Leasehold amortization	20	
Interest	50	
Other	40	(920)
Income before income tax		$ 80
Provision for income tax		(32)
Net Income		$ 48

Additional Information:
1. No assets were sold during the year.
2. The new equipment was purchased with a down payment of $20 and the remainder on a 5-year note.
3. Cash owner withdrawals amounted to $77 for the year.

EP 7.7   Prepare a Statement of Cash Flows in good form for the Waterstreet Company for the year-ended 12/31/X9 from the data below. Use the indirect method for cash provided by operating activities.

Waterstreet Company Comparative Balance Sheets
as of December 31, 19X9 and 19X8

	12/31/X9	12/31/X8
Cash	$ 68	$ 30
Current Note Receivable	20	10
Accounts Receivable	100	90
Inventory	210	200
Other Current Assets	30	20
Total Current Assets	$ 428	$ 350
Investments	143	140
Equipment	600	500
Accum. Depr. Equipment	(110)	(100)
Leasehold Improvements	34	60
Total Assets	$1,095	$ 950
Accounts Payable	$ 100	$ 80
Interest Payable	20	36
Taxes Payable	40	34
Total Current Liabilities	$ 160	$ 150
Noncurrent Note Payable	315	250
Total Liabilities	$ 475	$ 400
Owner's Capital	620	550
Total Equities	$1,095	$ 950

Waterstreet Company Income Statement
for the year-ended 12/31/X9

Sales		$800
Cost of Goods Sold		(500)
Gross Profit		$300
Operating Expenses:		
Wages and Salaries	$100	
Depreciation of equipment	25	
Leasehold Amortization	26	
Interest	29	
Other	44	(224)
Income from operations		$ 76
Investments Revenue		4
Income from operations before income tax		$80
Provision for income tax		(30)
Net Income		$ 50

Additional Information:
1. Sold equipment which cost $20,000 for $5,000. The book value was $5,000.
2. Equipment was purchased for cash.
3. An additional owner investment was made for $25.

EP 7.8 Prepare a Statement of Cash Flows in good form for the Yuba Company for the year-ended 12/31/X9. Use the indirect method for cash provided by operating activities.

Yuba Company Comparative Balance Sheets
as of December 31 19X9 and 19X8

	12/31/X9	12/31/X8
Cash	$ 35	$ 90
Current Note Receivable	50	60
Accounts Receivable	150	90
Supplies	30	25
Prepaid Items	10	5
Total Current Assets	$275	$270
Noncurrent Note Receivable	140	110
Equipment	579	420
Accum. Depr. Equipment	(340)	(300)
Leasehold Improvement	40	40
Total Assets	$694	$540
Current Note Payable	$ 84	$ 40
Accounts Payable	105	80
Wages Payable	15	10
Interest Payable	5	20
Total Current Liabilities	$209	$150
Noncurrent Notes Payable	100	100
Total Liabilities	$309	$250
Owner's Capital	385	290
Total Equities	$694	$540

Yuba Company Income Statement
for the year-ended 12/31/X9

Sales		$1,000
Operating Expenses:		
Wages and Salaries	$695	
Utilities and Rent	117	
Interest	16	
Depreciation on equipment	40	
Leasehold Amortization	10	(878)
Income from operations		$ 122
Interest Revenue		17
Income before income tax		$ 139
Provision for income tax		(55)
Net Income		$ 84

Additional Information:
1. The leasehold improvement was paid in cash.
2. Owner investment was $15.

Supplemental Problems

SP 7.9 Refer back to Luigi's Auto Parts Period 2 (Supplemental problem 4.17) and prepare a statement of cash flows in good form using the indirect method for cash provided by operating activities.

SP 7.10 Refer back to Irene's Sport Shop Period 2 (Supplemental problem 4.18) and prepare a statement of cash flows in good form using the indirect method for cash provided by operating activities.

SP 7.11 Refer back to Luigi's Auto Parts Period 4 (Supplemental problem 6.19) and prepare a statement of cash flows in good form using the indirect method for cash provided by operating activities.

SP 7.12 Refer back to Irene's Sport Shop Period 4 (Supplemental problem 6.20) and prepare a statement of cash flows in good form using the indirect method for cash provided by operating activities.

SP 7.13 Refer back to the Albert Company for the year-ended 12/31/X5 (Supplemental problem 6.17) and prepare a statement of cash flows in good form using the direct method for cash provided by operating activities.

SP 7.14 Refer back to the Brandywine Company for the year-ended 12/31/X2 (Supplemental problem 6.18) and prepare a statement of cash flows in good form using the direct method for cash provided by operating activities.

Preparer Problems

PP 7.1 Prepare a statement of cash flow worksheet for EP 7.5 using the indirect method.

PP 7.2 Prepare a statement of cash flow worksheet for EP 7.6 using the indirect method.

PP 7.3 Prepare worksheet journal entries for PP 7.1.

PP 7.4 Prepare worksheet journal entries for PP 7.2.

8

Variations in
Measuring and
Reporting
Inventories

CHAPTER PREVIEW

The objective of this chapter is to demonstrate the significance of inventory measurement and the effect of cost of goods sold on the Income Statement. In this chapter you can learn:

1. That in an inflationary price situation, different definitions of income may be needed;
2. That identification of the cost of ending inventory often necessitates certain assumptions and estimates;
3. What factors are initially included in the cost of inventory;
4. The different systems used to measure and report inventory and cost of goods sold;
5. The three different inventory flow assumptions possible under GAAP, their different income effects, and the significance of consistency in inventory measurement;
6. That, following the principle of conservatism, GAAP require ending inventory amounts that exceed realizable value be written down to at least their net realizable value.

With this knowledge, you should be able to interpret inventory and cost of goods sold appearing in the financial statements. You will understand the need to know the inventory method used before making comparisons between firms and have insight into the difficulties resulting from inflationary prices. Finally, the limitations of the financial reporting system first mentioned in Chapter 1 will become more apparent to you.

Significance of Inventory and Cost of Goods Sold

You may wonder why an entire chapter of this book is devoted to the single asset inventory and its associated expense, cost of goods sold. For a firm primarily in the business of manufacturing, distributing, or sales, inventory can be an extremely significant item. For example, as of 12/31/86, inventory on hand reported by General Motors amounted to approximately 7.2 billion dollars, which was 10 percent of total assets.[1] Of even more significance, GM's 1986 cost of goods sold was in excess of 88 billion dollars. It represented 86 percent of net sales and 88 percent of all the firm's cost and expenses that year. Accounting for inventory can be significant, and, as you will find out, can present some real problems.

Is My Profit Really Profit?

You may find it somewhat difficult to visualize 88 billion dollars. Try this example. Assume you own a firm which each year buys and sells one gizmo. At the beginning of the year you invested $5,000 cash in your firm. During the year you purchased one gizmo costing $5,000, paying cash. Before year-end, you sold it for $7,000 cash.

What was your net income or profit for the year? Would your answer be any different if the next gizmo, ordered from your supplier, was going to cost $6,000 because of inflation? Accountants following GAAP will report the current year's income as $2,000. Can you withdraw your profits from the business and still be as well-off as you were at the beginning? Or, for that matter, if you withdraw of your so called income, can you even continue in business?

The answer to these questions depends on how you precisely define income. The GAAP definition of income is simply the number of dollars, regardless of their purchasing power or the replacement cost of assets used. In a sense, GAAP "reasons" that your firm actually made or earned $2,000. It was $2,000 better off. The fact that inflation may have occurred is an outside or exogenous event not resulting from the firm's activities, and therefore not reported as such. If you were starting your firm next year, you would need a start up investment of $6,000, not $5,000.

The issues demonstrated by this simple example, and the question of what GAAP should consider and report as income, have been an active concern of accountants, academicians, and business people for decades. A further discussion, together with a description of proposed alternatives, is contained later in this text. At this point, it is only important that you understand the nature of the problem and its source, and that GAAP do not currently provide any adjustment of assets currently held for inflation in the conventional or primary financial statements.

---

[1] See 1986 Annual Report for General Motors Corporation and Consolidated Subsidiaries. Inventory was reported under the LIFO method.

What is My Profit this Year?

A related problem, also resulting from inflation, involves the timing and proper identification of reported profits. Assume you retire from the gizmo business and decide to purchase and sell widgets. This time you started your firm with an investment of $10,000 cash. Early in the year, you purchased one widget costing $1,000. Towards the end of the year you purchased a second which, because of inflation, cost $2,000. By the end of the year you had sold one of the widgets for $2,500. Which widget did you sell? What was the amount of your ending inventory, and what was this year's income?

Exhibit 8.1

Income Flow Assumptions

	First Widget Sold First (FIFO)	Second Widget Sold First (LIFO)
YEAR 1		
Sales	$ 2,500	$ 2,500
COGS	1,000	2,000
Gross Profit	$ 1,500	$ 500
Cash	$ 9,500	$ 9,500
Ending Inventory	2,000	1,000
	$ 11,500	$ 10,500
Your Capital*	$ 11,500	$ 10,500
YEAR 2		
Sales	$ 2,500	$ 2,500
COGS	2,000	1,000
Gross Profit	$ 500	$ 1,500
Cash	$ 12,000	$ 12,000
Inventory	0	0
	$ 12,000	$ 12,000
Your Capital*	$ 12,000	$ 12,000

* Note: There are no liabilities.

Study Exhibit 8.1 carefully. Can you see that each assumption could be correct, depending upon which widget had been the one sold? If the first widget was sold, your income statement would show a profit of $1,500. If the second was sold, your profit would be only $500.

To complete your understanding of the "timing" problem, assume that the event during the second year was the sale of the other widget, for $2,500.

Looking at the entire two year period, your total reported profit was clearly $2,000. But users require financial information more frequently, at least yearly, and often quarterly. How much of the $2,000 was earned the first year? The second year?

Timing of reported income depends upon which widget was assumed to have been sold the first year. You may find this grossly simplified example too trivial; and you may think that, with only two widgets, you could certainly tell which one went out to the customer first. You are right; with only two widgets, you would hardly have to make an assumption. But assume you didn't know which widget was sold first. Think of widgets as being individual nails or washers in a hardware store bin, or a tanker truckload of gasoline mixed with orders in a large storage tank. There are a great many cases where it is impossible, or far too costly, for a firm to specifically identify different items or batches in inventory.

Illustration 8.1

Relationship of Beginning Inventory, Net Purchases, Ending Inventory, and Cost of Goods Sold

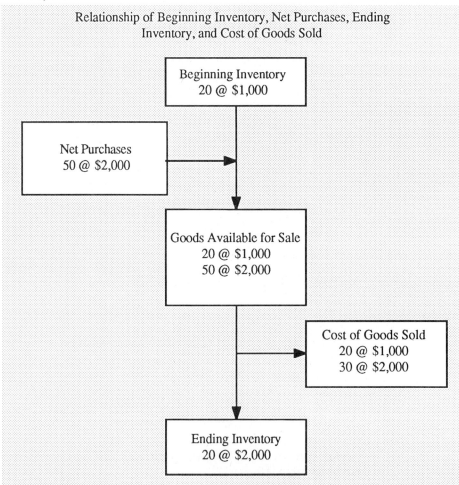

If you cannot tell which widget was sold, how do you determine the dollar amount of the first year's ending inventory and cost of goods sold? How do you measure the first year's profit? If the widgets were mingled in goods available for sale as shown in Illustration 8.1, you, or your accountant, would have to make a **cost flow** (or cost assignment) **assumption**. Regardless of the actual physical flow of the widgets sold, first you would have to assign a cost to the widgets remaining. This assignment would, in turn, result in an "assignment" of the cost of the widgets sold.

Remember that the total of beginning inventory plus net purchases is goods available for sale. Goods available is not affected in the current year by whatever cost flow assumption is used. If you were to assume a beginning inventory of 20 widgets costing $1,000 apiece and purchases during the year of 50 additional widgets costing $2,000 apiece, goods available would always equal $120,000, as shown in Exhibit 8.2. The inventory cost flow assumption that is made will affect, in the current period, only the division of goods available between ending inventory and cost of goods sold. In this example, if 50 widgets were sold, and if it were assumed the 50 represented the 20 from beginning inventory and 30 from those purchased, then the $120,000 would be split with $40,000 assigned to ending inventory and the remaining $80,000 to cost of goods sold.[2] Later in this chapter, you can learn about the various GAAP approved assumptions from which accountants may choose in measuring inventory. Before proceeding, make sure you see the potential significance of inventory cost flow assumption for reported income.

Exhibit 8.2

Schedule of cost of goods sold*

Beginning inventory	$ 20,000
Net purchases	100,000
Goods available for sale	$ 120,000
Less ending inventory	(40,000)
Cost of goods sold	$ 80,000

* Illustration of FIFO Inventory Valuation Method

---

[2] The 20 remaining widgets would be assumed to be the most recently purchased at a cost of $2,000 each.

Income for the Past or for the Future?

There is another reason for making a cost flow assumption even when inventory can be economically identified. Remember the unresolved issue of how much profit to report for gizmos under inflation? Think of the widget case, and assume you knew that the first widget had actually been the one shipped. Would an income statement reporting a $1,500 profit provide the best information to investors? Would this profit be repeatable in the future? Could the reporting of $1,500 profit be misleading to investors in much the same way that the inclusion of extraordinary gains as part of operating income could be misleading? Remember that the primary measurement objective for cost of goods sold is to match the costs of merchandise or products with the revenues that these goods or products generate in the same income reporting period.

Of the $1,500 of profit in the widget example (whether or not reported as earned in the first or second year), $1,000 represented a nonrepeatable **holding gain**. If the purpose of the income statement is to report on what management has done, how well they have acted as stewards or trustees with the investors' funds, then $1,500 reported profit would be appropriate. If, on the other hand, the income statement is to serve effectively as a basis for future decisions by investors, then the $500 profit might be more appropriate.

GAAP allow for either flow assumption as long as it is applied consistently. Many firms have elected the LIFO assumption (discussed below) which would result in the cost of the most recently acquired widget being applied to the one sold, and in a reported profit of only $500. These firms elect to make this assumption even when they know the actual physical movement of merchandise may have been just the opposite. Their reason for the election is that the income statement will provide more current (repeatable) cost information for investors.[3]

Another suggested alternative for meeting past and future income reporting objectives simultaneously involves reporting holding gains when they occur but segregating them in a similar manner to extraordinary items. This text will not explore these more advanced concepts. You should be aware of them, and you might wish to discuss them in class. At this point, you only need understand the details of the accountant's current treatment of inventories under GAAP.

Components of Net Purchases

Regardless of possible cost flow assumptions involved in determining ending inventory and cost of goods sold, inventory is first measured and recorded at its **full acquisition cost**. Full acquisition costs are all those costs related to making the merchandise available for sale at the intended selling location. These costs could include costs of acquisition,

---

[3] As discussed later in this chapter, another reason for electing the LIFO flow assumption involves tax savings or tax postponement. LIFO may be used for tax purposes only if it is used for financial reporting.

transportation to the point of sale, manufacture, packaging and storage. Full acquisition costs of all inventory acquired during a particular period or year are collectively known as **net purchases.**

It is important to understand what is included in the net purchases figure. Net purchases are determined by adding gross purchases and transportation-in or freight-in and then subtracting purchase returns and allowances and purchase discounts. As mentioned above, other costs such as costs of manufacturing, of packaging, and of storage may also be included.[4]

Gross purchases are the total of the invoice costs of all merchandise acquired during the year. **Purchase returns** represent the cost of those items acquired and subsequently returned to the supplier for whatever reason. **Transportation-in or freight-in** covers the cost of moving the merchandise from the supplier to the location where it is to be sold. Some items may be delivered by the supplier at no additional charge. For others, the purchaser may have to pay delivery costs which are then added to inventory costs. By including any freight-in costs, the accountant ensures that inventory is uniformly valued at the full cost of having it available for sale. Note that transportation out, or freight-out, involves part of shipping/selling expense and is not related to inventory measurement.

Exhibit 8.3

Net Purchases

Gross Purchases (55 units @ $1900)		$104,500
less:		
Purchase Returns & Allowances	$ 9,500	
(5 units @ $1,900)		
Purchase Discounts (*2/10, n30*)	1,900	(11,400)
		$ 93,100
Freight-in		6,900
Net Purchase (50 units @ $2,000)		$100,000

Purchase Discounts

Purchase discounts require further understanding of common business practices. When a supplier sells merchandise to your firm on account, it is making a short-term investment of assets in your firm. Since the supplier's primary business is not that of making loans, it wants to motivate you to pay as soon as possible. Many orders are, therefore, shipped with payment terms such as 2/10, n30. This code merely means you can take a two percent discount from the invoice price if you pay within ten days of the invoice date. The

---

[4] Inventory for manufacturing firms are covered in Managerial Accounting Information, 2nd Edition by A. Thompson Montgomery and Robert Fess, to be published by Kendall/Hunt Publishing Company, 1989.

full or net billed price must be paid between eleven and 30 days of the invoice date. After 30 days, the supplier may charge you interest on the unpaid bill.

Net purchases are illustrated in Exhibit 8.3. The gross purchases were 55 units purchased at $1,900 each. Of the 55 units, 5 were found to be defective and were returned to the supplier for a credit. Because the firm paid the bill by the tenth day, it took a 2 percent discount. The discount can be calculated as 2 percent of the remaining bill ($104,500 less 9,500). Therefore, purchase discounts taken offset gross purchases so as not to overstate inventory costs.[5]

Perpetual and Periodic Inventory Systems

Every firm must maintain records of total dollar amounts of its net purchase transactions to ensure appropriate and timely payment of its obligations to suppliers. The total of the inventory at the beginning of the year and net purchases is known as goods available for sale:

Beginning inventory + net purchases = Goods available for sale

Some firms, and especially those using computer systems, can afford to maintain detailed separate records for each distinct inventory item. Firms keeping these detailed records for each item and recording purchases and sales or shipments to this record continually throughout the year, are said to be on the **perpetual inventory system**. Many firms cannot afford the recordkeeping involved in a perpetual system. They keep records which together provide total costs of goods available for sale. Sales to customers at selling price are, of course, continually recorded to update the accounts for cash or accounts receivable and sales. The delivery of products to customers, that is, shipments, at cost is not continually recorded. At the end of the year, such firms take a physical inventory. The physical inventory involves counting all items still on hand. The physical inventory count is "costed," that is, costs are assigned. Cost of goods sold, items shipped or missing (theft and spoilage) is then calculated by taking the total of goods available and then subtracting the ending inventory at cost.

Firms which complete the updating of their inventory records only periodically or once a year (period) are said to follow the **periodic inventory system**.

---

[5] The method described in this text is the "Gross Method." Also acceptable under GAAP is the "net method." Under the net method gross purchases are recorded net of the available discount. If the discount is not taken, another account "discounts lost" is created and immediately expensed to the income statement.

Specific Identification

In "costing" ending physical inventory under the periodic system, or in "costing" day to day shipments recorded under the perpetual system, a firm must be able to assign costs to items. Some firms can afford to specifically identify each unit (or batch of similar units) in inventory with that unit's cost. For example, Boeing 747 planes are large enough, and sufficiently customized, that individual cost records for each plane are both economical and necessary. Hairpins, thumbtacks, and so forth are clearly not amenable to **specific cost identification.**

Cost Flow Assumptions

Where it is not feasible to specifically identify inventory items, or where the firm does not wish to measure inventory via the specific identification method, then a cost flow (cost assignment) assumption must be made. There are three different assumptions, any one of which may be elected under GAAP: FIFO, average cost, and LIFO. The following example will be used to demonstrate these methods:

John King owns a wine wholesale business. He sells domestic and imported wines by the case. The records show for one particular wine during the year as follows:

Beginning inventory	None
January purchase	500 cases costing $10 each
May purchase	750 cases costing $12 each
September purchase	250 cases costing $15 each
Goods available for sale	1,500 cases
Ending inventory	200 cases
Sales/Shipments	
March	480 cases selling for $18.50
July	765 cases selling for $19.25
November	55 cases selling for $25.34
	1,300 cases

FIFO Cost Flow Assumption

What was the proper measurement of ending inventory in dollars for this particular wine? Regardless of the actual physical movement of wine in the warehouse the accountant can assume that each lot is placed onto a conveyor belt as it arrives and that cases of wine are shipped from the opposite end of the conveyor. Most items in most firms actually physically move through inventory in this manner, in order to avoid spoilage or obsolescence.

Even though they may not move on a conveyor, the first items received are generally the first items shipped. This "conveyor belt" assumption is known as **first-in-first-out** or **FIFO.**

In John King's situation, he had three lots of wine purchased at different costs. His FIFO conveyor belt would contain:

Illustration 8.2

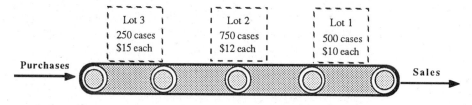

FIFO FLOW ASSUMPTION

How many cases were shipped (or disappeared) during the year? Note that under a periodic inventory system cost of goods sold must include all items delivered to customers, stolen, deteriorated, or otherwise disappeared. 1500 cases were available for sale. Two hundred remained on hand; therefore cost of goods sold would be 1,300 cases. Note that the actual quantity of items leaving inventory is a physical reality and is the same, regardless of the cost flow assumption.

Under the FIFO flow assumption, what would John King report as cost of goods sold and as ending inventory for this particular wine? Calculate your answer before proceeding.

Exhibit 8.4

FIFO Inventory Method

	Units	x	Unit Cost	=	Value
Beginning Inventory	0				0
January Purchase	500		$10		$ 5,000
May Purchase	750		12		9,000
September Purchase	250		15		3,750
Goods Available for Sale	1,500				$ 17,750
less Ending Inventory	(200)		15		(3,000)
Cost of Goods Sold	1,300				$ 14,750

In Exhibit 8.4, goods available for sale, again independent of any flow assumption, amounted to $17,750. If 1,300 cases were shipped under a FIFO flow assumption, you can see that the cost of goods sold would include the oldest units:

(January Purchases)	500 cases at $10	$ 5,000
(May Purchases)	750 cases at $12	9,000
(September Purchases)	50 cases at $15	750
Total		$ 14,750

Using the FIFO flow assumption, ending inventory of $3,000 (200 cases at $15) shown on the balance sheet would be reported in terms of the most recent costs. These could be a close approximation of current market costs, depending upon how recently purchased, and would make the balance sheet measurement more relevant. On the other hand, the income statement would reflect the oldest, and perhaps nonrepeatable costs. Operating income could be very misleading as a basis for forecasting. Gross profit would include inflation profit or inventory holding gains along with repeatable current trading profits. To see this clearly, assume John King had received $25,000 for the 1,300 cases sold this year. His gross profit under the FIFO flow assumption would have been $10,250. How much of this $10,250 trading profit was of repeatable profit in terms of current wine costs? In terms of current costs, John's cost of goods sold would have been $19,500 ($15 times 1,300 cases) and his trading profit only $5,500. Therefore, of his $10,250 gross profit, $4,750 represents a holding gain which he could not expect to recur unless he could raise selling prices faster than costs increase.

Sales		$ 25,000
Current cost of items sold		19,500
Trading Profit		$ 5,500
Holding gain:		
Current cost of items sold	$ 19,500	
Actual cost of items sold	(14,750)	4,750
Reported Gross Profit		$ 10,250

To review, in periods of increasing prices, FIFO tends to result in ending inventory on the balance sheet reported in near current costs. Cost of goods sold on the income statement is reported in terms of older nonrecurring costs. Therefore, gross profit and net income will include nonrepeatable holding gains. GAAP currently do not distinguish between trading profit and holding gains on the income statement.

Average Cost Flow Assumptions

A second inventory flow assumption that can be made is average cost. For this assumption, you can visualize all items placed in a big mixer and blended together. Each item shipped to customers would be a representative blend of all costs going into the mix.

Weighted Average Cost

Weighted average cost is a periodic cost method. The average cost per unit is based on beginning inventory and all purchases during the period.

Exhibit 8.5

Weighted Average Cost Method

	Units	x	Unit Cost	=	Value
Beginning Inventory	0				0
January Purchase	500		$10.00		$ 5,000
May Purchase	750		12.00		9,000
September Purchase	250		15.00		3,750
Goods Available for Sale	1,500		11.83*		$ 17,750
less Ending Inventory	(200)		11.83*		(2,366)
Cost of Goods Sold	1,300				$ 15,384

* Wt Avg Cost per unit $17,750 ÷ 1500 = $11.83 (Rounded)

Cost of goods sold would be $15,384 and ending inventory $2,366. Note that a simple average price per case[6] would not be appropriate. 1,500 total cases at $12.33 each would equal $18,495 even though there were only $17,750 of total costs to begin with. The average cost must be weighted to reflect the different cost proportions in the mix.

The weighted average cost assumption results in balance sheet inventory values which are neither the latest nor the oldest costs. A balance sheet figure for inventory is less meaningful since inventory costs are less current than under FIFO. Inventory costs on the income statement would represent the same "blend," and profit may include some holding gain. This "blend" of costs would be appropriate for homogeneous items with reasonably stable prices. Otherwise, all the pitfalls inherent in any average could exist.

Moving Average Cost

Moving average cost is a perpetual inventory method. It differs from weighted average in that a new average cost per unit is calculated at the time of each purchase. Cost of sales are deducted from the goods available at the time of the sales. In the John King example, average cost would be calculated three times.

---

[6] $10 + $12 + $15 = $37 $37 ÷ 3 = $12.33 (rounded)

Exhibit 8.6   Moving Average Cost Inventory Method

	Units	x	Unit Cost	=	Value
Beginning Inventory	0				0
January Purchase	500		$ 10.00		$ 5,000
Goods Available	500		10.00		$ 5,000 ÷ 500 = $10.00
March Shipment	(480)				
Inventory Remaining	20		10.00		$ 200
May Purchase	750		12.00		9,000
Goods Available	770				$ 9,200 ÷ 770 = $11.95*
July Shipments	(765)				
Inventory Remaining	5		11.95		$ 60
September Purchase	250		15.00		3,750
Goods Available	255				$ 3,810 ÷ 255 = $14.94*
November Shipment	(55)				
Ending Inventory	200		14.94		$ 2,988
Goods Available for Sale	1,500				$ 17,750
Ending Inventory	(200)		14.94		(2,988)
Cost of Goods Sold	1,300				$ 14,762

* Average Unit Cost rounded to nearest cent

Cost of goods sold must be calculated by subtracting ending inventory from goods available for sale. If you were to calculate cost of goods sold by multiplying unit cost times the number of units, it may be incorrect due to rounding differences. For example:

March	480	$ 10.00	$ 4,800
July	765	11.95	9,142
November	55	14.94	822
	1300		$ 14,764 14,762

Note that cost of goods sold is overstated by two dollars compared to Exhibit 8.6. Since cost of goods sold is generally a significantly larger amount than ending inventory, it is appropriate for the rounding difference to be absorbed by cost of goods sold. The more precision on the unit price, the smaller the rounding difference.

LIFO Flow Assumption

The third cost flow assumption for financial accounting purposes is known as **last-in-first-out** or **LIFO**. For this assumption you can visualize a big barrel. Items purchased are placed in the barrel in layers as they arrive. Items shipped are taken out of the top of the barrel. Physically very few items are actually moved on a LIFO basis. Actual physical LIFO flow is safe only where there is no risk of spoilage or obsolescence for items at the bottom of the barrel or pile. Items physically handled on a LIFO basis would be limited to natural resources such as crude oil, coal, or sand and gravel for construction, salt, and so forth.

Balance sheet inventory data could be much less current and therefore less meaningful and relevant under LIFO. Under the LIFO alternative, a firm's balance sheet could show inventory at costs as old and out of date as when the firm started in business, or at least as far back as when the item was last out of stock.

The income statement, on the other hand, would disclose the most recent costs. Very little holding gain would be mixed with trading profit, unless, of course, merchandise was not regularly replaced and the "barrel" was emptied of "old items" in a given year. LIFO is frequently used since it results in reported income that provides a better forecasting base. LIFO is limited to those firms which sell durable goods. Therefore, those firms selling perishable goods cannot use this method.

Periodic LIFO

Whether a firm follows periodic or perpetual procedures has no effect upon measurement of ending inventory or cost of goods sold under the FIFO flow assumption. However, firms electing LIFO, the use of the periodic or perpetual procedure can make a significant difference. Under **periodic LIFO**, information is not available regarding time when individual shipments (sales) occurred during the year. Therefore it may be assumed that all units sold had been shipped on the last day of the year. That would be after all purchases during the year had been received and their layers added to the "barrel" as shown below.

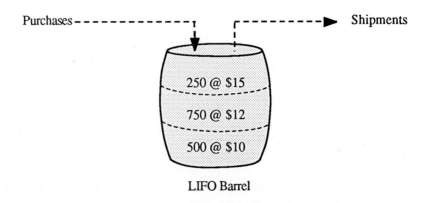

LIFO Barrel

In the John King example, under periodic LIFO ending inventory of 200 cases would be assumed to be those at the very bottom of the barrel, or the oldest units and would be reported at $2,000. Remember that LIFO valuation does not necessarily match the actual physical flow of inventory. LIFO valuation merely assumes that ending inventory contains the earliest cost.

Exhibit 8.7

Periodic LIFO Inventory Method

	Units	x	Unit Cost	=	Value
Beginning Inventory	0				0
January Purchase	500		$10		$ 5,000
May Purchase	750		12		9,000
September Purchase	250		15		3,750
Goods Available for Sale	1,500				$ 17,750
less Ending Inventory	(200)		$10		(2,000)
Cost of Goods Sold	1,300				$ 15,750

Cost of Goods sold:

March	480	250 @ $15	
		230 @ $12	$ 6510
July	765	520 @ $12	
		245 @ $10	8690
November	55	55 @ $10	550
	1300		$ 15,750

Perpetual LIFO

Perpetual LIFO on the other hand, could result in different amounts of ending inventory and cost of goods sold than under periodic LIFO. Suppose John King's firm followed perpetual LIFO. Under the perpetual system, information would be available on the date purchases arrived and shipments were made. Exhibit 8.8 shows the perpetual LIFO Method. Note that under perpetual LIFO, you know that only five cases of $10 cost wine remained, together with the other layers. Under periodic LIFO, you could only assume that all layers (purchases) were on hand before any shipments were made and therefore the 200 cases of $10 wine at the bottom of the "inventory barrel" were assumed to have been untouched. Ending inventory would be assumed and reported as $2,975 under perpetual LIFO, but only $2,000 under periodic LIFO. In this example, goods available either to be sold or retained in inventory amounted to $17,750 under all systems. Therefore, cost of goods sold would be $14,775 under perpetual LIFO and $15,750 under periodic LIFO. This difference could become significant if you consider a firm with hundreds or thousands of different items.

Exhibit 8.8

Perpetual LIFO Inventory Inventory Method

	Units	x	Unit Cost	=	Value
Beginning Inventory	0				0
January Purchase	500		$ 10.00		$ 5,000
Goods Available	500		10.00		$ 5,000
March Shipment	(480)				
Inventory Remaining	20		10.00		$ 200
May Purchase	750		12.00		9,000
Goods Available	770				$ 11,000
July Shipments	(765)				
Inventory Remaining	5		10.00		$ 50
September Purchase	250		15.00		3,750
Goods Available	255				$ 3,800
November Shipment	(55)				
Ending Inventory			5 @ $10		
	200		195 @ $15		$ 2,975
Goods Available for Sale	1,500				$ 17,750
Ending Inventory			5 @ $10		
	(200)		195 @ $15		(2,975)
Cost of Goods Sold	1,300				$ 14,775
Cost of Goods sold:					
March	480		480 @ $10		$ 4,800
July	765		15 @ $10		
			750 @ $12		9,150
November	55		55 @ $15		825
	1,300				$ 14,775

LIFO Pools and Dollar-Value LIFO

Even following LIFO, most firms with many products find the cost of maintaining a separate record for each individual product prohibitive. Two other modifications of LIFO can reduce these recordkeeping and computational costs. One modification involves the use of LIFO pools and the other involves dollar-value LIFO.

As their name implies, **LIFO pools** involve grouping substantially identical items as if they were a single unit and applying the LIFO approach to the common pool. dollar-value LIFO extends the inventory pooling approach to a similar (not necessarily nearly identical) items in inventory or even to the firm's entire inventory.[7] **Dollar-value LIFO** also differs from LIFO pools, in that layers are priced or costed using composite price indexes instead of individual unit or weighted average unit costs.

The methods of determining applicable price/cost indexes, and variations in applications of these indexes, will be discussed later in the chapter.

Review of Inventory Flow Assumptions

Before considering the factors influencing the choice among flow assumptions and the effect of such choices upon income, you might wish to review the various inventory flow assumptions already discussed. Exhibit 8.9 provides data for John King's inventory for the year. You can use this data to reinforce your knowledge of the methods of measuring ending inventory and cost of goods sold, following the various flow assumptions. Note in Exhibit 8.9 that, in a single year alternative flow assumptions can result in reported amounts for cost of goods sold ranging from $15,750 to $14,750.

Exhibit 8.9   Data for Review of Inventory Flow Assumption Alternatives

	PERIODIC			PERPETUAL		
	FIFO	WT AV	LIFO	FIFO	MOV AV	LIFO
Sales	$25,000	$25,000	$25,000	$25,000	$25,000	$25,000
Cost of Goods Sold	14,750	15,384	15,750	14,750	14,762	14,775
Gross Profit	$10,250	$9,616	$9,250	$10,250	$10,238	$10,225
Ending Inventory	$3,000	$2,366	$2,000	$3,000	$2,988	$2,975

---

[7] Limitations to the extent of the pool may be imposed by the IRS for tax purposes. these limitations generally control the financial accounting practices. If LIFO is elected for tax purposes, the IRS requires that there be conformity between financial accounting and tax accounting for inventory.

Choice Among Alternative Assumptions

Many factors beyond the scope of this text enter into a firm's initial choice of an inventory flow assumption. It is nevertheless worth noting that the LIFO choice often dominates due to tax considerations. If a firm wishes to elect LIFO for tax purposes (in order to minimize its taxable income during periods of inflationary prices) the IRS will only allow such an election if the firm also uses LIFO in its financial statements.[8] As mentioned earlier, LIFO often provides a more current cost picture in the income statement in periods of inflationary prices. Nonrepeatable holding gains are minimized and therefore do not "distort" potentially repeatable income. However, under the LIFO method ending inventory may be stated in out of date and unrealistic costs, and can seriously compromise the value and credibility of the balance sheet.

The LIFO choice can also prove potentially disastrous if the firm is ever forced to dip into its base stock (normally constant level of inventory). Under such circumstances, carefully postponed holding gains of perhaps significant magnitude will be included in both financial statements and income tax returns. Reported profits for the current period could be overstated, and misleading, especially in comparison to prior years when only trading profits appeared. The sudden "catch up" of postponed taxes on holding gains could generate a cash shortage at the very time when the firm needed to replace its base stock at higher current prices.

FIFO, on the other hand, has the advantage of maximizing reported income during periods of inflationary prices, since all realized holding gains are included in reported gross profit. It also results in balance sheet valuation of inventory in terms of current costs. Its disadvantage is the potentially misleading inclusion of possible nonrepetitive holding gains in reported net income, coupled with the necessity for the payment of taxes on such gains.

Average cost, being between FIFO and LIFO, shares the advantages and disadvantages of each. Since it does not require layering, it is simpler and less costly than either FIFO or LIFO.

There is no ideal method for all businesses, therefore the choice must be made considering the circumstances of the particular firm. However, a firm may not choose one method one year and a different method the next.

Although GAAP allow a firm to choose among the four alternative flow assumptions: FIFO, average cost, LIFO, or specific identification, they also provide that, once a given alternative is elected, it must be adhered to consistently from year to year.[9] Consistency among GAAP alternatives is a fundamental principle of financial accounting. Its importance is indicated by the fact that the annual auditor's opinion is required either to attest to consistency or to note the exception.

---

[8] IRS allows firms to include in its financial statements supplementary information explaining what the reported balance sheet amount for inventory would have been under other flow assumptions.

[9] GAAP allow a firm to change in infrequent special circumstances. However, the CPA opinion will advise you of the change in the year it occurs. The income effect of the change will also be disclosed, and any prior years' data published in the current statement will be restated under the new alternative.

Effect on Reported Income

You should now realize why the accountant's choice of an inventory flow assumption and a record keeping system has important implications for the user of financial statements. When prices are changing, two identical firms can have very different income statements and balance sheets, even with identical movements of inventory. In periods of inflationary prices, a FIFO firm is realizing and reporting inventory holding gain as part of gross profit. A LIFO firm may postpone indefinitely the reporting of this holding gain. In the identical firm situation, the FIFO firm during inflationary prices would be reporting higher profits than the LIFO firm when the only difference would be the accountant's inventory flow assumption.

A specific example might help you remember the income effect of electing different inventory flow assumptions. Assume that you are in a period of significant inflationary prices, and that during the year your firm has sold 500,000 widgets. Also assume that your goods available for sale consisted of 100,000 units costing $1 each in beginning inventory, 400,000 units costing $2 apiece purchased in April, and 500,000 units costing $3 apiece in November. Following the periodic inventory system, what would be your cost of goods sold under each alternative: FIFO, average cost, and LIFO?

Flow assumption	Cost of goods sold
FIFO	$ 900,000
Avg.Cost	1,200,000
LIFO	1,500,000

In this example, as compared with FIFO, the LIFO flow assumption would result in an additional $600,000 being included in cost of goods sold, with a corresponding reduction in reported net income of $600,000.

The financial statement reader must be careful not to make direct comparisons between or among companies unless he or she is certain the firms are all electing the same inventory cost flow assumption. Similar major intercompany variations can also result from different depreciation and amortization methods. These will be discussed in Chapter 9. The financial statement user can ascertain which valuation alternatives are being followed by a particular firm by consulting the statement footnotes. GAAP require that a firm disclose accounting method used in the preparation of its financial statements.

Lower of Cost or Market (LCM)

Regardless of the cost flow assumption used, there exists one overriding principle of ending inventory measurement. Under the principle of conservatism, GAAP require that ending inventory not be stated above its net realizable value. The cost of the ending inventory is first determined and recorded, following one of the previously described inventory methods. Then, before the balance sheet is released, the calculated inventory value is tested to ensure that it meets the LCM requirement.[10]

LCM means the **lower of cost or market**. However, "market" does not mean market value in the conventional sense. LCM refers to the lower of original cost or "recoverable cost." The objective of this GAAP standard is that inventory should not be reported at any amount greater than could be recovered or realized in the future. There is a formula for determining the "M" of LCM or "recoverable costs": "M (market)" or recoverable cost is one of three amounts:

a) **Net realizable value** (NRV): expected selling price less cost of completing the sale or finishing the item (if partially finished), packaging, and shipping;

b) **Replacement cost** (RC): current cost of obtaining a similar item;

c) Net realizable value less the firm's normal gross profit margin (NRV $- \pi$).

Recoverable cost is defined as:

RC when NRV $\geq$ RC $\geq$ (NRV $- \pi$)

NRV when NRV $<$ RC

NRV $- \pi$ when RC $<$ (NRV $- \pi$)

By definition, market will always be the middle value of NRV, RC, and NRV$-\pi$. For example, given the following three sets of facts:

Exhibit 8.10

		Market Determination		
	Market	Net Realizable Value *(Upper Limit)*	Replacement Cost	Net Realizable Value less Normal Profit Margin *(Lower Limit)*
Inventory A	90	100	90	70
Inventory B	100	100	105	70
Inventory C	70	100	60	70

In Inventory A, replacement cost is between the upper and lower limits; therefore, M would be the replacement cost of $90. In Inventory B, replacement cost exceeds the upper limit; therefore M is the upper limit of $100. In Inventory C, replacement cost is below the lower limit; therefore M is the lower limit of $70.

---

[10] GAAP provide exceptions for certain items having established mass markets. Examples would include agricultural commodities, precious metals, and marketable securities held as trading inventory by a broker. These items are carried in inventory at selling price, and any profit is recognized prior to sale. An exception also has effectively existed for firms on LIFO for tax purposes. The Tax Code specifically prohibits adjustments of inventory, as measured for tax purposes, to below LIFO cost. IRS does allow firms to adjust for LCM when using LIFO on financial statements.

The logic behind limiting the use of replacement cost as M may not be readily apparent. If replacement cost were less than original cost but still greater than NRV, and if it were used as M, then inventory would still be reported at greater than its recoverable cost, thus defeating the LCM objective. If replacement cost were less than both original cost and NRV less normal profit margin, and was still used as M, then the current year's inventory write down would create abnormal profits in the following year.

If recoverable cost (M) is equal to or greater than the already recorded inventory cost, no adjustment is made. If recoverable cost (M) is less, then an adjustment is made to reduce reported ending inventory to the recoverable cost amount.[11] The balancing reduction to owner's equity would be through an operating expense account, possibly entitled "loss on inventory revaluation."

Exhibit 8.11

Lower of Cost or Market

Item	Inventory Cost	Market	Lower of Cost or Market
Inventory A	100	90	90
Inventory B	105	100	100
Inventory C	66	70	66

As mentioned above, the LCM standard for inventory valuation is an example of the underlying accounting rule of conservatism. Conservatism, simply stated, means an avoidance of unpleasant surprises. If a loss is reasonably certain, recognize it now. Also, we do not recognize expected gains or profits until they actually occur. Suppose you had a store with an inventory of calculators. These calculators previously sold for $29.95, and you paid $18.00 each for those in your inventory. If they are now selling for $14.95, there is no way you are going to recover your $18.00 inventory cost for each calculator. You are probably going to sustain a loss, and conservatism requires that you recognize it in the current year by "writing down" your inventory.

Inventory measurement is just one example of the need for estimates and assumptions within the financial accounting system. Accountants know that they are working with estimates and assumptions. GAAP sensibly dictate that estimates should be on the conservative side to minimize profit. It attempts to ensure that most "surprises" encountered by the financial statement user will not be unpleasant. In the next chapter, you will see the need for still more estimating in the measurement of long lived assets.

---

[11] Note that GAAP allow LCM to be applied on either an item-by-item or on a major category basis. If applied on a category basis, a higher overall inventory valuation will usually result, since decreases in certain items may be offset by increases in others.

Other Aspects of Inventory Measurement and Reporting

The most important elements relating to the measurement and reporting of inventories have already been covered above. In addition, there are special inventory related topics with which you might wish to become familiar. They include:

- The method of estimating inventory at intervals during the year, or when inventory records are lost—the gross profit method,
- Special estimating procedures followed by many retailers—the retail method,
- Reporting inventory on consignment to others,
- Accounting for damaged and repossessed merchandise, and
- Computing dollar-value LIFO.

Gross Profit Method

Often, a firm desires to determine ending inventory and the cost of goods sold at interim points throughout the year. Normally, a complete physical inventory is too costly to be feasible more than once a year. How can a firm estimate cost of goods sold, at the end of a quarter? What information is readily available? Beginning inventory, net purchases, and net sales amounts for the current year are generally available. Similarly, sales and cost of goods sold for the prior year are available.

For example, the following information may be available for the Vance Company as of 3/31/X8:

19X7 Net sales	$400,000
19X7 Cost of goods sold	280,000
12/31/X7 Inventory	65,000
Net sales for first 3 months of 19X8	115,000
Net purchase for first 3 months of 19X8	75,000
Cost of goods sold for first 3 months of 19X8	?
3/31/X8 Inventory	?

Given these data, how could you reasonably estimate the cost of goods sold and the ending inventory for the first quarter of 19X8? If you assumed continuation of last year's gross profit, then 70 percent of $115,000 (first quarter 19X8 sales) would provide an estimate of cost of goods sold; and ending inventory could be estimated at $59,500 ($140,000 of goods available less $80,500 estimated cost of goods sold).

The **gross profit method** involves assuming continuation of the previous period's gross profit ratio. In most circumstances, this can represent a reasonable assumption for interim period estimating purposes. It can also be the only feasible method of estimating casualty loss (fire, major theft, and so forth) of inventory for firms following the periodic system, or those on perpetual systems whose records have been lost or destroyed. The gross profit method is not acceptable under GAAP for annual financial statement reporting.

Retail Inventory Method

Retail stores often use a more sophisticated version of the gross profit method known as the **LIFO Retail Inventory Method**. This method does not involve assuming continuation of a prior period gross profit ratio. Under the retail inventory method, the ratio is updated before application. The retail inventory method is sufficiently accurate to be acceptable for financial reporting and for tax purposes.

Unless retailers can justify complete computerized perpetual inventory records for other purposes, they usually cannot afford to keep necessary item-by-item records for use in "costing" the ending inventory. For other purposes, however, they do have readily available data on markups, selling prices, and markdowns. Markdowns may be viewed as reductions of originally intended selling prices. Inventory data are therefore maintained for the firm as a whole, or for major departments within the firm, at both cost and "selling."

Exhibit 8.12

LIFO Retail Inventory Method

	Cost	Retail
Net purchases during period	$ 250,000	$ 415,000
Net Markups		10,000
Net Markdowns		(5,000)
Total		$ 420,000
Add Beginning Inventory	50,000	80,000
Total	$ 300,000	$ 500,000
Net Sales during Period		400,000
Ending Inventory	$ 60,000*	$ 100,000

Cost to retail percentage:

$$\frac{\$300,000}{\$500,000} = 60\%$$

* $100,000 x 60% = $60,000 ending inventory at cost

Note that markdowns are not applicable to cost. Also note that this system generates a continually updated gross-profit ratio. At the end of the quarter, the firm can, with reasonable confidence, estimate the quarter's cost of goods sold as 60 percent of sales (300,000/500,000).

The more important application of the retail method is to obtain ending inventory at cost for use in the periodic inventory equation. If you had goods available for sale for the entire year at both cost and selling, and if you knew the firm had no records for "costing" each item in a physical inventory, what could you do? In retailing, selling prices are readily available with the merchandise. A physical inventory is taken and "priced" at selling price. Then this amount is converted to cost via the goods available ratio. Thereafter, the periodic inventory system proceeds as with any other firm. Ending inventory at cost would be ending inventory at retail times the cost to retail percentage or $60,000.

Many retailers using the retail method omit the deduction of markdowns in calculating goods available at selling. This method is called the conventional retail method. The slightly lower resulting goods available ratio is considered to be more conservative and also to yield an ending inventory estimate better approximating LCM.

Consignments

Sometimes Firm A will "loan" inventory to Firm B at its location to sell to customers. Firm B does not purchase form Firm A; it merely sells for A, as one of A's salespersons. Inventory "loaned" to another firm for sale is said to be on **consignment**. It remains on Firm A's balance sheet, possibly separately classified, until sale to a customer is made by Firm B. Cost of shipment to B would properly be included in the asset cost of inventory on consignment.

Damaged Goods

Inventory that is damaged and merchandise that is repossessed from customers is costed at its net realizable or recoverable value.

Computing Dollar-Value LIFO

Three techniques exist for computing dollar-value LIFO: the double extension technique; the link chain technique; and retail LIFO. The essential differences among the techniques involve the selection of LIFO pools and the method of computing or obtaining the appropriate LIFO index.[12] The following discussion will focus upon the double-extension technique. It will be assumed that all products under consideration are in a single LIFO pool.

Dollar-value LIFO is similar to strictly layered periodic LIFO for an individual product item except:

1. Each layer covers the result of an entire year's activity,
2. Each layer includes the cost of all items in the pool, and
3. The costs included in each layer are calculated in total for the layer via the use of an index.

A key concept to dollar-value LIFO, and one which provides the data base for succeeding years, is that of the base year or the year in which dollar-value LIFO was first adopted. Base year costs for each product are involved in computations in every subsequent year for

[12] For an excellent and thorough discussion of LIFO in general and dollar-value LIFO in particular, refer to "LIFO - An Implementation Guide" published by Arthur Young & Company, 277 Park Avenue, NY, 10172, 1980.

every product still in stock. New products subsequently added to the base year must be assigned a base year cost (which may be either their cost upon entering the pool or an estimate of what their costs would have been had they been in stock at the end of a base year).

The second key concept is that of the LIFO index which is calculated each year (period) as:

$$\frac{\text{Current Cost of Ending Inventory X 100}}{\text{Base Year Cost of Ending Inventory}} = \text{Current Period's LIFO Index}$$

Current costs used are usually the actual costs paid for the most recent purchase of each item. Note that the computation of the LIFO index need not represent 100 percent double costing of all items in ending inventories. A sample that is representative and based upon valid statistical methods may be used.

Exhibit 8.13

Dollar-Value LIFO

Year	Ending Inventory At Current Costs	÷	LIFO Index	=	Ending Inventory Base Year Cost
19X0	$ 500,000		100		$ 500,000
19X1	605,000		110		550,000
19X2	662,500		125		530,000
19X3	798,000		140		570,000

Year	Base Year	Base year Cost layers	x	LIFO Index	=	LIFO Cost
19X0	19X0	$ 500,000		100		$ 500,000
19X1	19X0	$ 500,000		100		$ 500,000
	19X1	50,000		110		55,000
		$ 550,000				$ 555,000
19X2	19X0	$ 500,000		100		$ 500,000
	19X2	30,000		110		33,000
		$ 530,000				$ 533,000
19X3	19X0	$ 500,000		100		$ 500,000
	19X1	30,000		110		33,000
	19X3	40,000		140		56,000
		$ 570,000				$ 589,000

To illustrate the operation of dollar-value LIFO over several years or periods, 19X0 will be taken as the base year.

As of the end of 19X0, dollar-value LIFO inventory was reported as $500,000 dollars since 19X0 was the base year.

As of the end of 19X1, ending inventory restated at base year cost ($605,000/1.10) was $550,000 indicating an overall quantity increase of $50,000 in terms of base year prices. This increment is added in terms of 19X1 costs ($50,000 x 1.10) at $55,000, and inventory is reported at $555,000. Two layers are carried forward to 19X2, the 19X0 layer of $500,000 and the 19X1 layer of $55,000.

As of the end of 19X2, ending inventory restated at base year costs ($662,500/1.25) was $530,000 indicating an overall quantity decrease of $20,000 in terms of base year costs. Following the LIFO approach, this decrement must be first subtracted from the most recently added (19X1) layer. The inventory layer reduction is made in terms of the costs in effect at the time the layer was added, not in terms of current year costs or base year costs.[13] The 19X1 layer is reduced to $30,000 ($50,000 – $20,000) at base year costs and then restated to 19X1 costs of $33,000 ($30,000 x 1.10). 19X2 ending inventory is reported as $533,000 and consists of 19X0 layer of $500,000 and the remaining 19X1 layer of $33,000.

As of the end of 19X3, ending inventory restated at base year costs ($798,000/1.40) was $570,000 indicating an overall increase of $40,000 in terms of base year costs when compared to beginning inventory at base year costs ($530,000). This third layer is added in terms of current costs ($40,000 x 1.40) of $56,000. Inventory is reported at $589,000 and consists of three layers: 19X0 at $500,000; 19X1 at $33,000; and 19X3 at $56,000.

Note from this example that total ending inventories at base year prices will always reconcile (after adjusting each layer by the applicable LIFO index) with ending inventory at dollar-value LIFO cost if computations are made correctly. Finally, you should observe from the 19X2 year's illustration that, as is true for simple LIFO, once a portion or all of a layer is peeled off, it cannot be reconstructed.

The use of dollar-value LIFO can significantly reduce the risk of liquidating the older cost LIFO base and being forced to recognize accumulated past holding gains when the base stock of a few items may be depleted. So long as the overall level of inventory is not significantly reduced, the stock depletion of individual items may be offset by other item increases within the dollar-value LIFO pool. The offsetting feature, coupled with the significant decrease in record keeping costs mentioned above, make dollar-value LIFO a widely used method.

---

[13] Had the quantity reduction in this example amounted to $75,000 in base year costs, $55,000 would have been peeled off in 19X1 prices and $25,000 in 19X0 prices.

Supplementary Information on Inflation and Changing Prices

As first mentioned in Chapter 2, GAAP encourage but do not require disclosure of supplementary information on the effects of changing prices for inventory.[14] Supplementary data includes:

- Ending Inventory measured/valued at the lower of current cost or recoverable amount on the statement date;

- Cost of goods sold measured/valued at current cost at the statement date; and

- Change in current cost measurement during the year.

Various measurement methods may be used to calculate **current cost** which may be applied on an individual item or group basis. Methods suggested, but not restricted to, are indexation of prices and direct pricing. Historical cost adjusted for constant purchasing power dollars may be substituted for current cost as long as the difference between current cost and constant purchasing power dollars is not material. Cost of goods sold reported under LIFO may be used as an approximation of current cost provided that the effect of any decrease in beginning inventory is excluded.

The meaning of the terms "constant dollar" and "current cost" will be discussed further in Chapter 15. This chapter will also cover the methods for calculating the inventory data requirements together with a discussion of the potential usefulness of supplementary data.

Preparer Procedures

You will find all accounts necessary for the preparer problems in this chapter in the complete chart of accounts at the beginning of the Odd-numbered Solutions—Appendix D—at the back of the book.

Exhibit 8.14

Additions to the Chart of Accounts

Current Asset Inventory Subaccounts
011   Gross Purchases
012   Freight in

Contra-Asset Inventory Subaccounts
202   Purchase Returns and Allowances
203   Purchase Discounts

Other Expenses
821   Discounts Lost
822   Loss on Inventory Revaluation

---

[14] For more precise criteria, and for amplification of the various topics covered in this section, see FASB Statement No. 89, Financial Accounting Standards Board, Stamford, CT 06905, Dec. 1986.

Additions to the Chart of Accounts

To accommodate transactions and adjustments in this chapter, the partial chart of accounts first introduced in Chapter 5 as Exhibit 5.1 must be expanded to include accounts in Exhibit 8.14.

New Transactions

Essentially the only new transactions introduced in this chapter involve the recording of inventory transactions to individual accounts for Gross Purchases, Freight in, Purchase Returns and Allowances, and Purchase Discounts, rather than directly to the inventory account itself. For example, suppose the following events related to a particular inventory purchase for 19X9:

Invoice cost	$1,000
Transportation in billed	90
Returns	150
Discounts taken	20

The appropriate journal entries would be:

	DR	CR
Gross Purchases	*1,000*	
Accounts Payable		*1,000*
To record purchase of inventory		
Freight-In	*90*	
Accounts Payable		*90*
To record freight-in cost for inventory purchase		
Accounts Payable	*150*	
Purchase Returns and Allowances		*150*
To record purchase returns		
Accounts Payable	*850*	
Cash		*833*
Purchase Discounts		*17*
To record payment of invoice taking discount		

Note that, although not illustrated throughout this book or its problems some firms record gross purchases net of available discount. From the above example the entries under the net method would be:

	DR	CR
Gross Purchases	*980*	
Accounts Payable		*980*
To record payment of inventory invoice		
Freight-In	*90*	
Accounts Payable		*90*
To record freight-in cost for inventory pruchase		
Accounts Payable	*147*	
Purchase Returns and Allowances		*147*
To record purchase returns		
Accounts Payable	*833*	
Cash		*833*
To record payment of inventory invoice		

If the payment was made after the discount had expired, the entry would be:

	DR	CR
Accounts Payable	*833*	
Discounts Lost	*17*	
Cash		*850*
To record payment after discount expired		

New Adjustments

Three new year-end adjustments were introduced in this chapter: two involving the closing of inventory related accounts to cost of goods sold and the recording of ending inventory. The third is necessary only when ending inventory must be adjusted downwards to reflect LCM.

For example, assume the following balances in the inventory-related accounts at year end:

Inventory (1/1/X9)	5,000 DR
Gross Purchases	30,000 DR
Freight-In	4,000 DR
Purchase Returns and Allowances	2,000 CR
Purchase Discounts	560 CR

The first entry would close (transfer the balances) of all inventory related accounts to cost of goods sold:

	DR	CR
Cost of Goods Sold	*36,440*	
Purchase Returns and Allowances	*2,000*	
Purchase Discounts	*560*	
Inventory (1/1/X9)		*5,000*
Gross purchases		*30,000*
Freight In		*4,000*
To close inventory accounts		

In effect, this entry assumes that all inventory has been sold. Ending inventory is then determined via the specific identification, FIFO, weighted average, or LIFO method from separate records (assumed to be $5,300 in this example) and reversed out of cost of goods sold back into the balance sheet with the following entry:

	DR	CR
Inventory (12/31/X9)	5,300	
Cost of Goods Sold		5,300
To record ending inventory		

Where an LCM adjustment is necessary (assume M were determined to be $4,900 in this example) the following entry is made:

Loss on Inventory Revaluation	400	
Inventory		400
To record LCM adjustment of inventory		

Chapter Overview

Based on the material presented in this chapter, you should be able to:

- Describe the significance of inventory measurement to overall asset measurement and income reporting;
- Describe the inventory measurement problems created by inflationary prices;
- Explain the basis for initial inventory (input) measurement;
- Describe the difference between a periodic and a perpetual inventory system, and the significance of this difference;
- Explain why cost flow assumptions may be necessary or desirable;
- Describe the three cost flow assumptions acceptable under GAAP, give examples of each, and explain the alternative effects of each on the balance sheet and income statement;
- Explain the importance of consistency as applied to inventory measurement;
- Describe Lower of Cost or Market and how it represents an application of the accounting principle of conservatism.

New Vocabulary and Concepts

Consignment	Moving average cost
Cost flow assumption	Net purchases
Current cost	Net realizable value (NRV)
Dollar-value LIFO	Periodic inventory (system)
FIFO	Periodic LIFO
Full acquisition cost	Perpetual inventory (system)
Gross profit method	Perpetual LIFO
Gross purchases	Purchase discounts
Holding gain	Purchase returns and allowances
LIFO pools	Replacement cost (RC)
LIFO Retail Method	Specific (cost) identification
LIFO	Transportation-in/freight-in
Lower of Cost or Market (LCM)	Weighted average cost

- Basis for initial measurement of inventory.
- Price changes and assumed inventory cost flows.
- Cost flow assumption/cost assumption.
- Effects of cost flow assumptions on financial statements.
- Consistency and conservatism.

Review Questions

1. (a) What is the current rationale under GAAP for excluding recognition of inflationary changes to existing assets, that is, for recognizing new higher prices only in a transaction? (b) Exogenous specific price decreases may be recognized under the Lower of Cost or Market rule. Explain.

2. (a) Explain why a firm might be forced to use an inventory cost flow assumption. (b) Explain why a firm might elect to use a cost flow assumption even when it did not need to.

3. (a) What are the components of net purchases? (b) Explain each component and how it affects net purchases.

4. (a) Once an inventory flow assumption is adopted by a firm, can it change to another? (b) If yes, when, and what must be disclosed? (c) How is the principle of "consistency" involved?

5. Describe what is meant by the specific (cost) identification system. Give an example of how it would work and a product where it typically might apply.

6. (a) Explain the weighted average cost flow assumption. (b) Explain why a simple unweighted average will not work.

7. Explain the FIFO cost flow assumption.

8. Explain the LIFO cost flow assumption.

9. Regardless of the flow assumption accountants may adopt, what are examples of items that usually physically follow the FIFO flow pattern? The LIFO pattern?

10. (a) What is trading profit and what is inventory holding gain? (b) How are each reported under FIFO? (c) Under LIFO?

11. (a) What is the difference between the perpetual and the periodic inventory systems? (b) How does this difference affect LIFO?

12. In periods of inflationary prices, what is the effect upon reported income of using FIFO as compared with weighted average cost and with LIFO?

13. What are some of the advantages and disadvantages of using specific identification and each of the three cost flow assumptions?

14. (a) What are LIFO pools? (b) What is dollar-value LIFO? (c) What are some of the advantages of each?

15. Is the possible LCM adjustment made as part of the initial determination of ending inventory, or is it made after the normal determination of ending inventory? Explain.

16. How does LCM relate to the accounting principle of conservatism?

Mini Cases and Questions for Discussion

MC 8.1   Becky and Lita are discussing the income statements of the Peter Company and the Paul Company. Becky says, "Peter's net income is $100,000 and Paul's is only $50,000. That means that Peter had twice as much profit as Paul."

"Not necessarily," replies Lita. "The statement footnotes say that Peter follows FIFO and Paul uses LIFO. In periods of inflation, that could explain the entire difference. In fact, it is possible that, if both use the same system, Paul might report more income than Peter!"

"That does not make sense," says Becky. "Both statements have CPA opinions that they are consistently following GAAP. How could a CPA approve Paul's statement if, as you say, Paul may be making more profit than Peter?" Discuss.

MC 8.2   Jack has read that many companies' reported earnings have been very high. "Business is not suffering," he says.

Phil disagrees. "A lot of profit during periods of inflation is 'phony profit'. Some firms with high reported profits aren't really doing well at all. It all has something to do with holding gains." Discuss.

MC 8.3 In a large corporation where the owners (stockholders) and management are different, it is possible that the owners' and management's preferences for a particular inventory cost flow assumption might differ. Also, in any firm, it is possible for owners and creditors to have different flow assumption preferences. Explain how these differences could occur and discuss their implications.

MC 8.4 Is a holding gain on inventory more like an unusual but periodically recurring gain on a long-lived asset disposition or more like a truly extraordinary item? Discuss.

MC 8.5 Income tax is generally based on "dollar income" in the same manner as GAAP income measures "dollar-value." No allowance for inflation or future replacement costs is currently incorporated in either system. Discuss.

MC 8.6 Assume that a very large piece of equipment has been sold for $850,000 on account at year-end. The profit of $150,000 has been included in last year's reported income. Early this year, the customer is unable to obtain anticipated financing. The equipment is returned unused and the sale is cancelled. How should the equipment be recorded in inventory? At what amount? How can the sale and profit be reversed on last year's closed and published statements? If the equipment is resold to another customer this year, should the sale and profit be included in this year's totals? If it is, wouldn't this result in double counting? Discuss.

MC 8.7 The LIFO method has been criticized as enabling firms to manipulate their reported income just by purchasing or deferring purchase of inventory at year end. Is this possible? How would it work? Discuss.

Essential Problems

EP 8.1 The following information is available for a particular firm:

Gross purchases	$473,000
Transportation-in	27,000
Purchase returns	32,000
Purchase discounts and allowances taken	8,000

What are net purchases for the year?

EP 8.2 The following data is available for 19X5 for Firms A, B, C, and D:

	Firm A	Firm B	Firm C	Firm D
Gross purchases	$600,000	$700,000	$800,000	$900,000
Transportation-in	60,000	65,000	70,000	75,000
Purchase returns	30,000	70,000	120,000	200,000
Purchase discounts & allowances taken	11,000	13,000	14,000	15,000

What are net purchases for each firm during 19X5?

EP 8.3 The following information is available for a particular firm:

Beginning inventory	$125,000
Ending inventory	140,000
Cost of goods sold	560,000
Gross purchases	590,000
Purchase returns	40,000
Purchase discounts and allowances taken	10,000

What was the cost of transportation during the year?

EP 8.4 For each of the following situations, determine the missing amount(s):

	A	B	C	D	E	F
Beginning inventory	$?	$100	$?	$175	$125	$ 75
Cost of goods sold	?	590	?	?	722	353
Ending Inventory	60	?	175	190	110	?
Freight-in	30	50	40	45	?	20
Goods available for sale	359	680	808	?	?	?
Gross purchases	300	600	?	850	750	?
Net purchases	309	580	658	?	?	368
Purchase discounts taken	6	?	12	12	13	7
Purchase returns	?	60	70	80	65	45

EP 8.5 Nordic Ski Wholesale Company uses the weighted average cost flow assumption to measure its inventory and cost of goods sold. Its fiscal year runs from June 1 through May 31. At the beginning of the current fiscal year June 1 its inventory of a particular type of ski consisted of 200 pairs, all purchased at a cost of $30 per pair. During the year, the following additional purchases were made:

July:	300 pairs costing $35 per pair
November:	150 pairs costing $40 per pair
January:	200 pairs costing $50 per pair

At year-end a physical inventory revealed 300 pairs still in stock. What amounts would properly be reported:(a) on the firm's ending balance sheet for inventory; and (b) on its income statement for cost of goods sold?

EP 8.6 Refer to the Nordic Ski Company data in EP 8.5 above. Suppose you knew the firm followed periodic inventory but did not know which flow assumption they were using. Their income statement showed cost of goods sold as $18,500. Calculate inventory FIFO and LIFO inventory method. Which method was the firm using?

EP 8.7   Refer to the Nordic Ski Company data in EP 8.5. Assume that, instead of periodic inventory, the firm used perpetual inventory. The 550 units were sold and shipped as follows:

September: 250 pairs
October: 100 pairs
December: 200 pairs

Determine cost of goods sold under the moving average method.

EP 8.8   Refer to the Nordic Ski Company data in EP 8.5 and in EP 8.7 above. Determine cost of goods sold and ending inventory, assuming the firm used Perpetual LIFO.

EP 8.9   You are trying to compare the profit performance of two firms, A and B. A's income statement showed cost of goods sold as $210,000 and reported operating income of $30,000. B's showed cost of goods sold as $160,000 and operating income as $70,000. Footnotes reveal that they are both following the same accounting methods except that A uses periodic LIFO and B follows periodic FIFO. From other information, you have calculated that B's cost of goods sold following periodic LIFO would have been $205,000. Determine B's operating income on the same basis as A for comparison purposes.

EP 8.10   Referring to the situation described in EP 8.9 above, suppose B's LIFO cost of goods sold was not obtainable. Instead you have the following additional information on A.

Reported ending inventory $70,000
Ending inventory if FIFO had been used: 95,000

What would A's operating income have been, determined on the same basis as B for comparison purposes?

EP 8.11   At year-end the cost of ending inventory for the Spindrift Company was determined to be $95,000, following periodic FIFO. An LCM calculation revealed that M was $97,000. (a) At what amount should ending inventory be reported on the balance sheet? Explain your reasoning. (b) If M had been determined to be $87,000, how should balance sheet inventory have been reported and why?

EP 8.12   Determine the amount of ending inventory that should appear on the ending balance sheet and the amount of loss on inventory revaluation (if any) that should be included in the income statement for each of the following six situations.

	A	B	C	D	E	F
Book inventory before adjustment	$100	$120	$140	$150	$165	$200
Net realizable value	150	130	100	130	175	140
Replacement cost	90	100	50	135	180	60
Net realizable value less normal profit	75	78	55	91	70	63

Supplementary Problems

SP 8.13 Integrative Problem: The following events occurred during Period 5 for Luigi's Auto Parts:

1) In anticipation of an impeding cash shortage, Luigi arranged for $20,000 in new long-term debt payable at the end of Period 20 with interest of $800 per period. The cash was received early in Period 5.

2) Luigi also contributed an additional $10,000 of his own cash to the firm.

3) The $5,000 current note (lawsuit settlement) was paid at the beginning of the period. No interest was required.

4) The $2,000 current note receivable was extended to mature at the beginning of Period 6.

5) Rent of $550 covering the previous and the current periods' rent receivable was collected.

6) The remaining special order merchandise priced at $2,000 for which customers had paid in advance, was received and delivered to customers.

7) The $700 of inventory property taxes due at the beginning of the period were paid.

8) Sales totaled $80,000, $20,000 for cash and the balance on account.

9) Receivable collections from customers totaled $56,000.

10) Inventory costing $54,000 was acquired on account.

11) Supplies costing $500 were acquired on account.

12) $500 was paid for utilities and services consumed during the period.

13) $4,500 was paid in advance covering the current period's rent.

14) Wages and salaries totaling $16,000 were paid including the $900 previously accrued.

15) $1,600 was paid for insurance covering Periods 5 through 8.

16) $30,000 plus the period's interest of $960 was paid to retire the maturing notes.

17) $53,000 was paid on accounts payable.

Adjustments were made for $100 of accrued interest on the $2,000 current notes receivable (A); $800 of inventory property tax due at the beginning of Period 6 (B); maturation of the $900 note due at the end of Period 6 (C); $50,000 of inventory delivered to customers (D); $300 of supplies used (E); $250 amortization of leasehold improvement (F); $75 of depreciation on equipment (G); $400 expiration of insurance (H); accrual of $36 interest payable on the $900 equipment note (I); accrual of $800 interest on the $20,000 new long term debt (J); and accrual of $300 of wages and salaries earned but unpaid (K).

Luigi's firm balance sheet as of the end of Period 5 is:

LUIGI'S AUTO PARTS BALANCE SHEET AS OF THE END OF PERIOD 5

ASSETS		EQUITIES	
Cash	$ 5,432	Current notes payable	$ 900
Current notes receivable	2,000	Accounts payable	16,500
Accounts receivable	50,000	Wages and salaries	300
Interest receivable	200	Interest payable	836
Inventory	39,000	Taxes payable	800
Supplies	260		
Prepaid items	1,200	Total Current Liabilities	$ 19,336
		Noncurrent note payable	20,000
Total Current Assets	$ 98,092		
Equipment	1,200	Total Liabilities	$ 39,336
Accum. depr. equip.	(300)		
Leasehold improvement	3,750	Luigi Cavelli,Capital	63,406
Total Assets	$ 102,742	Total Equities	$ 102,742

During Period 6, the following occurred affecting the financial position of Luigi's Auto Parts (Note: Items marked with an asterisk have been illustrated in previous periods.)

1) The current note receivable together with accrued interest was collected at the start of the period.

*2) The $800 of inventory property taxes due at the beginning of the period and previously accrued were paid. No further property taxes were anticipated as the law had been repealed effective with Period 6.

*3) The $836 of accrued interest was paid.

*4) The $900 current note payable plus $36 of interest was paid.

*5) Sales totaled $100,000, $25,000 for cash and the balance on account.

*6) Collections of receivables from customers totaled $65,000. All remaining receivables were expected to be collected in the following period.

*7) Wages and salaries totaling $20,000 were paid including $300 accrued from the prior period.

*8) The current period's rental of $4,500 was paid in advance.

*9) Current period's bills for utilities and services consumed totaling $500 were received and paid.

10) Prior to Period 6, for amplification, Luigi had recorded all merchandise purchase related transactions directly to inventory. Starting in Period 6 separate accounts were established for Gross Purchases, Freight in, Purchase Returns and Allowances, and Purchase Discounts. During Period 6, gross purchases of merchandise on account totaled $65,250 representing 45,000 average units.

11) Of the 45,000 average units purchased, 3,000 average units were determined to be defective and were returned to the supplier for full credit.

12) The firm was billed $3,300 for freight-in on merchandise purchases.

*13) 5,000 typical supplies units were purchased on account at a net purchase cost of $750.

14) $62,250 was paid on accounts payable, and $1,200 in purchase discounts were taken on merchandise purchases.

At the end of Period 6:

*A) $400 of prepaid insurance and $4,500 of prepaid rent had expired.

*B) $75 of depreciation expense on equipment was recorded.

*C) $250 of amortization of leasehold improvement was recorded.

*D) $800 of interest owed on the $20,000 noncurrent note was accrued.

*E) $1,200 of wages and salaries owed but unpaid were accrued.

F)   Beginning merchandise inventory and all accounts related to merchandise purchases were closed or expensed to cost of goods sold (a minus in the income box) as if there were no ending merchandise inventory.

G)   Ending inventory of 41,000 average units calculated on the periodic LIFO basis is reversed from cost of goods sold to inventory (a plus to inventory and a plus in the income box). You may assume that beginning inventory consisted of 39,000 average units.

H)   Supplies were carried on FIFO. You may assume that 2,500 typical units were on hand and unused at year-end, and that beginning supplies inventory consisted of 2,600 typical units.

Required:

a)   The effect on the beginning period balance sheet of those Period 6 transactions and adjustments that were introduced in earlier periods, and which are identified with and asterisk (*), has already been recorded in the partially completed balance sheet effect worksheet given below. Prepare a final balance sheet effect worksheet (per Balance Sheet Diagram 4.9) for Luigi's Store for Period 6 starting with the preliminary balances and recording the effect of Period 6 transactions (1), (10), (11), (12), and (14), and adjustments (F), (G), and (H). Identify starting balances as "(p)" and the effect of the remaining transactions and adjustments with their numbers or letters. Also identify all revenue and expense effects upon Luigi's capital in an income box. Provide necessary space on your worksheet by entering account titles as follows:

Account	Line number	Account	Line number
Cash	1	Current Notes Payable	1
Current Notes Receivable	5	Accounts Payable	3
Accounts Receivable	8	Wages and Salaries	9
Interest Receivable	10	Interest Payable	11
Inventory	13	Taxes Payable	13
Gross Purchase	17	Noncurrent Notes Payable	15
Freight in	21	Luigi Cavelli Capital	18
Purchase Returns	25		
Purchase Discounts	29		
Supplies	33		
Prepaid Items	36		
Equipment	38		
Accum. Depr. Equip.	40		
Leasehold Improvements	42		

PARTIALLY COMPLETED BALANCE SHEET EFFECT WORKSHEET
Luigi's Auto Parts Period 6
(b = Beginning Balance; p = Partially Completed Balance)

Cash	$	5,432	(b)			Current Notes Payable				
	–	800	(2)				$ 900	(b)		
	–	836	(3)				– 900	(4)	$ 0	(p)
	–	936	(4)			Accounts Payable				
	+	25,000	(5)				16,500	(b)		
	+	65,000	(6)				+ 750	(13)	17,250	(p)
	–	20,000	(7)			Wages and Salaries				
	–	4,500	(8)				+ 300	(b)		
	–	500	(9)	$ 67,860	(p)		– 300	(7)		
Current Notes Receivable							+ 1,200	(E)	1,200	(p)
		2,000	(b)	2,000	(p)	Interest Payable				
Accounts Receivable							836	(b)		
		50,000	(b)				– 836	(3)		
	+	75,000	(5)				+ 800	(D)	800	(p)
		65,000	(6)	60,000	(p)	Taxes Payable				
Interest Receivable							800	(b)		
		200	(b)	200	(p)		– 800	(2)	0	(p)
Inventory						Noncurrent Notes Payable				
		39,000	(b)	39,000	(p)		20,000	(b)	20,000	(p)
Gross Purchases										
		0	(b)	0	(p)					
Freight-in										
		0	(b)	0	(p)					
Purchase Returns										
		0	(b)	0	(p)	Luigi Cavelli, Capital				
Purchase Discounts							63,406	(b)	63,406	(p)
		0	(b)	0	(p)					
Supplies										
		260	(b)				Income			
	+	750	(13)	1,010	(p)					
Prepaid Items						– 36	(4)		
		1,200	(b)			+ 100,000	(5)		
	+	4,500	(8)			– 19,700	(7)		
	–	4,900	(A)	800	(p)	– 500	(9)		
Equipment		1,200	(b)	1,200	(p)	– 4,900	(A)		
Accum. Depr. Equipment						– 75	(B)		
		(300)	(b)			– 250	(C)		
	–	75	(B)	(375)	(p)	– 800	(D)		
Leasehold Improvement						– 1,200	(E)	72,539	(p)
		3,750	(b)							
	–	250	(C)	3,500	(p)					
TOTALS				$ 175,195	(p)	TOTALS			$ 175,195	(p)

b) Prepare a schedule of cost of goods sold for Luigi's Auto Parts for Period 6.

c) Prepare the firm's income statement for Period 6 in good form following the multiple step format.

d) Prepare the statement of owner's capital in good form for Period 6.

e) Prepare the firm's balance sheet in good form as of the end of Period 6.

f) Prepare the firm's statement of cash flow for Period 6 in good form using the indirect method for operation activities.

g) Determine for Luigi's Store as of the end of Period 6:

1) The amount of net working capital in the business;

2) The current ratio (to two decimals);

3) The quick ratio (to two decimals);

4) The long term debt ratio (to three decimals); and

5) The asset composition ratio (to three decimals).

SP   8.14 Integrative Problem: The following events occurred during Period 5 for Irene's Sport Shop:

1) In anticipation of an impending cash shortage, Irene arranged for $10,000 in new term debt payable at the end of Period 20 with interest of $350 per period. The cash was received early in Period 5.

2) Irene also contributed an additional $5,000 of her own cash to the firm.

3) The $10,000 current note (lawsuit settlement) was paid at the beginning of the period, interest was required.

4) The $1,000 current note receivable was extended to mature at the beginning of Period 6.

5) Rent of $750 covering the previous and current periods' rent receivable was collected.

6) The remaining special order merchandise priced at $2,000, for which customers have paid in advance, was received and delivered to customers.

7) The $1,200 of inventory property taxes due at the beginning of the period were paid.

8) Sales totaled $120,000, $48,000 for cash and the balance on account.

9) Receivable collections from customers totaled $73,000.

10) Inventory costing $68,000 was acquired on account.

11) Supplies costing $650 were acquired on account.

12) $700 was paid for utilities and services consumed during the period.

13) $6,600 was paid in advance covering the current period's rent.

14) Wages and salaries totaling $27,800 were paid including the $800 previously accrued.

15) $4,400 was paid for insurance covering Periods 5 through 8.

16) $35,000 plus the period's interest of $1,400 was paid to retire the maturing notes.

17) $56,545 was paid on accounts payable.

Adjustments were made for $25 of accrued interest on the $1,000 current note receivable (A);

$1,300 of inventory property tax due at the beginning of Period 6 (B); maturation of $2,000 note due at the end of Period 6 (C); $63,000 of inventory delivered to customers; $600 of supplies used (E); $1,150 amortization of leasehold improvement (F); $150 of depreciation on equipment (G); $1,100 expiration of insurance and $6,600 expiration of prepaid rent (H); accrual of $80 interest payable on $2,000 equipment note (I); accrual of $350 on the $10,000 new long term debt (J); and accrual of $1,000 of wages and salaries owed but unpaid (K).

Irene's firm's balance sheet as of the end of Period 5 is given below:

IRENE'S SPORT SHOP BALANCE SHEET AS OF THE END OF PERIOD 5

ASSETS		EQUITIES	
Cash	$ 6,000	Current notes payable	$ 2,000
Current notes receivable	1,000	Accounts payable	36,105
Accounts receivable	83,750	Wages and salaries	1,000
Interest receivable	50	Interest Payable	430
Inventory	55,000	Taxes payable	1,300
Supplies	200		
Prepaid items	3,300	Total Current Liabilities	$ 40,835
		Noncurrent note payable	10,000
Total Current Assets	$ 149,300		
Equipment	2,400	Total Liabilities	$ 50,835
Accum. depr. equip.	(600)		
Leasehold Improvement	12,650	Irene Morton, Capital	112,915
Total Assets	$·163,750	Total Equities	$ 163,750

During Period 6, the following events occurred affecting the financial position of Irene's Sport Shop: (Note: Items marked with an asterisk have been illustrated in previous periods.)

1) The current note receivable together with accrued interest was collected at the start of the period.

*2) The $1,300 of inventory property taxes due at the beginning of the period and previously accrued were paid. No further property taxes were anticipated as the law had been repealed effective with Period 6.

*3) The $430 of accrued interest was paid.

*4) The $2,000 current note payable plus $40 of interest was paid.

*5) Sales totaled $140,000, $56,000 for cash and the balance on account.

*6) Collections of receivables from customers totaled $80,750. All remaining receivables were expected to be collected in the following period.

*7) Wages and salaries totaling $29,700 were paid including $1,000 accrued from the prior period.

*8) The current period's rental of $6,600 was paid in advance.

*9) Current period's bills for utilities and services consumed totaling $900 were received and paid.

10)   Prior to Period 6, for simplification, Irene had recorded all merchandise purchase related transactions directly to inventory. Starting in Period 6 separate accounts were established for Gross Purchases, Freight-in, Purchase Returns and Allowances, and Purchase Discounts. During Period 6, gross purchases of merchandise on account totaled $78,750 representing 15,000 average units.

11)   Of the 15,000 average units purchased, 700 average units were determined to be defective and were returned to the supplier for full credit.

12)   The firm was billed $5,075 for freight-in on merchandise purchases.

*13) 10,000 typical supplies were purchased on account at a net purchase cost of $1,000.

14) $80,755 was paid on accounts payable, and $1,500 in purchase discounts were taken on merchandise purchases.

At the end of Period 6:

*A) $1,100 of prepaid insurance and $6,600 of prepaid rent had expired.

*B) $150 of depreciation expense on equipment was recorded.

*C) $1,150 of amortization of leasehold improvement was recorded

*D) $350 of interest owed on the $10,000 noncurrent note was accrued.

*E) $1,300 of wages and salaries owed but unpaid were accrued.

F)   Beginning merchandise inventory and all accounts related to merchandise purchases were closed or expensed to cost of goods sold (a minus in the income box) as if there were no ending merchandise inventory.

G)   Ending inventory of 12,000 average units calculated on the periodic LIFO basis is reversed from cost of goods sold to inventory (a plus to inventory and a plus in the income box) You may assume that beginning inventory consisted of 11,000 average units.

H)   Supplies were carried on FIFO. You may assume that 4,000 typical units were on hand and unused at year end, and that beginning supplies inventory consisted of 4,000 typical units.

PARTIALLY COMPLETED BALANCE SHEET EFFECT WORKSHEET
Irene's Sport Shop Period 6
(b = Beginning Balance; p = Partially Completed Balance

Cash	$ 6,000	(b)				Current Notes Payable				
−	1,300	(2)				$	2,000	(b)		
−	430	(3)				−	2,000	(4)	0	(p)
−	2,040	(4)								
+	56,000	(5)				Accounts Payable				
+	80,750	(6)					36,105	(b)		
−	29,700	(7)				+	1,000	(13)	37,105	(p)
−	6,600	(8)								
−	900	(9)	$ 101,780	(p)		Wages and Salaries				
							1,000	(b)		
Current Notes Receivable						−	1,000	(7)		
	1,000	(b)	1,000	(p)		+	1,300	(E)	1,300	(p)
Accounts Receivable										
	83,750	(b)				Interest Payable				
+	84,000	(5)					430	(b)		
−	80,750	(6)	87,000	(p)		−	430	(3)		
						+	350	(D)	350	(p)
Interest Receivable										
	50	(b)	50	(p)		Taxes Payable				
							1,300	(b)		
Inventory							1,300	(2)	0	(p)
	55,000	(b)	55,000	(p)						
Gross Purchases						Noncurrent Notes Payable				
	0	(b)	0	(p)			10,000	(b)	10,000	(p)
Freight in	0	(b)	0	(p)						
Purchase Returns										
	0	(b)	0	(p)		Irene Morton, Capital				
							112,915	(b)	112,915	(p)
Purchase Discounts										
	0	(b)								
Supplies	200	(b)								
+	1,000	(13)	1,200	(p)						
Prepaid Items										
	3,300	(b)								
+	6,600	(8)								
−	7,700	(A)	2,200	(p)						
Equipment	2,400	(b)	2,400	(p)						
Accum. Depr. Equip.										
	(600)	(b)								
−	150	(B)	(750)	(p)						
Leasehold Improvement										
	12,650	(b)								
−	1,150	(C)	11,500	(p)						
TOTALS			$ 261,380	(p)		TOTALS			$ 261,380	(p)

Income
−	40	(4)
+	140,000	(5)
−	28,700	(7)
−	900	(9)
−	7,700	(A)
−	150	(B)
−	1,150	(C)
−	350	(D)
−	1,300	(E) 99,710 (p)

Required:

a) The effect on the beginning period balance sheet of those Period 6 transactions and adjustments that were introduced in earlier periods, and which are identified with an asterisk (*), has already been recorded in the partially completed balance sheet effect worksheet given below. Prepare a final balance sheet effect worksheet (per Balance Sheet Diagram 4.9) for Irene's store for Period 6 starting with the preliminary balances and recording the effect of Period 6 transactions (1), (10), (11), (12), and (14), and adjustments (F), (G), and (H). Identify starting balances as "(p)" and the effect of the remaining transactions and adjustments with their numbers or letters. Also identify all revenue and expense effects upon Irene's capital in an income box. Provide necessary space on your worksheet by entering account titles as follows:

Account	Line number	Account	Line number
Cash	1	Current Notes Payable	1
Current Notes Receivable	5	Accounts Payable	3
Accounts Receivable	8	Wages and Salaries	9
Interest Receivable	10	Interest Payable	11
Inventory	13	Taxes Payable	13
Gross Purchase	17	Noncurrent Notes Payable	15
Freight in	21	Irene Morton, Capital	39
Purchase Returns	25		
Purchase Discounts	29		
Supplies	33		
Prepaid Items	36		
Equipment	38		
Accum. Depr. Equip.	40		
Leasehold Improvements	42		

b) Prepare a schedule of cost of goods sold for Irene's Sport Shop for Period 6.

c) Prepare the firm's income statement for Period 6 in good form following the multiple step format.

d) Prepare the statement of owner's capital in good form for Period 6.

e) Prepare the firm's balance sheet in good form as of the end of Period 6.

f) Prepare the firm's statement of cash flow for Period 6 in good form using the indirect method for operating activities.

g) Determine for Irene's Store as of the end of Period 6:

1) The amount of net working capital in the business;

2) The current ratio (to two decimals);

3) The quick ratio (to two decimals);

4) The long term debt ratio (to three decimals); and

5) The asset composition ratio (to three decimals).

SP 8.15 The Hadley Company retailed clothing. Based on the following data (000 omitted), what would Hadley estimate as its gross profit on its first quarterly interim income statement (for the three months ending 4/30/X4) and as its inventory on its interim balance sheet as of that date?

Sales for the fiscal year ending 1/31/X4	$ 800
Cost of goods sold for the same period	320
Sales for the first quarter ending 4/30/X4	160
Net purchases during the first quarter	70
Ending inventory as of 1/31/X4	100

SP 8.16 Answer the same questions asked in SP 8.15 for competitors A, B, and C based on the following data (000 omitted):

	A	B	C
Sales for previous year	$750	$850	$900
Cost of goods sold for previous year	315	323	360
Sales for current first quarter	177	195	225
Net purchases for current first quarter	75	70	90
Inventory at end previous year	105	135	120

SP 8.17 The Barking Seal was a retailer of jeans and shirts. At the start of the year, the merchandise on hand was priced to sell at $34,000, and the cost had been estimated at $22,000. During the year net purchases amounted to $140,000, and these new items had been priced to sell at $226,000. Sales during the first few months were slow. Markdowns of $15,000 were taken. At year-end, stock still on hand had a total selling price of $40,000. Following the LIFO retail method, ending inventory at cost should be reported at what amount?

SP 8.18 Determine cost of goods sold for each of the three firms X, Y, and Z following the LIFO retail method. Round your answer to the nearest hundred dollars. Data available includes (000 omitted):

	X	Y	Z
Beginning inventory at cost	$100	$200	$300
Beginning inventory at selling	160	300	465
Ending inventory at selling	150	320	500
Markdowns taken	60	200	375
Net purchases at cost	400	1,000	1,800
Net purchases at selling	600	1,500	3,000

SP 8.19 The Brinkley Company maintained its inventory following the dollar-value LIFO method. Its base year was 19X3 at which time its inventory was $100,000 at year-end current costs. The representative sample inventory at the end of 19X3 had a cost of $10,000. The following data is available relating to the firm's inventory for the years 19X4 and 19X5:

	19X4	19X5
Year-end cost of representative sample	$11,500	$12,550
Year-end cost of total inventory	92,000	162,500

(a) Determine applicable LIFO indexes for 19X4 and 19X5.

(b) Determine 19X4 ending inventory at dollar-value LIFO cost.

(c) Determine 19X5 ending inventory at dollar-value LIFO cost.

SP 8.20 The Rather Corporation maintained its inventory following the dollar-value LIFO method. Its base year was 19X1 at which time its inventory was $200,000 at year end current costs. The representative sample inventory at the end of 19X1 had a cost of $60,000. The following data are available relating to the firm's inventory over the next seven years:

Year	Base Year Cost Total Inventory	LIFO Index %	Representative Sample	Total Inventory	Dollar-Value LIFO Cost
19X2	$220,000	110	?	?	$222,000
19X3	?	120	?	228,000	190,000
19X4	200,000	?	75,000	?	202,500
19X5	?	?	81,000	310,500	?
19X6	?	?	84,000	350,000	?
19X7	?	?	96,000	384,000	?
19X8	?	?	105,000	455,000	?

(a) Complete the missing items for 19X2 through 19X4.

(b) Complete the missing items for 19X5.

(c) Complete the missing items for 19X6.

(d) Complete the missing items for 19X7.

(e) Complete the missing items for 19X8.

(f) Prepare a schedule showing the remaining inventory levels at the end of 19X8 at both base year costs and dollar-value LIFO costs. Identify each level by its cost year.

Preparer Problems

PP 8.1   Prepare journal entries for the following events. The firm uses temporary accounts for the elements making up net purchases. a) Merchandise is purchased at an invoice cost of $50,000. b) Defective merchandise invoiced at $4,000 is returned. c) A freight bill for $5,000 of transportation in is received. d) Accounts payable of $46,000 are settled, taking a purchase discount and paying only $45,080.

PP 8.2   Assume that the events in PP 8.1 above were the only elements of net purchases during a period. At the beginning of the period, inventory was $6,000. Ending inventory was determined to be $7,000. Prepare all entries to close the net purchases accounts and to record ending inventory.

PP 8.3   Prepare journal entries in good form for all non asterisk transactions and adjustments for Period 6 for Luigi's Auto Parts (SP 8.13).

PP 8.4   Prepare journal entries in good form for all transactions and adjustments for Period 6 for Irene's Sport Shop (SP 8.13).

How Much Capacity is Required to Compete?

Saul Goldman is a small West Coast wholesaler of janitorial service equipment. His industry is characterized by small local firms scattered around the country and by significantly larger firms, all currently located east of the Mississippi. Smaller firms such as Saul's average an annual sales volume of approximately $750,000. The larger firms average annual sales of about $8 million. Saul has been very successful, and is considering expanding his business and moving into the "big leagues." He understands that to compete successfully with the "majors" he would need to match their much larger investment in warehouse space and specially built material-handling equipment. He believes that with his knowledge of the business he could succeed as a large West Coast firm. One of the many things he needs to determine, before making a decision to proceed, is the actual capacity required to be a major wholesaler in his field. Saul needs to estimate:

- The total dollars of required investment in capacity assets if all were purchased at the same time, and

- The "age mix" of assets on hand at any time in a typical established firm.[1]

Saul has operating income data and balance sheets, abbreviated to highlight long-lived assets, for two of the major firms: Smith and Jones. This information is given in Exhibit 9.1. Saul is alarmed at the apparent disparity in capacity between these two firms. Study the data given for the Smith and Jones companies. As a first approximation, what would you recommend to Saul Goldman as the minimum investment in capacity assets required to support an $8-million sales volume? Are all long-lived assets being used reported on the balance sheet? How could you explain the disparity in amounts shown for the two firms? What is the accountant's intention in reporting long-lived assets; that is, what is reported and how is it measured? These issues will be discussed in this chapter.

Objectives of Long-Lived Asset Reporting

The accountant's objective in reporting long-lived assets is to disclose all of those properties or rights which:

- Were acquired in an exchange transaction and are owned or effectively controlled by the entity;

- Have demonstrable future usefulness or benefit to the firm extending beyond one year; and

- Can be measured with reasonable objectivity.

---

[1] Capacity assets have different useful lives. At any given point, a firm will have a mix of assets— with some near replacement, some partially through their useful life, and other relatively new.

Exhibit 9.1

SMITH COMPANY AND JONES COMPANY

Selected Data from Balance Sheets as of 12/31/X8 and from Income Statements for the year ending 12/31/X8 (000 omitted)

	SMITH	JONES
Net working capital	$ 400	$ 405
Land	100	50
Buildings	375	180
Less accumulated depreciation, Bldgs	(175)	(84)
Equipment	725	360
Less accumulated depreciation, Equip.	(425)	(211)
Property under capital lease	0	160
Less accumulated depreciation, Capital lease	0	(10)
Total Assets	$ 1,000	$ 850
Noncurrent mortgage notes	$ 350	$ 170
Noncurrent capital lease obligations	0	130
Total Long-Term Debt	$ 350	$ 300
Owner's Equity	650	550
Total Equities	$ 1,000	$ 850
Sales	$ 7,900	$ 8,100
Cost of goods sold	(4,740)	(4,860)
Depreciation	(95)	(42)
Rent and amortization	0	(69)
Interest	(31)	(15)
Other operating expenses	(2,644)	(2,784)
Income from operations	$ 390	$ 330

The term "**exchange transactions**," includes, in addition to those purchased, self-constructed assets. It also includes assets donated to the firm. The exchange transaction requirement specifically excludes intangibles (ideas or methods) acquired fortuitously or generated within the firm, and "value" increases resulting from such exogenous (external to the firm) events as inflation. Inflation is only recognized in the primary financial statements when it has been realized as a result of an exchange transaction (sale) with an outsider.

Recall from Chapter 2 that a firm's self-generated goodwill (as distinct from goodwill acquired in the process of purchasing another business) can not be recognized and reported. Self-generated goodwill, like future benefits from research and development, cannot be measured or verified with reasonable objectivity. If such items were to be included as assets, it could result in an unreasonable manipulation of financial data. The exchange transaction test also effectively excludes those items neither owned nor effectively controlled—those that are temporarily held on consignment or under simple operating lease agreements.

The term "capacity assets" will be used in this chapter to cover all property, plant, and equipment and all intangible and other assets that appear on a balance sheet. Even though intangible assets represent the right of use rather than physical resources possessed, they still provide the capacity or the capability to do business. A franchise or a patent would be a good example of an intangible capacity asset. By definition, capacity assets are nonmonetary, and may be viewed as collections of future benefits or services that have been acquired at a particular cost.

Capacity Assets Reported

In conformance with GAAP, the long-lived asset classification includes all assets owned or controlled by the firm which, when they were acquired, had an objectively measured future usefulness beyond one year.[2]

Examples of capacity assets that are normally included in the balance sheet are:

PROPERTY, PLANT, AND EQUIPMENT:

Land
Buildings
Equipment
Machinery
Vehicles
Furniture and fixtures
Properties held under capital lease

INTANGIBLE AND OTHER:

Leasehold improvements
Patents
Copyrights
Franchises
Goodwill
Deferred charges

Items held under capital lease are classified along with property, plant, and equipment, because leased items are effectively controlled (or essentially owned except for legal title), even though the lease grants intangible rights of use. Also note that deferred charges provide future rights in that, like prepaid items, they represent advanced payments made for services that otherwise would have to be purchased in future periods.

---

[2] This statement refers to all capacity assets that are material in amount. Following the principle of materiality, accountants would not normally record, and depreciate items such as wastebaskets and staplers, even though they have future value and provide capacity. Such immaterial items would normally be charged off to supplies expense when acquired, or initially recorded under supplies and expensed when used.

Capacity Assets Not Reported

As first discussed in Chapter 2, a firm may have many valuable resources which are not reported as assets by accountants. These **unreported assets** may be significant and essential to the firm's successful operation. Unreported assets involve intangible future benefits. They are omitted because their future benefits are uncertain or contingent on future events (for example, assets not presently owned or effectively controlled by the firm could be withdrawn by their owner); or because the benefits are not readily measurable. Examples of unreported assets include:

- Rights to use tangible assets under executory operating lease agreements where the item may be currently in the firm's possession, but the duration of future possession (and therefore the amount of benefit) is uncertain;

- Benefits accruing to the firm as a result of past expenditures for public relations, advertising, employee hiring and training, and development of new products and processes (results of research and development).

Off-Balance-Sheet Financing

Often when a tangible asset is owned by a firm, it must be financed, that is, acquired in exchange for a down payment and a long-term loan. In such a situation, the firm's balance sheet would reveal less liquidity and less remaining debt capacity as the result of the purchase. The balance sheet would disclose the new asset and a greater amount of long-term debt (higher long-term debt ratio). The accountant's definition of an asset was formerly restricted to something legally owned. "Effectively controlled" was not part of the definition. In recent years the practice of acquiring assets under a long-term noncancellable lease, with the lease term often covering the entire useful life of the asset, has become prevalent. Some firms may have entered into these capital leases and treated them as executory agreements to appear more liquid and to escape reporting the long-term obligation. Both the asset and the financing were excluded from the balance sheet; hence the term **off-balance-sheet financing.**

GAAP now requires long-term leases, which are, in substance, purchases, be included in the balance sheet. The asset that is effectively controlled is classified, along with property, plant, and equipment in an account called "**Properties held under capital lease.**" The associated liability is reported as "Obligations under capital leases." Capital leases will be discussed in more detail in Chapter 11. Ordinary leases which are not, in substance, purchases, are known as **operating leases.** Operating leases, since they are executory and do not represent effective control over the asset, are not reported in the balance sheet as either assets or as future obligations. For operating leases, only lease payments already earned by the lessor (no longer executory), and not yet paid by the lessee, will be reported as liabilities on the lessee's balance sheet.

Capacity Information Provided

Returning to Saul Goldman's analysis with respect to the Smith and Jones companies, one question was "Are all long-lived assets being used by a firm reported on the balance sheet?" What would you tell Saul to assist him in his analysis? Saul should realize that many essential intangible assets may be present but not reported by either firm. Saul could reasonably assume that the same intangibles would be omitted from both statements, and therefore not be a source of disparity. Saul was also concerned about the different totals for capacity assets appearing for the two firms when they both had essentially the same volume of business (sales). Is this difference important? How can you explain it? The book values, or original cost less depreciation and amortization, of Smith's and Jones' capacity assets were $600,000 and $445,000 respectively. Excluding the effect of accumulated depreciation, the totals would be $1,200,000 and $750,000. Smith appears to have almost twice the capacity assets of Jones. Several factors could contribute to this difference. Smith could have a significant amount of unused capacity. Smith might be able to handle $13 million of sales with no additional capacity assets required.

There is another possibility. Jones could be leasing much of his capacity on a sufficiently short-term basis that it escapes capital-lease treatment, that is, operating leases. If this were happening, Jones' income statement would reveal significant rental expense. Examine Exhibit 9.1. What would be a reasonable assumption for Saul to make regarding the disparity? Note that Jones has very high rental and amortization expense. Probably only a portion of this would relate to property under capital lease, since annual rental is $69,000 and the entire future capital-lease obligation is only $130,000. Also note that the sum of Jones' annual expenses related to capacity assets (depreciation, rent, amortization, and interest) is $126,000, which is identical to Smith's similar expenses. In essence rental and amortization costs substitute for depreciation expenses. Later you will see how different depreciation methods could make such a comparison misleading. But even then, there appears definite evidence that the disparity results from an ownership-versus-rental difference in practice, and not from significantly differing capacities.

Assuming both Jones and Smith are representative, can Saul use the reported amounts as an indication of the investment required? What do the reported amounts represent? Do all these amounts represent capital requirements for starting a business?

Initial Valuation of Capacity Assets

GAAP require that capacity assets be initially recorded at their fair market value at the date of acquisition. The initial valuation would include all reasonable and necessary costs involved in getting the asset into place and ready to provide service. What the accountant uses as evidence of these costs depends upon how the asset is acquired and from whom. Many capacity assets are acquired from nonrelated parties as a result of an expenditure. An expenditure involves an outflow of monetary items—cash, or a commitment to pay cash (new debt)—in exchange for goods or services received. If the item received has an expected useful life extending beyond the current accounting period, it is **capitalized**, or recorded as an asset. If not, then the expenditure results in an expense. When capacity assets are acquired as a result of an expenditure involving nonrelated parties, the original cost or historical cost, is considered adequate evidence of the fair market value and provides the initial basis for valuation.

As an example of costs included in initial asset valuation, assume that a manufacturer had the following expenditures related to putting a new machine "on line" in the factory:

$130,000	Invoice cost from machine-tool manufacturer,
2,000	Cost of insurance and trucking to bring machine to plant,
2,500	Contractor's cost for concrete foundation and electrical hookup,
500	Installation and tune-up,
1,000	Repair damage caused at the time of installation.
800	Cost of training machine operator.

What would be the initial capitalized cost of this asset? $135,000 would be recorded as the fair value of all reasonable and necessary costs to place this equipment in service. The $1,000 of repair and $800 of training would be expensed in the current period, because they were not reasonable and necessary costs of acquiring the asset.

Another example involves the acquisition of land with an old building to be razed to make room for a new building. Other expenditures incurred prior to the date of the new building completion are also listed:

Purchase price of land and old building	$200,000
Finder's fee paid to individual locating property and negotiating purchase	2,000
Cost of razing old building (net of salvage proceeds)	40,000
Cost of constructing new building	600,000
Construction insurance on new building during construction	6,000
Interest costs on construction financing	30,000
Costs of installing drainage tiles around building	20,000
Costs of paving and grading new parking lot	50,000
Costs of landscaping grounds	15,000

How much of these costs should be capitalized as assets under property and equipment, and what portion should be classified under land (nondepreciable) and under buildings (depreciable)? You should check your understanding of the concepts involved by attempting to answer both questions before reading the next paragraph.

In this example, all of the costs listed are properly capitalized as long-lived assets—they all involve costs necessary to acquire and prepare the assets for use.

Land should reflect $327,000 of costs. All of these items were necessary to acquire the land and to prepare it for intended use.[3] The remaining $636,000 of cost should be capitalized under buildings as necessary to complete the new building ready for use. Note that once the building was ready for use, further costs of insurance, interest, upkeep of landscaping, and so forth would all thereafter be treated as current operating expenses.

Exhibit 9.2

Initial Valuation of Assets

Land	
Purchase price of land and building	$200,000
Finders Fee	2,000
Net cost of razing old building	40,000
Drainage tiles	20,000
New parking lot paving and grading	50,000
Landscaping	15,000
	$327,000

Building	
Construction cost	$600,000
Insurance during construction	6,000
Interest on financing during construction	30,000
	$636,000

When a firm constructs its own asset, the insurance covering the period while the asset is under construction may also be capitalized as part of the asset's cost. The logic of GAAP is consistent. All costs (including interest costs on borrowed funds) which are directly related to acquiring and preparing an asset for use are properly capitalized into the asset's original cost.

Capacity Assets Acquired in Nonmonetary Exchanges

Capacity assets may be acquired for nonmonetary consideration. They may be contributed (invested) by the owner. They may be donated as a gift (rare), or by government to induce activity involving a desired product or service (environmental or health research, defense) or to encourage development at a particular geographic location. Where there is an exchange, and the item given up has a readily determinable **fair market value** (e.g., stock in a publicly traded corporation), the value of the item exchanged is assumed to indicate the value of the asset acquired. In others situations, additional evidence of fair market value, such as a professional appraisal, is required.

---

[3] In another situation where land and a building were acquired with the building to be used, the initial cost plus any finder's fee or commission would be allocated between land and building on the basis of FMV appraisals at the time of acquisition. See Basket Purchases.

The exchange of nonmonetary assets is divided into two categories: similar and dissimilar. A **dissimilar exchange** can be defined as an asset exchanged for another where the use of the assets is different. An exchange of equipment for a building would be considered dissimilar since the building would provide a different purpose in the firm's operations. Any gain or loss on the dissimilar exchange is recognized immediately. The new asset is valued at the fair market value (FMV) of the old or new asset, whichever is easier to verify. It is important to recognize that the "sticker price" or the price on the sales contract is not necessarily market value. If FMV cannot be determined, book value of the old asset is used.

Exhibit 9.3

Exchange of Dissimilar Assets				
Fair Market Value	$ 200	$ 185	?	$ 160
Book value of old asset	190	190	190	190
Gain or (loss)	$ 10	$ (5)	$ 0	$ (30)
Cash payment (boot)	0	0	0	15
Valuation of Asset	$ 200	$ 185	$ 190	$ 175

The **exchange of similar monetary assets** is treated differently. Since the new cost is considered a continuation of the old asset, gains will be not be reported.[4] The gain is presumed to reflect excessive past depreciation on the old asset. Although these gains will be deferred, losses are always reported immediately.[5] The loss represents a "catch up" depreciation.

Frequently an asset is acquired in exchange for another asset plus an additional payment called "**boot**." Boot may be a cash payment, the incurrence of a new liability, or a combination of both. In the case of a dissimilar exchange, the boot is added to the fair market value of the old asset to determine the valuation of the new asset.

Basket Purchase

Assets may be acquired as part of a **basket purchase**. Usually land and any building on it are sold together at one price. Accountants must divide or allocate the cost between two different accounts, since one is depreciated and the other is not (unless only a single asset survives as in the earlier example). An appraisal of or the assets would be required as a

---

[4] An exception to this rule is applied when cash is received rather than paid. In this case a portion of the asset is considered sold rather than exchanged. A partial gain then will be recognized using the following formula: Cash Received divided by (Cash Received + FMV of New Asset) times the Total Gain = Recognized Gain.

[5] Although the loss must be reported on the financial statements under GAAP, the losses are deferred for income taxes.

basis for the division of the "basket." Two or more assets with different useful lives but acquired together would be another example of a basket purchase requiring division.

For example, if land and building are acquired for $200,000, an appraisal would be made on the assets to determine how to allocate the $200,000 purchase price.

Exhibit 9.4

BASKET PURCHASE VALUATION

	Land Appraisal	Building Appraisal	Total
Situation A	$120,000	$80,000	$200,000
Situation B	154,000	66,000	220,000

$$\frac{\text{Asset Appraisal}}{\text{Total appraisals}} \times \text{Purchase Price} = \text{Initial Asset Valuation}$$

$$\text{Land} \quad \frac{\$154,000}{\$220,000} \times \$200,000 = \$140,000$$

$$\text{Building} \quad \frac{\$66,000}{\$220,000} \times \$200,000 = \underline{60,000}$$
$$\underline{\$200,000}$$

Situation A is simple since the total of the two appraisals equal the purchase price. Land should be recorded at $120,000 and Buildings at $80,000. Situation B is more complicated. the two appraisals do not equal the purchase price. The assets should be recorded at $140,000 for land and $60,000 for Buildings.

Apportionment of related acquisition costs can be extended to two other common situations. In the case where a "finder's fee" or commission is paid to an agent who locates an eventually acquired property, the fee or commission may properly be apportioned between the land and building costs.

Betterments

Additional reported capacity assets can result from **betterments**, or improvements, to existing assets. Ordinary repairs and maintenance to tangible capacity assets are treated as maintenance expense and are not capitalized. However, adding a new floor or wing to a building at a cost of $150,000 could hardly be considered maintenance or repair. The $150,000 would properly be capitalized in the building account. The cost of an improvement that increases the capacity or usefulness of an asset is usually added to the asset account.

However, some improvements merely prolong or extend the useful life of an asset without necessarily increasing its usefulness. For example, if your firm incurred an $4,800 charge for truck overhaul, part of which ($3,800) involved installation of a new engine. The new engine would extend the previously anticipated useful life of the truck to the firm to three years. Would you still expense the entire $4,800? Assuming materiality in this situation, accountants would expense only $1,000 and would capitalize $3,800 as a betterment. In this situation, the individual asset's capacity or usefulness has not been increased, only its useful life. Therefore, rather that add the $3,800 to the fixed-asset account, accountants would subtract it from accumulated depreciation:

Before betterment:	Truck	$10,000
	Accumulated depreciation	(6,000)
After betterment:	Truck	$10,000
	Accumulated depreciation	(2,200)

Note that under either approach, the book value of the truck is increased by the $3,800 cost of the betterment. Regardless of the method used for recording the betterment, a new depreciation schedule would be made for the remaining useful life of the asset:

Adjusted cost	$ 10,000
less accumulated depreciation	2,200
Book value	$ 7,800
less new salvage value	300
Remaining depreciable base	$ 7,500

$$\frac{\$7,500}{3 \text{ years*}} = \$2,500 \text{ depreciation per year}$$

* Remaining useful life

Cost Expirations of Capacity Assets

All capacity assets, except for land, are subject to wear and tear and obsolescence. As described in earlier chapters, the process of systematically allocating the expiration of cost value to the years of the asset's useful life is known as depreciation for tangible assets, and amortization for intangible and other assets. To provide more complete information relating to capacity assets, depreciation is accumulated in a separate valuation or contra-asset account shown on the balance sheet immediately beneath the related asset. Book value of a depreciable asset is the asset's reported initial value less its accumulated depreciation.

Annual amortization charges, rather than being reported in a separate amortization account, directly reduce the unamortized balance of the intangible asset. Such accounts therefore report current book value as a single figure.

Useful Life and Salvage Value

The net amount anticipated to be recovered in dollars upon disposition of the asset is known as **salvage value**. Other terms used synonymously by accountants are "residual value" or "scrap value."[6]

The period of time over which the total cost expiration occurs—the time elapsing from the date on which the asset is first placed in use until its final disposition—is referred to as its expected **useful life**, or service life. Note that useful life refers to the usefulness to the firm, that is, how long the company expects to use the asset. It does not refer to the total life of the asset to all users. The overall life of the asset itself may be many years greater than its useful life to the firm.

Are you clear on the intention of accountants with respect to depreciation and amortization? There is no intention to adjust the book value of capacity assets to reflect current market value. The intention is to match or to allocate the unrecoverable costs to the periods in which the related benefits (revenues) occur. Admittedly, such allocations are arbitrary. They represent the accountant's best judgement.

Alternative Allocation Methods

Up to this point, you have been introduced only to straight-line depreciation as one of the allocation methods acceptable under GAAP. The accountant's choice of straight-line theoretically implies that the asset's usefulness or benefits will be equal in each period and that directly associated costs (fuel and maintenance costs) will also be equal. On the other hand, the use of straight-line depreciation could theoretically imply that overall usefulness was increasing if related costs, and therefore total costs, were increasing over time.[7] Many situations do not fit either of these two patterns; GAAP therefore provides for alternatives. GAAP permits any systematic and rational method considered appropriate for the situation so long as it is consistently used. Three commonly used allocation methods, are discussed as alternatives to the straight-line method of depreciation: Productive Method, Sum-of-the-Years Digits, and Declining Balance.

Straight-Line Depreciation

As previously discussed, **straight-line depreciation** produces an equal depreciation allocation in each period of the asset's useful life. Exhibit 9.5 illustrates the depreciation schedule for a truck with a useful life of 5 years costing $85,000 and a salvage value of

---

[6] The use of the word "value" is unfortunate. Net recovered dollars would be more explicit.

[7] Remember that accountants try to match expenses with the revenues generated. Unless the asset's usefulness were actually increasing, to use straight-line depreciation when operating and repair costs were increasing over time might be considered misleading and a violation of the matching principle.

$10,000. Since the firm wants to produce annual statements, we will depreciate the truck over five periods. If the firm was making quarterly statements, we would depreciate the truck over twenty quarters (5 years x 4 quarters per year), and the quarterly depreciation would be $3,750.

Exhibit 9.5

Straight-Line Depreciation

Year	Depreciation Expense	Accumulated Depreciation	Book value End of Year
1	$15,000	$15,000	$70,000
2	15,000	30,000	55,000
3	15,000	45,000	40,000
4	15,000	60,000	25,000
5	15,000	75,000	10,000

$$\frac{\text{Cost - salvage value}}{\text{\# useful periods}} = \text{Depreciation per period}$$

$$\frac{\$85,000 - 10,000}{5 \text{ years}} = \$15,000 \text{ depreciation per year}$$

Units-of-Production Method

A realistic basis for depreciation would be to match cost expiration with usage. For example, a truck's useful life may be estimated as 200,000 miles rather than a specific number of years. Each year a check of the odometer would indicate the number of miles driven which could then be converted to the amount to be depreciated that year. This so-called **units-of-production method**, also called units-of-service or productive-output method, while appealing as logical, is not often used. Most assets do not have usage meters that are attached or readily attachable. Useful life estimation, in terms of usage or service output units, is difficult. Finally, the operation of this method could cost more than the benefit of the more precise information. Except for factory assets for manufacturers, depreciation is a period cost. Period costs are those charged to expense in the period incurred or expired, as distinct from product or capitalized costs which are held as assets until matched with specific sales. Therefore, accountants usually associate depreciation increments with the passage of time rather than with usage.

Exhibit 9.6

Units-of-Production Depreciation

Year	Miles	x	Depreciation per mile	=	Depreciation expense	Accumulated depreciation	Book Value end of year
1	35,000		$0.375		$13,125	$13,125	$71,875
2	55,000		$0.375		20,625	33,750	51,250
3	50,000		$0.375		18,750	52,500	32,500
4	45,000		$0.375		16,875	69,375	15,625
5	15,000		$0.375		5,625	75,000	10,000

$$\frac{\text{Cost - Salvage value}}{\text{Estimated useful life in miles}} = \text{Depreciation per mile}$$

$$\frac{\$85,000 - \$10,000}{200,000 \text{ miles}} = \$0.375 \text{ depreciation per mile}$$

Accelerated Depreciation

Where the usefulness of an asset is expected to decrease over time, straight-line or production method allocation might be inappropriate. And even if benefits are uniform, the costs of operation, especially repair and maintenance costs, often increase dramatically as an asset gets older. Such situations indicate the desirability of allocating more depreciation in the early years and less in the later years, for better overall cost matching. The combined effect of the related expenses would then more uniformly match the uniform benefits. Any method where more depreciation expense is allocated in the early years of useful life and less in the later years is known as an **"accelerated" depreciation method.**[8]

Sum-of-the-Years' Digits Method

One of the two more common variations of accelerated depreciation is known as the **"sum-of-the-years' digits"** (or SYD) method. To understand this method, imagine an asset with a five-year life and $75,000 to be depreciated over those five years. First, obtain the sum of the digits of the useful life. Second, divide the total amount to be depreciated ($75,000) by this sum (15) to find "depreciation per unit"—$5,000 each, in this example. Then, each year, depreciate an amount equal to the depreciation unit times the years' digit. The years' digits is the number of periods left to depreciate (or the number of years in inverse order).

---

[8] Accelerated depreciation is acceptable for tax purposes regardless of the pattern of other costs and benefits. It is almost always desirable to take advantage of accelerated depreciation for tax purposes. It is not necessary or even desirable that depreciation for financial reporting purposes be the same as tax depreciation.

Exhibit 9.7

Sum-of-the-Years' Digits Depreciation

Year	Years remaining	Depreciation x per digit =	Depreciation expense	Accumulated depreciation	Book Value end year
1	5	$5,000	$25,000	$25,000	$60,000
2	4	5,000	20,000	45,000	40,000
3	3	5,000	15,000	60,000	25,000
4	2	5,000	10,000	70,000	15,000
5	1	5,000	5,000	75,000	10,000

Sum of years' digits = 1 + 2+ 3 + 4+ 5 = 15

or

$$\frac{n(n+1)}{2} = \frac{5(5+1)}{2} = 15$$

$$\frac{Cost - salvage\ value}{Sum\text{-}of\text{-}years'\ digits} = Depreciation\ per\ digit$$

$$\frac{\$85,000 - \$10,000}{15} = \$5,000\ depreciation\ per\ digit$$

Assume, as shown in Exhibit 9.7, that the asset had originally cost $55,000 and had an expected salvage value of $10,000 after five years of use. The amount to be depreciated would be $45,000. Book value after five years following the SYD method shown above would be $10,000. The asset would then be fully depreciated. Have you noticed in Exhibits 9.5, 9.6, and 9.7 that regardless of depreciation method used, when the asset is fully depreciated, that the book value equals salvage value?

Declining-Balance Method

Another commonly used accelerated-depreciation method is known as **declining-balance** depreciation. Under this method, a fixed percentage rate is applied each year to the book value of the asset at the beginning of the year. In the final year, sufficient depreciation is taken to reduce the book value to, but not below, salvage value and the process is terminated. The fixed percentage rate may be calculated by a formula[9] or arbitrarily

---

[9] This depreciation rate is not used often, because it is not acceptable for tax purposes.

$$Depreciation\ rate\ (\%) = \sqrt[n]{\frac{Salvage\ Value}{Acquistion\ Cost}} \times 100,\ where\ n = years\ of\ useful\ life.$$

chosen. When the rate is arbitrarily chosen, declining-balance depreciation ignores salvage value until the final year when the amount of depreciation is selected to make book value equal salvage value. In contrast to straight-line and SYD the amount of declining-balance depreciation is not determined on the basis of the amount to be depreciated (initial book value less salvage value). Instead it is calculated on the declining book value.

A common arbitrary rate, often also used for certain assets for tax purposes, is 200 percent of the straight-line rate, or **double-declining-balance** (or DDB). DDB is one of a great number of different declining balance methods. DDB is merely a declining-balance method using a 200 percent rate. An example of the application of double-declining balance is shown in Exhibit 9.8 for an asset which cost $55,000. Assume the useful life is five years, and the estimated salvage value is $10,000. The straight-line rate would be 20 percent. Therefore the double-declining rate would be 40 percent.

Exhibit 9.8

Double-Declining-Balance Depreciation

Year	Book Value Begin Year	x	Rate	Depreciation = Expense	Accumulated Depreciation	Book Value End Year
1	$85,000		0.4	34,000	34,000	51,000
2	51,000		0.4	20,400	54,400	30,600
3	30,600		0.4	12,240	66,640	18,360
4	18,360		0.4	7,344	73,984	11,016
5	11,016	–	10,000	1,016*	75,000	10,000

$$\frac{1}{\text{\# of useful periods}} \times 200\% = 1/5 \times 2 = 0.4 \text{ Rate}$$

* Note that, in the final year of useful life, depreciation is the amount necessary to reduce book value to salvage value.

Income Effect of Different Methods

Just as LIFO and FIFO cause comparability problems between firms electing the different methods, straight-line and accelerated depreciation cause similar difficulties. Compared with a firm which has elected straight-line depreciation, another firm which has elected an accelerated method would have greater depreciation expense in the early years of the asset's useful life and less in the last few years. The comparison in Exhibit 9.9 assumes that each firm acquires assets costing $85,000 with a five-year useful life and $10,000 salvage value; it also assumes that each firm's income before depreciation equaled $60,000 each year.

Exhibit 9.9

Income Statement Effect of Depreciation Methods

	FIRM A (Straight-line)		FIRM B (Years' digits)		FIRM C (Double-declining)	
Year	Depr. expense	Operating income	Depr. expense	Operating income	Depr. expense	Operating income
1	$15,000	$45,000	$25,000	$35,000	$34,000	$26,000
2	15,000	45,000	20,000	40,000	20,400	39,600
3	15,000	45,000	15,000	45,000	12,240	47,760
4	15,000	45,000	10,000	50,000	7,344	52,656
5	15,000	45,000	5,000	55,000	1,016	58,984

Note that for the first two years, both accelerated methods result in reported income being less than under straight-line. And note that, even though the firms are actually experiencing constant profits, under accelerated-depreciation methods, two are reporting substantially increased profits each successive year.[10]

In theory, a firm would not elect accelerated depreciation with all other revenues and expenses constant. In practice, GAAP allow it. Also one method could have been elected in different circumstances in the past, and continued into the present, following the GAAP principle of consistency. Can you see where a comparison of firms' performance, when one is using straight-line depreciation and the others accelerated methods, might lead to disastrously incorrect conclusions?

The user of financial statements must be careful not to accept reported income comparisons between two companies, unless they are both using the same depreciation and amortization methods. The balance sheet footnotes disclose the method(s) being used.

Amortization of Intangibles

Although the foregoing discussion and examples have focused on depreciating tangible fixed assets, the information is equally applicable to intangible assets. Intangible assets can be very significant in amount and income statement effect. Any of the various methods of depreciation may be used for amortizing capital leases and other intangible assets. The only difference from depreciation is that amortization is not reported in a contra-asset account for "accumulated amortization." Instead, amortization is generally subtracted each year directly from the beginning unamortized balance of the asset. The balance reported therefore represents current book value rather than original cost.

---

[10] This difference is only extreme when a firm has mostly new assets. Where some of a firm's assets are being replaced each year, high early years' depreciation offsets low later years' depreciation on older assets and the difference between accelerated and straight-line depreciation for all assets together may be minimal.

Depletion

Recall from earlier discussions that land or real property is never depreciated or amortized, since land itself never decreases in value or usefulness. However, in those cases where natural resources are permanently removed from the land—ore is mined; rock, sand, or gravel is quarried, and so forth, the future usefulness or resale value of the land is often impaired. The value of the land is separated from the value of the natural resources and the natural resources are treated as "**wasting assets.**"

Where natural resources are treated as a wasting asset, the book value is systematically reduced in a manner very similar to depreciation on a units-of-production or service-life basis. The incremental reduction of wasting assets each year is known as **depletion** or depletion expense. Depletion per unit of natural resources is calculated based on an estimate of total estimated units to be removed. Total depletion is then allocated each year in proportion to the quantity of resources extracted via the use of an accumulated depletion contra-asset account and also a charge to depletion expense in the same manner as for depreciation.

To illustrate depletion, assume a firm acquired land for $250,000 with $200,000 of the price representing the value of 800,000 tons of minerals expected to be extracted. If 40,000 tons of mineral were removed and sold in the first year, depletion expense of $10,000 (five percent of $200,000) would be recorded. Land would then be valued at $50,000 and minerals at $190,000. Note that depletion for financial accounting purposes reflects cost expiration and is calculated using the production method.[11]

If the minerals extracted during the year are not all sold, a portion of the depletion will be capitalized into minerals inventory. Of the 40,000 tons mined, if only 35,000 tons were sold, $1,250 [(5,000 ÷ 40,000) x $10,000] would be capitalized in inventory and the remaining $8,750 [(35,000 ÷ 40,000) x $10,000] would be expensed for depletion.

Group and Composite Depreciation

Companies may find it expedient to account for certain capacity assets on a **group** (similar items) or **composite** (dissimilar items) basis. Group or composite depreciation or amortization is merely a process where a number of assets are treated collectively as if they were a single unit. A weighted-average useful life based on cost times life of the individual assets is used to determine depreciation for the entire lot.

The advantage of using either the group or composite methods is twofold. Depreciation records are simplified, and the methods allow deferral on gains or losses on disposal of assets within the group. Any resultant gain or loss is treated as an adjustment to the accumulated depreciation account.

---

[11] Tax depletion is based upon a percentage of gross income derived from extractive operations; it may accumulate far beyond asset cost; and it is beyond the scope of this text.

Change of Accounting Estimate

Once initial estimates of useful life and salvage value have been made, consistency does not require that they be adhered to blindly if subsequent events indicate that they are incorrect. When new information indicates that the original estimates are incorrect, the estimates are revised for current and subsequent years. Note that accountants do not attempt to rewrite history. If the useful life is extended over the original estimate, they will prorate remaining depreciation over the new remaining life. Similarly, revised depreciation amounts in current and subsequent years could result from a reduction of estimated useful life or a change in expected salvage value. Should an asset be **fully depreciated**—book value equals salvage value—and it turns out to have more years of useful life, no change can be made. The asset continues on the books until it is disposed of. A **change of accounting estimate** described above should be undertaken whenever the new information becomes available. A new depreciation schedule is produced and followed for the remaining useful life. Note, however, that a change in estimate should not be confused with a change in accounting method.

Change in Accounting Method

A **change in accounting method** would involve a changeover from straight-line to an accelerated depreciation method, or vice versa, for an existing asset already partially depreciated. It would also include a change from FIFO to LIFO or vice versa as discussed in Chapter 8. Consistency requires adherence to one method once adopted. Note, however, that to adopt a different depreciation method for a new depreciable asset at the time of its acquisition is not a change of method. A method change involves a switch from a method already in use for a particular asset. The reasons for making a change of method are many and almost always unique to the firm's situation at the time. A discussion of possible reasons is beyond the scope of this book. GAAP only allow for changes in infrequent cases where circumstances have clearly made an alternative method preferable. Changes in accounting method are always considered sufficiently significant to be noted in the auditor's opinion and justified in statement footnotes, together with data showing the effect of the change. The opinion, or a footnote cited in the opinion, must disclose the income effect of the change in the year of adoption. Also, any prior years' data accompanying the current financial statements must be restated (on a pro forma basis) to reflect the methods adopted.

Deferred Income Tax

Firms are allowed to use different depreciation methods for financial statements and tax returns. This difference results in different depreciation schedules and earlier recognition of depreciation in computing taxable income. The accelerated portion of the depreciation is in effect only a postponement of income taxes (assuming tax rates remain the same) since more taxes are paid in later years when the depreciation tax deduction is smaller. GAAP require provision for income taxes to be accrued on the income statement distinguishing the current from the deferred portion.[12]

The tax accrued but not currently payable—the amount of tax postponed—is recorded as a long-term debt on the balance sheet and identified as Deferred Income Taxes.[13] In the later years of the asset's useful life when the current tax liability is greater than the current year's tax provision, the difference will represent a payment of postponed taxes and deferred income taxes will be correspondingly reduced.

Since the difference in timing of depreciation expense recognition between financial statements and tax returns is only one of the timing differences leading to deferred income tax, the subject together with illustrations of appropriate accounting entries will be covered as a separate topic in this book. For now you need only be aware that the use of different depreciation methods and different estimated useful lives between financial statements and tax returns is allowable, that such differences can lead to postponement of tax payments, and that postponed taxes are shown as a deferred income tax liability on the balance sheet.

Disposition of Capacity Assets

To complete your general understanding of capacity assets, there is one further area to be introduced—disposition of capacity assets. A tangible asset continues to be disclosed on the balance sheet until it is disposed of, even if fully depreciated. When disposition occurs, depreciation is first updated to the date of disposition. This is necessary, since ordinarily depreciation on all assets is updated only at the close of the period, when statements are to be prepared.

The updated book value is then removed from the accounts (both the entire asset cost and its related accumulated depreciation) and the salvage-value inflow is recorded. In a sense, this is a simple exchange of assets, except that rarely is an asset sold for precisely its book value. If salvage value exceeds book value, total assets increase. Owner's equity is therefore increased through a gain on disposition. Conversely, a loss on disposition is recorded as a loss. Note that gains and losses on disposition of long-lived assets are operating items and are not considered extraordinary.

Intangible assets are disclosed on the balance sheet until their unamortized cost is reduced to zero, or until they are disposed of, whichever occurs first. Disposal of intangible assets follows the same steps as for tangible assets.

Consider the following illustration of equipment disposition. The original cost of the equipment was $60,000 and it has been depreciated at a rate of $6,000 per year. At the beginning of the current year, $36,000 of depreciation has been accumulated. It is sold for $22,000 on July 1 (transaction 2). An additional $3,000 representing one-half of a year's depreciation is first recorded and charged to depreciation expense (adjustment 1). Accumu-

---

[12] FASB Statement No. 96 requires adjustments to deferred taxes for future rate changes.

[13] If the reversal of the tax postponement is within one year, the debt would be a current liability.

lated depreciation is now $39,000 and updated book value is $21,000. There would be a gain on disposition of $1,000. Balance Sheet Diagram 9.1 shows the effects of this transaction and adjustment.

DIAGRAM 9.1

Effect of Long-Lived Asset Disposition
(b indicates beginning balance)

Current Assets:		Current Liabilities:
Cash	+ $22,000 (2)	
		Long-Term Debt:
Long-Lived Assets:		**Owners' Equity:**
Equipment	$60,000 (b)	
	– 60,000 (2)	Income
		– 3,000 (1)
Accum. depr.	(36,000)(b)	+ 1,000 (2)
	– 3,000 (1)	
	+ 39,000 (2)	

Another example involves an intangible asset—a patent—with an original cost of $51,000 that was being amortized equally over the patent's 17-year useful life. At the beginning of the current year, the patent had been amortized down to $21,000. It was sold at the end of April for $17,500. An adjustment is made to reflect four month's amortization of $1,000. Then the sale is recorded indicating a loss on dispositions of $2,500. Balance Sheet Diagram 9.2 shows the effects of the adjustment and the transaction.

DIAGRAM 9.2

Effect of Intangible Asset Disposition
(b indicates beginning balance)

Current Assets:		Current Liabilities:
Cash	+ $17,500 (2)	
		Long-Term Debt:
Long-Lived Assets:		**Owners' Equity:**
Patent	$21,000 (b)	
	– 1,000 (1)	Income
	– 20,000 (2)	– 1,000 (1)
		– 2,500 (2)

Limitations of Balance Sheet Information

Have you forgotten Saul Goldman? Saul still wants to know how much investment in capacity assets appears to be required for an $8-million-volume level. Turn back to Exhibit 9.1. Assuming Smith does not have excess capacity and is a representative firm, what can you tell Saul? How reliable would your estimate be in terms of current cost? Would you estimate have been any more or less reliable had one of the material capacity assets been an intangible asset?

Since the original cost information for all of Smith's reported capacity assets is disclosed, you could tell Saul, "Approximately $1,2000,000 of capacity assets would be required," Note that you cannot tell him:

- Whether the assets were new or used when purchased, or

- How recent, and therefore relevant in an inflationary economy, these figures are.

Even with footnote information on depreciation methods employed, you have no information on useful lives or salvage values. "Roughly 55 percent depreciated" therefore doesn't mean much. The Saul Goldman questions were not designed to trick you. Instead, they should have focused your attention on the actual information available with respect to capacity assets. More importantly, you should be aware of the information not available and the inferences that should not be drawn.

Supplementary Information on Inflation and Changing Prices

As first mentioned in Chapter 2, GAAP encourage but do not require disclosure of supplementary information on the effects of changing prices for property, plant, and equipment.[14] Supplementary data includes:

- Property, plant, and equipment measured/valued at the lower of curent cost at the measurement date or recoverable value of the assets' remaining useful life;

- Depreciation and depletion measured/valued at the lower of current cost at the statement date; and

- Changes in current cost measurement during the year.

Current costs may be measured at the current cost of a replacement asset with the same remaining useful life. If the useful life is different, then the current cost of the replacement asset must be depreciated down to the remaining useful life of the asset owned. An alternative method would be to measure the current cost of an used asset of the same age and condition as the asset owned. Historical costs adjusted in constant purchasing power dollars may be used as a substitute for current cost as long as the difference is not material.

The precise definitions of the terms "constant dollars" and "current cost" will be discussed further in Chapter 15. In that chapter, you can also learn how these values are determined and how they might be useful to you in analyzing a firm's financial statements.

---

[14] For more precise criteria, and for amplification of the topics covered in this section, see FASB Statement No. 89, Financial Accounting Standards Board, Stamford, CT 06905, Dec., 1986.

Preparer Procedures

To accommodate transactions and adjustments presented in this chapter, the partial chart of accounts first introduced in Chapter 5 and augmented in Chapters 6 and 8 must be further expanded to include accounts for:

Exhibit 9.3

Additions to Chart of Accounts

Long-lived assets

110	Land
111	Buildings
113	Furniture and fixtures
121	Patents
123	Copyrights
124	Trademarks

Contra-assets

212	Accumulated depreciation - buildings
214	Accumulated depreciation - office furniture and fixtures

Other revenues

715	Gain on disposition of property and equipment

Other expenses

824	Loss on disposition of property and equipment
825	Loss on disposition of intangibles

You will find the accounts necessary for the preparer problems in this chapter in the chart of accounts covering all items introduced in this text at the beginning of appendix D at the back of the book.

New Transactions and Adjustments

New transactions introduced involve acquisitions of long-lived assets (other than investments, properties under capital lease, and goodwill) and dispositions of same. New adjustments merely involved depreciation and amortization of newly introduced assets. Note in the following illustrations that most transactions involving long-lived asset dispositions require compound entries (more than two accounts involved) and often concurrently involve an adjustment updating book values to the point of sale:

Building and land costing $250,000 acquired, paying $25,000 down and giving two promissory notes—one for $25,000 plus interest, maturing in six months, and one for $200,000 plus interest, maturing in ten years. The land alone was appraised at $60,000. The journal entry (without accompanying explanation) recording the acquisition would be:

	D R	C R
Land	60,000	
Buildings	190,000	
Cash		25,000
Current Notes Payable		25,000
Noncurrent Notes Payable		200,000

An attorney's bill is received for $1,000 covering legal services related to the above acquisition. The fee is to be prorated between the land and the building:

Land	240	
Buildings	760	
Accounts Payable		1,000

Annual depreciation on buildings is $30,000, on equipment $64,000, and on office furniture and fixtures $19,000:

Depreciation Expense	113,000	
Accumulated Depreciation on Buildings		30,000
Accumulated Depreciation on Equipment		64,000
Accumulated Depreciation on O.F.F.		19,000

A franchise has an unamortized cost of $64,000 on 12/31/X4. It has been previously amortized on a straight-line basis at $8,000 per year. On 9/30/X5, it is sold for $59,000:

Cash	59,000	
Amortization Expense	6,000	
Franchise		64,000
Gain on Sale of Intangible Asset		1,000

A piece of equipment costing $130,000 has a book value of $45,000 on 12/31/X8. Depreciation is on a straight-line basis at $9,000 per year. On 4/31/X9, the equipment is sold for $40,000:

Cash	40,000	
Depreciation Expense	3,000	
Accumulated Depreciation—Equipment	85,000	
Loss on Disposition of Prpt. & Equip.	2,000	
Equipment		130,000

Equipment costing $90,000 and with a book value of $25,000, together with $75,000 cash, is traded in on a similar piece of equipment:

Equipment (New)	100,000	
Accumulated Depreciation—Equipment	65,000	
Cash		75,000
Equipment (Old)		90,000

Assume in transaction 6 above that the two items of equipment were not similar and that the new equipment had a fair market value of $93,000:

Equipment (New)	93,000	
Accumulated Depreciation—Equipment	65,000	
Loss on Disposition of Equip.	7,000	
Cash		75,000
Equipment (Old)		90,000

Chapter Overview

From the material in this chapter, you should be able to:

- Describe the GAAP standards for recognition of a capacity asset, and explain why some intangible items with future benefits for the firm are not reported as assets;

- Define the standards for the initial measurement and reporting of capacity assets under different types of acquisition;

- Explain the intention of depreciation and amortization, their different applicability, and their different balance sheet presentation;

- Describe the four most common methods for systematically recording asset expiration, calculate depreciation or amortization by each method, and explain the rationale behind the choice of a particular method;

- Describe and contrast the different income effects of each alternative method and the significance of these differences to comparative statement analysis;

- Explain the information provided with respect to capacity assets on the balance sheet and cite the limitations of, and possibly inappropriate inferences from, such information;

- Describe the accounting treatment of capacity-asset dispositions, and determine the gain or loss on a given disposition;

- Explain with examples the difference between a change of accounting method and a change of accounting estimate, and give the requirements for disclosure (if any) of such changes in the financial statements.

- Briefly explain the significance of such related items as: trade-ins, basket purchases, arm's-length transactions, betterments, changes in estimates, group or composite depreciation, and deferred income taxes.

New Vocabulary and Concepts

Accelerated depreciation	Fair market value
Basket purchase	Fully depreciated
Betterment	Group depreciation
Capital leases	Off-balance-sheet financing
Capitalize	Operating leases
Change in accounting estimate	Production method
Change in accounting method	Salvage value
Composite depreciation	Sum-of-the-Years' digits method
Declining-balance method	Unreported assets
Depletion	Useful life
Double-declining-balance method	Wasting asset

• Criteria for identification as capacity asset.

• Basis for initial measurement and reporting of capacity assets.

• Objective of depreciation and amortization.

• Rationale for selecting each of four standard methods of depreciation/amortization.

• Income statement effect of each method.

• Difference between change of accounting estimate and change in accounting method.

Review Questions

1. An asset acquired by a firm and having future benefits to the firm extending beyond one year still must meet three tests or qualifications to be capitalized and reported as a capacity asset. Describe these three qualifications and the rationale for each.

2. List at least four tangible and four intangible capacity assets and explain how each meets the qualifications for asset treatment.

3. List several long-lived assets which are not measured and reported as such by accountants, and explain why each does not "qualify."

4. (a) Describe what is meant by "off-balance-sheet financing." (b) Describe a recent change in GAAP related to items previously part of off-balance-sheet financing. (c) How was the definition of an asset altered by this change?

5. (a) How does "fair market value at the time of acquisition" relate to the initial measurement and recording of nonmonetary assets? (b) Is fair market value always the same as "original cost"? (c) If not, explain the possible source of the difference and which amount is used as the initial measurement of capacity assets.

6. What is an expenditure?

7. How is the basis for measurement of and recording a new capacity asset determined when: (a) It is acquired with an expenditure? (b) It is acquired via a nonmonetary exchange? (c) It is acquired by donation? (d) It is self-constructed? (e) It is acquired as part of a basket purchase? (f) It is acquired as part of a transaction involving a trade-in? (g) It is acquired from a related party (non-arm's-length)? Give an example illustrating your reply to each question.

8. What costs are included in the initial valuation of a capacity asset?

9. What is a betterment and how is it handled by accountants?

10. Does useful life refer to the useful life of the asset? If not, to what does useful life refer?

11. A particular asset's useful life with proper care and maintenance is 18 years. The firm will not need it after seven years and will sell it to another user at that time. What is the useful life of this asset for depreciation purposes? Explain.

12. (a) Define period and product costs. (b) Explain why a wholesaler would treat merchandise purchases and capacity-asset purchases as one or the other, and why.

13. (a) Explain how you would determine the amount to be depreciated/amortized or the depreciation or amortization base for any capacity asset. (b) Would this same amount be useful for all four depreciation methods? Explain.

14. What is the difference between straight-line and accelerated depreciation?

15. Under what circumstances would straight-line depreciation be preferable to an accelerated method?

16. Under what circumstances would an accelerated method of depreciation be preferable to straight-line?

17. A firm acquires an auto costing $13,000. Salvage value is estimated at $1,000 and useful life to the firm as ten years, during which it is expected to be driven 180,000 miles. The car was driven 15,000 miles during its second year. What would second-year depreciation expense be, and why, if: (a) straight-line depreciation were being used? (b) production depreciation were being used? (c) sum-of-years' digits depreciation were being used? (d) double-declining-balance depreciation were being used?

18. (a) Does GAAP allow for changing depreciation methods once started? (b) Does GAAP allow for changing depreciation estimates once started? (c) What is the difference between depreciation methods and depreciation estimates?

19. An asset costing $6,000 with six-year life and zero salvage was being depreciated on a straight-line basis. At the end of three years it was determined that only two more years of useful life remained. Explain if, how, and why: (a) The first three years' depreciation expense and total accumulated depreciation would be modified following GAAP.

20. In the early years of useful life and in comparison with straight-line, will a firm using accelerated depreciation report higher or lower operating income, all other things being equal?

21. Why is it difficult to estimate the age of long-lived assets subject to amortization by using the balance sheet figures?

22. Why is it difficult to estimate the age of long-lived assets subject to depreciation by using the balance sheet figures?

23. Properly recording the disposition of a capacity asset may involve three steps:

    Step 1: ?

    Step 2: Estimate the asset balance (and accumulated depreciation) from the asset accounts and record the proceeds of the sale.

    Step 3: ?

    a) What are steps (1) and (3)? b) When might steps (1), or (3), or both, be unnecessary? Explain.

24. (a) What is deferred income tax? (b) How is deferred income tax related to the accounting for capacity assets?

Mini-Cases and Questions for Discussion

MC **9.1** Sam Fisher is very disturbed. "Who says consistent accounting?" he asks. "Look at these two statements! Two retailers with identical delivery trucks. I know. I sold them both to these guys less than a week apart. They cost $6,000, and would you believe it? After one year Mel's Surplus Store depreciated it by $1,000. The exclusive Maison Fifi Lingerie Shop took $2,000 depreciation the first year. How can you wear out a truck hauling around lingerie? It doesn't make sense!"

       Can you explain to Sam that higher depreciation may be perfectly logical for Maison Fifi? Obsolescence may be a more important factor than wear and tear. Fifi may need to have newer trucks to maintain its image. Discuss.

MC **9.2** Coleen Murphy is skeptical about accounting terms. "How can accountants talk about a loss on disposition of a long-lived asset?" she asks. "If they had estimated the useful life and salvage value accurately, there wouldn't be any so-called loss. Such a loss is just the accountant's estimating error, and should be considered extra depreciation that year. And the same thing applies to gains upon disposition. Take off too much depreciation, and you're bound to have a gain. It should be a reduction of depreciation, not a separate gain." Discuss.

MC **9.3** Can reported income be manipulated through choice of depreciation methods or estimates? Could hidden "reserves" of depreciation expense increases and decreases be created for use in a year when the firm wanted to report lower earnings (labor contract negotiations are going on) or higher earnings (it needs to raise more capital)? Discuss.

MC **9.4** Isn't a capital lease still an executory contract? Aren't all executory contracts off the balance sheet? Discuss.

MC **9.5** Why are general financing costs (interest) excluded in measuring and recording capacity assets? Why are cash discounts not taken (but not interest) included in the measurement of inventory? Discuss.

MC **9.6** A owns land originally costing $5,000 and on its books at that amount. It sells the land to B for the current fair market value of $25,000. a) Would the $20,000 gain be reported if B were nonrelated? b) Would the $20,000 gain be reported if B were related (a wholly owned subsidiary company)? Discuss.

MC **9.7** Refer to MC 9.6 above. A has recorded the sale and the gain. How should the following be reported by A if, during the following year: a) A repurchases the land from B (not related) for $25,000. b) B completely defaults on a $20,000 note given A as part of the original sale. A takes back the property. c) A repurchases the land from B (closely related) for $30,000. Discuss.

MC **9.8** Assume that a firm buys an asset costing $100,000 which it intends to use for five years and then resell. It estimates that, because of rapid inflation affecting this type of asset, resale value in five years will be $105,000. Should the asset be depreciated? How much? Discuss.

MC 9.9 A firm has capacity assets costing $600,000, on which it has been regularly taking $25,000 of annual depreciation. During all of 19X4, the firm was shut down by a strike. There were no 19X4 revenues. Should the 19X4 Income Statement (loss statement?) add insult to injury by recording $25,000 of depreciation expense? a) If yes, wouldn't inclusion be a violation of "matching"—shouldn't expenses be matched with revenues? b) If not, wouldn't omission be a violation of "consistency"—don't costs expire (aging and obsolescence) whether or not the asset is used? Discuss.

MC 9.10 A seasonal resort wishes to prepare interim (quarterly) income statements. During one-half of the year (offseason), funds from operations are negative. The overall yearly profit is excellent. Should 50 percent of annual depreciation be allocated to the two off-season quarterly reports? If not, how much should be allocated? If you advocate zero depreciation for these two quarters, are you being consistent with your position in MC 9.9 above? Discuss.

MC 9.11 An expenditure resulting in rights to use goods or services entirely within the next year or period that is capitalized as an asset is classified under prepaid items as current. Its expiration over the ensuing year would then represent both a cash outflow as part of cash from operations and an expense on the income statement.

If the rights to the use of the identical goods or services over a period of several years were acquired (four years for example) the resulting asset would be classified as long-lived. The portion to be used or consumed within the forthcoming period would not be reclassified to current, whereas any portion of long-term debt that will be paid during the forthcoming period is reclassified. The expiration or consumption of these long-lived rights, while reported as a current expense on the income statement, is excluded from cash from operations. Yet if these same four years of rights had been acquired one year at a time, their expiration or use would be included in cash from operations per above.

Is this differing treatment an inconsistency or simply an appropriate result of mutually exclusive definitions/classifications? Discuss.

Essential Problems

EP 9.1 The Sisich Bottling Company has just acquired a new bottling machine for its line of soft drinks. The machine cost $260,000 at the factory in Chicago. Related costs were

Freight bill to truck the machine to Sisich Company	$4,000
Insurance coverage while being transported	400
Contractor's bill for installing concrete base for machine	500
Electrician's bill for installing power lines to machine	1,600
Rigger's bill for unloading machine and installing in factory	1,300
Maintenance during first year of operation	900
Repair of damage to machine while being installed	700
Cost of training machine operator	600
Cost of materials consumed during period that machine was being adjusted and made ready for operation	300

Determine the amount to be added to the equipment account.

EP 9.2   The Waspin Company on January 1 purchased an old office building for refurbishing and use. The cost of the building and land was $240,000. Related events during the year were as follows:

Land was appraised at	$ 60,000
Building was appraised at	200,000
Real estate commission paid	12,000
Contractor's bill for remodeling	45,000
Landscape bill for landscaping grounds	9,000
Insurance on premises for first year	1,000
Watering and gardening bill last half of year after landscaping completed	300

Assuming the building is ready for use and is occupied on July 1, what would be the appropriate total additions to the land account and to the building account?

EP 9.3   On January 1, 19X0, the McDaniel Company purchased three different pieces of equipment: A, B, and C. Each cost $50,000, each had an estimated five-year useful life, and each had an estimated salvage value of $5,000. The firm elected to depreciate—A on straight-line, B sum-of-years' digits, and C on double-declining balance. On the 12/31/X0 balance sheet, accumulated depreciation was shown as $15,000, $20,000 and $9,000 for the three assets. Which accumulated depreciation related to which asset?

EP 9.4   Refer to the McDaniel Company in EP 9.3. One of the firm's annual income statements, prepared during the life of these assets, showed combined depreciation expense for all three as $25,200.

  a) Prepare a depreciation schedule for each asset covering the five years. For each year show the current year's depreciation expense, accumulated depreciation at year-end, and the net book value of the asset as carried on the year-end balance sheet.

  b) Which year had combined depreciation expense of $25,200?

EP 9.5   On a 12/31/X8 balance sheet, two particular long-lived assets—P and Q—were show as:

Equipment P	$74,000
Accumulated depreciation on P	(57,000)
Intangible asset Q	11,000

The following day, these assets were sold at a gain of $2,000. How much did the company receive on the sale of these two assets?

EP 9.6   On a 12/31/X0 balance sheet, the Littlejohn Company had only two long-lived assets, as follows:

Truck	$18,000
Accumulated depreciation on truck	(6,000)
Intangible asset	9,000

The truck was being depreciated at $4,000 per year and the intangible asset was being amortized at $3,000 per year. On 7/1/X1 the company sold both of these long-lived assets at a combined net loss of $5,000. How much did the company receive on the sale os these two assets?

EP 9.7 A capital lease acquired on 1/1/X3 had accumulated depreciation of $30,600 on 12/31/X4. If double-declining balance was being used and the capital lease had a five-year life, what was the original value of the lease?

EP 9.8 An asset acquired on 1/1/X5 had accumulated depreciation of $30,000 and a book value of $20,000 on 12/31/X7. If the asset had a six-year useful life and sum-of-years' depreciation was being used, what was the expected salvage value?

EP 9.9 A recently acquired asset (1/1/?) had an accumulated depreciation of $21,875 and a book value of $28,125 on 12/31/X9. The asset was expected to have an eight-year life and double-declining balance was being used. When was the asset acquired?

EP 9.10 An asset acquired on 1/1/X2 was sold for $15,000. The asset had originally cost $59,000 and had been expected to have a salvage value after ten years of useful life of $4,000. Annual depreciation expense was rounded to the nearest hundred dollars.

a) If the asset had been sold at midyear and a gain of $3,000 had been realized on the sale, what depreciation method was used and when was the asset sold?

b) If, instead, the same midyear sale had resulted in a gain of only $1,050, what depreciation method was used and when was the asset sold?

EP 9.11 On 12/31/X7 a firm's equipment account showed $200,000 with accompanying accumulated depreciation of $80,000. During the first two weeks of the following year, $30,000 was spent improving the machine. 19X7 depreciation expense on this equipment on a straight-line basis was $20,000 and its original salvage was estimated at $60,000. The improvement was not expected to extend the original useful life or increase its salvage value and was capitalized into the asset account.

a) What depreciation expense on equipment should be reported for 19X8?

b) What was the net book value and the total accumulated depreciation that should appear on the 12/31/X8 balance sheet?

EP 9.12 On 12/31/X2 the Heidi Company's balance sheet reported a building at a cost of $700,000 and with accumulated depreciation of $400,000. Depreciation expense was being taken on a straight-line basis at $20,000 per year. During the first six months of 19X3 the building was closed for extensive renovations costing $200,000. The renovations were not expected to extend the building's useful life more than six months or increase its originally estimated salvage value of $100,000. It was decided to take depreciation on the building and improvements for only the last half of 19X3.

a) What was depreciation expense related to the building for 19X3?

b) If the firm elected to capitalize the betterment in the asset account, what would be the amounts reported for the building and its accumulated depreciation on the 12/31/X3 balance sheet?

c) If the firm elected the alternative treatment for capitalizing the betterment, what would be the amount reported for the building and its accumulated depreciation as of 12/31/X3?

Supplementary Problems

SP 9.13 The George Company traded in their old truck along with $18,500 to acquire a new model. The "sticker price" on the new truck was $22,000 and a trade-in allowance of $12,000 was given on the old truck even though "blue book" estimated fair market value on the old truck at $7,500.

    a)   How much should the George Compay record the new truck for?

    b)   What if the George Company had exchanged the old truck for a copier machine?

SP 9.14 Assume the same information for the George Company in SP 9.13, except the fair market value of the old truck was $5,500.

    a)   How how much shcould the George Company record the new truck for?

    b)   What if the George Company had exchanged the old truck for a copier machine?

SP 9.15 Bruce Hatch started his trucking business three years ago, and it is now the beginning of the fourth year. When he started, he elected straight-line depreciation as the simplest. His trucks cost $56,000, had an estimated four-year life in the business, and an anticipated salvage value of $8,000. He is trying to compare his income statement with that of a competitor of the same size. The footnotes to the competitor's statement reveal that it is using years' digits depreciation. Bruce had decided that accelerated depreciation would have been better for him. He will use it on new trucks in the future. How should he mentally adjust his third year operating income for comparability with his competitor's statement?

SP 9.16 Refer to the data given in SP 9.15 above. Suppose instead that both Bruce's trucks and his competitor's trucks had six-year lives, and his competitor was using double-declining balance. How much of an adjustment to his third year operating income should Bruce mentally make for comparison purposes?

SP 9.17 Integrative Problem: The following events occurred during Period 7 for Luigi's Auto Parts:

    1)   Sales totaled $110,000, $25,000 for cash and the balance on account.

    2)   Collections of receivables from customers totaled $70,000.

    3)   Merchandise inventory costing $75,000 was purchased on account.

    4)   Wages and salaries totaling $21,000 were paid including the $1,200 previously accrued.

    5)   The period's rent of $4,500 was paid in advance.

    6)   Supplies costing $800 were purchased on account.

    7) $1,600 of interest was paid covering the current period's interest costs and those accrued from the prior period.

    8) $550 was paid for utilities and services currently consumed and billed.

    9) $73,800 was paid on accounts payable.

Adjustment were made for LIFO ending inventory of $51,000 (A); FIFO ending supplies inventory of $475 (B); $400 expiration of prepaid insurance and $4,500 expiration of prepaid rent (C); $75 of depreciation on equipment (D); $250 amortization of leasehold improvement (E); and accrual of $400 of wages and salaries earned but yet not paid (F).

Luigi's firm's balance sheet as of the end of Period 7 is as follows:

LUIGI'S AUTO PARTS BALANCE SHEET AS OF THE END OF PERIOD 7

ASSETS		EQUITIES	
Cash	$ 1,360	Accounts Payable	$20,000
Accounts Receivable	75,000	Wages and Salaries	400
Inventory	51,000	Total Current Liabilities	$20,400
Supplies	475		
Prepaid Items	400	Noncurrent Note Payable	20,000
Total Current Assets	$128,235	Total Liabilities	$40,400
Equipment	1,200		
Accum. Depr. Equip.	(450)		
Leasehold Improvement	3,250	Luigi Cagelli, Capital	91,835
Total Assets	$132,235	Total Equities	$132,235

At the beginning of Period 8, Mr. Cavelli was once again running short of cash. His quick ratio was currently 3.7 to 1 and his receivables averaged less than one month's sales. He therefore was reasonable solvent. He had concluded that, if he moved to a better and larger location, he could significantly expand his volume and profits. The following events occurred during Period 8: (Note: Items marked with an asterisk have been illustrated in prior periods.)

*1) Mr. Cavelli invested $50,000 in the business to assist during the transition period.

2) The $20,000 noncurrent note was retired early in Period 8 to make way for more long-term debt financing. In addition to the face value, $200 of interest accrued up to the time of retirement and a prepayment penalty (additional interest expense) of 5 percent or $1,000 were also paid.

3) Land and a reasonable new store were purchased at the beginning of Period 8 for a total cost of $145,000. Luigi was able to finance all but $10,000 of the cost with a 30-period first-mortgage note for $120,000 at four percent interest per period and a second-mortgage note for $15,000 covering 20 periods at five percent interest per period. At the time of the purchase, the land was appraised at $25,000.

4) The old cash register was sold at the beginning of the period for $1,000 cash.

5) New registers and other equipment were purchased at the start of the period for $20,000, $4,000 to be paid on account within 30 days and the balance covered by a note payable maturing in 10 periods with interest at five percent per period.

*6) Sales for the period were temporarily down because of the move to the new location. Sales totaled $90,000 with $20,000 for cash and the balance on account.

*7) Collections on customer receivables totaled $80,000.

*8) Merchandise inventory consisting $45,000 was purchased on account. Inventory purchases were added directly to the inventory account.

*9) Supplies costing $450 were purchased on account.

*10) Wages and salaries totaling $26,000 were paid including the $400 previously accrued.

*11) $2,775 representing one-half period's interest on the two mortgage loans was paid.

*12) The final period's rent on the old store of $4,500 was prepaid at the beginning of the period. At the end of the period the premises were turned over to the landlord in good condition.

*13) Bills for utilities and services currently consumed in the amount of $650 were received and recorded.

14) Moving expenses classified as miscellaneous and totalling $4,000 were paid in cash.

15) $5,000 was spent refurbishing the newly acquired building and preparing it for use.

*16) $60,000 was paid on accounts payable.

At the end of Period 8:

*A) Merchandise inventory was adjusted to reflect ending inventory at LIFO of $42,000.

*B) Supplies inventory was adjusted to reflect ending supplies on hand under FIFO of $300.

*C) The remaining prepaid insurance of $400 and the prepaid rent of $4,500 had expired.

*D) The second half of the period's interest on the two mortgage loans was accrued.

*E) Wages and salaries totaling $1,300 earned but not yet paid were accrued.

*F) One period's interest was accrued on the register and equipment note.

*G) As the leased building had been vacated, the remaining unamortized leasehold improvement was written off.

H) The newly refurbished building was expected to have a useful life of 40 periods and a salvaged value of $25,000. It was to be depreciated on the DDB basis with a full period's depreciation taken in Period 8 and each period's depreciation expense rounded to the nearest $100.

I) The new equipment was expected to have a useful life of 15 periods and a salvage value of $8,000. It was to be depreciated on the SYD basis with a full period's depreciation taken in Period 8.

Required:

a) Prepare a depreciation schedule showing, for Periods 8 through 20, each period's depreciation expense and remaining book value for both the new building and the new equipment.

b) The effect on the beginning period balance sheet of those Period 8 transactions and adjustments that were introduced in earlier periods, and which are identified with an asterisk (*), has already been recorded in the partially completed balance sheet effect worksheet given below. Prepare a final balance sheet effect worksheet (per Balance Sheet Diagram 4.9) for Luigi's store for Period 8 starting with the preliminary balances and recording the effect of Period 8 transaction (2), (3), (4), (5), (14), and (15), and adjustments (G), (H), and (I). Identify starting balances as "(p)" and the effect of the remaining transactions and adjustments with their numbers or letters. Also identify all revenue and expense effects upon Luigi's capital in an income box. Provide necessary space on your worksheet by entering account titles as follows:

Account	Line number	Account	Line number
Cash	1	Accounts Payable	1
Accounts Receivable	8	Wages and Salaries	4
Inventory	10	Interest Payable	6
Supplies	12	Noncurrent Notes Payable	8
Prepaid Items	14	Luigi Cavelli, Capital	29
Land	16		
Buildings	19		
Accu. Depr. Bldgs.	23		
Equipment	26		
Accum. Depr. Equip.	30		
Leasehold Improvement	34		

c) Prepare the firm's income statement for Period 8 in good form following the multiple-step format.

d) Prepare the statement of owner's capital in good form for Period 8.

e) Prepare the firm's balance sheet in good form as of the end of Period 8.

f) Prepare the firm's statement of Cash Flows for Period 8 in using the indirect method for operating activities.

g) Determine for Luigi's firm as of the end of Period 8:

   1) The amount of net working capital in the business;

   2) The current ratio (to two decimals);

   3) The quick ratio (to two decimals);

   4) The long-term debt ratio (to three decimals); and

   5) The asset composition ratio (to three decimals).

PARTIALLY COMPLETED BALANCE SHEET EFFECT WORKSHEET

Luigi's Auto Parts—Period 8
(b = Beginning Balance; p = Partially Complete Ending Balance)

Cash $ 1,360 (b)		Accounts Payable
+ 50,000 (1)		$ 20,000 (b)
+ 20,000 (6)		+ 45,000 (8)
+ 80,000 (7)		+ 450 (9)
− 26,000 (10)		+ 650 (13)
− 2,775 (11)		− 60,000 (16) $ 6,100 (p)
− 4,500 (12)		Wages and Salaries
− 60,000 (16) $ 58,085 (p)		400 (b)
Accounts Receivable		− 400 (10)
75,000 (b)		+ 1,300 (E) 1,300 (p)
+ 70,000 (6)		Interest Payable
− 80,000 (7) 65,000 (p)		0 (b)
Inventory		+ 2,775 (D)
51,000 (b)		+ 800 (F) 3,575 (p)
+ 45,000 (8)		Noncurrent Notes Payable
− 54,000 (A) 42,000 (p)		20,000 (b) 20,000 (p)
Supplies		Luigi Cavelli, Capital
475 (b)		91,835 (b)
+ 450 (9)		+ 50,000 (1) 141,835 (p)
− 625 (B) 300 (p)		
Prepaid Item		Income
400 (b)		+ 90,000 (6)
+ 4,500 (12)		− 25,600 (10)
− 4,900 (C) 0 (p)		− 2,775 (11)
Equipment		− 650 (13)
1,200 (b) 1,200 (p)		− 54,000 (A)
Accum. Depr. Equip.		− 625 (B)
(450) (b) (450) (p)		− 4,900 (C)
Leasehold Improvement		− 2,775 (D)
3,250 (b) 3,250 (p)		− 1,300 (E)
		− 800 (F) (3,425) (p)
TOTAL $ 169,385 (p)		TOTAL $ 169,385 (p)

SP 9.18 Integrative Problem: The following events occurred during Period 7 for Irene's Sport Shop:

1) Sales totaled $150,000, $60,000 for cash and the balance on account.

2) Collections of receivables from customers totaled $85,000.

3) Merchandise inventory costing $84,500 was purchased on account.

4) Wages and salaries totaling $31,700 were paid including the $1,300 previously accrued.

5) The period's rent of $6,600 was paid in advance.

6) Supplies costing $950 were purchased on account.

7) $700 of interest was paid covering the current period's interest costs and those accrued from the prior period.

8) $1,000 was paid for utilities and services currently consumed and billed.

9) $100,450 was paid on accounts payable.

Adjustments were made for LIFO ending inventory of $65,000 (A); FIFO ending supplies inventory of $500 (B); $1,000 expiration of prepaid insurance and $6,600 expiration of pre-paid rent (C); $150 of depreciation on equipment (D); $1,150 amortization of leasehold improvement (E); and accrual of $600 of wages and salaries but not yet paid (F).

Irene's firm's balance sheet as of the end of Period 7 is given below:

IRENE'S SPORT SHOP BALANCE SHEET AS OF THE END OF PERIOD 7

ASSETS		EQUITIES	
Cash	$ 26,625	Accounts Payable	$ 20,000
Accounts Receivable	92,000	Wages and Salaries	600
Inventory	65,000	Total Current Liabilities	$ 20,600
Supplies	500		
Prepaid Items	1,100	Noncurrent Note Payable	10,000
Total Current Assets	$185,225	Total Liabilities	$ 30,600
Equipment	2,400		
Accum. Depr. Equip.	(900)		
Leasehold Improvement	10,350	Irene Morton, Capital	166,475
Total Assets	$197,075	Total Equities	$197,075

At the beginning of Period 8, Ms. Morton's business had been so successful that she decided to acquire a larger store in a nearby fashionable shopping center. The following events occurred during Period 8: (Note: Items marked with an asterisk have been illustrated in prior periods.)

*1)   Ms. Morton invested $110,000 in the business to assist during the transition period.

2)   The $10,000 noncurrent note was retired early in Period 8 to make way for more long-term debt financing. In addition to the face value, $50 of interest accrued up to the time of retirement and a prepayment penalty (additional interest expense) of five percent or $500 were also paid.

3)   Land and a reasonably new store were purchased at the beginning of Period 8 for a total cost of $450,000. Irene was able to finance all but $90,000 of the cost with a twenty-period first-mortgage note for $270,000 at four percent interest per period and a second-mortgage note for $90,000 covering fifteen period at five percent interest per period. At the the time of the purchase, the land was appraised at $90,000.

4)   The old cash registers were sold at the beginning of the period for $2,000 cash.

5)   New registers and other equipment were purchased at the start of the period for $35,000, $7,000 to be paid on account within thirty days and the balance covered by a note payable maturing in 8 periods with interest at 5 percent per period.

*6)   Sales for the period were temporarily down because of the move to the new location. Sales totaled $145,000 with $60,000 for cash and the balance on account.

*7)   Collections on customer receivables totaled $84,000.

*8)   Merchandise inventory costing $80,000 was purchased on account. Inventory purchases were added directly to the inventory account.

*9)   Supplies costing $1,300 were purchased on account.

*10) Wages and salaries totaling $34,100 were paid including the $600 previously accrued.

*11) $7,650 representing one-half period's interest on the two mortgage loans was paid.

*12) The final period's rent on the old store of $6,600 was prepaid at the beginning of the period. At the end of the period the premises were turned over to the landlord in good condition.

*13) Bills for utilities and services currently consumed in the amount of $1,250 were received and recorded.

14) Moving expenses classified as miscellaneous and totaling $3,000 were paid in cash.

15) $10,000 was spent refurbishing the newly acquired building and preparing it for use.

*16) $69,550 was paid on accounts payable.

At the end of Period 8:

*A)   Merchandise inventory was adjusted to reflect ending inventory at LIFO of $70,000.

*B)   Supplies inventory was adjusted to reflect ending supplies on hand under FIFO of $1,000.

*C)   The remaining prepaid insurance of $1,100 and the prepaid rent of $6,600 had expired.

*D)   The second half of the period's interest on the two mortgage loans was accrued.

*E)   Wages and salaries totaling $1,500 earned but not yet paid were accrued.

*F)   One period's interest was accrued on the register and equipment note.

*G)   As the leased building had been vacated, the remaining unamortized leasehold improvement was written off.

*H)   The newly refurbished building was expected to have a useful life of 50 periods and a salvage value of $100,000. It was to be depreciated on the DDB basis with a full period's depreciation taken in Period 8 and each period's depreciation expense rounded to the nearest one hundred dollars.

I) The new equipment was expected to have a useful life of 16 periods and a salvage value of $14,600. It was to be depreciated on the SYD basis with a full period's depreciation taken in Period 8.

Required:

a) Prepare a depreciation schedule showing, for Periods 8 through 20, each period's depreciation expense and remaining book value for both the new building and the new equipment.

b) The effect on the beginning period balance sheet of those Period 8 transactions and adjustments that were introduced in earlier periods, and which are identified with an asterisk (*), has already been recorded in the partially completed balance sheet effect worksheet given below. Prepare a final balance sheet effect worksheet (per Balance Sheet Diagram 4.9) for Irene's store for Period 8 starting with the preliminary balances and recording the effect of Period 8 transaction (2), (3), (4), (5), (14), and (15), and adjustments (G), (H), and (I). Identify starting balances as "(p)" and the effect of the remaining transactions and adjustments with their numbers or letters. Also identify all revenue and expense effects upon Irene's capital in an income box. Provide necessary space on your worksheet by entering account titles as follows:

Account	Line number	Account	Line number
Cash	1	Accounts Payable	1
Accounts Receivable	8	Wages and Salaries	4
Inventory	10	Interest Payable	6
Supplies	12	Noncurrent Notes Payable	8
Prepaid Items	14	Irene Morton, Capital	29
Land	16		
Buildings	19		
Accum. Depr. Bldgs.	23		
Equipment	26		
Accum. Depr. Equip.	30		
Leasehold Improvement	34		

c) Prepare the firm's income statement for Period 8 in good form following the multiple-step format.

d) Prepare the statement of owner's capital in good form for Period 8.

e) Prepare the firm's balance sheet in good form as of the end of Period 8.

f) Prepare the firm's statement of Cash Flows for Period 8 using the indirect method for operating activities.

g) Determine for Irene's firm as of the end of Period 8.

1) The amount of net working capital in the business;

2) The current ratio (to two decimals);

3) The quick ratio (to two decimals);

4) The long-term debt ratio (to three decimals); and

5) The asset composition ratio (to three decimals).

PARTIALLY COMPLETED BALANCE SHEET EFFECT WORKSHEET

Irene's Sport Shop—Period 8
(b = Beginning Balance; p = Partially Complete Ending Balance)

Cash $ 26,625 (b)	Accounts Payable
+ 110,000 (1)	$ 20,000 (b)
+ 60,000 (6)	+ 80,000 (8)
+ 84,000 (7)	+ 1,300 (9)
− 34,100 (10)	+ 1,250 (13)
− 7,650 (11)	− 69,550 (16) $ 33,000 (p)
− 6,600 (12)	
− 69,550 (16) $ 162,725 (p)	Wages and Salaries
	600 (b)
Accounts Receivable	− 600 (10)
92,000 (b)	+ 1,500 (E) 1,500 (p)
+ 85,000 (6)	
− 84,000 (7) 93,000 (p)	Interest Payable
	0 (b)
Inventory	+ 7,650 (D)
65,000 (b)	+ 1,400 (F) 9,050 (p)
+ 80,000 (8)	
− 75,000 (A) 70,000 (p)	Noncurrent Notes Payable
	10,000 (b) 10,000 (p)
Supplies	
500 (b)	Irene Morton, Capital
+ 1,300 (9)	166,475 (b)
− 800 (B) 1,000 (p)	+ 110,000 (1) 276,475 (p)
Prepaid Item	
1,100 (b)	
+ 6,600 (12)	
− 7,700 (C) 0 (p)	
Equipment	
2,400 (b) 2,400 (p)	
Accum. Depr. Equip.	
(900) (b) (900) (p)	
Leasehold Improvement	
10,350 (b) 10,350 (p)	
TOTAL $ 338,575 (p)	TOTAL $ 338,575 (p)

Income box:

Income		
+ 145,000	(6)	
− 33,500	(10)	
− 7,650	(11)	
− 1,250	(13)	
− 75,000	(A)	
− 800	(B)	
− 7,700	(C)	
− 7,650	(D)	
− 1,500	(E)	
− 1,400	(F)	8,550 (p)

Preparer Problems

Journalize the following transactions and adjustments in good form:

PP 9.1 On 5/23/X7 the firm purchased land and building in exchange for $20,000 cash and a 20-year mortgage note for $270,000 plus interest. The building was appraised at $260,000.

PP 9.2 On 3/7/X2 the firm acquired land, buildings, and equipment in exchange for $30,000 cash and a 15-year mortgage note for $270,000 plus interest. The buildings and equipment were appraised at $90,000 and $180,000 respectively.

PP 9.3 A building acquired on 1/1/X2 at a cost of $275,000 was being depreciated, assuming a 5-year life on the double-declining basis. Record the depreciation for the year 19X4.

PP 9.4 A building acquired on 12/28/X3 at a cost of $400,000 was estimated to have a 25-year life and a $20,000 salvage value. Record depreciation for the year 19X9 following the years' digits method.

PP 9.5 Equipment costing $230,000 and with a book value of $40,000 on 12/31/X6 was sold on 3/1/X7 for $40,000. Depreciation had been taken on a straight-line basis at a rate of $24,000 per year.

PP 9.6 Equipment costing $80,000 and with a book value of $6,000 on 12/31/X8 was sold on 7/5/X9 for $2,000. Depreciation had been taken on a straight-line basis at a rate of $7,400 per year.

PP 9.7 A new truck was acquired on 10/22/X6 in exchange for $6,000 cash. A $5,000 noncurrent interest-bearing note, and the trade-in of an old truck. The old truck cost $15,000 and had a book value of $8,000 on 12/31/X5. The old truck was being depreciated on a straight-line basis at a rate of $1,800 per year.

PP 9.8 A new machine tool with a fair market value of $135,000 was purchased on 1/8/X7 in exchange for $15,000 cash, a mortgage note for $115,000 plus interest, and the trade-in of a truck. The truck had cost $20,000 and had a book value on 12/31/X6 of $8,000. It had been depreciated on a straight-line basis at an annual rate of $3,000.

PP 9.9 Prepare journal entries in good form for all non-asterisked transactions and adjustments given for Period 8 for Luigi's Auto parts in SP 9.17. Identify each entry with its appropriate number or letter code.

PP 9.10 Refer to SP 9.18. For Period 8 for Irene's Sports Shop prepare journal entries in good form identified with appropriate number or letter code for:
    (a) All non-asterisked transactions and adjustments.
    (b) All asterisked transactions and adjustments.

10

Owners' Equity
for Partnerships
and Corporations

Chapter Preview

The objective of this chapter is to introduce you to accounting for businesses with more than a single owner, partnerships and corporations. In this chapter you can:

1. Learn that the basic financial accounting system is essentially the same for sole proprietorships, partnerships, and corporations, with the only significant difference occurring within owners' equity;

2. Learn about partnership agreements and their control over the accountant's distribution of income and losses among partners;

3. Become familiar with some of the distinctive features of corporations including limited liability, the concept of "permanent" contributed capital, and owner withdrawal limitations designed to protect creditors;

4. Learn how to interpret the stockholders' equity section of a corporate balance sheet;

5. Learn how various stockholder related transactions, including stock sale, stock splits, stock dividends, cash dividends, and the purchase and resale of treasury stock are recorded and reported; and

6. Become familiar with the relationships among stockholder claims, par value, book value, and market values.

With this knowledge you will have completed the basic understanding of financial accounting for proprietorships, partnerships, and corporations.

Partnerships

Jan Ford is thinking of going into partnership with Pat Ward. The Potted Planter has been successful and Pat has been considering opening stores in three more shopping centers. Jan would invest $250,000 in the business now with an additional payment of $50,000 to be made during the first year.

The **partnership agreement** provides that, in the event of dissolution, net assets would be allocated in direct proportion to owners' equity balances at the time of dissolution. As partners might have different amounts of capital in the business, and also might be contributing different effort and skill, a simple 50-50 split of profits might not be a fair method of compensation.

The agreement provides that any business profits will be divided as follows:

- Profits up to an amount equal to 10 percent of yearly average owners' equity will be allocated proportionally to average annual investment of each partner (compensates for investment);
- Profits in excess of this amount will be apportioned on the basis of 70 percent to Pat and 30 percent to Jan up to $100,000, in recognition of Pat's experience, and the remainder of the profits will be divided equally.

Pat prepared the firm's financial statements after the first year of operation. Note the abbreviated statements in Exhibit 10.1 show partnerships equity only in total and does not reflect the individual partner shares.

Exhibit 10.1

The Potted Planter
Abbreviated Balance Sheets

	12/31/X6	1/1/X6
Total Current Assets	$ 960	$ 800
Total Long-Lived Assets (net)	740	700
Total Assets	$ 1,700	$ 1,500
Total Current Liabilities	$ 500	$ 450
Total Long-Term Debt	350	350
Total Liabilities	$ 850	$ 800
Total Partners' Equity	850	700
Total Equity	$ 1,700	$ 1,500

Potted Planter Income Statement
for the Year Ending 12/31/X6

Sales	$ 3,000
Cost of Goods Sold	1,700
Gross Profits	$ 1,300
Operating Expenses	1,100
Net Income	$ 200

Partners' Equity Still Just Owners' Equity

It is important that you understand that it makes no difference how partners allocate shares. Total owners' equity for a partnership is equivalent to owner's equity for a proprietorship. Recall the basic balance sheet equality which was first introduced in Chapter 2. Total partners' equity is still simply total assets minus total liabilities.

$$\textbf{Total Assets} - \textbf{Total Liabilities} = \textbf{Partners' Equity}$$

The accounting system itself essentially remains the same for a proprietorship and for a partnership. Neither proprietorships or partnerships pay income taxes. The only difference is that, instead of a single account for the owner's capital (equity), there would be a capital account for each partner. The sum of all partners' shares after closing would still be equal to owners' equity. Accounting procedures will differ only with respect to transactions affecting owners' equity directly, and for closing revenue and expense accounts.

Income, instead of being closed to a single owner's capital account, will be allocated to several partners' accounts following the proportions specified in the partnership agreement. Note that GAAP are not involved in this apportionment. GAAP merely require the accountant to follow the partners' wishes. It is the partners' business to divide as they choose.

Division of Partners' Shares

The division of owners' equity makes no difference to the firm or to the accounting system. It does make a difference to the partners. They want and need information on where they stand.

Returning to the example involving Pat and Jan, beginning partners' equity was $700,000. Jan's and Pat's contributions were $450,000 and $250,000 respectively. A more detailed beginning balance sheet would then show partners' equity as:

Pat Ward, Capital	$ 450,000
Jan Ford, Capital	250,000
Total Partners' Equity	$ 700,000

Partner withdrawals in a partnership, as with sole proprietorships, are known as **drawings**.

To better illustrate income allocation using the proposed partnership formula given above, assume the following additional information:

- Jan's initial contribution was $250,000 with the additional $50,000 invested a few months later;

- Pat's drawings during the year for personal use were $100,000, and

- Jan made no drawings during the year.

Following the proposed agreement, the $200,000 net income would be divided as shown in Exhibit 10.2. Note that ending partners' equity is $850,000 reflecting $476,250 for Pat and $373,750 for Jan.

Exhibit 10.2

The Potted Planter
Statement of Partners' Capital
for the Year Ending 12/31/X6

	Pat Ward	Jan Ford	Total	Remaining profit to be divided
Beginning partners' capital	$ 450,000	$ 250,000	$ 700,000	
Additional investments	0	50,000	50,000	
Partner withdrawals	(100,000)	—	(100,000)	
Partners' capital before profit allocation	$ 350,000	$ 300,000	$ 650,000	$ 200,000
Average investment basis*	$ 400,000	$ 275,000	$ 675,000	
Profit allocation:				
10% average investment	40,000	27,500	67,500	$ 132,500
70/30 allocation up to $100,000	70,000	30,000	100,000	32,500
50/50 allocation for balance	16,250	16,250	32,500	
Total profit allocation	$ 126,250	$ 73,750	$ 200,000	
Ending partners' capital**	$ 476,250	$ 373,750	$ 850,000	

* per partnership agreement: simple average investment = (Beginning partner capital + partner capital before profit allocation) ÷ 2
** balance before profit allocation + profit allocation

Partnership Equity Classifications

The balance sheet would include one line for each partner and show total partners' equity. The ending balance sheet for Pat and Jan in the partners' equity section would disclose:

Pat Ward, Capital	$ 476,250
Jan Ford, Capital	373,750
Total Partners' Equity	$ 850,000

A **partnership** is just a multiple proprietorship. Each partner has a share of the overall "proprietorship."

Multi-Step Partnership Allocations

Pat and Jan already have a two-step allocation agreement. With an investment basis of $650,000, 10 percent of this amount, or the first $65,000 of profits, were to be allocated in proportion to average investment. The remainder, as a second step, was split 70-30. Many agreements are more complex. They may produce allocations for different contributions of capital, experience, contacts or customers, and time devoted to the business. In fact, they may provide anything the partners can agree upon that is workable.[1]

One of the reasons for partnership agreement complexity involves salaries. In the case of both proprietorships and partnerships, owners' payments to themselves or uses of assets are not treated as salaries. Wages and salaries expense for these types of firms will not include any renumeration to the owner(s). All assets taken by the owner(s) are recorded as withdrawals, or drawings. Therefore, where partner contributions of time and skill differ, allocations in lieu of salaries, which are agreed upon in advance, must be incorporated into the partnership agreement. This is why partnership agreements frequently allow for changes in profit distribution over time.

Liability Limitations

In addition to treating salaries as withdrawals, proprietorships and partnerships have another thing in common—unlimited liability. **Unlimited liability** simply means general partners in a partnership are personally responsible for all of the obligations of a business.[2] A creditor who is unable to obtain payment from the assets of the firm has legal claim on the personal assets of all the general partners. In law, there is no distinction between the firm, the individual proprietor, or the general partners.

Both proprietorships and partnerships are therefore artificial entities (as opposed to legal entities) for business and accounting purposes. Neither is subject to taxation. Therefore, no provision for income taxes is included in a proprietorship's or partnership's financial statements. Reported net income is always "before taxes." A proprietor is subject to income tax on the sum of the proprietorship's income and his or her other personal earnings. A partner's taxable income will be his or her share of partnership income plus all other personal earnings.

---

[1] Minimum provisions in partnership agreements would contain the following: accounting methods to be followed, limitations on drawings, division of profits or losses, procedures in event of partner's death, management responsibilities, division on liquidation (The divorce clause), and transfer of partner's interest.

[2] A partnership may have some members who are limited partners. Limited partners may not participate in the management of the firm and may have limited liability. Generally, limited partners cannot lose more than their investment.

Corporations

Corporations are a third and quite distinct legal form of business that are chartered to do business by individual states. Unlike the owners of proprietorships or partnerships, corporate owners have **limited liability**. In law, a corporation is a separate legal entity distinct from its owners. Corporate owners are known as **stockholders** or as **shareholders**, and their liability for the corporation's debts is generally limited to what they have already contributed or invested.

There are many advantages and disadvantages of the corporate form of business. Most are not relevant to understanding financial accounting. One advantage, in addition to owners' limited liability, is that ownership in a corporation is readily transferable to another. If either Jan or Pat died, were disabled, or just wished to withdraw, the partnership would have to be dissolved. The net assets might have to be sold and the proceeds divided. Addition of any new partners would also necessitate a new partnership agreement.

One possible disadvantage of the corporate form worth noting results from the fact that the corporation is a legal entity. As such, a corporation itself is subject to income taxation. A corporation's financial statements therefore include a provision for income taxes and reported net income is "after taxes." After-tax earnings are distributed to stockholders in the form of dividends. These distributions are taxable income to the recipients who are separate legal entities from the business. Corporate profits are taxed twice. Hence, the term double taxation of corporate profits.[3]

Corporate owners own "shares" in the corporation. These shares are known as **common stock** or capital stock. Stock can be transferred—sold, given, or bequeathed—from one owner to another with no effect on the corporation's continuity of operation. Under the terms of a corporation's charter and corporation law, holders of **voting stock** have a voice in management and share in net assets and profits in proportion to the number of shares owned. The term common stock or voting stock is used to designate ownership shares with the rights described above. Common stockholders vote each year to elect a **Board of Directors**.[4] The directors, as the elected representatives of the owners, oversee the management of the business. They hire the corporation president and define his or her job as well as other jobs and responsibilities. They also hire or engage the independent auditor to report to them and the stockholders.[5]

Existing owners of a corporation's common stock generally have preemptive rights to purchase any new stock issues in proportion to their existing holdings. A **preemptive right** is like a first option or first right of refusal. Thus, an existing stockholder is guaranteed the opportunity to maintain his or her proportionate ownership share in the event additional common stock is issued or sold.

---

[3] Some smaller corporations, meeting certain standards under the Internal Revenue Code, can elect to be taxed as partnerships thus avoiding double taxation.

[4] In rare cases a corporation may also have some common stock which is nonvoting or shares receiving diminished voting rights. This is outside the scope of this book.

[5] Usually the Board of Directors recommends to the stockholders the selection of a particular CPA firm to be engaged as the firm's auditor for the forthcoming year. The stockholders then vote to ratify this selection.

Significance of Limited Liability to Creditors

The stockholders' limited liability feature in a corporation may be advantageous to the stockholder. However, it is a different story for the creditor. Assume, for a moment, that you are a creditor of a business. Suppose the firm's balance sheet revealed the following information:

Total Assets	$ 700,000
Total Liabilities	300,000
Owners' Equity	400,000

As a creditor of this business, would you feel secure? You know that, in liquidation, your claim comes first. There would have to be liquidation losses in excess of $400,000 before you would suffer any loss on your claim. Suppose the firm were a partnership or a proprietorship, and suppose the owner(s) withdrew $399,000 of choice assets. As long as the personal net worth of the owner(s) was adequate, you would not be concerned. You have a direct claim against the personal assets of the owner(s) in addition to the business' assets.

Now suppose this same firm were a corporation, and the owners could withdraw as dividends $399,000 of choice assets. Where would that leave you as a creditor? Your answer should be obvious (and perhaps not printable). To protect creditors, only a portion of stockholders' equity can be withdrawn as dividends.

As a potential corporate creditor, you need to know how much cannot be withdrawn by the owners. The various state laws provide protection to corporate creditors in this matter. Owners may not withdraw assets for their benefit if the result would be to reduce total stockholders' equity below a certain minimal amount. This minimal amount is generally equal to **contributed capital**. Contributed capital is distinct from profits (earnings) retained in the business. The use of the word "capital" can be confusing, since capital normally implies something of value, an asset. The term "contributed capital" for a corporation refers to that portion of total assets invested by stockholders and contributed by gifts or donations.[6] It does not refer to the specific assets themselves.

Stockholders' Equity Classifications

Before proceeding, make sure that you have a clear understanding of owners' equity. It makes no difference whether a firm is a proprietorship, a partnership, or a corporation. The total owners' equity merely reflects that amount of total assets not claimed by creditors. For a partnership, total partners' equity is divided among the partners, and their individual shares are separately stated. For a corporation, total stockholders' equity is classified on a different basis. Corporate stockholders' equity on the balance sheet is divided into several accounts to differentiate contributed capital from past earnings retained in the business.

---

[6] If the corporation is being liquidated, any remaining portion of such assets may be withdrawn after all creditor claims have been satisfied.

Basic Division Between Contributed Capital and Retained Earnings

Corporations generally have thousands of separate stockholders. Furthermore, the roster of stockholders is constantly changing, as individuals buy and sell stock shares. It would be ridiculous to try to disclose individual shares in a large corporation's balance sheet. There is, however, an important distinction within stockholders' equity of a different kind. Creditors wish to know the amount of contributed capital, which is their safety factor. Stockholders and directors also are interested in the proportion of assets that could legally be withdrawn by the stockholders as dividends. **Dividends** are merely formal owner withdrawals by corporate stockholders.

GAAP therefore provide for this essential separation of total corporate stockholders' equity. The corporate balance sheet will show, for example:

Contributed capital	$ 750,000
Retained earnings	100,000
Total stockholders' equity	$ 850,000

Contributed capital is generally reported in several subdivisions (as illustrated in Exhibit 10.4) which can reflect different types of stock and related accounts. Total contributed capital is also known as the legal or stated capital. It represents a share of total reported assets not subject to claims by creditors. Assets representing contributed capital generally are not available for dividends.

Illustration 10.1

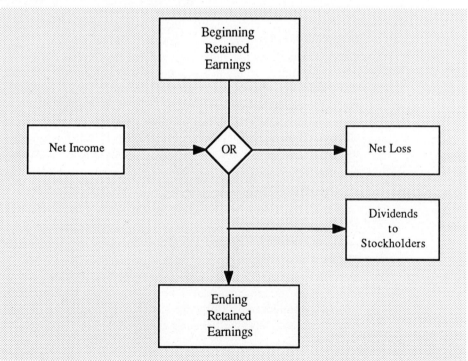

Retained earnings, which may also be reported in subdivisions, identifies the remaining share of total assets that may be withdrawn as dividends. Retained earnings represents total accumulated profits or earnings since the corporation's inception, less amounts previously withdrawn in dividends or assigned to contributed capital via stock dividends. Total retained earnings are increased by net income and reduced by net losses or dividends as pictured in Illustration 10.1.

A word of caution, although it is common to speak of dividends being paid from or out of retained earnings, remember the balance sheet equality. All equities merely represent claims against or shares in assets. Retained earnings is the residual share of total assets after all prior claims.

Total Assets – Total Liabilities – Contributed Capital = Retained Earnings

Any dividends of cash or other assets that are voted by the Directors to be distributed in the future will eventually reduce total assets. At the time dividends are voted (declared) by the Directors, the declaration is reflected by an immediate reduction of retained earnings and a corresponding increase in a dividends payable liability.

Exhibit 10.3

BALANCE SHEETS FOR THREE LEGAL FORMS OF THE SAME BUSINESS
as of 12/31/X6

The Potted Planter (*Proprietorship*)

Current Assets	$ 960,000	Current Liabilities	$ 500,000
Long-lived Assets (net)	740,000	Long-term Debt	350,000
		Total Liabilities	$ 850,000
		Pat Ward, Capital	850,000
Total Assets	$1,700,000	Total Equities	$1,700,000

The Potted Planter (Partnership)

Current Assets	$ 960,000	Current Liabilities	$ 500,000
Long-lived Assets (net)	740,000	Long-term Debt	350,000
		Total Liabilities	$ 850,000
		Pat Ward, Capital	476,250
		Jan Ford, Capital	373,750
Total Assets	$1,700,000	Total Equities	$1,700,000

The Potted Planter, Inc. (*Corporation*)

Current Assets	$ 960,000	Current Liabilities	$ 500,000
Long-lived Assets (net)	740,000	Long-term Debt	350,000
		Total Liabilities	$ 850,000
		Contributed Capital	750,000
		Retained Earnings	100,000
Total Assets	$1,700,000	Total Equities	$1,700,000

Exhibit 10.3 illustrates the essential similarity and differences between balance sheets for the three forms of business. The balance sheets appear in abbreviated form for Pat and Jan as a partnership (same as Exhibit 10.2), as a proprietorship (assuming one partner bought out the other), and as a corporation. Study this exhibit to obtain a clear picture of the differences within owners' equity.

Note that under the corporate form, Pat and Jan's joint $750,000 investment is reported as contributed capital. Retained earnings would contain net income of $200,000 less dividends (withdrawals) of $100,000. In the corporate example, the dividends would have been distributed according to the number of shares of stock owned. You will rarely find the term "contributed capital" shown on a balance sheet. It is used in this exhibit (in place of the detailed accounts described below that collectively comprise capital) to focus your attention on the fundamental distinction between contributed capital accounts and retained earnings accounts.

Contributed Capital

Contributed capital consists of the stockholders' investment in shares of stock. Categories of stock include common and preferred stock. There may be more than one class of stock for each of these categories. Each class of stock will be recorded in separate accounts. Often the balance sheet will only differentiate between common and preferred stock. In this case, the details of different classes of stock will be disclosed in the footnotes that accompany the financial statements.[7]

Contributed capital will be decreased only for retiring stock and liquidating dividends. Both will be discussed further in the chapter.

Common Stock

As mentioned above, the basic ownership and control of a corporation is vested in its voting common stockholders. The share of a firm's assets that represent common stock-holders' contributed capital is usually disclosed in two accounts identified as common stock and additional paid-in capital.

The stockholders' equity section of The Potted Planter's Balance Sheet as of 12/31/X8 (Exhibit 10.4) shows the common stock with a par value of $10 per share. Stock may be issued with or without a par value. If the stock is "no-par" stock, the corporation may issue the stock with or without a stated value.

Par value is the legal capitalization per share of stock issued by the firm. Par value is determined in the firm's corporate charter and is printed on each stock certificate. Therefore, the minimum amount of contributed capital per share of stock will be par value. If

---

[7] Not all stock have the same rights. Some may have restricted voting and/or preemptive rights. Note the Xerox Class B Common Stock does not have preemptive rights (Appendix A).

the shares of stock are issued for greater than par value, the excess amount will go into additional paid-in capital.

Issue amount − Par or stated value = Additional paid-in capital

No-par stock may be issued with a stated value set by the board of directors. The stated value becomes the legal capitalization per share of stock issued. The allocation of the proceeds from issuing a share of stock is the same as for par value stock. When no-par stock does not have a stated value, the entire proceeds are considered legal capital and are added to the stock account. No additional paid-in capital is used.

Legal capital is a cushion for creditors and is not available for dividends. You should recognize there is no correlation between legal capital and the market price of stock, except that most states do no allow stock to be issued at less than par or stated value. Although it is rare, if stock is issued at less than par or stated value, a discount is created which is a contra-equity account. The stockholders become contingently liable for this amount. To avoid this situation, par or stated value is generally set at a nominal amount.

Exhibit 10.4

The Potted Planter, Inc.
Stockholders' Equity Section of Balance Sheet
as of 12/31/X8

Preferred stock 12% $100 par (10,000 shares authorized, issued and outstanding)	$1,000,000	
Common stock $10 par (500,000 shares authorized, 220,000 shares issued, 212,000 shares outstanding)	2,200,000	
Additional paid-in capital[a]	700,000	$3,900,000
Retained Earnings:		
Appropriated for self insurance	$ 350,000	
Appropriated for contingencies	150,000	
Unappropriated retained earnings[b]	400,000	
Total Retained Earnings		900,000
Less treasury stock (8,000 shares at cost)		(200,000)
Total Stockholders' Equity		$4,600,000

[a] $300,000 contributed by preferred stockholders;
$400,000 contributed by donors and common stockholders.

[b] $200,000 restricted by treasury stock acquisition.

Additional Paid-in capital

Additional paid-in capital or paid-in capital in excess of par is an arbitrary classification and may be viewed as an "overflow" account. It is used to record any investments by owners in excess of the par or stated value of the stock issued to them. For example, if the Potted Planter issued and sold one more share of its common stock for $60, cash would be increased by $60. Only the par amount $10 would be added to the common stock account. The excess over par would be recorded in the "overflow" account, additional paid-in capital, to balance.

Additional paid-in capital is also used to record other issues of additional stock where the valuation in the exchange exceeds par or stated value. Examples would include the exchange of the firm's stock for new long-lived assets, where either the stock or the asset is objectively valued above the stock's par value. Another possibility involves convertible long-term debt or convertible debentures. Convertible debt is debt that allows the creditor to exchange debt for a fixed number of shares of common stock and thus become a shareholder. Where debt is converted and the book value of the exchanged debt exceeds the par value of the stock issued, the excess represents additional paid-in capital. Note that these last two examples of stock issued in exchange for long-lived assets, and debt conversion, represent two common investing and financing activities not involving cash flow which will be discussed in Chapter 7. Examples of these transactions involving additional paid-in capital would include:

1. 10,000 shares of stock with par value of $10 is sold for $130,000. Cash is increased by $130,000. Common stock is increased by $100,000 (par value portion only). Additional paid-in capital is increased $30,000 to balance.

Proceeds from issue	$ 130,000
Common stock ($10 par x 10,000 shares)	100,000
Additional paid-in capital	$ 30,000

2. 10,000 shares of common stock with stated value of $5 are exchanged for land with a fair market value of $75,000. Land is increased by $75,000. Common stock is increased by $50,000 (stated value only). Additional paid-in capital is increased $25,000 to balance.

Fair market value of land	$ 75,000
Common stock ($5 stated value x 10,000 shares	50,000
Additional paid-in capital	$ 25,000

3. Long-term debt with a book value of $400,000 is exchanged for 30,000 shares of $10 par common stock. Long-term debt is reduced by $400,000 to record its extinguishment. Common stock is increased by $300,000 (par value only). Additional paid-in capital is increased $100,000 to balance. Debt conversion will be discussed further in Chapter 12.

Book value of debt	$ 400,000
Common stock ($10 par x 30,000 shares)	300,000
Additional paid-in capital	$ 100,000

Additional paid-in capital also accumulates any excess of market price over par in a stock dividend, or any profit realized on the resale of treasury stock. Finally, although they are rare, gifts made to a corporation increase the account for the asset received and additional paid-in capital.

Preferred Stock

Common stockholders in a corporation are in a relatively high risk position, as are all business owners. Whether or not there are profits, creditors still demand and receive interest on their long-term investments. But common stockholders can receive dividends only if there have been profits, and there is enough cash in the business to pay them. In the event of serious trouble and liquidation, common stockholders are entitled only to the amount remaining after creditors and liquidation costs are paid in full. Often this residue can prove to be little or nothing.

When a corporation wishes to obtain more capital, it may not desire, or be able to, incur more debt. At the same time, it may be difficult to persuade existing and potential owners to risk an additional investment in common stock. Preferred stock is often the compromise solution. **Preferred stock** is not debt and, unlike interest on debt, preferred dividends need not be declared and paid every year. On the other hand, preferred stock generally has a fixed dividend rate higher, at least at the time the preferred stock is issued, than the normal interest rate on debt because of its greater risk to investors. Preferred stockholders are entitled to receive dividends before dividends may be paid to the common stockholders. In addition to the preference as to dividends, preferred stockholders receive preference in liquidation. If anything remains after the creditors' claims and liquidation costs are paid, preferred stockholders receive their claims in full before any distribution to common stockholders.[8] Preferred stock is normally nonvoting. It represents an ownership claim that is safer than common stock. Preferred stock is therefore shown in the stockholders' equity section above capital stock.

Preferred stock may have other features. It may be cumulative—entitled to both current and also passed or omitted dividends (known as "dividends in arrears") to be paid before common dividends; it may be convertible—exchangeable for common stock at a fixed rate; or it may have many other rarer features.

Note, in Exhibit 10.4, that the preferred stock is shown at $100 par and at 12 percent. The 12 percent indicates that the preferred stockholders are first entitled to receive $120,000 in dividends on their 10,000 shares (12 percent x $100 par x 10,000 shares) each year that the directors declare dividends.

---

[8] The preferred stockholders' claims per share in liquidation are determined at the time the preferred is originally authorized. The liquidation claim may be greater than par value for par plus additional paid-in capital.

Authorized, Issued, and Outstanding

Exhibit 10.4 also discloses the number of shares of stock that are authorized, issued, and outstanding. **Authorized shares** represent the number currently authorized for possible issuance in the corporate charter by the state of incorporation. Although not a difficult process, if a corporation wishes to issue more shares than presently authorized, it would first have to obtain additional authorization from the government of the state of incorporation. The number of shares **issued** represents the total sold or otherwise distributed to stockholders.[9] Finally, the number of shares currently **outstanding** is also reported. The difference between the number of shares issued and outstanding is the shares that have been reacquired and are being held temporarily before resale or other use. Temporarily reacquired stock is known as **treasury stock** which is illustrated in Exhibit 10.4.

Retained Earnings

Retained earnings accounts collectively represent:

- The amount of stockholders' equity in excess of contributed capital.

- The share in or claim against total assets other than that represented by creditors and contributed capital.

- Net assets in the business representing accumulated past net income or earnings not yet distributed (therefore retained).

Note, as illustrated in Exhibit 10.4, that retained earnings may be divided among two or more accounts. The firm's directors may decide publicly to designate a portion of total retained earnings as "not available" in the foreseeable future for dividends in anticipation of possible loss contingencies or future losses. By resolution of the board, a portion of retained earnings is then classified as an **appropriation** and transferred to a separate retained earnings account. Such appropriations have little significance since they are voluntary and may be reversed by board resolution at anytime. Where some retained earnings are appropriated, the balance sheet will disclose the nature of the appropriation and any remaining balance of retained earnings available for dividends is designated as "**unappropriated.**"

Appropriations may also be created from legal **restrictions**. These restrictions include treasury stock and contractual agreements. Contractual agreements may include loan restrictions. A creditor may demand a larger safety factor than contributed capital. The company may agree, and contract to restrict dividends by a certain amount until the loan is paid. Treasury stock will be discussed later in this chapter. When these appropriations are increased, unappropriated retained earnings are decreased. An alternative treatment for legal

---

[9] Although uncommon, stock can be reacquired and "retired," or cancelled. This action will be reflected by a reduction in the stock account and a reduction in the number of shares reported as issued.

restrictions is to footnote the restrictions in the financial statements rather than create appropriations (Exhibit 10.4). The footnotes must disclose the source of the restriction, the amount , and the pertinent provisions of the restriction.

The amount available for dividends is therefore limited to unappropriated retained earnings less any footnoted restrictions. Remember that nothing on the right side of a balance sheet represents an asset. The retained earnings shown, and any parts thereof, are merely a representation of a source, claim, or share in total assets. The firm must have adequate liquidity (available cash) to distribute cash dividends to stockholders.

Changes in Stockholders' Equity Accounts

Changes in stockholders' equity accounts reflecting sale of new stock, issuance of stock in exchange for long-lived assets, and debt conversion have already been described. Other changes that may occur involve declaration of cash dividends, stock dividends, stock splits, and the acquisition and resale of treasury stock.

Cash Dividends

You have probably already correctly concluded that, in the case of a corporation, revenue and expense accounts (summarized as income) are closed to unappropriated retained earnings at year-end. Similarly, dividends reduce unappropriated retained earnings.

Two conditions must be met, before a dividend can be declared by the Board of Directors. There must be adequate earned resources (profits) not previously withdrawn, appropriated, or restricted in unappropriated retained earnings. And, since most dividends are in cash, there must be adequate liquidity so that a dividend will not cause a cash shortage. Cash dividends become a legal liability when declared and are a current liability of the corporation until actually paid. Therefore the accountant will treat a dividend declaration as a transaction. Retained Earnings is reduced by the amount of the dividend, and Dividends Payable, as a current liability, is correspondingly increased.

As an example of a cash dividend, assume the Potted Planter Board of Directors declared cash dividends for both preferred and common stock on March 15, to be paid to stockholders of record as of April 30.[10] Remember that the Board of Directors cannot declare and pay dividends for common stock before the preferred dividends. On March 15 the accountant would record the dividends by increasing dividends payable and reducing retained earnings. The preferred dividends were $120,000, which represents 12 percent times the preferred stock of $1,000,000 (par value x number of shares x dividend rate). Common dividends declared were $0.45 per share (200,000 shares outstanding).

---

[10] When stock is sold among stockholders, the firm is notified of the new owner "of record" so that future dividends, annual reports, and so forth can be sent to the current owner.

Diagram 10.1   Effect of a Cash Dividend

Current Assets:		Current Liabilities:	
Cash	− 210,000 (3)	Dividends payable	+ $120,000 (1)
			+ 90,000 (2)
			− 210,000 (3)
		Long-term Debt:	
Long-lived Assets:		**Stockholders' Equity:**	
		Unappropriated Retained earnings	
			− 120,000 (1)
			− 90,000 (2)

(1) Preferred dividends declared
(2) Common dividends declared
(3) Payment of the preferred and common dividends

When the dividends are paid on April 30, the payment would be recorded with another entry to decrease cash and decrease dividends payable by $210,000. The payment of the dividend liability is a cash flow and considered a financing activity on the Statement of Cash Flows.

Liquidating Dividends

Liquidating dividends are not true dividends since they decrease contributed capital rather than retained earnings. These dividends are relatively rare and represent a return of capital invested by the stockholders rather than a distribution of profit. Liquidating dividends must be approved by the state of incorporation and must be clearly disclosed to the stockholder to avoid misrepresentation.[11]

Stock Dividends

Stock dividends involve distributions, rather than sales, of additional shares of stock where the amount distributed is less than 20-25 percent of the amount of stock outstanding. The purpose is to **capitalize retained earnings**, to transfer some past earnings

---

[11] Since liquidating dividends represent a return of the stockholders' original investment, they are not considered taxable income to the stockholders. These dividends do reduce the cost basis of the stockholders' investment. The cost basis will be used by the stockholder to determine whether a gain or loss is realized when the stock is resold.

not yet distributed to contributed capital. Stock dividends may be thought of as a form of compulsory investment or involuntary stock sale to existing stockholders.

Rather than distribute cash dividends and require the owners to use the dividends to purchase more stock, the new stock is just issued and mailed. The market value of the number of shares distributed is transferred from retained earnings to the contributed capital accounts for common stock (Preferred stock is usually not involved). The market value of the stock dividend is distributed with the par value portion (number of stock dividend shares times par value) added to the capital stock account. Any excess of market value over par increases additional paid-in capital. Note that a stock dividend has no cost to the firm in assets distributed and no effect on total stockholders' equity beyond the cost of the paperwork to distribute the dividend. The individual stockholder's proportionate claim and voting power is unchanged. If the market doesn't dilute the stock price fully for the additional shares, the stockholders benefit by an increased value of their invested shares. The firm's dividend policy may play a part in the overall increase in the market value of the stock. If the dividend policy per share stays the same after the stock dividend, then individual stockholders will receive more dividends on their investment. The market price should reflect the increased dividends.

The Potted Planter declared and distributed a 10 percent stock dividend on its 200,000 outstanding shares in July when the market price was $12. 20,000 shares were distributed. If you were holding 100 shares before the stock dividend, you would receive 10 additional shares. So long as the market price stayed above $10.91, you would gain. The accountants would record the effect of earnings capitalization as shown on Balance Sheet Diagram 10.2. Retained earnings will be decreased by $240,000 on the declaration date and Common Stock Distributed and Additional Paid-in Capital will be increased. On the date of distribution, the Common Stock Distributed is eliminated and Common Stock is increased.

Diagram 10.2   Effect of 10 Percent Stock Dividend

Current Assets:	Current Liabilities:
	Long-term Debt:
Long-lived Assets:	Stockholders' Equity:
	Common Stock + 200,000 (c)
	Common Stock Distributable
	+ 200,000 (a)
	− 200,000 (b)
	Addition Paid-in Capital
	+ 40,000 (a)
	Unappropriated
	Retained Earnings − 240,000 (a)

(a) Dividend declared
(b) Date of record
(c) Date of distribution

The stock dividend may be calculated:

200,000	shares of stock outstanding
x 0.10	stock dividend
20,000	new shares issued
x $12	market price per share
$240,000	decrease Unappropriated Retained Earnings
200,000	increase Common Stock ($10 par x 20,000 shares)
$40,000	increase Additional Paid-in Capital

Deficits

For creditor protection, dividends may not be declared if they would reduce total stockholders' equity below the amount shown as contributed capital. In other words, dividends cannot legally be declared in excess of the amount shown in retained earnings.[12] But what about losses, that is, negative net income?

Suppose the Potted Planter, Inc. had a net loss of $80,000 during 19X6. What will appear on the ending balance sheet? You are correct if you guessed:

Contributed Capital	$ 750,000
Retained Earnings (Deficit)	(80,000)
Total Stockholders' Equity	$ 670,000

Negative retained earnings is known as a **deficit**. When a corporation is in a deficit position, it may not declare any dividends. The $80,000 deficit advises you that the company would need over $80,000 of net income in the future before its directors could consider declaring any dividend. The deficit also advises creditors that the contributed capital has been impaired. The impairment was not for the benefit of the owners. Unfortunately, there are no laws to protect creditors against business losses.

Stock Splits

A **stock split** is a proportionate increase in the number of common shares held by existing shareholders, and a corresponding decrease in par or stated value per share. A stock split has no effect on any of the dollar amounts in the various stockholders' equity accounts. If The Potted Planter's directors were to split the stock 4 for 1 in 19X5 (refer to Exhibit 10.4) and you held 800 shares, you would receive an additional 2,400 shares in the mail, or else exchange your 800 $10 par shares for 3,200 $2.50 par shares. You would now have 3,200 shares instead of 800, but would still have the same claim in liquidation, voting power, and proportionate share of any dividends. The accountant would merely

---

[12] Some states also restrict dividends that would imperil the firm's liquidity even if not reducing total stockholders' equity below minimums.

change the common stock explanatory note to read "$2.50 par, 880,000 shares issued, 848,000 outstanding." Except to record the paperwork expenses, no dollar amounts on the balance sheet change as a result of a stock split.

At this point you may be wondering "Why split stock?" Think of what will happen to the market price of your Potted Planter stock, which you may assume is $32 per share. With the same earnings potential but four times as many shares outstanding, the market price will drop to around $8. For the moment, assume that the market price reflected full dilution at $8. What would be your benefit? Stock is normally traded, to reduce paperwork costs, in lots or batches of 100 shares. Before the split, had you wanted to sell 100 shares at the market price, you would have had to find a buyer willing to invest $3,200 in The Potted Planter stock. After the split, you could sell a 100 share block to anyone willing to invest $800. The minimum cost to play the game has been reduced. More players can afford to buy the stock, and your liquidity (chance to sell without suffering loss) is therefore increased. This increase in liquidity for existing shareholders is generally the primary objective of a stock split in the first place.

What would be your second or other possible benefit from a stock split? If The Potted Planter split 4 for 1, the actual market may not fully dilute. If the price stopped falling at $8.50 per share, and you held 800 shares, you would be $1,600 ahead (800 shares at $32 vs. 3,200 shares at $8.50). Often the market does not fully dilute when a stock splits. More people able to play mean more buyers, and the price is bid up accordingly. So there can be sort of a magic effect to a stock split, something for nothing.

It is important to remember that a stock split results in no change in any stockholders' equity accounts. Only the par value and the number of shares are affected. The note accompanying the common stock caption is changed accordingly. For example, a corporation with 10,000 shares of $10 par common stock issued and outstanding that subsequently split its stock 5 for 1 would disclose on its balance sheet:

Before split: Common Stock ($10 par, 10,000 Shares issued & outstanding) $100,000
After split: Common Stock ($2 par, 50,000 Shares issued & outstanding) $100,000

Note also that treasury stock participates in the stock splits, since the par value on it must change also.

Treasury Stock

Occasionally, a corporation will need, for various reasons, to purchase from existing stockholders shares of its outstanding common stock. These shares may be used for stock options, for employee plans, to maintain the market price of stock, to increase Earnings per Share, to decrease the threat of takeover attempts, stock dividends, or the conversion of preferred stock or Bonds Payable to common stock.

A firm's own stock which it has repurchased is known as treasury stock. Treasury stock generally is not treated as an asset. Instead accountants generally record treasury stock at its cost as a contra-equity item within the stockholders' equity section. Shares of common stock outstanding will be the number of shares issued less the number of treasury shares. Treasury stock generally has no rights until reissued.[13]

It is conceivable that a company could accumulate enough treasury stock so that total stockholders' equity would fall below the amount of contributed capital. This would subvert the protection for creditors. Consequently, a corporation may not legally purchase treasury stock costing more then its reported retained earnings. Nor can the firm subsequently declare dividends (reducing retained earnings) if such dividends plus treasury stock would impair the contributed capital. The accountant therefore discloses this limitation by indicating the amount of the restriction on retained earnings. Retained earnings restrictions are generally disclosed in one of two ways: Either they are simply footnoted on the financial statement, or they can be shown in a separate appropriation account. An example of the first approach is shown for The Potted Planter in Exhibit 10.4. You can see that The Potted Planter currently holds treasury stock costing $200,000. Therefore retained earnings are restricted by $200,000. This restriction is disclosed in a footnote to unappropriated retained earnings.

When The Potted Planter treasury stock was first acquired, cash was reduced $200,000 and the contra account treasury stock was increased (thus reducing total stockholder's equity by $200,000) to balance.[14] Also, unappropriated retained earnings were noted to reflect the dividend restriction.

Look again at Exhibit 10.4. What is the balance sheet telling you as a stockholder? Can you see that the balance sheet, in accounting language, is providing you with the following message from the directors:

"$900,000 of our total assets came from past earnings and are presently not committed for distribution to stockholders. Of these $900,000 share of total assets, $200,000 cannot be distributed unless all of our treasury stock is resold. Another $350,000 we do not currently plan even to consider for distribution. We are self insuring ourselves in certain areas, and will need to have this amount of capital readily available to cover possible losses. We also are reserving other assets for unforeseen contingencies. $200,000 of assets may be considered for distribution as dividends at some time in the future."

When treasury stock is disposed of, the restriction applicable to the stock distribution is eliminated. The treasury stock account is also reduced in proportion to the cost of the amount of stock disposed. When proceeds received from the resale of treasury stock are in excess of its purchase cost, the excess is not considered revenue or gain. Instead, it is added to additional paid-in capital, like any original contribution in excess of par. When

---

[13] Treasury stock does not enjoy voting or preemptive rights or rights in liquidation of the firm. Depending on the future use of the stock (e.g. to be issued for employee plans) treasury stock may participate in dividends. This subject is beyond the scope of this text.

[14] Although beyond the scope of this text and not illustrated, GAAP allow treasury stock to be carried at a par rather than cost with an adjustment for the difference made to additional paid-in capital at the time of treasury stock acquisition.

resale proceeds received are less than the purchase cost of the treasury stock, the difference is deducted from additional paid-in capital, treasury stock. Losses on the reissuance of treasury stock in excess of previous "profits" on treasury stock transactions are deducted from retained earnings so as not to impair contributed capital.[15]

Balance Sheet Diagram 10.3 illustrates the effect of the following treasury stock transactions for The Potted Planter:

(1) 12,000 shares of treasury stock acquired for cash at a cost of $12.50 per share on 10/1/X8.

(2) 1,000 shares of treasury stock are subsequently sold for $13.00 per share on 11/15/X8.

(3) 3,000 shares of treasury stock are later sold for $12.00 per share on 8/1/X9.

Diagram 10.3   Effect of Treasury Stock Transactions

Current Assets:			Current Liabilities:		
Cash	−	150,000 (1)	**Long-term Debt:**		
	+	13,000 (2)			
	+	36,000 (3)			
Long-lived Assets:			**Stockholders' Equity:**		
			Additional Paid-in Capital		
				+	500 (2)
				−	500 (3)
			Unappropriated Retained Earnings*		
				−	1,000 (3)
			Treasury Stock**	−	150,000 (1)
				+	12,500 (2)
				+	37,500 (3)

* Footnoted to restrict retained earnings by:
   $150,000 after (1)
   $137,500 after (2)
   $100,000 after (3)

** Contra-equity account increased by a minus

---

[15] Treasury stock may be reissued at less than par value since it was previously issued stock and the original issue value still remains in the common stock and additional paid-in capital accounts.

Retire Stock

The stockholders must approve the purchase of outstanding stock with the intent of retiring it. The stock is first placed into "treasury" and then retired. This treasury stock does not participate in any **stock rights**. When the stock is retired, all capital accounts must be decreased by the amount of the original issuance. If the stock was repurchased for less than the original issued amount, the difference will be added to the account Additional Paid-in Capital–Retirement of Stock. For example, $10 par stock originally sold for $16 and repurchased at $15 would increase Additional Paid-in Capital–Retirement of Stock by $1 as illustrated in Balance Sheet Diagram 10.4

Diagram 10.4   Retire Treasury Stock for less than the Amount Issued

Current Assets:		Current Liabilities:		
Cash		Long-term Debt:		
Long-lived Assets:		Stockholders' Equity:		
		Common Stock	–	10
		Additional Paid-in Capital, Common	–	6
		Additional Paid-in Capital, Retirement of Stock	+	1
		Treasury Stock	+	15

If the stock in the example above had originally sold for $13, then the $2 difference would reduce retained earnings so that the company's contributed capital would not be compromised.

Diagram 10.5   Retire Treasury Stock for greater than the Amount Issued

Current Assets:		Current Liabilities:		
Cash		Long-term Debt:		
Long-lived Assets:		Stockholders' Equity:		
		Common Stock	–	10
		Additional Paid-in Capital, Common	–	3
		Retained Earnings	–	2
		Treasury Stock	+	15

Stock Subscriptions

Stock subscriptions are installment contracts to sell a specific number of shares of stock at a specified price. Upon acceptance of the contract, the firm increases a Subscriptions Receivable account by the entire contract amount and increases Common Stock Subscribed by par value times the number of shares. The difference increases Additional Paid-in Capital. When payment is made, subscriptions receivable is decreased and cash is increased. The SEC requires subscriptions receivable to be listed as a contra-equity account; however, for financial reports firms may list subscriptions receivable (assuming payment will be made within the current period) as a current asset. This treatment can be justified since the receivable is the result of a legal contract.[16] It depends on the state laws what treatment will be used if the buyer defaults on the contract.

After full payment has been made, the stock is issued and common stock subscribed is decreased and common stock increased.

Diagram 10.6   Stock Subscriptions

Current Assets:			Current Liabilities:		
Cash	+ 14 (2)				
Subscriptions Receivable	+ 14 (1)				
	− 14 (2)		Long-term Debt:		
Long-lived Assets:			Stockholders' Equity:		
			Common Stock	+ 10 (2)	
			Common Stock Subscribed	+ 10 (1)	
				− 10 (2)	
			Additional Paid-in Capital	+ 4 (1)	

(1) Acceptance of contract
(2) Full or last payment of contract

Stock Options, Rights, and Warrants

Before concluding the discussion of stock, you should be familiar with the terms stock options, stock rights, and stock warrants. Stock options and stock rights both involve the privilege of purchasing a specific number of shares at a specific price over a specified period of time. Stock options are often granted to executives as incentive compensation or

---

[16] Various treatments for default of a stock subscription contact include: forfeiture of payments, issue stock in proportion of the amount paid, return the amount paid less any costs incurred to the purchaser, or return of all payments. Defaults will not be covered in this book.

may be included as a "sweetener" along with the sale of other securities, bonds, or preferred stock. Stock rights are generally "options" granted to existing shareholders under their preemptive rights to purchase additional issue of stock.

Stock warrants are the certificates issued by the corporation granting options or rights. In common usage, the term warrants is used to differentiate options granted as sweeteners from options under preemptive rights (stock rights) or for other purposes (stock options).

Stock options fall into two categories: compensatory and noncompensatory. Noncompensatory stock options are generally offered to eligible full-time employees based on a percentage of their salaries. The offer price must not be less than would be offered to existing stockholders and there is a time limit to exercise the option.

Compensatory stock options are often limited to key officials and managers as additional compensation. The difference between the offered price and the market price is considered a compensation cost and will be expensed over an appropriate period of time not to exceed the option time limit.

Stock options require disclosure on the balance sheet. Disclosure includes: type of plan, how many shares are involved, and the terms of the options.

The Statement of Retained Earnings

In Chapter 4 you learned that a Statement of Owner's Capital is included with the financial statements for a proprietorship. This statement summarizes all changes occurring to the owner's equity (capital) during the year—additional investment, net income or loss, and owner withdrawals. A similar statement is prepared for a partnership and is known as the **Statement of Partners' Capital**. It is similar to Exhibit 10.2.

Exhibit 10.5

The Potted Planter Statement of Retained Earnings
for the Year Ending 12/31/X8

Unappropriated retained earnings 12/31/X7		$ 300
add: 19X8 Net income		500
Decreasing appropriation for contingencies		51
		$ 851
less: Preferred cash dividends declared	$ 120	
Common cash dividends declared	90	
Common stock dividends declared	240	
Loss on treasury stock	1	(451)
Unappropriated retained earnings 12/31/X8		$ 400

For a corporation (except in liquidation), the stockholders can only anticipate possibly withdrawing assets up to the amount identified as unappropriated retained earnings.

They cannot normally withdraw assets that represent contributed capital. Therefore, for a corporation, the statement of owner's capital is replaced by one that focuses exclusively on retained earnings.

Exhibit 10.5 illustrates a corporate **Statement of Retained Earnings**. Note that this statement essentially describes in words and numbers the same flows pictured in Illustration 10.1 with the addition of changes in appropriations and the loss in treasury stock.

What is Stock Worth?

The value of stock can be stated in many ways. As discussed in the chapter, par value or stated value are legal capitalization terms. Book value is the adjusted historical cost value of common stock on the balance sheet. The most objective value of the stock is the market price. **Market price** is the value investors are willing to pay to purchase the stock on the open market.

Book Value per Share

One measure often used by financial analysts is the **book value of common stock**. Recall that the term book value is also used with respect to an asset. A truck costing $15,000, with $7,000 of accumulated depreciation, is said to have a book value of $8,000. Book value can be thought of as meaning the "net amount currently assigned (reported) by accountants." What is the net amount of common stockholders' equity on Exhibit 10.4?

The book value of the firm to all owners (stockholders) is the total stockholders' equity or $4,600,000. Preferred stockholders have a claim against, or share in, total assets. In this simplified example, you may assume that the preferred claim is equal to the preferred stock par value. Exhibit 10.4 shows this amount to be $1,000,000. Preferred stockholders usually have no claim against retained earnings.[17] If The Potted Planter's preferred stockholders have a $1,000,000 claim or share in total assets, what is the common book value, or book value of all the common stock of the firm?

Remember, you are assumed to own 110 shares (100 + 10 stock dividend) of The Potted Planter's common stock. The fact that, as of 12/31/X8, all common stock had a book value of $3,600,000 may be interesting to you in some abstract fashion, but you might be more interested in the book value of your stock. From Exhibit 10.4, calculate the book value of your stock.

---

[17] In circumstances where preferred stock is cumulative, preferred stockholders would have claims against retained earnings in the case where previous years' preferred dividends had not been paid-in full. This claim for back dividends is called "dividends in arrears" and would be disclosed parenthetically on the balance sheet or in the footnotes.

Book value per share is generally understood to mean "per share of common stock outstanding."

$$\text{Book value per share} = \frac{\text{Total stockholders' equity} - \text{preferred claims}}{\text{Number of common shares outstanding}}$$

The book value of a Potted Planter common share on 12/31/X8 would be $16.98 (rounded). The book value of the 110 shares of your stock would be $1,868.

Market Value

Market value of stock is based on expectations of the company's future performance rather than on book value. The financial statements along with information released about the company and the market contribute to create expectations of risk, future earnings, and dividends. Additional measures of earnings (earnings per share) and dividends (dividend yield) will be discussed in Chapter 13.

Summary of Changes in Stockholders' Equity Accounts

To assist you to bring together the various elements of corporate equity accounting introduced in this chapter, Exhibit 10.6 summarizes the various events which can alter the balances in the stockholders' equity accounts. Remember that some of these changes merely involve a reallocation of dollars among different accounts. Stock splits, stock dividends, and changes to appropriations do not affect the total of stockholders' equity. As you study Exhibit 10.6, for each item visualize an event which would result in the specific change.

Exhibit 10.6   Summary of Changes Which May Occur in Stockholders' Equity Accounts

Preferred Stock

Increased by:
Par value of proceeds from sale of preferred stock

Common Stock

Increased by:
Par or stated value of proceeds from sale of common stock
Par or stated value portion of stock issued as stock dividend
Par or stated value portion of stock issue as part of conversion of long-term debt*
Proceeds of sale of no-par common stock

Additional Paid-in Capital

Increased by:
Excess over par for new preferred stock sold or issued on debt conversion
Excess over par or stated value of new common stock sold or distributed as stock dividend, or distributed as part of long-term debt conversion

Gifts to corporation
Gains from sale of treasury stock
Gains resulting from retirement of stock
Compensatory stock options not exercised

Decreased by:
Losses on treasury stock transactions up to the amount of
previous gains

Common Stock Distributable	*Increased by:* Declaration of stock dividend
	Decreased by: Issuance of stock dividend
Common Stock Subscribed	*Increased by:* Acceptance of installment stock contract
	Decreased by: Issue stock certificates on installment contract
Appropriated Retained Earnings	*Increased by:* Voluntary appropriations established or increased by directors Appropriations recognizing restriction of retained earnings resulting from contractual obligation or treasury stock purchase**
	Decreased by: Reduction or elimination of voluntary appropriations by directors Reduction or elimination of appropriation recognizing legal restrictions**
Unappropriated Retained Earnings	*Increased by:* Net income Reduction or elimination of any appropriation
	Decreased by: Net loss (negative net income) Declaration of cash dividend Declaration of stock dividend Creation of or increase in any appropriation Losses on treasury stock transactions exceeding any previous gains Stock retired at less than original cost

* Bond conversion is covered in Chapter 12.

** Alternative to simply footnoting retained earnings with respect to the amount of
the restriction.

Preparer Procedures

To accommodate transactions and adjustments introduced in this chapter, the partial chart of accounts first introduced in Chapter 5 and augmented in Chapters 6, 8, and 9 must be further expanded to include accounts for:

Exhibit 10.7

Additions to Chart of Accounts

Current Assets

008	Subscriptions Receivable

Current Liabilities

307	Dividends Payable

Partners' and Stockholders' Contributed Capital*

510	Partner A Capital
511	Partner B Capital
512	Partner C Capital
520	Preferred Stock
521	Additional Paid-in capital—Preferred
522	Common Stock
523	Additional Paid-in Capital—Common
524	Additional Paid-in Capital—Treasury Stock
525	Additional Paid-in Capital—Stock Options
526	Common Stock Subscribed
527	Common Stock Distributable

Stockholders' Retained Earnings

530	Appropriated for Contingencies
531	Appropriated for Self Insurance
532	Appropriated for Treasury Stock
533	Appropriated for Dividend Restrictions
540	Retained earnings (Unappropriated)

Contra-Equities

611	Treasury Stock
612	Deferred Compensation Expense

Other Accounts**

920	Partner A Withdrawals (drawings)
921	Partner B Withdrawals (drawings)
922	Partner C Withdrawals (drawings)
930	Dividends Declared

* Note that a single firm's chart would have either 510-512 or 520-527.

** Note that a single firm's chart would have either 920-922 or 930.

New Transactions

New transactions introduced in this chapter all involve owners' equity accounts. Since owners' equity is assumed to have a credit balance, all owners' equity accounts for a partnership and a corporation normally have credit balances. The contra-equity accounts, drawings in a partnership, dividends declared, and treasury stock in a corporation have debit balances. In a partnership, owner withdrawals are recorded by crediting the appropriate asset account for the item withdrawn, usually cash or inventory, and debiting the particular partner's drawing account. The drawing account at year-end is then closed to the individual partner's capital account. For a corporation, cash dividends become a current liability at the time they are formally declared by the Board of Directors. The entry recording the declaration of a $50,000 cash dividend would be:

	DR	CR
Dividends Declared	50,000	
Dividends Payable		50,000

The dividends declared account at year-end is closed to unappropriated retained earnings, or retained earnings if there are no appropriations.

Issuance of new stock would involve credits to the appropriate stock account and to additional paid-in capital in the case of par or stated value stock issued at greater than par or stated value. The balancing debit will be to cash for stock sold, or to the appropriate asset account for stock issued in exchange for an asset, or to retained earnings for a stock dividend. For example, the sale for cash of 10,000 shares of $5 par common stock for $85,000 would be recorded as:

Cash	85,000	
Common Stock		50,000
Additional Paid-in Capital—Common		35,000

No-par stock would be issued as:

Cash	85,000	
Common Stock		85,000

Declaration of a 10 percent stock dividend on 300,000 outstanding shares when the market price was $46 and par is $10 would be recorded as:

Retained Earnings	1,380,000	
Common Stock Distributable		300,000
Additional Paid-in capital—Common		1,080,000

When the stock is distributed the following entry would be made:

	DR	CR
Common Stock Distributable	*300,000*	
Common Stock		*300,000*

Acquisition of treasury stock will involve two entries, one debiting treasury stock and crediting cash and the other a memo entry (where restrictions àre footnoted) or an appropriation entry (where restrictions are appropriated). The latter may be illustrated for treasury stock acquired costing $40,000:

Treasury Stock	*40,000*	
Cash		*40,000*
Retained Earnings	*40,000*	
Appropriated for Treasury Stock		*40,000*

Disposition of treasury stock involves simple reversal of the acquisition entry in the amount of the cost of the stock resold. Proceeds in excess of cost are credited to additional paid-in capital. When a loss on treasury stock disposition exceeds prior net gains on treasury transactions the excess is debited to retained earnings. Treasury stock sold for $45,000 is recorded:

Cash	*45,000*	
Treasury Stock		*40,000*
Additional Paid-in Capital—Treasury Stock		*5,000*

Sales of Treasury Stock below cost will be debited to Additional Paid-in Capital—Treasury Stock. If the balance in the account is less than the loss, the difference will be a debit to Retained Earnings. If the credit balance in Additional Paid-in Capital was $2,000 and Treasury Stock was reissued for $6,000 less than its cost of $40,000 the following entry would be made:

Cash	*34,000*	
Additional Paid-in Capital—Treasury Stock	*2,000*	
Retained Earnings	*4,000*	
Treasury Stock		*40,000*

An additional entry would be made to reverse the appropriations for Treasury Stock Restriction. If no appropriation was made, then the footnote would be removed from Unappropriated Retained Earnings:

Appropriated for Treasury Stock	*40,000*	
Unappropriated Retained Earnings		*40,000*

Note, for all transactions affecting the stock account (treasury stock, stock dividends, stock splits, issue stock, retire stock) memorandum entries must be made to change the balance sheet note relating to the number of shares authorized, issued and outstanding.

No entry is made for noncompensatory stock options until they are exercised. When exercised the entry would be made:

	DR	CR
Cash	*150*	
Common Stock		*100*
Additional Paid-in Capital		*50*

Compensatory stock options require an entry at the time of the offer. The entry for the difference between the market price of $150 and the offer price of $110.

Deferred Compensation Expense	*40*	
Additional Paid-in Capital—Stock Options		*40*

If the "service" period for the options is 4 years, an annual entry would be made:

Compensation Expense	*10*	
Deferred Compensation Expense		*10*

When the option is exercised the following entry would be made:

Cash	*110*	
Common Stock		*100*
Additional Paid-in Capital		*10*

Chapter Overview

Based upon an understanding of the material covered in this chapter, you should be able to:

- Explain the essential similarities in accounting for proprietorships, partnerships, and corporations;

- Describe the basic differences between proprietorship, partnership, and corporate accounting;

- Define the role of the partnership agreement in the division of earnings and partners' equity, and determine such a division, given the essential facts;

- Explain the meanings of limited and unlimited liability and their effect upon GAAP for owners' equity accounting;

- Describe the essential difference between, and the intention behind, contributed capital and retained earnings classifications;

- Explain the functions of the several accounts possibly appearing as parts of contributed capital, including preferred stock, common stock, and additional paid-in capital;

- Explain the functions of the several accounts possibly appearing as parts of the retained earnings subsection, including voluntary appropriations, restrictions, unappropriated retained earnings, and treasury stock;

- Describe the content and purpose of the statement of retained earnings;

- Define and describe any relationships among par value, book value, and market value, all as applied to common stock;

- Explain the reasoning behind, and the accounting for, certain stockholder related events, including cash dividends, stock splits, stock dividends, and the purchase and resale of treasury stock;

- Describe and explain the various possible limitations upon the distribution of assets to stockholders as dividends.

New Vocabulary and Concepts

Additional paid-in capital	Partnership
Appropriation	Preemptive rights
Authorized (stock)	Preferred stock
Board of Directors	Retained earnings restrictions
Book value of common stock	Retained earnings
Book value per share	Statement of Partners' Capital
Capitalize retained earnings	Statement of Retained Earnings
Common stock	Stock dividend
Contributed capital	Stock options
Deficit	Stock rights
Dividend	Stock split
Drawings	Stock Subscriptions
Issued (stock)	Stock warrants
Limited liability	Stockholders/shareholders
Market price (of stock)	Treasury stock
Market value (of stock)	Unappropriated retained earnings
Outstanding (stock)	Unlimited liability
Par value/stated value	Voting stock
Partnership agreement	

- The necessity for partnership agreements.

- The common need for multi-step partnership agreements covering earnings allocations.

- The difference between contributed capital and retained earnings.

- The necessity for dividend limitations and their association with limited liability.

- The difference between book value and market value.

- Capitalization of retained earnings.

Review Questions

1. A partnership agreement should specify the division of net assets upon dissolution of the partnership. What other important provisions should be included in such an agreement?

2. How does the accountant determine the basis for allocating profits and equity among partners? How do GAAP apply in this determination?

3. What are the limits of owner liability to company creditors in a proprietorship? A partnership? A corporation?

4. What is the significance of limited liability to the corporation's owners? To its creditors?

5. (a) What is contributed capital? (b) What is its significance to creditors? (c) Why is it segregated from retained earnings in a corporate balance sheet?

6. What three different types of transactions could result in an increase in the balance reported for common stock?

7. What are the various possible limitations on dividend declarations?

8. What events can increase or decrease retained earnings?

9. (a) What is a statement of retained earnings? (b) What information does it provide?

10. If you owned 100 shares of a 12 percent $100 par value preferred stock, and if the common stockholders were receiving a dividend this year, how much dividend should you receive?

11. As a preferred stockholder, how much in the way of dividends can you expect to receive in the future?

12. What effect does par or stated value for stock have on recording new issues or stock dividends?

13. (a) What is the function of the additional paid-in capital account? (b) What events can result in an increase in additional paid-in capital? (c) Under normal (going concern) circumstances, could additional paid-in capital be reduced? If yes, under what conditions would this occur?

14. When a firm has preferred stock, how does one calculate the book value per share of common stock?

15. Explain the differences among par value, book value, and market value?

16. Why isn't treasury stock included, along with other purchased securities, in the appropriate asset accounts?

17. Why are retained earnings restricted by the cost of treasury stock acquired and not yet resold?

18. (a) What is the difference between an appropriation of retained earnings and a restriction? (b) What is the common effect of both on retained earnings?

19. If a company has 20,000 shares of $10 par common stock issued and outstanding, and then splits two for one, what dollar amount after the split will appear in the common stock account? What will appear after the split in the common stock footnote concerning par value and shares issued?

20. A stock dividend is said to have the effect of permanently capitalizing retained earnings. Explain.

21. What is the difference between the accountants' treatment of a stock split and a stock dividend?

Mini Cases and Questions for Discussion

MC 10.1   Bob, Mike, and Ted have decided to go into partnership. They are trying to work out a partnership agreement that will be fair to everyone. Bob states his position: "Look, you guys, I know I don't know much about business, and I'll only be around a few hours a week. But I'm putting up almost all of the money $200,000. I could get 12 percent if I invested it in real estate. This partnership couldn't get off the ground without my money."

"I can see that, Bob," says Mike. "But I'm the one who really has the management experience in this business. I'll be putting in 50 to 60 hours per week. Without my knowledge and effort, the business could never make a profit. I can make $60,000 in salary working for another firm."

"Don't forget me," says Ted. "I may know only how to sell, but without customers, all of your money and management skill wouldn't generate revenue. Sixty percent of our planned first year's sales are coming from customers that are already mine. I'll be bringing them along from my present job. I'm making $75,000 in straight commissions right now."

Assume that anticipated first year profits are $120,000 before any remuneration to partners. Can you suggest a fair partnership agreement? Discuss.

MC 10.2   Ann Mason is considering whether to lend $200,000 to the Ajax Corporation for a three year period. She is concerned about the safety of her loan in the event that the firm fails. A proforma balance sheet, projecting conditions after the loan was made, shows:

Current Liabilities	$100,000	Contributed Capital	$150,000
Long-term Debt	250,000	Retained Earnings	375,000
Total Liabilities	$350,000	Total Equities	$875,000

She says, "I would be comfortable with a long-term debt ratio of 0.4, but 0.625 is too risky. After all, the stockholders could take out all $375,000 in dividends."

Is there anything Ajax could do or suggest which might reduce Ann's concern? Discuss.

MC 10.3   Sally Yale is quite upset. She has just learned that a corporation can buy and sell its own stock in the market. "That's totally unfair," says Sally. "The company will always know good and bad news before it gets published for us in the financial statements. And it has all those internal forecasts which aren't available to me. It's like betting on a horse race after the race is over. You don't have the results yet, but one bettor does."

a)   Can the company usually "win" with its insider information?

b)   What prevents a company from taking unfair advantage of its "edge"?

c)   Couldn't the majority of stockholders, or even an effectively controlling minority, make nice profits and receive large dividends by taking advantage of unsuspecting and unknowledgeable outsiders?

Discuss.

MC 10.4 Book value per share of common stock and market value per share are rarely if ever the same. Often market value is higher than book value. What factors cause this situation? Also, occasionally, market value will be below book value. What could bring about this situation?

Discuss.

MC 10.5 Jerry Black is confused. He understands a stock split which effectively splits existing outstanding shares into smaller pieces. He sees clearly why a stock split should not, and does not, affect the dollar amounts in the balance sheet accounts.

What doesn't make sense to Jerry is the accountant's treatment of stock dividends. "Since a stock dividend is just a baby split, why shouldn't it be treated like all other splits?" Jerry asks you. "And why bring in the current market price? There is no attempt to have stock values in the owners' equity section report market values."

Discuss. See whether you can satisfy Jerry with a reason for this apparently disparate treatment.

MC 10.6 If someone has 100 shares of common stock in a corporation with 400,000 shares issued and outstanding, how significant is that person's "ownership voice"? Suppose he or she does not like what the firm is doing; what, realistically, are his or her choices? Discuss.

MC 10.7 Directors never have to declare, and often cannot declare, dividends even though large retained earnings are reported. What, then, is the significance of a voluntary appropriation, which can be eliminated by a simple resolution at the next directors' meeting?

Discuss.

Essential Problems

EP 10.1 The Pat and Mike Partnership Agreement calls for profits to be distributed as follows:

Step 1: 15 percent of simple average investment during the year excluding any apportionment of current year's profit.

Step 2: Remaining profits, up to a total of $80,000 divided 70 percent to Pat and 30 percent to Mike in lieu of salary.

Step 3: Any remaining profits to be divided equally.

Pat's capital account was $63,000 at the beginning of the year and $57,000 at year end, reflecting $6,000 of withdrawals. Mike's was constant at $40,000. a) Total profits were $120,000. b) The net worth loss was $10,000. Determine both the proportion of profits to be allocated to each partner and also each partner's year-end capital account balance.

EP 10.2 Refer to the partnership agreement in EP 10.1. Give the partners' profit shares and ending capital account balances if:

(a) Profits were $25,000

(b) Profits were $150,000

(c) Mike's capital account had started at $40,000 but he had withdrawn $20,000 during the year, and profits were $70,000.

EP 10.3 Given the following selected data in thousands of dollars from the Ferrara Corporation's financial statements as of 12/31/X9 (unless otherwise noted) determine the missing amounts.

Additional paid-in capital common	$60	Total Assets	$600
Total contributed capital	?	Additional paid-in capital preferred	15
Common stock	?	Total liabilities	200
19X9 dividends	40	Total stockholders' equity	?
19X9 net income	?	Unappropriated retained earnings	
Preferred stock	75	(12/31/X8)	20
Retained earnings—appropriated		Unappropriated retained	
(12/31/X8 earnings and X9)	20	(12/31/X9)	80

EP 10.4 The following selected data as of 12/31/X5 (unless otherwise noted) from the financial statements of six firms are given in thousands of dollars. Complete the missing amounts for each firm.

	A	B	C	D	E	F
Additional paid-in capital common	$ 25	$ 75	$ 30	$?	$ 50	$ 20
Additional paid-in capital preferred	?	30	20	10	15	10
Common stock	100	?	200	290	250	200
19X5 dividends	40	40	?	90	70	140
19X5 net income	?	110	200	100	?	250
Preferred stock	50	70	60	80	?	90
Retained earnings appropriated						
(12/31/X4 and X5)	20	?	40	60	30	40
Total assets	500	?	900	800	700	?
Total contributed capital	180	300	?	?	400	?
Total liabilities	200	100	300	?	150	100
Total stockholders' equity	?	500	?	550	?	?
Unappropriated retained earnings						
(12/31/X4)	60	?	175	?	80	100
Unappropriated retained earnings						
(12/31/X5)	?	150	?	40	?	?

EP 10.5   The stockholders' equity section of the Arnold Corporation's balance sheet as of 12/31/X8 is given below. In April of 19X9, Arnold sold 10,000 shares of $100 par 14 percent preferred stock. Proceeds of this sale were $1,150,000. In late June the company sold an additional 100,000 shares of its common stock to its existing common shareholders for $3,400,000. Net income for 19X9 was reported as $900,000. By year end the regular preferred dividend and a common dividend of $310,000 had been declared.

Common stock*	$2,000,000
Additional paid-in capital—common	300,000
Retained earnings	700,000
Total Stockholders' Equity	$3,000,000

* $10 par, 1,000,000 shares authorized. 200,000 shares issued and outstanding.

a) Give the contributed capital section of Arnold's balance sheet in good form as of 5/1/X9.
b) Give the contributed capital section of Arnold's balance sheet in good form as of 7/1/X9.
c) Give the stockholders' equity section of Arnold's balance sheet in good form as of 12/31/X9.
d) If 19X8 net income had been reported as $400,000, what was the corporation's book value per share as of 12/31/X8?
e) Assuming that the preferred liquidation claim was the same as par, what was the corporation's book value per share as of 12/31/X9?

EP 10.6   Data from the stockholders' equity sections as of 12/31/X8 for Corporations X, Y, and Z are given below together with related footnotes. Other data are also given:

	X	Y	Z
Common stock ($10 par)	$300,000	$ 450,000	$ 600,000
Additional paid-in capital common	$ 50,000	$ 75,000	$ 340,000
Retained earnings	$150,000	$1,200,000	$ 900,000
Common shares authorized (12/31/X8)	500,000 shares	800,000 shares	900,000 shares
Common shares issued and outstanding (12/31/X8)	?	?	?
Other Data:			
Shares $100 par preferred stock sold 4/1/X9	2,000 shares	4,000 shares	4,500 shares
Proceeds sale of preferred	$210,000	$ 700,000	$1,500,000
Shares common sold 7/1/X9	40,000 shares	90,000 shares	200,000 shares
Proceeds sale of common	$420,000	$1,200,000	$3,500,000
Preferred dividend rate	12%	13%	14%
19X8 net income	$ 40,000	$ 300,000	$ 500,000
19X9 net income	$ (5,000)	$ 400,000	$ 800,000
19X9 common dividends paid	$ 10,000	$ 148,000	$ 474,000
Preferred stock liquidation claim	$200,000	$ 500,000	$ 600,000

Required for each firm:
(a) Contributed capital section in good form of balance sheet as of 5/1/X9
(b) Contributed capital section in good form of balance sheet as of 8/1/X9
(c) Stockholders' equity section in good form as of 12/31/X9
(d) Book value per share as of 12/31/X8 and as of 12/31/X9

EP 10.7 The stockholders' equity section of the Arnold Corporations' balance sheet as of 12/31/X8 is given below. Assume on 1/15/X9 Arnold declared and distributed a ten percent stock dividend when the market price of the common was $18. Give the stockholders' equity section of Arnold's balance sheet in good form as of 2/1/X9 assuming (a) That the firm had no net income during January of 19X9 and (b) That January net income was $75,000.

Common stock*	$2,000,000
Additional paid-in capital—common	300,000
Retained earnings	700,000
Total Stockholders' Equity	$3,000,000

* $10 par, 1,000,000 shares authorized. 200,000 shares issued and outstanding.

EP 10.8 The stockholders' equity sections as of 12/31/X8 of the X, Y, and Z Corporations are given below. In March of 19X9, assume that the firms declared and issued common stock dividends of 10, 15, and 20 percent respectively when the market prices of their common stock were $10.50, $13.00, and $16.50. For each firm, prepare a balance sheet stockholders' equity section as of the end of the first quarter of 19X9 assuming (a) That the firm had no net income during the first quarter of 19X9 and (b) That 19X9 first quarter net income was $(2,000) loss, $125,000, and $250,000 respectively.

	X	Y	Z
Common stock ($10 par)	$300,000	$ 450,000	$ 600,000
Additional paid-in capital common	$ 50,000	$ 75,000	$ 340,000
Retained earnings	$150,000	$1,200,000	$ 900,000
Common shares authorized (12/31/X8)	500,000 shares	800,000 shares	900,000 shares

EP 10.9   The Arnold Corporation's stockholders' equity section as of 12/31/X8 given below. Assume that the following occurred during 19X9:

- On 1/15, 3,000 shares of treasury stock were acquired at a cost of $18 per share.

- On 5/15, at a Director's meeting it was duly resolved to appropriate $200,000 of retained earnings for contingencies.
- On 8/21, 2,000 shares of the treasury stock was resold to outsiders at a price of $20 per share.

Common stock*	$2,000,000
Additional paid-in capital—common	300,000
Retained earnings	700,000
Total Stockholders' Equity	$3,000,000

* $10 par, 1,000,000 shares authorized. 200,000 shares issued and outstanding.

a) Prepare in good form the stockholders' equity sections of Arnold's balance sheet as of the end of each of the first three quarters of 19X9 assuming no 19X9 net income. You may assume Arnold followed the practice of footnoting retained earnings restrictions.
b) Prepare for the same three statement sections, but assume that Arnold followed the practice of establishing a separate appropriation for restrictions of retained earnings and that net income for each of the first three quarters of 19X9 was $200,000, $225,000, and $250,000 respectively.

EP 10.10   The stockholders' equity sections as of 12/31/X8 of the X, Y, and Z Corporations is given below. Assume that the following occurred during 19X9:

	X	Y	Z
Common stock ($10 par)	$300,000	$ 450,000	$ 600,000
Additional paid-in capital common	$ 50,000	$ 75,000	$ 340,000
Retained earnings	$150,000	$1,200,000	$ 900,000
Common shares authorized (12/31/X8)	500,000 shares	800,000 shares	900,000 shares
Loan agreement retained earnings restriction (2/15/X9)	$75,000	$600,000	$400,000
Treasury stock shares acquired 4/15/X9	1,000 shares	1,500 shares	2,000 shares
Price paid per share	$ 11	$ 12	$ 16
Reserve for self insurance established 7/20/X9	$20,000	$140,000	$ 90,000
Treasury stock shares sold 11/20/X9	600 shares	900 shares	1,000 shares
Selling price per share	$ 8	$ 14	$ 20
Net income (loss) 19X9			
First quarter	$(8,000)	$ 50,000	$100,000
Second quarter	$(2,000)	$100,000	$250,000
Third quarter	$ 1,000	$150,000	$250,000
Fourth quarter	$ 4,000	$100,000	$250,000

Required for each firm separately:

(a) Stockholders' equity sections of the firm's balance sheets as of the end of each quarter during 19X9 assuming no 19X9 income and footnoting any retained earnings restrictions.

(b) Stockholders' equity sections for the same four quarters including 19X9 income as given and providing an appropriation for any retained earnings restrictions.

Supplementary Problems

SP 10.11 Selected data from the Able Corporation's balance sheet as of 12/31/X0 were as follows:

Cash	$130,000	Total Liabilities	$220,000
Other Assets	840,000	Common Stock	400,000
		Additional Paid-in Capital	50,000
		Retained Earnings	300,000
Total Assets	$970,000	Total Equities	$970,000

The stock consisted of $10 par common stock with 40,000 shares issued and outstanding. During 19X1, the following major events occurred:

1. Able had net income of $200,000, all ending up as cash.

2. Able declared and then paid a cash dividend of $2 per share.

3. Able declared and distributed a 10 percent stock dividend when the market price was $45 per share.

4. After the stock dividend, Able split its common stock two for one.

How would you expect the accountant to report the effects of all of these events? Prepare a balance sheet for the Able Corporation as of 12/31/X1, reflecting the events given.

SP 10.12 Selected information from the Baker Corporation's 12/31/X0 balance sheet revealed:

		Total Liabilities	$ 200,000
		Common Stock*	300,000
		Additional Paid-in Capital	100,000
		Retained Earnings	600,000
Total Assets	$1,200,000	Total Equities	$1,200,000

* $10 par, 30,000 shares issued and outstanding.

During 19X1, the following events transpired:

1. Baker sold 5,000 shares of $100 par 14 percent preferred stock at $115 per share.

2. Baker split its common stock five for one.

3. The corporation received a gift of $50,000 cash.

4. After the stock split, the firm declared and issued a 10 percent stock dividend when the market price was $4 per share.

Prepare a balance sheet for the Baker Corporation as of 12/31/X1, reflecting these events.

SP 10.13 The Charlie Corporation's balance sheet, stockholders' equity section, was as follows as of 12/31/X0:

Preferred stock ($100 par; 12%)	$ 500,000
Additional paid-in capital on preferred stock	20,000
Common stock ($10 par; 200,000 shares)	2,000,000
Additional paid-in capital on common stock	810,000
Appropriation for self insurance	900,000
Unappropriated retained earnings	1,670,000
Total Stockholders' Equity	$5,900,000

During 19X1, the following events related to retained earnings occurred:

1. The company reported net income after taxes of $400,000.
2. The company declared a preferred dividend and a cash dividend of $1.50 per share on the common stock.
3. The company declared and distributed after the cash dividend a 5 percent stock dividend when the market price was $40 per share.
4. The directors voted to reduce the self insurance appropriation by $400,000.

What would be the 12/31/X1 balance in unappropriated retained earnings?

SP 10.14 Refer to the Charlie Corporation's 12/31/X0 statement in SP 10.13. Assume the following events occurred during 19X1.

1. The preferred dividend was declared and paid.
2. The common stock was split five for one.
3. After the split, a 10 percent stock dividend was declared and distributed when the market price was $9 per share.
4. After the stock dividend, a cash dividend of $.25 per share on the common was declared.
5. Reported net income after taxes for 19X1 was $300,000.

What would be the 12/31/X1 balance in unappropriated retained earnings?

SP 10.15 The Dawe Corporation's 12/31/X0 balance sheet stockholders' equity section was as follows:

Common stock ($5 par; 40,000 shares)	$200,000
Additional paid-in capital	60,000
Appropriated for treasury stock restriction	20,000
Unappropriated retained earnings	330,000
Treasury stock (400 shares)	(20,000)
Total Stockholders' Equity	$590,000

During 19X1 the company resold the 400 shares of treasury stock at a price of $55 per share. It subsequently purchased another 500 shares of treasury stock at a cost of $57 per share. Assume that no other events affecting owners' equity occurred during the year. Prepare the stockholders' equity section of the Dawe Corporation's 12/31/X1 balance sheet.

SP **10.16** Refer to the data given for the Dawe Corporation in SP 10.15. Assume that the following events took place in 19X1. The 400 shares of treasury stock had been resold at a price of $40 per share; and that, subsequently, 600 additional shares of treasury stock costing $38 per share had been acquired. Give the stockholders' equity section of the Dawe Corporation's 12/31/X1 balance sheet.

SP **10.17** Integrative Problem: The following events occurred during Period 9 for Luigi's Auto Parts:

1) Sales totaled $100,000, $25,000 for cash and the balance on account.
2) Collections of receivables from customers totaled $70,000.
3) Merchandise inventory costing $65,000 was purchased on account.
4) Wages and salaries totaling $27,500 were paid-including the $1,300 previously accrued.
5) Supplies costing $800 were purchased on account.
6) $2,000 was paid at the beginning of the period for insurance covering Periods 9 through 12.
7) $700 of bills for utilities and services consumed in the current period were received and recorded.
8) $9,925 of interest was paid covering the current period's interest costs (on the two mortgage notes and the equipment note) including the $3,575 previously accrued.
9) $56,600 was paid on accounts payable.
10) $7,900 was withdrawn by Luigi for personal use.

Adjustments were made for LIFO ending inventory of $47,000 (A); FIFO ending supplies inventory of $450 (B); $500 expiration of prepaid-insurance (C); $5,900 of depreciation on buildings and $1,400 depreciation on equipment (D); and accrual of $800 of wages and salaries earned but not yet paid (E).

Luigi's firm's balance sheet as of the end of Period 9 is given below:

LUIGI'S AUTO PARTS BALANCE SHEET AS OF THE END OF PERIOD 9

ASSETS		EQUITIES	
Cash	$ 9,960	Accounts Payable	$ 20,000
Accounts Receivable	70,000	Wages and Salaries	800
Inventory	47,000	Total Current Liabilities	$ 20,800
Supplies	450		
Prepaid Items	1,500	Noncurrent Notes Payable	151,000
Total Current Assets	$128,910	Total Liabilities	$171,800
Land	25,000		
Buildings	125,000		
Accum. Depr. Bldgs.	(12,200)		
Equipment	20,000		
Accum. Depr. Equip.	(2,900)	Luigi Cavelli, Capital	112,010
Total Assets	$283,810	Total Equities	$283,810

During Period 10, the following events occurred affecting the financial position of Luigi's Auto Parts (Note: Items marked with an asterisk have been illustrated in previous periods):

*1) Sales totaled $125,000, $30,000 for cash and the balance on account.

*2) Collections on customer receivables totaled $90,000.

*3) Merchandise inventory costing $72,000 was purchased on account. Inventory purchases were added directly to the inventory account.

*4) Supplies costing $600 were purchased on account.

*5) Wages and salaries totaling $27,200 were paid-including the $800 previously accrued.

*6) $680 of bills for utilities and services consumed in the current period were received and recorded.

*7) $78,280 was paid on accounts payable.

 8) At the beginning of the period, Luigi decided that he could no longer devote the long hours necessary to be the sole manager responsible for all of the management of the business. He wished to have someone take responsibility for financial management and allow him to concentrate on merchandising operations; and yet he knew he could not afford a a salaried financial executive at the current level of operations. He was also concerned about the high level of interest costs (currently $6,350 per period) and his firm's very high long-term debt ratio (0.574 at the end of Period 9). He realized that his firm's creditors only went along with so much debt since his firm was a proprietorship and therefore his personal assets could also be attached.

 Tony Sorbo, who currently held the second mortgage note for $15,000 on the building, he knew to be a competent financial manager. Luigi approached Tony, and he agreed to become a general partner in the firm. The firm would be renamed "Luigi and Tony's Auto Parts," and the partnership agreement provided:

 • Effective at the beginning of Period 10, Tony (as Partner B) would personally and solely assume liability for one half of the $120,000 first mortgage note (you may assume this arrangement was acceptable to the creditor), and this $60,000 claim plus Tony's $15,000 second mortgage claim would be converted to a partnership share in the same amount. The beginning balance of Luigi's proprietorship capital would be transferred to his partner's capital account (Partner A).

 • Profits or losses of the partnership would be allocated in three steps:

Step 1: In recognition of partners' investment, each period the amount of capital invested by each partner is defined as the beginning partner share of owners' equity plus additional investments less withdrawals during the period. Profits or losses up to 3 percent of total partners' capital invested (as defined) and rounded to whole dollars are allocated in proportion to partners' respective shares (rounded to the nearest percent).

Step 2: In lieu of salary or commission, and in recognition of Luigi's intended greater contribution of time, profits or losses up to $10,000 per period in excess of the amount allocated in Step 1 are to be apportioned 75 percent to Luigi as Partner A (rounded to whole dollars) with the balance to Tony as Partner B.

Step 3: Any profit in excess of that allocated in Steps 1 and 2 is apportioned equally between the partners (rounded to whole dollars).

 9) During the period, Luigi withdrew $4,083 for personal use.

At the end of Period 10:

*A)   Merchandise inventory was adjusted to reflect ending inventory at LIFO of $46,000.

*B)   Supplies inventory was adjusted to reflect ending supplies on hand under FIFO of $380.

*C)   Prepaid items was adjusted to reflect expiration of $500 of prepaid-insurance.

*D)   Wages and salaries totaling $600 earned but not yet paid were accrued.

*E)   Depreciation of $5,600 on buildings and $1,300 on equipment was recorded.

*F)   Interest of $2,400 for the period on the remaining $60,000 first mortgage note and interest of $800 on the equipment note was owed and accrued.

 G)   The firm's earnings were apportioned to partners per the partnership agreement (see transaction 8 above).

Required:
 a)   Prepare a balance sheet effect worksheet for the partnership for Period 10 starting with the Period 9 ending balances identified as (b). Record the effect of all transactions and all adjustments (except adjustment G) for the period identified with their numbers or letters. Record partner withdrawals to the partner's capital accounts and record all revenues and expenses in an income box. Provide necessary space on your worksheet by entering account titles as follows:

Account	Line number	Account	Line number
Cash	1	Accounts Payable	1
Accounts Receivable	8	Wages and Salaries	7
Inventory	12	Interest Payable	11
Supplies	16	Noncurrent Notes Payable	14
Prepaid Items	20	Luigi Cavelli, Capital	17
Land	23	Tony Sorbo, Capital	20
Buildings	25		
Accum. Depr. Bldgs.	27		
Equipment	30		
Accum. Depr. Equip.	32		

 b)   Prepare the firm's income statement for Period 10 in good form following the multiple step format.
 c)   Prepare the statement of partner's capital in good form for the period indicating allocation of partner's profit shares per the partnership agreement.
 d)   Prepare the firm's balance sheet in good form as of the end of Period 10.
 e)   Prepare the firm's statement of cash flows for Period 10 in good form using the indirect method for operating activities.
 f)   Determine for Luigi and Tony's firm as of the end of Period 10:
      1. The amount of net working capital in the business;
      2. The current ratio (to two decimals);
      3. The quick ratio (to two decimals);
      4. The long-term debt ratio (to three decimals); and
      5. The asset composition ratio (to three decimals).

SP   10.18 Integrative Problem: The following events occurred during Period 9 for Irene's Sport Shop:

1) Sales totaled $160,000, $65,000 for cash and the balance on account.
2) Collections of receivables from customers totaled $90,000.
3) Merchandise inventory costing $85,000 was purchased on account.
4) Wages and salaries totaling $40,700 were paid-including the $1,500 previously accrued.
5) Supplies costing $300 were purchased on account.
6) $4,800 was paid at the beginning of the period for insurance covering Periods 9 through 12.
7) $1,400 of bills for utilities and services consumed in the current period were received and recorded.
8) $25,750 of interest was paid covering the current period's interest costs (on the two mortgage notes and the equipment note) including the $9,050 previously accrued.
9) $51,700 was paid on accounts payable.
10) $50,000 was withdrawn by Irene for personal use.

Adjustments were made for LIFO ending inventory of $75,000 (A); FIFO ending supplies inventory of $400 (B); $1,200 expiration of prepaid-insurance (C); $14,200 of wages and salaries earned but not yet paid (E). Irene's firm's balance sheet as of the end of Period 9 is given below:

IRENE'S SPORT SHOP BALANCE SHEET AS OF THE END OF PERIOD 9

ASSETS		EQUITIES	
Cash	$ 33,225	Accounts Payable	$ 75,000
Accounts Receivable	98,000	Wages and Salaries	800
Inventory	75,000	Total Current Liabilities	$ 75,800
Supplies	400		
Prepaid Items	3,600	Noncurrent Notes Payable	388,000
Total Current Assets	$210,225	Total Liabilities	$463,800
Land	90,000		
Buildings	370,000		
Accum. Depr. Bldgs.	(29,000)		
Equipment	35,000		
Accum. Depr. Equip.	(4,650)	Irene Morton, Capital	207,775
Total Assets	$671,575	Total Equities	$671,575

During Period 10, the following events occurred affording the financial position of Irene's Sports Shop: (Note: Items marked with an asterisk have been illustrated in previous periods.)

*1) Sales totaled $200,000, $80,000 for cash and the balance on account.
*2) Collections on customer receivables totaled $110,000.
*3) Merchandise inventory costing $120,000 was purchased on account. Inventory purchases were added directly to the inventory account.
*4) Supplies costing $1,350 were purchased on account.

*5) Wages and salaries totaling $39,400 were paid-including the $800 previously accrued.

*6) $1,600 of bills for utilities and services consumed in the current period were received and recorded.

*7) $147,850 was paid on accounts payable.

8) At the beginning of the period, Irene decided that she could no longer devote the long hours necessary to be the sole manager responsible for all of the management of the business. She wished to have someone take responsibility for merchandising operations and allow her to concentrate on general and financial management; and yet she knew she could not afford a salaried merchandising executive at the current level of operations. She was also concerned about the high level of interest costs (currently $16,700 per period) and her firm's very high long-term debt ratio (.651 at the end of Period 9). She realized that her firm's creditors only went along with so much debt since her firm was a proprietorship and therefore her personal assets could also be attached. Janet Chang, who currently held the second mortgage note for $90,000 on the building, she knew to be a competent merchandising manager. Irene approached Janet, and she agreed to become a general partner in the firm. The firm would be renamed "Irene and Jan's Sports Shop," and the partnership agreement provided:

* Effective at the beginning of Period 10, Janet (as Partner B) would personally and solely assume liability for one third of the $270,000 first mortgage note (you may assume this arrangement was acceptable to the creditor), and this $90,000 claim plus Janet's $90,000 second mortgage claim would be converted to a partnership share in the same amount. The beginning balance of Irene's proprietorship capital would be transferred to her partner's capital account (Partner A).

* Profits or losses of the partnership would be allocated in three steps:

Step 1: In recognition of partners' investment, each period the amount of capital contributed by each partner is defined as the beginning partner share of owners' equity plus additional investments less withdrawals during the period. Profits or losses up to four percent of total partners' capital contributed (as defined) and rounded to whole dollars are allocated in proportion to partners' respective shares (rounded to the nearest one percent).

Step 2: In lieu of salary or commission, and in recognition of Janet's intended greater contribution of merchandising expertise, profits or losses up to $12,000 per period in excess of the amount allocated in Step 1 are to be apportioned 60 percent to Janet an Partner B (rounded to whole dollars) with the balance to Irene as Partner A.

Step 3: Any profit in excess of that allocated in Steps 1 and 2 apportioned equally between the partners (rounded to whole dollars).

9) During the period, Irene withdrew $7,775 for personal use.

At the end of Period 10:

*A) Merchandise inventory was adjusted to reflect ending inventory at LIFO of $95,000.

*B) Supplies inventory was adjusted to reflect ending supplies on hand under FIFO of $750.

*C) Prepaid items was adjusted to reflect expiration of $1,200 of prepaid-insurance.

*D) Wages and salaries totaling $1,400 earned but not yet paid were accrued.

*E)   Depreciation of $13,600 on buildings and $2,100 on equipment was recorded.

*F)   Interest of $7,200 for the period on the remaining $180,000 first mortgage note and interest of $1,400 on the equipment note was owed and accrued.

G)   The firm's earnings were apportioned to partners per the partnership agreement (see transaction 8 above).

Required:

a)   Prepare a balance sheet effect worksheet for the partnership for Period 10 starting with the Period 9 ending balances identified at (b). Record the effect of all transactions and all adjustments (except adjustment G) for the period identified with their numbers or letters. Record partner withdrawals to the partner's capital accounts and record all revenues and expenses to an income box. Provide necessary space on your worksheet by entering account titles as follows:

Account	Line number	Account	Line number
Cash	1	Accounts Payable	1
Accounts Receivable	8	Wages and Salaries	7
Inventory	12	Interest Payable	11
Supplies	16	Noncurrent Notes Payable	14
Prepaid Items	20	Irene Morton, Capital	17
Land	23	Janet Chang, Capital	20
Buildings	25		
Accum. Depr. Bldgs.	27		
Equipment	30		
Accum. Depr. Equip.	32		

b)   Prepare the firm's income statement for Period 10 in good form following the multiple step format.

c)   Prepare the statement of partner's capital in good form for the period indicating allocation of partner's profit shares per the partnership agreement.

d)   Prepare the firm's balance sheet in good form as of the end of Period 10.

e)   Prepare the firm's cash flows for Period 10 in good form following the indirect method for operating activities.

f)   Determine for Irene and Janet's firm as of the end of Period 10.

   1.   The amount of net working capital in the business;
   2.   The current ratio (to two decimals);
   3.   The quick ratio (to two decimals);
   4.   The long-term debt ratio (to three decimals); and
   5.   The asset composition ratio (to three decimals).

SP 10.19 Integrative Problem: The following events occurred during Period 11 for Luigi and Tony's Auto Parts:

1) Sales totaled $130,000, $30,000 for cash and the balance on account.
2) Collections of receivables from customers totaled $95,000.
3) Merchandise inventory costing $80,000 was purchased on account.
4) Wages and salaries totaling $27,600 were paid-including the $600 previously accrued.
5) Supplies costing $720 were purchased on account.
6) $750 of bills for utilities and services consumed in the current period were received and recorded.
7) $6,400 of interest was paid covering the current period's interest costs on the $60,000 building mortgage note and on the $16,000 equipment note and also including the $3,200 previously accrued.
8) $80,470 was paid on accounts payable.
9) $20,977 was withdrawn by partners, $11,836 by Luigi and $9,141 by Tony.

   Adjustments were made for LIFO ending inventory of $48,000 (A); FIFO ending supplies inventory of $400 (B); $500 expiration of prepaid-insurance (C); $5,400 of depreciation on buildings and $1,200 depreciation on equipment (D); accrual of $1,500 of wages and salaries earned but not yet paid (E); and profit allocation of $8,025 to Luigi and $3,725 to Tony (F).

Luigi and Tony's firm's balance sheet as of the end of Period 11 is given below:

LUIGI AND TONY'S AUTO PARTS BALANCE SHEET AS OF THE END OF PERIOD 11			
ASSETS		**EQUITIES**	
Cash	$ 9,950	Accounts Payable	$ 16,000
Accounts Receivable	80,000	Wages and Salaries	1,500
Inventory	48,000	Total Current Liabilities	$ 17,500
Supplies	400		
Prepaid Items	500	Noncurrent Notes Payable	76,000
Total Current Assets	$138,850	Total Liabilities	$ 93,500
Land	25,000		
Buildings	125,000		
Accum. Depr. Bldgs.	(23,200)		
Equipment	20,000	Luigi Cavelli, Capital	113,025
Accum. Depr.Equip.	(5,400)	Tony Sorbo, Capital	73,725
Total Assets	$280,250	Total Equities	$280,250

During Period 12, the following events affected the financial position of Luigi and Tony's Auto Parts: (Note: Items marked with an asterisk have been illustrated in previous periods.)

*1) Sales totaled $150,000, $40,000 for cash and the balance on account.

*2) Collections of customer receivables totaled $115,000.

*3) Merchandise inventory costing $88,000 was purchased on account. Inventory purchases were added directly to the inventory account.

*4) Supplies costing $1,000 were purchased on account.

*5) Wages and salaries totaling $30,600 were paid-including the $1,500 previously accrued.

*6) $800 of bills for utilities and services consumed in the current period were received and recorded.

*7) $1,600 representing one half of the current period's interest costs were paid.

*8) $88,850 was paid on accounts payable.

9) In anticipation of future expansion and the need to raise additional capital, and for certain tax advantages, Luigi and Tony incorporated the business at the beginning of the period. The new corporation was named the LUTON Corporation. Its charter authorized the sale of 20,000 shares of $100 par preferred stock, with a claim against assets in the event of liquidation of $125 per share, and with a noncumulative dividend of 2.5 percent per period. The corporation was also authorized to issue 200,000 shares of $5 par voting common stock.

Legal fees and other costs of incorporation including the printing of necessary stock certificates amounted to $1,200, were paid, and were written off as miscellaneous expense during the period.

10) The partners agreed to issue themselves 36,000 shares of common stock in exchange for their capital interests at the start of the period with 22,000 shares going to Luigi and 14,000 shares to Tony.

11) Additional capital was raised through the sale of 1,000 shares of preferred stock to relatives and friends early in the period at a price of $110 per share.

12) At the end of the period, the preferred dividend of $2,500 was declared and paid.

13) At the end of the period, to conserve cash for expansion, the Directors declared and distributed a five percent stock dividend. Since there was no established market value for the stock, the Directors voted to capitalize the stock dividend at the par value of $5 per share.

14) A cash dividend on the common stock outstanding after the stock dividend of $0.05 per share was declared to be paid early in Period 13.

At the end of Period 12:

*A) Merchandise inventory was adjusted to reflect ending inventory at LIFO of $46,000.

*B) Supplies inventory was adjusted to reflect the expiration of $500 of prepaid-insurance.

*C) Prepaid items were adjusted to reflect the expiration of $500 of prepaid-insurance.

*D) Wages and salaries totaling $900 earned but not yet paid were accrued.

*E) Depreciation expense of $5,100 on buildings and $1,100 on equipment was recorded.

*F) Utilities cost estimated at $50 consumed but not yet billed was accrued.

*G) Interest owed of $1,600 and unpaid was accrued. H) Corporate income taxes payable early in Period 13 were estimated to be $2,900.

Required:

a) The effect on the beginning period balance sheet of those Period 12 transactions and adjustments that were introduced in earlier periods, and which are identified with any asterisk (*), has already been recorded in the partially completed balance sheet effect worksheet given below. Prepare a final balance sheet effect worksheet for the LUTON Corporation for Period 12 starting with the Preliminary Balances and recording the effect of Period 12 transactions (9) through (14) and adjustment (H). Provide necessary space on your worksheet by entering account titles as follows:

Account	Line number	Account	Line number
Cash	1	Accounts Payable	1
Accounts Receivable	6	Wages and Salaries	3
Inventory	8	Interest Payable	5
Supplies	10	Taxes Payable	7
Land	12	Dividends Payable	10
Buildings	14	Noncurrent Notes Payable	13
Accum. Depr. Buildings	16	Luigi Cavelli, Capital	16
Equipment	18	Tony Sorbo, Capital	17
Accum. Depr. Equipment	20	Preferred Stock	22
		Addtl. Paid-in capital, Preferred	25
		Common Stock	28
		Addtl. Paid-in capital, Common	32
		Retained Earnings	35

b) Prepare the firm's income statement for Period 12 in good form following the multiple step format.

c) Prepare the statement of retained earnings in good form for Period 12.

d) Prepare the firm's balance sheet in good form as of the end of Period 12.

e) Prepare the firm's statement of cash flows in good form following the indirect method for operating activities.

f) Determine for the LUTON Corporation for Period 12:

1. The amount of net working capital in the business at the end of the period;

2. The period end current ratio (to two decimals);

3. The period end quick ratio (to two decimals);

4. The period end long-term debt ratio (to three decimals);

5. The period end asset composition ratio (to three decimals); and

6. The book value per share at the end of the period.

PARTIALLY COMPLETED BALANCE SHEET EFFECT WORKSHEET
LUTON Corporation Period 12
(b = Beginning Balance; p = Partially Complete Ending Balance)

Cash			Accounts Payable		
$	9,950	(b)	$	16,000	(b)
+	40,000	(1)	+	88,000	(3)
+	115,000	(2)	+	1,000	(4)
−	30,600	(5)	+	800	(6)
−	1,600	(7)	−	88,850	(8)
−	88,850	(8) $ 43,900 (p)	+	50	(F) $ 17,000 (p)

Accounts Receivable			Wages and Salaries		
	80,000	(b)		1,500	(b)
+	110,000	(1)	−	1,500	(5)
−	115,000	(2) 75,000 (p)	+	900	(D) 900 (p)

Inventory			Interest Payable		
	48,000	(b)		0	(b)
+	88,000	(3)	+	1,600	(G) 1,600 (p)
−	90,000	(A) 46,000 (p)	Noncurrent Notes Payable		

Supplies				76,000	(b) 76,000 (p)
	400	(b)	Luigi Cavelli, Capital		
+	1,000	(4)		113,025 (b)	113,025 (p)
−	800	(B) 600 (p)	Tony Sorbo, Capital		

Prepaid Items				73,725 (b)	73,725 (p)
	500	(b)	Preferred Stock		
−	500	(C)		0 (b)	0 (p)

Land			Addtl. Paid–in Capital, Preferred		
	25,000	(b) 25,000 (p)		0 (b)	0 (p)

Buildings			Common Stock		
	125,000	(b) 125,000 (p)		0 (b)	0 (p)

Accum. Depr. Buildings			Addtl. Paid–in Capital, Common		
	(23,200)	(b)		0 (b)	0 (p)
−	5,100	(E) (28,300)(p)		0 (b)	0 (p)

Equipment			Retained Earnings		
	20,000	(b) 20,000 (p)		0 (b)	0 (p)

Accum. Depr. Equipment			Income		
	(5,400)	(b)	+	150,000	(1)
−	1,100	(E) (6,500)(p)	−	29,100	(5)
			−	800	(6)
			−	1,600	(7)
			−	90,000	(A)
			−	800	(B)
			−	500	(C)
			−	900	(D)
			−	6,200	(E)
			−	50	(F)
			−	1,600	(G) 18,450 (p)

TOTALS	$ 300,700 (p)	TOTALS	$ 300,700 (p)

SP **10.20** Integrative Problem: The following events occurred during Period 11 for Irene and Jan's Sport Shop:

1) Sales totaled $220,000, $50,000 for cash and the balance on account.

2) Collections of receivables from customers totaled $160,000.

3) Merchandise inventory costing $120,000 was purchased on account.

4) Wages and salaries totaling $48,900 were paid-including the $1,400 previously accrued.

5) Supplies costing $700 were purchased on account.

6) $1,550 of bills for utilities and services consumed in the current period were received and recorded.

7) $17,200 of interest was paid covering the current period's interest costs (on the $180,000 building mortgage note and on the $28,000 equipment note) including the $8,600 previously accrued.

8) $97,250 was paid on accounts payable.

9) $22,000 was withdrawn by partners, $15,236 by Irene and $6,744 by Janet.

Adjustments were made for LIFO ending inventory of $103,000 (A); FIFO ending supplies inventory of $400 (B); $1,200 expiration of prepaid-insurance (C); $13,100 of depreciation on buildings and $1,950 depreciation on equipment (D); accrual of $2,500 of wages and salaries earned but not yet paid (E); and profit allocation of $14,275 to Irene and $16,275 to Janet (F). Irene and Jan's firm's balance sheet as of the end of Period 11 is given below:

IRENE AND JAN'S SPORT SHOP
BALANCE SHEET AS OF THE END OF PERIOD 11

ASSETS		EQUITIES	
Cash	$ 52,850	Accounts Payable	$ 75,000
Accounts Receivable	118,000	Wages and Salaries	2,500
Inventory	103,000	Total Current Liabilities	$ 77,500
Supplies	400		
Prepaid Items	1,200	Noncurrent Notes Payable	208,000
Total Current Assets	$275,450	Total Liabilities	$285,500
Land	90,000		
Buildings	370,000		
Accum. Depr. Bldgs.	(55,700)	Irene Morton, Capital	214,275
Equipment	35,000		
Accum. Depr. Equip.	(8,700)	Janet Chang, Capital	206,275
Total Assets	$706,050	Total Equities	$706,050

During Period 12, the following events occurred affecting the financial position of Irene and Jan's Sport Shop: (Note: Items marked with an asterisk have been illustrated in previous periods.)

*1) Sales totaled $230,000, $55,000 for cash and the balance on account.

*2) Collections of customer receivables totaled $165,000.

*3) Merchandise inventory costing $150,000 was purchased on account. Inventory purchases were added directly to the inventory account.

*4) Supplies costing $2,000 were purchased on account.

*5) Wages and salaries totaling $57,000 were paid-including the $2,500 previously accrued.

*6) $1,500 for bills for utilities and services consumed in the current period were received and recorded.

*7) $4,300 representing one half of the current period's interest costs were paid.

*8) $128,600 was paid on accounts payable.

9) In anticipation of future expansion and the need to raise additional capital, and for certain tax advantages, Irene and Janet incorporated the business at the beginning of the period. The new corporation was named the MORCHAN Corporation. Its charter authorized the sale of 50,000 shares of $100 par preferred stock, with a claim against assets in the event of liquidation of $110 per share, and with a non cumulative dividend of three percent per period. The corporation was also authorized to issue 500,000 shares of $10 par voting common stock.

Legal fees and other costs of incorporation including the printing of necessary stock certificates accounted to $2,500, were paid, and were written off as miscellaneous expense during the period.

10) The partners agreed to issue themselves 40,800 shares of common stock in exchange for their capital interests at the start of the period with 20,800 shares going to Irene and 20,000 shares to Janet.

11) Additional capital was raised through the sale of 2,000 shares of preferred stock to relatives and friends early in the period at a price of $105 per share.

12) At the end of the period, the preferred dividend of $6,000 was declared and paid.

13) At the end of the period, to conserve cash for expansion, the Directors declared and distributed a two percent stock dividend. Since there was no established market value for the stock, the Directors voted to capitalize the stock dividend at the par value of $10 per share.

14) A cash dividend on the common stock outstanding after the stock dividend of $0.05 per share was declared to be paid early in Period 13.

At the end of Period 12:

*A) Merchandise inventory was adjusted to reflect ending inventory at LIFO of $133,000.

*B) Supplies inventory was adjusted to reflect ending supplies on hand under FIFO of $1,250.

*C) Prepaid items were adjusted to reflect the expiration of $1,200 of prepaid-insurance.

*D) Wages and salaries totaling $900 earned but not yet paid were accrued.

*E) Depreciation expense of $5,100 on buildings and $1,100 on equipment was recorded.

*F) Utilities cost estimated at $50 consumed but not yet billed was accrued.

*G) Interest owed of $1,600 and unpaid was accrued. H) Corporate income taxes payable early in Period 13 were estimated to be $2,900.

Required:

a) The effect on the beginning period balance sheet of those Period 12 transactions and adjustments that were introduced in earlier periods, and which are identified with any asterisk (*), has already been recorded in the partially completed balance sheet effect worksheet given below. Prepare a final balance sheet effect worksheet for the LUTON Corporation for Period 12 starting with the Preliminary Balances and recording the effect of Period 12 transactions (9) through (14) and adjustment (H). Provide necessary space on your worksheet by entering account titles as follows:

Account	Line number	Account	Line number
Cash	1	Accounts Payable	1
Accounts Receivable	6	Wages and Salaries	3
Inventory	8	Interest Payable	5
Supplies	10	Taxes Payable	7
Land	12	Dividends Payable	10
Buildings	14	Noncurrent Notes Payable	13
Accum. Depr. Buildings	16	Luigi Cavelli, Capital	16
Equipment	18	Tony Sorbo, Capital	19
Accum. Depr. Equipment	20	Preferred Stock	22
		Addtl. Paid-in capital, Preferred	25
		Common Stock	28
		Addtl. Paid-in capital, Common	32
		Retained Earnings	35

b) Prepare the firm's income statement for Period 12 in good form following the multiple step format.

c) Prepare the statement of retained earnings in good form for Period 12.

d) Prepare the firm's balance sheet in good form as of the end of Period 12.

e) Prepare the firm's statement of cash flows for Period 12 in good form following the indirect method for operating activities.

f) Determine for the LUTON Corporation for Period 12:

1. The amount of net working capital in the business at the end of Period 12;
2. The period end current ratio (to two decimals);
3. The period end quick ratio (to two decimals);
4. The period end long-term debt ratio (to three decimals);
5. The period end asset composition ratio (to three decimals);
6. The book value per share at the end of the period.

PARTIALLY COMPLETED BALANCE SHEET EFFECT WORKSHEET
MORCHAN Corporation Period 12
(b = Beginning Balance; p = Partially Complete Ending Balance)

Cash		Accounts Payable	
$ 52,850 (b)		$ 75,000 (b)	
+ 55,000 (1)		+ 150,000 (3)	
+ 165,000 (2)		+ 2,000 (4)	
− 57,000 (5)		+ 1,500 (6)	
− 4,300 (7)		− 128,600 (8)	
− 128,600 (8)	$ 82,950 (p)	+ 100 (F)	$ 100,000 (p)
Accounts Receivable		**Wages and Salaries**	
118,000 (b)		2,500 (b)	
+ 175,000 (1)		− 2,500 (5)	
− 165,000 (2)	128,000 (p)	+ 500 (D)	500 (p)
Inventory		**Interest Payable**	
103,000 (b)		0 (b)	
+ 150,000 (3)		+ 4,300 (G)	4,300 (p)
− 120,000 (A)	133,000 (p)	**Noncurrent Notes Payable**	
Supplies		208,000 (b)	208,000 (p)
400 (b)			
+ 2,000 (4)		**Irene Morton, Capital**	
− 1,150 (B)	1,250 (p)	214,275 (b)	214,275 (p)
Prepaid Items		**Janet Chang, Capital**	
1,200 (b)		206,275 (b)	206,275 (p)
− 1,200 (C)	0 (p)	**Preferred Stock**	
Land 90,000 (b)	90,000 (p)	0 (b)	0 (p)
Buildings		**Addtl. Paid–in Capital, Preferred**	
370,000 (b)	370,000 (p)	0 (b)	0 (p)
Accum. Depr.–Bldgs.		**Common Stock**	
(55,700)		0 (b)	0 (p)
− 12,600 (E)	(68,300)(p)	**Addtl. Paid–in Capital, Common**	
Equipment		0 (b)	0 (p)
35,000 (b)	35,000 (p)	**Retained Earnings**	
Accum. Depr.–Equip.		0 (b)	0 (p)
(8,700) (b)		**Income**	
− 1,800 (E)	(10,500)(p)		

Income:

+	230,000	(1)
−	54,500	(5)
−	1,500	(6)
−	4,300	(7)
−	120,000	(A)
−	1,150	(B)
−	1,200	(C)
−	500	(D)
−	14,400	(E)
−	100	(F)
−	4,300	(G) 28,050 (p)

TOTALS	$ 761,400	TOTALS	$ 761,400 (p)

Preparer Problems

PP 10.1 Prepare journal entries in good form for the transactions given in EP 10.5 and for closing income summary and dividends declared to retained earnings.

PP 10.2 Prepare the same entries required in PP 10.1 for the X, Y, and Z Corporations from data given in EP 10.6.

PP 10.3 Prepare the journal entry required for the stock dividend in EP 10.7.

PP 10.4 Prepare journal entries for each firm's stock dividend from data given in EP 10.8.

PP 10.5 Prepare journal entries to record the three 19X4 events given in EP 10.9. Assume that the firm footnotes retained earnings restrictions.

PP 10.6 Prepare journal entries to record for each firm the two treasury stock transactions and the two independent appropriations from data given in EP 10.10 assuming that the firm uses appropriations for all retained earnings restrictions.

PP 10.7 Prepare journal entries for all asterisked transactions and adjustments for Period 10 for Luigi's and Tony's Auto Parts from data given in SP 10.17.

PP 10.8 Prepare journal entries for Period 10 for Irene's and Jan's Sports Shop from data given in SP 10.18 for (a) All asterisked transactions and adjustments, and, (b) All non asterisked transactions and adjustments.

PP 10.9 Prepare journal entries for all asterisked transactions and adjustments for Period 12 for the Luton Corporation from data given in SP 10.19.

PP 10.10 Prepare journal entries for Period 12 for MORCHAN Corporation from data given in SP 10.20 for (a) All asterisked transactions and adjustments and (b) All non asterisked transactions and adjustments.

11

Measurement of Assets
and Asset Valuation

Chapter Preview

The objective of this chapter is to complete your understanding of asset measurement in conformance with GAAP. In this chapter you can:

1. Become familiar with the concept of consolidation and the purpose of consolidated financial statements;

2. Review the basic principles of asset measurement incorporated in GAAP;

3. Learn how accountants apply these principles to the initial valuation of specific assets not covered in previous chapters;

4. Learn how accountants apply these principles to the measurement of specific assets subsequent to their acquisition;

5. Complete your understanding of those adjustments to assets (reflecting revenue and expenses) which are included in income from operations;

6. Review all changes that can occur to all common asset accounts; and

7. Complete your understanding of those adjustments to assets that do not involve cash flows, and therefore are not part of cash from operating activities.

With this knowledge, you will be qualified to read and correctly interpret the asset side of most published balance sheets. You will also have the necessary background to learn about and be able to intelligently use more sophisticated tools of balance sheet analysis pertaining to assets.

Asset Measurement Under GAAP

Remember, from previous chapters, that the accountant's basis for the initial measurement of assets is the fair market value of the asset at the time of its acquisition. When a new asset is acquired from an unrelated party in an arm's length transaction, the cost can be assumed to represent the fair value. In related party transactions, verification of fair value is required.

Subsequent to acquisition, GAAP require that all assets be reduced to reflect expirations of usefulness or unrecoverable amounts. Remember that property, plant, and equipment, except land, are systematically depreciated down to salvage (recoverable) value and that, following the principle of conservatism, anticipated losses are recognized when the loss becomes reasonably certain (LCM for inventory, for example).

Accountants, following the principle of **full disclosure**, recognize all measurable assets which the firm owns, has a legal claim upon, or effectively controls, as of the statement date. Adjustments at year-end recognizing accrued interest and rent receivable are examples of the implementation of this principle.

What are These Items?

Grace Wong has been assigned by her firm to analyze the Omega Corporation's financial statements including the footnotes that are part of the financial statement package. Grace's firm is considering the purchase of the Omega Corporation. The current phase of her study focuses on Omega's assets. Her firm wishes to know exactly what assets it would be acquiring, and how they are currently measured (valued) by Omega.

Exhibit 11.1 gives the asset portion of Omega's most recent balance sheet and contains additional information related to Omega's assets selected from the statement footnotes. Grace understands that, on the balance sheet, monetary assets are shown at or near current value and nonmonetary items are shown at adjusted original cost. These generalized asset measurement and reporting objectives were first presented in Chapter 2. She has marked with an asterisk the items requiring clarification on Omega's balance sheet. These items will be discussed in the chapter.

Consolidated Financial Statements

Before proceeding with asset measurement, the meaning of the term "consolidated statement" requires clarification. Many of the financial statements you will read will be consolidated statements. It is important that you understand that they differ from a single firm's statements only with respect to the entity being reported upon. Basic accounting principles of measurement and reporting are not affected.

Exhibit 11.1

Omega Corporation
Asset Portion of Consolidated Balance Sheet as of 12/31/X1 ($ in thousands)

Cash		$ 35
*Marketable securities[1]		120
Current receivables:		
Notes receivable	$ 95	
*Discount on notes receivable	(5)	
Accounts receivable	200	
*Allowance for bad debts	(3)	
Accrued interest receivable	15	302
Inventory[2]		425
Supplies		12
Prepaid items		30
Total Current Assets		$924
*Investments and funds[3]		874
Property, plant, and equipment:		
Land	$ 220	
Buildings and equipment[4]	759	
less Accumulated depreciation for bldgs and equip.	(260)	
*Property under capital lease[5]	600	
less Accumulated depreciation for capital lease	(200)	1,119
Intangible and other:		
*Deferred charges[6]	$ 10	
*Goodwill	175	185
Total Assets		$3,102

1. Cost $136,000.
2. At LCM using FIFO.
3. Investments and funds include:

Acme Corporation Bonds (11 % maturing 12/31/X9)	190,000
Premium on Acme Bonds	10,291
Baker Corporation Bonds (8% maturing 12/31/X5)	218,000
Discount on Baker Bonds	(14,094)
Carter Corporation Preferred Stock (Market value $46,000)	39,000
Dungeness Corp. Common Stock (3% ownership, market $50,000)	41,000
Edwards, Corporation Common Stock (25% ownership, market $340,000, includes $18,000 equity in Edwards' undistributed earnings)	310,000
Noncurrent Note Receivable (2% maturing 12/31/X9)	130,000
Discount on Noncurrent Note Receivable	(70,000)
Bond Sinking Fund	19,803
Total	$874,000

4. At cost using straight-line depreciation.
5. Leased for three years on 1/1/X1 paying $100,426 on signing and providing for three annual payments at year-end of $208,200 each.
6. Unamortized costs of long-term debt financing.

For various reasons, many large corporations have acquired all, or at least more than half, of the voting common stock of another corporation. In such cases the acquiring corporation is known as a **parent** corporation. The other corporation which is legally controlled (through ownership of a majority of stockholder votes) by a parent is known as a **subsidiary** corporation. Sometimes a parent with 100 percent control will legally merge with its wholly owned subsidiary. Legal or statutory merger involves transferring all the assets and liabilities from the wholly owned subsidiary to the parent. The subsidiary thereafter ceases operating as a separate legal entity and a parent subsidiary relationship no longer exists.[1]

Where a parent subsidiary relationship exists, and there is no statutory merger, the parent is required by GAAP to prepare consolidated financial statements in addition to preparing its own regular statements. **Consolidated statements** can be viewed as statements showing "what we would look like if we were merged." All assets owned, effectively controlled, or involving claims against those outside of the new "family" and all established legal claims from those outside of the new "family," are combined into a consolidated balance sheet. The statement reports on paper the effective "economic entity," the parent and the subsidiaries it legally controls. The parent and its subsidiaries, however, continue as legally separate entities with independent sets of accounting records.

Actual preparation of consolidated statements is sufficiently intricate so that a significant portion of advanced accounting courses are spent on these techniques. For our purposes, we can assume that consolidated statements merely represent a combination of parent and subsidiary information with "intrafamily" items eliminated. An example of an "intrafamily" elimination would be a situation where a subsidiary owed the parent $50,000 at year-end. The subsidiary would have $50,000 of Notes Payable and the parent would have $50,000 of Notes Receivable. On a combined balance sheet for the "family," $50,000 would be eliminated from both combined receivables and combined payables as part of the preparation of a consolidated statement. The $50,000 would not be collectible from, or payable to, anyone outside the "family." Consolidated statements are discussed more fully in Chapter 14. Grace Wong can assume that the fact that Omega's statement is consolidated need not affect her understanding of the basic asset measurement principles employed by accountants.[2]

Current Marketable Securities

Securities—stocks, bonds, and notes—that are readily salable are known as marketable securities. Marketable securities are purchased by the firm as a short-term investment of excess idle cash (where the securities' conversion into cash could occur within one year as a normal part of business) and are classified as current assets. Those securities which are either

---

[1] A statutory merger could also involve the parent and wholly owned subsidiary transferring assets and liabilities of both into a third corporation, which would then be the surviving entity.

[2] The method of consolidation, however, could affect whether certain assets are restated to more recent costs and whether goodwill is recognized.

not readily marketable or are expected to be held longer than one year are classified as long-lived assets under investments (see below). Most current marketable securities are usually in the form of U.S. Treasury bills or short-term notes.[3] Marketable securities are initially recorded at cost. Recall that cash equivalents, those securities maturing within 90 days of the date of purchase, will either be classified with cash or included in marketable securities.

Market prices of securities fluctuate. On 12/31/X1, Omega's current Marketable Securities which cost $136,000 had a market value of $120,000. Following the accounting principle of conservatism, Marketable Securities are reported at the lower of cost or market. Marketable Securities were written down to $120,000 and a loss of $16,000 was reported on the income statement for 19X1. The original cost of $136,000 was disclosed in a footnote.

Diagram 11.1

Omega Corporation 19X1

Current Assets:		Current Liabilities:
Marketable Securities	136,000 (b)	**Long-term Debt:**
–	16,000	
		Owners' Equity:
Long-lived Assets:		Income –16,000 Loss on Mkt Sec.

Note that, like inventory (with LCM), the "usefulness" of current marketable securities is in their short-term sale value (plus, of course, interest earned). Supplies, prepaid items, fixed assets, and intangibles are not normally adjusted downwards, because their usefulness is internal and is not affected by declines in market prices.

Current marketable securities are treated as a group. Prices of some securities held may rise and others fall. Only if the recoverable value of the entire group or portfolio taken as a whole declines below current book value of the whole, is a loss recognized and recorded. A loss would directly reduce the balance reported for Marketable Securities and be reflected as "Loss on Current Marketable Securities" on the income statement. No valuation contra account is involved.

A decline in the market value of the portfolio of current marketable securities, which has been previously recorded as a loss, may reverse. The combined market value may subsequently increase. Any increase in the market value of current marketable securities as a

---

[3] Recall that bonds, notes receivable, and treasury bills as distinct from preferred or common stock are monetary. Since stock does not provide for a specific commitment of cash inflow(s) at specific date(s), it is not monetary by definition. Since the use of stock as a vehicle for short-term investment of excess cash is rare, most firms, current marketable securities portfolios contain all monetary items.

group, above previously reported book value, represents a gain. Where the gain represents a recovery of previously recorded loss—that is, does not result in book value being above cost—a holding or recovery gain is recognized in the accounts. Marketable Securities is increased, and a nonextraordinary gain is reflected on the income statement. Note that GAAP and conservatism preclude any increase in marketable securities, or reflected revenue, above original cost unless and until the securities are actually sold.

For example, if Omega's portfolio of current marketable securities recovered in 19X2, and the portfolio of current value was $126,000 on 12/31/X2, the accountant would make a year-end adjustment to increase marketable securities by $6,000 and report a gain in marketable securities. Note that cost would still be footnoted.

Diagram 11.2   Omega Corporation 19X2

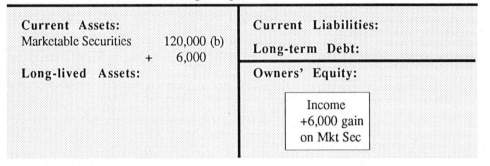

If the market value of the portfolio rose to $150,000 in 19X3, the 12/31/X3 balance sheet would report marketable securities at the lower of cost or market, $136,000. A gain of $10,000 would be reported in the income statement in 19X3. Market value of $150,000 would be footnoted.

Diagram 11.3   Omega Corporation 19X3

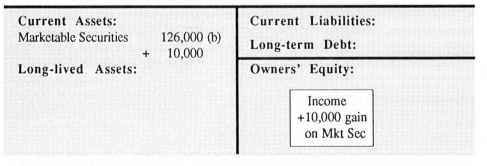

The standards for marketable securities are different from those for inventory. LCM requires that inventory be written down for losses. Inventory may not be written back up to cost if the market recovers. Marketable securities can and must be written up (but not above cost) to record any recovery of loss.

Allowance for Bad Debt

Usually a firm will have accounts receivable from many different customers. Unfortunately, not all of these accounts will prove to be collectible. If the accountant were to wait until an account proved to be uncollectible (all collection efforts have failed) before reducing accounts receivable, assets at the end of a given period and income for that period could be overstated, violating the matching principle. Both accounts receivable and net income would reflect a forthcoming cash receipt that would never be realized.[4]

To avoid such overstatement, the accountant establishes a contra-asset account designated as allowance for bad debts. As individual receivables prove to be uncollectible during the year, they are written off, which reduces both accounts receivable and the allowance for bad debts. At year-end, as part of the adjusting process, the accountant estimates the portion of accounts receivables that, based on experience, will turn out in the future to be uncollectible. The accountant then makes an adjusting entry for whatever amount is necessary to achieve the desired balance. The balancing minus to income will be identified as bad debt expense on the income statement. Note that bad debts are so common that the term "loss" is not even used. Two methods are used to determine bad debts: aging of accounts receivable and the percentage ending accounts receivable method.

Aging of Accounts Receivable Method

Recall that Omega Corporation's 12/31/X1 accounts receivable was $200,000 and of these $200,000 of receivables, $3,000 was the estimate for future bad debts. The 12/31/X1 balance sheet reveals under current assets:

Accounts Receivable	$200,000
less allowance for Bad Debts	(3,000)
Account Receivable (net)	$197,000

Assume during 19X2 that the following transpired:

(1) Receivables totaling $196,600 were collected from sales made in 19X1.
(2) Receivables resulting from sales made in 19X1 totaling $3,400 proved to be uncollectible and were written off during 19X2.
(3) 19X2 credit sales totaled $1,200,000.
(4) Collections on 19X2 credit sales totaled $950,000.
(5) Receivables resulting from sales made in 19X2 totaling $100 proved to be uncollectible and were written off during 19X2.

The effects of these transactions are shown on Balance Sheet Diagram 11.4.

---

[4] Ignoring potential bad debts and only writing them off when they materialize is known as "direct write off method" and is not acceptable under GAAP where uncollectibles are material in amount.

Diagram 11.4

Effects of Write-offs and Bad Debt Expense
Aging of Accounts Receivable Method (b = beginning balance)

Current Assets:		Current Liabilities:
Cash	+ $196,600 (1)	
	+ 950,000 (4)	**Long-term Debt:**
Accounts receivable	200,000 (b)	
	− 196,600 (1)	**Stockholders' Equity:**
	− 3,400 (2)	
	+1,200,000 (3)	Income
	− 950,000 (4)	+1,200,000 (3)
	− 1,000 (5)	− 4,268 (A)
Allowance for uncollectibles	(3,000)(b)	
	+ 3,400 (2)	
	+ 100 (5)	
	− 4,268 (A)	

Note that, after reflecting these events, the balance in accounts receivable is $249,000 and the balance in the allowance for bad debts is $500 positive. Assume that, of the remaining $249,000 of receivables, the accountant estimates that $3,768 of receivables are not expected to be collectible, even though all accounts already identified as worthless have been weeded out. How much of an adjustment to allowance for bad debts (and bad debt expense) will be necessary to achieve the desired balance?

Exhibit 11.2

Aging of Accounts Receivable

Customers	Total	1-30 days	31-60 days	61-90 days	over 90
B. Able	$ 1,000		$ 1,000		
A. Becker	4,000	$ 4,000			
etc. (list each account)	244,000	199,000	25,000	$15,000	$5,000
Totals	$249,000	$203,000	$26,000	$15,000	$5,000
Percentage estimated bad debts		0.25%	1.0%	5%	45%
Estimated Bad Debts	$3,768	$508	$260	$750	$2,250

You are correct if you recognize that an adjustment for $4,268 is required, as shown as adjusting entry (A). The year's reported bad debt expense of $4,268 will represent $100 of 19X2 receivables that were written off already plus $3,768 of 19X2 receivables that are expected to prove uncollectible plus $400 of under anticipated uncollectibles for the prior year.

Percentage Ending Account Receivable Method

An alternative method of determining bad debt expense is the percentage of ending accounts receivable as shown in Exhibit 11.3. Note that regardless of the method used, bad debt expense should be about the same.

Exhibit 11.3

Percentage Ending Accounts Receivable Method

Year	Ending A/R	Write-offs	− Recoveries	= Net write-offs
19X9	$140,000	$2,408	$ 5	$2,403
19X0	190,000	3,294	13	3,281
19X1	200,000	3,400	0	3,400
Total	$530,000			$9,084
Average	$176,667			$3,028

$$\frac{\$3,028}{\$176,667} = .01714 \text{ or } 1.714\%$$

19X2	249,000	Accounts receivable
	x 1.714	Percentage rate
	$ 4,268	Bad debt expense

To complete your understanding of the way accountants handle uncollectible receivables, you should note that occasionally a specific account that has been declared uncollectible and written off later turns out to be wholly or partially recoverable. In such situations, the accountant first reinstates the amount believed collectible by reversing the write-off (increasing both accounts receivable and the allowance for bad debts). After reinstatement, the receivable collection can be processed routinely.

Investments in Stock

Stock acquired and held as long-lived investments are accounted for under one of four methods: cost, lower of cost or market, equity, or consolidated statements. The **cost method** is used for stock where there is no readily available market price. Stock is recorded at its original value until it is sold.[5]

---

[5] The stock would be reduced in value for a liquidating dividend as discussed in Chapter 10.

Lower of Cost or Market

Lower of cost or market is applied when the stock purchased is marketable and the ownership share represents less than 20 percent of the outstanding stock. Lower of cost or market for investments differs from accounting for current marketable securities:

- Only losses on individual securities that are considered to be permanent (for example, an investee goes into bankruptcy) are written off as a reduction to current income;

- **Permanent losses** reduce the cost based "ceiling" above which the portfolio of long-term securities may not be valued on the balance sheet; and

- Temporary market decreases in value are placed in a contra-asset valuation account to the stock investment and a contra-equity valuation account to stockholders' equity. The valuation accounts are decreased as the market value recovers.

If the market value of the Dungeness Corporate stock held by Omega were to drop to $40,000 in 19X2, the stock investment would then be reported as of 12/31/X2 as $40,000 ($41,000 less allowance of $1,000) as illustrated in Diagram 11.5.

Diagram 11.5   Omega Corporation 19X2

Current Assets:		Current Liabilities:	
Long-term Assets:		Long-term Debt:	
Dungeness Stock Investment	41,000	Owners' Equity	
Allowance for temporary market decline	– 1,000	Temporary losses in investments	–1,000

The allowance and **temporary loss** accounts would be decreased and then eliminated as the market recovers. Income is not affected by temporary losses and loss recovery on noncurrent portfolios. Only permanent losses in these portfolios are recognized as losses on the income statement.

Where a firm owns any bonds or preferred stock; or the common stock amounting to less than 20 percent of the total outstanding voting common stock of another firm; interest and dividends are recognized as assets and as revenue only when they are earned (interest) or declared (dividends). This approach is consistent with conservatism and the realization principle, and is known as the cost method of investments revenue recognition.

Equity Method

When one firm owns 20 to 50 percent of another firm's voting common stock, it is presumed to exert significant influence over the timing of dividend declaration.[6] If the cost methods cited above (dividends not recognized until declared) were to be followed, the investor firm could readily manipulate its reported earnings from period to period through controlling the timing of dividend declaration.

To avoid such potential abuse, GAAP require a firm with a significant influence to follow the **equity method** of accounting for its common stockholdings. Each period the investing firm must "pick up" its equity (share) of the current period's earnings (or losses) in its investment account regardless of whether any dividends are declared.[7] This **equity pickup** is simultaneously recognized as income (or loss) in the investor's income statement. Thus the timing of dividends received under the equity method has no effect on reported earnings.

Diagram 11.6

Equity Method 19X2
(b = beginning balance)

Current Assets:			Current Liabilities:	
Cash	+	6,000 (1)		
Long-lived Assets:			Long-term Debt:	
Edwards Stock				
Investment		310,000 (b)		
	−	6,000 (1)		
	+	25,000 (2)	Owners' Equity:	
			Income	
			+ 25,000 (2)	
			Investment	
			Revenue	

(1) Received $6,000 in dividends from the $18,000 not previously distributed.
(2) Equity pickup ($100,000 net income x 25%)

---

[6] Significant influence is only certain when legal control exists (50 plus percent of the voting common stock). However, for corporations where common stock is held by numerous individual stockholders, 20 percent can represent effective control. GAAP require presumption of significant influence between 20 and 50 percent, and presumption of no significant influence below 20 percent, unless there is evidence to the contrary. In this text and in the text problems you may assume that the 20 percent cut line is absolute, that 20 percent or more represents significant influence and less than 20 does not.

[7] In situations where the dividends are never expected (for example a foreign subsidiary in a nation prohibiting the "export" of dividends), no equity pickup is required.

Where the equity method is used, the investment account will already include an amount for "dividends receivable someday," and the earnings will have already been recognized as revenue on current or prior income statements. Therefore, dividends received on common stock accounted for under the equity method are treated as simple collections of previously recorded "receivables." The investments account is reduced and cash is increased by the amount of the dividend.

Balance Sheet Diagram 11.6 illustrates the balance sheet effect of dividends of $6,000 received and $25,000 of equity pickup for the Edwards Stock held by Omega in 19X2. You should note that permanent losses will be recorded the same way under the equity method as in the cost and lower of cost or market methods.

Consolidated Method

The stock investments must be reported under the **consolidated method** when more than 50 percent of the outstanding stock is owned. Consolidated statements will be covered in Chapter 14.

Effects on Cash from Operating Activities

Note that equity pickup itself and permanent losses on noncurrent marketable securities investments (regardless of method used) do not involve cash flow. In calculating cash from operating activities, permanent losses on investments must be reversed (added back) to income. Since only dividends received under the equity method do involve cash inflow, the portion of equity pickup not matched by dividends received must be reversed (subtracted for profit, added for losses) to income as part of the cash from operating activities calculation.

Present Value

Knowledge of the concept of present value is essential to your understanding the basis of asset measurement. The **present value** of any item can be thought of as its current or **principal** value as distinct from its future value (principal plus interest). Note that, in this sense, future value excludes any future effects of taxation; inflation; changes in market prices; or wear, tear, and obsolescence. Future value only involves principal and accumulated interest.

Although the concept of present value can be used to value nonmonetary goods and services involving fixed monetary payments, it is easier initially to understand in terms of money. If you have $1 today, its present value is $1. If you can obtain 10 percent interest, the future value of your dollar one year from now is $1.10, and five years from now would be $1.61.[8]

---

[8] Note that the concepts of present and future value both assume the effects of compound interest. In the second year you would earn $0.11 interest on your $1.10, and end up with $1.21, and so forth.

The future value of something is the sum of principal invested today plus compound interest. Any specific payment or receipt due on a specified future date can be viewed as the future value of some amount of principal invested today. The amount of principal that could be invested today and accumulate enough interest to exactly equal the payment or receipt on the payment date is defined as the present value of the future payment or receipt. Referring to the earlier example the present value of a payment or receipt of $1.61 five years from today when the interest rate is 10 percent, is $1.You could invest $1 today at 10 percent compound interest and have exactly $1.61 in five years.

Notice that the present value of something can be thought of as its principal value. Also note that the interest or discount rate applicable is unique to the individual firm involved. If your obtainable interest rate is 10 percent, then the present value of $1.61 five years from now discounted at 10 percent is $1. If another firm can obtain a 12 percent interest return on its investments, then the present value to that firm of $1.61 five years from now discounted at 12 percent would be $0.91 (rounded). That firm would only have to invest $0.91 of principal now to have a future value of $1.61 five years from now. A more detailed discussion of present value, and of simple techniques for determining it, is contained in Appendix B.

Notes Receivable

Promissory notes between unrelated parties generally provide for rental charges for the borrowed funds in the form of interest. Promissory notes can be written in three different ways:

- All interest separately stated from the principal (**face value**) of the note. These notes are known as interest bearing notes.

- All interest added to the principal and included in the face value of the note. The practice of incorporating or including interest with the principal is called "capitalizing" the interest. These notes are known as **noninterest bearing notes**, since no additional interest is specified.

- A portion of the interest is separately stated, and the remainder is capitalized into the face value.

Assume you were making a one year loan of $1,000 to someone. Suppose reasonable interest rates for loans of similar risk and duration were 10 percent annually. Your total expected cash receipts at the end of the year would be $1,100 ($1,000 principal plus interest). A promissory note covering this loan could be written in different ways:

Note A: "I owe you $1,000 (face value) payable in one year plus 10 percent interest"—an interest bearing note.

Note B: "I owe you $1,100 (face value) payable in one year"—a noninterest bearing note.

Note C: "I owe you 1,040 (face value) payable in one year plus $60 interest."

Observe that Note A has no interest capitalized into the face value; Note B has all of the interest capitalized; and Note C has some of the interest capitalized and some stated separately. Assume you would be indifferent as to which note you accepted in exchange for the loan. How could the accountant initially record each of these notes so that unearned interest is excluded, and so that these essentially identical loans do not appear to be different?

Recall that an agreement between two parties where neither has performed its obligations is known as executory. At the time the $1,000 loan agreement is signed, the agreement is fully executory. At the start of the loan period, when you have provided the borrower with $1,000 to use, you are entitled to have only the $1,000 principal returned. After one year, you have earned $100 in interest and are entitled to claim $1,100.

Note A, at the time of making the loan, would be recorded by the accountant as "Notes Receivable $1,000," replacing the $1,000 cash reduction—a simple exchange of assets. No unearned interest is included in this $1,000 measurement.

Note B, at the time of the loan, would be recorded and shown in two parts. Notes Receivable would disclose the face value of $1,100. Since the face value is greater than the present claim or present value, a contra-asset—**discount on notes receivable**—of $100 is required, in order to reduce the book value of the note by the $100 of unearned interest. Note C would be initially recorded at $1,040 with a $40 contra account representing the discount or amount of unearned interest. Discount on notes receivable merely represents the amount of interest, capitalized into the face value, that is not yet earned.[9]

The use of the contra account results in all three possible notes initially recorded at the amount of their monetary claim excluding unearned interest or at their net present value:

		Book Value
Note A: Note receivable		$1,000
Note B: Note receivable	$1,100	
Less discount on notes receivable	(100)	1,000
Note C: Note receivable	$1,040	
Less discount on notes receivable	(40)	1,000

In this example, it was assumed that all three notes covered the same one year loan at ten percent. It was therefore easy to determine or impute the amount of interest capitalized in Notes B and C which required separate disclosure. If you were asked to record another note receivable which was noninterest bearing, matured in one year, and had a face value of $5,400 following GAAP, you would need to identify the capitalized interest and show it as a discount. Without other information on the specific loan, you would need to impute the

---

[9] The term "discount" or more appropriately "discounted" can also be used as an offset to notes receivable that have been pledged or assigned to another party in exchange for cash, and where the other party has "recourse," can demand payment from the firm if the note proves uncollectible.

interest.[10] If other loans of similar risk and maturity were being regularly made at 8 percent annual interest, how much of the $5,400 would you impute as being interest?

In the case of short-term (one year or less) receivables, compounded interest is not a factor. You can assume simple annual interest. The $5,400 noninterest bearing loan, in a situation where eight percent was the "going rate," would comprise $5,000 of principal and $400 of **imputed interest.**[11]

What would be the appropriate amount of imputed interest, if any, in the case of a one year note with a face value of $9,500, which provided for annual interest of $310? Assume, in this situation, that the "going rate" of interest was nine percent. Is this note a simple **interest bearing note** or is it part of the interest capitalized in the face value?

The amount of $310 represents only slightly more than three percent annual interest. If the going rate were nine percent for similar loans, approximately six percent was capitalized. What would be the exact amount of capitalized interest which should initially be recorded as a discount? The total proceeds would be $9,810 (9,500 + 310). At a nine percent annual interest rate, $9,000 (9810 ÷ 1.09) would be the principal. Therefore this note would be similar to Note C in the earlier example and is calculated when the stated interest is less than the prevailing market rate of interest. Interest of $310 is stated and $500 of imputed interest is capitalized. The note will initially be recorded and reported as:

Notes receivable	$9,500
Less discount on notes receivable	(500)
	$9,000

In the examples of the $5,400 and $9,500 notes, the principal amounts of $5,000 and $9,000 were the present value of these notes discounted at eight percent and nine percent, respectively. Remember that present value can be viewed as the amount or "value" of something excluding interest. Discounted means separating or factoring out interest at the assumed or imputed appropriate rate.

GAAP require that all assets be initially recorded at their present value, that is, with all future interest factored out. Note from the earlier discussion that the term "present value" (or discounted present value) has this very specific meaning. It should not be used in place of, or confused with, such terms as "current value." When receivables extend beyond one year, compound interest or interest earned enters the picture as illustrated in

---

[10] Essentially you would be first "inferring" the existence of capitalized interest and its amount. You would then be ascribing or "imputing" this inferred interest to the note. Accountants use the term "impute" to cover the entire process.

[11] Let X equal principal. Then X + 0.08X = $5,400; and X = $5,000. The method of determining imputed interest on notes running beyond one year is described in Appendix B.

the brief introduction to present value. Discounting for, or separating out, compound interest is covered in Appendix B. It is important that you see clearly that:

- Accountants initially measure and report receivables at both their present value (excluding any capitalized interest) and the receivable's face or maturity value.

- Unearned interest capitalized into the face value (face value minus present value) is shown separately in a valuation contra-asset called "discount on notes receivable."

- Any interest not capitalized and not yet earned is executory.

In the Omega example, the $5,000 discount on the current note receivable represents executory (unearned) interest capitalized into the $95,000 face value of the note. Similarly, the $130,000 noncurrent note receivable (included in the investments account) has $70,000 of executory interest as of 12/31/X1. Observe that the stated or nominal interest rate of two percent on this note is below current interest rates, and therefore some interest must have been capitalized into the face value (like Note C illustrated above). GAAP require that where the stated value of interest is zero (a so called noninterest bearing note similar to Note B above) or else where the stated value is unreasonably below the prevailing rate of interest for similar notes, that the difference between the prevailing rate and the stated rate be inferred and factored out as a discount.

When a promissory note is deliberately written with all or some of the interest capitalized into the face value, the intention is to reduce the interest payments required of the borrower during the life of the note and to defer the balance of accumulating interest until the note's maturity. In effect, the face value includes both the principal originally borrowed and a "balloon" interest payment at maturity. The **effective interest cost** to the borrower will still be the prevailing rate at the time the note was written.

Suppose you accepted a $15,000 note due in four years when the prevailing rate of interest—the going rate that you could obtain from other borrowers—was 15 percent. If the borrower wished to pay annual interest payments of only five percent, and to defer the balance to the note's maturity, the discount on the note would be $4,282 (rounded) as calculated in Exhibit 11.4.

Exhibit 11.4

$15,000 x .05	=	$750
$750 x 2.8550*	=	$2,141
$15,000 x .5718**	=	8,577
Present value		$10,718
Face value		15,000
Discount		$4,282

* Present value factor for a stream of payments where $n = 4$, $i = 15$
** Present value of a single payment where $n = 4$, $i = 15$.

Amortization of Discounts

Return for a moment to the simplified examples of Notes A, B, and C described above. Remember that each was received in exchange for a $1,000 one year loan. Note A had a face value of $1,000 and called for an additional payment of 10 percent interest that you may assume was the prevailing rate. The present value of Note A on signing was $1,000. No interest was included in the face value.

Note B had a face value of $1,100 and provided for no additional interest payments. Since the prevailing rate was 10 percent, it may be inferred that $100 of the face value represented imputed interest. Note C had a face value of $1,040 and called for an additional payment of $60 of interest. $40 of interest may therefore be inferred as capitalized into the note's face value.

Diagram 11.7   Initial Recording of Receivables

Current Assets:		Current Liabilities:
Cash	−$3,000	
Notes Receivable	+ 3,140	Long-term Debt:
Discount on notes receivable	− 140	
Long-lived Assets:		Stockholder's Equity:

Note	Face Value	−	Discount	= Present value (Cash)
A	$1,000		0	$1,000
B	1,100		$100	1,000
C	1,040		40	1,000
Totals	$3,140		$140	$3,000

The effect of the initial recording of these three loans is shown on Balance Sheet Diagram 11.7. Notes are conventionally shown at their face value, and the contra-asset account (Discount On Notes Receivable $140) of interest included in the face value of two of the notes that was executory as of the date of the initial transaction.

If statements were to be prepared nine months later, as part of the adjusting process, it would be necessary to accrue the $225 ($75 x 3 loans) representing interest now owed (no longer executory) on these notes. The interest can be calculated: Present value times interest rate times time ($1,000 x .10 x 9/12 = $75). Balance Sheet Diagram 11.8 shows the effect of the three necessary adjustments. Adjustment(A) should be already familiar. $75 of accrued interest receivable on Note A is shown as an asset and $75 is added to income (interest revenue on the income statement).

Diagram 11.8   Accrued Interest Receivable After Nine Months
                                       (b = beginning balance)

Current Assets:		Current Liabilities:	
Notes receivable	$ 3,140 (b)		
Discount on notes receivable	(140) (b)	**Long-term Debt:**	
	+ 75 (B)		
	+ 30 (C)	**Stockholders' Equity:**	
Accrued interest receivable	+ 75 (A)		
	+ 45 (C)	Income	
		Interest revenue + 75 (A)	
		Interest revenue + 75 (B)	
Long-lived Assets:		Interest revenue + 75 (C)	

Adjustment (B) for Note B, merely reduces the discount by $75. Only $25 of the capitalized interest in Note B is still executory. For adjustment (C), $30 of capitalized interest in Note C is no longer executory, and the discount is reduced accordingly. $45 of stated interest on Note C has now been earned and is also accrued. The income statement will reflect the $225 of interest earned. At the end of the nine month period, the discount on notes receivable will show an unamortized balance of $35 representing $25 of still executory interest incorporated in the face value of Note B and $10 in Note C.

If a balance sheet were to be prepared three months later, at the time of maturity of the notes, but prior to payment received, it would disclose the three notes as:

Notes Receivable	$3,140
Accrued interest receivable	160

No discount would be reported since all the interest would be earned.

Notes Receivable Discounted

When a company wants to obtain cash without borrowing, it may sell or "discount" its note(s) receivable to a bank. This may be done with or without recourse. When the bank purchases the note, the customer is notified to pay the bank on the maturity date. When a company sells a note "with recourse" it is guaranteeing payment should the customer default. When notes are sold with recourse, this must be disclosed in the financial statements, because it is a contingent liability, a liability that might occur at a future date.

At the time the note is discounted, a contra-asset "Notes Receivable Discounted" is created and cash is increased. If the note is discounted on the day it is written, then no interest would be earned and the cash proceeds from the bank would be principal plus interest on the note less the bank discount. Balance Diagram 11.9 shows the effect of a one year note for $1,000 at the market rate interest of 10 percent accepted from a customer in settlement of his accounts receivable. The bank agreed to discount the note at 12 percent on the date the note was accepted.

Diagram 11.9   Discounted Notes with Recourse

Current Assets:			Current Liabilities:
Cash	+	968 (2)	
			Long-term Debt:
Note receivable	+	1,000 (1)	
	–	1,000 (3)	
Note receivable			Owners' Equity
discounted	–	1,000 (2)	
	+	1,000 (3)	
Accounts receivable	–	1,000 (1)	
Long-lived Assets:			

Owners' Equity box:

> Income
> –   32 (2)
> Loss on sale
> of note

(1) Accept note from customer
(2) Sell note to bank
(3) Customer pays bank $1,100

$1,000	face value of note
x .10	interest rate
$1,100	maturity value of note
(132)	less discount ($1,100 x .12)
$968	Proceeds on note
(1000)	Present value of note
$32	Loss on sale of note

Should the customer default on the note, the company would owe the bank the note's maturity value plus any bank service charges.

Bond Investments

Bonds are similar to noncurrent promissory notes but are more negotiable, and therefore are sometimes easier for a firm to use when it wishes to obtain long-term debt. Bonds commonly are issued in $1,000 denominations (face value representing the amount to be paid at maturity) and usually have a fixed long-term maturity and a fixed or stated interest rate.[12] The firm insuring its bonds in exchange for a long-term loan of cash will disclose such bonds as a long-term liability under Bonds Payable. Omega, in this situation, is the creditor or investor in these bonds, which therefore represent monetary assets (claims for future cash payments) to Omega. Bonds may be purchased either from the issuing company or in the market from a previous bondholder. Bonds, whether held as an investment or issued as long-term debt, are conventionally disclosed in the balance sheet at their face value of $1,000 each. In the Omega example, Acme and Baker bonds have a face value of $408,000 and are classified as part of investments.

When bonds have a stated interest rate below the prevailing rate at the time they are originally sold (or later resold among bondholders) they will be sold at a discount. The bond buyer will not pay (lend) the full face or par value of the bond since that stated interest rate is not competitive. Instead, the bond will sell at a discount (for less than par) with the discount representing a final balloon interest payment sufficient so that, together with the stated interest, the entire cash flow will yield the buyer the prevailing rate of interest on the discounted amount invested.

The bond discount shown in Exhibit 11.1 on the $218,000 par value Baker Corporation Bonds owned by Omega is exactly analogous to the $70,000 discount on the noncurrent note receivable. Both discounts represent unearned interest as of 12/31/X1 included in the par/face values of the respective bonds and notes.

A bond premium is the exact opposite of a bond discount. Where the fixed stated interest on a bond is higher than it needs to be (higher than the prevailing rate on the day of sale) the seller will demand and receive enough additional principal (loan) above the par or face value so that the **effective yield** (rate of return) to the buyer or lender will be the prevailing rate. Although the bondholder will be receiving higher than necessary interest payments (in terms of the par or face value) over the life of the bond, part of these payments will actually be a return of the extra principal (premium) invested. At maturity, only the par value (principal) will be paid to the bondholder.

In the Omega example, Grace recognizes that the premium on the Acme Corporation bonds held as an investment and shown in Exhibit 11.1 represents the amount that will be returned in increments over the remaining life of the bond as part of the stated interest payments to be received.

Bond Acquisition

Bonds are purchased to yield the prevailing market rate of interest. This is the present value of the stream of interest payments and the face value or maturity value of the bonds discounted at the market rate of interest.

The Acme Corporation bonds were purchased on 1/1/X1 and have a face value of $190,000. they will mature on 12/31/X9 and have a stated interest rate of 11 percent.

---

[12] A bond's stated rate of interest may also be called the coupon rate.

Interest payments are made on 6/30 and 12/31 of each year. To calculate the present value of the stream of interest payments, first you must find the semiannual interest payment.

Face value x stated interest x time = interest payment

The Acme bonds interest payment is $10,450 ($190,000 x .11 x 6/12). The prevailing market rate of interest was 10 percent at the time of acquisition. Therefore the present value of the bonds was $201,101 (rounded). Note that since the interest payments are semiannual there will be 18 payments (9 years x 2) and the market interest rate for each period will be 5 percent (10% ÷ 2).

PV interest payment + PV face value = Purchase price

Acme Corporation Bonds:

$10,450 x	11.6896*	=	$122,156
$190,000 x	.4155**	=	78,945
Purchase Price/Present Value		=	$201,101

*   stream of payments where i = 5, n = 18
** single payment where i = 5, n =18

The Baker bonds were purchased at a discount because the present value was less than the face value of the bonds. Diagram 11.10 illustrates the acquisition of the Acme and the Baker bonds by Omega.

Baker Corporation Bonds:

$8,720 x	7.7217	=	$ 67,333
218,000 x	.6139	=	133,830
Purchase Price/Present value		=	$201,163

Bond Amortization

Discounts and premiums are amortized on the payment dates. Two methods are used to amortize bonds: straight-line and effective yield. Straight-line produces a constant revenue, while the effective yield produces a constant rate of return on the investment. GAAP recommends the yield method, but allows the straight-line method if the difference between the two methods is not material.[13]

---

[13] Present value involves compound interest that is curvilinear, therefore straight-line (linear) amortization can only result in a net book value that approximates present value.

Diagram 11.10   Acquisition of Bond Investments and Amortization
                            of Bond Premiums and Discounts—Effective Yield Method

Current Assets:		Current Liabilities:
Cash	$ 201,101 (1)	
	− 201,163 (2)	
	+ 10,450 (3)	
	+ 8,720 (5)	
	+ 10,450 (7)	
	+ 8,720 (9)	Long-term Debt:
Long-lived Assets:		
Bond Investment	+ 190,000 (1)	Stockholders' Equity:
	+ 218,000 (2)	
Bond premium	+ 11,101 (1)	
	− 395 (4)	
	− 415 (8)	
Bond discount	− 16,837 (2)	
	+ 1,338 (6)	
	+ 1,405 (10)	

	Income
+	10,450 (3)
−	395 (4)
+	8,720 (5)
+	1,338 (6)
+	10,450 (7)
−	415 (8)
+	8,720 (9)
+	1,405 (10)

1 Purchase Acme Bonds 1/1/X1
2 Purchase Baker Bonds 1/1/X1
3 Acme Interest Payment 6/30/X1
4 Acme Amortization 6/30/X1
5 Baker Interest Payment 6/30/X1
6 Baker Amortization 6/30/X1
7 Acme Interest Payment 12/31/X1
8 Acme Amortization 12/31/X1
9 Baker Interest Payment 12/31/X1
10 Baker Amortization 12/31/X1

Straight-line Method

Straight-line amortization on the Acme Bonds would be $617 (rounded) per period and $1,234 ($617 + 617) each year.

Bond Premium ÷ Number of Periods = Straight-line Amortization

$$\$11,101 \div 18 = \$617 \text{ per period (rounded)}$$

The interest revenue would be $9,833 ($10,450 – 617) per period and $19,666 per year. Interest revenue is decreased by the amortization of Bond Premium. Baker Bonds would be amortized by $1,684 ($16,837 ÷ 10 periods) per period and $3,368 each year. Bond revenue would be $20,808 (($8,720 x 2) + 3,368) per year under the straight-line method. Bond revenue is increased by amortization of Bond Discount.

Effective Yield Method

Amortization of the Acme Bond premium under the effective yield method is the difference between the interest payment and interest revenue. Interest revenue is the market rate of interest times the present value of the bonds at the beginning of the period.

Exhibit 11.5

Effective Yield Method
Acme Bonds 19X1

Date	Beginning Book Value	Interest Revenue	Interest Payment*	Premium Amortization	Ending Book Value
6/30/X1	$201,101	$10,055	$10,450	$395	$200,706
12/31/X1	200,706	10,035	10,450	415	200,291

* $190,000 x .055

Acme Bonds	$ 190,000
Premium	10,291
PV at 12/31/X1	$ 200,291

The Baker Bond amortizations schedule is presented in Exhibit 11.6. Note that when the bonds are fully amortized on the date of maturity, that the book value of the bonds is the maturity value.

Exhibit 11.6

Effective Yield Method
Baker Corporation Bonds Investment

Date	Beginning Book Value	Interest Revenue	– Interest Payment	= Discount Amortization	Ending Book Value
1/30/X1	$201,163	$10,058	$8,720	$1,338	$202,501
12/31/X1	202,501	10,125	8,720	1,405	203,906
6/30/X2	203,906	10,195	8,720	1,475	205,381
12/31/X2	205,381	10,269	8,720	1,549	206,930
6/30/X3	206,930	10,347	8,720	1,627	208,557
12/31/X3	208,557	10,428	8,720	1,708	210,265
6/30/X4	210,265	10,513	8,720	1,793	212,058
12/31/X4	212,058	10,603	8,720	1,883	213,941
6/30/X5	213,941	10,697	8,720	1,977	215,918
12/31/X5	215,918	10,796	8,720	2,082*	218,000

* difference due to rounding

Note on Balance Sheet Diagram 11.10 that $2,743 of discount amortization on bonds investment is an accrual of interest earned. It will be included in the income statement as part of interest revenue along with interest payments actually received (or otherwise accrued). Premium amortization on bonds represents a return of the extra principal initially paid, therefore it reduces interest revenue on the income statement. In determining cash from operating activities under the indirect method, that portion of interest revenue representing amortization of asset discounts must be reversed (subtracted) from net income. Conversely, that portion of interest revenue not reported as such (offset by amortization of asset premiums) must be reversed (added back) to reported income in calculating cash from operating activities.

Bond Sinking Fund

Bonds may have many different features. These features will be discussed more thoroughly for bonds as liabilities in Chapter 12. One possible feature is the requirement that the issuing firm make periodic deposits of cash in escrow or savings each year so that, together with accumulated interest, sufficient cash will be available to redeem the bonds at maturity. Bonds having such a provision are called sinking fund bonds. In this illustration, Omega must have bonds payable with a sinking fund provision. The **bond sinking fund** represents a long-lived asset investment. Note that the sinking fund is classified as long-lived since it is not available to pay current liabilities. Also note that it is not offset against the related bonds on the liability side of the balance sheet.[14]

As interest accumulates in the sinking fund each period, it is recognized and recorded as an increase to the sinking fund account and as interest revenue on the income statement. Balance Sheet Diagram 11.11 shows the effect of reporting $1,800 as sinking fund interest earned. Note that it does not represent cash flow. In determining cash from operating activities, any portion of recorded interest revenue representing interest accumulated in

Diagram 11.11   Record Bond Sinking Fund Interest 19X2

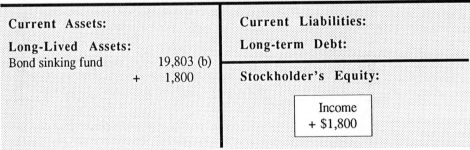

Current Assets:		Current Liabilities:	
Long-Lived Assets:		Long-term Debt:	
Bond sinking fund	19,803 (b)		
+	1,800	Stockholder's Equity:	
		Income + $1,800	

---

14 The GAAP rule of "no offsetting" and its one minor allowable exception will be covered as part of the discussion of liabilities in Chapter 12.

a sinking fund must be reversed or subtracted from income as not representing an inflow of cash.

Any gains or losses on the sale of specific securities within the sinking fund will be reported on the income statement in the period in which they occur and in the sinking fund account accordingly.[15] Gains or losses are also noncash flow. Therefore, they too must be eliminated to find cash from operating activities.

Property Held Under Capital Lease

Certain types of leased property, even though not actually owned by the lessee, are included as assets along with property, plant, and equipment.[16] Grace is concerned with how such property is valued or measured for balance sheet purposes.

All lease payments beyond the initial down payment upon signing are viewed as representing both principal and executory interest. The initial value of property held under capital lease would be the principal value (present value) of all required lease payments.

The principal value of the lease payments is the present value at the time of signing the lease discounted at the firm's borrowing rate or the interest rate it would have to pay if it had purchased the property with a mortgage loan. You may assume that Omega's borrowing rate is 12 percent.

Capital leases or financing leases are generally long-term, extending over most of the useful life of the asset. They are noncancelable, and they generally provide that the lessee assume all of the normal responsibilities of ownership such as payment of insurance, property taxes, and maintenance. They may also provide for bargain purchase (below expected market value) by the lessee at the end of the lease term.[17] In the Omega example, an unrealistically short-term three year lease is used to simplify the illustration.

You may assume that Omega signed a three year lease agreement on 1/1/X1 that qualified as a capital lease. The lease terms provided for a payment on signing of $100,426 and for three annual payments of $208,000 each on 12/31/X1, 12/31/X2, and 12/31/X3. The present value of all four payments discounted at Omega's assumed rate of 12 percent would be $600,000 (rounded).[18]

---

[15] Although not illustrated, sinking funds may also exist for purposes other than bond retirement.

[16] Accounting for capital leases by the lessor is beyond the scope of this text and therefore is not illustrated. Briefly the lessor, depending on certain criteria specified by the FASB, will treat the leased Asset either as an immediate sale with both gross profit and future unearned interest income or else as an exchange of inventory for a receivable that includes future unearned interest.

[17] The precise FASB criteria for distinguishing a capital lease from an operating lease are beyond the scope of this text.

[18] The method of calculating the present value of a series of payments is covered in Appendix B.

The property under capital lease therefore was recorded as an asset valued at $600,000 with a corresponding cash reduction of $100,426 and increased liabilities of $499,574. The initial value must be depreciated to zero over the life of the lease to reflect expiration of usefulness by an appropriate depreciation method—straight-line, SYD, DDB, and so forth. Note there is no salvage value since capital leases represent rights to use property, plant and equipment rather than ownership. In the Omega example, straight-line depreciation over the three year lease life is being used with a resultant book value of $400,000 on 12/31/X1.

Intangibles and Other

Intangible assets are long-lived assets, but have no physical substance. The initial value reported on the balance sheet is either the purchase price or the legal costs associated with registering the rights. Intangible assets rarely contain any research and development costs since GAAP generally requires these costs to be expensed when incurred. Typical intangible assets include copyrights, patents, franchises, leaseholds, leasehold improvements and goodwill.

Copyrights are a right granted by the government to publish and sell artistic materials (e.g. computer programs) over the author's life plus 50 years. Generally the useful life is less and therefore amortization would be over a shorter period.

Patents have a 17 year legal life granted by the government and should also be amortized over their useful life. Costs associated with successfully defending patents are added to the asset and amortized over the remaining useful life.

Franchises are recorded only if the company granting the franchise owes additional services to the franchised firm. Maximum amortization is 40 years although it is generally amortized over a much shorter period.

Leaseholds are purchased lease rights and should be amortized over the remaining life of the lease. Leasehold improvements are improvements made to leased property and should be amortized over their useful life or remaining life of the lease, whichever is shorter.

Goodwill

Recall from Chapter 2 that goodwill represents the amount paid in excess of fair market value of the net assets to acquire a firm. In this example, one or more of Omega's acquired firms was purchased and the unamortized balance of the amount originally paid for goodwill is $175,000.[19]

19 It is possible for one firm to acquire another and to have no goodwill recorded regardless of the price paid. This occurs under pooling of interests accounting as distinct from purchase accounting. These subjects, together with a discussion of how goodwill is initially measured under purchase accounting, are covered in Chapter 14.

Goodwill is very real for the going concern. Goodwill covers a trained and functioning team of employees and managers, established relationships with financial creditors and suppliers, and customer satisfaction and recognition which result in superior earnings. Although goodwill is very real, it has proven to be impossible to measure objectively for the ongoing firm itself. Therefore GAAP prohibit an entity from recording its own goodwill.

The value of goodwill may be arbitrarily agreed upon by the buyer and seller or a more objective formula based on expected earnings may be used. Generally goodwill is determined by capitalizing the excess of expected earnings over the industry average earnings at the industry's normal rate of return. For example, if the industry's rate of return was 20 percent and the Omega's expected excess income per year was $50,000, the goodwill would be calculated as $250,000 ($50,000 ÷ 20%).

In the Omega example, you may assume purchased goodwill originally amounted to $250,000 three years ago and is being amortized on a straight-line basis over 10 years.[20] Note that, like the write-off of any long-lived asset, goodwill amortization is a noncash expense and therefore must be reversed (added back) to income in calculating cash from operating activities.

Deferred Charges

Deferred charges were described in Chapter 2 as equivalent to long-term prepaid items. A typical example of items appearing as deferred charges, as illustrated for Omega, are the unamortized underwriting costs associated with issuing bonds payable or otherwise obtaining long-term debt. For Omega you may assume that its bonds payable covered a period of 20 years and were issued 10 years ago. You may also assume that the costs of issuance were $20,000. Since these costs were just as much a part of the borrowing costs as the interest payments over the 20 years, they are initially capitalized and subsequently amortized on a straight-line basis of $1,000 per year. Ten years have passed since issuance of the bonds, and a total of $10,000 has been amortized leaving the $10,000 unamortized balance appearing on Omega's balance sheet. The amortization of these deferred charges, since they relate to financing costs, are included on Omega's income statement as part of reported interest expense.

Note that the annual adjustment for amortization of deferred charges is a noncash flow expense. Therefore, that portion of interest expense representing deferred charge amortization must be reversed (added back) to net income in determining cash from operating activities.

---

[20] Although goodwill purchased after October 31, 1970 must be amortized over a period not to exceed 40 years, it should be amortized over an appropriate period of time. This may be significantly shorter than 40 years.

Organizational Costs

Incorporation costs for a company are called organizational costs and are classified as "Other Assets." Costs included are legal costs, fees to the state of incorporation, initial promoter and accountants' fees, costs to print stock certificates, and so forth. Although these costs should benefit the firm over its entire life, it is customary to amortize the costs over a five year period, which is the minimum time allowed for tax purposes.

Financial Instrument Disclosure

Disclosure requirements for financial instruments have developed in an ad hoc fashion. The FASB has proposed a statement on financial instruments and off-balance sheet financing which addresses the issue of lack of adequate disclosure of financial instruments created due to market volatility, deregulation, and tax law changes. The proposed statement defines a **financial instrument** as "any contract which is both a (recognized or unrecognized) financial asset of one entity and a (recognized or unrecognized) financial liability or equity of another entity."[21] Financial instruments would be defined as cash, receivables, payables, debt, and equity securities (stock), financial futures, forward contracts, options, interest rate and currency swaps, collateralized mortgage obligations, financial guarantees, and so forth. The proposed disclosure include:

- Estimate of the amount and probability of credit risk including the maximum possible losses;
- Amounts of future cash receipts and payments divided into categories of current (within one year), one to five years, and over five years;
- Amount of interest-bearing financial instruments divided into categories of current (within one year), one to five years, and over five years;
- Estimate of current market values of financial instruments;
- Amount of future cash receipts and payments and amount of interest bearing financial instruments reported by foreign currencies, if material;
- Concentration of credit risk with any one company, if it exceeds 10 percent of total assets; and
- Concentration of credit risk within one industry or geographic region, if significant in amount.

Financial instruments expected to be sold before their maturity would be exempt from this disclosure proposal.

---

[21] "Disclosures about Financial Instruments," *Proposed Statement of Financial Accounting Standards*, Financial Accounting Standards Board, Stamford, CT, November, 1987, para 5

Review of Asset Changes

Exhibit 11.7 reviews the assets discussed in this chapter. For each asset, the common transactions and adjustments which may affect its balance are also given. Review this exhibit carefully. For each numbered transaction or adjustment, make sure that you can visualize a specific example and identify the rest of the entry that might be involved, that is, the other balance sheet balancing effect(s).

Exhibit 11.7   Summary of Changes Affecting Assets covered in Chapter 11

Accounts	Effect
Marketable Securities	*Increased by:* Acquisition of temporary investments Adjustment reflecting recovery (up to cost) of previously recorded loss in market value
	Decreased by: Sales of temporary investments Adjustments reflecting loss in market value
Notes Receivable	*Increased by:* Loans made to outsiders Notes accepted from customers in settlement of accounts receivable Notes purchased as temporary investments
	Decreased by: Collections of cash Sales or "discounting" to outsiders
Discount on Notes Receivable (Contra-asset)	*Negative balance increased by:* Amount of interest included in note face value
	Negative balance decreased by: Adjustment for amount of capitalized interest earned
Notes Receivable Discounted (Contra-asset)	*Negative balance increased by:* Selling notes to the bank with recourse
	Negative balance decreased by: The bank collecting on the note Default of the note

Exhibit 11.7 (continued)

Accounts receivable	*Increased by:* Sales to customers on account *Decreased by:* Collections of cash Write-off of uncollectible accounts Acceptance of promissory note receivable in settlement
Allowance for Bad Debts (contra-asset)	*Negative balance increased by:* Adjustment allowance Reinstatement of all accounts written off *Negative balance decreased by:* Adjustment down to desired allowance Write-off of uncollectible accounts
Investments	*Increased by:* Acquisitions of long-lived investments Share of "significantly influenced" investee's earnings Adjustment reflecting recovery of temporary loss in market value *Decreased by:* Sales of long-term investments Redemption of bonds or preferred stock Share of "significantly influenced investee's losses Dividends received from "significantly influenced investees" Adjustment for permanent loss in market value Adjustment for temporary loss in market value
Investments Premium	*Increased by:* Amount of premium paid on acquisition *Decreased by:* Adjustment for amount of interest "returned" by investee Sale or redemption of bonds
Investments Discount (Contra-asset)	*Negative balance increased by:* Amount of interest included in face value not yet earned *Negative balance decreased by:* Adjustment for amount of capitalized interest earned Sale or redemption of Bonds Investment
Funds	*Increased by:* Deposits of cash Adjustment accruing interest Realized gains on sale of specific securities

Exhibit 11.7 (continued)

Funds

Decreased by:
Use of fund proceeds for intended purpose
Transferring any residual cash to cash account
Loss on funds investments

Capital Leases

Increased by:
Acquisitions

Decreased by:
Expiration or sale of lease

Intangibles

Increased by:
Acquistion costs
Legal defense costs
Costs of assets developed by the firm

Decreased by:
Amortization adjustment
Write-off of asset
Sale of asset

Deferred Charges

Increased by:
Payments of cash for services
Acquisition of future services on account

Decreased by:
Amortization adjustments as benefits expire or are used
Sale or redemption of Bonds Payable

Goodwill

Increased by:
Actual purchase of goodwill in another firm

Decreased by:
Required amortization

Organization Costs

Increased by:
Costs of incorporation

Decreased by:
Amortization adjustments

Preparer Procedures

To accommodate transactions and adjustments introduced in this chapter, the partial chart of accounts first introduced in Chapter 5 and augmented in subsequent chapters is expanded to include accounts introduced in this chapter in Exhibit 11.8.

Exhibit 11.8   Additions to Chart of Accounts

Current Monetary Assets
    007   Dividends Receivable

Long-lived Assets
    100   Noncurrent Notes Receivable
    101   Bond Investments
    102   Bond Investments Premium
    103   Preferred Stock Investments
    104   Common Stock Investments
    105   Other Investments
    106   Sinking Funds
    114   Properties Held Under Capital Lease
    125   Deferred Charges
    126   Goodwill

Contra-assets
    200   Discount on Current Notes Receivable
    202   Notes Receivable Discounted
    205   Allowance for Bad Debts
    210   Discount on Noncurrent Notes Receivable
    211   Discount on Bond Investments

Current Liabilities
    306   Current Capital Lease Obligations

Long-term Debt
    403   Noncurrent Capital Lease Obligations

Contra-equities
    601   Discount on Noncurrent Notes Payable
    610   Temporary Loss on Investments

Revenues
    714   Gain on sale of Investments

Expenses
    820   Loss on Current Marketable Securities
    821   Loss on Investments

You will find all accounts necessary for the preparer problems in this chapter in the complete chart of accounts at the beginning of Appendix D.

Gains and losses on Marketable Securities

Asset revaluations reflecting external circumstances involve direct adjustments to the asset account, and a corresponding expense or revenue item. A decline in market value of marketable securities below current book value would be a charge to an operating loss account, and a credit to marketable securities. A recovery of market value would result in a debit to marketable securities, with a ceiling of cost recovery, and a corresponding credit to gain on securities.

A $12,000 decline in the market value of a firm's portfolio of current marketable securities below their existing book value would be journalized:

	DR	CR
Loss on Marketable Securities	*12,000*	
Current Marketable Securities		*12,000*

A recovery (gain up to but not exceeding original cost) of $7,000 on marketable securities as a group during a year would be journalized:

Marketable Securities	*7,000*	
Gain on Marketable Securities		*7,000*

Gains and Losses on Investments

A temporary loss of market value on investments and a recovery gain is not treated as expense or revenue. Instead, a contra-equity account Temporary Loss on Investments is used. A $23,000 temporary loss would be recognized with:

Temporary Loss on Investments	*23,000*	
Investments		*23,000*

If market increased by $20,000 during the year a full recovery of this temporary losses would be journalized:

Investments	*23,000*	
Temporary Loss on Investments		*23,000*

A permanent loss on investments of $11,000 would be recognized on the income statement. Note that recovery of a permanent loss may not be recognized unless the asset was sold under GAAP, since it would be considered a write up above the cost basis. A $11,000 permanent loss would be journalized:

Loss on Investments	*11,000*	
Investments		*11,000*

Accounts Receivable and Allowance for Bad Debts

Accounts declared uncollectible are written off to the allowance account. Accounts totaling $3,000 deemed to be uncollectible would be journalized:

	DR	CR
Allowance for Bad Debts	*3,000*	
Accounts Receivable		*3,000*

For any accounts already written off that subsequently prove collectible this entry would be reversed and the collection would be recorded:

Accounts Receivable	3,000	
Allowance for Bad Debts		3,000
Cash	3,000	
Accounts Receivable		3,000

At the end of the period the allowance for bad debts will normally have accumulated a debit balance. An adjusting entry is then made to force the desired credit balance (estimate for uncollectibles) and to charge bad debt expense. Assuming the year-end balance before adjustment in the allowance account was $8,000 debit and that the estimate of ending receivables that would prove uncollectible in the future was $1,500, the adjustment entry would be:

Bad Debt Expense	9,500	
Allowance for Bad Debts		9,500

Equity Pickup

When investments are reported under the equity method a proportionate share of an investee's earnings must be recognized, the investments account is charged directly with a matching credit to revenue. Dividends received would be credited to investments where the proportionate share of earnings had been previously recognized.

Assume a firm held voting stock in Corporations X and Y and had significant influence over X but not over Y. If X had $100,000 of earnings, paid $40,000 in dividends, and the firm held 30 percent of X's stock, the events would be journalized following the equity method as follows:

	DR	CR
Common Stock Investments	*30,000*	
Investments Revenue		*30,000*
Cash	*12,000*	
Common Stock Investments		*12,000*

If Y paid $60,000 in dividends and the firm owned 10 percent of Y's stock, the revenue would be recognized following the cost method as follows:

Cash	*6,000*	
Investments Revenue		*6,000*

Notes Receivable and Bond Investments

All asset accounts by convention normally have debit balances. Contra-asset accounts normally have credit balances. Examples of contra-asset accounts include discount on notes receivable, allowance for bad debt accounts, discount on bonds owned as investments, and accumulated depreciation.

Assets are reported at their fair market value excluding any unearned interest. Therefore, when interest is included in the face value of notes receivable or bonds are purchased at a discount, the asset will be initially recorded at face value together with a contra account which effectively offsets the unearned interest component. For example, assume that a $6,660 current note receivable, with $600 of interest included in the face value, is accepted as deferred payment for a $6,000 account receivable. This transaction would be journalized as:

Current Notes Receivable	*6,600*	
Discount on Current Notes Receivable		*600*
Accounts Receivable		*6,000*

Similarly, bonds acquired at a discount for $140,000 with a maturity value of $150,000, would be recorded:

Bond Investment	*150,000*	
Cash		*140,000*
Discount on Bond Investment		*10,000*

Bonds purchased at a premium for $175,000 with a maturity value of $160,000 would be recorded:

	DR	CR
Bond Investment	*160,000*	
Premium on Bond Investment	*15,000*	
Cash		*175,000*

Interest receivable is accrued as earned. Where not already included in the receivable's face value, the debit is to interest receivable and the credit is to interest revenue. Where some or all of the interest is already included in the face value, the debit is to note or bond discount and the credit to interest revenue for the portion earned. Assume a firm has three different one year notes receivable:

Note A: $5,000 face value (no capitalized interest) plus 8 percent interest;

Note B: $6,540 face value ($540 of interest capitalized), no additional interest;

Note C: $8,320 face value ($320 of interest capitalized) plus $240 interest.

To record accrual of earned revenue in these notes after six months, the following separate journal entries could be made:

A. *Interest Receivable*	*200*	
Interest Revenue		*200*
B. *Discount on Current Notes Receivable*	*270*	
Interest Revenue		*270*
C. *Discount on Current Notes Receivable*	*160*	
Interest Receivable	*120*	
Interest Revenue		*280*

Similar entries would be appropriate for bonds held as investments. Interest of $8,000 was received on the bonds and the premium on bond investments was amortized as a reduction of interest revenue. The appropriate journal entries would be:

Cash	*8,000*	
Interest Revenue		*8,000*
Interest Revenue	*15,000*	
Bond Investments Premium		*15,000*

Sinking Funds

Accrual of interest ($15,000) and an annual contribution to a sinking fund ($20,000) could be journalized with the following compound entry:

	DR	CR
Sinking Funds	*35,000*	
Cash		*20,000*
Interest Revenue		*15,000*

Properties Held Under Capital Lease

Initial recording of property under capital lease by the lessee is similar to that for acquisition of any other asset in exchange for both a current and a noncurrent obligation. Assume that an item with a present value of $90,000 was acquired under a nine year capital lease; and that the present value of the current obligation (payment to be made on signing plus first year's payment) was $12,000 and of the noncurrent obligation $78,000; the entry would be:

Properties under Capital Lease	*90,000*	
Current Capital Lease Obligation		*12,000*
Noncurrent Capital Lease Obligations		*78,000*

The leased property is then amortized to zero over the life of the lease. Assuming SYD depreciation was being used, the first year's entry would be:

Depreciation Expense	*18,000*	
Accumulated Depreciation for Capital Lease		*18,000*

Chapter Overview

Based on the material covered in this chapter, you should be able to:

- Explain the purpose and significance of consolidated financial statements;
- Describe the basic standards for the initial measurement of all reported assets;
- Explain the concept of present value and how it relates to asset measurement;
- Describe and give examples of how GAAP are specifically applied to the initial measurement of note receivable, bonds, capital leases, deferred charges, goodwill, and assets acquired for other than cash;
- Describe and give examples of recognition of expenses, losses, or revenue reductions related to marketable securities, accounts receivable, investments, bond premium, properties under capital lease, deferred charges and goodwill;
- Describe and give examples of recognition of revenue and gains related to marketable securities, notes receivable, bond discounts, and sinking funds;
- For any asset or contra-asset introduced so far in this text, describe those transactions and adjustments that can increase and decrease its reported amount on the balance sheet;
- Describe all possible asset-related items that might affect cash from operating activities.

New Vocabulary and Concepts

Bond sinking fund	Financing leases
Bonds	Full disclosure
Consolidated financial statements	Imputed interest
Consolidated method	Interest bearing notes
Cost method	Noninterest bearing notes
Discount on notes receivable	Parent
Effective interest cost	Permanent losses (investments)
Effective yield	Present value
Equity method	Principal
Equity pickup	Subsidiary
Face value	Temporary losses (investments)
Financial instrument	

- The reason for and content of consolidated financial statements.
- Present value and the need to segregate interest.
- Significant influence and recognition of proportionate share of another's earnings.
- Temporary vs. permanent losses relating to noncurrent marketing securities.

Review Questions

1. A parent and a subsidiary's balance sheets could be simply added together in a combined statement. A combined statement without further adjustment would not be a consolidated statement and would not be acceptable under GAAP.(a) What is the essential difference between a combined and a consolidated balance sheet? (b) What is the intent of adjustments or eliminations in consolidation? (c) Give an example of a possible elimination.

2. Do GAAP require that consolidated statements be prepared to include all firms where significant influence is determined to exist? If not, what are the criteria for necessary consolidation?

3. What is the difference between the standards for valuing marketable securities as a group and the LCM valuation rule as applied to inventory?

4. (a) What is the purpose of the Allowance for Bad Debts account? (b) Why not reduce Accounts Receivable directly for anticipated uncollectibles? (c) Why does the accountant anticipate losses on receivables? Why doesn't the accountant just wait until the losses are certain?

5. (a) What is the purpose of a contra-asset discount on notes receivable or on bonds owned as an investment? (b) What does the amount of unamortized discount reported on a particular balance sheet represent? (c) What term or concept describes the basis for the initial measurement of monetary assets? What does the initial book value of a monetary asset represent?

6. Discount on receivables and bonds owned as investments is systematically amortized. (a) What is the basis for amortization—how much and when? (b) What is the effect of such amortization upon income?

7. Sometimes a bond premium valuation account appears with bonds owned as an investment.
   (a) What is the purpose of this bond premium account?
   (b) What does the amount of unamortized premium represent?
   (c) Bond premium is amortized systematically as a reduction of interest revenue. Why?

8. For some common stock investments, no additional asset and accompanying revenue are recognized until a dividend is actually declared. For others, a proportionate share of new earnings is recognized each year, whether or not there have been any dividends declared. What is the reason behind this apparently inconsistent treatment?

9. Assume a particular capital lease agreement provides for equal payments over the 20 years of the lease term. Must the firm use 20 year straight-line depreciation with respect to its capital lease asset account? If not, what standards apply to such depreciation?

10. (a) What are some common examples of deferred charges? (b) How do deferred charges as a long-lived asset differ from prepaid items as a current asset?

11. (a) What are the various relationships or conditions that can result in the existence of goodwill, whether or not the goodwill is measured and reported by accountants? (b) Under GAAP it is not acceptable for a firm to capitalize its own goodwill. Why is it not acceptable?

12. (a) What is goodwill arising from consolidation? (b) Purchased goodwill? (c) What does the amount so reported on a balance sheet represent? (d) What is done with this amount over future years?

Mini Cases and Questions for Discussion

MC 11.1   A land development company recently acquired a large tract of land, which it intended to sub-divide into parcels and to sell. The transaction involved the firm's receiving title to 50,000 acres, in exchange for a cash payment of $100,000 and a 10 year promissory mortgage note for $400,000 at one percent annual interest. The usual interest rate for such mortgages was eight percent.

The company's accountants originally recorded the land as inventory, at a value of $500,000, and reported a noncurrent note of $400,000. The firm's CPA would give a "clean" (no exceptions) opinion only if the land were initially valued at $312,120, and the liability shown at $400,000, together with a $187,880 discount.

What are the issues involved? Discuss.

MC 11.2 Jose Grenados is studying to be an investment analyst. He understands the primary need for consistency in the measurement and reporting of information. He has been very favorably impressed with GAAP, but now he is not so sure. "How can accountants preach consistency and then be so inconsistent?" he asks. "They use LCM for inventory and something else for marketable securities. They pick up future dividends on some stocks and not on others. They treat some leases one way and others another. How can this be considered consistent reporting?" Discuss.

MC 11.3 Goodwill, in some cases, can represent the most valuable asset in a firm. This is regularly demonstrated by the numerous cases where a firm is sold for many times its accounting book value. If it can be so important, why don't accountants recognize a firm's own goodwill? If accountants are so dead set against goodwill, why do they then go ahead and report goodwill arising out of a purchase or consolidation? And finally, if they do recognize and report goodwill, why do they amortize it when, in reality, it might continue to exist, or even grow?

Essential Problems

EP 11.1 On its 12/31/X1 balance sheet, the Archer Company disclosed accounts receivable of $400,000 and an allowance for bad debts of $16,000. During 19X2 the following events occurred:

1. Of 19X1 ending receivables, $383,000 were collected and the balance was determined to be uncollectible.
2. 19X2 sales on account totalled $2,500,000.
3. Collections of 19X2 receivables totalled $2,000,000.
4. $75,000 of 19X2 receivables were written off.
5. Of 19X2 ending accounts receivable, the firm's accountant estimated $17,000 would prove uncollectible.
   a) Give the amounts that should appear on the 12/31/X2 balance sheet.
   b) What amount of bad debt expense would be reported on the 19X2 income statement?

EP 11.2 The following data with respect to accounts receivable are available for the A,B,C, and D Companies:

	A	B	C	D
Accounts receivable 12/31/X4	$100,000	$200,000	$300,000	$400,000
Allowance for bad debts	2,000	6,000	12,000	20,000
19X4 ending receivables collected during 19X5	97,500	193,000	290,000	385,000
19X4 ending receivables written off during 19X5	2,500	7,000	10,000	15,000
19X5 credit sales	900,000	1,200,000	2,100,000	2,400,000
Collections of 19X5 receivables during 19X5	775,000	930,000	1,800,000	2,016,000
Amount of 19X5 ending receivables estimated to be uncollectible after aging accounts receivable	2,200	7,230	10,400	15,000

a) For each firm give the amounts that should appear on its 12/31/X5 balance sheet for accounts receivable and for bad debts.
b) For each firm give the amount that should be reported for bad debt expense on its 19X5 income statement.

EP 11.3 The Fox Company had an account receivable of $8,000 from one of its customers, the George Company. George had requested extended time to make payment and had given Fox a six month promissory note with a face value of $8,400, including 10 percent interest.

a) How should this note be first reported on the Fox Company's balance sheet?
b) How should it be reported three months later, if straight-line amortization was used?
c) How much revenue (if any) should be reported after three months?

EP 11.4 The following one year notes receivable were received by the A,B,C, and D companies on 1/1/X6 in exchange for cash loans made to assist suppliers:

	A	B	C	D
Face value of note	$ 5,800	$ 7,400	$11,100	$15,000
Stated interest rate	none	8%	2%	14%
Interest included in face value	$ 800	$ 400	$ 1,200	none

For each firm:

a) Indicate how the note should be first reported on the firm's balance sheet (as of 1/1/X6).

b) Indicate what a balance sheet as of 3/31/X6 should report with respect to the note and the amount of related interest that should appear on the first quarter's income statement, if the straight-line method is used for amortization.

c) Assuming the note had not been collected by 12/31/X6, indicate the appropriate balance sheet disclosure as of 6/30/X6, 9/30/X6, and 12/31/X6 and the amount of related interest revenue that should appear on the second, third, and forth quarter income statements.

EP 11.5 The Easy Company has a group of current marketable securities purchased during 19X1 at a cost of $90,000. The market value of this group taken together was:

$93,000 on 12/31/X1
80,000 on 12/31/X2
88,000 on 12/31/X3

Assume that these securities were held through 19X3, and continued to be classified as current, since they were readily available for conversion into cash. How would marketable securities be valued on the balance sheet as of 12/31/X1, 12/31/X2, and 12/31/X3? What would be the effect on operating income of the changing market values in the years 19X1, 19X2, and 19X3?

EP 11.6 The following data in thousands of dollars relate to the portfolio of current marketable securities acquired on 6/1/X4 and held by the A, B, C, and D companies.

	A	B	C	D
Portfolio cost (each year)	$20	$30	$40	$50
Portfolio market value 12/31/X4	22	20	42	47
Portfolio market value 12/31/X5	20	25	38	52
Portfolio market value 12/31/X6	16	34	35	46
Portfolio market value 12/31/X7	18	28	44	51

For each firm:

a) Give the amount that should be included in current assets on the firm's balance sheets as of 12/31/X4, 12/31/X5, 12/31/X6, and 12/31/X7.

b) Give the amount of gain or loss (if any) that should be recognized in the firm's 19X4, 19X5, 19X6, and 19X7 income statements relating its current marketable securities.

EP 11.7   The Sorbo Company held a portfolio of common stocks costing $100,000 and purchased on 9/15/X2 as a long-term investment. The stock is reported under the lower of cost or market method. You also have the following information with respect to these investments subsequent to their acquisition:

- 12/31/X2 market value $105,000
- 12/31/X3 market value $90,000
- $6,000 loss during 19X4 deemed permanent
- 12/31/X4 market value $98,000
- 12/31/X5 market value $100,000

a) Determine the amount that should appear in the firm's investments account (assuming no other investments) on its balance sheets as of 12/31/X2, 12/31/X3, 12/31/X4, and 12/31/X5.

b) What amount of gain or loss (if any) related to these investments should be reported in the firm's 19X2, 19X3, 19X4, and 19X5 income statements?

c) What amount (if any) should be shown in the firm's 19X2, 19X3, 19X4, and 19X5 year-end balance sheets for temporary loss on investments?

EP 11.8   The following information in thousands of dollars is available with respect to the portfolios of long-term investment securities of the X, Y, and Z companies that were acquired during 19X4:

	X	Y	Z
Portfolio cost	$100	$200	$300
Market value 12/31/X4	90	210	275
Market value 12/31/X5	95	205	290
Loss during 19X6 deemed permanent	8	10	20
Market value 12/31/X6	92	200	280
Market value 12/31/X7	105	185	295

For each firm:

a) Determine the amount that should appear in the firm's investments account on its balance sheets as of 12/31/X4, 12/31/X5, 12/31/X6, and 12/31/X7 if the investments were reported under the lower of cost or market method.

b) Determine the amount of gain or loss (if any) related to these investments that should be reported in the firm's 19X4, 19X5, 19X6, and 19X7 income statements.

c) Determine the amount (if any) related to these investments that should be reported as a temporary loss in the firm's 19X2, 19X3, 19X4, and 19X5 year-end balance sheets.

EP 11.9   The Mike Company owns 40,000 shares of the Nice Corporation's common stock purchased several years ago at a cost of $350,000. Nice has a total of 100,000 shares of common stock outstanding. Except for Mike's shares, the others are widely distributed. Mike is considered to have significant influence over Nice.

On 12/31/X0, Mike's balance sheet showed Nice's stock in the investment account at $412,000. During 19X1, the Nice Corporation declared and paid a cash dividend of $0.50 per share. Nice also reported $150,000 of net income for 19X1.

a) What should be the balance in Mike's investment account for Nice's stock as of 12/31/X1?

b) In Mike's 19X1 income statement, how much investment revenue should be reported attributable to the Nice Corporation?

c) In determining Mike's cash from operating activities for 19X1, what adjustment should be made (if any) to reported income with respect to revenue reported from the Nice Corporation?

EP 11.10 The Peter Company in its investments portfolio held common stock in the X, Y, and Z Corporations acquired on 1/1/X5. Stock in all three corporations was widely held among hundreds of stockholders. You may assume the company had no other investments. You have the following additional data with respect to these investments:

	X	Y	Z
Number of common shares outstanding	40,000 shs	50,000 shs	60,000 shs
Shares held by Peter Company	4,000 shs	15,000 shs	18,000 shs
Cost of Peter Company's investment	$16,000	$150,000	$360,000
Investee's 19X5 earnings/share	$4	$2	$3
12/31/X5 market value of Peter's investment	$28,000	$145,000	$387,000
Investee's 19X6 earnings/share	$5	$3	$4
Investee's 19X6 dividends/share	$2	none	$1
12/31/X6 market value of Peter's investment	$45,000	$180,000	$435,000

a) What was the balance in the company's investments account as of 12/31/X5?

b) How much revenue on investments should be reported in the company's 19X5 income statement?

c) What adjustments (if any) to 19X5 reported income is necessary related to investments revenue as part of calculating 19X5 cash from operating activities?

d) What was the balance in the company's investments account as of 12/31/X6?

e) How much revenue on investments should be reported in the company's 19X6 income statement?

f) What adjustment (if any) to 19X6 reported income is necessary related to investments revenue as part of calculating 19X6 cash from operating activities?

EP 11.11 The Ruth Company purchased bonds in the X and Y corporations on 1/1/X0, when the market rate of interest for these bonds was 12 percent. Both bonds pay interest on 6/30 and 12/31 each year. You have the following information with respect to these investments:

	X	Y
Maturity value of bonds	$50,000	$75,000
Stated annual interest rate	14%	10%
Maturity date	12/31/X6	12/31/X9

a) How should these bonds and their related premium and discount be reported on Ruth's 12/31/X1 balance sheet, assuming Ruth used the effective yield method for amortization?

b) What should be reported as interest revenue on these bonds for 19X1?

EP   11.12 Bonds were purchased from the ABC and XYZ Corporations on 1/1/X1 when the market rate of interest for these bonds was 12 percent. Interest is paid on 6/30 and 12/31 each year on these bonds.

	ABC	XYZ
Maturity value	$100,00	$200,00
Stated interest rate	10%	14%
Maturity date	12/31/X5	12/31/X8

a) Show the balance sheet presentation of its investment in the ABC Corporation and in the XYZ Corporation bonds as of 12/31/X1, 12/31/X2, 12/31/X3 using the effective yield method.

b) What should be reported as interest revenue on the ABC bonds and the XYZ bonds separately and in total by the firm on its 19X1, 19X2, and 19X3 income statements?

EP   11.13 The George Company leased special equipment under a 20 year lease on 1/1/X5. Twenty years is the effective life of the equipment. At the end of the lease, George has the option of purchasing the equipment for $1. You may assume that the lease qualifies as a capital lease. The total of all 20 equal annual payments, required at the end of each year, under the lease is $200,000. The discounted present value of the total of these payments at 12 percent, which you may assume is appropriate for the George Company, is $74,694.

In initially recording this transaction, how much will the accountant show as:

a) The asset amount?

b) Using straight-line depreciation, what would the book value of the capital lease be on 12/31/X5?

EP   11.14 The A, B, C, and D Corporations each acquired equipment under capital lease on 1/1/X2. The following data relate to these four corporations and their leased equipment:

	A	B	C	D
Duration of lease	5 yrs.	8 yrs.	10 yrs.	12 yrs
Method of depreciation to be used	SYD	St. line	DDB	St.line
Down payment on signing	$ 10,000	$ 15,000	$ 6,000	$ 25,000
Future payments	200,000	150,000	120,000	480,000
Present value of future payments	134,088	84,138	60,226	216,824

For each corporation separately indicate the book value for properties under capital lease as of 1/1/X2, 12/31/X2, 12/31/X3, and 12/31/X5. You may round yearly depreciation to the nearest dollar and, in this problem, ignore the liabilities and expenses related to the leased property.

Supplementary Problems

SP 11.15 On 1/1/X3 the Homer Company acquired land and a building in exchange for a $20,000 down payment and a 20 year mortgage note with a face value of $400,000 and a stated annual interest payment of two percent. The note was an interest only note requiring annual interest and the face value at maturity. The land at the time of acquisition was appraised at $25,000. What initial value (cost) should be reported in the buildings account on the firm's balance sheet if the firm's incremental borrowing rate was 15 percent?

SP 11.16 On 1/1/X1 the Joye Corporation acquired land and a building in exchange for a $50,000 down payment and an interest only mortgage note requiring annual interest payments for the balance. What initial value (cost) should be reported in the buildings account on the firm's balance sheet under each of the following different situations:

	(a)	(b)	(c)	(d)
Face value of mortgage	$500,000	$700,000	$750,000	$900,000
Years until maturity	20	15	30	20
Stated annual interest rate	12%	3%	5%	8%
Joye's incremental borrowing rate	12%	12%	13%	14%
Appraised value of land 1/1/X1	$100,000	$75,000	$50,000	$125,000

SP 11.17 Integrative Problem: The following events occurred during Period 13 for the LUTON corporation:

1) Sales totaled $180,000, $45,000 for cash and the balance on account.
2) Collections of receivables from customers totaled $130,000.
3) Merchandise inventory costing $120,000 was purchased on account.
4) Wages and salaries totaling $38,900 were paid including the $900 previously accrued.
5) Supplies costing $900 were purchased on account.
6) $2,800 was paid at the beginning of the period for insurance covering Periods 13 through 16.
7) $950 of bills for utilities and services consumed in the current period were received and recorded.
8) $4,800 of interest was paid covering the current period's interest cost (on the building mortgage and equipment notes) and the $1,600 previously accrued.
9) The $2,900 of taxes payable for Period 12 were paid.
10) $103,850 was paid on accounts payable.
11) The preferred dividend of $2,500 and a cash dividend on the common of $9,450 ($.25 per share) were declared and paid along with the $1,890 common dividend previously declared.
12) $140,000 of excess cash at the beginning of the period was invested in marketable securities.

Adjustments were made for LIFO ending inventory of $61,000 (A); FIFO ending supplies inventory of $300 (B); $700 expiration of prepaid insurance (C); $4,800 of depreciation on buildings and $1,000 depreciation on equipment (D); accrual of $2,000 of wages and salaries earned but not yet paid (E); accrued interest receivable on marketable securities of $3,500 (F); and provision for corporate income taxes for the period of $4,000 (G).

The LUTON Corporation's balance sheet as of the end of Period 13 is given below:

LUTON CORPORATION BALANCE SHEET AS OF END OF PERIOD 13

ASSETS		EQUITIES	
Cash	$ 18,110	Accounts payable	$ 35,000
Marketable securities	140,000	Wages and salaries	2,000
Accounts receivable	80,000	Taxes payable	4,000
Interest receivable	3,500	Total Current Liabilities	$ 41,000
Inventory	61,000		
Supplies	300		
Prepaid items	2,100	Noncurrent notes payable	76,000
Total Current Assets	$305,010	Total Liabilities	$117,000
Land	25,000	Preferred stock*	100,000
Buildings	125,000	Addtl. paid-in capital–pfd.	10,000
Accum. depr. bldgs.	(33,100)		
Equipment	20,000	Common stock**	189,000
Accum. depr. equip.	(7,500)	Addtl. paid-in capital–com.	6,750
		Retained earnings	11,660
Total Assets	$434,410	Total Equities	$434,410

* $100 par; 20,000 shares authorized; 1,000 shares issued and outstanding.
** $5 par; 200,000 shares authorized; 37,800 shares issued and outstanding.

During Period 14, the following events occurred affecting the financial position of the LUTON Corporation: (Note: Items with an asterisk have been illustrated in previous periods.)

*1) Sales totaled $200,000, $50,000 for cash and the balance on account.

*2) Collections of customer receivables totaled $130,000.

*3) Merchandise inventory costing $125,000 was purchased on account. Inventory purchases were added directly to the inventory account.

*4) Supplies costing $2,100 were purchased on account.

*5) Wages and salaries totaling $44,000 were paid including the $2,000 previously accrued.

*6) $1,000 of bills for utilities and services consumed in the current period were received and recorded.

*7) The period's interest costs on long-term debt of $3,200 were paid.

*8) The prior period's income tax liability of $4,000 was paid.

*9) $118,200 was paid on accounts payable.

*10) The period's preferred dividend of $2,500 and a cash dividend of $13,230 ($0.35 per share) on the common were declared and paid.

*11) $4,500 of interest on marketable securities was collected including the $3,500 previously accrued.

12) Early in the period, marketable securities costing $100,000 were sold for $115,000.

13) At the beginning of the period, a note receivable with a face value of $10,600 was accepted in settlement of a customer's accounts receivable of $10,000. The note would mature at the end of Period 15 and included interest of $300 per period in its face value.

14) During the period, accounts receivable totaling $2,800 were determined to be uncollectible and were written off.

15) 15,000 shares of the Ajax Corporation's common stock were purchased as a long-term investment early in Period 14 at a cost of $80,000. The shares acquired equaled 25 percent of the firm's outstanding voting stock and represented significant influence over Ajax.

16) LUTON also purchased as a long-term investment at the beginning of the period, 40 $1,000 denomination bonds of the Baker Corporation. The bonds will mature at the end of Period 33, have a stated or coupon rate of interest of two percent per period, and were acquired at a cost of $800 each.

17) $800 representing the period's interest on the Baker Corporation bonds was received at the end of Period 14.

18) At the beginning of Period 14, the company acquired a small nearby warehouse under a 20 period capital lease terminating at the end of Period 33. The lease required a $10,000 payment within 10 days of signing and payments of $5,000 per period payable on the first day of each period starting with Period 16, with the last payment to be made at the start of Period 33. LUTON's borrowing rate was four percent per period, and the present value of the capital lease on signing was $70,862 (19 future $5,000 payments discounted at four percent per period less the first period's (Period 15) $5,000 payment discounted at four percent plus the $10,000 immediate payment). The current portion ($10,000) of the total capital lease obligation was paid within a few days of signing.

At the end of Period 14:

*A) Merchandise inventory was adjusted to reflect ending inventory at LIFO of $66,000.

*B) Supplies inventory was adjusted to reflect ending supplies on hand under FIFO of $900.

*C) Prepaid items were adjusted to reflect the expiration of $700 of prepaid insurance.

*D) Wages and salaries totaling $3,000 earned but not yet paid were accrued.

*E) Depreciation expense of $4,600 on buildings and $900 on equipment was recorded.

*F) Utilities cost estimated at $100 consumed but not yet billed was accrued.

*G) Corporate income taxes payable early in Period 15 were estimated to be $7,000.

H) The remaining portfolio of marketable securities that had cost $40,000 had a current market value of $35,000.

I) $300 of interest included in the face value had been earned on the note receivable from a customer.

J) An aging of ending accounts receivable indicated that accounts totaling $1,800 were not expected to prove collectible.

K) The Ajax Corporation's Period 14 earnings totaled $40,000. The corporation did not, however, declare any common dividends during the period.

L) One period's amortization totaling $400 of the discount on the Baker Corporation bonds held as long-term investments was recorded (straight-line amortization may be assumed acceptable).

M) One period's straight-line depreciation of the warehouse capital lease was recorded (rounded to the nearest $10).

Required:
a) The effect on the beginning period balance sheet of those Period 14 transactions and adjustments that were introduced in earlier periods, and which are identified with an asterisk (*), has already been recorded in the partially completed balance sheet effect worksheet given below. Prepare a final balance sheet effect worksheet for the LUTON Corporation for Period 14 starting with the preliminary balances and recording the effect of Period 14 transactions (12) through (18) and adjustments (H) through (M). Identify starting balances as "(p)" and the effect of the remaining transactions and adjustments with their numbers or letters. Also identify all revenue and expense effects upon retained earnings with a double asterisk (**). Provide necessary space on your worksheet by entering account titles as follows:

Account	Line number	Account	Line number
Cash	1	Accounts Payable	1
Marketable Securities	7	Wages and Salaries	2
Notes Receivable	10	Taxes Payable	3
Notes Receivable Discount	12	Current Cap. Lse. Obligations	4
Accounts Receivable	15	Noncurrent Notes Payable	7
Allowance for Bad Debts	18	Noncurrent Cap. Lse. Obligations	8
Inventory	21	Preferred Stock	26
Supplies	22	Addtl. Paid-in Capital—Pfd.	27
Prepaid Items	23	Common Stock	28
Investments	24	Addtl. Paid-in Capital—Com.	29
Bond Investments Discount	28	Retained Earnings	30
Land	31		
Buildings	32		
Accum. Depr. Buildings	33		
Equipment	34		
Accum. Depr. Equipment	35		
Properties Under Cap. Lse.	36		

b) Prepare the firm's income statement for Period 14 in good form following the multiple step format.
c) Prepare the statement of retained earnings in good form for Period 14.
d) Prepare the firm's balance sheet in good form as of the end of Period 14.
e) Prepare the firm's statement of cash flows for Period 14 in good form following the indirect method for operating activities.
f) Determine for the LUTON Corporation for Period 14:
   1) The amount of net working capital in the business at the end of the period;
   2) The period end current ratio (to two decimals);
   3) The period end quick ratio (to two decimals);
   4) The period end long-term debt ratio (to three decimals);
   5) The period end asset composition ratio (to three decimals);
   6) The book value per share at the end of the period (preferred claim in liquidation is $125 per share); and
   7) Earnings per share for the period.

SP 11.20 Integrative Problem: The following events occurred during Period 13 for the MORCHAN Corporation:

PARTIALLY COMPLETED BALANCE SHEET EFFECT WORKSHEET
LUTON Corporation Period 14
(b = beginning balance; p = Partially Complete Ending Balance)

Cash	$ 18,110	(b)			Accounts Payable			
	+ 50,000	(1)				$ 35,000	(b)	
	+ 130,000	(2)				+ 125,000	(3)	
	− 44,000	(5)				+ 2,100	(4)	
	− 3,200	(7)				+ 1,000	(6)	
	− 4,000	(8)				− 118,000	(9)	
	− 118,200	(9)				+ 100	(F)	$ 45,000 (p)
	− 15,730	(10)			Wages and Salaries			
	+ 4,500	(11)	$ 17,480 (p)			2,000	(b)	
Marketable Securities						− 2,000	(5)	
	140,000	(b)	140,000 (p)			+ 3,000	(D)	3,000 (p)
Accounts Receivable					Taxes Payable			
	80,000	(b)				4,000	(b)	
	+ 150,000	(1)				− 4,000	(8)	
	− 130,000	(2)	100,000 (p)			+ 7,000	(G)	7,000 (p)
Interest Receivable					Noncurrent Notes Payable			
	3,500	(b)				76,000	(b)	76,000 (p)
	− 3,500	(11)	0 (p)					
Inventory	61,000	(b)			Preferred Stock			
	+ 125,000	(3)				100,000	(b)	100,000 (p)
	− 120,000	(A)	66,000 (p)		Addtl. Paid-in Capital—Pfd.			
Supplies	300	(b)				10,000	(b)	10,000 (p)
	+ 2,100	(4)			Common Stock			
	− 1,500	(B)	900 (p)			189,000	(b)	189,000 (p)
Prepaid Items					Addtl. Paid-in Capital—Com.			
	2,100	(b)				6,750	(b)	6,750 (p)
	− 700	(C)	1,400 (p)		Retained Earnings			
Land	25,000	(b)	25,000 (p)			11,600	(b)	
Buildings	125,000	(b)	125,000 (p)			− 15,730	(10)	

Accum. Depr. —Bldgs			
	(33,100)	(b)	
	− 4,600	(E)	(37,700)(p)
Equipment	20,000	(b)	20,000 (p)
Accum. Depr.—Equip.			
	(7,500)	(b)	
	− 900	(E)	(8,400)(p)

Income		
+ 200,000	(1)	
− 42,000	(5)	
− 1,000	(6)	
− 3,200	(7)	
+ 1,000	(11)	
− 120,000	(A)	
− 1,500	(B)	
− 700	(C)	
− 3,000	(D)	
− 5,500	(E)	
− 100	(F)	
− 7,000	(G)	

TOTALS	$ 449,680	TOTALS	$ 449,680

1) Sales totaled $250,000, $50,000 for cash and the balance on account.
2) Collections of receivables from customers totaled $125,000.
3) Merchandise inventory costing $150,000 was purchased on account.
4) Wages and salaries totaling $55,200 were paid including the $500 previously accrued.
5) Supplies costing $1,500 were purchased on account.
6) $5,600 was paid at the beginning of the period for insurance covering Periods 13 through 16.
7) $1,650 of bills for utilities and services consumed in the current period were received and recorded.
8) $12,900 of interest was paid covering both the current period's interest cost (on the building mortgage and equipment notes) and the $4,300 previously accrued.
9) the $5,000 of taxes payable for Period 12 were paid.
10) $93,150 was paid on accounts payable.
11) The preferred dividend of $6,000 and a cash dividend on the common of $20,808 ($0.50 per share) were declared and paid along with the $2,081 common dividend previously declared.
12) $240,000 of excess cash at the beginning of the period was invested in marketable securities.

Adjustments were made for LIFO ending inventory of $158,000 (A); FIFO ending supplies inventory of $1,550 (B); $1,400 expiration of prepaid insurance (C); $12,100 of depreciation on buildings and $1,650 depreciation on equipment (D); accrual of $1,300 of wages and salaries earned but not yet paid (E); accrued interest receivable on marketable securities of $7,000 (F); and provision for corporate income taxes for the period of $9,900 (G).

The MORCHAN Corporation's balance sheet as of the end of Period 13 is given below:

MORCHAN CORPORATION BALANCE SHEET AS OF END OF PERIOD 13

ASSETS		EQUITIES	
Cash	$ 18,711	Accounts Payable	$ 160,000
Marketable Securities	240,000	Wages and Salaries	1,300
Accounts Receivable	203,000	Taxes Payable	9,900
Interest Receivable	7,000		
Inventory	158,000	Total Current Liabilities	$ 171,200
Supplies	1,550	Noncurrent Notes Payable	208,000
Prepaid Items	4,200		
Total Current Assets	$632,461	Total Liabilities	$ 379,200
Land	90,000	Preferred Stock*	200,000
Buildings	370,000	Addtl. Paid-in Capital Pfd.	10,000
Accum. Depr. Bldgs.	(80,400)	Common Stock**	416,160
Equipment	35,000	Addtl. Paid-in Capital Com.	12,550
Accum. Depr. Equip.	(12,150)		
		Retained Earnings	17,001
Total Assets	$1,034,911	Total Equities	$1,034,911

* $100 par; 50,000 shares authorized; 2,000 shares issued and outstanding.
** $10 par; 500,000 shares authorized; 41,616 shares issued and outstanding.

During Period 14, the following events occurred affecting the financial position of the MORCHAN Corporation: (Note: Items marked with an asterisk have been illustrated in previous periods.)

*1)   Sales totaled $275,000, $50,000 for cash and the balance on account.

*2)   Collections of customer receivables totaled $192,100.

*3)   Merchandise inventory costing $192,000 was purchased on account. Inventory purchases were added directly to the inventory account.

*4)   Supplies costing $350 were purchased on account.

*5)   Wages and salaries totaling $58,800 were paid including the $1,300 previously accrued.

*6) $1,600 of bills for utilities and services consumed in the current period were received and recorded.

*7)   The period's interest costs on long-term debt of $8,600 were paid.

*8)   The prior period's income tax liability of $9,900 was paid.

*9) $180,150 was paid on accounts payable.

*10) The period's preferred dividend of $6,000 and a cash dividend of $2,081 ($0.05 per share) on the common were declared and paid.

*11) $8,500 of interest on marketable securities was collected including the $7,000 previously accrued.

12)   Early in the period, marketable securities costing $190,000 were sold for $180,000.

13)   At the beginning of the period, a note receivable with a face value of $5,400 was accepted in settlement of a customer's accounts receivable of %5,000. The note would mature at the end of Period 15 and included interest of $200 per period in its face value.

14)   During the period, accounts receivable totaling $5,900 were determined to be uncollectible and were written off.

15)   20,000 shares of the Acme Corporation's common stock were purchased as a long-term investment early in Period 14 at a cost of $100,000. The shares acquired equaled 30 percent of the firm's outstanding voting stock and represented significant influence over Acme.

16)   MORCHAN also purchased as a long-term investment at the beginning of the period, fifty $1,000 denomination bonds of the Zukor Corporation. The bonds would mature at the end of Period 38, had a stated or coupon rate of interest of four percent per period, and were acquired at a cost of $1,100 each.

17) $2,000 representing the period's interest on the Zukor Corporation bonds was received at the end of Period 14.

18)   At the beginning of Period 14, the company acquired a nearby warehouse under a 25 period capital lease terminating at the end of Period 38. The lease required a $20,000 payment within ten days of signing and payments of $10,000 per period payable on the first day of each period starting with Period 16, with the last payment to be made at the start of Period 38. MORCHAN's borrowing rate was three percent per period, and the present value of the capital lease on signing was $179,646 (24 future $10,000 payments discounted at three percent per period less the first period's Period 15 -$10,000 payment discounted at three percent plus the $20,000 immediate payment). The current portion ($20,000) of the total capital lease obligation was paid within a few days of signing.

At the end of Period 14:

*A) Merchandise inventory was adjusted to reflect ending inventory at LIFO of $210,000.

*B) Supplies inventory was adjusted to reflect ending supplies on hand under FIFO of $400.

*C) Prepaid items were adjusted to reflect the expiration of $1,400 of prepaid insurance.

*D) Wages and salaries totaling $2,500 earned but not yet paid were accrued.

*E) Depreciation expense of $11,600 on buildings and $1,500 on equipment was recorded.

*F) Utilities cost estimated at $200 consumed but not yet billed was accrued.

*G) Corporate income taxes payable early in Period 15 were estimated to be $4,000.

H) The remaining portfolio of marketable securities that had cost $50,000 had a current market value of $49,000.

I) $200 of interest included in the face value had been earned on the note receivable form a customer.

J) An aging of ending accounts receivable indicated that accounts totaling $6,750 were not expected to prove collectible.

K) The Acme Corporation's Period 14 earnings totaled $20,000. The corporation did not, however, declare any common dividends during the period.

L) One period's amortization totaling $200 of the premium on the Zukor Corporation bonds held as long-term investments was recorded (straight-line amortization may be assumed acceptable).

M) One period's straight-line depreciation of the warehouse capital lease (rounded to the nearest $10) was recorded.

Required:

a) The effect on the beginning period balance sheet of those Period 14 transactions and adjustments that were introduced in earlier periods, and which are identified with as asterisk (*), has already been recorded in the partially completed balance sheet effect worksheet given below. Prepare a final balance sheet effect worksheet for the MORCHAN Corporation for Period 14 starting with the preliminary balances and recording the effect of Period 14 transactions (12) through (18) and adjustments (H) through (M). Identify starting balances as "(p)" and the effect of the remaining transactions and adjustments with their numbers or letters. Also identify all revenue and expense effects upon retained earnings with a double asterisk (**). Provide necessary space on your worksheet by entering account titles as follows:

Account	Line number	Account	Line number
Cash	1	Accounts Payable	1
Marketable Securities	7	Wages and Salaries	2
Notes Receivable	10	Taxes Payable	3
Notes Receivable Discount	12	Current Cap. Lse. Oblig.	4
Accounts Receivable	15	Noncurrent Notes Payable	7
Allowance for Bad Debts	18	Noncurrent Cap. Lse. Oblig.	8
Inventory	21	Preferred Stock	26
Supplies	22	Addtl. Paid-in Cap. Pfd.	27
Prepaid Items	23	Common Stock	28
Investments	24	Addtl. Paid-in Cap.Com.	29
Bond Inv. Premium	28	Retained Earnings	30
Land	31		
Buildings	32		
Accum. Depr. Buildings	33		
Equipment	34		
Accum. Depr. Equipment	35		
Properties Under Cap.Lse.	36		

PARTIALLY COMPLETED BALANCE SHEET EFFECT WORKSHEET
MORCHAN Corporation Period 14
(b = Beginning Balance; p= Partially Complete Ending Balance)

Cash	$ 18,711	(b)		Accounts Payable		
	+ 50,000	(1)		$ 160,000	(b)	
	+ 192,100	(2)		+ 192,000	(3)	
	− 58,800	(5)		+ 350	(4)	
	− 8,600	(7)		+ 1,600	(6)	
	− 9,900	(8)		− 180,150	(9)	
	− 180,150	(9)		+ 200	(F)	$ 174,000 (p)
	− 8,081	(10)		Wages and Salaries		
	+ 8,500	(11) $ 3,780 (p)		1,300	(b)	
Marketable Securities				− 1,300	(5)	
	240,000	(b) 240,000 (p)		+ 2,500	(D)	2,500 (p)
Accounts Receivable				Taxes Payable		
	203,000	(b)		9,900	(b)	
	+ 225,000	(1)		− 9,900	(8)	
	− 192,100	(2) 235,900 (p)		+ 4,000	(G)	4,000 (p)
Interest Receivable				Noncurrent Notes Payable		
	7,000	(b)		208,000	(b)	208,000 (p)
	− 7,000	(11) 0 (p)				
Inventory	158,000	(b)		Preferred Stock		
	+ 192,000	(3)		200,000	(b)	200,000 (p)
	− 140,000	(A) 210,000 (p)		Addtl. Paid–in Capital—Pfd.		
Supplies	1,550	(b)		10,000	(b)	10,000 (p)
	+ 350	(4)		Common Stock		
	− 1,500	(B) 400 (p)		416,160	(b)	416,160 (p)
Prepaid Items				Addtl. Paid–in Capital—Com.		
	4,200	(b)		12,550	(b)	12,550 (p)
	− 1,400	(C) 2,800 (p)		Retained Earnings		
Land	90,000	(b) 90,000 (p)		17,001	(b)	
Buildings	370,000	(b) 370,000 (p)		− 8,081	(10)	

Income
+ 275,000	(1)
− 57,500	(5)
− 1,600	(6)
− 8,600	(7)
+ 1,500	(11)
− 140,000	(A)
− 1,500	(B)
− 1,400	(C)
− 2,500	(D)
− 13,100	(E)
− 200	(F)
− 4,000	(G)

Accum. Depr. —Bldgs			
	(80,400)	(b)	
	− 11,600	(E)	(92,000)(p)
Equipment	35,000	(b)	35,000 (p)
Accum. Depr.—Equip.			
	(12,150)	(b)	
	− 1,500	(E)	(13,650)(p)

TOTALS	$1,082,230	TOTALS	$1,082,230

    b) Prepare the firm's income statement for Period 14 in good form following the multiple step format.

    c) Prepare the statement of retained earnings in good form for period 14.

    d) Prepare the firm's balance sheet in good form as of the end of period 14.

    e) Prepare the firm's statement of cash flows for Period 14 in good form following the indirect method for operating activities.

    f) Determine for the MORCHAN Corporation for Period 14:

        1) The amount of net working capital in the business at the end of the period;

        2) The period end current ratio (to two decimals);

        3) The period end quick ratio (to two decimals);

        4) The period end long-term debt ratio (to three decimals);

        5) The period end asset composition ratio (to three decimals); and

        6) The book value per share at the end of the period (preferred claim in liquidation is $110 per share).

Preparer Problems

PP 11.1 Give the necessary transactions and adjusting entries during 19X2 for the Archer Company (Problem EP 11.1)

PP 11.2 Give the necessary journal entries relating to accounts receivable and bad debt allowance for 19X5 from the data given in EP 11.2 for all companies separately.

PP 11.3 Refer to EP 11.3, (a) journalize the acquisition of the note. (b) Journalize the accrued revenue after three months.

PP 11.4 Based on the data supplied in EP 11.4, for each of the four firms separately:

    a) Journalize the acquisition of the note.

    b) Journalize the interest accrued at the end of the first quarter.

PP 11.5 Refer to EP 11.5. Give any necessary adjusting entries reflecting gains or losses on marketable securities for the years 19X1, 19X2, and 19X3.

PP 11.6 Refer to EP 11.6. For each of the four firms separately, give any necessary adjusting entries reflecting gains or losses on marketable securities for the years 19X4, 19X5, 19X6, and 19X7.

PP 11.7 Refer to EP 11.9. Give the necessary entries during 19X1 relating to the investment in the Nice Corporation.

PP 11.8 Refer to EP 11.10. For the years 19X5 and 19X6 separately, give all necessary entries relating to the investments in the X,Y, and Z Corporations' stocks.

PP 11.9 Refer to EP 11.11. Give all necessary 19X1 entries relating to the two bond investments assuming interest was paid.

PP 11.10 Refer to EP 11.12. Give all necessary entries for 19X1 relating to their holdings of ABC and XYZ Corporations' bonds assuming interest had not yet been paid/received.

PP 11.11 Refer to SP 11.15. Give the entry recording the acquisition of the land and building.

PP 11.12 Refer to SP 11.16. For each of the four separate situations, give the entry recording the acquisitions to the land and building.

PP   **11.13** Refer to SP 11.17. Give the appropriate transaction and adjustment entries identified by number or letter for all non asterisked items for Period 14 for the corporation.

PP   **11.14** Refer to SP 11.18. Give appropriate transactions and adjustment entries identified by number or letter for Period 14 for the corporation as follows:

    a)   All non asterisked transactions and adjustments:

    b)   All asterisked transactions and adjustments.

Appendix Problems

AP   **11.15** The Marina Corporation's cash records showed the following transactions and other data since the last bank reconcilation:

• Total deposits	$14,000	• Cash on hand	$ 600
• Total checks drawn	11,000	• Cash account balance	16,000

The bank's statement indiciated the following activitiy and balance since the last reconciliation:

• Deposits received	$13,000	• Service charges on NSF check	$ 5
• Total checks cashed	9,000	• Interest credited	60
• NSF check returned	1,400	• Balance in account	15,050

    a)   Prepare a bank reconciliation in good form.

    b)   Prepare any journal entries indicated as necessary as a result of the reconiliation process.

AP   **11.16** The La Costa Company's cash records showed the following transactions and other data since the last bank reconciliation:

• Total deposits	$105,000	• Cash account balance	$25,000
• Total checks drawn	95,000	• Note receivable given to bank	
• Cash on hand	900	for collection	9,000

The bank's statement indiciated the following activitiy and balance since the last reconciliation:

• Deposits received	$102,000	• Checks cleared and returned	$91,000
• Note collected	9,000	• Service charges on NSF check	15
• Interest credited	100	• Balance in account	31,385
• NSF checks returned	2,800		

    a)   Prepare a bank reconciliation in good form.

    b)   Prepare any journal entries indicated as necessary as a result of the reconiliation process.

APPENDIX

Bank Reconciliation

If you have a bank checking account, you are already familiar with the desirability and necessity of reconciling your checkbook with your bank's statement of your account each month. A business must similarly update and correct the balance in its cash account (cash on hand and in banks) each month. The process of comparing one's own records with the bank's, to explain differences and to locate any errors made by either party, is known as bank reconciliation.

At the start of the reconciliation process, you should have:

1. Your cash account records, indicating bank deposits made, checks drawn, the amount of cash you believe you have available in the bank, and also the amount of cash you have on hand.

2. Your bank's monthly statement of your account, indicating beginning balance, deposits made, checks cleared, other additions and subtractions to your account, and the ending balance.

3. Cancelled checks that you have drawn and which have cleared your account each month and been returned to the bank.

Exhibit 11.9 contains information that might appear on a typical bank statement. Note that it indicates your firm's account has been charged (reduced) $5,400.50 for six of your checks which have cleared the bank with your statement. Two other charges to your account—$3.00 identified as a bank service charge and $500.00 identified as a NSF (insufficient funds) check were recorded.

Exhibit 11.9 Example of Information contained on Monthly Bank Statement

Beginning balance		$10,000.00
Deposits received:	$1,200.00	
	800.00	
	500.00	
	3,500.00	6,000.00
Notes collected:		400.10
Checks paid:	$1,400.00	
	700.00	
	1,600.00	
	900.00	
	800.50	(5,400.50)
NSF Check		(500.00)
Service charge on NSF check		(3.00)
Interest credit		45.00
Ending balance		$10,541.60

The $500.00 NSF check is an example of a check previously received from a customer and deposited at the bank. The $500.00 was originally credited (added) to your account by the bank at the time of deposit, as part of the $6,000.00 of deposits shown as received. When your bank was unable to collect on the check from the customer's bank, it charged your account and returned the check to you. You, of course, now have an additional receivable claim against your customer for this $500.00 and will be attempting to collect it, separately from the bank reconciliation process.

In addition to the $6,000.00 of deposits shown as received, Exhibit 11.9 also shows that the bank has credited your account for $400.10 representing a note which you have given the bank to collect for you (for collection) and for $45.00 of interest earned on your average balance. The bank indicates, on its statement, that your ending balance after all this activity is $10,541.60.

You may assume your cash account shows a balance of $10,799.50 ($10,499.50 in the bank and $300.00 cash on hand). Your accounts show checks drawn since the last reconciliation totaling $6,300.50, and deposits sent to the bank totaling $6,800.00.

Reconciling involves correcting the separate amounts for any discovered errors and updating for information (amounts) not yet received and processed. To adjust the bank's balance to the correct balance of total cash in the firm, two items must be added. Any cash on hand ($300.00 in this example) must be added, since the bank knows nothing about it. Similarly, any deposits in transit—recorded on the firm's books but not yet received and processed by the bank—must also be added to the bank's statement balance ($800.00 in this example). Also any outstanding checks—checks that have been drawn and deducted on the firm's books but have not yet been presented to the bank for payment—must be deducted from the bank's statement balance, since these funds are no longer available to the firm (outstanding checks totaling $900.00 in this example).

Exhibit 11.10 shows an example of a bank reconciliation incorporating the above data. Note that the $10,541.60 balance per bank statement has been adjusted for cash on hand, deposits in transit, and outstanding checks. The adjusted amount, $10741.60, is identified as the corrected cash balance. To prove the accuracy of this amount, it is reconciled, in turn, with the amount appearing in the firm's books.

Exhibit 11.10   Example of Bank Reconciliation

From bank statement		From firm's accounts	
Balance per statement	$10,541.60	Balance per books	$10,799.50
Add:		**Add:**	
Cash on hand	300.00	Note proceeds	400.10
Deposits on hand	800.00	Interest credited	45.00
	$11,641.60		$11,244.60
Deduct:		**Deduct:**	
		NSF deposit	500.00
Outstanding checks	900.00	Service charge	3.00
Correct cash balance	$10,741.60	Correct cash balance	$10,741.60

The bank statement provides information concerning events not yet recorded in the firm's accounts. After reconciliation is complete, appropriate entries must be made to record this additional information. As part of the reconciliation process, additional deposits not previously recorded and interest earned are added to the original book balance ($400.10 collected on a note and $45.00 of interest, in this example).

Exhibit 11.10 shows these adjustments. It also shows deductions for charges (reductions) not previously recorded in the firm's books such as NSF (bad) checks received from customers and service charges assessed by the bank ($500.00 and $3.00 in this example). This total is identical to that previously arrived at by adjusting the bank's statement balance, and the reconciliation is complete.

The reconciliation process in the above example has revealed the following journal entries to be necessary to update the firm's accounts:

	DR	CR
(1) Cash	$400.10	
Notes Receivable		$400.10
To record collection and deposit of note by bank.		
(2) Accounts Receivable	500.00	
Cash		500.00
To record reversal of collection arising out of customers NSF check.		
(3) Miscellaneous Expense	3.00	
Cash		3.00
To record bank service charge.		
(4) Cash	45.00	
Interest Revenue		45.00
To record interest earned.		

The reconciliation process could also uncover errors of recording in the firm's books, which would then both be shown as an adjustment to the firm's book balance on the reconciliation and would also generate a correcting entry. Although rare, bank reconciliation can also uncover errors made by the bank. Bank errors would be shown as adjustments to the bank statement balance on the reconciliation, and the bank would then be advised to change its records accordingly.

12

The Measurement
and Reporting
of Liabilities

Chapter Preview

The objective of this chapter is to complete your understanding of liability measurement and reporting in conformance with GAAP. In this chapter, you can:

1. Learn of the objectives of liability measurement and reporting under GAAP;

2. Develop an understanding of the distinction among different types of liabilities and which ones are reported on the balance sheet;

3. Learn that there may be several items disclosed as liabilities that do not represent obligations to creditors; and develop an understanding of what these items do represent, and why they are classified as liabilities;

4. Discover that liability discount and premium accounts are the counterpart of those accounts for bonds and receivables discussed in Chapter 11;

5. Learn how accountants measure, classify, and report certain liabilities not previously discussed;

6. Discover various ways debt can be eliminated other than by payment at maturity;

7. Review all changes that can occur to common liability accounts; and

8. Complete your understanding of those adjustments to debt that do not involve cash flow.

With this knowledge you will be qualified to read and interpret correctly the liability section of most published balance sheets. Together with your existing knowledge of assets (Chapter 11) and owners' equity (Chapter 10), you will be prepared to analyze financial statements by employing the approaches and tools to be presented in Chapter 13.

Objectives of Liability Measurement and Reporting

Recall, from Chapter 11, that measurement and reporting objectives for assets include reporting all measurable assets which the firm actually owns, has legal claims to, or effectively controls as of the balance sheet date. Resources, benefits, or gains that might come in the future are specifically not included since they are either executory or represent speculation. Specifically, future unearned interest is excluded in computation of total assets.

GAAP standards for liability measurement are consistent with these objectives. All measurable obligations of the firm that legally exist as of the balance sheet date are disclosed. Future obligations that are executory, or which may develop in the future, are not included in the balance sheet. Interest that is not yet owed is specifically excluded. Liabilities are measured and reported at the present value of the stream of payments owed. The arithmetic technique for determining present value, where a liability extends beyond one year and compound interest is involved, is covered in Appendix B.

Note also that GAAP specifically prohibit offsetting liabilities with associated assets.[1] Remember from Chapter 11 that Omega has accumulated $19,803 in a sinking fund escrow account specifically established to retire $50,000 of sinking fund bonds at maturity. Omega cannot use these funds for any other purpose; therefore it might seem logical to show the sinking fund as an offset to the debt with only the net amount unfunded included in total liabilities. The reason behind the no-offset rule is Omega's bank or escrow agent could "go under" or disappear with the assets, and Omega's liability would still be $50,000 to the bondholders at maturity as shown.

In previous chapters, liabilities such as current notes payable, accounts payable, various accrued liabilities, and noncurrent notes payable have been introduced. Their measurement and reporting should now be familiar and will not be discussed further. This chapter will address additional possible liabilities and liability accounts not previously covered.

How Much Does This Firm Really Owe to Others?

Grace Wong is continuing her investigation of the Omega Corporation's balance sheet. After satisfying herself that she understood the basis of valuation for the firm's reported $3,102,000 of assets (Exhibit 11.1), she turns to the firm's liabilities. Exhibit 12.1 gives Omega's liabilities as reported in its balance sheet as of 12/31/X1.

Grace believes liabilities represent the amounts of resources contributed by and owed to (claimed by) creditors. Again, she has marked with an asterisk the 11 items about which she has questions. If her firm buys the Omega Company, it will assume responsibility for Omega's debts. She would like to be sure that all the firm's liabilities as of 12/31 are shown, that those liabilities represent all the resources owed to the creditors,

---

[1] The only exception to the offsetting rule is for government tax anticipation certificates that a firm may acquire to accumulate interest on monies being set aside to pay taxes. These certificates may be offset against accrued tax liabilities.

and that she knows how the liabilities are measured. Each asterisked item will be discussed, and the chapter will focus on this exhibit.

Exhibit 12.1

OMEGA CORPORATION
Liability Portion of Consolidated Balance Sheet as of 12/31/X1
($ in thousands)

Current notes payable	$20
* Less discount on notes payable	(2)
Accounts payable	210
Accrued wages and salaries payable	12
Accrued interest payable	13
Taxes payable	27
* Current capital lease obligations	166
* 5% serial bonds (maturing 12/31/X2)	10
* Estimated product warranties	8
* Accrued pension costs	9
Unearned revenue	4
Other current liabilities	3
Total Current Liabilities	$480
Mortgage note payable (maturing 6/30/X6)	30
* Less discount on mortgage note payable	(3)
5% serial bonds (10,000 maturing 12/31/X3 and 10,000 maturing 12/31/X4)	20
8% sinking fund bonds payable (maturing 12/31/X3)	50
* Less discount on bonds payable	(1)
10 1/2% bonds payable (maturing 12/31/X5)	100
* Premium on bonds payable	2
* Noncurrent capital lease obligations	186
* Deferred income tax	11
Total liabilities	$875
* Minority interest	$100

* Indicates items Grace Wong wants to clarify

Statement footnotes:
   The company is defendant in a lawsuit in the amount of $500,000.
   The company has a contract to purchase 2,000,000 gizmos over the next four years at a price of $4 each. Current market price is $4.75.

Estimated and Contingent Liabilities

Omega's $8,000 of estimated product warranties brings up the issue of different types of liabilities which may be reported on the balance sheet. Up to this point, you have been exposed only to liabilities which have the following characteristics:

1. They were the result of a past transaction or event. Performance by the creditor has been completed.

2. Except for unearned revenue they were all monetary (represented an obligation to pay specific amounts of cash at specific times). In the case of unearned revenue, even though the primary obligation is not monetary, the amount and the recipient are certain.

GAAP require that all of these liabilities be **"booked"** or recorded in the accounts. Either all liabilities will be included on the balance sheet, disclosed in footnotes, or else the auditor's opinion, included with the financial statements, will advise you of the exception.

Estimated Liabilities

Recall that in Chapter 4, an adjusting entry was entered at period-end to accrue the portion of utilities expense and the associated liability for the power consumed during the current period but not yet billed. **Estimated liabilities**, where the amount of the obligation is not known precisely, and even where the payee may not be known, are included on the balance sheet. Estimated liabilities are included because they are not executory or future related, the money or service is owed.

Contingent Liabilities

Contingent liabilities are contingent or dependent on something happening in the future. They can be divided into three categories:

- probably (likely to occur)
- reasonable possible (neither slight nor likely)
- remote (slight chance of occurrence)

All contingent liabilities, regardless of the probability of occurrence, are fully disclosed in the financial statement footnotes. Those contingencies which are both probable and can be estimated by the date the statements are prepared are booked as liabilities and expenses for the current period.

Omega's potential loss of $500,000 in a lawsuit, as footnoted, was not booked because the outcome could not be estimated.

Purchase Commitments

Businesses are expected to make **purchase commitments** on an ongoing basis. They are executory and most are not reported or disclosed. However, formal, noncancelable purchase commitments which are material in amount and where the price has been established, must be footnoted in the financial statements. Both the commitment and current market prices must be disclosed. Note that Omega's purchase commitment for $8,000,000 is for less than the current market price of $4.75 per gizmo. GAAP require that in the case where the current market price drops below the purchase commitment price, the loss, even though contingent, must be immediately recognized.

Warranty Costs

Estimated product **warranty costs** are nonmonetary liabilities since warranties are obligations to provide goods or services. It should be noted that this obligation exists as of the balance sheet date. It is not contingent or dependent upon the firm's continuing to sell the product or any other future occurrence.

In the situation where products are sold under warranty, the sale has been completed, and the firm has an existing obligation to the customer until the warranty period expires. In the Omega example, based on past experience, the accountant has statistically estimated that $8,000 of warranty expenses next year will be related to sales completed during this year. An adjusting entry is made at year-end, establishing this liability and charging warranty expense. The actual customers involved are not known, any more than actual customers who will fail to pay are known in estimating uncollectible receivables. Nevertheless, the amounts and timing can be reasonably estimated.

The accrual of estimated warranty expense is another example of the matching principle. Estimated repair or replacement costs reduce final profit on any group of warranted products sold. They represent an obligation to provide goods or services related to completed transactions and are properly matched with the revenues recognized in the year in which the products are sold. If they were not matched, next year's profits would be reduced by expenses which would be a result of this year's sales.

Minority Interest

Another nonmonetary item appearing on Exhibit 12.1 for the Omega Corporation is $100,000 of **minority interest**. Minority interest can appear only on a consolidated financial statement, and then only when one or more of the consolidated subsidiaries is (are) less than 100 percent owned. Minority interest represents the ownership claim of other stockholders of the subsidiaries that have been consolidated. If a subsidiary is not wholly owned, some outside stockholders have owners' equity claims against the subsidiary's assets. When the subsidiary's assets and liabilities are combined with the parent's on a consolidated statement, the minority claim is included along with its "share" of the subsidiary's total assets. Minority interest indicates that not all of the combined net assets are claimed, or owned, solely by the parent stockholders. It is sometimes included on the stockholders' or owners' equity section, in which case "owners" would mean all owners as distinct from creditors. Other firms follow Omega's example of disclosing it between liabilities and owners' equity. Grace Wong should recognize that the $100,000 minority interest represents a "nonfamily claim" against certain subsidiary dividends and subsidiary assets in the case of the subsidiary's liquidation. It does not represent any obligation or liability of Omega.

Obligations Under Pension Plans

When a firm establishes an employee pension plan, with or without its being involved in a union contract, it is customary to establish a separate pension fund or trust as a distinct accounting and legal entity. The fund's assets and its estimated liabilities to employees are not shown on the company's balance sheet. The fund is then used to make required pension payments to retired employees from cash invested and accumulated interest earned by the fund on its investments.

Pension plans can be divided into two classifications: defined benefit plans and defined contribution plans. Under defined contribution plans the firm's obligation is limited to making agreed upon contributions or payments to the fund. However, under defined benefit plans, the firm is under obligation to pay agreed upon benefits regardless of future events. The risk is obviously higher under defined benefit plans. Pension plans can also be contributory (employees pay into the fund) or noncontributory (firm pays all costs).

Pension costs are determined by applying a discount rate to actuarial tables. The discount rate is the interest rate selected to determine the present value of the future pension costs and liability.

A firm generally has two types of liabilities for its pension fund: current service costs and prior service costs. **Current service costs** are the amounts necessary to operate the plan if employee benefits were only to accrue from the date of the implementation of the plan. Current service costs each year are a current liability until paid and are a part of operating expenses.

When most pension plans are originally adopted, or when benefits are subsequently increased, the employee accrued benefits are made retroactive to the start of employment rather than just to the date the plan was instituted or upgraded. The corresponding retroactive costs are known as **prior service costs**.

A firm's required annual pension fund contribution or "funding" is comprised of both the full current service cost and also prior service costs. The remaining past service cost liability not yet picked up must also be disclosed in the statement footnotes. Any portion of total required payments not yet made is reported as a current liability—$9,000 in the Omega example. Any contributions to the fund in excess or in advance of the required payments will be disclosed as an asset—prepaid pension expense.

Deferred Tax Liabilities

The accounting for deferred taxes requires calculation of the future tax obligation of **temporary differences** between tax income and accounting income based on the tax rates expected at the time the taxes will ultimately be paid. As tax laws/rates change, estimates of deferred taxes on the firm's books must be adjusted to reflect those tax changes. The liability for deferred taxes will be either current or noncurrent depending on when the liability is expected to reverse or be paid.

Temporary differences include **timing differences** between accounting and taxable income such as differences between recognition of revenue and expenses.[2]

An example of revenue deferred for tax purposes would be installment sales. In most cases, GAAP require recognition of all revenue from installment sales at the time of the sale; whereas the IRS may allow installment sales revenue to be recognized at the time of payment, that is on the cash basis, even if the taxpayer is otherwise on the accrual basis for tax computation. Note that the effect of this timing difference is to postpone taxes as compared to when they would have been payable had there been no timing differences between GAAP and the tax code for tax reporting.

Of often greater significance and magnitude are timing differences related to expense recognition. The major example of expenses recognized earlier for tax purposes and later for financial accounting purposes involves depreciation. For tax purposes, depreciable assets may often be depreciated to zero in less time than the useful life used in financial statements. Accelerated depreciation for many items is allowable for tax purposes whereas straight-line may be appropriately used for financial reporting. Here again the effect is to postpone taxes.

Temporary differences also include differences between tax bases or values of assets and/or liabilities and their reported amounts on the balance sheet. The differences in tax bases will be discussed in Chapter 14 under the purchase method.

To avoid misleading users of financial statements, GAAP require **interperiod tax allocation** eliminating temporary differences between financial statements and tax returns. Provision for taxes on the income statement is shown at the amount that would have been payable had there been no temporary differences. In the years where the tax provision is greater than the actual tax liability, the amount of postponed taxes is accrued as a liability—deferred income taxes. In the years where the actual tax liability is greater than the reported tax provision, the difference is reversed. The balance of deferred taxes may be viewed as a noninterest loan from the government resulting from temporary differences.

Tax benefits arising from net operating loss carryforwards can only be recognized to offset deferred tax liabilities. These loss carryforwards may or may not be treated as an extraordinary item.

---

2 In tax language, revenue or gain is referred to as income or gain; expense or loss is referred to as a deduction or loss; and the difference (income) is referred to as taxable income. To avoid confusion the accounting terminology will be used exclusively in this chapter even referring to tax regulations.

Bonds Payable

In Chapters 2 and 11, bonds were described as negotiable debt instruments with maturity usually in excess of 10 years and having a stated rate of interest fixed prior to issuance (stated on the bond certificate).

Many different types of bonds exist. Bonds may be secured by liens on particular pieces of property and equipment (**mortgage bonds**), or they may be unsecured and represent simple long-term indebtedness (**debentures**). Bonds issued at one time by a firm may have a single common maturity date, often 10 to 30 years from date of issue, or they may have their maturities staggered over several years (**serial bonds**). Bonds may be registered like stock with the issuing company sending interest checks to the bondholder of record, or they may be "bearer" bonds with interest coupons attached (**coupon bonds**). With a coupon bond, the bondholder "clips" a coupon on the interest date and has it redeemed by his or her bank.

Bonds may carry a provision for early redemption at the option of the issuer (callable bonds). **Callable bonds** may specify a call price, or early redemption price slightly higher than the bond's face value. This **call premium** for early redemption is intended to compensate the creditor for costs of locating another equally safe investment at possibly a lower interest return.[3] Bonds may also be accompanied by warrants or rights to buy the issuing firm's stock at an advantageous price; or the bonds themselves may be convertible (exchangeable) at the bondholder's option into a given number of stock shares (convertible debentures). A single bond issue may have more than one of the above features. For example, a convertible debenture issue could be unsecured and convertible by definition, and could also be callable and be issued as an unregistered coupon bond.

Initial Bond Valuation

As previously mentioned, bonds carry a fixed rate of interest that is stated on the bond certificate and often stated in the bond's indenture agreement.[4] Prevailing (competitive) market interest rates for bonds of any particular risk continually move up and down in response to numerous factors beyond the scope of this text. Even though the issuing firm will make its best estimate to the interest rate required, the interest rate must be set or

---

[3] Usually the reason bonds are called is that market interest rates have declined since the bonds were originally issued, and the issuer is able to replace the old high interest rate issue with new bonds having a lower interest rate.

[4] A bond indenture agreement may be viewed as a "master contract" covering all bonds of a particular issue and detailing the rights and obligations of the issuing firm and of the bondholder.

"locked in" prior to the date the bonds are offered for sale. When bonds are actually sold there may be a discrepancy between the stated rate and the prevailing market rate.[5]

Recall from Chapter 11 that a bond purchaser (lender) will demand and receive the prevailing market rate of interest on the day the bond is sold regardless of the stated rate on the bond. The bond will sell to yield, as a return on investment to the buyer, the prevailing interest rate. Bonds, therefore, are issued at the present value of all the bond's future cash flows discounted at the prevailing market rate of interest.

Bonds Issued at a Discount

Bonds whose stated rate is below the prevailing rate will sell at a discount. The discount will be just sufficient to make the sum and timing of all cash flows coming to the investor equivalent to an investment return at the prevailing interest rate. Remember that the bondholder will receive the stated interest plus the full face value at maturity regardless of the bond purchase/selling price. The amount of the discount, when paid as part of the face value at maturity, will be like a balloon interest payment making up for the too-low (below prevailing rate) interest payments during the life of the bond.

Omega Corporation's 50, $1,000 face value, 4 year bonds with an 8 percent interest rate compounded semiannually, were sold on 1/1/X0 when the market rate was 9 percent. The bonds sold for $48,352, the present value of all cash flows. Note that these bonds were issued for only 4 years for illustrative purposes.

Exhibit 12.2

	Issue Bonds at a Discount	
Present value of:		
Semiannual interest payments	$2,000 x 6.5959*	$13,192
Bond maturity value	$50,000 x .7032**	35,160
		$48,352
	Discount	$ 1,648

semiannual interest payment = maturity value x stated interest rate x time

$2,000 = $50,000 x .08 x 6/12

Semiannual market rate = .09 x 6/12 = 0.045

* PV factor of a stream of payments where i=.045, n=8

** PV factor of a single payment where i=.045, n=8

---

[5] The "time clock" for when interest payable starts accruing is also stated on the bond. If the bond is sold at a date later than anticipated, it will be sold "plus accrued interest." The buyer will give the issuer that amount of interest that the buyer will receive covering the period between the bond's planned issuance and the date they are actually sold. Accounting for accrued interest at the time of sale is not covered in this text.

Bonds Issued at a Premium

When a bond's stated interest rate is greater than the prevailing rate at the date of sale, it will sell at a premium or greater than the face value of the bond. Since the bondholder only receives the face value at maturity, the higher-than-required fixed interest payments will effectively represent both interest and a gradual return of the premium over the life of the bond. On 1/1/X1 Omega Corporation's 10 1/2 percent 5 year bonds were issued for $101,929 when the market interest rate was 10 percent. Interest is paid on 6/30 and 12/31 of each year.

Exhibit 12.3

Issue Bonds at a Premium

Present value of:		
Semiannual interest payments	$5,250 x 7.7217*	$ 40,539
Bond maturity value	$100,000 x .6139**	61,390
		$101,929
	Premium	$ 1,929

Semiannual interest payment = $100,000 x .105 x 6/12 = $5,250
Semiannual market interest rate = .10 x 6/12 = 0.05
* PV factor of a stream of payments where i=.05, n=10
** PV factor of a single payment where i=.05, n=10

Amortization of Bond Discount and Premium

In the same manner that bond premiums and bond discounts for bonds held as investments are amortized to interest revenue by the bondholder (Chapter 11), premiums and discounts on bonds payable are amortized over the life of the bonds to interest expense by the issuer. The two methods for amortizing bond discounts and premiums are the straight-line method and the effective yield method. Straight-line produces a constant expense, while effective yield produces a constant rate of expense. GAAP recommend the yield method, but allows the straight-line method if the difference between the two methods is not material.[6]

Straight-Line Method

Straight-line amortization on the 8 percent sinking fund bonds would be $206 per period or $412 per year.

Bond discount ÷ number of periods = straight-line amortization

---

[6] Present value involves compound interest that is curvilinear, therefore straight-line (linear) amortization can only result in a net book value that approximates present value.

The bond discount (or premium) must be amortized at each payment date, and at year-end to determine interest expense. Bond discount amortization is added to the interest payment to calculate interest expense. Semiannual interest expense for the sinking fund bonds would be $2,206 or $4,412 per year.

Exhibit 12.4

Straight-line Discount Amortization

Payment Date	Beginning Book Value	Interest Expense	Interest − Payment	Discount = Amortization	Ending Book Value
6/30/X0	$48,352	$2,206	$2,000	$206	$48,558
12/31/X0	48,558	2,206	2,000	206	48,764
6/30/X1	48,764	2,206	2,000	206	48,970
12/31/X1	48,970	2,206	2,000	206	49,176
6/30/X2	49,176	2,206	2,000	206	49,382
12/31/X2	49,382	2,206	2,000	206	49,588
6/30/X3	49,588	2,206	2,000	206	49,794
12/31/X3	49,794	2,206	2,000	206	50,000

Amortization of the premium on the 10 1/2 percent bonds would be $193 per period or $386 per year. Amortization of the premium reduces interest expense. Therefore interest expense per period would be the interest payment less the premium amortization or $5,057. Interest expense per year would be $10,114.

Exhibit 12.5

Straight-line Premium Amortization

Payment Date	Beginning Book Value	Interest Expense	Interest − Payment	Premium = Amortization	Ending Book Value
6/30/X1	$101,929	$5,057	$5,250	$193	$101,736
12/31/X1	101,736	5,057	5,250	193	101,543
6/30/X2	101,543	5,057	5,250	193	101,350
12/31/X2	101,350	5,057	5,250	193	101,157
6/30/X3	101,157	5,057	5,250	193	100,964
12/31/X3	100,964	5,057	5,250	193	100,771
6/30/X4	100,771	5,057	5,250	193	100,578
12/31/X4	100,578	5,057	5,250	193	100,385
6/30/X5	100,385	5,057	5,250	193	100,192
12/31/X5	100,192	5,058	5,250	192*	100,000

* difference due to rounding

Effective Yield Method

GAAP recommend using the effective yield method since it produces a constant rate of interest per period. Exhibits 12.6 and 12.7 present schedules for amortization of premiums and discounts using the effective yield method. Note that beginning book value times the market interest rate equals the market interest or interest expense. The difference between the interest expense and the interest payment will be the amortization of the discount or premium.

Exhibit 12.6

Effective Yield Amortization of a Premium
10 1/2 % Bonds Payable

Payment Date	Beginning Book Value	Interest Expense*	Interest – Payment	Premium = Amortization	Ending Book Value
6/30/X1	$101,929	$5,096	$5,250	$154	$101,775
12/31/X1	101,775	5,089	5,250	161	101,614
6/30/X2	101,614	5,081	5,250	169	101,445
12/31/X2	101,445	5,072	5,250	178	101,267
6/30/X3	101,267	5,063	5,250	187	101,080
12/31/X3	101,080	5,054	5,250	196	100,884
6/30/X4	100,884	5,044	5,250	206	100,678
12/31/X4	100,678	5,034	5,250	216	100,462
6/30/X5	100,462	5,023	5,250	227	100,235
12/31/X5	100,235	5,012	5,250	235**	100,000

* Beginning book value x market interest rate x time
** Difference due to rounding

The 10 1/2 percent bonds were issued at a premium. Therefore, interest expense, regardless of the method used will be less than the interest payment. However, under the effective yield method, the interest expense decreases as the book value declines thus creating a constant cost of capital at present value. Note that the interest expense for 19X1 would be $10,185 ($5,096 + 5,089).

Interest expense for the 8 percent sinking fund bonds will be greater than the interest payment because they were issued at a discount. Discount amortization is added to the payment to determine interest expense. Interest expense on the sinking fund bonds was $4,393 ($2,192 + 2,201) in 19X1. Note that the interest expense was higher since the book value of bonds issued at a discount increases over time.

Exhibit 12.7

Effective Yield Amortization of a Discount
8% Sinking Fund Bonds Payable

Payment Date	Beginning Book Value	Interest Expense*	− Interest Payment	= Discount Amortization	Ending Book Value
6/30/X0	$48,352	$2,176	$2,000	$176	$48,528
12/31/X0	48,528	2,184	2,000	184	48,712
6/30/X1	48,712	2,192	2,000	192	48,904
12/31/X1	48,904	2,201	2,000	201	49,105
6/30/X2	49,105	2,210	2,000	210	49,315
12/31/X2	49,315	2,219	2,000	219	49,534
6/30/X3	49,534	2,229	2,000	229	49,763
12/31/X3	49,763	2,239	2,000	237**	50,000

* Beginning book value x market interest rate x time
** difference due to rounding

Cash From Operating Activities

Interest payments are the only part of interest expense which is cash flow. Therefore, to determine cash from operating activities from reported income under the indirect method, bond premium amortization must be subtracted, and bond discount amortization and amortization for deferred charges must be added back. Recall from Chapter 11 that deferred charges are bond issue costs which were stated separately from the proceeds of the bonds.

Exhibit 12.8

Bond Interest Expense

	Reported Income	Cash from Operating Activities
8% sinking fund bonds:		
interest payment	$ 4,000	$ 4,000
*discount amortization	393	
10 1/2% bonds:		
interest payment	10,500	10,500
*premium amortization	(315)	
*Deferred charges amortization	1,000	
Totals	$15,578	$14,500

*noncash flow adjustments to interest expense

Other Contra-Liability Accounts

The Omega balance sheet in Exhibit 12.1 disclosed contra-liability accounts (discounts) for current notes payable and for the noncurrent mortgage note payable. As covered in Chapter 11, debt discounts represent executory interest capitalized into the face value of the debt instrument (bonds, debentures, or promissory notes).

In the same manner as for discounts on bonds payable, discounts on other debt instruments are amortized to reflect interest earned (no longer executory) by the creditor, with a corresponding increase to reported interest expense. Again, as for bond discount amortization, the amortization of discounts on any debt instrument does not represent cash flow and must therefore be reversed in the calculation of cash from operating activities.

Fully Amortized Loans

So far in this text all loans illustrated have been interest-only loans. With an **interest-only loan**, the borrower has the use of the entire principal over the entire loan period.[7] Interest may be paid periodically or accumulated and paid at maturity, but no portion of the principal is payable until maturity—hence the term "interest-only."

You may be already familiar with a second type of loan known as a fully amortized loan. Most consumer loans—personal loans, auto and appliance loans, and residential home mortgages—are fully amortized loans. Under a **fully amortized loan**, periodic payments of equal amounts include both payment of interest and repayment of principal. When the final payment is made, the entire obligation is satisfied.[8]

As with any loan, interest applies to the outstanding loan balance. Since the loan balance is systematically reduced with each payment under a fully amortized loan, the portion representing interest declines with each payment. The opposite is true for the principal repayment portion. Given the amount of each payment and the applicable interest rate, for any payment period you can calculate the portion of that period's payment representing interest and principal. You merely determine that period's interest owed on the outstanding loan balance and subtract the interest from the loan payment to determine the principal (PV) of the current loan payment. The ending balance represents the loan balance for the following period.

---

[7] Commercial bank loans that require compensating balances as noted in Chapter 2 would be an exception.

[8] It is, of course, possible to have a partially amortized loan—part of principal amortized and part payable at maturity. Also, some long-term loans have varying interest rates over the life of the loan. Accounting for these variations is more appropriately covered in intermediate accounting.

Exhibit 12.9

Fully Amortized Loan Payment Schedule

Monthly Payment	Payment Amount	Interest – Expense*	Principal = Amortization	Ending loan balance
First	$166.07	$50.00	$166.07	$4,883.93
Second	166.07	48.84	117.23	4,766.70
Third	166.07	47.67	118.40	4,648.30
Thirty-fifth	166.07	3.27	162.80	164.43
Thirty-sixth	166.07	1.64	164.43	0
Totals	$5,978.52	$978.52	$5,000.00	

* loan balance x interest rate x time = interest expense

The following situation is reflected in Exhibit 12.9. Your firm has purchased a used pickup truck on 1/1/X1 costing $6,000, paying $1,000 down and giving a three-year fully amortized promissory note for the balance. The effective annual interest rate (the rate being applied to the unpaid balance) is 12 percent or one percent per month. The necessary 36 equal monthly payments were determined by using present value analysis as introduced in Chapter 11 and through the use of calculations described in Appendix B.[9]

The payment schedule shown in Exhibit 12.9 was constructed period by period as described above. During the first month, the entire $5,000 loan was outstanding. Therefore, interest owed was $50 (one percent of $5,000) and the remaining principal repayment portion was $116.07 ($166.07 payment – 50.00 interest). This process continues, step by step through the remaining periods. Note that, by the last payment, the interest portion is only $1.64 on the remaining loan balance of $164.43.

Capital Lease Obligations

Assume that your firm had acquired equipment under a capital lease on 1/1/X1, and that the lease terms specified the following lease payments:[10]

- Payment on signing $10,000
- Payment at end of first year $20,820
- Payment at end of second year $20,820
- Payment at end of third year $20,820

[9] Let X equal the amount of each payment. If one percent interest per month were factored out, that if the present value discounted at one percent per period of a stream of X payments over 36 periods were determined, and the resultant present (principal) value exactly equalled $5,000, then the payment of X each period would provide the lender with both a return of the $5,000 loan principal and a 12 percent annual interest return on the outstanding balance. The PV factor of a stream of payments for 36 periods discounted at one percent is 30.1075. Therefore: 30.1075 X = $5,000. The payment then would be $166.07 (rounded).

[10] Normally capital leases cover more than three years. A three-year lease is used here to simplify the illustration.

Recall from Chapter 11 that the leased asset and the associated lease obligation are initially recorded at the present value (PV) of the total of all lease payments discounted at the firm's **incremental borrowing rate**. A firm's incremental borrowing rate is the rate it would currently be required to pay if it were financing the asset as a purchase with a mortgage loan. Assume your firm's borrowing rate is 12 percent. Using the PV factor of 1.0000 for the payment on signing (already in the present), and the PV factor of 2.4018 for a three-year stream of payments at 12 percent, the present value would be $60,000 (rounded).

The asset would be initially recorded as "properties held under capital lease— $60,000." Cash would be decreased by $10,000 and the accompanying liability would be $50,000 (the present value of the future lease payments). However, the $50,000 new liability must be divided into current and noncurrent obligations. To determine the current and noncurrent obligations, a payment schedule identifying interest and principal portions of each lease payment must be prepared. Exhibit 12.10 presents such a schedule with interest calculated at 12 percent on the outstanding present value (loan principal) balance.

Exhibit 12.10

Capital Lease Schedule

Year	PV lease Obligation	Interest Expense*	– Payment	= Current Obligation	Noncurrent Obligation
19X1	$50,000	$6,000	$20,820	$14,820	$35,180
19X2	35,180	4,222	20,820	16,598	18,582
19X3	18,582	2,238**	20,820	18,582	0

* PV of lease obligation x incremental borrowing rate = interest expense
** difference due to rounding

With the lease payment schedule completed the effect of the initial signing of the capital lease can be seen as transaction (1) on the balance sheet Diagram 12.1.[11] Note that the current capital lease obligation includes the present value (principal) portion of the first year's lease payment due on 12/31/X1. The noncurrent capital lease obligation includes the present value (principal portions) of the remaining lease payments.

Transaction (2) shows the effect of making the first year's payment on 12/31/X1 for $20,820. Note that, just as for any fully amortized obligation, the maturing present value (principal portion) of the coming year's lease payment is reclassified in adjusting entry (A). The asset account is also depreciated (via the straight-line method in this example) in adjusting entry (B).

If the lease payment had not been made on 12/31/X1, then the $6,000 of interest which had accrued would have been recognized as an adjusting entry. The accrued interest

---

11 Note that signing of a contract normally does not affect the balance sheet since it is executory. Capital leases are an exception to the rule of excluding executory items. The present value or principal portions of a capital lease are picked up as if they were not executory. Executory interest, however, is excluded.

Diagram 12.1   Balance Sheet Effects of Capital Lease Obligation in 19X1

Current Assets:			**Current Liabilities:**		
Cash	– 10,000	(1)	Current Capital Lease		
	– 20,820	(2)	Obligations	+ 14,820	(1)
				– 14,820	(2)
				+ 16,598	(A)
Long-lived Assets:			**Long-term Debt:**		
Properties Held under			Noncurrent Capital		
Capital Lease	+ 60,000	(1)	Lease Obligations	+ 35,180	(1)
Accum. Depr.,				– 16,598	(A)
Lease	– 20,000	(B)			

Stockholders' Equity

	Income	
–	6,000	(2)
–	20,000	(B)

would increase interest expense and the current capital lease obligation. Note that interest payable would not be affected.

The interest paid on a capital lease will be included in the calculation for cash from operating activities. However, the principal portion (PV) paid will be considered an investing activity. Recall that the depreciation on the lease is noncash flow and must be added back to net income to determine cash from operating activities.

Maturing Long-Term Debt

In the same way that maturing principal portions of forthcoming capital lease payments are reclassified to current liability status, noncurrent notes and bonds all have maturities that eventually come within one year of the balance sheet date. At that time, unless a refunding (replacement with other long-term debt) agreement has been signed, the maturing debt must be reclassified.

Early Debt Extinguishment

Debt can be retired in advance of the maturity date—**early debt retirement**. It can be replaced by other new debt (debt refinancing or **refunding**). Also debt can be retired through an exchange for ownership interest (stock)—a **debt conversion**. Under each of these three alternatives, the bondholder is paid any interest accrued/owed from the date of the last interest payment through the date of extinguishment. To direct your attention to the appropriate accounting for the debt principal and any associated premium, discount, or deferred charges, in the discussion that follows early extinguishment is assumed to occur immediately following the interest payment date (no accrued interest owed). You should remember that, when early debt extinguishment occurs between payment dates, interest through the date of extinguishment must also be accrued and paid.

Early Debt Retirement

Some long-term notes and bonds carry a call provision for early repayment by the issuing firm. Early repayment can be a benefit to the issuing firm when market interest rates decline and the debt can be refinanced at a lower interest cost. However it can be a hardship or penalty for the creditor who now must locate a new, equally safe investment with perhaps a lower return.

Diagram 12.2

Early Debt Retirement
(b) = beginning balance ($ in thousands)

Current Assets:			Current Liabilities:		
Cash	−	1,050 (1)			
			Long-term Debt:		
Long-lived Assets:			Bonds Payable		1,000 (b)
Deferred Charges		30 (b)		−	1,000 (1)
	−	30 (1)			
			Bond Discount		(80) (b)
				+	80 (1)
			Owners' Equity		
				Income	
			−	160 (1)	
				loss on	
				early	
				retirement	

Early debt retirement, for the foregoing reasons, often involves a prepayment penalty charge on loans or an early call premium on callable bonds. Upon retirement, all related items are removed from the balance sheet. These would include the book value of the liability—face value and any unamortized premium or discount—and related unamortized deferred charges. If the sum of the cash paid as part of the retirement (that is, face value plus repayment penalty or call premium) plus the unamortized deferred charges that are eliminated, exceeds the book value of the debt eliminated, there is a loss on early debt retirement. If the sum is less than the net debt eliminated, there is a gain. Gains or losses on early debt retirement are presumed to be material in amount and are reported as extraordinary items.

Diagram 12.2 gives an example of the balance changes resulting from early debt retirement. A $1,000,000 bond issue with $80,000 of unamortized discount is retired with a payment of $1,050,000 cash. The $1,000,000 is the maturity value of the bonds, and $50,000 is the call premium or prepayment penalty. The $30,000 of deferred charges were related to the bond issue and, therefore, are also eliminated by the early retirement. The assets used or expiring exceed the net liabilities eliminated by $160,000. This amount therefore represents the extraordinary loss on early retirement.

Note also that a firm may retire outstanding debt through purchase of bonds or debentures in the open market. Where the market price is below the sum of the face value and call premium, a portion or all of the call-premium cost (and even more if the bonds are selling at a discount) can be saved through open-market purchase.

Refunding

Early retirement may be part of a replacement of old debt with new debt—a refinancing or a refunding of debt. New debt may be sold and the cash proceeds used to retire old debt. There also may be a direct exchange of debt instruments, new bonds or notes exchanged for old, with no cash changing hands. Regardless of the method used, GAAP require that the old debt and associated unamortized premium, or discount, and deferred charges, be treated as an independent early retirement. Therefore, a gain or loss on refunding may be realized just as for early retirement, as described above.

Debt Conversion

Some bond issues provide the bondholders with the option of exchanging their bonds for shares of stock at a fixed number of shares per bond.[12] The exchange of debt for ownership interest is called debt conversion. Bonds or debentures which have a conversion privilege are known as **convertible debentures (or CVD's)**.

Where a CVD is converted, the accountant removes from the liability account(s) the amount of net liability (the book value) represented by the CVD's converted. The bonds payable liability is removed along with the associated unamortized premium or discount. Any related unamortized deferred charges are also extinguished.

To complete recording a CVD conversion, the accountant will restore the balance sheet equality by increasing owners' equity by the amount of the net CVD liability

---

12 In more advanced texts you may learn that preferred stock can also be convertible on a fixed conversion ratio to common stock. Convertible preferred will not be discussed further in this text.

removed. Conversion represents a mere exchange of equities.[13] In the case of a corporation with par or stated value stock, the net CVD claim is added to common stock in the amount of the new par stock issued in conversion. Any excess goes to additional paid-in capital. Recall from Chapter 7 that debt conversion is a noncash flow financing activity on the statement of cash flows. As an example of a bond conversion, assume the following facts pertain to the Deck Corporation:

5% Bonds Payable* ($1,000 bonds)	$500,000
Bond discount	(10,000)
Common Stock** ($10 par)	1,000,000

*   Conversion ratio: 90 shares of stock per bond
** Current market price per share $15

In response to the $15 market price, the bondholders exchange (convert) each $1,000 bond into 90 shares of stock with a market value of $1,350.

The bonds payable and bond discount accounts, are $450,000 and $40,000, respectively, for common stock and additional paid-in capital. Of the $490,000 net book value of debt extinguished by the conversion, $450,000 (500 bonds x 90 shares x $10 par) is added to common stock representing the par value of additional shares issued. The balance of $40,000, representing an excess over par, is added to additional paid-in capital.

Diagram 12.3   The effects of Debt Conversion

Current Assets:	Current Liabilities:
Long-lived Assets:	**Long-term Debt:**
	Bonds Payable 500,000 (b)
	– 500,000 (1)
	Bond Discount (10,000) (b)
	+ 10,000 (1)
	Owners' Equity
	Common Stock 1,000,000 (b)
	+ 450,000 (1)
	Addtl. PIC + 40,000 (1)

---

[13] If associated deferred charges are involved, then the amount of the face value of the CD's converted together with any related premium or discount less any associated deferred charges is added to stockholders' equity.

Conversion increases the firm's debt capacity. It also has an effect on net income. Annual interest expense in the amount of $25,000 in this example is no longer required. Since interest is tax-deductible, taxable income will increase $25,000. At a 40-percent income-tax rate, taxes would increase $10,000. Therefore, the after-tax savings on conversion would be $15,000.

Review of Liability Changes

Exhibit 12.11 lists the liabilities discussed in this chapter. For each liability, the common transactions and adjustments that may affect its balance are also given. For each transaction or adjustment, make sure you can:

1. Visualize a specific example.
2. Identify the other half of the entry that might be involved.

Exhibit 12.11

Changes Affecting Balance Sheet Liabilities and Contra-Liabilities*
Does not include changes to correct for error or to record extraordinary items

Account	Effect
Current Note Payable	*Increased by:* Issuing promissory note as part of a loan purchase Currently maturing portion of long-term notes Issuing promissory note to replace accounts receivable *Decreased by:* Retirement by payment of cash Replacement with long-term note
Discount on Current Notes Payable (Contra-liability)	*Negative balance increased by:* Interest included in note face value not yet owed *Negative balance decreased by:* Adjustment for amount of interest owed Retirement or replacement of note
Current Obligations under Capital Lease	*Increased by:* Executing lease agreement containing current payment provision Maturing "principal" portion of noncurrent capital-lease obligation Accrual of current interest portion of capital-lease obligation *Decreased by:* Payments of cash

Various Accrued or Estimated Liabilities (Rent, interest, wages, taxes, etc.)	*Increased by:* Adjustment accruing estimated owed to date *Decreased by:* Payment of cash Reversal to avoid double counting Adjustment reflecting new estimate
Noncurrent Notes and Bonds Payable	*Increased by:* Issuing debt instrument as part of loan or purchase Issuing debt instrument as replacement for other liability *Decreased by:* Portion maturing to current classification Early retirement by payment of cash Replacement by other noncurrent debt Debt conversion
Premium on Bonds Payable	*Increased by:* Portion of proceeds of bond issue to be returned to creditor as part of higher interest *Decreased by:* Adjustment for amortization Early retirement or replacement of bonds Conversion of bonds
Noncurrent Obligations under Capital Lease	*Increased by:* Executing lease agreement *Decreased by:* Maturing "principal" portion to current classification
Deferred Income Tax	*Increased by:* Adjustment reflecting amount of tax liability deferred *Decreased by:* Reversal of previously deferred tax liability Adjustment for amount of previously deferred tax liability no longer owed

Preparer Procedures

This section will cover preparer procedures related to the liabilities that were introduced in this chapter. Then a distinct subsection will be devoted to payroll accounting.

Exhibit 12.12   Additions to Chart of Accounts

Current Liabilities
    310   Estimated Warranty Costs

Long-term Debt
    401   Bonds Payable
    402   Bond Premium
    410   Deferred Income Taxes

Contra-Equities
    600   Discount on Current Notes Payable
    602   Bond Discount

Expenses
    810   Warranty Repairs

The complete chart of accounts to be used in conjunction with the preparer problems for Chapter 12 may be found in Appendix D at the back of the book.

Liabilities Involving Discounts or Premiums

A liability originally issued at a premium or discount involves a compound entry. The sale of a $1,000 bond at a premium for $1,150 would be journalized:

	DR	CR
Cash	1,150	
Bond Payable		1,000
Bond Premium		150

The sale of a $1,000 bond at a discount for $900 would be journalized:

Cash	900	
Bond Discount	100	
Bond Payable		1,000

Both bond premium and bond discount are amortized by adjustment to interest expense, but with opposite effects. Adjustment to amortize $40 of bond premium and $50 of bond discounts would be journalized:

	DR	CR
Bond Premium	40	
Interest Expense		40
Interest Expense	50	
Bond Discount		50

Note that bond premium amortization reduces annual interest expense, whereas amortization of bond discount increases it.

Discounts on current and noncurrent notes payable are treated the same as are bond discounts. Each period they are amortized by a debit to interest expense and a credit to the appropriate discount account.

Capital Lease Obligation

A capital lease is originally journalized by the lessee with the asset value equal to the sum of the discounted present value of all required lease payments (for example, $130,000). The present value of the current lease payment (for example, $30,000) is recorded as a current liability. The present value of the noncurrent payments (for example, $100,000) is recorded as a noncurrent liability.

Properties under Capital Lease	130,000	
Current Capital Lease Obligations		30,000
Noncurrent Capital Lease Obligations		100,000

Thereafter, the asset and liability components of capital leases are treated separately. Interest is the difference between the present value of the current payment and its stated value (for example, $35,000 – 5,000) and must be accrued:

Interest Expense	5,000	
Current Capital Lease Obligations		5,000

Fully Amortized Loan Obligations

As mentioned in the chapter, accounting for obligations under fully amortized loans is very similar to that for capital lease obligations. The initial obligation is shown at its present (principal) value with the current and noncurrent portions separately classified.

Assuming the data used above to illustrate accounting for a capital lease obligation were applicable to a fully amortized loan, the initial entry would be:

	DR	CR
Cash	130,000	
Current Notes Payable		30,000
Noncurrent Notes Payable		100,000

Interest, the difference between current payments due and the present (principal) value of these payments, is accrued to interest payable rather than to the current notes payable account:

Interest Expense	5,000	
Interest Payable		5,000

Maturing Debt Reclassification

Reclassification of the principal portion of maturing noncurrent debt merely involves debiting the long-term debt account and crediting the current liability. For example, if the maturing principal portions of a capital lease obligation and of a noncurrent note were $8,000 and $10,000 respectively, the reclassification entries would be:

Noncurrent Capital Lease Obligations	8,000	
Current Capital Lease Obligations		8,000
Noncurrent Notes Payable	10,000	
Current Notes Payable		10,000

Estimated Liabilities

The allowance for estimated warranty expense, and for other similar liability accruals made for matching purposes, is usually a single year-end adjustment; for example:

Warranty Repairs Expense	14,000	
Estimated Warranty Costs		14,000

At the start of the next year, this entry (together with all other adjusting accruals involving anticipations) is reversed, to avoid the possibility of double-counting:

Estimated Warranty Costs	14,000	
Warranty Repairs Expense		14,000

Note that this reversal affects the next year's expense account which will thus open with a $14,000 credit, or "negative" balance. Suppose during this "next" year, total warranty repairs charged to the expense account amounted to $89,000, of which only $75.000 related to current year's sales. The $89,000 is charged to the expense account initially having a $14,000 credit balance. The ending balance would be $75,000 debit, properly identifying the $75,000 of "additional" expense applicable to the current year. Of course, estimates are never perfect in an actual situation. The amount of the year-end accrual ($14,000 above) is determined as the balance necessary to update the accounts and compensate for the prior year's estimation error. Warranty repairs expense in any one year on the income statement is therefore understood to include:

- Actual expenses of the current year applicable to current revenues, plus
- Estimated expenses expected to occur next year, but applicable to the current year's revenues, plus or minus
- Prior year's estimation error.

Deferred Income Tax

Each year, income tax is calculated on two bases:

1. Provision (amount that would be due) for taxes assuming all permanent differences between accounting income and taxable income and assuming no temporary differences, and

2. Actual current tax liability after allowing for temporary differences.

Assume the provision amounted to $174,000, but the actual current year's liability was only $136,000 because of depreciation tax-shield differences. The item $38,000 would need to be deferred as a future "liability." the entry recording income tax obligations would be:

	DR	CR
Provision for Income Taxes	174,000	
Taxes Payable		136,000
Deferred Income Tax		38,000

In subsequent years when the temporary differences were reversed, the amounts previously deferred would be presumed as being paid as part of the current liability. Assume the provision amount to $205,000 with the actual current liability in that year equaling $230,000. $25,000 of the deferred liability is now payable. The journal entry would call for:

Provision for Income Taxes	205,000	
Deferred Income Tax	25,000	
Taxes Payable		230,000

Note that, each year, the provision for income taxes appearing on the income statement is normalized to include taxes temporarily postponed and to exclude previously postponed taxes now due.

Early Debt Retirement or Refunding

In the case of early debt retirement or refunding, the first step is to update all accounts related to the debt being extinguished. Then the related amounts are eliminated in conjunction with the cash payment—maturity value plus call premium—and a balancing gain or loss is recorded.

For example, assume that four hundred $1,000 six-percent bonds were called and redeemed on 4/1/X1 with a call premium of $50 each. Also assume that interest is payable semi-annually on 6/30 and 12/31, and that, associated with this bond issue as of 12/31/X0, are $19,200 of unamortized bond discount and $6,400 of unamortized deferred charges. Deferred charges are being amortized at $1,600 per year, and bond discount is being amortized at $4,8000 annually. Two entries—one accruing the interest liability and one updating amortization—would be required before the entry recording the extinguishment.

	DR	CR
Interest Expense	6,000	
Interest Payable		6,000
Interest Expense	1,600	
Bond Discount		1,200
Deferred Charges		400
Bonds Payable	400,000	
Interest Payable	6,000	
Extraordinary Loss on Debt Extinguishment	44,000	
Cash		426,000
Bond Discount		18,000
Deferred Charges		6,000

Debt Conversion

Debt conversion also first involves updating amortization of debt discount or premium and any deferred charges and also accruing any interest payable through the conversion date. Then the debt and related amounts are eliminated, and the net debt amount is added to capital stock and paid-in capital.

For example, assume the same six-percent bond issue described above under debt retirement were extinguished on 4/1/X1 by conversion to common stock. Assume the bonds or debentures are convertible into 50 shares of $10 par stock for each $1,000 bond. The two entries accruing interest and updating amortization would be the same as shown above for early retirement.

The entry recording would then be as follows:

	DR	CR
Bonds Payable	400,000	
Bond Discount		18,000
Deferred Charges		6,000
Common Stock		200,000
Additional Paid-in Capital		176,000

Payroll Accounting

Payroll accounting can be divided into two separate parts: first, the determination and recording of the actual payroll liability based on employee earnings, and then the recording of the employer's additional payroll-tax liability.

An employee's gross earnings (wage or salary plus overtime) may be subject to the following deductions:

- Federal income taxes (amount varies, depending upon the number of the individual employee's authorized dependents);
- State income taxes (amount varies, depending upon the number of the individual employee's authorized dependents);
- Federal Social Security (F.I.C.A.) taxes (apply only up to a certain maximum amount of employee annual earnings);
- State disability insurance taxes (apply only up to a certain maximum amount of annual earnings, different from F.I.C.A. ceilings);
- Other voluntary deductions (may be a fixed amount per payroll period, or a proportion of earnings, sometimes with a ceiling).

For each separate employee, the accountant must determine:

- Gross earnings for the payroll period;
- Applicable federal and state income taxes, based on the individual employee's earnings and claimed dependents;
- Applicable F.I.C.A. taxes (beyond the cumulative year's earnings ceiling, no taxes are applicable);
- Applicable state disability taxes (beyond a different cumulative year's earnings, and in some states, no taxes are applicable);
- Applicable other deductions (as authorized by each employee separately).

Assume that a total weekly payroll amounted to $60,000 of wages and $30,000 of salaries earned. And assume that the totals of individually determined deductions were:
- $18,000 of federal income taxes to be withheld;
- $4,500 of state income taxes to be withheld;
- $5,400 of F.I.C.A. taxes to be withheld;
- $900 of state disability taxes to be withheld;
- $450 of union dues withheld.

The above totals are for all employees. The individual employee's deductions will have been separately recorded in the payroll ledger and reported to the employee along with his or her paycheck.

The entry recording the week's employee payroll liability would be:

	DR	CR
Wages Expense	60,000	
Salaries Expense	30,000	
Employee Federal Income Taxes Payable		18,000
Employee State Income Taxes Payable		4,500
F.I.C.A. Employee Taxes Payable		5,400
State Disability Taxes Payable		900
Union Dues Payable		450
Cash (take-home pay)		60,750

The employer's payroll tax liability could include:

- F.I.C.A. taxes (exactly matches employee contribution);
- Federal unemployment (F.U.T.A.) taxes;
- State unemployment taxes;
- State disability taxes.

Assume, for the same weekly payroll period as above, that these taxes amounted to $5,400, $3,600, $900, and $1,800, respectively. The appropriate journal entry would then be:

Payroll Tax Expense	11,700	
F.I.C.A. Taxes Payable		5,400
F.U.T.A. Taxes Payable		3,600
State Unemployment Taxes Payable		900
State Disability Taxes Payable		1,800

Note also that employer payroll costs often include expenses which are not payroll taxes as such. Examples would include cost of health insurance, supplementary unemployment benefits, pension-fund contributions, and the like. These "fringe benefit" items would be journalized in a manner similar to that for payroll taxes.

Chapter Overview

- State the standards for the initial valuation of liabilities in conformance with GAAP;
- Describe the differences among estimated liabilities and contingent liabilities; give examples of each; state how and why each is disclosed in the financial statements;
- Explain the meaning of present value and how it relates to liability measurement;
- Describe how amortization of liability contra accounts affects income and specifically interest expense, and explain the rationale for such treatment;
- Explain the difference between a fully amortized and an interest-only loan, how a payment schedule is constructed for a fully amortized loan, and how this schedule may be used;
- Explain how capital lease obligations are accounted for over several periods;
- Describe three different ways noncurrent debt may be extinguished or exchanged prior to maturity, and explain with examples the possible effect of each transaction on the balance sheet and income statement;
- Explain the meaning of minority interest and the reasons for disclosing it, either within or separate from stockholders' equity; and
- Describe those liability changes that do not involve a cash flow; explain which of these are involved in adjusting income to determine cash from operating activities; and state whether the adjustment to income is an addition or subtraction.

New Vocabulary and Concepts

"Booked"	Incremental borrowing rate
Callable bonds	Interest-only loans
Callable Premium	Interperiod tax allocation
Contingent liabilities	Minority interest
Convertible debenture (CVD)	Mortgage bonds
Coupon bonds	Prior service costs (pensions)
Current service costs (pensions)	Purchase commitments
Debentures	Refunding
Debt conversion	Serial bonds
Early debt retirement	Temporary differences (taxes)
Estimated liabilities	Timing differences (taxes)
Fully amortized loan	Warranty costs

Review Questions

1. (a) What are the basic objectives/requirements of liability measurement and reporting under GAAP? (b) What are the similarities to the standards for assets?

2. What does the amount of unamortized discount on notes or bonds payable represent?

3. Discount on payables is amortized to what account? As an increase or decrease?

4. What does unamortized premium on bonds payable represent?

5. (a) To what account is premium on bonds payable amortized? (b) Is the effect to increase or decrease the balance in this account? Explain.

6. (a) What is a fully amortized loan: (b) How does it differ from and interest-only loan? (c) Explain with an example covering several periods how a payment schedule is constructed for a fully amortized loan.

7. (a) Why doesn't the timing of maturation of noncurrent capital-lease obligation coincide with the amortization of the related leased asset? (b) What is the basis for reclassifying portions of the noncurrent capital-lease obligation to a current liability?

8. Why is there a difference between the currently maturing portion of a capital-lease obligation and the actual lease payment to be made? What does this difference represent?

9. Give examples of estimated and contingent liabilities, and explain the difference.

10 Why are estimated liabilities "booked" and contingent liabilities only footnoted?

11. (a) What is deferred income tax? (b) What situation could bring about an increase in deferred income tax? (c) A decrease?

12. (a) What is a tax shield? (b) What is its effect?

13. (a) What is minority interest? (b) In what circumstances and in which financial statements does it appear?

14. (a) What is a CVD? (b) What is meant by debt conversion?

15. If a corporation has, on 12/31/XO, $100,000 of long-term debt in the form of CVD's (liabilities) together with unamortized premium of $11,000, and on 1/1/X1 all of these bonds are converted, how much will be added to corporate owners' equity?

16. Why is there often a penalty payment or a call premium given to the creditor as part of early debt extinguishment?

17. What accounts may be involved in the early retirement of bonds?

18. What are the sources of possible gain or loss on early debt extinguishment?

Mini-Cases and Questions for Discussion

MC 12.1 One way of viewing a bond premium is as an extra payment or gift given by the buyer to obtain the bond. The bond obligation—interest payments plus maturity principal payment— is the same with or without a premium. Why don't accountants recognize all bond premium received as revenue or as a gift at the time of sale of the bond? Discuss.

MC 12.2 Accountants normally disclose ling-term liabilities at their present value. That is, their "principal" value excluding explicit or implicit interest at the going rate for similar obligations at the time incurred. How can this be true when:

    a)   Bonds and notes are shown at their face of maturity value regardless of whether interest is included therein?

    b)   Capital lease obligations are not shown at the sum of all payments?

    c)   Some notes with explicit interest have discounts and others do not?

Discuss.

MC 12.3 Future-interest obligations are excluded from liability measurement, as they are executory. Why, then, is Bond Premium shown as a liability? It doesn't even represent payments which will be made, as these are already part of the bond obligation. Discuss.

MC 12.4 When a bond is subject to early extinguishment (early retirement for refunding), association premium or discount may not be carried forward to future years. A gain or loss on early extinguishment may result. However, when a bond is converted, the book value is carried forward in owners' equity and no gain or loss is recognized. Isn't this inconsistent? Discuss.

Essential Problems

EP 12.1 The Harwich Corporation reported the following liabilities on its 12/31/X3 balance sheet:

Current notes payable	$116,000
Discount on current notes	(16,000)
Noncurrent notes payable	272,000
Discount on noncurrent notes	(72,000)
10% Bonds Payable	500,000
Bond discount	(60,000)

The current note was noninterest-bearing and matured on 12/31/X4. The noncurrent note had a stated interest of four percent payable on 12/31 of each year, $72,000 (as of 12/31/X3) of imputed interest capitalized into its face value, and will mature on 12/31/X6. The bond interest is payable semi-annually on 6/30 and 12/31 and they will mature fifteen years from 12/31/X3.

    Assuming that Harwich had no other liabilities requiring payment of interest, that straight-line amortization of discounts was acceptable, and that all required interest payments as of 12/31/X3 had been made, for the first quarter of 19X4 give:

    a)   The amounts that should appear on the firm's end-of-quarter balance sheet for these liabilities and related interest assuming that all payments were made on the dates specified.

b) The amount that should be reported on the quarterly income statement as interest expense.

c) In determining the first quarter's cash from operating activities, what adjustments (if any) related to these obligations should be made to reported net income?

EP 12.2 Urich Corporation issued a one year noninterest bearing note on January 1, 19X5 for $12,000. A noncurrent 3 year note was issued for $250,000 with a 4 percent stated interest on March 31, 19X5. Interest on the note is to be paid on 12/31 each year. 10% 15 year bonds payable were issued on July 1. Interest payments are made on 6/30 and 12/31 of each year on the bonds. You may assume that the market rate of interest was 12 percent and applicable for all three debt instruments. Using the effective yield method and assuming that all payments were made on time for each quarter of 19X5 give:

a) The amounts that should appear on the firm's end-of-quarter balance sheet for these liabilities and related interest.

b) The amount that should be reported on the quarterly income statement as interest expense.

c) In determining 19X5 cash from operating activities, what adjustments (if any) related to these obligations should be made to reported net income?

EP 12.3 The Glander Corporation as of 12/31/X7 reported as long-term debt bonds payable of $800,000 and associated bond premium of $80,000. These bonds had a stated interest rate of 14 percent payable semi-annually, and would mature in 20 years. You may assume straight-line amortization is acceptable.

a) How should these bonds and their associated premium be reported in the firm's 12/31/X8 balance sheet?

b) How much interest expense should be reported for 19X8 related to these bonds?

c) In determining 19X8 cash from operating activities, what adjustment (if any) related to these bonds should be made to reported net income?

EP 12.4 The following data are related to bond obligations of four different firms os of 12.31.X4:

	Firm A	Firm B	Firm C	Firm D
Bonds Payable	$600,000	$700,000	$800,000	$900,000
Market interest rate	12%	12%	12%	12%
Stated interest rate	14%	13%	12%	11%
Years until maturity	20	15	10	8

For each firm;

a) Show how the bonds and associated premium should be reported on the 12/31/X5 balance sheet.

b) Give the amount that should be reported as 19X5 interest expense related to these bonds.

c) In determining 19X5 cash from operating activities, what adjustments (if any) related to these bonds should be made to reported not income? Explain.

EP 12.5   Assuming on 1/1/X1 your firm purchased a used car paying $750 down and signing a fully amortized three-year promissory note for the balance. The loan agreement provided for payments of $100 at the end of each month , and the effective annual interest rate was 18 percent. If the loan principal amounted to $2,766 (rounded), prepare a partial (first six months) loan repayment schedule rounded to the nearest cant indicating what portion of each payment represented principal and what portion interest.

EP 12.6   Prepare the same partial repayment schedule required in EP 12.5 for each of the following fully amortized loans:

	Loan principal*	Monthly payment	Effective interest	Loan term	Loan balance**
a)	$2,124	$100	12%	2 yrs	$1,125
b)	7,186	200	15%	4 yrs	5,769
c)	5,106	150	18%	4 yrs	4,149
d)	8,298	300	18%	3 yrs	6,009

*   Rounded to nearest dollar.
** At the end of first year rounded.

EP 12.7   The Beaver Company acquired equipment under a capital lease signed on 1/1/X2. The lease contract called for payment of $15,635 with in 10 days of signing and $50,000 per year for eight years payable on 12/31 starting with 12/31/X2. At the same time, Beaver's incremental borrowing rate was 15 percent, and the present value of the eight year-end payments was $244,365. The equipment was to be amortized on a straight-line basis. What amount should be reported for:

- Properties held under capital lease?
- Current capital lease obligations?
- Noncurrent capital lease obligations?
- The interest expense for the year (related to this lease)?
- Amortization expense for the year (related to this lease)?

a) As of 1/1/X2 assuming the initial payment had not yet been made.

b) As of 12/31/X2 assuming the initial payment and the first annual payment had been made.

EP 12.8   The Boxer Corporation acquired plant and equipment under a capital lease on 1/1/X3. The lease called for a payment of $57,842 within 10 days of signing and $180,000 per year for 20 years payable on 12/31 each year starting with 12/31/X3. At the time of signing the lease, Boxer's increments borrowing rate was 14 percent. The plant and equipment was to be amortized on a straight-line basis. Assuming all required payments were made, what amounts should be reported for:

- Properties under capital lease?
- Current capital lease obligation?
- Noncurrent capital lease obligations?
- Interest expense for the year (related to the lease)?

a) As of 1/1/X3.

b) As of 12/31/X3 first year.

c) As of 12/31/X4.

d) As of 12/31/X5.

EP 12.9 The equity of the Dagwood Corporation's 12/31/X0 balance sheet was as follows ($ in thousands):

Total Current Liabilities	$150
7% convertible debentures	600
Discount on debentures	(80)
Total Liabilities	$ 670
Common stock	1,200
Additional paid-in capital	400
Retained earnings	900
Total Equities	$3,170

The common stock had a par value of $10 per share. Each $1,000 face value CVD was convertible into 25 shares of common stock.

The market price of Dagwood's stock climbed above $40 per share, and half of the bondholders converted their bonds on 1/1/X1. Give the balance in the following accounts after this conversion;

a) 7% convertible debentures;
b) Discount on debentures;
c) Common stock;
d) Additional paid-in capital.

EP 12.10 Data from the equity portions of the balance sheets for the X, Y, and Z Corporations as of 12/31/X1 are given below ($ in thousands):

	X	Y	Z
Total Current Liabilities	$ 200	$ 300	$ 400
9% convertible debentures	500	700	600
Premium on debentures	60	0	0
Discount on debentures	0	(30)	(90)
Total Liabilities	$ 760	$ 970	$ 910
Common stock	2,000	2,500	3,000
Additional paid-in capital	280	650	790
Retained earnings	820	950	330
Total Equities	$3,860	$5,070	$5,030
Other data included:			
Par value of common stock	$1	$5	$10
Each $1,000 CVD convertible to	200 shs	100 shs	50 shs
Percent bondholders voluntarily converting	100%	50%	40%
Call premium per $1,000 CVD	$30	$40	$50
CVD maturity date	12/31/X6	12/31/X6	12/31/X7

Assuming that the conversions took place on 4/30/X2, for each firm separately give the balances in the following accounts as of 12/31/X2:

a) 9% convertible debentures;
b) Premium on debentures;
c) Discount on debentures;
d) Common Stock;
e) Additional paid-in capital;
f) Interest expense (assuming no other interest except on the debentures).

Supplementary Problems

SP **12.11** The following selected data were taken from the Foxwater Corporation's 12/31/X1 financial statements and accompanying footnotes:

9% bonds payable[a]	$800,000
Bond premium	56,000
Common stock[b]	1,200,000
Additional pail-in capital	450,000
Deferred charges[c]	16,000

[a] Convertible debentures: each $1,000 debenture entitled to receive 80 shares of common stock if converted; maturing 12/31/X9; interest payable semi-annually on 6/30 and 12/31 with call premium of $40 per bond

[b] $10 par; issued and outstanding shares have not changed for past several years.

[c] Unamortized costs of convertible debenture issue.

In the spring of 19X2 when the market price of the common was $14, the company formally called the debentures effective 6/30/X2. By 6/30 60 percent of the bondholders had elected to convert and the balance of the issue was retired.

a) How much cash did the firm give to the bondholders in June of 19X2? Explain the various sums making up the total disbursement.

b) What were the balances in the common stock and additional paid-in-capital accounts after the conversion/retirement?

c) How much gain or loss on the conversion/retirement would be reported on the 19X2 income statement and how would it be reported?

d) Assuming that income tax was at a rate of 35 percent and was based on reported income from operations before taxes, what would be the effect of the conversion/retirement on 19X2 income from continuing operations? Explain.

SP **12.12** Refer to the information given for the Foxwater Corporation in SP 12.11. Answer the same four questions for each of the following three situations considered independently assuming all facts were the same as originally given except:

	Percent CVD interest rate	Conversion ratio	Common market price	Unamortized deferred charges	Bondholders electing conversion
I	10%	90 for 1	$15	$48,000	80%
II	8%	75 for 1	$14	36,000	10%
III	11%	100 for 1	$11	24,000	50%

SP **12.13** The following selected data ere taken from the Gemini Corporation's 12/31/X4 financial statements and accompanying footnotes:

10% bonds payable[a]	$900,000
Bond discount	60,000
Deferred charges[b]	10,000

[a] Maturing on 12/31/X9; interest payable semi-annually on 6/30 and 12/31; callable with call premium of $50 per $1,000 bond.
[b] Unamortized costs of bond issue.

The company refunded these bonds with a new 20-year issue of eight percent bonds that were sold at a price of $980 per bond with associated charges of $35,000 on 7/1/X5. The proceeds of the new issue were used to call and retire old bonds with accrued interest as of 9/30/X5.

a) Assuming the company sold just enough new bonds so that its new cash proceeds would be just sufficient to cover the incremental cash costs (excluding interest) of the refunding, how may bonds were sold?

b) Was there a gain or loss on this refunding and how would it be reported in the 12/31/X5 financial statements?

c) How should the firm's bond liability and related items be reported on its 12/31/X5 balance sheet?

d) How much interest was paid to, or earned by, all bondholders during 19X5?

e) How much interest expense would be reported on the firm's 19X5 income statement?

SP **12.14** Refer to the information given for the Gemini Corporation in SP 12.13. Answer the same five questions for each of the following three situations assuming all facts were the same as originally given except:

	Interest rate old bonds	Number old $1,000 bonds	Call premium old bonds	Unamortized deferred charges	Interest rate new bonds	Selling price new bonds	Associated charges new issue
I	9%	1000	$40	$4,800	8%	$1,000	$60,000
II	12%	800	$50	$6,000	10%	1,050	$40,000
III	11%	750	$60	$7,200	10%	950	$80,000

SP **12.15** On 1/1/X1 the Casella Corporation sold 2,000 twenty-year $1,000 bonds with a stated annual interest (coupon) rate of 12 percent payable semi-annually on 6/30 and 12/31. At the time of sale, bonds of similar risk and maturity were selling to yield 14 percent (going market rate of interest). $40,000 of issue costs were incurred as part of the bond financing.

a) What would be the effect of this sale on the firm's balance sheet as of 1/1/X1?

b) How should the liability and associated costs be reported on the firm's balance sheet as of 12/31/X1?

c) How much interest expense related to these bonds should be reported on the firm's 19X1 income statement?

SP   12.16 Refer to the information given for the Casella Corporation in SP 12.15. Answer the same questions for each of the three following situations considered independently assuming that all facts were the same as originally given except:

	Number bonds sold	Maturity	Stated interest rate	Bonds sold to yield	Issue costs
I	1,000	25 yrs	8%	10%	$50,000
II	600	15 yrs	10%	12%	$30,000
III	800	20 yrs	14%	12%	$40,000

SP   12.17 The Oliver Corporation acquired equipment under capital lease on 1/1/X4. The lease specified payment of $10,000 on signing and $40,000 per year on the first day of each of the next 10 years. At the time of signing, the firm's incremental borrowing rate was 14 percent, and the firm elected to use straight-line amortization.

   a) How would the leased equipment and associated obligations appear on the firm's 1/1/X4 balance sheet immediately prior to the making of the payment on signing?

   b) How should the equipment and associated obligations be reported on the firm's 12/31/X4 balance sheet assuming the first annual payment had not yet been made?

   c) How much interest expense related to this lease should be reported on the firm's 19X4 income statement?

   d) How should the equipment and associated obligations be reported on the 12/31/X5 balance sheet assuming the first and second annual payments had been made?

SP   12.18 Refer to the information given for the Oliver Corporation in SP 12.17. Answer the same four questions for each of the following three situations assuming that all facts were the same as originally given except:

	Lease term	Annual payments	Incremental borrowing rate	Amortization method elected
I	10 yrs.	$40,000	12%	St. line
II	15 yrs.	30,000	13%	SYD
III	20 yrs.	20,000	15%	DDB

SP   12.19 Integrative Problem: The following events occurred during Period 15 for the LUTON Corporation:

   1) Sales totaled $210,000, $50,000 for cash and the balance on account.

   2) Collections of receivables from customers totaled $150,000.

   3) Merchandise inventory costing $130,000 was purchased on account.

   4) Wages and salaries totaling $51,500 were paid including the $3,000 previously accrued.

   5) Supplies costing $1,,500 were purchased on account.

   6) $1,200 of bills for utilities and services consumed in the current period were received and recorded.

   7) $3,200 of interest was paid covering the current period's interest obligations on notes payable.

   8) The $7,000 of taxed payable for Period 14 were paid.

   9) $127,700 was paid on accounts payable.

   10) The preferred dividend of $2,500 was declared and paid.

11) $900 of interest was collected on current marketable securities.
12) The note receivable from a customer with a face value of $10,600 (including interest of $300 per period for Periods 14 and 15) matured and was collected.
13) Accounts receivable totaling $3,120 proved uncollectible and were written off.
14) Dividends of $6,000 were received on the Ajax Corporations common stock held as an investment and representing significant influence over Ajax's dividend decisions.
15) $800 representing the period's interest in the Baker Corporation bonds held as an investment was received.
16) LUTON declared and paid a common dividend of $18,900 ($.50 per share).

Adjustments were made for LIFO ending inventory of $70,000 (A); FIFO ending supplies inventory of $900 (B); $700 expiration of prepaid insurance (C); $4,400 of depreciation on building and $800 depreciation on equipment (D); $3,200 of bad debt expense resulting in an ending bad debt allowance of $1,880 (E); $12,000 representing the current period's share of the Ajax Corporation's reported earnings of $48,000 (F); $400 of discount amortization on the Baker Corporation bonds held as a long-term investment (G); $3,540 of depreciation on properties held under capital lease (H); accrual of $1,500 of wages and salaries earned but not yet paid (I); reclassification of $2,566 of capital lease obligation to current representing the principal portion of the $5,000 payment due at the beginning of Period 16 (J); accrual of $2,434 of current capital lease obligation representing interest expense (K); reclassification to current of the $16,000 note payable on equipment maturing at the end of Period 16 (L); and provision for corporate income taxes for the period of $5,500 (M).

The LUTON Corporation's balance sheet as of the end of Period 15 is given below:

LUTON CORPORATION--BALANCE SHEET AS OF END PERIOD 15			
ASSETS		**EQUITIES**	
Cash	$18,780	Current notes payable	$16,000
Marketable securities	35,000	Accounts payable	50,000
Accounts receivable	94,080	Wages and salaries	1,500
Allowance for bad debt	(1,880)	Taxes Payable	5,500
Inventory	70,000	Current cap. lse. obligation	5,000
Supplies	900	Total Current Liabilities	$78,000
Prepaid items	700	Noncurrent notes payable	60,000
Total Current Assets	$217,580	Noncurrent cap. lse. obligation	58,296
Investments	136,000	Total Liabilities	$196,296
Investments discount	(7,200)		
Land	25,000		
Buildings	125,000	Preferred stock*	100,000
Accum. depr. bldgs.	(42,100)	Addtl. paid in cap.—pfd.	10,000
Equipment	20,000	Common stock**	189,000
Accum. Depr. equip.	(9,200)	Addtl. paid in cap.—com.	6,750
Properties under capital lease	70,862	Retained earnings	26,816
Accum. depr. lease	(7,080)		
Total Assets	$528,862	Total Equities	$528,862

  * $100 par; 20,000 shared authorized; 1,000 shared issued and outstanding.
** $5 par; 200,000 shared authorized; 37,800 shares issued and outstanding.

During Period 16, the following events occurred affecting the financial position of the LUTON Corporation: (Note Items marked with as asterisk have been illustrated in previous periods.)

*1) Sales totaled $220,000, $55,000 for cash and the valance on account.
*2) Collections of customer receivables totals $160,000.
*3) Accounts receivable totaling $3,260 proved uncollectable and ere written off.
*4) Merchandise inventory costing $140,000 was purchased on account.
*5) Supplies costing $2,000 were purchased on account.
*6) $1,300 of bills for utilities and services consumed in the current period were received and recorded.
*7) Wages and salaries totaling $50,500 were paid including the $1,500 previously accrued.
*8) The $5,500 of taxes payable for Period 15 were paid.
*9) The $2,500 preferred dividend was declared and paid.
*10) $133,300 was paid on accounts payable.
*11) $800 representing the period's interest on the Baker Corporation bonds held as an investment was received.
12) The remaining portfolio of current marketable securities (that had originally cost $40,000 and had been written down to $35,000 to reflect loss of overall market value in an earlier period) were sold for $33,000.
13) The $16,000 current note payable on equipment matured and was paid together with $800 of interest.
14) The $5,000 current capital lease payment due at the beginning of the period was paid.
15) 2,000 shares of the Charles Corporation's common stock were purchased as a long-term investment at a cost of $20,000. The shares represented less than five percent of the firm's outstanding voting common stock and did not represent significant influence over dividend decisions.
16) The Charles Corporation reported $2 per share of earnings for the period and declared and paid a dividend on its common stock of $1.25 per share.
17) At the start of Period 16, LUTON sold, for $1,150 each, 50 $1,000 face value 30-period bonds with a stated interest rate of four percent per period.
18) Issue costs of the 50 bonds paid totaled $6,000, were paid and recorded as deferred charges.
19) The $60,000 first mortgage note due in Period 38 was retired with a payment of $63,000 covering principal, $2,400 of interest, and a $600 early retirement penalty.
20) A pickup and delivery truck was acquired at the beginning of the period for a down payment of $1,676 and a promissory note maturing at the end of Period 25 with a face value of $11,000. The note provided for interest payments of one percent ($110) per period payable at the end of each period. LUTON's borrowing rate (cost) was four percent, and the present value of the note discounted at four percent per period was $8,324.

At the end of Period 16:
*A) Merchandise inventory was adjusted to reflect ending inventory at LIFO of $78,000.
*B) Supplies inventory was adjusted to reflect ending supplies on hand under FIFO of $1,350.
*C) Prepaid items were adjusted to reflect $700 expiration of prepaid insurance.

*D) Wages and salaries totaling $1,000 earned but not yet paid were accrued.

*E) Depreciation expense of $4,100 on buildings and $700 on the older equipment was recorded.

*F) An aging of accounts receivable indicated that accounts totaling $1,920 were not expected to prove collectible.

*G) The firm's $15,000 share of the Ajax Corporation's reported earnings was recorded as income since LUTON's investment in Ajax common stock represented significant influence over Ajax's dividend decisions. Ajax did not declare any common dividends during the period.

*H) One period's $400 amortization of the discount on the Baker Corporation's bonds held as a long-term investment was recorded.

*I) One period's straight-line depreciation of the warehouse capital lease amounting to $3,540 was recorded.

J) $2,000 of interest owed on the firm's 50 30-period bonds was accrued.

K)   The period's amortization of premium on bonds payable of $250 was recorded.

L)   The period's amortization of $200 of deferred charges was recorded.

M) $400 of straight-line depreciation on the new pickup truck was recorded. The truck's useful life was estimated as 20 periods with a salvage value of $2,000.

N) $110 of interest owed on the $11,000 pickup truck noncurrent note payable was accrued.

O) $270 amortization (rounded) of the discount on the $11,000 noncurrent note payable was recorded.

P)   The $2,668 principal portion of the $5,000 capital lease payment due at the beginning of Period 17 was reclassified to current.

Q)   The $2,332 interest portion of the Period 17 $5,000 capital lease payment was accrued.

R)   An income statement provision for income taxes of $6,500 was recorded. Because of temporary timing differences between the firm's income statement and its tax return, the actual tax liability for the period was estimated to be $5,300. It was not expected to be paid within the next year.

Required:

a) Prepare a schedule of payments required under the warehouse capital lease (see transaction 18 for Period 14 in SP11.19) starting with the initial payment on signing and continuing through the payment due at the start of Period 21. For each payment indicate the amount, when it is due, the interest and principal portions, and the remaining loan balance after the payment is made.

b) The effect on the beginning period balance sheet of those Period 16 transactions and adjustments that were introduced in earlier periods, and which are identified with an asterisk (*), has already been recorded in the partially completed balance sheet worksheet given below. Prepare a final balance sheet worksheet for LUTON Corporation for Period 16 starting with the preliminary balances and recording the effect of Period 16 transactions (12) through (20) and adjustments (J) through (R). Identify opening balances as "(p)" and the effect of the remaining transactions and adjustments with their numbers or letters. Provide necessary space on your worksheet by entering account titles as follows:

Account	Line number	Account	Line number
Cash	1	Current Notes Payable	1
Marketable Securities	11	Accounts Payable	3
Accounts Receivable	13	Wages and Salaries	4
Allowance for Bad Debts	14	Interest Payable	5
Inventory	15	Taxes Payable	8
Supplies	16	Current Cap. Lse. Obligations	10
Investments	17	Noncurrent Notes Payable	14
Investments Discount	19	Notes Payable Discount	17
Land	20	Noncurrent Cap. Lse. Oblig.	20
Buildings	21	Bonds Payable	22
Accum. Depr. Buildings	22	Bond Premium	24
Equipment	23	Deferred Income Taxes	27
Accum. Depr. Equipment	25	Preferred Stock	29
Properties Under Capital Lse.	27	Addtl. Paid-in Capital—Pfd.	30
Accum. Depr. Lease	28	Common Stock	31
Deferred Charges	31	Addtl. Paid-in Capital—Com.	32
		Retained Earnings	33

c)   Prepare the firm's income statement for Period 16 in good form following the multiple-step format.

d)   Prepare the statement of retained earnings in good form for Period 16.

e)   Prepare the firm's balance sheet in good form as of the end of Period 16.

f)   Prepare the firm's statement of cash flows for Period 16 in good form using the indirect method for cash from operating activities.

g)   Determine for the LUTON Corporation for Period 16:

1)   The amount of net working capital in the business at the end of the period;

2)   The period-end current ratio (to two decimals);

3)   The period-end quick ratio (to two decimals);

4)   The period-end long-term debt ratio (to three decimals); and

5)   The period-end asset composition ratio (to three decimals).

PARTIALLY COMPLETED BALANCE SHEET EFFECT WORKSHEET
LUTON Corporation Period 16
(b = beginning balance; p = Partially Complete Ending Balance)

Cash	$	18,780	(b)		Current Notes Payable				
	+	55,000	(1)			$	16,000	(b) $ 16,000	(p)
	+	160,000	(2)		Accounts Payable				
	−	50,500	(7)				50,000	(b)	
	−	5,500	(8)			+	140,000	(4)	
	−	2,500	(9)			+	2,000	(5)	
	−	133,300	(10)			+	1,300	(6)	
	+	800	(11) $ 42,780 (p)			−	133,300	(10) 60,000	(p)
Marketable Securities					Wages and Salaries				
		35,000	(b) 35,000 (p)				1,500	(b)	
Accounts Receivable						−	1,500	(7)	
		94,080	(b)			+	1,000	(D) 1,000	(p)
	+	165,000	(1)		Taxes Payable		5,500	(b)	
	−	160,000	(2)			−	5,500	(8) 0	(p)
	−	3,260	(3) 95,820 (p)		Current Cap. Lse. Oblig.				
Allowance for Bad Debts				(3,800) (b)			5,000	(b) 5,000	(p)
		(1,880)	(3)		Noncurrent Notes Payable				
	+	3,260	(3)				60,000	(b) 60,000	(p)
	−	3,260	(F) (1,820) (p)		Noncurrent Cap. Lse. Oblig.				
Inventory		70,000	(b)				58,296	(b) 58,296	(p)
	+	140,000	(4)						
	−	132,000	(A) 78,000 (p)						
Supplies		900	(b)						
	+	2,000	(5)						
	−	1,550	(B) 1,350 (p)						
Prepaid Itms		700	(b)		Preferred Stock				
	−	700	(C) 0 (p)				100,000	(b) 100,000	(p)
Investments		136,000	(b)		Addtl. Paid–in Capital—Pfd.				
	+	15,000	(G) 151,000 (p)				10,000	(b) 10,000	(p)
Investments Discount					Common Stock				
		(7,200)	(b)				189,000	(b) 189,000	(p)
	+	400	(H) (6,800) (p)		Addtl. Paid-in Capital—Com.				
Land		25,000	(b) 25,000 (p)				6,750	(b) 6,750	(p)
Buildings		125,000	(b) 125,000 (p)		Retained Earnings				
Accum. Depr. —Bldgs.							66,569	(b) 66,569	(p)
	−	(42,100)	(b)						
	−	4,100	(E) (46,200) (p)						
Equipment		20,000	(b) 20,000 (p)						
Accum. Depr.—Equip.									
		(9,200)	(b)						
	−	700	(E) (9,900) (p)						
Properties Under Capital Lease									
		70,862	(b) 70,862 (p)						
Accum. Depr.—Lease									
		(7,080)	(b)						
	−	3,540	(H) (10,620)(p)						

Income				
+ 220,000 (1)	−	700 (C)
− 1,300 (6)	−	1,000 (D)
− 49,000 (7)	−	4,800 (E)
− 2,500 (9)	−	3,200 (F)
+ 800(11)	+	15,000 (G)
− 132,000 (A)	−	400 (H)
− 1,550 (B)	−	3,540 (I)

TOTALS	$ 755,196		TOTALS	$ 775,196

SP **12.20** Integrative Problem: The following events occurred during Period 15 for the MORCHAN Corporation:

1) Sales totaled $300,000, $60,000 for cash and the balance on account.

2) Collections of receivables from customers totaled $208,600.

3) Merchandise inventory costing $240,000 was purchased on account.

4) Wages and salaries totaling $64,000 were paid including the $2,500 previously accrued.

5) Supplies costing $2,000 were purchased on account.

6) $1,900 of bills for utilities and services consumed in the current period were received and recorded.

7) $8,600 of interest was paid covering the current period's interest obligations on notes payable.

8) The $4,000 of taxes payable for Period 14 were paid.

9) $167,900 was paid on accounts payable.

10) The preferred dividend of $6,000 was declared and paid.

11) $1,400 of interest was collected on current marketable securities.

12) The note receivable from a customer with a face value of $5,400 (including interest of $200 per period for Periods 14 and 15) matured and was collected.

13) Accounts receivable totaling $6,400 proved uncollectible and were written off.

14) Dividends of $3,600 were received on the Acme Corporation's common stock held as an investment and representing significant influence over Acme's dividend decisions.

15) $2,000 representing the period's interest on the Zukor Corporation bonds held as an investment was received.

16) MORCHAN declared and paid a common dividend of $16,646 ($0.40 per share).

Adjustments were made for LIFO ending inventory of $300,000 (A); FIFO ending supplies inventory of $800 (B); $1,400 expiration of prepaid insurance (C); $11,100 of depreciation on buildings and $1,350 depreciation on equipment (D); $7,150 of bad debt accounts expense resulting in an ending bad debts allowance of $7,500 (E); $16,600 representing the current period's share of the Acme Corporation's reported earnings of $55,300 (F); $200 of premium amortization on the Zukor Corporation bonds held as a long-term investment (G); $7,190 of depreciation of properties held under capital lease (H); accrual of $3,500 of wages and salaries earned but not yet paid (I); reclassification of $5,211 of capital lease obligation to current representing the principal portion of the $10,000 payment due at the beginning of Period 16 (J); accrual of $4,789 of current capital lease obligation representing interest expense (K); reclassification to current of the $28,000 note payable on equipment maturing at the end of Period 16 (L); and provision for corporate income taxes for the period of $5,000 (M).

The MORCHAN Corporation's balance sheet as of the end of Period 15 is given below:

MORCHAN CORPORATION —BALANCE SHEET AS OF END OF PERIOD 15

ASSETS		EQUITIES	
Cash	$ 24,634	Current notes payable	$ 28,000
Marketable securities	48,000	Accounts payable	250,000
Accounts receivable	250,000	Wages and salaries	3,500
Allowance for bad debts	(7,500)	Taxes payable	5,000
Inventory	300,000	Current cap. lse. obligation	10,000
Supplies	800	Total Current Liabilities	$ 296,500
Prepaid items	1,400	Noncurrent notes payable	180,000
Total Current Assets	$ 617,334	Noncurrent cap. lse. oblig.	154,435
Investments	168,000	Total Liabilities	$ 630,935
Investments premium	4,600		
Land	90,000	Preferred Stock*	200,000
Buildings	370,000	Addtl. paid-in cap.—pfd.	10,000
Accum. depr. bldgs.	(103,100)	Common stock**	416,160
Equipment	35,000	Addtl. paid-in cap.—com.	12,550
Accum. depr. equip.	(15,000)	Retained earnings	62,455
Properties under capital lease	179,646		
Accum. depr. lease	(14,380)		
Total Assets	$1,332,100	Total Equities	$1,332,100

* $100 par; 50,00 shares authorized; 2,000 shares issued and outstanding
** $10 par; 500,000 shares authorized; 41,616 shares issued and outstanding

During Period 16, the following events occurred affecting the financial position of the MORCHAN Corporation: (Note: Items marked with an asterisk have been illustrated in previous periods.)

*1) Sales totaled $325,000, $65,000 for cash and the balance on account.
*2) Collections of customer receivables totaled $116,400.
*3) Accounts receivable totaling $3,600 proved uncollectible and were written off.
*4) Merchandise inventory costing $195,000 was purchased on account.
*5) Supplies costing $2,200 were purchased on account.
*6) $1,950 of bills for utilities and services consumed in the current period were received and recorded.
*7) Wages and salaries totaling $70,700 were paid including the $3,500 previously accrued.
*8) The $5,000 of taxes payable for Period 15 were paid.
*9) The $6,000 preferred dividend was declared and paid.
*10) $124,150 was paid on accounts payable.
*11) $2,000 representing the period's interest on the Zukor Corporation bonds held as an investment was received.
12) The remaining portfolio of current marketable securities (that had originally cost $50,000 and had been written down to $48,000 to reflect loss of overall market value in the earlier period) were sold for $45,000.

13) The $28,000 current note payable on equipment matured and was paid together with $1,400 of interest.

14) The $10,000 current capital lease payment due at the beginning of the period was paid.

15) 500 shares of the Castle Corporation's common stock were purchased as a long-term investment at a cost of $10,000. The shares represented less than one percent of the firm's outstanding voting common stock and did not represent significant influence over dividend decisions.

16) The Castle Corporation reported $3.00 per share of earnings for the period and declared and paid a dividend on its common stock of $1.50 per share.

17) At the start of Period 16, MORCHAN sold, for $900 each, 230 $1,000 face value 20-period bonds with a stated interest rate of three percent per period.

18) Issue costs for the 230 bonds totaled $5,000, were paid, and were recorded as deferred charges.

19) The $180,000 first mortgage note due in Period 28 was retired with a payment of $189,900 covering principal, $7,200 of interest, and a $2,700 early retirement penalty.

20) A pickup and delivery truck was acquired at the beginning of the period for a down payment of $3,000 and a promissory note maturing at the end of Period 27 with a face value of $10,000. The note provided for interest payments of one percent ($100) per period payable at the end of each period. MORCHAN's borrowing rate (cost) was three percent, and the present value of the note discounted at three percent per period was $8,000 (rounded).

*A) Merchandise inventory was adjusted to reflect ending inventory at LIFO of $330,000.

*B) Supplies inventory was adjusted to reflect ending supplies on hand under FIFO of $1,300.

*C) Prepaid items were adjusted to reflect $1,400 expiration of prepaid insurance.

*D) Wages and salaries totaling $2,800 earned but not yet paid were accrued.

*E) Depreciation expense of $10,700 on buildings and $1,200 on the older equipment was recorded.

*F) An aging of ending accounts receivable indicated that accounts totaling $11,700 were not expected to prove collectible.

*G) The firm's $12,000 share of the Acme Corporation's reported earnings was recorded as income since MORCHAN's investment in Acme common stock represented significant influence over Acme's dividend decisions. Acme did not declare any common dividends during the period.

*H) One period's $200 amortization of the premium on the Zukor Corporation's bonds held as long-term investments was recorded.

*I) One period's straight-line depreciation on the warehouse capital lease amounting to $7,190 was recorded.

J) $6,900 of interest owed on the firm's 230 20-period bonds was accrued.

K) The period's amortization of discount on bonds payable of $1,150 was recorded.

L) The period's amortization of $250 of deferred charges was recorded.

M) $600 of straight-line depreciation on the new pickup truck was recorded. The truck's useful life was estimated as 15 periods with a salvage value of $3,000.

N) $100 of interest owed on the $10,000 pickup truck noncurrent note payable was accrued.

O) $167 amortization (rounded) of the discount on the $10,000 noncurrent note payable was recorded.

P) The $5,367 principal portion of the $10,000 capital lease payment due at the beginning of Period 17 was reclassified to current.

Q) The $4,633 interest portion of the Period 17 $10,000 capital lease payment was accrued.

R) An income statement provision for income taxes of $10,000 was recorded. Because of temporary tiing differences between the firm's income statement and its tax return, the actual tax liability for the period was estimated to be $9,200. The deferral was not expected to be paid within the next year.

Required:

a) Prepare a schedule of payments required under the warehouse capital lease (see transaction 18 for Period 14 in SP 11.20) starting with the initial payment on signing and continuing through the payment due at the start of Period 21. For each payment indicate the amount, when it is due, the interest and principal portions, and the remaining "loan" balance after the payment is made.

b) The effect on the beginning period balance sheet of those Period 16 transactions and adjustments that were introduced in earlier periods, and which are identified with an asterisk (*), has already been recorded in the partially completed balance sheet worksheet given below. Prepare a final balance sheet worksheet for the MORCHAN Corporation for Period 16 starting with the preliminary balances and recording the effect of Period 16 transactions (12) through (20) and adjustments (J) through (R). Identify opening balances as "(p)" and the effect of the remaining transactions and adjustments with their numbers or letters. Provide necessary space on your worksheet by entering account titles as follows:

Account	Line number	Account	Line number
Cash	1	Current Notes Payable	1
Marketable Securities	11	Accounts Payable	3
Accounts Receivable	13	Wages and Salaries	4
Allowance for Bad Debts	14	Interest Payable	5
Inventory	15	Taxes Payable	8
Supplies	16	Current Cap. Lse. Obligations	10
Investments	17	Noncurrent Notes Payable	14
Investments Premium	19	Notes Payable Discount	17
Land	20	Noncurrent Cap. Lse. Oblig.	20
Buildings	21	Bonds Payable	22
Accum. Depr. Bldgs.	22	Bond Discount	24
Equipment	23	Deferred Income Taxes	27
Accum. Depr. Equip.	25	Preferred Stock	29
Properties Under Capital Lse.	27	Addtl. Paid-in Capital—Pfd.	30
Accum. Depr. Lease	28	Common Stock	31
Deferred Charges	31	Addtl, Paid-in Capital—Com.	32
		Retained Earnings	33

    c)   Prepare the firm's income statement for Period 16 in good form following the multiple-step format.

    d)   Prepare the statement of retained earnings in good form for Period 16.

    e)   Prepare the firm's balance sheet in good form as of the end of Period 16.

    f)   Prepare the firm's statement of cash flows in good form for Period 16 using the indirect method for cash for operating activities.

    g)   Determine for the MORCHAN Corporation for Period 16:

       1)   The amount of net working capital in the business at eh end of the period;

       2)   The period-end current ratio (to two decimals);

       3)   The period-end quick ratio (to two decimals);

       4)   The period-end long-term debt ratio (to three decimals); and

       5)   The period-end asset composition ratio (to three decimals).

Preparer Problems

PP 12.1   Refer to EP 12.1. Prepare the necessary adjusting journal entry or entries relating to interest expense for the quarter.

PP 12.2   Refer to EP 12.4. Assume that the bonds were sold for cash on 12/31/X4 and that issue expenses related to the sale and paid on 12/31/X4 were as follows:

Firm A	Firm B	Firm C	Firm D
$6,000	$6,750	$8,000	$9,000

Give the necessary journal entries for each firm:

    a)   To record the sale and related costs on 12/31/X4.

    b)   Assuming interest payments were made semi-annually on 6/30 and 12/31, to record all interest-related expense associated with these bonds during 19X5 and at year-end.

PP 12.3   Refer to EP 12.7. Give the necessary journal entries:

    a)   To record acquisition of the equipment on 1/1/X2.

    b)   To record the first year's payment on 12/31/X2.

    c)   To make all adjustments related to this capital lease for 19X2.

PP 12.4   Refer to EP 12.8. Give the necessary journal entries:

    a)   To record acquisition of the plant and equipment on 1/1/X3.

    b)   To record the first year's payment on 12/31/X3.

    c)   To make all adjustments related to this capital lease for 19X3.

PP 12.5   Refer to EP 12.9. Give the necessary journal entry to record the bond conversion on 1/1/X1.

PP 12.6   Refer to EP 12.10. Give the necessary journal entry for each firm separately to record the bond conversion on 4/30/X2.

PARTIALLY COMPLETED BALANCE SHEET EFFECT WORKSHEET
MORCHAN Corporation Period 16
(b = beginning balance; p = Partially Complete Ending Balance)

Cash	$ 24,634	(b)		Current Notes Payable			
	+ 65,000	(1)			$ 28,000 (b)	$ 28,000	(p)
	+ 116,400	(2)		Accounts Payable			
	− 70,700	(7)			250,000	(b)	
	− 5,000	(8)			+ 195,000	(4)	
	− 6,000	(9)			+ 2,200	(5)	
	− 124,150	(10)			+ 1,950	(6)	
	+ 2,000	(11) $ 2,184 (p)			− 124,150 (10)	$ 325,000	(p)
Marketable Securities				Wages and Salaries			
	48,000	(b) 48,000 (p)			3,500	(b)	
Accounts Receivable					− 3,500	(6)	
	250,000	(b)			+ 2,800 (D)	2,800	(p)
	+ 260,000	(1)		Taxes Payable	5,000	(b)	
	− 116,400	(2)			− 5,000 (G)	0	(p)
	− 3,600	(3) 390,000 (p)		Current Cap. Lse. Oblig.			
Allowance for Bad Debts					10,000 (b)	10,000	(p)
	(7,500)	(b)		Noncurrent Notes Payable			
	+ 3,600	(3)			180,000 (b)	180,000	(p)
	− 7,800	(F) (14,400) (p)		Notes Payable Discount			
Inventory	300,000	(b)			(1,666) (b)	(1,666)	(p)
	+ 195,000	(4)		Noncurrent Cap. Lse. Oblig.			
	− 165,000	(A) 330,000 (p)			154,435 (b)	154,435	(p)
Supplies	800	(b)					
	+ 2,200	(5)					
	− 1,700	(B) 900 (p)		Preferred Stock			
Prepaid Itms	1,400	(b)			200,000 (b)	200,000	(p)
	− 1,400	(C) 0 (p)		Addtl. Paid–in Capital—Pfd.			
Investments	168,000	(b)			10,000 (b)	10,000	(p)
	+ 12,000	(G) 180,000 (p)		Common Stock			
Investments Premium					416,160 (b)	416,160	(p)
	(4,600)	(b)		Addtl. PIC—Com.			
	− 200	(H) (4,200) (p)			12,550 (b)	12,550	(p)
Land	90,000	(b) 90,000 (p)		Retained Earnings			
Buildings	370,000	(b) 370,000 (p)			129,986 (b)	129,986	(p)
Accum. Depr. —Bldgs.							
	(103,100)	(b)					
	− 10,700	(E) (113,800) (p)					
Equipment	35,000	(b) 35,000 (p)					
Accum. Depr.—Equip.							
	(15,000)	(b)					
	− 1,200	(E) (16,200) (p)					
Properties Under Capital Lease							
	179,646	(b) 179,646 (p)					
Accum. Depr.—Lease							
	(14,380)	(b)					
	− 7,100	(I) (21,480) (p)					
Deferred Charges							
	4,500	(b)					
	− 250	(H) 4,250 (p)					
TOTALS		$1,467,260		TOTALS		$ 1,467,260	

Income

+ 325,000 (1)		− 1,400 (C)	
− 1,950 (6)		− 2,800 (D)	
− 67,200 (7)		− 11,900 (E)	
− 6,000 (9)		− 7,800 (F)	
+ 2,000 (11)		+ 12,000 (G)	
− 165,000 (A)		− 2000 (H)	
− 1,700 (B)		- 7,1900 (I)	

PP   12.7   Prepare in good form the two journal entries necessary to record the weekly payroll and the employer's payroll tax and other related liabilities, given the following data:

Salaries earned	$60,000
Income taxes to be withheld	12,000
F.I.C.A. taxes to be withheld	3,600
Union dues to be withheld	300
Employer F.U.T.A. taxes	2,400
Employer health plan costs	4,800

PP   12.8   Prepare in good form the two journal entries necessary to record the weekly payroll and the employers' payroll tax and other related liabilities given the following data:

Salaries and wages earned	$35,000
Income taxes to be withheld	7,000
F.I.C.A. taxes to be withheld	2,100
State disability taxes to be withheld	350
Union dues to be withheld	300
Employee pension-fund contribution	1,050
Employer F.U.T.A. taxes	1,400
Employer state disability taxes	1,050
Employer pension-fund contributions	1,050
Employer health plan costs	1,575

13

Financial
Statement
Analysis

Chapter Preview

The objective of this chapter is to expand your awareness of the information content of financial statements, and to enhance your ability to use and analyze them intelligently. In this chapter you can:

1. Develop an understanding of return on investment as the basic criterion of economic efficiency;

2. Learn how various measures incorporating both income statement and balance sheet data may be used to evaluate the efficiency of a firm's operating management;

3. Learn that other measures, together with the statement of cash flows, may be used to evaluate a firm's financial management and its recent financial activities;

4. Understand why different users of accounting information may have differing perspectives or interests, and learn the important distinction between return on investment for the firm as a whole and return for the individual investor; and

5. Reinforce your perspective of the limitations of financial statement analysis as being just one of several necessary parts of any investment decision.

With this information, you will have a working knowledge of the major financial statements. In subsequent business courses, you will be able to read, understand, and interpret the statements with reasonable proficiency and with confidence.

What Can Financial Statements Tell Me?

Since financial statements essentially report on the results of a firm's management activities, statement analysis can be viewed as an evaluation of management's performance. However different analysts have different objectives and, therefore, may focus upon one particular aspect of management rather than the overall performance of the firm.

Three Components of Overall Management

Overall management may be viewed as a combination of operating management, financial management, and tax management. These three aspects although interrelated, may be considered separately. Operating management refers to managing the resources already available within the firm effectively and efficiently without regard for the manner by which the resources were financed (obtained). Effectiveness refers to the selection and accomplishment of objectives. Information relating to management's effectiveness is generally not contained in financial statements and is beyond the scope of this text. Efficiency refers to the concept of return on investment, or outputs generated by certain inputs.

Financial management involves anticipating the need for obtaining necessary resources at minimal cost. It also involves maintaining, in the long-run, an optimal capital structure for the firm (as first discussed in Chapter 3) and thus maximizing the return on owners' equity. The objective of tax management is simply to minimize the firm's tax liabilities. This objective is achieved not only through the skilled preparation of tax returns, but, more importantly, through coordinating the timing and the legal form of the actions taken by operating and financial managers to lessen adverse tax consequences.

Four Differing Analysts' Viewpoints

As the various different tools of financial statement analysis are introduced in this chapter, you will be asked to consider their usefulness to four individuals:

1. Mr. John Chandler is an older man unable to work because of partial paralysis. Mr. Chandler is financially dependent on the income from his savings and investments. His primary objectives are safety of principal and consistent income. These factors are of much greater importance to John than any potential for spectacular growth of his investments.

2. Ms. Prudence Parkinson is a young fast-rising executive. Ms. Parkinson is interested in an investment with major growth potential and is willing to accept considerable risk in her investments. Since her salary currently covers all her needs, current income from investments is a secondary consideration.

3. Mr. Jack Jordan is the absentee owner of Jack's Motel. Mr. Jordan personally built and for many years operated the motel. During the last few years, he has semi-retired to a different state. He employs a resident manager whom he supervises by mail, phone, and an occasional visit. Mr. Jordan is concerned that his motel continues to run profitably.

4. Ms. Becky Silverman is the purchasing agent for a large manufacturer. Becky is concerned over the ability of a supplier to finance a potential major increase in volume.

In the following sections, you will be introduced to measures of investment safety, efficient use of resources, return on owner's investment, and detailed operating performance. Their significance to each of the four analysts will be reviewed. The Columbia Corporation will be analyzed for purposes of illustration in Exhibit 13.1 on the following pages. Exhibit 13.2 provides other data for comparative evaluation.

Investment Safety

Although investments are never perfectly safe, some may be safer than others. There are four common tools of safety analysis: the current ratio, the quick ratio, the long-term debt ratio, and times interest earned. Columbia's current ratio (as of 12/31/X1) is 3.00, and its quick ratio is 2.00. The previous year these ratios were the same. The company appears to be maintaining adequate solvency.

One of the risks of excessive debt is the inability to raise additional cash in emergencies. Recall that debt capacity has been defined as the ability of the firm to obtain more cash if necessary, with minimum difficulty. If a firm should need additional funds, creditors may not be willing to provide them when the firm is already too heavily in debt. The ideal and the maximum allowable long-term debt ratios, or debt-to-equity ratios, for a firm vary by industry. Assume the normal industry long-term debt ratios in Columbia's case are 0.100, ideal and 0.300, maximum. From Exhibit 13.1, what is your opinion of Columbia's debt capacity? How much cash does it appear that the firm could borrow without exceeding its debt limits?

Columbia's long-term debt ratio of 0.123 over the past two years is nearly ideal. There appears to be adequate debt capacity; the firm could borrow $115,000 of additional net working capital before reaching its upper limit of debt. This amount is determined by letting X equal total long-term debt plus owners' equity if the firm were to borrow up to the 0.3 debt limit. 0.7 X would equal owners' equity. With no additional owner investment, 0.7X would equal $399,000 (present owners' equity) and X would equal $570,000 (rounded). Maximum debt (0.3X) would be $171,000 (rounded). Present long-term debt is only $56,000. Therefore the difference of $115,000 is potentially "available."

Another risk of excessive debt is the necessity of making high interest payments each year. Remember that interest must be paid whether or not the firm's operations are profitable. Times interest earned is a ratio used to measure the risk of interest obligations. **Times interest earned** is calculated by taking earnings from operations before deduction for interest expense and taxes—**EBIT**—and dividing by annual interest expense.

$$\text{Times Interest Earned} = \frac{\textbf{EBIT}}{\textbf{Annual Interest}}$$

Exhibit 13.1

COLUMBIA CORPORATION
Comparative Balance Sheets as of 12/31/X0 and 12/31/X1
($ in thousands)

	12/31/X1	12/31/X0
Assets:		
Cash	$ 85	$ 50
Marketable securities	55	75
Receivables:		
Notes receivable	5	10
Accounts receivable	107	94
Less allowance for uncollectibles	(2)	(4)
Inventory[a]	113	100
Supplies	4	10
Prepaid items	8	5
Total Current Assets	$375	$340
Investments	35	25
Land	60	60
Plant and Equipment	205	200
Less accumulated depreciation[b]	(95)	(60)
Total Assets	$580	$565
Equities:		
Current notes payable	$ 10	$ 20
Accounts payable	101	85
Other current liabilities	14	10
Total Current Liabilities	$125	$115
Bonds payable	60	60
Less Bond Discount	(4)	(5)
Total Liabilities[c]	$181	$170
Preferred stock (12% $100 par)[d]	100	100
Common stock ($10 par)[e]	150	150
Additional paid-in capital[f]	40	40
Retained earnings[g]	126	122
Less treasury stock	(17)	(17)
Total Stockholders' Equity	$399	$395
Total Equities	$580	$565

[a] At LCM following FIFO.
[b] Straight-line depreciation used for all fixed assets.
[c] Damages amounting to $250,000 against the company and not covered by insurance have been awarded to an injured employee. Company is appealing the court's decision.
[d] 1,000 shares issued and outstanding.
[e] 15,000 shares issued. 14,000 shares outstanding.
[f] $15,000 from preferred stock.
[g] $17,000 restricted by cost of treasury stock.

**Exhibit 13.1
(continued)**

COMPARATIVE INCOME STATEMENTS FOR YEARS ENDING
12/31/X0 AND 12/31/X1
($ in thousands)

	19X1	19X0
Sales	$850	$745
Less cost of goods sold	440	385
Gross Profit	$410	$360
Less other operating expenses		
Wages and salaries	188	178
Utilities	9	9
Supplies	4	4
Insurance	6	6
Depreciation	35	35
Bad debts	8	7
Miscellaneous	3	7
Interest	5	5
Total Expenses	258	251
Income before income taxes	$152	$109
Less provision for income taxes	61	43
Income from operations	$ 91	$ 66
Extraordinary flood damage to building	0	44
Net Income	$ 91	$ 22
Earnings per share before extraordinary items	$5.64	$3.86
Earnings per share after extraordinary items	$5.64	$0.71

A firm that barely manages to cover its interest, and therefore has zero income from operations before taxes, would have times interest earned of 1. There is no absolute standard for an adequate times interest earned rate which would indicate safety. Earnings could be reinvested in assets and the firm could have inadequate cash to make interest payments. Furthermore, earnings could decline in the future and make coverage of interest payments difficult. Since the future ability to cover interest is of concern, the preferable definition of EBIT, given, above excludes the results of nonrecurring extraordinary items. Subject to these qualifications, you may consider a rate of three or more "times" as adequate safety. Does Columbia's recent performance indicate adequate safety with respect to existing interest obligations?

Columbia has $5,000 of annual interest cost and EBIT of $157,000 in 19X1 and $114,000 in 19X0. Times interest earned rates are therefore 31 and 23, respectively, which appear to provide more than adequate safety. The company therefore does not appear to have to much debt, either in terms of its capital structure or as a source of high interest requirements.

Exhibit 13.2   Statement of Cash Flows for the Year Ending 12/31/X1
                                                  ($ in thousands)

Operating activities:
    Net Income $ 91
    Depreciation   35
    Bond discount amortization   1
    Increase Accounts Receivable (net)   (15)
    Increase Inventory   (13)
    Decrease Supplies   6
    Increase Prepaid Items   (3)
    Increase Accounts Payable   16
    Increase other Current Liabilities   4
Cash provided by operating activities $122
Investing Activities:
    Proceeds Sale of Marketable Securities $20
    Collection on Notes Receivable   5
    Purchase Investments   (10)
    Purchase Equipment   (5)
Cash provided by investing activities   10
Financing Activities:
    Paid current notes payable   (10)
    Paid Preferred Dividends   (12)
    Paid Common Dividends   (75)
Cash used in financing activities   (97)
Increase in cash $ 35
Beginning Cash   50
Ending Cash $ 85

Other Data for Comparative Evaluation

	Industry average 19X1	Columbia Corporation 19X0
Current ratio	2.90	3.00
Quick ratio	1.80	2.00
Debt ratio	0.300	0.123
Times interest earned	20 times	23 times
Asset turnover	1.40 times	1.42 times
Receivables turnover	9.00 times	8.27 times
Average days' receivables	41 days	44 days
Inventory turnover	3.80 times	4.05 times
Average days' sales in inventory	96 days	90 days
Property and equipment turnover	4.50 times	4.08 times
Return on investment	25%	26%

Operating Effectiveness and Efficiency

In evaluating a company's future, you must consider many factors not revealed by the financial statements. Some of these other factors would include:

- The firm's projects or services and future demand for them;
- The firm's employee relations; and
- The overall economic future.

Management must be effective in choosing the firm's objectives. Evaluation of such choices is beyond the scope of this book. Given objectives, management must be efficient in achieving them. Financial statements can provide information as to management's efficiency.

Efficient Use of Resources

Various efficiency rates (or ratios) measure performance over a specific time period, usually a year. The numerator is the amount of a specific output generated or earned during the year, such as sales, profit, interest, and so forth. The denominator represents resources (inputs) used or invested during the year to generate the output. A single quantity of resources measured as of one instant in time, as reported in a balance sheet, is therefore inappropriate to use in the denominator.

Asset Turnovers

An important group of efficiency measures are known as "turnovers." Consider a measure of the firm's efficiency of overall asset usage in generating revenue. The objective of having assets in the firm is to generate revenue and, hopefully, profit. The **asset turnover** rate indicates the degree of achievement of the revenue objective. It is calculated by dividing sales (revenue) for the year by average total assets in use during the year.

$$\text{Asset Turnover (times)} = \frac{\text{Net Sales}}{\text{Average Total Assets}}$$

Net Sales is commonly used, rather than total revenues. To use Gross Sales would result in including some revenues that were not actually earned, that is, some that were subsequently "cancelled" by sales returns or reduced by sales discounts. To include other secondary revenues or gains would diffuse the focus on the primary operations of the firm.

The denominator includes average total assets employed and not just the amount reported on a single balance sheet. Some analysts use more sophisticated weighted-average techniques to account for seasonality and other variables. For our purposes, in this and all other efficiency measures, average resources employed will be determined as a simple average for the year, that is, one-half the sum of total assets at the beginning of the period plus those at the end of the period.

$$\text{Simple Average} = \frac{\text{Balance at beginning of period} \quad \textbf{plus} \quad \text{Balance at end of period}}{2}$$

What was Columbia's asset turnover for 19X1? For the Columbia Corporation, asset turnover would be 1.48 for 19X1. This can be interpreted as "Each dollar of average assets employed has generated $1.48 of sales." The higher the turnover, the better the efficiency of asset usage. Acceptable asset turnover varies greatly by industry. Companies requiring large investments in capacity assets may be fortunate to "turn" assets one or more times per year. Therefore, turnover can be evaluated meaningfully only in comparison with other firms, an industry standard, or as a trend indicator that compares performance to that of prior periods for the same firm.

The turnover concept as a measure of efficiency can also be applied to specific assets or groups of assets. **Receivables turnover** is used as a measure of the timeliness of receivable collections. Note that this ratio refers to accounts receivable, and not all receivables. Accounts receivable turnover is calculated by dividing total credit sales by average net receivables.

$$\text{Receivables Turnover (times)} = \frac{\text{Credit Sales}}{\text{Average Net Accounts Receivable}}$$

This ratio measures the number of dollars of credit sales resulting from dollars invested in receivables, that is, invested as a short-term creditor in the customer's business through the customer's accounts payable. The numerator should therefore include only credit sales (sales made on account). In practice, information on credit sales is not always available, although most nonretail firms make substantially all sales on account. Therefore, total net sales is often used in the numerator as an acceptable substitute.

$$\frac{\text{Estimator of}}{\text{receivables turnover}} = \frac{\text{Net Sales}}{\text{Average Net Accounts Receivable}}$$

For Columbia, receivables turnover was 8.72 for 19X1. For every average dollar invested accounts receivable, sales of $8.72 were realized. The higher the turnover, the shorter the time during which assets were invested in customers. Desirable receivables turnover for a particular firm is influenced by industry patterns and the credit policy of the firm. In some industries, especially where cash discounts are offered, early collection is normal, and desirable turnover may be as high as 11 to 12 times.[1] In other industries or firms,

---

[1] Recall from Chapter 8 that often payment terms of 2/10 N/30 (two percent discount granted if invoice paid within 10 days otherwise payment in full due within 30 days) are offered. In such situations it is not uncommon to have all or almost all receivables collected on average within 30 days and thereby achieve an 11 or 12 times receivables turnover.

where the privilege of slow payment is part of the inducement to purchase, and early collections are not rigorously pushed, acceptable turnover might be as low as 5 to 6 times.[2]

Rather than using receivables turnover, the efficiency of receivable collections is often evaluated in terms of average days' receivables. **Average days' receivables** is calculated by dividing receivables turnover into 365, or into the number of days in the period.

$$\text{Average Days' Sales in Receivables} = \frac{365}{\text{Receivables Turnover}}$$

For Columbia, in 19X1, average days' receivables was 42 (rounded). This indicates that, on the average, receivables were paid within 42 days of sale, or that the average investment involved in making a credit sale was for a period of 42 days. In the case of average days' receivables, the lower the number, the more rapidly receivables were being collected.[3]

Turnover measures are also applied to investment in inventories. **Inventory turnover** measures the cost of items delivered to customers as compared to the average dollars invested in inventory.

$$\text{Inventory Turnover (times)} = \frac{\text{Cost of Goods Sold}}{\text{Average Inventory}}$$

Note that the effect of varying amounts of gross profit is excluded by using the cost of sales generated as the numerator, and not sales. Inventory is generally measured at cost. Therefore, both the numerator and denominator of this ratio are in terms of cost dollars.

What was Columbia's inventory turnover for 19X1? For Columbia, 19X1 inventory turnover was 4.13 times. This ratio (or rate) may be interpreted as indicating that, for each dollar invested in inventory, $4.13 of sales at cost (before gross profit margin) were generated. Since gross profit is generated on each dollar cost of sales or each inventory "turn," a higher inventory turnover rate indicates a higher return on dollars invested in inventory. Too low an inventory turnover in a firm could indicate unnecessary dollars tied up in slow-moving inventory. Turnover could also be too high, indicting the possibility of excessive expenses of reordering in small lots or of out-of-stock conditions and lost sales.

As with other turnover measures, inventory turnover can only be evaluated against industry standards or prior years' performance. Overall inventory turnover in a supermar-

---

[2] Terms of net 60 days could lead to this result.

[3] In situations where the proportion of cash sales are material and yet receivables turnover has been calculated using total net sales (both cash sales and credit sales) as the numerator, the formula given for average days' receivables can yield misleading results. In such situations the average days' receivables formula should be modified to:

$$\text{Average Days' Receivables} = \frac{365}{\text{Receivables Turnover*}} \quad X \quad \frac{\text{Net Credit Sales}}{\text{Total Net Sales}}$$
* Calculated Using Total Net Sales

ket could be 20 or more times per year after averaging very rapid turnover of produce and dairy products with lower turnover of packaged and canned goods. A manufacturer of giant hydroelectric turbines and other heavy equipment would be fortunate to "turn" once a year.

$$\text{Number of Average Days' Sales in Inventory} = \frac{365}{\text{Inventory Turnover}}$$

Inventory turnover can also be expressed in terms of **average days' sales in inventory.** This measure is calculated by dividing 365 by inventory turnover. Columbia's 88 days indicates that average inventory during the year amounted to 88 days' sales. The smaller the number of days' sales of inventory on hand, the smaller the investment committed to inventory, and the higher the turnover.

Although similar to the asset turnover ratio, a more specific ratio is the **property and equipment turnover.** This ratio is an indicator of the efficiency of use of capacity assets, and is determined by dividing sales of the year by the average book value of property and equipment in use during the year.

$$\text{Property, Plant and Equipment Turnover (times)} = \frac{\text{Net Sales}}{\text{Average Net Property Plant and Equipment}}$$

For Columbia, property, plant and equipment turnover was 4.59 times for 19X1, indicating that approximately $4.59 in sales were generated for each average dollar invested in property, plant and equipment. This same turnover ratio may also be used as an indicator of capacity utilization. In years where a significant excess capacity existed, this ratio would be lower than when the firm was operating at nearer full capacity.

Return on Investment (ROI)

An overall measurement of efficient asset usage relates to the ultimate objective of the firm. Companies are in business to earn the maximum return on the owners' investment, subject to legal and social constraints. Since assets are the sole source of earnings, an overall measure is **return on investment** or total assets. Return on investment is calculated by dividing EBIT[4] by average total assets.

$$\text{Return on Investment (ROI)} = \frac{\text{EBIT}}{\text{Average Total Assets}}$$

---

[4] Return on investment is derived from two ratios, the asset turnover and profit margin on sales where investment is defined as Total Assets and profit as either net income or EBIT.

$$\text{ROI} = \frac{\text{Sales}}{\text{Investment}} \times \frac{\text{Profit}}{\text{Sales}} = \frac{\text{Profit}}{\text{Investment}}$$

Some analysts use net income rather than EBIT and ending total assets rather than average total assets. This is less precise. Assets generate earnings regardless of who supplied the assets (creditor or owners) and regardless of how these overall "earnings" are divided among governments (taxes), creditors (interest), and owners (profits). Therefore EBIT, which indicates earnings before various distributions is the appropriate amount to measure efficiency of asset usage. Obviously, the higher the return on investment, the greater will be the earnings potentially available for the owner. Columbia's 19X1 return on investment was 27 percent (rounded).[5]

What are your conclusions with respect to Columbia's efficient use of assets in 19X1 as compared with industry averages and with 19X0? Exhibit 13.3 includes the most recent (19X1) data as determined above. From Exhibit 13.3 you can see that Columbia is better than the industry average and has improved over the previous year in all measurements except for receivables. Receivables turnover is, however, only slightly below industry average and has improved over the previous year. Columbia appears to be managing its assets efficiently.

Exhibit 13.3   Data for Comparative Evalualtion including Most Recent Year

	Industry average 19X1	Columbia Corporation 19X1	Columbia Corporation 19X0
Current ratio	2.90 to 1	3.00 to 1	3.00 to 1
Quick ratio	1.80 to 1	2.00 to 1	2.00 to 1
Long-term debt ratio	0.300	0.123	0.123
Times interest earned	20 times	31 times	23 times
Asset turnover	1.40 times	1.48 times	1.42 times
Receivable turnover	9.00 times	8.72 times	8.27 times
Average days' receivables	41 days	42 days	44 days
Inventory turnover	3.80 times	4.13 times	4.05 times
Average days' sales in inventory	96 days	88 days	90 days
Property and equipment turnover	4.50 times	4.59 times	4.08 times
Return on investment	25%	27%	26%

Efficient Financial Management

Occasionally a business may be unsuccessful even with expert operating management. Many business managers are skilled in operating but naive when it come to proper financial management. As cited in earlier chapters, a firm with profitable operations can grow too fast and possibly become insolvent. Such a failure is the result of improper (or poor) financial management.

5   $$\frac{\$152,000 + \$5,000}{1/2 \ (\$565,000 + \$580,000)} = 27.42\%$$

In addition to maintaining adequate solvency and liquidity, financial management involves taking advantage of optimal **financial leverage or trading on equity**. Trading on equity can be understood as making money on other people's money. Since interest is tax-deductible, the "after-tax cost" of debt financing may be only five to seven percent. If the funds borrowed can be used to generated EBIT of 27 percent, as in the Columbia example, these earnings, after provision for interest and taxes, are available to the owners. The benefits of trading on equity are a reward to the owner for assuming the risks of debt. Remember that interest is usually payable at least annually, and principal is payable at maturity regardless whether EBIT is positive or negative. If debt obligations cannot be met, the firm may be liquidated and the owners could lose their entire investment.

In a particular line of business or industry, it is therefore not only possible for a firm to have too much debt but also to have too little debt. The proportion of debt financing is also referred to as financial leverage.[6] A firm with too little financial leverage is not taking adequate advantage of trading on equity. The determination of optimal financial leverage for a given firm is a responsibility of financial management and is not covered in this text. It is cited here so that you may understand that, in financial statement analysis, you must also be concerned about excessive conservatism in financing, that is, too little debt.

Measures of Owner Return

As cited previously, return to the owners of a business is the final result of good operating, financial, and tax management. Good operating management results in optimal EBIT. Good tax management ensures minimal taxes. Efficient financial management ensures optimal leverage and therefore optimal interest with respect to achievable EBIT. The combined result is the ultimate objective of the owner, optimal return on the owner's investment.

In Chapter 10 you were introduced to several measures of ownership interest and return. Recall that the amount of "owners" investment in a corporation is normally identified as the residual share of total assets assigned to the common stockholders. If preferred shareholders exist, even though they are legally owners rather than creditors, computations of book value of owners' investment, book value per share of stock, is based on the residual income after preferred claims.

Simple EPS is determined as net income available to common stockholders, net income less the preferred dividend, divided by the weighted average number of common shares outstanding during the year (period):

$$\text{Simple EPS} = \frac{\text{Net income–Preferred dividend}}{\text{Weighted-average Common Shares Outstanding}}$$

---

[6] Leverage involves not only optimal debt, but often an optimal mix of debt, preferred stock, and common stock.

For Columbia, 19X1 EPS was $5.64 ($91,000 less $12,000, divided by 14,000 shares) and this amount is included on the income statement (see Exhibit 13.1)

Weighted average was not calculated for Columbia Corporation for 19X1 since the balance of shares of stock did not change during the year. The weighted average number of shares of stock can be calculated in two ways. The first method recognizes the number of shares outstanding during each portion of the year (note the portions of the year add to a full year) and multiplies those shares times the weighting, or portion of the year. If 6,000 shares of stock were issued by Columbia Corporation on April 1, 19X2, Columbia's weighted average number of shares outstanding for 19X2 would be 18,500 shares as calculated below.

Shares Balance	x	Month/ Year	=	Weighted
14,000	x	3/12	=	3,500
20,000	x	9/12	=	15,000
		12/12		18,500

The alternative method for determining weighted average calculates a weighting for individual blocks of shares. The 14,000 shares outstanding at the beginning of 19X2 were outstanding all year while the 6,000 shares issued on April 1 were outstanding for only 9 months. Note that the weighted average number of shares is the same regardless of the method used.

Balance	x	Month/ Year	=	Weighted
14,000	x	12/12	=	14,000
6,000	x	9/12	=	4,500
20,000				18,500

GAAP also require disclosure of EPS before the effect of extraordinary items or discontinued operations. For Columbia in 19X1, there was no difference, but note in Exhibit 13.1 how misleading the $0.71 19X0 EPS figure could be by itself.

For corporations with substantial amounts of convertible debentures or convertible preferred stock outstanding, the potential dilution of EPS upon conversion could be significant. Many more stock shares could be outstanding without a proportionate increase in earnings. Where the potential dilution is significant (defined as more than three percent) GAAP prohibit the disclosure of simple EPS, as being potentially misleading. Instead, accountants will report two earnings amounts, each before and after effects of extraordinary items. These amounts are known as primary earnings per share and fully diluted earning per share.

Fully diluted EPS assumes that all rights, options, warrants, and conversion privileges have been exercised. It discloses the worst that could happen to EPS. Primary EPS is difficult to compute and is beyond the scope of this text. It will be equal to or greater than fully diluted EPS. It is calculated on the basis of an assumption that only certain options and debt conversions with a high probability of occurring will take place. Primary EPS discloses the dilution that probably will occur.

In evaluating the firm's performance for all common stockholders instead of on a per-share basis, earnings available for the common stockholders are compared to the average book value of the common stock.

$$\text{Return on Common Equity} = \frac{\text{Net Income} - \text{Preferred Dividend}}{\text{Average Common Equity}}$$

Recall, from Chapter 10, that the book value of the common stock is total stockholders' equity less all preferred claims.[7] The average would be one-half the sum of the beginning and ending amounts for the period.

If industry average return were 26 percent, calculate Columbia's 19X1 return, and evaluate it with respect to the industry. Columbia's return on common equity of 28 percent (rounded) compares very favorably with the industry average.

The market price of the common stock is influenced by EPS and anticipated future earnings. Analysts often view market price in terms of EPS. The ratio is called the price/earnings ratio.

$$\text{Price/Earnings (P/E) Ratio} = \frac{\text{Market price per share}}{\text{Earnings per share}}$$

Columbia would be said to be selling at approximately "ten times earnings" assuming the common stock market price was $55 on 12/31/X1.

An important measure to the individual investor is the potential return on his or her investment as measured by the current market price per share.

Since the preferred dividend is fixed in amount, even if not paid each year, a potential preferred stock investor can simply determine the potential return by dividing the preferred dividend by the market price of the preferred. In the Columbia example, assuming that the current market price of the preferred was $80 per share, the potential return on investment would be 15 percent since the preferred dividend is $12 per share.

$$\text{Preferred Dividend Yield} = \frac{\text{Annual Preferred Dividend Per Share}}{\text{Market Price Per Share}}$$

---

[7] Preferred claims in liquidation are contractual, unique to each firm, and may include arrearage if the preferred is cumulative. For simplication in the Columbia example it is assumed that the preferred stock is noncumulative and that the claim in liquidation is equal to the original preferred stock contribution.

To evaluate **dividend yield** on common stock, since common dividends are not fixed in amount, you will have to determine if a dividend pattern exists and compare the expected dividend to the current market price of the common. Columbia's common dividend yield would be approximately 10 percent (($75,000 ÷ 14,000) ÷ $55).

$$\textbf{Common Dividend Yield} = \frac{\textbf{Annual Common Dividend Per Share}}{\textbf{Market Price Per Share}}$$

Should They Buy Columbia's Stock?

To review and apply the tools of analysis so far presented, consider whether John Chandler or Prudence Parkinson should acquire any of Columbia's stock assuming current prices are $80 per share for the preferred and $55 per share for the common. Exhibit 13.3 indicated that for the past several years Columbia's ratios and return equalled or exceeded industry average (except for receivables which were very close). Columbia's recent Statement of Cash Flow indicates a high annual dividend payout—over 70 percent of cash from operating activities each year.

Since John is primarily concerned with income security he might consider buying Columbia's preferred stock with a dividend yield of 15 percent. He would make this decision in light of other alternative investment opportunities available of similar risk and might be advised to delay an investment in Columbia for other reasons (see below).

Prudence, on the other hand, would only be interested in Columbia's common stock if at all. The current year's common dividend of $5.36 per share (rounded) would provide a dividend yield of approximately 10 percent. However, dividend yield is not her primary objective, and there is little evidence of Columbia being a spectacular growth company.

Footnote (C) in Exhibit 13.1 indicates that John should wait until the lawsuit is resolved. The firm has already lost its case in the first trial. It is appealing the decision. If it loses the appeal, the $250,000 of awarded damages could drastically alter the firm's financial picture and its prospects.

In analyzing financial statements, you should always study the statement footnotes carefully. Footnotes will disclose material contingent liabilities and purchase commitments. Footnotes will also inform you of the firm's measurement elections for inventory (LIFO vs FIFO) and depreciation (accelerated vs. straight-line). Recall, from Chapters 8 and 9, how differences in accounting methods can invalidate simple direct comparison between firms using different measurement systems.

Finally, in analyzing financial statements, remember that they contain only some of the information relevant to an investment decision. Important factors mentioned earlier in this chapter, such as the future markets for the firm's products or services, and the overall economic picture, must be evaluated from separate information.

Is My Manager Doing a Good Job?

In Chapter 1 you learned that financial statement information is of interest to many people other than potential preferred and common stockholders. Statement analysis of operations is of particular interest to managers and absentee owners such as Jack Jordan. Recall that Jack is interested in monitoring the performance of the resident manager of his motel.

Jack wants to analyze the 19X3 income statement. He also has the average motel guidelines statement prepared for a typical firm by the motel association of which he is a member. He is comparing these two statements with earlier years' statements for his motel. Exhibit 13.4 gives the representative income data for 19X3 from the trade association and the actual data for Jack's motel. It also includes the motel's income statements for the years 19X2 and 19X1.

In earlier chapters, you learned that converting amounts to percentages aided in the comparison of similar data. Exhibit 13.4 also includes percentages for each reported item. Sales each year is expressed as a percentage change over the prior year (horizontal analysis as first discussed in Chapter 6). All other items are given as a percent of the current year's sales (vertical analysis as discussed in Chapter 6). Study Exhibit 13.4 carefully. If you were Jack Jordan, which items would you note for discussion with your manager assuming that differences of greater than one percent were potentially significant?

Exhibit 13.4

JACK'S MOTEL INCOME STATEMENTS
for Years Ending 12/31/X1, 12/31/X2, and 12/31/X3
and Trade Association 19X3 Data
($ in thousands)

	Trade assoc.		Jack's Motel					
	19X3		19X3		19X2		19X1	
Room Rentals	$960	+13%	$920	+ 5%	$880	+16%	$760	+14%
Wages and Salaries	298	31%	312	34%	299	34%	251	33%
Supplies	77	8%	83	9%	70	8%	68	9%
Laundry	106	11%	56	6%	70	8%	76	10%
Utilities	86	9%	83	9%	79	9%	68	9%
Insurance	77	8%	73	8%	70	8%	61	8%
Office supplies	10	1%	10	1%	9	1%	7	1%
Landscaping	19	2%	18	2%	18	2%	15	2%
Pool maintenance	9	1%	10	1%	9	1%	7	1%
Interest	57	6%	56	6%	53	6%	46	6%
Depreciation	96	10%	101	11%	97	11%	83	11%
General maintenance	67	7%	36	4%	44	5%	38	5%
Restaurant revenue[a]	115	12%	56	6%	79	9%	91	12%
Operating income	$173	18%	$138	15%	$141	16%	$131	17%

[a] Restaurant and bar operation leased to concessionaire for a base rental plus a percentage of gross revenue.

Analyzing Operating Performance

Earlier in this chapter you learned that return on assets and various asset turnovers were some of the measures of the efficiency of operating management. Detailed analysis of the income statement provides further information on the operating management of the business. To maximize return on investment, operating management strives to maximize revenues and to control costs. Exhibit 13.4 reveals to Jack that his manager is apparently doing an excellent job of cost control in most areas. This judgment is based both upon results reported for the past three years and upon a comparison with the trade association's data. The only expense categories requiring further investigation would appear to be wages and salaries, laundry, and general maintenance since they differ from industry averages by more than one percent.

Jack is more concerned about operating income than specific expense items. His operating income, as a percent of sales, is steadily declining and is substantially below the industry average—3 percent (or $27,600) under average. Jack's manager may not be doing as good a job at generating revenues as he is in controlling costs. Both revenue items are prime candidates for further investigation. Restaurant revenue is dropping sharply. If it were at industry average, it alone would bring in $56,000 more profit, and would result in Jack's bottom line being above industry average.

Also note that, in 19X3, sales increased only 5 percent over the prior year. The industry average increase was 13 percent. If sales had increased 13 percent, there would be an additional $74,000 of sales revenue. And if the motel were running at the industry average of 18 percent operating income, this would have meant $13,320 in additional profit.

Possibly Interrelated Factors

Although income statement analysis can only highlight items for further investigation, it is important that Jack also look for possible interrelationships among trouble spots. Let us review the items pinpointed by Exhibit 13.4:

- Sales growth has fallen off by more than 50 percent;
- Bar and restaurant revenues have fallen 50 percent in the past three years despite an overall 21 percent increase in room rentals;
- Laundering expenses have dropped to almost half of the industry average in the past three years;
- General maintenance expense is declining, and is significantly below industry average; and
- Wages and salaries are slightly higher than industry average.

Even though you certainly cannot draw firm conclusions without further investigation, you can see possible interrelationships in these factors that might merit separate investigation. The higher wages and salaries do not appear related to the other items. They may simply reflect the fact that Jack has a hired general manager, whereas most trade association motels have owner-managers.

Cost cutting and cost control can go too far. It is possible that the significant "savings" in laundry and general maintenance are turning away customers. Sheets and towels with holes, plumbing and doors that do not work, and peeling paint are not conducive to attracting or holding guests. Jack Jordan might be well advised to make one of his periodic visits soon.

Income Statement Ratios (Vertical Analysis)

You can see the advantage of converting income statement line items to percentages of sales, for analysis purposes. Two particular items, when converted to percentages, are commonly referred to with specific titles. The **gross profit ratio** is merely a firm's gross profit or gross margin expressed as a percent of sales. A change of difference in gross profit ratio can signal:

- Different selling prices—raised prices or significant discounting; and/or

- Different product costs, which may or may not indicate different quality.

The **operating ratio** is simply the firm's net income expressed as a percent of sales. It indicates the final result of management's profit-directed activities. Comparisons of operating ratios between two firms can be distorted by differing financial leverage patterns, different current tax situations, or even extraordinary items.

As an extreme example, consider two firms with the following abbreviated income statements ($ in thousands):

	Firm A	Firm B
Sales	$900	$950
Operating expenses (except for interest)	747	797
Interest expense	3	14
Income from operations before taxes	$150	$139
Provision for taxes	38	56
Income from operations	$112	$ 83
Extraordinary gain	40	0
Extraordinary loss	0	60
Net income	$152	$ 23
Operating ratio	16.9%	2.4%

Firm A has practically no debt (leverage) as indicated by lower interest expense, lower proportionate taxes, and an extraordinary gain. Firm B has significantly higher debt and interest, a higher tax rate, and a large extraordinary loss. A simple comparison of operating ratios indicates that Firm A is performing seven times as well as Firm B. Try calculating EBIT for both firms. Most analysts will also determine EBIT and compare the ratio or percentage of EBIT to sales. EBIT to sales is a better indicator of repeatable operating performance. In the foregoing example, both firms have a similar EBIT to sales of 16 and 17 percent.

Items Bypassing the Income Statement

There are two types of events, in addition to owner transactions and donations, which bypass the income statement. They affect owners' equity directly and are not included in the determination of net income.

Both of these bypassing events reflect adjustments. One type first discussed in Chapter 6 is known as a **prior period adjustment**. When an event that clearly should have been recognized in prior years is discovered to have been omitted from the statements, GAAP provide for direct adjustment to owner's capital or retained earnings. GAAP provide specific tests before an item can be treated as a prior period adjustment.[8] Otherwise, income could be manipulated through arbitrarily treating certain items as past adjustments.

The second bypassing adjustment involves temporary revaluations of long-term investments. Recall, from Chapter 11, that a permanent loss of market or recoverable value will be recorded as a write-down of the asset and an expense on the income statement. Recall, where a decline in value is believed to be temporary, the write-down is not reflected in net income. Instead a contra-equity account is set up within owners' equity to carry the balancing adjustment. Subsequent recovery of the market or recoverable value of investments, up to but not above original cost, would result in a write-up of the asset, and a corresponding decrease or elimination of the investments revaluation account.

Except for temporary revaluation of investments, prior period adjustments, owner transactions (including treasury stock transactions), donations and foreign currency translation adjustments, all events affecting owners' equity will be reported as revenue, expense, gain, or loss, on the income statement.[9] The income statement primarily is a report on the operating management of the business. Financial management activities are reported on the Statement of Cash Flows.

How Good is This Supplier's Financial Management?

The fourth and final analyst viewpoint illustrated in this chapter is that of Becky Silverman, a purchasing agent for a large manufacturer. Her firm has just been awarded a con-

---

[8] An item must be clearly identifiable with activities of a specific prior year and completed then and not the result of subsequent events. Further, it must not be something essentially controlled by management, and it must not have been susceptible to reasonable estimation at the time.

[9] Foreign currency translation adjustments are reported in a contra-equity account as are temporary gains and losses on investments.

tract for limited production of a new item. There's a very good change that a much larger order will follow within a few months. Becky is responsible for procuring a critical component part that is to be made by one or more outside suppliers. She has obtained bids from the Giant Corporation and the Little Company. Little's bid is substantially lower, and Becky would like to give them the order.

Before committing to the Little Company, Becky wishes to evaluate the financial management activities of this supplier. Little can readily handle the first small order, but if the expected larger order comes through, Little would be required to expand its capacity. Becky is seeking assurance that the Little Company management could cope with the expected larger order. Could they recognize the need for, and obtain, necessary new capital? Would they maintain solvency during rapid expansion, so that there would be no risk that their creditors might interfere with production?

Exhibit 13.5 includes Statement of Cash Flows for the Little Company over the past three years, plus some additional selective information. Study this exhibit. See whether you can assist Becky in answering the following questions:

1. Has the potential supplier maintained adequate solvency, especially during periods of expanding volume? Has it been increasing cash to accompany increased volume? Or has it been operating with more limited solvency?

2. Has the potential supplier maintained desirable liquidity, especially during periods of expansion?

3. Has the potential supplier been reasonably profitable over the past few years? Little's industry standard for return on investment is 26 percent. Profitability is generally essential if new owners' equity capital is to be raised for expansion.

4. Has Little a regular practice of paying out in dividends a certain proportion of each year's earnings? What proportion of earnings are regularly retained and reinvested?

5. Has Little been expanding its capacity assets, or at least replacing assets as they have worn out?

6. Has the firm been maintaining a good proportion between debt and owners' equity as part of raising new capital? The optimal long-term debt ratio in Little's industry is 0.300.

7. Does the potential supplier currently generate sufficient cash for operating activities to assist significantly in the financing of new expansion? Becky estimates that the larger follow-up order would require Little to obtain $350,000 of additional resources for investment in cash and other assets.

Solvency

The Little Company has apparently managed to maintain solvency very well, especially during rapid growth. Over the past two years, sales volume has increased 89 percent and total assets have grown 80 percent. During this period, the current ratio has been held at 2.5 to 1 or above. Approximately one-third of new asset investment has been in the form of new net working capital.

Debt Capacity

The Little company, again during a period of rapid growth, has managed to maintain more than adequate debt capacity. If anything, the firm has been overly cautious in maintaining a 0.254 debt ratio when its industry's optimum is 0.3. Little could immediately raise $70,000 in new long-term debt, and still be within the industry standard.[10]

Exhibit 13.5

LITTLE COMPANY
Statements of Cash Flows and Selected Data
($ in thousands)

	X3	X2	X1
Cash from Operating Activities:			
Net Income	$171	$119	$85
Depreciation and Amortization	50	45	30
Increase Accounts Receivable, Inventory	(120)	(115)	(90)
Increase Current Payables	55	40	40
Cash from Operating Activities	$166	$89	$65
Investing Activities			
Proceeds in Sale of Plant, Property, and Equipment	5	10	5
Purchase of Plant, Property, and Equipment	(170)	(170)	(120)
Financing Activities			
Proceeds in New Debt	60	140	0
Payments on Debt Principal	(10)	(20)	(10)
Proceeds New Stock Issues	37	19	104
Cash Dividends	(68)	(48)	(34)
Changes in Cash	$20	$20	$10
Beginning Cash	95	75	65
Ending Cash	$105	$95	$75
Additional Selected Data:			
Current ratio	2.60	2.50	3.00
Long-term debt ratio	.254	.239	.100
Total assets	$900	$700	$500
Sales	$845	$595	$448
Sales growth	42%	33%	25%
EBIT	$261	$196	$135
Total long-term debt	$200	$140	$ 30
Total stockholders' equity	$844	$644	$444

---

[10] To determine this amount: If long-term debt of 0.3 is desirable, then owners' equity must be 0.7; let X equal total long-term debt and owners' equity; in thousands, present owners' equity of $630 equals 0.7 X; X equals $900; optimal long-term debt equals $900 times 0.3 equals $270; $270 minus present long-term debt of $200 equals $70 of "available" debt capacity.

Profitability

Little has been quite profitable. Return on investment has been 30 percent, 33 percent, and 33 percent, in 19X1, 19X2, and 19X3, respectively. This is well above industry averages. Return on owners' equity has been an exceptional 22 percent, 27 percent, and 31 percent, over these same three years.

Dividend Policy

Little appears to have an established policy of distributing 40 percent of earnings as dividends. This practice, coupled with high earnings (see above), should make it relatively simple for the firm to sell more stock if capital is required for expansion.

Asset Replacement/Expansion

When a firm's Statement of Cash Flows indicates net property, plant, and equipment acquisition is equal to or greater than annual depreciation, the firm is probably at least regularly replacing capital assets as they wear out or become obsolescent.[11] Little is apparently replacing its property plant and equipment as they expire. It appears also that capacity is being significantly expanded. Net acquisitions exceeded annual depreciation and amortization by $85,000, $115,000, and $115,000 over the past three years.

Maintenance of Optimal Capital Structure

Little's financial managers appear to be doing an excellent job of maintaining a desirable capital structure or balance of debt to owners' equity. In 19X1, new long-term capital of $155,000 was acquired, of which $51,000 was the result of retained earnings—$85,000 net income less $34,000 of dividends. The remaining $104,000 came from the sale of new stock.

In 19X2 and 19X3, new long-term capital was acquired:

	Reinvested earnings	Stock sale	New net debt	Total
19X2	$ 71	$19	$120	$210
19X3	103	37	50	190

Note that, in 19X2, substantially more new debt brought the debt ratio form 0.100 to 0.239. In 19X3 the proportion of new debt and new stock was controlled so that the debt

---

[11] If inflation has resulted in a significant increase in replacement costs, or if most depreciation represents the final years' charges under an accelerated method, then such a conclusion may not be accurate.

ratio was maintained at 0.254. It appears the firm has "targeted" this more conservative leverage proportion. Given its apparent target, the firm appears to be managing its financial affairs very well.

Owners' Commitment

The Little Company's owners (stockholders) have been making a continuing significant commitment of resources to the firm in the form of both reinvested earnings and new stock. These investments have been:

	19X3	19X2	19X1
Reported income	$171,000	$119,000	$85,000
Less dividends	68,000	48,000	34,000
Income reinvested	$103,000	$ 71,000	$51,000
Additional (stock) investment	37,000	19,000	104,000
Total additional owner investment	$140,000	$ 90,000	$155,000

Potential for Raising Additional Capital

Becky Silverman is concerned whether Little could raise an additional $350,000 of new capital should the larger order materialize. An analysis of Little's current situation and recent "track record" would indicate no real difficulty in the firm's obtaining this capital. $166,000 is currently being generated from operations. As mentioned above, the company could take on $70,000 of new debt and still be at the optimal debt-equity mix. The remaining $114,000 should be readily obtainable from the sale of stock or a mix of debt and stock.

Furthermore, Little's management has demonstrated the ability to cope with rapid expansion without impairing solvency. Little's financial ability to handle the potential large forthcoming order should not be a major concern for Becky. She should, of course, satisfy herself with respect to other nonfinancial concerns that are not within the scope of this book. Such significant nonfinancial considerations could include the availability of adequate additional raw materials, skilled labor, and special tools, which might prove to be in short supply even if the capital were available to pay for them.

The Little Company example has been introduced to demonstrate the information content of financial statements and especially the Statement of Cash Flows. All the foregoing findings and conclusions concerning the Little Company were derived from the data appearing in Exhibit 13.5.

Limitations of Financial Statement Analysis

In concluding this discussion of statement analysis, it is important to review and emphasize inherent limitations. You should already be aware of the following:

1. In any investment decision, qualitative information not measured and reported by accountants can be very significant. Examples would include, but not be limited to:

    a) The quality of the firm's management and work force, and the selection and training programs needed to ensure maintenance or improvement of this quality;

    b) The quality of its labor relations and its prospects for continued operation at competitive labor costs;

    c) The quality of its products or services and of research directed towards new and improved products in a rapidly changing world; and

    d) The environment of the firm, including overall economic forecasts, industry forecasts, and the future share of the market that the firm might reasonably anticipate.

2. It may prove difficult to make comparisons of data between or among different firms using different accounting methods. Also contributing to comparison difficulties is the diversification of firms into different markets and industries. With two firms involved in different combinations of activities, except for overall return on owners' investment, comparison of other data becomes relatively meaningless.

Financial statement analysis, therefore, may have limited value except for trend analysis for the same firm consistently applying the same accounting methods. Even in these situations, you should remain constantly aware that ratio analysis and the underlying data refer to history. An extrapolation of past data into a forecast has all the limitations of any prediction.

The foregoing cautions are not intended to lead to a conclusion that statement analysis is futile. Some analysis is probably better than none. You should merely remember that statement analysis can provide information which at best is only a starting point for decision analysis.

Chapter Overview

Based upon the information contained in this chapter, you should be able to analyze a firm's financial statements and arrive at tentative conclusions and recommendations concerning the firm's:

- Solvency and debt capacity, employing and correctly interpreting its current, quick, and long-term debt ratios;
- Adequate but not excessive proportion of debt, employing and correctly interpreting long-term debt and times interest earned ratios;
- Efficiency of asset usage, employing and correctly interpreting: asset turnover; receivables turnover or average days' receivable; inventory turnover or average days' sales in inventory; property and equipment turnover; and return on investment;
- Degree of trading on equity and amount of financial leverage employed, assuming no preferred stock;
- Adequacy of return on owners' investment, relative to the return on common equity;
- Operating performance through use of income statement percentages particularly the gross profit ratio, the operating ratio, and EBIT to sales; and
- Financial management activities as disclosed by the Statement of Cash Flows.

You should also be able to:

- Calculate the return on an individual shareholder's investment in terms of simple EPS and dividends per share;
- Explain the significance of primary and fully diluted EPS and when they are reported;
- Describe those events or adjustments which change the balance of owners' equity but which are not included on the income statement as parts of net income; and
- Describe and explain some of the significant limitations of financial statement analysis.

New Vocabulary and Concepts

Asset turnover	Inventory turnover
Average days' receivables	Operating ratio
Average days' sales in inventory	Prior period adjustment
Dividend yield	Property and equipment turnover
EBIT	Receivables turnover
Financial leverage/trading on equity	Return on investment
Fully diluted EPS	Simple EPS
Gross profit ratio	Times interests earned

Review Questions

1. (a) What is EBIT (b) Explain, with examples, why EBIT may be a more useful earnings measure than net income for certain types of financial analysis.

2. For each of the items listed below, explain: (a) its meaning and usefulness; (b) how it is calculated; and (c) whether a higher or lower figure is considered favorable in most situations:
   - times interest earned
   - asset turnover
   - receivables turnover
   - average days' receivables
   - inventory turnover
   - average days' sales in inventory
   - property and equipment turnover
   - return on investment
   - return on common equity
   - simple earnings per share

3. What are the objectives of, and distinctions among, operating management, financial management, and tax management?

4. (a) What is financial leverage? (b) What is trading on equity? (3) How do they relate?

5. (a) What is the difference between return on owners' investment and return to a particular owner on his/her investment? (b) What causes this difference?

6. (a) What are the purposes of reporting primary and fully diluted earnings per share? (b) When would they replace simple EPS on the income statement? (c) Generally what is the difference in the meaning of primary and fully diluted EPS?

7. How can an income statement "signal" items that are probably adequately controlled and require no immediate further investigation? Give examples.

8. How can an income statement "signal" items that may be unsatisfactory and which require further investigation? Give examples.

9. (a) What is the gross profit ratio? (b) How is it calculated? (c) What are the possible factors that could lead to differences in gross profit ratios in the same firm for different periods? (d) Differences between firms in different industries?

10. What is the operating ratio and what is its significance?

11. How does the statement of cash flows, in conjunction with the balance sheet, provide information relating to recent changes in the firm's solvency? debt capacity? financial leverage?

12. (a) How can you tell from the statement of cash flows, or preferably from several years' statements, whether a firm is replacing its capacity assets as they wear out or become obsolete? (b) How can you tell whether it is expanding its capacity?

13. What is the source of cash for investment in new or replacement assets other than sale of existing assets, new debt, or additional owner investment from outside of the business?

14. How can you tell from the statement of cash flows, or preferably from several years' statements, whether the firm's owners are significantly committing capital for the future?

Mini-Cases and Questions for Discussion

MC 13.1   At a recent conference of financial executives, one speaker stated: Most people really don't appreciate the value of good financial management. A good financial manager can take only average results from the operating management and transform them to very good results for the common stockholder. An absence of financial management can lead adequately operating management into insolvency. Is this merely a meaningless self-serving declaration, or does it essentially represent the truth? Discuss.

MC 13.2   Two financial analysts are having a disagreement. One says, "I don't know why you don't use net income to average total assets as the measure of efficient asset usage. After all, net income is the final result. It represents what really happened. How can you ignore interest, taxes, and extraordinary items? They are real and they happen."

The second analyst replies, "That isn't the point. Net income represents the combined result of several different types of management, government action, and even acts of God. By using EBIT, I can somewhat pinpoint responsibility to operating management."

Who is correct? Discuss.

MC 13.3   Linda Drake is a militant looking for a cause. She has just learned about trading on equity and is bursting with righteous indignation. "This is a perfect example of capitalist exploitation," she shouts. "Making money on other people's money is a real rip-off. It is completely unfair!"

You realize that many corporations' bonds and shares of preferred stock are held by banks, insurance companies, and pension funds. You also know that common stock in the same corporations is also held by aged widows. Are these aged widows really "ripping off" big banks and insurance companies? What are the factors that make creditors and preferred stockholders content to allow common stockholders to make money on their money? Discuss.

MC 13.4   Two financial analysts are in disagreement. John maintains that the income statement of a firm or, especially a series of annual statements, provide the best measure of a firm's performance. Harry takes exception to this. He believes net income to be a relatively meaningless figure, and prefers to rely on cash from operating activities as reported on the statement of cash flows. Harry points out that net income includes very arbitrary estimates of such things as depreciation and amortization, and therefore is not a reliable performance indicator.

Who do you think is right? Discuss.

MC 13.5   Mary is a commercial loan officer with a local bank. She believes a series of statements of cash flows, together with a projected (or pro forma) statement of cash flows, provide the best information when she is evaluating a request for a short-to-medium-term—one to five years—commercial loan. She is concerned with an applicant's ability to repay, without difficulty, any loan, with interest. She feels that in many cases net income understates the firm's debt-repayment capacity. Do you agree with Mary? Why? Discuss.

MC 13.6   Many credit analysts do not place much reliance on the times interest earned figure. They reason that a high figure does not necessarily indicate debt safety, especially in the short-run. They also know that a very low figure does not necessarily indicate inadequate cash flow to meet interest obligations. Discuss.

MC 13.7   Is it possible that the various turnovers in a firm—asset, receivables, and inventory—could be **too** high? Specifically, could there be any reason why a retailer might be content with—and even prefer—a relatively low receivables turnover? Are major retailers really retailers, or could they be considered financial institutions? Discuss.

Essential Problems

EP 13.1   Exhibit 13.6 includes the recent balance sheets and income statements for the Francine Corporation. For this company, calculate the following:

a) Current ratio as of 12/31/X1,

b) Quick ratio as of 12/31/X1,

c) Long-term debt ratio as of 12/31/X1,

d) Times interest earned during 19X1.

EP 13.2   Exhibit 13.7 includes the recent balance sheets and income statements for the Naomi Corporation. Calculate the four items required in EP 13.1, for the Naomi Corporation.

EP 13.3   Determine the following data for 19X1 for the Francine Corporation:

a) Asset turnover,

b) Receivables turnover (assume all sales are on account),

c) Average days' receivables (based on 365-day period),

d) Inventory turnover,

e) Average days' sales in inventory (based on 365-day period),

f) Property and equipment turnover,

g) Return on investment.

EP 13.4   Determine the six items of information required in **EP 13.3**, for the Naomi Corporation (Exhibit 13.7).

EP 13.5   Determine the following items for 19X1 for the Francine Corporation (Exhibit 13.6).

a) Return on total stockholders' equity,

b) Return on common equity.

EP 13.6   Determine the following items for 19X1 for the Naomi Corporation (Exhibit 13.7).

a) Return on total stockholders' equity,

b) Return on common equity.

EP 13.7   Assume that the Francine Corporation (Exhibit 13.6) regularly paid out 40 percent of its net income in dividends. Also assume that you could purchase Francine common stock on the open market for $60 per share. Calculate, for 19X1, the following:

a) Simple earnings per share,

b) Dividends per share,

c) Earnings yield,

d) Dividend yield.

EP 13.8   Assume that the Naomi Corporation (Exhibit 13.7) regularly paid out 60 percent of net income in dividends, and that the common stock's market price was $80 per share. Calculate, for the Naomi Corporation for 19X1, the following:

a) Simple earnings per share,

b) Dividends per share,

c) Earnings yield,

d) Dividend yield.

Exhibit 13.6

FRANCINE CORPORATION
Balance Sheets as of 12/31/X0 and 12/31/X1 and
Income Statement for 19X1
($ in thousands)

	12/31/X1	12/31/X0
Assets		
Cash	$ 50	$ 40
Marketable securities	60	90
Accounts receivable (net)	210	190
Inventory	280	260
Other current assets	25	30
Total Current Assets	$ 625	$610
Investments	75	75
Equipment	398	300
Less accumulated depreciation	(180)	(180)
Property under capital lease	95	105
Total Assets	$1,013	$910
Equities		
Accounts payable	$ 140	$120
Other current liabilities	60	50
Total Current Liabilities	$ 200	$170
Noncurrent notes payable	105	115
Less discount	(10)	(15)
Total Liabilities	$ 295	$270
Preferred stock ($100 par 14%) [1]	100	100
Common stock ($10 par) [2]	300	300
Additional paid-in capital [3]	60	60
Retained earnings [4]	258	180
Total Equities	$1,013	$910
Income Statement		
Sales	$1,800	
Cost of goods sold	1,080	
Gross profit	$ 720	
Interest	13	
Depreciation on equipment	30	
Amortization on capital lease	10	
Other operating expenses	451	
Operating income before taxes	$ 216	
Income taxes	8	
Net Income	$ 130	

1. $120 per share liquidation claim.
2. Common shares outstanding: 30,000 shares, both years.
3. All on common stock.
4. Dividends declared and paid $52

Exhibit 13.7

NAOMI CORPORATION

Balance Sheets as of 12/31/X0 and 12/31/X1 and
Income Statement for 19X1
($ in thousands)

	12/31/X1	12/31/X0
Assets		
Cash	$ 30	$ 40
Marketable securities	80	10
Accounts receivable (net)	465	451
Inventory	325	313
Other current assets	40	30
Total Current Assets	$ 940	$844
Land	120	90
Plant and equipment	544	400
Accumulated depreciation	(270)	(250)
Intangible assets	54	60
Total Assets	$1,388	$1,144
Equities		
Accounts payable	$ 207	$148
Other current liabilities	80	90
Total Current Liabilities	$ 287	$238
Bonds payable	250	200
Premium on bonds	18	20
Total Liabilities	$55	$458
Preferred stock ($100 par 12%) [1]	200	200
Common stock ($10 par) [2]	275	265
Additional paid-in capital [3]	105	35
Retained earnings [4]	253	186
Total Equities	$1,388	$1,144
Income Statement		
Sales	$2,200	
Cost of goods sold	1,275	
Gross profit	$ 925	
Interest	14	
Depreciation on fixed assets	50	
Amortization of intangible assets	6	
Other operating expenses	621	
Operating income before taxes	$ 234	
Income taxes	66	
Net Income	$ 168	

1. $110 per share liquidation claim.
2. Common shares outstanding:26,500 shares 12/31/X0 and 27,500 shares 12/31/X1.
3. All on common stock.
4. Dividends declared and paid $101

EP 13.9   Exhibit 13.8 contains income statements for the Sugarman Corporation for the years 19X0, 19X1, and 19X2.

a) Has the gross profit ratio improved?

b) Has the operating ratio improved?

c) If you were owner/manager of Sugarman, which items would you wish to investigate further and why?

Exhibit 13.8

SUGARMAN CORPORATION
Income Statements for the Years Ending
12/31/X0, 12/31/X1, 12/31/X2
($ in thousands)

	19X2	19X1	19X0
Sales	$780	$625	$500
Less cost of goods sold	359	275	210
Gross profit	$421	$350	$290
Other operating expenses			
Wages and salaries	101	75	65
Utilities	47	44	35
Depreciation	31	31	25
Insurance	23	25	20
Supplies	16	19	10
Maintenance	8	19	30
Interest	8	0	5
Operating income before taxes	$187	$137	$100
Income taxes	56	41	30
Net Income	$131	$96	$70

EP 13.10   Exhibit 13.9 contains income statements for the Tilamook Corporation for the years 19X0, 19X1, and 19X2.

a) What is happening to the gross profit ratio? What factors could be causing this change?

b) What is happening to the operating ratio? What factors appear to be responsible for the changing operating ratio?

c) If you were the owner-manager of Tilamook, which items would you wish to immediately investigate further, and why?

Exhibit 13.9

TILAMOOK CORPORATION
Income Statements for the Years Ending
12/31/X0, 12/31/X1, and 12/31/X2
($ in thousands)

	19X2	19X1	19X0
Sales	$505	$500	$400
Less cost of goods sold	222	230	196
Gross profit	$283	$270	$204
Other operating expenses			
Wages and salaries	60	65	48
Utilities	51	40	24
Rent	25	25	20
Insurance	15	15	8
Supplies	10	5	4
Maintenance	20	20	16
Interest	32	25	20
Operating income before taxes	$70	$75	$64
Income taxes	15	15	12
Net Income	$55	$60	$52

SP 13.11 Compare the income statements of the Sugarman and Tilamook Corporations (Exhibits 13.8 and 13.9) for the year 19X0. Assuming that both firms are in the same business:
  a) Which firm appears to be doing a better job?
  b) Which are the relatively favorable and unfavorable items in each firm?
  c) What differences in accounting methods might exist which could change your conclusions?

SP 13.12 Refer to SP 13.13 above. Answer the same questions for the years 19X1 and 19X2.

SP 13.13 Using the ratio calculated for the Franchine and Naomi Corporations (Exhibits 13.6 and 13.7) and using the information below, answer questions a through d.
  • Both firms are in the same industry;
  • Francine pays 40 percent of net income in dividends, and has a current market price of $60 per share;
  • Naomi pays 60 percent of net income in dividends, and the current market price of the stock is $80 per share;
  a) Explain which firm has the better performance.
  b) Which firm would be preferable for an individual first investing in the common stock today.
  c) Which firm would appear a safer investment for a creditor? For an owner? Explain.
  d) Which firm is doing a better job of financial management if optimal financing leverage in this industry was a long-term debt ratio of 0.300?

SP **13.14** Compute and compare the Statement of Cash Flows of the Francine and Naomi Corporations (Exhibits 13.6 and 13.7).

a) Which firm is investing more in replacement or expansion of its capacity assets?

b) Which firm is reinvesting more earnings?

c) Which firm is doing more to improve its solvency?

d) Which firm is increasing its indebtedness more than the other?

SP **13.15** Integrative Problem The following events occurred during Period 17 for the LUTON Corporation:

1) Sales totaled $250,000, $65,000 for cash and the balance on account.

2) Collections of receivables from customers totaled $90,000.

3) Accounts receivable totaling $1,920 proved uncollectible and were written off.

4) Merchandise inventory costing $232,000 was purchased on account.

5) Wages and salaries totaling $53,000 were paid including the $1,000 previously accrued.

6) Supplies costing $2,000 were purchased on account.

7) $3,200 was paid for insurance covering Periods 17 through 20.

8) $1,400 of bills for utilities and services consumed in the current period were received and recorded.

9) The $5,300 of taxes payable for Period 16 were paid.

10) Interest of $4,220 was paid (covering the current period's bond and noncurrent note payments) including the $2,110 previously accrued.

11) The $5,000 current capital lease obligation previously accrued was paid.

12) $800 representing the period's interest on the Baker Corporation bonds held as an investment was received.

13) The $2,500 preferred dividend was declared to be paid early in Period 18.

14) $95,400 was paid on accounts payable.

Adjustments were made for LIFO ending inventory of $160,000 (A); FIFO ending supplies inventory of $1,750 (B); $800 expiration of prepaid insurance (C); $3,900 of depreciation on buildings and $1,000 depreciation on equipment (D); $3,900 of bad debt expense resulting in a bad debt allowance of $3,800 (E); $400 of discount amortization on the Baker Corporation's bonds held as a long-term investment (F); $3,540 depreciation of properties held under capital lease (G); $200 amortization of deferred charges related to the earlier sale of bonds (H); accrual of $3,000 of wages and salaries earned but not yet paid (I); reclassification of $2,775 of capital lease obligation to current representing the principal portion of the $5,000 payment due at the beginning of Period 18 (J); accrual of $2,225 of current capital lease obligation representing interest expense (K); provision for income taxes of $5,000, $4,000 payable in Period 18 with the balance deferred (L); $250 amortization of premium on bonds payable (M); and $270 amortization of the discount on the $11,000 noncurrent note payable (N).

The LUTON Corporation's balance sheet as of the end of Period 17 is given below:

LUTON CORPORATION—BALANCE SHEET AS OF END OF PERIOD 17

ASSETS		EQUITIES	
Cash	$ 12,984	Accounts Payable	$200,000
Accounts Receivable	188,900	Wages and Salaries	3,000
Allowance for Uncollectibles	(3,800)	Taxes Payable	4,000
Inventory	160,000	Current Cap. Lse. Obligations	5,000
Supplies	1,750	Dividends Payable	2,500
Prepaid Items	2,400	Total Current Liabilities	$214,500
Total Current Assets	$362,234	Noncurrent Notes Payable	11,000
Investments	171,000	Notes Payable Discount	(2,136)
Investments Discount	(6,400)	Noncurrent Cap. Lse. Obligations	52,853
Land	25,000	Bonds Payable	50,000
Buildings	125,000	Bond Premium	7,000
Accum. Depr. Bldgs.	(50,100)	Deferred Income Taxes	2,200
Equipment	30,000	Total Liabilities	$335,417
Accum. Depr. Equip.	(11,300)	Preferred Stock*	100,000
Properties under Capital Lease	70,862	Addtl. Paid in Capital—pfd.	10,000
Accum. Depr. Lease	(14,160)	Common Stock**	189,000
Deferred Charges	5,600	Addtl. Paid in Capital—com.	6,750
		Retained Earnings	66,569
Total Assets	$707,736	Total Equities	$707,736

* $100 par; 20,000 shares authorized; 1,000 shares issued and outstanding.
** $5 par; 200,000 shares authorized; 37,800 shares issued and outstanding.

The LUTON Corporation's income statement for Period 17 is also included below:

LUTON CORPORATION—INCOME STATEMENT FOR PERIOD 17

Net Sales		$250,000
Cost of Goods Sold		(150,000)
Gross Profit		$100,000
Operating Expenses		
Wages and Salaries	$55,000	
Supplies	1,600	
Insurance	800	
Utilities	1,400	
Bad Debts	3,900	
Depreciation on buildings and equipment	4,900	
Depreciation on lease	3,540	(71,140)
Operating Profit		$28,860
Other Revenue and (Expense)		
Investments Revenue	$1,200	
Interest Expense	(4,555)	(3,355)
Income from Operations Before Taxes		$25,505
Less Provision for Income Taxes		(5,000)
Net Income		$20,505

During Period 18, the following events occurred affecting the financial position of the LUTON Corporation: (Note: Items marked with an asterisk were illustrated in previous periods.)

*1) Sales totaled $275,000, $85,000 for cash and the balance on account.

*2) Collections of receivables from customers totaled $174,900.

*3) Accounts receivable totaling $4,000 proved uncollectible and were written off.

*4) Merchandise inventory costing $225,000 was purchased on account. Inventory purchases were added directly to the inventory account.

*5) Supplies costing $2,000 were purchased on account.

*6) Wages and salaries totaling $53,000 were paid including the $3,000 previously accrued.

*7) Bills for utilities and services currently consumed in the amount of $1,500 were received and recorded.

*8) The $4,000 of taxes payable for Period 17 were paid.

*9) The $5,000 capital lease payment due at the beginning of the period and previously accrued was paid.

*10) The previous period's referred dividend of $2,500 was paid.

*11) The current period's $2,500 preferred dividend was declared and paid.

*12) A dividend of $30,000 was received on the Ajax Corporation's common stock. The stock was held as a long-term investment and represented 25 percent of the outstanding stock and significant influence over Ajax's dividend decisions.

*13) The current period's bond interest payment of $2,000 was made.

*14) A $28,350 cash dividend on the LUTON common stock outstanding at the beginning of Period 18 was declared to be paid early in Period 19.

*15) $230,500 was paid on accounts payable.

*16) At the start of the period, the Baker Corporation bonds (with a face value of $40,000 and unamortized discount of $6,400) that had been held as a long-term investment were sold for $42,000.

17) Near the end of the period, the creditor holding the $11,000 face-value truck note (noncurrent) agreed to convert his creditor claim to an ownership interest. The period's stated interest of $110 was first accrued in preparation for the conversion.

18) One period's amortization of $270 of the discount on the $11,000 note was also recorded in preparation for the conversion.

19) The $11,000 face-value noncurrent note and accrued interest were exchanged for 1,800 shares of newly issued LUTON common stock. Both Luigi and Tony had formerly waived their preemptive rights on this new stock issue.

20) During the period, the directors decided that the 2,000 shares of the Charles Corporation's common stock carried as a long-term investment at their cost of $20,000 (current market value was $23,000) should be available for immediate sale to cover any cash needs that might arise. It was therefore decided to reclassify these assets as current. The 2,000 shares did not represent significant influence over the Charles Corporation's dividend decisions.

21) The Charles Corporation reported earnings of $3 per share for the period and paid dividends that were received of $2 per share.

At the end of Period 18:

*A) Merchandise inventory as adjusted to reflect ending inventory at LIFO of $220,000.

*B) Supplies inventory was adjusted to reflect ending supplies on hand under FIFO of $2,050.

*C) Prepaid items were adjusted to reflect $800 expiration of prepaid insurance.

*D) Wages and salaries totaling $5,000 earned but not yet paid were accrued.

*E) Depreciation expense of $3,700 on buildings and $900 on the equipment and the truck was recorded.

*F) An aging of ending accounts receivable indicated that accounts totaling $4,000 were not expected to prove collectible.

*G) The Ajax Corporation reported earnings of $100,000 for the period. LUTON's common stock investment in Ajax represented 25 percent of Ajax's voting common stock and significant influence over Ajax's dividend decisions. An adjustment was made to pick up LUTON's share of the Ajax earnings.

*H) One period's straight-line depreciation of the warehouse capital lease of $3,540 was recorded.

*I) The period's amortization of $200 of deferred charges was recorded.

*J) The $2,886 principal portion of the $5,000 capital lease payment due at the beginning of Period 19 was reclassified as current.

*K) The $2,114 interest portion of the Period 19 $5,000 capital lease payment was accrued.

*L) $250 amortization of premium on bonds payable was recorded.

*M) A $21,000 provision for income taxes for the period was determined to be appropriate. However, because of a reversal of temporary timing differences, the current tax liability payable early in Period 19 was $21,900.

Required:

a) The effect on the beginning period balance sheet of those Period 18 transactions and adjustments that were introduced in earlier periods, and which are identified with an asterisk (*), has already been recorded in the partially completed balance sheet effect worksheet given on the following page. Prepare a final balance sheet effect worksheet for the LUTON Corporation for Period 18 stating with the preliminary balances and recording the effect of Period 18 transactions (16) through (21) and adjustment (M). Identify opening balances as "(p)" and the effect of the remaining transactions and the adjustment with their numbers and letters to identify all revenue and expense effects upon retained earnings in an income box. Provide necessary space on your worksheet by entering account titles as follows:

Account	Line number	Account	Line number
Cash	1	Accounts Payable	1
Marketable Securities	4	Wages and Salaries	2
Accounts Receivable	6	Taxes Payable	3
Allowance for Bad Debts	7	Interest Payable	5
Inventory	8	Current Cap. Lse. Obligations	8
Supplies	9	Dividends Payable	9
Prepaid Items	10	Noncurrent Notes Payable	10
Investments	11	Notes Payable Discount	12
Investments Discount	14	Noncurrent Cap. Lse. Oblig.	15
Land	16	Bonds Payable	16
Buildings	17	Bond Premium	17
Accum. Depr. Bldgs.	18	Deferred Income Taxes	18
Equipment	19	Preferred Stock	20
Accum. Depr. Equip.	20	Addtl. Paid-in Capital—Pfd.	21
Properties Under Cap. Lse.	21	Common Stock	22
Accum. Depr. Lease	22	Addtl. Paid-in capital—Com.	24
Deferred Charges	23	Retained Earnings	26

b) Prepare the firm's income statement for Period 18 in good form following the multiple-step format.

c) Prepare the statement of retained earnings in good form for Period 18.

d) Prepare the firm's balance sheet in good form as of the end of Period 18.

e) Prepare the firm's statement of cash flows for Period 18 in good form using the indirect method for cash from operating activites.

f) Determine for the LUTON Corporation for Period 17 the following data for analysis:
1) The amount of net working capital in the business at the end of the period;
2) The period-end current ratio (to two decimals);
3) The period-end quick ratio (to two decimals);
4) The period-end long-term debt ratio (to three decimals);
5) The period-end asset composition ratio (to three decimals);
6) The book value per share at the end of the period (preferred claim in liquidation is $125 per share);
7) Earnings per share for the period (preferred dividend $2,500 per period);
8) EBIT (earnings before interest and taxes);
9) Times interest earned;
10) Asset turnover (Period 16 ending total assets were $550,396.)
11) Receivables turnover using credit sales (Period 16 ending net receivables were $94,000;
12) Average days' receivables (assume one period equals 91 days);
13) Inventory turnover (Period 16 ending inventory was $78,000);
14) Average days' inventory (assume one period equals 91 days);
15) Property and equipment turnover (Period 16 ending net property and equipment was $183,842);
16) Return on investment;
17) Return on common equity (Period 16 ending common equity was $229,314.

g) Determine for the LUTON Corporation for Period 18 the same 17 items required in (f) above. Note that in calculating period 18 EPS, beginning shares should be weighted three and ending shares one.

h) Compare each of the 17 items of data for the firm for Periods 17 and 18 (requirements "f"

PARTIALLY COMPLETED BALANCE SHEET EFFECT WORKSHEET
LUTON Corporation Period 18
(b = beginning balance; p = Partially Complete Ending Balance)

Cash	$	12,984	(b)		Accounts Payable				
+		85,000	(1)			$	200,000	(b)	
+		174,900	(2)		+		225,000	(4)	
−		53,000	(6)		+		2,000	(5)	
−		4,000	(8)		+		1,500	(7)	
−		5,000	(9)		−		230,500	(15) $ 198,000 (p)	
−		2,500	(10)		Wages and Salaries				
−		2,500	(11)				3,000	(b)	
+		30,000	(12)		−		3,000	(6)	
−		2,000	(13)		+		5,000	(D) 5,000 (p)	
−		230,500	(15) $ 3,384 (p)		Taxes Payable	4,000	(b)		
Accounts Receivable					−		4,000	(G) 0 (p)	
		188,900	(b)		Current Cap. Lse. Oblig.				
+		190,000	(1)				5,000	(b)	
−		174,900	(2)		−		5,000	(9)	
−		4,000	(3) 100,000 (p)		+		2,886	(J)	
Allowance for Bad Debts		(3,800) (b)			+		2,114	(K) 5,000 (p)	
+		4,000	(3)		Dividends Payable				
−		4,200	(F) (4,000) (p)				2,500	(b)	
Inventory	160,000	(b)			−		2,500	(10)	
+		225,000	(4)		+		28,350	(14) 28,350 (p)	
−		165,000	(A) 220,000 (p)		Noncurrent Notes Payable				
Supplies	1,750	(b)					11,000	(b) 11,000 (p)	
+		2,000	(5)		Notes Payable Discount				
−		1,700	(B) 2,050 (p)				(2,136)	(b) (2,136) (p)	
Prepaid Itms	2,400	(b)			Noncurrent Cap. Lse. Oblig.				
−		800	(C) 1,600 (p)				52,853	(b)	
Investments	171,000	(b)			−		2,886	(J) 49,967 (p)	
−		30,000	(12)		Bonds Pay.	50,000	(b) 50,000 (p)		
+		25,000	(G) 166,000 (p)		Bonds Prem.	7,000	(b)		
Investments Discount					−		250	(L) 6,750 (p)	
		(6,400)	(b) (6,400) (p)		Def. Inc. Tax	2,200	(b) 2,200 (p)		
Land	25,000	(b) 25,000 (p)			Prf Stock	100,000	(b) 100,000 (p)		
Buildings	125,000	(b) 125,000 (p)			Addtl. Paid–in Capital—Pfd.				
Accum. Depr. —Bldgs.							10,000	(b) 10,000 (p)	
		(50,100)	(b)		Com. Stock	189,000	(b) 189,000 (p)		
−		3,700	(E) (53,800) (p)		Addtl. PIC—Com.				
Equipment	30,000	(b) 30,000 (p)					6,750	(b) 6,750 (p)	
Accum. Depr.—Equip.					Ret. Earn.	66,569	(b) 66,569 (p)		
		(11,300)	(b)						
−		900	(E) (9,200) (p)						

Income	
+ 275,000 (1)	− 800 (C)
− 50,000 (6)	− 5,000 (D)
− 1,500 (7)	− 4,600 (E)
− 2,500(11)	− 4,200 (F)
− 2,000(13)	+ 25,000 (G)
− 28,350(14)	− 3,540 (H)
− 165,000 (A)	- 200 (I)
− 1,700 (B)	− 2,114 (K)
	+ 250 (L)

Properties Under Capital Lease				
	70,862	(b) 70,862 (p)	
Accum. Depr.—Lease				
	(14,160)	(b)	
−	3,540	(H) (17,700)(p)	
Deferred Charges			
	5,600	(b)	
−	300	(I) 5,400 (p)	
TOTALS		$ 755,196	
TOTALS		$ 775,196	

and "g" above) and determine whether each item considered independently was improved, essentially unchanged, or worse. The industry average long-term debt ratio is 0.2, and you may assume greater solvency and liquidity are improvements.

i) Considering all available information for the firm for Periods 17 and 18:

1) Was the financial position improved and, if yes, how was this improvement accomplished?

2) Was the operating performance improved?

3) Was the firm more profitable?

4) Assuming that one period equalled 91 days, what one item appears to be alarmingly out of control?

SP 13.16 Integrative Problem:

The following events occurred during Period 17 for the **MORCHAN** Corporation:

1) Sales totaled $350,000, $70,000 for cash and the balance on account.

2) Collections of receivables from customers totaled $242,500.

3) Accounts receivable totaling $7,500 proved uncollectible and were written off.

4) Merchandise inventory costing $195,000 was purchased on account.

5) Wages and salaries totaling $74,300 were paid including the $2,800 previously accrued.

6) Supplies costing $1,000 were purchased on account.

7) $6,000 was paid for insurance covering Periods 17 through 20.

8) Bills for utilities and services currently consumed in the amount of $2,000 were received and recorded.

9) The $9,200 of taxes payable for Period 16 were paid.

10) Interest of $14,000 was paid covering the current period's and and noncurrent note payments and also including the $7,000 previously accrued.

11) The $10,000 current capital lease obligation previously accrued was paid.

12) $2,000 representing the period's interest on the Zukor corporation bonds held as an investment was received.

13) The $6,000 preferred dividend was declared to be paid early in Period 18.

14) $200,000 was paid on accounts payable.

Adjustments were made for LIFO ending inventory of $350,000 (A); FIFO ending supplies inventory of $500 (B); $1,500 expiration of prepaid insurance (C); $10,200 of depreciation on buildings and $1,650 depreciation on equipment (D); $8,400 of bad debt expense resulting in an ending allowance of $12,600 (E); $200 of premium amortization on the Zukor Corporation's bonds held as a long-term investment (F); $7,190 depreciation of properties held under capital lease (G); $250 amortization of deferred charges related to the earlier sale of bonds (H); accrual of $3,500 of wages and salaries earned but not yet paid (I); reclassification of $5,528 of capital lease obligation to current representing the principal portion of the $10,000 payment due at the beginning of Period 18 (J); accrual of $4,472 of current capital lease obligation representing interest expense (K); provision for income taxes of $11,000, $9,500 payable in Period 18 with the balance deferred (L); $1,150 amortization of discount on bonds payable (M); and $167 amortization of the discount on the $10,000 noncurrent note payable (N).

The MORCHAN Corporation's balance sheet as of the end of Period 17 is given below:

MORCHAN CORPORATION—BALANCE SHEET
AS OF END OF PERIOD 17

ASSETS		EQUITIES	
Cash	$8,634	Accounts Payable	$323,000
Accounts Receivable	420,000	Wages and Salaries	3,500
Allowance for Uncollectibles	(12,600)	Taxes Payable	9,500
Inventory	350,000	Current Cap. Lse. Obligations	10,000
Supplies	500	Dividends Payable	6,000
Prepaid Items	4,500	Total Current Liabilities	$352,000
Total Current Assets	$771,034	Noncurrent Notes Payable	10,000
Investments	190,000	Notes Payable Discount	(1,666)
Investments Premium	4,200	Noncurrent Cap. Lse. Obligations	143,540
Land	90,000	Bonds Payable	230,000
Buildings	370,000	Bond Discount	(20,700)
Accum. Depr. Bldgs.	(124,000)	Deferred Income Taxes	2,300
Equipment	46,000	Total Liabilities	$715,474
Accum. Depr. Equip.	(18,450)	Preferred Stock*	200,000
Properties under Capital Lease	179,646	Addtl. Paid-in Capital—Pfd.	10,000
Accum. Depr. Lease	(28,760)	Common Stock**	416,160
Deferred Charges	4,500	Addtl. Paid-in Capital—Com.	12,550
		Retained Earnings	129,986
Total Assets	$1,484,170	Total Equities	$1,484,170

* $100 par; 50,000 shares authorized; 2,000 shares issued and outstanding.
** $10 par; 500,000 shares authorized; 41,616 shares issued and outstanding.

The MORCHAN Corporation's income statement for Period 17 is also included below:

MORCHAN CORPORATION—INCOME STATEMENT FOR PERIOD 17

Net Sales		$350,000
Cost of Goods Sold		(175,000)
Gross Profit		$175,000
Operating Expenses		
Wages and Salaries	$75,000	
Supplies	1,800	
Insurance	1,500	
Utilities	2,000	
Uncollectible Accounts	8,400	
Depreciation for buildings and equipment	11,850	
Depreciation for Lease	7,190	(107,740)
Operating Profit		$67,260
Other Revenue and (Expense)		
Investments Revenue		$1,800
Interest Expense	(13,039)	(11,239)
Income From Operations Before Taxes		$56,021
Less Provision for Income Taxes		(11,000)
Net Income		$45,021

During Period 18, these events occurred affecting the financial position of **MORCHAN** Corporation: (Note: Items marked with an asterisk have been illustrated in previous periods.)

*1) Sales totaled $400,000, $80,000 for cash and the balance on account.

*2) Collections of receivables from customers totaled $252,200.

*3) Accounts receivable totaling $7,800 proved uncollectible and were written off.

*4) Merchandise inventory costing $250,000 was purchased on account. Inventory purchases were added directly to inventory account.

*5) Supplies costing $2,400 were purchased on account.

*6) Wages and salaries totaling $77,500 were paid including the $3,500 previously accrued.

*7) Bills for utilities and services currently consumed in the amount of $2,300 were received and recorded.

*8) The $9,500 of taxes payable for Period 17 were paid.

*9) The $10,000 capital lease payment due at the beginning of the period and previously accrued was paid.

*10) The previous period's preferred dividend of $6,000 was paid.

*11) The current period's $6,000 preferred dividend was declared and paid.

*12) A dividend of $9,000 was received on the Acme Corporation's common stock. The stock was held as long-term investment and represented 30 percent of the outstanding stock and significant influence over Acme's dividend decisions.

*13) The current period's bond interest payment of $6,900 was made.

*14) A $20,808 cash dividend on the MORCHAN common stock outstanding at the beginning of Period 18 was declared to be paid early in Period 19.

*15) $232,700 was paid on accounts payable.

 16) At the start of the period, the Zukor Corporation bonds (with a face value of $50,000 and unamortized premium of $4,200) that had been held as a long-term investment were sold for $60,000.

 17) Near the end of the period, the creditor holding the $10,000 face-value truck note (noncurrent) agreed to covert his creditor claim to an ownership interest. The period's stated interest of $100 was first accrued in preparation for the conversion.

 18) One period's amortization of $167 of the discount on the $10,000 note was also recorded in preparation for the conversion.

 19) The $10,000 face-value noncurrent note and accrued interest were exchanged for 584 shares of newly issued MORCHAN common stock. Both Irene and Janet had formerly waived their preemptive rights on this new stock issue.

 20) During the period, the directors decided that the 500 shares of the Castle Corporation's common stock carried as a long-term investment at their cost of $10,000 (current market value was $12,000) should be available for immediate sale to cover any cash needs that might arise. It was therefore decided to reclassify these assets as current. The 500 shares did not represent significant influence over the Castle Corporation's dividend decisions.

 21) The Castle Corporation reported earnings of $4 per share for the period and paid dividends that were received of $3 per share.

At the end of Period 18:

*A) Merchandise inventory was adjusted reflect ending inventory at **LIFO** of $400,000.

*B) Supplies inventory was adjusted to reflect ending supplies on hand under **FIFO** of $900.

*C) Prepaid items were adjusted to reflect $1,500 expiration of prepaid insurance.

*D) Wages and salaries totaling $6,000 earned but not yet paid were accrued.

*E) Depreciation expense of $9,800 on buildings and $1,500 on the equipment and the truck was recorded.

*F) An aging of ending accounts receivable indicated that accounts totaling $14,400 were not expected to prove collectible.

*G) The Acme Corporation reported earnings of $50,000 for the period. **MORCHAN**'s common stock investment in Acme represented 30 percent of Acme's voting common stock and significant influence over Acme's dividend decisions. An adjustment was made to pick up **MORCHAN**'s share of the Acme earnings.

*H) One period's straight-line depreciation of the warehouse capital lease of $7,190 was recorded.

*I) The period's amortization of $250 of deferred charges was recorded.

*J) The $5,694 principal portion of the $10,000 capital lease payment due at the beginning of Period 19 was reclassified as current.

*K) The $4,306 interest portion of the Period 19 $10,000 capital lease payment was accrued.

*L) $1,150 amortization of discount on bonds payable was recorded.

M) A $28,000 provision for income taxes for the period was determined to be appropriate. However, because of a reversal of temporary timing differences, the current tax liability payable early in Period 19 was $28,500.

Required:

a) The effect on the beginning period balance sheet of those Period 18 transactions and adjustments that were introduced in earlier periods, and which are identified with an asterisk (*), has already been recorded in the partially completed balance sheet effect worksheet given below. Prepare a final balance sheet effect worksheet for the **MORCHAN** Corporation for Period 18 starting with the preliminary balances and recording the effect of Period 18 transactions (16) through 21) and adjustment (M). Identify opening balances as "(p)" and the effect of the remaining transactions and the adjustment with their numbers and letter. Also identify all revenue and expense effects upon retained earnings in an income box. provide necessary space on your worksheet by entering account titles as follows:

Account	Line number	Account	Line number
Cash	1	Accounts Payable	1
Marketable Securities	4	Wages and Salaries	2
Accounts Receivable	6	Taxes Payable	3
Allowance for Bad Debts	7	Interest Payable	5
Inventory	8	Current Cap. Lse. Obligations	8
Supplies	9	Dividends Payable	9
Prepaid Items	10	Noncurrent Notes Payable	10
Investments	11	Notes Payable Discount	12
Investments Premium	14	Noncurrent Cap. Lse. Obligations	15
Land	16	Bonds Payable	16
Buildings	17	Bond Discount	17
Accum. Depr. Bldgs.	18	Deferred Income Taxes	18
Equipment	19	Preferred Stock	20
Accum. Depr. Equip.	20	Addtl. Paid-in Capital—Pfd.	21
Properties Under Cap. Lse.	21	Common Stock	22
Accum. Depr. Lease	22	Addtl. Paid-in Capital—Com.	24
Deferred Charges	24	Retained Earnings	26

b) Prepare the firm's income statement for Period 18 in good form following the multiple-step format.

c) Prepare the statement of retained earnings in good form for Period 18.

d) Prepare the firm's balance sheet in good form as of the end of Period 18.

e) Prepare the firm's statement of cash flows for Period 18 in good form following the indirect method for csh from operating activities.

f) Determine for the **MORCHAN** Corporation for Period 17 the following data for analysis:

1) The amount of net working capital in the business at the end of the period;

2) The period-end current ratio (to two decimals);

3) The period-end quick ratio (to two decimals);

4) The period-end long-term debt ratio (to three decimals);

5) The period-end asset composition ratio (to three decimals);

6) The book value per share at the end of the period (preferred claim in liquidation is $110 per share);

7) Earnings per share for the period (preferred dividend $6,000 per period);

8) EBIT (earnings before interest and taxes);

9) Times interest earned;

10) Asset turnover (Period 16 ending total assets were $1,449,860);

11) Receivables turnover using credit sales (Period 16 ending net receivables were $378,300);

12) Average days' receivables (assume one period equals 91 days);

13) Inventory turnover (Period 16 ending inventory was $330,000);

14) Average days' inventory (assume one period equals 91 days);

15) Property and equipment turnover (Period 16 ending net property and equipment was $533,476);

16) Return on investment;

17) Return on common equity (Period 16 ending common equity was $509,675).

g) Determine for the **MORCHAN** Corporation for Period 18 the same 17 items of data required in (f) above. Note that in calculating Period 18 EPS, beginning shares should be weighted three and ending shares one.

h) Compare each of the 17 items of data for the firm for Periods 17 and 18 (requirements "f" and "g" above) and determine whether each item considered independently was improved, essentially unchanged, or worse. The industry average long-term debt ratio is 0.3, and you may assume greater solvency and liquidity are improvements.

i) Considering all available information for the firm for Periods 17 and 18:

1) Was the financial position improved and, if yes, how was the improvement accomplished?

2) Was the operating performance improved?

3) Was the firm more profitable?

4) Assuming that one period equalled 91 days, what one item appears to be alarmingly out of control?

PARTIALLY COMPLETED BALANCE SHEET EFFECT WORKSHEET
MORCHAN Corporation Period 18
(b = beginning balance; p = Partially Complete Ending Balance)

Cash	$	8,634	(b)		
	+	80,000	(1)		
	+	252,200	(2)		
	–	77,500	(6)		
	–	9,500	(8)		
	–	10,000	(9)		
	–	6,000	(10)		
	–	6,000	(11)		
	+	9,000	(12)		
	–	6,900	(13)		
	–	232,700	(15)	$ 1,234	(p)
Accounts Receivable		420,000	(b)		
	+	320,000	(1)		
	–	252,200	(2)		
	–	7,800	(3)	480,000	(p)
Allowance for Bad Debts		(12,600)	(b)		
	+	7,800	(3)		
	–	9,600	(F)	(14,400)	(p)
Inventory		350,000	(b)		
	+	225,000	(4)		
	–	200,000	(A)	400,000	(p)
Supplies		500	(b)		
	+	2,400	(5)		
	–	2,000	(B)	900	(p)
Prepaid Itms		4,500	(b)		
	–	1,500	(C)	3,000	(p)
Investments		190,000	(b)		
	–	9,000	(12)		
	+	15,000	(G)	196,000	(p)
Investments Premium		(4,200)	(b)	(4,200)	(p)
Land		90,000	(b)	90,000	(p)
Buildings		370,000	(b)	370,000	(p)
Accum. Depr. —Bldgs.		(124,000)	(b)		
	–	9,800	(E)	(133,800)	(p)
Equipment		46,000	(b)	46,000	(p)
Accum. Depr.—Equip.		(18,450)	(b)		
	–	1,500	(E)	(19,950)	(p)
Properties Under Capital Lease		179,646	(b)	179,646	(p)
Accum. Depr.—Lease		(28,760)	(b)		
	–	7,190	(H)	(35,950)	(p)
Deferred Charges		4,500	(b)		
	–	250	(H)	4,250	(p)
TOTALS				$1,571,130	

Accounts Payable					
	$	323,000	(b)		
	+	250,000	(4)		
	+	2,400	(5)		
	+	2,300	(7)		
	–	232,700	(15)	$ 345,000	(p)
Wages and Salaries		3,500	(b)		
	–	3,500	(6)		
	+	6,000	(D)	6,000	(p)
Taxes Payable		9,500	(b)		
	–	9,500	(G)	0	(p)
Current Cap. Lse. Oblig.		10,000	(b)		
	–	10,000	(9)		
	+	5,694	(J)		
	+	4,306	(K)	10,000	(p)
Dividends Payable		6,000	(b)		
	–	6,000	(10)		
	+	20,808	(14)	20,808	(p)
Noncurrent Notes Payable		10,000	(b)	10,000	(p)
Notes Payable Discount		(1,666)	(b)	(1,666)	(p)
Noncurrent Cap. Lse. Oblig.		143,540	(b)		
	–	5,694	(J)	137,846	(p)
Bonds Pay.		230,000	(b)	230,000	(p)
Bonds Disc.		(20,700)	(b)		
	+	1,150	(L)	(19,550)	(p)
Def. Inc. Tax		2,300	(b)	2,300	(p)
Prf Stock		200,000	(b)	200,000	(p)
Addtl. Paid–in Capital—Pfd.		10,000	(b)	10,000	(p)
Com. Stock		416,160	(b)	416,160	(p)
Addtl. PIC—Com.		12,550	(b)	12,550	(p)
Ret. Earn.		129,986	(b)	129,986	(p)

Income			
+ 400,000	(1)	– 1,500	(C)
– 74,000	(6)	– 6,000	(D)
– 2,300	(7)	– 11,300	(E)
– 6,000	(11)	– 9,600	(F)
– 6,900	(13)	+ 15,000	(G)
– 20,808	(14)	– 7,190	(H)
– 200,000	(A)	– 250	(I)
– 2,000	(B)	– 4,306	(K)
		– 1,150	(L)

| TOTALS | $ 1,571,130 |

14

Business Combinations
Segment and
Interim Reports

Chapter Preview

The objective of this chapter is to acquaint you with the several ways a business combination may occur and with the different forms it can take, and specifically to enable you to understand and properly interpret consolidated financial statements. Another objective of this chapter is to acquaint you with the availability and meaning of segment information and interim reports. In this chapter you can:

1. Learn that business combinations can come about through acquisition of one firm by another or through the pooling of interests of two firms;

2. Discover that the accounting treatment of a business combination is distinctly different, depending upon whether the combination is deemed a purchase or a pooling, and learn the significance of the differences;

3. Develop an understanding of the objectives of consolidated financial statements and of the principles of consolidation involved in their preparation;

4. Learn how accountants meet the need for information relating to individual segments of a business and to more timely reporting of financial information;

5. Become familiar with the content, usefulness, and limitations of segment information and interim reports;

6. Review and expand your knowledge of the importance of financial statement footnotes and of their common information content.

With this information, you will have completed the introduction of consolidated financial statements as they are currently prepared.

All in the Family

The Gargantuan Corporation actually is a **holding company**. It owns all or most of the voting stock of several other corporations which are engaged in various businesses. By itself, Gargantuan does little except make investments and collect interest and dividends. The balance sheet and income statements of the company without consolidation are given in Exhibit 14.1.

Exhibit 14.1

GARGANTUAN CORPORATION
Balance Sheet and Income Statement for Year Ending 12/31/X1
($ in thousands)

Assets

Cash	$	45
Office Supplies		3
Total Current Assets	$	48
Investments		25,412
Total Assets	$	25,460

Equities

Accounts Payable	$	20
Other current liabilities		5
Total Current Liabilities	$	25
Long-term debt		0
Total Liabilities	$	25
Common stock (no par)		23,000
Retained earnings		2,435
Total Equities	$	25,460

Income Statement

Investments revenue	$	6,076
Office expenses		200
Wages and salaries		1,000
Operating income	$	4,876
Income taxes		632
Net income	$	4,244

Exhibit 14.2

GARGANTUAN CORPORATION
Consolidated Balance Sheet as of 12/31/X1
($ in thousands)

Assets

Cash		$ 2,075
Marketable securities		1,740
Accounts receivable (net)		6,300
Inventory		10,125
Supplies		3,280
Prepaid items		2,450
Total Current Assets		$ 25,970
Investments (unconsolidated)*		5,750
Property and equipment:		
Land	4,560	
Buildings	8,230	
Accumulated depreciation	(4,460)	
Equipment	12,720	
Accumulated depreciation	(8,380)	
Properties under capital lease	3,600	16,270
Intangible and other assets:		
Patents and copyrights	1,475	
Deferred charges	2,270	
Consolidated goodwill	1,920	5,665
Total Assets		$ 53,655

Equities

Current notes payable		$ 2,120
Accounts payable		5,290
Other current liabilities		1,870
Total Current Liabilities		$ 9,280
Bonds payable		6,000
Less unamortized discount		(255)
Total Liabilities		$ 15,025
Minority interest		4,350
Common stock		23,000
Retained earnings		11,280
Total Equities		$ 53,655

* For various reasons to be discussed later in the chapter some investments representing legal control may still not be consolidated. Also investments not representing control are never involved in the consolidation process.

To read consolidated financial statements merely requires knowledge of the basic principles of consolidation, the new accounts that may arise out of consolidation, and some new vocabulary.

Business Combinations

For various reasons, two corporations may decide to work together as one. This "corporate marriage," often referred to as a **business combination**, **merger**, or **acquisition**, can come about in one of two ways. The firms may just join forces, with the owners of each company continuing as proportionate owners of the combination. This type of combination is known as a **pooling of interests**. The second way in which corporations may merge is to have one company buy the other company for consideration other than common stock. Where one firm acquires control of another by buying out the other, the merger is known as a **purchase**, or an acquisition.

Regardless of how the merger is accomplished, the combination may subsequently continue in one of two legal forms. The assets and liabilities of the controlled company may be transferred to the controlling corporation, and the controlled corporation extinguished—a **statutory merger**. Or the assets and liabilities of both may be transferred to a third corporation—a **statutory consolidation**. In either case, there is a single surviving corporation.

As an alternative to a statutory (legal) merger or consolidation, the two corporations may continue to operate as separate legal entities regardless of whether the merger was accomplished via purchase or pooling. There are definite economic, legal, tax, and even operating advantages in certain situations, if the two firms continue as legally distinct operations.

Recall that, when one corporation owns more than 50 percent of the voting stock of another corporation, the controlling corporation is known as the parent. The corporation which is legally controlled by the parent is known as the subsidiary. The subsidiary must be included in the parent's consolidated financial statements. When a parent owns 100 percent of the voting common stock of the subsidiary, the subsidiary is known as a **wholly owned subsidiary**. When a subsidiary is not wholly owned, the stockholders other than the parent are collectively known as the minority stockholders or just the **minority**.

Note that the parent-subsidiary relationship is determined by the percentage of interest in the voting common stock. Ownership of notes, bonds, and preferred stock have no bearing on whether or not a subsidiary relationship exists. GAAP require that a parent publish financial statements, including the details of assets and liabilities of its subsidiaries.[1] These more inclusive statements are known as consolidated statements.

---

[1] Consolidation is not required in the case of certain foreign subsidiaries where local government regulations impair effective control. In balance sheets of the parent, the investment in such cases would be disclosed as "investment in unconsolidated subsidiary."

It is important to understand that consolidated statements are prepared for an artificial entity. In a consolidation, both the parent and subsidiary are continuing as distinct legal entities. Each maintains separate accounting records and prepares separate statements. The "consolidated entity" exists only on paper. There are no accounting "books" for the consolidation. Even though the two firms are not "legally married" in the sense of living in one corporate home, they operate as one under a single top management. The artificial legal entity is a very real operating entity. Accountants, therefore, report on this operating entity. Consolidated financial statements can be viewed as a "living together relationship on paper."

Consolidated Statements for Poolings

In a pooling, the accounting book values from each firm's separate statements are combined in the consolidated statement. However, a simple combined statement—one statement added to the other line by line—may not result in a final consolidated statement. In the case of a balance sheet, further adjustment is always necessary. For income statements and statement of cash flows, further adjustments may be necessary, depending upon the particular circumstances.

Exhibit 14.3 presents an example of the steps necessary to arrive at a consolidated balance sheet following the pooling treatment. Note that, as a first step, the book values of the various assets and equities are simply added together on a combined statement.

Elimination of Intercompany Ownership in a Pooling

Now consider the $175,000,000 of combined "family" assets, and in particular the $21,000,000 shown as investments coming from the parent's balance sheet. Remember, from Chapters 2 and 3, that reported assets are properties and rights or claims against others. On the parent's separate balance sheet, the $21,000,000 of investments was properly included as a claim against a separate corporation's assets. But on the combined balance sheet, the $21,000,000 does not represent a claim against other's (outsiders') assets.

On the combined balance sheet the $21,000,000 claim is now inside the family. It is against assets which are now also included on the "family balance sheet" and, if reported, would represent double-counting and result in overstatement of "family total assets." The $21,000,000 must be eliminated. If the parent investments also included some portion not in subsidiaries, only the portion related to subsidiaries would be eliminated.

Exhibit 14.3   Balance Sheet Consolidation following Pooling Treatment
($ in thousands)

	Parent	Subsidiary	Simple combined statement	Elimina- tions	Consolidated balance sheet
Assets					
Cash	$ 6,000	$ 4,000	$ 10,000		$ 10,000
Accounts receivable	17,000	9,000	26,000	$ 650 (c)	25,350
Inventory	16,000	12,000	28,000		28,000
Investments (a)	21,000	0	21,000	21,000 (b)	0
Other assets (net)	40,000	50,000	90,000		90,000
Total Assets	$100,000	$75,000	$175,000		$153,350
Equities					
Accounts payable	$ 18,000	$10,000	$ 28,000	$650 (c)	$ 27,350
Noncurrent liabilities	22,000	14,000	36,000		36,000
Common stock—$10 par	50,000	15,000	65,000	15,000 (b)	50,000
Additional paid-in capital	5,000	6,000	11,000	6,000 (b)	5,000
Retained earnings	5,000	30,000	35,000		35,000
Total Equities	$100,000	$75,000	$175,000		$153,000

(a) Parent acquired 100 percent of voting stock of subsidiary in exchange for additional shares of parent's common stock.

(b) Elimination of intercompany investment at book value of subsidiary's contributed capital.

(c) Elimination of intercompany debt.

The essential difference between a combined statement and a properly completed consolidated statement is simply the elimination of items which, on a family statement, are now inside the family. Note that eliminations are made only on the consolidated working papers. Nothing is eliminated from the "books" of either company. Also note that all balance sheet eliminations reduce an equal amount from combined assets and combined equities, thus maintaining the balance sheet equality.

Contributed Common Capital claims totaling $21,000,000 coming from the subsidiary's balance sheet do not represent outside claims on the family statement. They must also be eliminated. Elimination of **intercompany ownership** from the combined total is always necessary in the preparation of a consolidated balance sheet. For subsidiaries qualifying for pooling treatment, the intercompany investment elimination is simple and straightforward, since the parent's investment is originally recorded as its share (100 percent on Exhibit 14.3) of the subsidiary's book value of contributed common capital. In subsequent years following acquisition (under the equity method discussed in Chapter 11) the parent will have picked up and included in its investment account, its share of any subsidiary retained earnings since acquisition which were not distributed in dividends. These amounts will also be eliminated from combined investments and combined retained earnings in order to avoid double counting. Note that, in a pooling, only subsidiary retained earnings since acquisition are subject to elimination. Subsidiary retained earnings prior to acquisition are added to parent earnings on the consolidated statement.

In essence, the parent has acquired or "bought" earnings by simply issuing stock. This makes sense only if the parent is now a "partnership" of previously separate owners who have merely combined their past earnings. It is inappropriate if the parent has essentially bought out the subsidiary's owners.[2]

Elimination of Intercompany Debt

Balance sheet elimination also requires removal of any **intercompany debt**. Assume, in the case of the example in Exhibit 14.3, that parent owed subsidiary $650,000 at year-end for products purchased and resold to customers. Parent's separate $18,000,000 of accounts payable properly includes this $650,000 of intercompany debt, and subsidiary's separate $9,000,000 of accounts receivable properly includes the $650,000 claim. In this example, $650,000 of receivables and payables are now "inside" the family and must be eliminated from both accounts. Other common possible intercompany debts or claims necessitating elimination might include:

• Interest receivable and payable;

• Rents;

• Dividends receivable and payable.

Elimination of Intercompany Nonownership Investment

It is possible that either the parent or the subsidiary might hold bonds or preferred stock of the other. In such cases, the amounts of intercompany investments would be eliminated from the combined investments account and from the appropriate combined equity accounts.

Elimination of Intercompany Profit in Inventory

It is possible that the parent and/or the subsidiary has purchased products from the other during the year, some of which remain in inventory at year-end (that is have not passed

---

[2] Accountants have very specific and complicated tests to determine whether a merger qualifies as a pooling of interests. If it does not qualify, GAAP require that the merger be treated as a purchase (see below).

through to outside customers). In such situations, the seller's gross profit will be included in combined inventory and retained earnings. Since this gross profit has not yet been realized through sale to outsiders, intercompany gross profit in unsold inventory must be eliminated from the parent's portion of the combined inventory account. The corresponding elimination is usually made to parent's retained earnings.[3]

Elimination of Intercompany Transactions and Accruals

Eliminations may also be necessary to complete consolidated income statements and consolidated statement of cash flows. Here again the basic concept is unchanged, The statements are first combined (added together). Then any transactions and accruals occurring during the year between the firms must be eliminated since they do not represent events occurring between the family and outsiders. Suppose the subsidiary had sold products during the year to the parent costing $5,000,000. The subsidiary would properly include the five million on its income statement as part of sales. The parent would properly include this amount on its income statement as part of its cost of goods sold. On the consolidated income statement, five million would have to be eliminated from both combined sales and combined costs of goods sold as not representing exchanges with outsiders. Other common income statement eliminations include matching revenues on one statement and expenses on the other for:

- Services performed
- Interest earned
- Rent earned

Note that eliminations of intercompany transactions and accruals will always involve equal amounts from combined revenue and combined expense accounts. Therefore, income statement eliminations will not change combined net income. Consolidated net income will remain the sum of the parent's and the subsidiary's separately reported net incomes under the pooling method. However, combined income for a purchase will rarely, if ever, be the same, as will be explained below.

Similarly, on the combined statement of cash flows, eliminations would be necessary for such items as:

- Sale or purchase of assets within the family;
- Issuance or retirement of debt within the family;
- Dividends within the family.

Both consolidated income statements and consolidated Statement of cash flows, under the pooling treatment, merely involve combinations less eliminations for intercompany

---

[3] In purchase consolidations with a minority interest (discussed below) where the subsidiary is the seller, the intercompany profit elimination may be pro-rated between parent's retained earnings and minority interest. This also applies to poolings with a small remaining minority interest, which are beyond the scope of this text.

transactions and accruals. The actual preparation of a consolidated statement of cash flows from the previously consolidated balance sheets, income statement, and statement of retained earnings is as simple as for a single firm. No additional special procedures are required.

Consolidated Statements for Purchases

A merger may essentially involve the parent's purchase of control of the company from the subsidiary's stockholders. Parent's cash, debt securities, or other considerations may be given to the subsidiary's stockholders in exchange for their controlling stock. The subsidiary's original common stockholders do not retain proportional voting interest in the new family. Where mergers do not qualify as a pooling, accountants treat them as a purchase.

Purchase treatment is essentially quite different from pooling treatment, even though the accountant's procedures are similar. Recall that, under a pooling, no new basis for accounting is deemed to exist. Original accounting book values are carried forward in the new family. Where the merger represents a purchase in the open market, a restatement of assets acquired to fair market value at the time of acquisition becomes appropriate.

Accounting book values may be well below market values or replacement costs after several years of inflation. Recall, from Chapters 2 and 3, that a firm may have significant intangible assets that are not capable of objective measurement and therefore are not measured and disclosed as assets under GAAP. These intangible assets (which are not reported by a firm as its own assets) can include:

- The firm's human capital (resulting from investment in hiring and training employees);

- Customer goodwill (resulting from investment in advertising, public relations, and good customer service);

- Creditor and supplier goodwill (resulting from long-term satisfactory past relationships); and

- Technical knowledge (resulting from past investment in research and development).

Although these intangibles, collectively referred to as "goodwill," and not "booked" for a firm by its accountants, they have real value in the marketplace. A new firm starting in business would have to invest many years of time and perhaps many millions of dollars to create similar goodwill. Therefore, when a company is sold, the selling owners seek recompense for the current market value of their assets plus compensation for any existing goodwill.

Elimination of Intercompany Ownership in a Purchase

Assume your family owned all of the stock of a corporation whose balance sheet looks like Exhibit 14.4. Also assume that, in addition to the current values of the assets which are noted on the exhibit, you believe your firm's goodwill to be worth at least $100,000. Would you willingly sell all of your stock for its book value of $595,000? You would be foolish, in this example, to not attempt to obtain at least $1,455,000 for your stock ($1,355,000 current value of net assets plus $100,000 for goodwill).

Exhibit 14.4

Your Corporation
Most Recent Balance Sheet Data
($ in thousands)

Assets		Equities	
Cash	$ 95	Total liabilities	$255
Receivables	205	Common stock	400
Inventory (LIFO)	190[a]	Additional paid-in capital	80
Investments	60[b]	Retained earnings	115
Fixed assets (net)	300[c]		
Total Assets	$ 850	Total Equities	$850

Current book value of total assets	$ 850,000
Add inventory replacement adjustment	170,000
Add unrecognized gain on securities	370,000
Add fixed asset replacement adjustment	220,000
Current (replacement) value of total assets	$1,610,000
Less Total Liabilities	255,000
Current (replacement) value of Net Assets	$1,355,000

[a] Current replacement cost, $360,000.
[b] Cost $60,000; current market value, $430,000.
[c] Replacement cost of equivalent capacity, $520,000.

Most subsidiaries acquired in a purchase cost the parent more than the common book value of the net assets acquired, for reasons similar to those above. Assume you were a good negotiator and sold your corporation to the Acquisition-Happy Conglomerate Corporation in exchange for $500,000 and a five-year interest-bearing note for $1,000,0000. Exhibit 14.5 shows both firms after the acquisition, and how they might be consolidated following the purchase treatment.

As with any consolidation of balance sheets, the first step is simple combination, and the second is elimination of intercompany ownership. Following the purchase, the entire parent's share (100 percent, in this example) of the subsidiary's stockholders' equity is eliminated, not just the subsidiary's contributed capital. In Exhibit 14.5 this amount totaled $595,000 and is also eliminated from the combined investment account. The balance in the combined investment account in this example still represents intercompany investment of $905,000. Note that any other parent investments (not shown in this example) in nonvoting stock, nonsubsidiary companies, and unconsolidated subsidiaries are not involved in intercompany ownership elimination. Also not involved in ownership eliminations would be any subsidiary investments (unless they are in the family).

Exhibit 14.5   Example of Balance Sheet Consolidation following Purchase Treatment
($ in thousands)

	Parent	Subsidiary	Simple combina-tion	Eliminations and adjustments	Consolidated balance sheet
Assets					
Cash	$ 140	$ 95	$ 235		$ 235
Receivables	350	205	555		555
Inventory	200	190	390	+170 (c)	560
Investments	1,500	60	1,560	−595 (a)	430
				−905 (b)	
				+370 (c)	
Prop. and Equip. (net)	800	300	1,100	+220 (c)	1,320
Goodwill	0	0	0	+145 (d)	145
Total Assets	$2,990	$850	$3,840		$3,245
Equities					
Total liabilities	$1,200	$255	$1,455		$1,455
Common stock	1,000	400	1,400	−400 (a)	1,000
Additional paid-in capital	350	80	430	− 80 (a)	350
Retained earnings	440	115	555	−115 (a)	440
Total Equities	$2,990	$850	$3,840		$3,245

Eliminations and adjustments with 100-percent ownership:
a.   First eliminate intercompany investment at total subsidiary book value (contributed capital plus retained earnings).
b.   Balance in investments account applicable to subsidiary represents excess paid over accounting book value of net assets acquired. It is eliminated and replaced by (c) and (d) below.
c.   Any acquired assets are written up to current fair market value.
d.   Balance of excess payment identified as goodwill.

The $905,000 excess over book value represents payment for "undervalued assets" plus goodwill. It is eliminated and replaced by writing up subsidiary inventory by $170,000, investments of subsidiary by $370,000, and subsidiary fixed assets net by $220,000. The balance of $145,000 does not represent "asset understatement" and is therefore assumed to represent acquired goodwill. It is shown as such on the consolidated balance sheet.

Recall that GAAP do not allow a firm to attempt to measure and report its own self-generated or self-developed goodwill. Such a measurement would be too subjective. However, when a firm is purchased or sold, any existing goodwill which is paid for may be readily identified and estimated. GAAP therefore provide that purchased goodwill may be reported. GAAP also require that any such purchased goodwill must be amortized to zero over a period of not less than 10 and no more than 40 years. The requirement for arbitrary amortization of **purchased goodwill** reflects the inability of accountants to objectively verify its continued existence after acquisition, and the inappropriateness of writing it all off as a loss in the first few weeks or years after acquisition.

Other Eliminations in a Purchase

The only essential difference between pooling and purchase accounting pertains to the elimination (and reclassification for a purchase) of intercompany ownership. All other eliminations are the same regardless of purchase or pooling accounting. To review, in addition to intercompany ownership eliminations:

- From the combined balance sheets, eliminate:

    1. Any intercompany debt,

    2. Any intercompany nonownership investment, and

    3. Any intercompany profit in inventory.

- From the combined income statements and statement of cash flows, eliminate all intercompany transactions and accruals.

Essential Differences Between Poolings and Purchases

Whether a business combination is treated as a pooling or as a purchase may have significant differences in future reported consolidated income and in asset valuations on the consolidated balance sheets.

Differences in Reported Income

The essential difference between purchase and pooling treatments with respect to the consolidated income statement does not involve eliminations. Significant difference can exist with respect to reported net income under the two treatments.

Under a pooling treatment, consolidated net income would be the sum of the two firms' incomes. Under pooling, any gain on the sale, subsequent to merger, of your investments portfolio (realizing the difference between the $60,000 of book value and the $430,000 of current market value) would be reported as part of consolidated net income. However, under the purchase treatment, your firm's assets would have already been revalued in consolidation. Any subsequent realization of gain on asset disposition up to market value at the time of acquisition would be excluded from consolidated net income as already recognized at the time of consolidation. Furthermore, consolidated net income would normally be lower in future years under the purchase method as opposed to pooling accounting.

Under purchase accounting, consolidated assets were written up to reflect recognition of the $905,000 paid in excess of original cost book values. $905,000 of "additional assets" would not be reported under the pooling treatment (assuming you had received stock instead of cash plus debt for your corporation). Under purchase accounting, the additional $905,000 will be systematically written off as additional expense over future years on the consolidated income statement in the form of higher cost of goods, higher depreciation expense, and amortization of goodwill.

Differences in Asset Valuations

As mentioned previously, under pooling no new basis for accounting is deemed to exist. Original asset book values of both firms are carried forward onto the consolidated balance sheet. Under purchase accounting, however, a new basis of accounting for the subsidiary's assets is deemed to exist, and they are written up on the consolidated balance sheet to their fair market value at the time of acquisition or to the excess paid over subsidiary's book value, whichever is lower.

Implications of Purchase vs. Pooling Treatments

To summarize, under the pooling treatment, consolidated net income is maximized. Retained earnings from both firms are combined on the consolidated balance sheet which means you can acquire retained earnings in exchange for stock. Future earnings, both operating and gains on historical cost measured assets acquired, can similarly be acquired and reported.[4]

Under purchase accounting, consolidated net income is often considerably lower than it would have been under the pooling treatment. Past subsidiary earnings are not added to

---

[4] You may wish to explore and tentatively connect with this point the highly publicized 1972 incident involving ITT, the Hartford Fire Insurance Company (a "pooled" subsidiary), Dita Beard, Attorney General John Mitchell and the antitrust division of the Department of Justice, the Sheraton Hotel Corporation (another ITT subsidiary), and the original planning for the 1972 Republican National Convention.

consolidated retained earnings on the balance sheet. Future consolidated income does not include gains realized between the historical-cost book value of the subsidiary's assets and their fair market value at the date on which control was acquired. Future income is reduced by goodwill amortization and other expenses reflecting the difference between the purchase cost and old book value.

Is it any wonder that parent corporations desiring to report high earnings prefer pooling to purchase treatment? There is evidence that some mergers have taken place to take advantage of the accountant's pooling treatment and to buy earnings; and that they would not have occurred had appropriate purchase treatment been required.

Unresolved Issues

Most business combinations are not clearly poolings or purchases. Although some outright purchases are obvious, a true pooling of near-equal partners is very rare. Many accountants maintain that all business combinations should be treated as purchases. They maintain that a business combination is still the result of a bargained transaction even if only securities are eventually exchanged.

Supporters of pooling argue that it is difficult to measure the value of securities given in exchange, especially when, as is often the case, the exchange agreement is based on anticipated stock values resulting from the combination. Pooling defenders are also concerned that partners to a pooling or a near-pooling, combination could immediately manipulate asset values if they were required to use the purchase method.

Minority Interest

A parent-subsidiary relationship exists when the parent controls 50 percent or more of the subsidiary's voting stock. A subsidiary does not have to be wholly owned in order to be consolidated. Recall that consolidated statements must be prepared when over 50 percent of the stock in a company is owned. Consolidation, when there are minority stockholders, follows basically the same steps as in the 100 percent ownership case. The only essential differences are:

1. Only the parent's share of the subsidiary common shareholders' equity is eliminated as intercompany investment. Any balance remaining in the combined investments account that is applicable to the subsidiary common stock represents and is treated as excess of cost over book value of the net assets acquired. Any balance remaining in subsidiary common shareholders' equity represents "outside of family" (minority) claims. These claims are combined into a single amount and shown along with other equities on the consolidated balance sheet as "minority interest."

2. The combined net income (after adjustments for additional appreciation and goodwill amortization) is designated "Income Before Minority Interest" or given some similar title; and two additional lines are added to the statement. The first indicates the minor-

ity stockholders' share of the subsidiary's net income and is shown as a deduction. The second is labeled net income and represents the parent stockholders' share or claim.

The consolidated balance sheets and income statements for the Xerox Corporation, contained in Appendix A at the back of the book, adequately demonstrate the disclosure of the minority of consolidated assets and consolidated income as "outside shareholders' interests."

Interpreting Consolidated Financial Statements

In interpreting a consolidated balance sheet, you now know that, regardless of purchase or pooling treatment, reported consolidated assets will include only properties held or controlled (capital leases) by the "family" plus rights and claims against outsiders who are not family members. Similarly, all liabilities and minority interest shown will represent claims by outside creditors and stockholders. And the consolidated income statement and statement of cash flows will reflect only transactions and accruals involving outsiders.

Purchase vs. pooling treatment will affect the accounting measurement of assets, retained earnings, and consolidated revenues and expenses subsequent to acquisition of control. Reference to the statement footnotes will tell you whether the pooling or purchase treatment has been followed.

Statutory Mergers

At the beginning of this chapter, it was pointed out that a merger could take the form of assets and equities being legally combined in a single corporation. In such cases, a parent-subsidiary relationship would no longer exist and consolidated financial statements would be irrelevant. In the event of a statutory merger, the subsidiary assets and equities are transferred onto the books of the surviving corporation. If conditions for a pooling are met, the transfer is at accounting book value. Otherwise assets and liabilities are recorded at fair market values, together with possible purchased goodwill. In essence, under either treatment, the same original eliminations and adjustments are made at the point of acquisition as with a consolidation. In a statutory merger, however, they are actually made in the surviving corporation's accounts instead of only on consolidated working papers. After acquisition, the financial statements would be essentially similar except that they would not be labeled as "consolidated." They would be for one legal entity—the surviving corporation.

Segment Reporting

Large corporations often operate throughout the world and are highly diversified into different lines of business through mergers and acquisitions. When data related to many different types of businesses are combined on a single set of financial statements, the aggregated amounts may have little meaning and no comparative value in relation to other firms. For instance, of what real significance would wage and salaries expense be in relation to anything else if the income statement combined an automated steel mill, a large lettuce farm, four movie companies, a cosmetics manufacturer and a chain of fast food restaurants?

GAAP require that firms disclose, as supplementary information, certain key data concerning each of its major **segments** of different types of business. Segment data may also be thought of as information concerning artificial entities, since a segment of an overall business could be a part of one corporation, the sum of parts of several corporations, or even the sum of several corporations (a sort of miniconsolidation). The detailed GAAP guidelines for identification of segments for reporting purposes are beyond the scope of this text. Generalized information for your overall understanding is included below. You may think of a segment as a distinctly different type of business.

Identifying Segments

GAAP require segment reporting by industry and **geographic location**. A separately reportable segment is one which:

- Generates 10% or more of total revenue, or
- Generates 10% or more of earnings, or
- Uses separately identifiable assets representing at least 10% of all segmentable assets.[5]

Think of a firm that obtained 50 percent of its revenue from selling tractors and the other 50 percent from selling food. Assume that it had a large French subsidiary selling tractors and home appliances, again on a 50-50 basis. Segment reporting by industry would separate the tractor, appliance, and food operations but would include both U.S. and French operations. The disclosure of geographic data would separate the domestic from the French operations.

Segment Information Reported

The intent of segment reporting is to provide meaningful operating and financial data which allows the reader to identify the areas of operation and the company's exposure risk to changes in the economy. For each **reportable segment**, GAAP require that supplementary information be provided with respect to the following:

- revenue,
- earnings from continuing operations,
- book value of identifiable (with the particular segment) assets,
- aggregate related depreciation, depletion, and amortization expense, and
- amount of capital expenditures—additions to fixed assets.

---

5 Some assets are not readily "segmentable"; that is they are common to several different segments of the business and therefore cannot be readily and specifically identified with one particular segment. Neither a corporate headquarters building nor a factory producing products for two or more distinct segments would be "segmentable" assets.

In addition, GAAP also require the disclosure of certain other information of a technical nature that is beyond the scope of this text and will not be discussed here.

It is important to note that total segment revenue might exceed total firm revenue. This could result from the fact that each segment will be reported on the basis of included both revenue from outsiders and revenue from other segments. Total firm revenue, of course, excludes intersegment revenue. Total segment operating profit may not match total firm profit. This difference in profit should be expected, because overall corporate or home-office revenues and expenses and all interest expense are specifically excluded in the calculation of segment profit.

Information concerning **major customers** must also be disclosed. Any single customer, foreign government, or domestic government agency providing at least ten percent of the firm's revenue is defined as a major customer. Such customers must be identified, together with revenues derived therefrom.

Exhibit 14.6

FARWELL CORPORATION
Abbreviated Financial Statement Data for Year Ending 12/31/X9
($ in thousands)

Net working capital	$10,000
Capacity assets (net)	50,000
Total	$60,000
Long-term debt (net)	$24,000
Stockholders' equity	36,000
Total	$60,000
Sales	$30,800
Operating expenses*	26,200
Income from operations before taxes	$ 4,600
Provision for income taxes	900
Net income	3,700

* interest expense was $2,000

Analysis of Segment Information

Exhibits 14.6 and 14.7 provide one example of the usefulness of segment information. Assume you are interested in the performance of the Farwell Corporation. You might be an officer of the company, a creditor, or a stockholder. Study the abbreviated statements contained in Exhibit 14.6. Can you see that a reader of these statements might find little cause for alarm? The operating ratio (net income as a percent of sales) is an apparently respectable 12 percent; and the return of long-term assets (EBIT as a percent of net working capital plus noncurrent assets) is an adequate 11 percent.

Exhibit 14.7 reveals that the appliance industry requires 36 percent of the assets to generate only 25 percent of the total revenue, with a resultant $2,300,000 operating loss.

Exhibit 14.7

FARWELL CORPORATION
Supplementary Segment Information for Year Ending 12/31/X9
($ in thousands)

	Tractors	Appliances	Food	Other	Total
Revenue	$12,300	$ 7,700	$10,800	0	$30,800
Operating Income/loss	3,700	(2,300)	3,200	0	4,600
Identifiable assets (at book value)	$13,500	$18,000	$13,500	$5,000	$50,000
Related expense (Depreciation and Amortization)	1,100	1,500	1,150	250	4,000
Additions to capacity assets	$ 1,100	$ 2,000	$ 2,400	$ 500	$ 6,000

Assuming that food and tractor revenues were not dependent on the appliance business, discontinuation and liquidation of the appliances segment could result in an additional $2,300,000 of profit with $18,000,000 less of capital invested. Note also that Exhibit 14.7 reveals an additional $2,000,000 of investment in the appliance business during the past year!

This admittedly extreme example is designed to demonstrate how segment reporting can disclose significant information that is hidden in combined totals. The firm's management normally has such information in far more detail as a product of its internal managerial accounting system. However, the management might not wish to disclose this information to creditors or stockholders. The GAAP requirement of segment reporting is intended to ensure that all interested parties have reasonable access to important information that otherwise could be buried in overall company totals.

In addition to the relative performance of different segments in comparison to each other, segmental information can provide a limited basis for comparative analysis with other firms, or other firm's segments, in the same line of business. Furthermore, data on a firm's **foreign operations** and their locations can give the investor the opportunity to estimate relative potential benefits and risks in those nations and their possible significance to the firm. Certain nations may be politically stable, undergoing rapid growth, and may present great opportunities for future earnings. Others may be the opposite, and may even hold a high risk of nationalization or expropriation of the firm's assets and business. Also, a firm with a high proportion of foreign operations may be especially vulnerable to gains and losses on currency revaluations.

Information concerning major customers also reveals degrees of relative stability or vulnerability of the firm's future business. Heavy dependence for a large portion of revenue upon a government agency or another firm is significant investor information. Future prospects of the firm will be linked to any analysis and projection of the anticipated volume of activity of its major customers.

GAAP provide that segment information may be presented in one of several ways. You may find it incorporated in the financial statements and footnotes, in separate schedules included as part of the statement "package," or entirely in the statement footnotes.

Footnote Disclosure

Appendix A contains complete financial statements for both the Xerox Corporation and the AT&T Company. There is general agreement that financial statements are prepared for the knowledgeable reader. Business activities are often too complex to reduce to a few meaningful numbers. At this point, you should have an understanding of accounting adequate to read and understand the contents of both corporations' statements. Turn to Appendix A and study the statements. You should find it interesting and informative. When you have a need to study financial statements as the basis for an important decision, study the footnotes. Many times the statement footnotes contain significant information that is equally important as that contained in the statements themselves. Footnotes are considered an integral part of financial statements, and they are covered by the auditor's examination and report.

Auditor's Report

A prime reason for reading footnotes is that they contain the auditor's report or certificate. This report is essential to give a statement credibility for you. Of even more importance, it will highlight any significant changes, departures from GAAP, or auditor's reservations as to the adequacy of the audit or the fairness of disclosure. If there are any exceptions or changes in accounting method, these must be noted in the report so your attention may be directed to the relevant footnote.

Choice of Accounting Methods

Throughout this text you have learned that there are various measurement and reporting options within GAAP than can produce significantly different results. For example, a firm can elect LIFO or FIFO for inventory and cost-of-goods-sold valuation. These differences can make comparisons with other firms, which may elect different measurement options, difficult, dangerous, and occasionally meaningless. The statement footnotes will tell you exactly which accounting method the firm has elected.

Accounting Changes

Changes in accounting methods can make comparisons difficult, not just with other firms, but with data for the same firm from prior years. GAAP require that significant **accounting changes** (changes in accounting methods) be made retroactive on any prior years' data included in the current report. The footnotes will contain details of any accounting changes so that you may take them into consideration in making comparisons to prior years' data.

Supplementary Information

Footnotes generally contain expansion of information only summarized on the report. This additional detail is often essential in evaluating statements. A single summary figure on the balance sheet can be relatively meaningless. For example, if you wish to analyze a firm's position, and a significant portion of total assets were investments, you couldn't do much with a single line "investments $43,742,000." The footnotes will often contain a breakdown of the investments account, allowing you to evaluate the individual components.

Contingencies and Commitments

Finally, footnotes will disclose all material contingencies and commitments. Contingencies and commitments could radically alter your assumptions concerning the firm's future prospects. Remember, as a financial statement user making a decision, the historical information contained in the statements is valuable only as a basis for forecasting the future. The future is relevant to your decision. A firm might be currently involved with products and services that you believe are obsolescent. The existence of future contract commitments would influence your judgement as to how quickly the firm could switch to a different growing line of business. Major legal action pending against the firm could also severely impact the future.

Interim Reports

The pace of change in the modern world continues to accelerate. Today investors desire more current updates on their investee's activities than just an annual report. **Interim reports** are essentially abbreviated and estimated financial statements for a period shorter than one year. They may be prepared semiannually, quarterly, or even monthly. Presently the quarterly reporting cycle appears to be the most common practice.

Interim reports appear to be growing in significance as a basis for investor decisions. There is even some evidence that the financial community has already made its major business decisions before the annual report is released.

Interim reports, hereafter discussed as quarterly reports, can be oriented in two quite different ways. They can focus on the events occurring in the particular quarter as if it were a distinct reporting period or they can report the quarter as an integral part of the annual report. An example of statement differences resulting from these two approaches can be seen with respect to the cost of an annual major maintenance program. Assume that the firm schedules this annual maintenance each August during the firm's vacation shutdown. Following the distinct period approach, all maintenance costs would appear as expenses during the third quarter. GAAP encourage the alternative approach. Quarterly reports are considered to be just part of a picture which will eventually encompass the entire annual accounting period. In the case of the annual maintenance costs, they would be accrued or deferred, as appropriate, so as to reasonably apportion them to each of the four quarters in order to match revenue patterns. Of course, for those costs that cannot be readily identified and matched with the benefits of particular periods, GAAP require that they be charged to the period when incurred.

Of necessity, more items will require estimates on quarterly reports. If the firm is on periodic inventory, it probably would not wish, and could not afford, to take a complete physical inventory at the end of each quarter. Instead it may estimate cost of goods sold based on sales using the prior year's average gross profit percentage.

Interpreting Interim Reports

The same matching principle applicable to all accounting is also the objective of quarterly reporting. Revenues are reported in the quarter earned, and expenses are allocated to quarters to achieve the optimal matching with revenues.

Exhibit 14.8

BOLGER ENTERPRISES, INC.
Selected Interim Report and Annual Report Data
($ in thousands)

	Most recent quarter (Winter 19X8)	Same quarter prior year (Winter 19X7)	Prior quarter (Fall 19X7)	Prior year total (19X7)
Revenue	$36,000	$30,000	$40,000	$130,000
Operating expenses	29,000	26,000	28,000	106,000
Income before taxes	$ 7,000	$ 4,000	$ 12,000	$ 24,000
Provision for income taxes	1,500	800	2,500	4,900
Net income	$ 5,000	$ 3,200	$ 9,500	$ 19,100

Only in the rare case of a firm whose revenues are linear throughout the year (no seasonality) can you meaningfully compare just one quarter to the previous quarter.

Comparisons need to be made to the same quarter in prior years. Alternatively, cumulative year-to-date amounts can be compared to similar cumulative amounts for prior years. Seasonality can have a major impact on interim reports.

Exhibit 14.8 demonstrates the usefulness of interim-report information. Assume you have been an investor in Bolger Enterprises, and that the 19X7 Annual Report, which you received in March of 19X8, indicated only average performance for the previous year. Also assume you were seriously considering selling your stock in Bolger and investing your funds elsewhere. Could Bolger's interim report for the first quarter of 19X8 influence your decision?

In this example, you might wish to hold your Bolger stock instead of selling it. The interim report indicates that sales increased 20 percent over the same quarter last year and net income increased 72 percent! It appears that Bolger's 19X8 performance may no longer be just "average."

Exhibit 14.8 also demonstrates the potential danger of the comparison of data to previous quarters. Assuming that the fall quarter is the largest and most profitable each year, and that Fall 19X7 was about the same as Fall 19X6, to compare Winter 19X8 with Fall 19X7 could be very misleading.

Chapter Overview

Based upon the material covered in this chapter, you should be able to:

- Explain the difference between a purchase and a pooling in terms of how a merger is effected;
- Explain the basic steps of consolidation following the pooling treatment;
- Explain the basic steps of consolidation following the purchase treatment;
- Describe the essential differences between purchase and pooling accounting, and explain the significance of these differences to future consolidated income reported for the combination;
- Describe the basic guidelines for segment disclosure for industries, geographic location, and major customers, and explain why disclosure is required for each;
- Describe the major categories or types of information you can expect to find included as part of financial statement footnotes;
- Explain the basic revenue and expense reporting objectives of interim reports, and the constraints relating to their appropriate use in trend analysis.

New Vocabulary and Concepts

Accounting changes	Merger
Acquisition	Minority stockholders
Business combination	Pooling of interests
Eliminations (in business combinations)	Purchase
Foreign operations	Purchased goodwill
Geographic location	Segments
Holding company	Separately reportable segment
Intercompany debt	Statutory consolidation
Intercompany ownership	Statutory merger
Interim reports	Wholly owned subsidiary
Major customers	

- Requirements for consolidation.
- Purchase vs. pooling: difference as to method of acquisition and as to accounting method of consolidation.
- Necessary eliminations in consolidation.
- Segment information.
- Matching and interim reports.

Review Questions

1. (a) What is a parent? (b) What is a subsidiary? (c) Explain the requirements for a parent-subsidiary relationship.

2. Can minority interest exist in the case of a wholly owned subsidiary?

3. (a) What is the difference between a consolidation and a statutory merger? (b) What is the difference in the accountant's treatment of each?

4. Explain two essentially different ways in which two corporations can merge.

5. In a pooling, how (at what amount) is the investment in the subsidiary originally carried on the parent's books?

6. In a pooling consolidation, is it possible to have investment in excess of book value which would be used to revalue assets and/or become goodwill? Explain.

7. What happens to subsidiary retained earnings at the time of acquisition in a pooling consolidation? Explain.

8. Although handled differently for poolings and purchases, why is intercompany investment always eliminated in consolidation?

9. In addition to intercompany investment, what major eliminations are made in consolidation, regardless of purchase or pooling treatment? Give examples.

10. What is done in a purchase consolidation with any excess paid over the book value of net assets obtained?

11. (a) On a consolidated balance sheet, what happens to any minority share of the subsidiary's book value at the time of acquisition? (b) What happens to the minority's share of the subsidiary's earnings since acquisition, on the consolidated balance sheet? (c) On the consolidated income statement?

12. On a consolidated balance sheet, none of the subsidiary's owners' equity appears as such. Where does it go?

13. In balance sheet consolidation, there may also be eliminations affecting the following items:

    a) Current notes receivable
    b) Accounts receivable
    c) Rent or interest payable
    d) Prepaid items
    e) Investments in bonds, noncurrent notes, or preferred stock

    f) Current notes payable
    g) Accounts payable
    h) Interest or rent payable
    i) Bonds or notes payable
    j) Preferred stock

    For each of these possible "targets of elimination," describe the situation where an elimination would be appropriate, the amount to be eliminated, and the reason for the elimination.

14. In income statement consolidation, there may be eliminations affecting the following items:

    a) Sales
    b) Cost of goods sold
    c) Rent revenue

    d) Rent expense
    e) Interest revenue
    f) Interest expense

    For each of these possible "targets of elimination," describe the situation when an elimination would be appropriate, the amount to be eliminated, and the reason for the elimination.

15. What is the difference in the accountant's treatment of a combination, between purchase treatment and pooling treatment? What is the potential effect of the differing treatments upon future income statements?

16. What is the basis for determining separately reportable segments of a business enterprise?

17. What are the three tests needed to qualify a reportable segment?

18. What minimum information must be reported for each reportable segment?

19. (a) When must foreign operations be separately disclosed? (b) What must be disclosed for significant foreign operations?

20. (a) When must major customers be disclosed? (b) What must be disclosed with respect to qualifying major customers?

21. What are five significant separate types of information that are included as part of statement footnotes?

22. In many firms, the comparison of two successive quarterly reports can prove misleading. Explain why this is possible.

Mini-Cases and Questions for Discussion

MC 14.1 Mr. Robert Curley sometimes takes things too literally. He perceives consolidated financial statements as essentially violating the underlying principles of accounting. "First of all, financial statements are prepared for business entities," he states. "A parent and its subsidiaries do not comprise an entity. Furthermore, even in the case of a wholly owned subsidiary, not all the assets on a consolidated balance sheet are either owned or controlled by the parent. Subsidiary creditors have prior claims on all subsidiary assets, and minority stockholders have a claim, too. Showing minority interest as an equity is like two wrongs trying to make a right. A consolidated balance sheet shows them as having a claim against total consolidated assets!"

Discuss Mr. Curley's position. Is he correct? If he is correct, would it still be reasonable to prepare consolidated financial statements?

MC 14.2 Ann Jackson can see no reason for different treatments between purchase and pooling, "Take a business combination where everything actually happens the same except the composition of the surviving owners—the same sales, the same expenses, the same funds flows, the same everything," she says. "Yet if the surviving owners' names are different, the accountants will report lower net income than if the names are the same. Income supposedly earned by the corporation independent of who its owners are. What possible justification is there for different accounting treatments?" Discuss.

Essential Problems

Note. In all Essential Problems below, the parent will be designated "P" and the subsidiary as "S."

EP 14.1 P purchases 100 percent of the voting common stock of S for $140,000. P has no other investments. The common book value and total owners' equity of S at the time of acquisition by P is $100,000. P's owners' equity immediately prior to acquiring S is $600,000. You may assume all of S's assets were on the firm's books at current costs. On the consolidated balance sheet immediately following acquisition:

   a) P's investments will be included at what amount?

   b) Goodwill will be what amount?

   c) Consolidated owners' equity, including minority interest, will total how much?

EP 14.2 Answer the same questions as in EP 14.1, assuming:

   • P purchases 80 percent of S's common stock for $200,000;

   • The common book value and total owners' equity of S at the time of acquisition was $187,5000;

   • P's owners' equity immediately prior to acquiring S was $700,000.

EP 14.3   P purchased 75 percent of the common stock of S for $150,000. P also has as an investment a 10 percent ownership in Q costing $30,000. The common book value and total owners' equity of S at the time of acquisition was $160,000. Since acquisition, S has $40,000 of accumulated retained earnings. P's current owners' equity totals $900,000. On a current consolidated balance sheet, what amounts should appear as:

  a) Investments?

  b) Goodwill?

  c) Minority interest?

  d) Consolidated owners' equity, including minority interest?

EP 14.4   Refer to EP 14.3. Answer the same questions, based on the same information, but assume that P's proportional interest in S was 60 percent at a cost of $150,000.

EP 14.5   P's and S's combined balance sheet, after only the elimination of intercompany common stock investment, appeared as follows:

Cash	$ 400	Accounts payable	$ 700
Accounts receivable (net)	900	Other current liabilities	500
Inventory	800	Bonds payable	400
Investments	300	Less bond discount	(40)
Property and equipment	1,200	Minority interest	200
Accumulated depreciation	(500)	Common stock	1,000
Consolidated goodwill	200	Retained earnings	540
Total Assets	$3,300	Total Equities	$3,300

During the previous year, S had sold merchandise costing $300 to P for $500. All the merchandise purchased from S had been sold by P at the end of the year. P had paid S for all merchandise delivered except for $40 not as yet paid. In P's investments account were some of S's bonds with a maturity value of $100 and a net book value of $90. Complete the preparation of the P and S consolidated balance sheet.

EP 14.6   Refer to EP 14.5, and start with the same partially finished consolidated balance sheet for P and S given in that problem. Assume that, during the previous year, P had sold merchandise costing $300 to S for $400. S had resold all of this merchandise to customers. S had performed various services for P during the year, which were billed at $200. All but $20 of these services have been paid for at year end. In S's investments account at year end were some of P's bonds with a face value of $50 and a net book value of $45. Complete the preparation of the P and S consolidated balance sheet.

EP 14.7 The combined income statement for P and S before any elimination was as follows:

Sales		$1,800
Cost of goods sold		1,100
Gross profit		$ 700
Other operating expenses:		
Wages and salaries	$ 400	
Depreciation	130	
Interest	15	
Rent	140	685
Other revenues		90
Operating income		$ 105
Less income taxes		40
Net income		$ 65

During the year, S had sold P merchandise costing $300, for $500. S had also paid P $10 of interest on notes held by P. Complete the preparation of the P and S consolidated income statement. You may assume S is a wholly owned subsidiary, and that P has sold all merchandise purchased from S.

EP 14.8 Refer to EP 14.7, and start with the same partially completed income statement for P and S given in that problem. During the year P had sold S merchandise costing $400 for $700. S had paid P $12 of interest on notes held by P. Warehouse space rented from S cost P a total of $68 for the year. Complete the preparation of the P and S consolidated income statement. You may assume S is a wholly owned subsidiary, and that P has sold all merchandise purchased from S.

EP 14.9 P acquired 100 percent of the voting stock of S in exchange for 10,000 shares of additionally issued P $10-par common stock. At the time of acquisition, S's owners' equity was:

Common stock	$100,000
Additional paid-in capital	70,000
Retained earnings	300,000
	$470,000

You may assume that P had no other investments, and that a consolidated balance sheet was to be prepared before S had any subsequent earnings. You may also assume that P's year-end retained earnings equaled $100,000 and that the combination with S qualified as pooling.

a) What was the balance in P's investments account immediately prior to consolidation?

b) What eliminations (amounts) in consolidation should be made from:
  i) combined investments?
  ii) combined common stock?
  iii) combined additional paid-in capital?
  iv) combined retained earnings?

c) What amount of retained earnings should be reported on the consolidated balance sheet?

EP 14.10 P acquired 100 percent of the voting stock of S in exchange for 80,000 shares of P's additionally issued $5-par common stock. At the time of acquisition, S's owners' equity was:

Common stock	$ 500,000
Additional paid-in capital	300,000
Retained earnings	200,000
	$1,000,000

You may assume that P had no other investments; that S had $100,000 of net income between
acquisition and the year end when consolidated statements were to be prepared on a pooling
basis; that between acquisition and year end, S paid out $40,000 in dividends; and that P's
retained earnings at year end amounted to $750,000.

   a) What was the balance in P's investments account immediately prior to consolidation?

   b) What eliminations (amounts) in consolidation should be made from:

     i) combined investments?

     ii) combined common stock?

     iii) combined additional paid-in capital?

     iv) combined retained earnings?

   c) What amount of retained earnings should be reported on the consolidated balance
sheet?

15

**Changing Prices
and
Supplementary Data**

Chapter Preview

The objective of this chapter is to introduce current GAAP recommendations for reporting supplementary information on the effects of inflation and changes in specific prices. In this chapter you can:

1. Become familiar with the differences between general and specific inflation and the effects on each;

2. Develop an understanding of the effect of general inflation on monetary items and how to calculate this effect;

3. Learn the differences between current cost and constant dollar accounting and the different definitions of income inherent in each;

4. Become familiar with supplementary current cost information and how it is determined.

5. Learn how supplementary constant dollar information may be estimated; and

6. Develop a familiarity with possible uses and interpretations of supplementary current cost data.

From the information contained in this chapter you will be better able to deal with the limitations of conventional or primary financial statements; and you be able to interpret the different types of inflation-adjusted information currently used by firms.

Is Reported Net Income Really Income

Assume that a service business was started on 1/1/X2 with $100,000 cash. In January, 19X2, a piece of equipment was purchased for $40,000 cash, and $50,000 was invested in a one-year certificate of deposit (CD) paying 12 percent annual interest. For simplification, you may assume that the equipment had a four-year useful life and zero salvage. You may also assume that the CD was purchased on 1/1/X2 with principal and accumulated interest to be received on 1/1/X3. During 19X2, cash sales were $200,000 and cash expenses (not including depreciation) were $166,000.

You may also assume, for simplification, that the firm was taxed as a corporation at an average 40 percent income tax rate on income as measured in the primary financial statements following GAAP; and that the taxes had not been paid by year-end. Assume no general inflation and no price/cost changes relating to the equipment, what was the 19X2 net income?

Balance Sheet Diagram 15.1 illustrates the effect of each of these events and the fact, following GAAP, that the 19X2 net income would be reported as $18,000.

Diagram 15.1

Effects of First Year's Events
As of 12/31/X2

Cash	$ 100,000 (1)	Taxes Payable $ 12,000 (C)
	− 50,000 (2)	
	− 40,000 (3)	Income
	+ 200,000 (4)	$ 200,000 (4)
	− 166,000 (5)	− 166,000 (5)
		+ 6,000 (A)
Marketable Securities		− 10,000 (B)
	50,000 (2)	− 12,000 (C)
Interest Receivable		+ 18,000 π
	6,000 (A)	
Equipment	40,000 (3)	
Accum. Deprec.		Owners' Capital 100,000 (1)
	(10,000) (B)	+ 18,000 (π)
Total Assets	$130,000	Total Equities $130,000

With assumed absence of both general inflation and specific price changes, income as reported in the primary financial statements accurately measures what most individuals define as income—increase in owner wealth or the amount earned after maintaining capital. To differentiate them from inflation-adjusted statements, note that conventional historical cost statements are known as "**primary financial statements.**" Under the assumption of no inflation and no price changes, $18,000 would clearly represent distributable income.

The owners could withdraw it from the business for personal use and still leave the firm as well off as it was at the outset. Exhibit 15.1 presents the firm's 12/31/X2 balance sheet.

Exhibit 15.1

Service Firm's Balance Sheet as of 12/31/X2
(Prepared following GAAP for primary financial Statements)

Current Assets		Current Liabilities	
Cash	$ 44,000	Taxes payable	$12,000
Marketable securities	50,000	Total Liabilities	$12,000
Interest receivable	6,000		
Total Current Assets	$100,000		
Equipment	40,000		
Accumulated depreciation	(10,000)	Owners' Capital	118,000
Total Assets	$130,000	Total Equities	$130,000

General Inflation

In periods of general inflation, the prices of most items and services increase in different proportions, and the price of some items might even decline. The term **general inflation** refers to the average overall increase in the prices of all items taken as a whole (or a representative sample of all items used for measurement purposes). It can also be viewed as the decline in the average or general purchasing power of the dollar or monetary unit of measurement. If, in one year, the general inflation rate is 10 percent, at year-end, on the average, it will take 110 monetary units (dollars) to purchase what could have purchased with 100 monetary Units (dollars) the previous year.

Exhibit 15.2

Service Firm's Balance Sheet as of 12/31/X2
(Prepared following constant dollar accounting*)

Current Assets		Current Liabilities	
Cash	$ 44,000	Taxes payable	$12,000
Marketable securities	50,000	Total Liabilities	$ 12,000
Interest receivable	6,000		
Total Current Assets	$100,000		
Equipment	40,000		
Accumulated depreciation	(11,000)	Owners' Capital	121,000
Total Assets	$133,000	Total Equities	$133,000

* Prepared using year-end inflation index.

Returning to the example of the service business, assume that during 19X2 the general inflation rate had been 10 percent and also that the cost of the equipment had risen 10 percent. For simplification, assume that the firm could sell its equipment or purchase equipment in equivalent condition for $33,000 on 1/1/X3, if it chose to do so. Under these conditions, would the 19X2 reported income of $18,000 really represent income? Would the firm's wealth have increased by $18,000 during the year?

Exhibit 15.2 illustrates the firm's 12/31/X2 financial position, adjusted to reflect general inflation or general price-level changes. The firm's position is restated in terms of constant dollars or constant dollar accounting. Note that the term constant dollar can be confusing, since dollars do not constantly maintain their purchasing power in periods of inflation. Instead, during inflation dollars lose general purchasing power or can be viewed as shrinking in size. **Constant dollar** accounting refers to the measurement and reporting of items on financial statements in terms of dollars, each of which has the same current general purchasing power.

Note in Exhibit 15.2 that the firm's ending position is measured in terms of current purchasing power dollar equivalents. Equipment has been revalued to reflect the number of year-end current dollars (with smaller general purchasing power) it would now take to acquire it. The revalued amount is also adjusted to reflect 25 percent depreciation. In terms of **nominal dollars**, owners' capital is $21,000 greater than the original capital of $100,000. The owners are apparently $21,000 better off.

Exhibit 15.3

Service Firm's 19X2 Income Statement

	Nominal Dollars	Constant Dollars
Sales	$200,000	$200,000
Interest revenue	6,000	6,000
Total Revenue	$206,000	$206,000
Depreciation	10,000	11,000
Other operating expenses	166,000	166,000
Income Before Taxes	$ 30,000	$ 29,000
Provision for income taxes	12,000	12,000
Income from Continuing Operations*	$18,000	$17,000**

*   Normally identified as net income when no extraordinary or discontinued items. Identified as income from continuing operations here since this measure is focused upon throughout the Chapter.

**   Before determining gain or loss on net monetary items as discussed below.

If you define wealth (or capital to be maintained) in terms of the general purchasing power of the dollars invested, on 12/31/X2 capital would have to be $110,000 in terms of current smaller "constant" dollars for capital maintenance. It would require $110,000 in terms of current dollars to purchase as much as could have purchased for $100,000 last year. Exhibit 15.2 reveals owners' capital as $121,000. Therefore the firm only had a real profit after taxes (measured in constant dollars) of $11,000 rather than the $18,000 (measured in nominal dollars) reported in the primary financial statements. The income tax liability is $12,000 ($30,000 income before tax times 40 percent) even though "real" income is only $11,000! The tax rate of 40 percent based on nominal dollar income is actually an effective rate of 52 percent of real income. Furthermore, if the reported $18,000 nominal dollar profit is withdrawn as distributable income, the general purchasing power of the firm would decline. Owners' capital would then be only $103,000 (in constant dollars) rather than the necessary capital maintenance of $110,000.

Effects of General Inflation

What really happened during 19X2 in terms of constant dollars? Exhibit 15.3 reveals income from continuing operations (or net income in this example) as $17,000 in constant dollars, since depreciation would be $11,000. An **unrealized holding gain** of $4,000 (measured in constant dollars) was created on equipment. Since there were no owner withdrawals, the sum of these two items is reflected in owners' capital in Exhibit 15.2.

But how is $17,000 of current income reconcilable with a net increase of only $11,000 in overall wealth? The answer is that the firm also experienced a $6,000 loss in year-end purchasing power on its net monetary items as described below.

Gain or Loss on Net Monetary Items

Note in comparing Exhibits 15.1 and 15.2 that only the nonmonetary items are adjusted to reflect changes in the purchasing power of dollars. Since they reflect cash or claims for cash that are fixed in dollar amounts **monetary items** are not adjusted. Monetary items are fixed in terms of dollars regardless of the purchasing power of such dollars.

If a firm holds monetary assets during inflation, it will experience a loss of purchasing power on these assets—the shrinking dollar. Conversely, monetary liabilities held during the period will result in a gain in the sense that the fixed dollar obligations can be settled in the future with less sacrifice of purchasing power—smaller dollars. Since such gains and losses offset each other, net monetary assets held during a year will result in a loss and net monetary liabilities will result in a gain.[1]

The calculation of the $6,000 loss (in terms of year-end dollars) is shown in Exhibit 15.4 For simplification, it is assumed that all changes (service revenues, expenditures, and

---

[1] Most firms hold net monetary liabilities—the total of current monetary liabilities and long-term debt exceeds total current monetary assets. During periods of inflation a firm may incur considerable expense to operate with the least feasible amount of monetary assets and to ensure that any excess cash is earning a return. Conventional statements report the costs of this activity as a current expense but do not report the benefit gain (or a minimum loss) on the holding of net monetary items.

interest earned) occurred at year-end, and therefore were not themselves subject to gain or loss. You can interpret Exhibit 15.4 as revealing that, at year-end the firm would have needed to have $94,000 of net monetary assets in order to maintain the purchasing power of its beginning $60,000 and its acquired $28,000. Since it ended with only $88,000 of general purchasing power, it experienced a loss of $6,000.

Exhibit 15.4   Simplified Computation of Purchasing Power Gain or Loss on
Net Monetary Items[a]

	Nominal Dollars	Conversion Factor	Constant Dollars
Balance 1/1/X2	$60,000[b]	$\dfrac{110^c}{100}$	$66,000
Increase in net monetary assets during the year	$28,000[d]	$\dfrac{110^e}{110}$	28,000 $94,000
Balance 12/31/X2	$88,000	$\dfrac{110^e}{110}$	88,000
Purchasing Power Loss On Net Monetary Items			$ 6,000

Notes: a Expressed in year-end constant dollars
 b Cash and marketable securities.
 c 10% inflation during year.
 d $34,000 net cash revenue plus $6,000 receivable minus $12,000 payable.
 e To simplify illustration, all revenues and expenditures are assumed to
   occur at year-end and therefore already to be in end-of-year constant dollars.

To review, constant dollar accounting is essentially the same as conventional historical cost accounting except that the measuring units are restated in terms of current (constant) dollars. Conventional historical cost accounting (the primary financial statements) reports a firm's position and performance in terms of adjusted costs expressed in nominal dollars. Constant dollar accounting reports the same items adjusted to common current measuring units. Note that, under constant dollar accounting, the current costs of non-monetary items are not recognized.[2] The current cost of equivalent equipment as of 12/31/X2 was not necessarily $33,000. It could, for example, have actually remained constant at $30,000, reflecting no special price on new equipment.

---

[2] A significant reduction in current costs (and possible recovery value) of an asset such as inventory would be recognized, however, via an LCM adjustment in the primary statements before adjustment to constant dollars.

Exhibit 15.5

More Realistic Computation of Purchasing Power Loss on
Net Monetary Assets*

	Nominal Dollars	Conversion Factor	Constant Dollars
Balance 1/1/X2	$60,000	$\dfrac{104}{100}$	$62,400
Increase in net monetary assets during the year	$28,000	**	28,000
			$90,400
Balance 12/31/X2	$88,000	$\dfrac{104}{110}$	83,200
Purchasing Power Loss On Net Monetary Items			$ 7,200

   *   Expressed in 19X2 average (mid-year) dollars.
**   Assumed to already be in 19X2 average dollars.

Specific Inflation

Whereas the term general inflation refers to the average of price changes for all items, **specific inflation** refers to the specific price change of a specific asset or type of asset. The **current cost** of an item reflects the effect of specific inflation (or deflation) of its price, regardless of the degree of general inflation.

Returning to the example of the service firm, recall that, for purposes of demonstrating constant dollar accounting, the actual current cost of equipment as of 12/31/X2 was effectively ignored. In essence it was assumed that the current cost had risen at exactly the general inflation rate, that the current cost of acquiring equipment having the same service potential or usefulness was $33,000.

To account for specific inflation GAAP recommend accounting for current cost. You may initially conceive of current cost (or lower recoverable amounts) at the time of their use or sale at year-end, regardless of the existence of any general inflation.

To understand accounting for current cost, you should assume all the same facts for the firm as given above except that the current cost (new) of the equipment as of 12/31/X2 has increased to $50,000, and the cost of equivalent equipment as of 12/31/X2 to $37,500—a specific inflation rate of 25 percent. The firm's 19X2 income statement and year-end balance sheet prepared following current cost accounting is given in Exhibit 15.6.

Effects of Specific Inflation

Compare the income statement in Exhibit 15.6 with those shown in Exhibit 15.3. Note that the only difference among all three statements is the reporting of the expiration or use of nonmonetary assets—only depreciation in this simplified example. Sales, interest received, operating expenses, and taxes are all assumed to reflect current prices and constant dollars.[3] Note especially that since taxes are imposed on taxable income measured in conventional nominal dollars, provision for taxes is not adjusted.

Exhibit 15.6

Service Firm's Balance Sheet 12/31/X2
(Prepared on a Current Cost Basis)

Cash	$ 44,000	Taxes payable	$12,000
Marketable securities	50,000	Total Liabilities	$12,000
Interest receivable	6,000		
Total Current Assets	$100,000		
Equipment	50,000		
Accumulated depreciation	(12,500)	Owners' Capital	125,500*
Total Assets	$137,500	Total Equities	$137,500

Income Statement

Sales	$200,000
Interest revenue	6,000
Total Revenue	$206,000
Depreciation	11,250
Other operating expenses	166,000
Income Before Taxes	$28,750
Provision for income taxes	12,000
Income from Continuing Operations*	$16,750**

* Reflects income, unrealized holding gain on equipment, and additional catch-up depreciation as discussed below.

** Normally identified as net income when no extraordinary on discontinued items. Identified as income from operations here since this measure is focused upon throughout the Chapter.

Current depreciation expense is reported at $10,000 on the conventional statement, reflecting expiration of original asset cost in nominal dollars. In the general-price-level-adjusted statement, it is reported as $11,000 reflecting the same expiration restated to constant dollars. In the current cost statement it reflects expiration in terms of specific current prices at the time of use, regardless of the general inflation rate. In this illustration, depreciation expense is based on the average current cost of the asset during the year—$45,000.

As compared to Exhibit 15.1 and 15.2, the current cost balance sheet as of 12/31/X2 in Exhibit 15.6 reflects the current cost of equipment as of the balance sheet

---

[3] If inventory were involved, cost of goods sold must also be adjusted for current cost.

date; and owners' capital reflects the result of $16,750 of current cost-measured income, $10,000 of unrealized holding gains, and $1,250 of additional catch-up depreciation.

Beginning retained earnings			$100,000
Add:	Net income	$16,750	
	Unrealized gain	10,000	26,750
Subtract:	Catch-up depreciation		1,250
Ending retained earnings			$125,500

Note that the $1,250 additional or **catch-up depreciation** reflects expiration measured in current costs as of the balance sheet date (year-end), whereas depreciation expense for the year is measured in terms of average (mid-year) costs.

Different Definitions of Income

Which income figure most accurately reflects the performance of firm during 19X2:

- $18,000 reported on the primary statement?
- $17,000 reported on the constant dollar statement?
- $16,750 reported on the current cost statement?

Each of these amounts reflects an accurate estimate of the firm's income depending upon the definition of income and capital maintainence.

Nominal capital can be defined as the number of dollars invested ignoring both any unrealized effects of inflation upon nonmonetary assets held and also any changes in the purchasing power of monetary items. If income is defined in terms of increased nominal dollars after maintaining nominal capital, then income was $18,000. If income is defined as an increase in wealth after maintaining the general purchasing power of the capital invested, then $17,000 is the more accurate estimate. If you define income in terms of increased wealth in nominal dollars after maintaining your present capacity to continue in the same line of business then $16,750 provides this measure.

There is general agreement among accountants that conventionally reported income, during periods of inflation, is a poor indicator of either distributable income or increased wealth. Constant dollar-measured income is probably more consistent with the commonly held notion of income—what is left after maintaining one's investment. An investor sacrifices current consumption (current purchasing power over consumable items) in anticipation of future gains. It is unlikely that such an investor would perceive a gain except in excess of the equivalent original sacrifice (current ability to purchase and consume the same items originally deferred).

Constant dollar accounting maintains the objectivity of the conventional system. Primary statement data are merely indexed by an objectively verifiable common factor for all firms. Also, constant dollar income further adjusted to reflect monetary gains or losses and to eliminate unrealized holding gains, can provide a good indicator of realized distributable income. Assuming, of course that "distributable" is defined in terms of maintaining the general purchasing power of the capital invested as distinct from the replacement costs of specific assets. However, the concept of constant dollar purchasing power measurement can be confusing to the average statement user, especially when the dollar valuation of an item whose special price has not increased is still adjusted upward (to reflect cost in terms of more smaller-sized dollars).

Current cost accounting has the appeal to the user of simplicity and ready understandability. When specific prices of certain assets increase at a greater rate than the general inflation rate, additional capital (current purchasing power sacrifice) is necessary for a firm to enter the business requiring such assets. For existing firms already in the business to claim depreciation against this higher required investment is a departure from the basic capital maintenance concept of income.[4]

Income measured on a current cost basis, especially when adjusted for purchasing power gains or losses and catch-up depreciation (reflecting insufficient current cost depreciation expense taken in current and prior years), can be a most meaningful measure of a particular portion of a firm's profits. Such measurement would disclose that portion of income that could be distributed and still have the firm remain in it s present line of business without infusion of additional capital.

Reporting Supplemental Information

GAAP recommend but do not require supplementary information on the effects of inflation and changing prices. Although current cost is recommended, constant dollar cost may be used if the difference is not material. GAAP do not discourage firms from experimenting with other forms of disclosure.

For each current year, GAAP recommend:

1. Income form continuing operations restated on a current cost basis (excluding gain or loss on net monetary items), including disclosure of cost of goods sold and depreciation at current cost.

2. Purchasing power gain or loss on net monetary items.

3. Current cost of inventory, property, plant, and equipment at year-end.

4. Changes during the year in current costs of inventory, property, plant, and equipment net of the effect of general inflation.

5. Foreign currency translation adjustments on a current cost basis, if material.

6. Footnotes explaining the basis selected from among allowable alternatives for the foregoing inflation adjustments.

7. Data for the preceding five years for all of the above plus restatement of net sales and other operating revenues and earnings per share on the current cost basis.

---

[4] Further, if tax depreciation were to be allowed on the basis of current or replacement cost measurements for the assets where inflation rates exceeded the general rate, then the government would be effectively subsidizing existing firms to the disadvantage of new firms (in essence providing a barrier to entry in the economic sense). Perhaps the expectation that the future adoption of current cost accounting as the basis for financial accounting might, in turn, lead to its adoption for tax purposes could partially explain the almost unanimous support for the current cost approach among existing business managers.

Obtaining Current Cost Data

To complete supplementary disclosure requirements, a firm must first estimate the current costs of inventories, property, plant, and equipment as of the beginning and as of the end of the current year.[5] Whereas the current cost of inventories is their current replacement or manufacturing cost; the current cost of property, plant, and equipment is not defined as the replacement cost of the asset. Rather it is defined as the current cost of obtaining the equivalent usefulness or service potential to the asset presently owned. Exhibit 15.7 presents primary statement data for the Jones Company.

Exhibit 15.7

Jones Company Primary Financial Statement Data
($ in thousands)

	As of 12/31/X9	As of 12/31/X8
Balance Sheet Data:		
Cash	$ 20	$ 15
Accounts receivable	160	140
Inventory[a]	190	170
Land[b]	75	75
Plant and equipment[c]	625	625
Accumulated depreciation[d]	(230)	(199)
Total Assets	$840	$826
Current liabilities[e]	$225	$194
Long-term debt[e]	100	162
Owners' capital	515	470
Total Equities	$840	$826
Income Statements:		
Net sales	$950	$900
Cost of goods sold	570	540
Depreciation expense	31	31
Other operating expenses	159	160
Income Before Tax	$190	$169
Provision for income tax	76	68
Net Income	$114	$101

a On LIFO, 19X8 ending inventory acquired during 19X6.
b Acquired 6/30/X1.
c Plant $225,000 acquired 6/30/X2, Equipment $400,000 acquired 6/30/X3.
d Depreciation 5% per year; plant depreciated 40% as 12/31/X9 and equipment 35%.
e All monetary.

[5] The amount to be used as the current cost is the estimated current cost or the recoverable value whichever is lower.

GAAP allow a wide range of approaches to the estimation of current costs including, but not necessarily limited to:

- Estimating current cost of an equivalent new asset and deducting proportionate depreciation;

- Estimating current cost of an equivalent used asset, or

- Estimating cost of an asset with different usefulness and adjusting for such differences.

Current cost data may be obtained from current manufacturing standard costs, suppliers' price lists or quotations, recent invoices, or from internally or externally generated specific indexes for the particular type of asset involved.

Reporting Current Cost Information

Exhibit 15.8 gives the necessary current cost data as estimated for the Jones Company. Exhibit 15.9 gives the required disclosures of current cost information together with the method under which certain items were determined.

Exhibit 15.8

Estimated Current Cost Data for the Jones Company
($ in thousands)

	Estimated Current Cost 12/31/X9	Estimated Current Cost 12/31/X8
Current Costs		
Inventories	$360	$238
Land	160	140
Plant	480	400
Equipment	870	700
Other Data		
12/31/X8 Inventory Units*		34,000
19X9 Sales Units*		67,000
12/31/X9 Inventory Units*		36,400

* Typical units or units of average product mix.

Note that, just as for the constant dollar accounting adjustments previously described, the amounts reported in the primary financial statements for purchases (or current production), changes in net monetary items, and all revenues and expenses (other than cost of goods sold and depreciation) are assumed to be in average 19X9 current cost constant dollars. Adjustments to year-end current costs are only required for inventory, property, plant, and equipment. Costs of goods sold and depreciation are estimated in terms of the simple average of current costs during the year.

Exhibit 15.9   Jones Company Supplementary Cost Information as of 12/31/X9
                                        ($ in thousands)

		Current Cost
1. Inventory 12/31/X9		$360[a]

2. Cost of Goods Sold

Inventory 12/31/X8	$ 7.00/unit	
Inventory 12/31/X9	9.89/unit	
	$16.89	
Average Current Cost $16.98 ÷ 2	$8.45	
Cost of goods sold at average current cost		$566
($8.45 X 67,000)		

3. Property, Plant and Equipment

Land	$160[b]
Plant	480[b]
Equipment	870[b]
Total	$1,510

4. Current Cost Depreciation on Plant and Equipment

Plant and equipment current cost 12/31/X8	$1,100[b]
Plant and equipment current cost 12/31/X9	1,350[b]
	$2,450
Average current cost $2,450 ÷ 2	$1,225
Current Cost Depreciation (5%)	$ 61

5. Income form Continuing Operations on a Current Cost Basis

Net Sales	$950
Cost of Goods Sold (from 2 above)	566
Depreciation Expense (from 4 above)	61
Other Operating Expenses	159
Income Before Taxes	$164
Provision for Income Taxes	76
Income from Continuing Operations	$ 88

**Exhibit 15.9
(continued)**

6. Increase in Current Costs—Net of Inflation

	Increase in Current Cost	Inflation Component	Increase Net of Inflation
Inventory (Schedule 6a) Property, Plant	$ 98	$ 37	$ 61
Equipment (Schedule 6b)	185	121	64
Totals	$283	$158	$125

Schedule 6a: Increase in Current Cost of Inventories Net of Inflation

	Current Cost Nominal Dollars	Conversion Factors	Current Cost Constant Dollars
Balance 12/31/X8	$238[a]	$\dfrac{216.8(\text{X9 average})}{202.9(\text{X8 yr. end})}$	$254
Acquisitions	590	(d)	590
Costs of Goods Sold	(566)	(d)	(566)
Balance 12/31/X9	(360)[a]	$\dfrac{216.8(\text{X9 average})}{230.5(\text{X9 yr. end})}$	(339)
Increase	$ 98		$ 61

Inflation Component ($98 – 61) = $37

Schedule 6b: Increase in Current Cost of Property, Plant and Equipment—Net of Inflation

	Current Cost Nominal Dollars	Conversion Factors	Current Cost Constant Dollars[e]
Balance 12/31/X8	$890[f]	$\dfrac{216.8(\text{X9 average})}{202.9(\text{X8 yr. end})}$	$951
Net Additions[g]	None	(d)	None
Depreciation Expense	(61)	(d)	(61)
Balance 12/31/X9	(1,104)[f]	$\dfrac{216.8(\text{X9 average})}{230.5(\text{X9 yr. end})}$	(954)
Increase	$ 185		$ 64

Inflation Component ($185 – 64) = $121

Exhibit 15.9 (continued)

    a Current cost data estimated by management. Since firm on LIFO, primary statement cost of goods sold approximates current costs. For firms on FIFO (illustrated for X-Ray Corporation in the odd-numbered essential problems in this chapter), primary statement ending inventory will approximate current costs.

    b Current cost data estimated by management.

    c As determined from primary financial statements.

    d Assumed to be in average 19X9 dollars.

    e Measured in average 19X9 dollars.

    f Current cost net book value assuming same percentage accumulated depreciation as on primary financial statements.

    g The conventionally reported costs of any additions would be assumed to be in current cost constant dollars. Any dispositions should be recorded at their estimated current-cost constant-dollar value at the date of disposition.

The two additional items required along with current cost data are, first the increases in current cost of inventory, property, plant and equipment measured in nominal dollars, and, second, the same figure(s) reported in constant dollars (net of the effect of the current year's general-inflation rate). The usefulness of these data will be discussed below.

Significance of Changes in Current Costs

Recall that capital maintenance must be maintained before a firm should be considered as having earned any profit. Regardless of profit measurement, the firm that wants to maintain its current operating capacity in its present line of business should focus upon income from operations measured in current dollars. This amount would reveal that portion of currently generated cash from operating activities possibly distributable to owners. However, to retain sufficient cash flow for replacement of inventories and expiring assets there are further considerations. The year's cost of goods sold and depreciation expense measured in current cost signal desirable retention of only a portion of cost expiration. Since both cost of goods sold and depreciation expense are calculated in terms of average current costs for the year, any increase in replacement costs by year-end over the average will not have been provided for. Further, prior year's depreciation probably is inadequate in terms of the year-end costs, and additional catch-up depreciation will have to be taken into account.

The reported increase in current costs of inventory, property, plant and equipment measured in current purchasing power or constant dollars, for Jones was $103,000 for 19X9, which indicates the amount of asset price increases occurring during the year not attributable to, or in excel of, the general inflation rate. The specific price inflation rate for the same period (measured following average-year index differences) was only 19 percent.[6]

---

[6] Ignoring the minor change in actual physical inventory, year-end asset costs of $1,555,000 divided by beginning costs of $1,280,000 equaled 1.2148. Assumed CPI-U (average year indexes for 19X9 and 19X8 were 216.8 and 181.5 respectively. Therefore 216.8 divided by 181.5 equals 1.1945.

Adjusting Primary Statement Data to Constant Dollars

In adjusting data from primary statements to a constant dollar basis, the U. S. **Urban Consumer Price Index (CPI-U)** is used. Note that this index reflects the changes in purchasing power of the investment alternative (consumption) as previous discussed.

The prices of a representative sample of consumer items were averaged and converted into a comparative index based on the prices in year 1967. A new index was implemented in January, 1988 using 1982-1984 as 100. A comparison between the two indices is presented in Exhibit 13.10 for selected years. Note that the conversion factor from the old index to the new is 0.3338279.

Exhibit 13.10   Consumer Price Index for All Urban Consumers
(CPI-U)

Selected Years	Old Index	New Index*
1967	100.0	33.4
1972	125.3	41.8
1977	181.5	60.6
1981	272.4	90.9
1985	322.2	107.6
1987	340.4	113.6
Dec 1986	331.1	110.5
April 1987	337.6	112.7
Dec 1987	345.7	115.4
April 1988	350.8	117.1

* New index is based on 1982-1984;

Old index x 0.3338279 = New index

To convert the reported cost of an item in nominal dollars as of 1977 to 1987 constant dollars, a conversion index is multiplied by the 1977 amount. The conversion index is simply a fraction whose numerator is the current index and whose denominator is the index at the time of the asset acquisition:

$$\text{Conversion Index} = \frac{\text{Current CPI-U Index}}{\text{CPI-U Index at Time of Acquisition}}$$

For example, the 1987 constant dollar valuation of an item acquired in June 1977, at a cost of $50,000 would be $89,815:

$$\$50,000 \ \times \ \frac{340.4}{189.5} = \$89,815 \text{ (rounded)}$$

Firms electing to supply minimum required data for are required to use the average level of CPI-U for the current year for:

- Inventory
- Property, plant and equipment
- Cost of goods sold
- Depreciation, depletion, and amortization expense
- Income from operations assuming all other primary statement data are already reported in constant dollars
- Purchasing power gain or loss on net monetary items

Exhibit 15.11 gives the required disclosures of constant dollar information for the Jones Company for 19X9 together with the method of calculation. Note that inventories and property, plant, and equipment are adjusted from their acquisition/reporting date to 19X9 average dollars. Also note that accumulated depreciation and depreciation expense simply are restated in the same proportions as in the primary financial statements. Purchases (or current production), changes in net monetary items, and all revenues and expenses (other than costs of goods sold and depreciation) are assumed to be in average 19X9 dollars as disclosed in the primary statements.

Note that Exhibit 15.11 reveals that, in terms of constant dollars, Jones had $21,000 less income than reported in the primary statements; and that this $21,000 reduction was offset by a $23,000 gain on net monetary liabilities held during the year.

Interpreting Supplementary Data

In terms of the primary statements, the Jones Company for 19X9 appeared to have had a reasonably good year. Return on investments can be calculated as approximately 13.6 percent, and return on ending owners' investment as approximately 22.1 percent.[7]

---

[7] For simplification, return on investment was calculated using net income rather than the more appropriate but not available EBIT (see Chapter 13); and total assets and owners' equity at year-end were used rather than the more appropriate averages for the year. These simplifying assumptions will be used throughout this section.

Exhibit 15.11   Supplementary Data for Jones Company as of 12/31/X9 in Constant Dollars
(Average 19X9 $ in thousands)

	Nominal Dollars	Conversion Factors	Average 19X9 Dollars
1. Inventory 12/31/X9	$170	$\dfrac{216.8(\text{X9 average})}{170.5(\text{X6 average})}$	$216
	$\underline{20}$	*	$\underline{20}$
	$\underline{\underline{\$190}}$		$\underline{\underline{\$236}}$

* Assumes acquired at average 19X9 prices

2. Cost of Goods Sold

	Nominal Dollars	Conversion Factors	Average 19X9 Dollars
Inventory 12/31/X8	$170	$\dfrac{216.8(\text{X9 average})}{170.5(\text{X6 average})}$	$216
19X9 acquisitions	590	*	590
Inventory 12/31/X8	(190)		(236)
Cost of Goods Sold	$\underline{\underline{\$570}}$		$\underline{\underline{\$570}}$**

* Assumes acquired at average 19X9 prices
** Same as nominal since firm on LIFO

3. Property, Plant and Equipment

	Nominal Dollars	Conversion Factors	Average 19X9 Dollars
Land	$ 75	$\dfrac{216.8(\text{X9 average})}{121.3(\text{X1 average})}$	$134
Plant	225	$\dfrac{216.8(\text{X9 average})}{125.3(\text{X2 average})}$	389
Equipment	400	$\dfrac{216.8(\text{X9 average})}{133.1(\text{X3 average})}$	652
Total	$\underline{\underline{\$700}}$		$\underline{\underline{\$1,175}}$

4. Accumulated Depreciation

	Nominal Dollars		Average 19X9 Dollars	
Plant	$ 90	(40%)	$156	(40%)
Equipment	140	(35%)	228	(35%)
Total	$\underline{\underline{\$230}}$		$\underline{\underline{\$384}}$	

5. Depreciation Expense	$ 31	(5%*)	$ 52	(5%*)

* Percent of cost depreciation during year

Exhibit 15.11
(continued)

6. Income from continuing operations

Net sales	$950	$950
Cost of goods sold	570	570
Depreciation expense	31	52
Other operating expenses	159	159
Income Before Tax	$190	$169
Provision for income tax	76	76
Income From Operations	$114	$ 93

7. Gain/Loss on Net Monetary Items

Net monetary liabilities 12/31/X8	$201	$\frac{216.8(\text{X9 average})}{202.9(\text{X8 yr. end})}$	$215
Decrease during year	(56)	*	(56)
			$159
Balance 12/31/X9	$145	$\frac{216.8(\text{X9 average})}{230.5(\text{X9 yr. end})}$	$136
Purchasing Power Gain on Net Monetary Items			$ 23

* Assumed to be in 19X9 averaged dollars.

CPI-U Indexes Assumed for Illustrative Purposes

19X1	Average	121.3		19X8	Average	195.4
19X2	Average	125.3		19X8	Year-end	202.9
19X3	Average	133.1		19X9	Average	216.8
19X4	Average	147.1		19X9	Year-end	230.5
19X5	Average	161.2				
19X6	Average	170.5				
19X7	Average	181.5				

Using Constant Dollar Data

If one is to consider the realities of general inflation and the need to at least maintain the general purchasing power of the dollars invested in the firm, then return on investment would be 8.1 percent and return on ending owners' investment only 11.3 percent.[8] Since Jones' overall income in constant dollars was only $93,000 (including purchasing power

[8] Based on income measured as $93,000 ($70,000 of constant dollar income plus $23,000 gain on net monetary liabilities); total assets as $1,151,000 (adjusted to constant dollars); and owners' equity of $826,000 (adjusted to balance increase in total assets).

gains on net monetary items), if it were to distribute the full $114,000 of conventionally reported income, it would actually be returning capital to its owners—reducing the wealth of the firm as measured in terms of general purchasing power—in the amount of $21,000.

A further analysis of the components of owners' equity (beyond the scope of this text) could reveal that portion of accumulated past retained earnings that could be distributed without impairing the original purchasing power of the contributed capital.[9]

Using Current Cost Data

Using current cost data, Jones' return on investment was only 1.9 and its return on ending owners' investment was 2.4 percent.

It may be assumed that the firm's managers and statement users are vitally interested in determining the amount of additional capital that will be necessary for the firm to maintain its wealth in terms of existing productive/service capacity.

The current year's asset specific inflation in excess of general inflation (not picked up in current cost of goods sold and current cost of depreciation) was reported as $103,000. Therefore the firm needed a constant dollar income of $196,000 ($93,000 + $103,000) to maintain its productive capacity, assuming no earnings distributions (dividends) are made.

In terms of maintaining productive or operating capacity, even if the Jones Company does retain 100 percent of reported 19X9 earnings, it would eventually require an additional $103,000 of capital to replace existing assets. And this analysis is, of course, ignoring any catch-up depreciation.

Five-Year Summaries

Although not illustrated for the Jones Company, the previously cited additional GAAP requirement for summary information for the preceding fives years can prove invaluable in estimating the seriousness of the potential catch-up depreciation problem. From such information you can also determine for a given firm:

- Whether its earnings have been sufficient during the period to maintain the general purchasing power of the capital invested and/or to provide for replacement at current costs of its expiring assets;
- Whether it has retained sufficient income during the period to maintain the general purchasing power of the capital invested;
- Whether it has retained sufficient income during the period for re-placement at current costs of its expiring assets; and
- How the market has evaluated the firm's performance in comparison to similar firms.

---

[9] Increments of contributed capital and accumulated retained earnings would have to be separately restated to current dollars (in the same manner as increments of property, plant and equipment are revalued) and then summed to arrive at the current purchasing power of the capital originally invested (or earnings reinvested). Any excess of the current balance sheet constant dollar figure over the current purchasing power of capital originally invested would indicate potentially distributable earnings.

Chapter Overview

Based on the material covered in this chapter, you should be able to:

- Describe the difference between general and specific inflation and how index numbers may be relevant and applicable to each;

- Define the terms nominal dollar, constant dollar, and current cost dollar as they apply to financial accounting measurement, and describe the concept of income related to each;

- Describe the minimum requirements for supplementary inflation-adjusted data that must be disclosed for the current year by very large firms;

- Explain the concept of gain or loss on net monetary items and how the amount is determined for a given year;

- Describe the source and type of input data used and the method of calculating constant dollar measurements for inventory; property, plant, and equipment; accumulated depreciation; cost of goods sold; and depreciation expense;

- Explain how changes in current costs of inventory, property, plant, and equipment are determined in both nominal dollars and net of general inflation; and

- Explain in general terms the potential usefulness of required supplementary inflation-adjusted data to both a company's directors and also to its financial statement readers.

New Vocabulary and Concepts

Catch-up depreciation	Nominal capital
Constant dollars	Nominal dollars
Consumer Price Index (CPI-U)	Primary financial statements
Current cost	Specific inflation
General inflation	Unrealized holding gain
Net monetary items	

- Gain or loss on net monetary items
- Maintenance of nominal capital
- Maintenance of general purchasing power of capital invested
- Maintenance of present physical capacity to do business
- Changes in current costs of inventory, plant, and equipment in nominal dollars and net of general inflation.

Review Questions

1. (a) What is general inflation? (b) What measurement of general inflation is used in calculating required supplementary inflation-related data? (c) How does general inflation affect the purchasing power of dollars or other monetary units?

2. (a) What is specific inflation? (b) How is specific inflation measured? (c) How does specific inflation differ from general inflation?

3. (a) What is constant dollar accounting? (b) What type of inflation does it reflect? (c) How does it differ from historical cost accounting as disclosed in the primary financial statements?

4. (a) Under constant dollar accounting, can a specific nonmonetary asset whose current cost has actually declined be reported at a higher amount than on the primary financial statements?

5. (a) Can a firm with the same number of dollars of monetary assets and the same number of dollars of lonerary liabilities at thge end of the year as the beginning have experienced a gain or loss on net monetary items? (b) If yes, how is this possible? (c) Under what circumstances woud a firm expeience a gain on net monetary items? (d) A loss? (e) How is a firm's gain or loss on net monetary items calculated?

6. (a) What is the difference between nominal dollars and constant dollars? Explain with examples. (b) Do primary financial statements report in nominal or constant dollars?

7. (a) What is accounting for current cost? (b) What type of inflation does it reflect? (c) How does it differ from historical cost accounting? (d) From constant dollar accounting? (e) Is current cost reported in nominal, current or constant dollars? Explain.

8. (a) What data are used in the preparation of current cost information? (b) What is their source? (c) Can current cost information be considered as objective as either primary financial statement or constant dollar information? Explain

9. (a) What is an index number? (b) What index numbers are used for constant dollar accounting? (c) Explain with examples how index numbers are used in determining constant dollar information. (d) Can index numbers also be used in determining current cost information? (e) If yes, what type of index numbers and how are they used?

10. (a) What are changes in current cost of inventory, property, plant, and equipment expressed in nominal dollars? (b) How is the amount of this changes calculated? (c) What is the meaning of this change expressed net of general inflation? (d) How is it calculated?

11. (a) What are present GAAP recommendations for inflation-adjusted information to be disclosed for the current year? (b) Is this information incorporated in the primary financial statements? (c) If not, how is it disclosed?

12. How is income effectively defined under (a) historical cost? (b) constant dollar? (c) current cost? (d) Which income concept most closely matches the average person's intuitive idea of income? Explain.

13. What is the relationship between distributable income and (a) Net income as reported on the primary financial statements? (b) Net income as determined on a constant dollar basis? (c) Net income as determined on a current cost basis?

Essential Problems

EP 15.1 Exhibit 15.12 provides basic primary financial statement and current cost data for the X-Ray Corporation for the years 19X7 and 19X8. Exhibit 15.11 provides simplified assumed CPI-Uindexes for the appropriate years. Give the necessary supplementary constant dollar information required to be included with X-Ray's 19X8 financial statements for:

a) Ending inventory.

b) Cost of goods sold.

c) Property, plant, and equipment.

d) Accumulated depreciation.

e) Depreciation expense.

f) Income from continuing operations.

Exhibit 15.12

Selected Data for the X-Ray Corporation
($ in millions)

	19X8		19X7	
	Historical Costs[a]	Current Costs[b]	Historical Costs[a]	Current Costs[b]
Assets				
Cash	$ 10	$ 10	$ 7	$ 10
Receivables (net)	40	40	38	40
Inventory[c]	60	60	50	50
Prop., plant, and equip[d]	205	470	205	409
Accum. depreciation[e]	(56)	(129)	(48)	(98)
Total Assets	$259	$451	$252	$411
Equities				
Current payables	$ 40	—	$ 35	—
Long-term debt	70	—	88	—
Total liabilities	$110	—	$123	—
Stockholders' equity	149	—	129	—
Total Equities	$259		$252	
Income				
Sales	$300			
Cost of goods sold [f]	180			
Depreciation	8			
Other operating expenses	62			
Provision for taxes	20			
Net Income	$ 30			

a From primary financial statements
b Estimated by management.
c Inventory carried under FIFO; acquired uniformly during fourth quarter of current year. Average units 12/31/X7 and 12/31/X8 = 250,000. 19X8 sales = 864,000 average units.
d Includes land acquired in mid 19X1 costing $5,000,000 and plant and equipment constructed/acquired in mid 19X2 costing $200,000,000. Current cost of land estimated at $9,000,000 as of 12/31/X7 and $10,000,000 as of 12/31/X8.
e Plant and equipment depreciated at four percent per year with full year's depreciation taken in 19X2.
f 19X7 portion acquired during fourth quarter of 19X7.

EP 15.2 Exhibit 15.14 provides basic data for the Yoke Corporation for the years 19X7 and 19X8. Also using Exhibit 15.13, give the same six items of information that are required for the X-Ray Corporation in EP 15.1.

EP 15.3 For the X-Ray Corporation (Exhibits 15.12 and 15.13), determine in average-year dollars the gain or loss on net monetary items for 19X8.

EP 15.4 For the Yoke Corporation (Exhibits 15.13 and 15.14), determine in average-year dollars the gain or loss on net monetary items for 19X8.

EP 15.5 For the X-Ray Corporation (Exhibit 15.12), give the necessary supplementary current cost information in nominal dollars required to be included with its 19X8 financial statements for:

    a) Ending inventory

    b) Cost of goods sold

    c) Property, plant, and equipment

    d) Accumulated depreciation

    e) Depreciation expense

    f) Income from continuing operations

EP 15.6 For the Yoke Corporation (Exhibit 15.14), give the same six items of information that are required for the X-Ray Corporation in 15.5.

EP 15.7 For the X-Ray Corporation (Exhibits 15.12 and 15.13), give the necessary supplementary current cost information required to be included with its 19X8 financial statements for:

    a) Changes in current costs separately and in total of inventories and of property, plant, and equipment in nominal dollars.

    b) The general inflation component of each of these changes.

    c) The changes net of general inflation.

EP 15.8 For the Yoke Corporation (Exhibits 15.13 and 15.14), give the same nine items of information that are required for the X-Ray Corporation in EP 15.7.

Exhibit 15.13   Assumed Simplified CPI Indices for Chapter Essential Problems

19X1	Average	120	19X7	Average	189
19X2	Average	129	19X7	Fourth-quarter average	192
19X3	Average	139	19X7	Year-end	196
19X4	Average	150	19X8	Average	204
19X5	Average	162	19X8	Fourth-quarter average	207
19X6	Average	175	19X8	Year-end	210

Exhibit 15.14   Selected Data for the Yoke Corporation ($ in millions)

	19X8 Historical Costs[a]	19X8 Current Costs[b]	19X7 Historical Costs[a]	19X7 Current Costs[b]
Assets				
Cash	$ 15	$ 15	$ 10	$ 10
Receivables (net)	85	85	75	75
Inventory[c]	50	53	40	42
Prop., plant, and equip.[d]	310	578	310	483
Accum. depreciation[e]	(96)	(179)	(74)	(114)
Total Assets	$364	$552	$361	$496
Equities				
Current payables	$ 90	—	$ 80	—
Long-term debt	18	—	70	—
Total liabilities	$108	—	$150	—
Stockholders' equity	256	—	211	—
Total Equities	$364		$361	
Income				
Sales	$500			
Cost of goods sold [f]	200			
Depreciation	22			
Other operating expenses	178			
Provision for taxes	40			
Net Income	$ 60			

a   From primary financial statements
b   Estimated by management.
c   Inventory carried under FIFO; acquired uniformly during fourth quarter of current year. Average units 12/31/X7 and 12/31/X8 = 80,000. 19X8 sales = 354,000 average units.
d   Includes land acquired in mid 19X3 costing $10,000,000 and buildings constructed in mid 19X3 costing $160,000,000; and equipment acquired in mid 19X5 costing $140,000,000. Current cost of land estimated at $21,000,000 as of 12/31/X7 and $25,000,000 as of 12/31/X8. Current cost of buildings estimated at $243,000,000 as 12/31/X7 and $280,000,000 as 12/31/X8.
e   Building depreciated at five percent per year with full year's depreciation taken in 19X5.
f   19X7 portion acquired during fourth quarter of 19X7. Balance acquired uniformly throughout 19X8.

A

1987 Annual Report: Financial Section

AT&T

Xerox Corporation

Financial Section

Hard Work Begins to Pay Off

Nineteen eighty-seven was a year of visible accomplishments and continuing challenges. As the year closed, we could see measured progress toward the company's long-term financial objectives and our goal of maximizing shareowner value.

Perhaps above all else, the encouraging results of 1987 are a testimonial to the decisive actions we took at the end of 1986. These steps were taken to reduce costs and expenses and improve our competitive position, and included a substantial charge against earnings to cover the cost of restructuring our business. These actions were costly in more than a financial sense; they had a significant impact on both our employee body and our business. Recognizing this, we made concerted efforts to ease employees' transitions to new endeavors and to preserve the continuity of operations. The progress we made in 1987 is a credit to AT&T people who adapted quickly and creatively to changes in their company and jobs.

Positive benefits from these moves came sooner than anyone expected, principally in the form of lower costs, which were a strong contributor to our 1987 earnings per share of $1.88. In addition to this traditional bottom-line result, other mea-

surements complete the story of our progress this year:

–Return on average shareowners' equity reached a post-divestiture record of 14.4 percent.

–Our stock price increased eight percent from its January opening to $27.00 at year-end.

–We covered all capital expenditures and dividends from internally generated sources. In addition, our cash balance continued to increase, growing to a healthy $2.8 billion.

However, we are not complacent. While we were pleased to see quarter-to-quarter revenue increases during 1987, revenues for the year in total decreased slightly. To attain our objectives, growth in revenues is essential. We also need to continue our progress in cost improvement. In the year ahead these will be our highest financial priorities.

The day-to-day operations of the company reflected our heightened em-

This new regional headquarters building being constructed in Chicago symbolizes AT&T's confidence in its future. Earnings for 1987 were the best since divestiture and demand for AT&T stock remained strong, even in the wake of October's stock market crash.

phasis on quality, not just in our products and services but in the efficiency of our internal operations.

Our annual productivity growth in manufacturing operations continued to average 10 percent, about double the productivity growth rate for durable goods manufacturing in the United States.

Progress has been made through the use of Just-In-Time (JIT) manufacturing initiatives. At AT&T's plant in Shreveport, Louisiana, for example, office communications systems that took three-and-a-half weeks to produce were rolling through the JIT assembly line in two-and-a-half hours.

Other efficiency improvements during 1987 included the centraliza-

tion and consolidation of support operations throughout the company. The new Contract Services Organization improved the terms and conditions on a wide range of goods and services purchased by our business units. The provisioning of computer services was also centralized, making progress toward increasing efficiency and eliminating duplication.

The sophisticated data networking technology we offer our large customers was also deployed internally to improve the productivity of our operations. Customers calling national 800 numbers in response to AT&T product promotions are now assisted by our people using state-of-the-art systems integration technology delivered by AT&T's own computers.

Along with the substantial cost reductions brought about by our restructuring activities, our data networking technology will aid us in achieving and maintaining a competitive edge.

Management's Discussion and Analysis

Because of the extraordinary internal change AT&T experienced in recent years, we have focused increased attention on financial controls and the ability to measure and assess performance. In addition to the marketing and customer service efforts and restructuring activities that are a central part of AT&T's story in 1987, internal actions were taking place to enhance the company's financial reporting and analysis process.

We are implementing uniform financial systems throughout the company. We are developing our own billing system to provide improved information about revenues and customer accounts. We are expanding reported information about sources of AT&T's revenues to focus on revenue contributions from the major areas of our business.

These and other actions are providing improved information for financial statement users both within and outside AT&T.

The discussions that follow explain trends in AT&T's results of operations and financial position in 1987 compared with prior years and include for the first time an analysis of our major revenue streams.

Operating Revenues

Although total operating revenues were greater than we expected in 1987, a decrease was experienced from the 1986 level. The growth in overall sales of services and products was more than offset by the continuing reduction in rental revenues.

The increase in sales of services in both 1987 and 1986 was due primarily to volume growth in sales of telecommunications services. Service revenues from equipment installation and maintenance activities also increased in 1987 and 1986.

The increase in sales of products in 1987 reflected growth in sales of certain telecommunications network products, microelectronics and special design products and consumer products. Sales of products decreased in 1986 from 1985, primarily as a result of declines in telecommunications network products and business and data products. Rental revenues declined during the past three years as expected, due to the continuing trend of customers deciding to purchase rather than lease telecommunications equipment.

Major Revenue Streams

AT&T operates predominantly in one industry, that of information movement and management. We offer a full range of data systems and communications network products and services. Our revenues are received from four major areas of the business: Telecommunications Services; Business, Data and Consumer Products; Telecommunications Network Systems; and Other.

Approximately half of AT&T's total revenue stream is derived from the sale of **telecommunications services.** These services are provided via the public switched long distance network in the United States and throughout the world, and by individual customer long distance circuits, called private line service.

Revenues from telecommunications services, net of access charge payments to local telephone companies to connect with their networks, increased substantially in 1987 and 1986 as a result of increased calling volumes, particularly for international calling and 800 services. This strong volume growth reduced the decline in gross toll revenues stemming from the significant price reductions taken in those years.

In addition to the strong growth experienced in international and basic 800 services on the public switched network, new services such as Pro-America, Megacom, and 800 Readyline continued to receive broad acceptance. Private line revenues remained essentially stable in 1987 due to price restructuring.

We have significantly lowered our long distance prices since divestiture to reflect reductions in our access charge payments and other expenses, as well as to reflect rate of return limitations. We reduced prices by about 16% in 1987 and by another 3.5% on January 1, 1988. In total, prices have been cut by about 36% since January 1984. The Federal Communications Commission (FCC) lowered our authorized interstate rate of return to 12.20% from 12.75% on January 1, 1987.

Future growth opportunities for telecommunications service revenues will depend on overall market growth and on the introduction of new and enhanced services, including digital services. International services in particular are expected to provide significant growth opportunities; however, we expect intense competition to continue, both domestically and internationally. The extent to which AT&T benefits from the market's overall growth will depend on two factors. One is our ability to meet customer needs successfully. The other is the extent to which AT&T is permitted to compete equally with other long distance companies. Now constrained by a polarized regulatory process, AT&T is the only fully-regulated carrier in an increasingly competitive marketplace.

Because strong competition now exists in telecommunications services, we continue to seek regulatory changes at both the state and federal levels. Some form of lessened regulation has been implemented in 31 state jurisdictions. At the federal level, the FCC has proposed to cap prices as an alternative to rate of return regulation. The alternative would not cause prices to increase. We support this proposal as a transitional form of regulation that would benefit both shareholders and customers.

Traders on the floor of the Tokyo Stock Exchange on November 17, 1987, the day AT&T became the 48th American company to be listed among the 1,500 companies trading on this busy exchange.

The second major contributor to AT&T's revenues is the **business, data and consumer products** area, which sells, installs, maintains and rents communications and computer products for office and home use. Revenues in this category reflect mixed trends. Product sales in this area decreased slightly in 1987 over 1986, as growing revenues from consumer products, newer business systems, and recently introduced data products did not fully offset the declines in older business systems and older data products revenues.

Solid successes have occurred in consumer products sales as we revamped our product line, adding to our high-quality product offerings. Market acceptance was good for recently introduced small-to-medium-sized PBXs and data products.

The business, data and consumer products market continues to be highly competitive. To meet this competition, we are strengthening and focusing our marketing and customer service activities, as well as continuing to invest heavily in new product development.

Business, data and consumer product sales declined in 1986 primarily because of soft market conditions and competitive pressures. This decline followed the strong demand experienced in 1985 for business products.

Service revenues from installation and maintenance contracts associated with business, data and consumer products have grown over the three-year period, due to increased business activity and our focus on making customers aware of the value of these services. In contrast, rental revenues declined each year as customers decided to purchase equipment rather than enter into short-term rental arrangements.

Future trends in the business, data and consumer products area are expected to include a gradual growth in product sales and service revenues, which are often sold together in business contracts, and a continued decline in the revenue contribution of rentals.

The **telecommunications network systems** area represents slightly less than one-fifth of AT&T's total revenue stream and includes sales of equipment and related

Revenues

Dollars in millions	1987	1986	1985
Telecommunications Services			
Public Switched Network	**$30,302**	$31,609	$32,461
Private Line	**4,845**	4,825	4,249
Less: Access Charges	**17,611**	19,593	21,521
	17,536	16,841	15,189
Business, Data and Consumer Products			
Sales	**3,155**	3,212	4,009
Services	**1,439**	1,392	963
Rentals	**3,728**	4,796	5,789
	8,322	9,400	10,761
Telecommunications Network Systems	**6,179**	6,185	6,585
Other Revenues			
Sales	**872**	781	641
Services	**684**	875	1,241
Rentals	**5**	5	0
	1,561	1,661	1,882
Total Revenues	**$33,598**	$34,087	$34,417

services to industry users of telecommunications equipment. This equipment includes switching systems, transmission equipment, cable, wire, and other products used by telephone companies and other large communications equipment users.

Revenues in this area of the business held constant in 1987 despite increased competition and the desire of some of our customers to diversify supply channels. Switching systems and cable and wire sales increased over 1986 levels, while transmission equipment and some other product sales were down. Sales in 1986 declined from 1985 levels largely because the operating telephone companies' equal access construction requirements created unusually high demand in 1985.

To respond to competition, the company is developing increasingly sophisticated and "feature rich" product offerings, enhancing customer service and support functions, and actively exploring new domestic and international markets. AT&T is committed to maintaining its leadership position in the telecommunications network equipment market. Because of the long-term prospects for revenue expansion in this market, the company will aggressively pursue new sales opportunities, both in this country and overseas. In the short term, however, sales may remain flat as competitive pressures continue to limit growth in AT&T's traditional markets.

The last major category of revenues, **other revenues**, represents a relatively small portion of our total revenue stream but one that features growth in product sales. These revenues include sales by AT&T Microelectronics (formerly called Components and Electronic Systems), which produces silicon chips, power supply devices, custom devices and other electronic components. In addition, other revenues include the sales of

special design products and related special services by AT&T's Federal Systems unit to the U.S. government. Sales of custom devices and special design products increased significantly over the three-year period.

Service revenues in the other category are primarily Shared Network Facilities Agreement (SNFA) revenues, which declined as expected during the three-year period. These revenues arose out of the January 1, 1984 Bell System divestiture and represent payments from telephone companies to AT&T for leased facilities, which were formerly jointly owned by the telephone companies and AT&T. As these arrangements are of a transitional nature, SNFA revenues are expected to continue decreasing each year.

The other services category also includes revenues from shareholder services provided by our American Transtech unit and other miscellaneous revenues. Rental revenues in the other category represent minor leasing activities.

Costs and Expenses

Total costs and expenses decreased 10.8% in 1987 reflecting network modernization, force reductions, more efficient manufacturing and services operations and improved inventory management. The substantial 1987 improvements were partially offset by increased marketing and sales expenses and costs associated with the development and implementation of an internal revenue, billing and customer account management program.

Total costs and expenses in 1986 increased 7.4% from 1985, due to charges for business restructuring and inventory and asset writedowns,

which were partially offset by reductions in pension expense associated with the adoption of Statement of Financial Accounting Standards No. 87 (FAS 87), "Employers' Accounting for Pensions." See Notes (B) and (L) to the financial statements.

Volume growth coupled with cost containment resulted in a steady improvement in the gross margin on sales of services. Our cost of services as a percent of service revenues was 44.7% in 1987 and 46.9% in 1986, compared with 52.3% in 1985.

Cost of products decreased to 58.8% of product revenues in 1987 from 70.7% in 1986 and 62.9% in 1985, from across-the-board cost reductions and productivity improvement efforts.

Product margins in 1987 and 1986 reflected the effects of price discounting, and in 1986 and 1985 were also significantly affected by charges for the writedown of inventory values.

Cost of rentals as a percent of rental revenues increased to 47.3% and 43.7% in 1987 and 1986, respectively, from 33.4% in 1985. The increases in both years are primarily attributable to higher depreciation rates on rental equipment in recognition of shorter depreciable lives.

Selling, general and administrative expenses increased slightly to 33.1% of total operating revenues in 1987, compared with 32.5% in 1986 and 32.3% in 1985. Savings from downsizing efforts were offset by increases in marketing and sales expenses and the development and implementation costs for customer billing and related support functions.

We are assuming increased responsibility for long distance services billing and account management functions, which currently are performed primarily by local telephone companies. Over the long term, this effort will further improve our ability to manage all aspects of our customer relationships. Additionally, we will be better positioned to control costs associated with billing and account management activities.

We continued to make significant expenditures for research and development in each of the past three years. The increase of 7.7% in 1987 reflects our commitment to new product and service development, as well as higher depreciation expenses for certain equipment used in research.

The provision for business restructuring of $2.2 billion in 1986 represented the estimated cost to reduce the workforce and consolidate various facilities and factories over a several year period. The programs and plans affect all AT&T business units and support organizations.

Significant progress has been made in resizing activities, and actions are proceeding according to plans. To date, the company has closed and consolidated clean rooms and support facilities used to produce semiconductors in Kansas City, Missouri, and in Allentown and Reading, Pennsylvania; also, on January 20, 1988, the closing of AT&T's Winston-Salem, North Carolina work location was announced.

At year-end 1987, the remaining business restructuring reserve totaled $1.2 billion and we believe the reserve remains adequate for the completion of our force and facility consolidation activities. About one-half of our force reduction activities had been completed by year-end; coupled with force additions in certain strategic growth areas of the business, the net decrease in our workforce during 1987 was 13,900.

Other Income and Interest Expense

Other income–net decreased in 1987 primarily due to the unusually high miscellaneous income reflected in 1986 results. During 1986, other income–net included an award for damages paid by the Republic of Iran and an increase in the value of our equity investment in Olivetti. These items were the principal reason for the increase in other income from the 1985 level. See Note (C) to the financial statements.

Interest expense related to debt has declined over the three-year period as a result of our continuing efforts to reduce financing costs through retirements and refinancing of debt. The growth in total interest expense in 1987 was primarily caused by increases in interest on accrued liabilities other than short- and long-term debt.

Provision for Income Taxes

In 1987, income tax expense increased significantly as a result of substantially higher earnings compared with 1986. The 1986 provision for income taxes was reduced by $1.4 billion as a result of charges for business restructuring and other major actions. This reduction was reflected almost entirely in deferred taxes. During 1987, we incurred $2.8 billion in expense for income, property and other taxes, as compared with $1.5 billion in 1986 and $2.6 billion in 1985.

Federal income tax expense in 1987 was reduced from what it otherwise would have been as a result of provisions enacted by the 1986 Tax Reform Act. Earnings in 1987 benefited by approximately 14 cents per share from the new tax law. The most significant benefit came from the re-

duction in the statutory federal income tax rate from 46% to 40%. We expect to receive additional benefits from the 1986 Tax Reform Act in 1988, due largely to a further reduction in the statutory federal income tax rate to 34%.

The recently issued Statement of Financial Accounting Standards No. 96 (FAS 96), "Accounting for Income Taxes," must be adopted no later than 1989. Under the new statement, deferred taxes are computed based on the enacted tax rates for the years in which these taxes will be payable or refundable.

While the impact is not currently estimable, it is expected that there will be a significant positive effect on net income in the year the standard is adopted. In years subsequent to adoption, net income may be impacted, possibly by substantial amounts, as a result of increases or decreases in statutory income tax rates.

Change in Depreciation Method

In 1986, the cumulative prior years' effect of a change in depreciation method from group to unit for factory machinery and laboratory equipment reduced net income by $175 million or $.16 per share. We implemented this change to provide improved assignment of costs to products and better identification of service lives. See Note (B) to the financial statements.

Net Income

Net income in 1987 grew primarily as a result of higher operating income due to growth in long distance revenues and cost reduction efforts, combined with the effect of the 1986 special charges.

Results in 1986 were reduced by $1.7 billion for charges for business restructuring, a change in accounting for depreciation, and a writedown of assets and inventory. These actions reduced 1986 earnings by $1.59 per share, resulting in only a small profit of five cents per share. We are seeing the benefits from restructuring activities in our earnings and expect improvements to continue in the future.

Our interstate earnings on telecommunications services in 1987, 1986, and 1985 were within the limit allowed by the FCC.

Dividends on preferred shares were reduced by $63 and $24 million in 1987 and 1986, respectively, through the redemption of $830 and $545 million of preferred stock during these years.

Working Capital and Liquidity

Funds from operations amounted to $6.1 billion in 1987, enabling us to

cover expenditures for capital investments and dividends from internally generated sources for the second consecutive year. These expenditures accounted for 80.7% of funds from operations in 1987, compared with 68.3% and 106.8% in 1986 and 1985, respectively. Our strong cash position allowed us to reduce preferred shares and retire debt outstanding of $1.2 billion in 1987 and $2.4 billion in 1986.

In 1987, funds from operations declined despite the substantial growth in net income, primarily due to the payment of liabilities related to carrying out our business restructuring and downsizing actions.

The increase in working capital (excluding cash and temporary investments, debt maturing within one year, dividends payable and deferred income taxes) in 1987, follows the significant decrease experienced in 1986. This 1986 decrease was partly the result of reserves created for business restructuring, but also reflected our success in improving the management of receivables and inventories.

With almost $2.8 billion in cash and temporary cash investments, strong cash flow from operations, and reduced long-term liabilities, we are in a position to meet our capital requirements internally and have the flexibility to take advantage of appropriate investment and financing opportunities as they arise. For example, we announced in January, 1988, an agreement to purchase, over the next three years, up to a 20% interest in Sun Microsystems, Inc., a computer company. This action should provide strategic benefits to both parties. We also increased our ownership in our joint venture with N.V. Philips from 50% to 60% in January, 1988.

Capital Investment

During 1987, expenditures for capital investment, including net additions to property, plant and equipment and the net change in investments, amounted to $3.6 billion. In 1986 and 1985, these expenditures totaled $3.6 and $4.6 billion, respectively.

Approximately $2.7 billion was spent in 1987 for expansion and continuing quality enhancement of our long distance network. We plan to invest approximately $3 billion in our worldwide network in each of the years 1988 and 1989. Digital route miles will nearly double to 88,000 worldwide by 1991. Capital spending for the network has increased in each of the past three years and total gross expenditures were approximately $7.8 billion during this period.

Investment to modernize our domestic and offshore manufacturing facilities has been primarily to attain world-class standards. Such state-of-the-art processes as surface mount technology and Just-In-Time manufac-

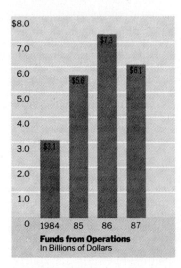

Funds from Operations
In Billions of Dollars

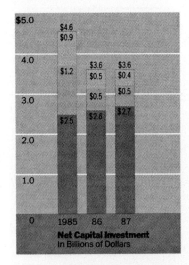

Net Capital Investment
In Billions of Dollars

R&D, Selling & Support, & Other

Manufacturing

Telecommunications

turing are being implemented. Investment in our manufacturing facilities was approximately $500 million during each of the years 1987 and 1986, a decrease from the 1985 level. Gross expenditures have amounted to some $2.2 billion since the beginning of 1985.

Other significant capital expenditures have been incurred for research and development equipment supporting new and existing products and services. In addition, we have invested capital in programs designed to enhance product distribution channels, customer service and support functions, and sales force productivity.

In 1987, property, plant and equipment–net declined by 1.9% as capital additions were more than offset by depreciation and retirements.

Investments increased by 6.8% in 1987, primarily as a result of favorable changes in foreign exchange rates and profits generated from our investments. These increases were partially offset by the sale of our interest in a real estate joint venture.

The 38.3% increase in 1987 in other assets consisted primarily of prepaid pension costs and capitalized software development costs.

Financing Activity and Capitalization

Strong cash flow from operations during 1987 permitted us to continue efforts toward increased financial flexibility. We redeemed $830 million of preferred stock and retired $417 million of long-term debt. Our external financing was limited to $343 million. Consequently, for the second consecutive year, we have reduced our utilization of external sources of financing.

As a ratio to total capital, debt decreased to 35.2% from 35.8% , preferred shares declined to 0.4% from 4% , and common shareowners' equity increased to 64.4% from 60.2% at December 31, 1987 and 1986, respectively. However, total capital remained relatively unchanged in 1987 as financing activity was offset by retained earnings generated from our operations.

In 1987, debt retirements consisted of regularly scheduled repayments. Over the past three years, $2.9 billion of long-term debt has been retired, including the call of $1.9 billion of high-cost debt, a portion of which was refinanced in 1986. Total debt outstanding has decreased by $2.4 billion since divestiture.

In 1988, we will implement the Statement of Financial Accounting Standards No. 94 (FAS 94), "Consolidation of All Majority-owned Subsidiaries." The new accounting standard will require that the accounts of AT&T Credit Corporation, a wholly-owned finance subsidiary accounted for under the equity method, be included in our consolidated financial statements. This accounting change will increase the consolidated debt ratio, but will not affect net income. If FAS 94 had been adopted in 1987, the debt ratio would have been 38% instead of 35.2% at year-end.

The Statement of Financial Accounting Standards No. 95 (FAS 95), "Cash Flow Reporting," will also be adopted in 1988. The new standard requires reporting cash flows from operating, investing and financing activities. This will necessitate a change in our presentation of the Consolidated Statements of Funds Flow, but will not affect our financial position or results of operations.

Preferred shares subject to mandatory redemption declined $830 and $545 million in 1987 and 1986, respectively, primarily through the exercise of optional redemption provisions.

Total common shareowners' equity increased by 6.7% in 1987 as a result of growth in earnings from operations. The return on average common equity was 14.4% in 1987, compared with 0.3% and 10.1% in 1986 and 1985, respectively.

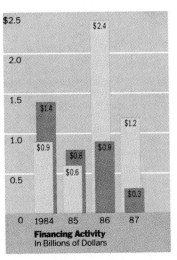

Financing Activity
In Billions of Dollars

■ Redemptions & Retirements
■ External Financing

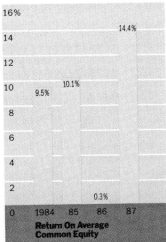

Return On Average Common Equity

Report of Management

The accompanying financial statements, which consolidate the accounts of American Telephone and Telegraph Company and its subsidiaries, have been prepared in conformity with generally accepted accounting principles.

The integrity and objectivity of data in these financial statements, including estimates and judgments relating to matters not concluded by year-end, are the responsibility of management as is all other information included in this Annual Report unless indicated otherwise. To this end, management maintains a system of internal accounting controls. Our internal auditors monitor compliance with it in connection with an annual plan of internal audits. The system of internal accounting controls, on an ongoing basis, is reviewed, evaluated and revised as necessary in view of the results of internal and independent audits, management recommendations, changes in the Company's business, and other conditions which come to management's attention. Management believes that the Company's system, taken as a whole, provides reasonable assurance (1) that financial records are adequate and can be relied upon to permit the preparation of financial statements in conformity with generally accepted accounting principles and (2) that access to assets is permitted only in accordance with management's authorizations. Recorded assets are compared with existing assets at reasonable intervals and appropriate action is taken with respect to any differences. Management also seeks to assure the objectivity and integrity of the Company's financial data by the careful selection of managers, by organizational arrangements that provide an appropriate division of responsibility, and by informational programs aimed at assuring that its policies, standards, and managerial authorities are understood throughout the organization. Management is also aware that changes in operating strategy and organizational structures can give rise to disruptions in internal controls. Special attention is given to controls while these changes are being implemented.

These financial statements have been examined by Coopers & Lybrand, Independent Certified Public Accountants. Their examinations are performed in accordance with generally accepted auditing standards and include selective tests of transactions and a review of internal accounting controls.

The Audit Committee of the Board of Directors, which is composed of Directors who are not employees, meets periodically with management, the internal auditors, and the independent auditors to review the manner in which they are performing their responsibilities and to carry out its oversight role with respect to auditing, internal accounting controls, and financial reporting matters. Both the internal auditors and the independent auditors periodically meet alone with the Audit Committee and have free access to the Audit Committee at any time.

Robert M. Kavner
Senior Vice President and Chief Financial Officer

James E. Olson
Chairman of the Board and Chief Executive Officer

Report of Independent Certified Public Accountants

To the Shareowners of American Telephone and Telegraph Company:

We have examined the consolidated balance sheets of American Telephone and Telegraph Company and subsidiaries at December 31, 1987 and 1986, and the related consolidated statements of income and funds flow for the years ended December 31, 1987, 1986 and 1985. Our examinations were made in accordance with generally accepted auditing standards and, accordingly, included such tests of the accounting records and such other auditing procedures as we considered necessary in the circumstances.

In our opinion, the financial statements referred to above present fairly the consolidated financial position of American Telephone and Telegraph Company and subsidiaries at December 31, 1987 and 1986, and the consolidated results of their operations and changes in their financial position for the years ended December 31, 1987, 1986 and 1985, in conformity with generally accepted accounting principles consistently applied during the three-year period, except for the changes, with which we concur, in the methods of accounting for depreciation and pensions as described in Notes B and L to the consolidated financial statements.

Coopers & Lybrand

1251 Avenue of the Americas
New York, New York
February 8, 1988

AT&T and Subsidiaries

Consolidated Statements of Income

Years ended December 31

Dollars in millions (except per share amounts)	1987	1986	1985
Sales and Revenues			
Sales of services, net of access charges (A)	**$19,659**	$19,108	$17,393
Sales of products	**10,206**	10,178	11,235
Rental revenues	**3,733**	4,801	5,789
Total operating revenues	**33,598**	34,087	34,417
Operating Costs and Expenses			
Cost of services	**8,796**	8,954	9,097
Cost of products	**6,000**	7,196	7,066
Cost of rentals	**1,766**	2,099	1,936
Selling, general and administrative expenses	**11,107**	11,071	11,104
Research and development expense (A)	**2,453**	2,278	2,228
Provision for business restructuring	**—**	2,157	—
Total operating costs and expenses (B) (L) (M)	**30,122**	33,755	31,431
Operating income	**3,476**	332	2,986
Other income–net (C)	**334**	402	252
Interest expense (K)	**634**	613	692
Income before income taxes	**3,176**	121	2,546
Provision for income taxes (D)	**1,132**	(193)	989
Income before cumulative effect of a change in depreciation method	**2,044**	314	1,557
Cumulative prior years' effect (to December 31, 1985) of a change in depreciation method (B)	**—**	(175)	—
Net Income	**2,044**	139	1,557
Dividends on preferred shares	**23**	86	110
Income applicable to common shares	**$ 2,021**	$ 53	$ 1,447
Weighted average common shares outstanding (millions)	**1,073**	1,071	1,058
Earnings per Common Share before cumulative effect of a change in depreciation method	**$ 1.88**	$ .21	$ 1.37
Cumulative prior years' effect of a change in depreciation method (B)	**—**	(.16)	—
Earnings per Common Share	**$ 1.88**	$ .05	$ 1.37

The notes on pages 30 through 35 are an integral part of the financial statements.

AT&T and Subsidiaries

Consolidated Balance Sheets

At December 31

Dollars in millions (except per share amounts)	1987	1986
Assets		
Current Assets		
Cash and temporary cash investments	$ 2,785	$ 2,602
Receivables less allowances (K)	7,689	7,820
Inventories (A)	3,157	3,519
Deferred income taxes	1,175	1,477
Other current assets	164	154
Total current assets	14,970	15,572
Property, plant and equipment–net (E) (F)	20,681	21,078
Investments (G)	1,063	995
Other assets	1,712	1,238
Total Assets	$38,426	$38,883
Liabilities and Shareowners' Equity		
Current Liabilities		
Accounts payable	$ 4,680	$ 4,625
Payroll and benefit related liabilities	2,332	2,499
Debt maturing within one year (H)	669	740
Dividends payable	323	338
Other current liabilities	2,571	3,015
Total current liabilities	10,575	11,217
Other Liabilities and Deferred Credits		
Long-term debt including capital leases (F) (H)	7,243	7,309
Other liabilities	1,034	1,144
Deferred income taxes	3,433	3,065
Unamortized investment tax credits	1,342	1,423
Other deferred credits	262	263
Total other liabilities and deferred credits	13,314	13,204
Preferred shares subject to mandatory redemption (J)	82	912
Common Shareowners' Equity (I)		
Common shares–par value $1 per share	1,074	1,072
Authorized shares: 1,500,000,000		
Outstanding shares: 1,073,674,000 at Dec. 31, 1987;		
1,071,987,000 at Dec. 31, 1986		
Additional paid-in capital	8,605	8,544
Retained earnings	4,776	3,934
Total common shareowners' equity	14,455	13,550
Total Liabilities and Shareowners' Equity	$38,426	$38,883

The notes on pages 30 through 35 are an integral part of the financial statements.

AT&T and Subsidiaries

Consolidated Statements of Funds Flow

Years ended December 31

Dollars in millions	1987	1986	1985
Funds (cash and temporary cash investments) at January 1...............	**$ 2,602**	$ 2,214	$ 2,140
Sources of Funds			
From operations:			
Net income	**2,044**	139	1,557
Depreciation	**3,724**	3,925	3,232
Net (increase) decrease in working capital, detailed below	**(73)**	2,661	13
Noncurrent portion of provision for business restructuring.....	**—**	1,159	—
Deferred income taxes–net	**643**	(391)	855
Less: Equity investment income in excess of dividends	**17**	24	23
Other adjustments for non-cash items	**238**	359	61
Total from operations before cumulative prior years' effect of a change in depreciation method	**6,083**	7,110	5,573
Cumulative prior years' effect of a change in depreciation method	**—**	175	—
Total from operations	**6,083**	7,285	5,573
From external financing:			
Increase in long-term debt including capital leases	**53**	729	141
Issuance of common shares......	**63**	64	671
Increase in short-term borrowing–net (H)	**227**	108	—
Total from external financing......	**343**	901	812
From other sources:			
Decrease in investments–net......	**74**	31	—
Sales to affiliate of long-term receivables–net (G)......	**—**	—	408
Total from other sources......	**74**	31	408
Total Sources of Funds	**6,500**	8,217	6,793
Uses of Funds			
Additions to property, plant and equipment–net (K)......	**3,662**	3,629	4,178
Dividends paid......	**1,320**	1,381	1,374
Retirement of long-term debt including capital leases	**417**	1,893	569
Increase in investments–net	**—**	—	402
Increase in other assets......	**281**	477	123
Decrease in short-term borrowing–net	**—**	—	22
Redemption of preferred shares	**830**	545	37
Other–net	**(193)**	(96)	14
Total Uses of Funds	**6,317**	7,829	6,719
Funds (cash and temporary cash investments) at December 31	**$ 2,785**	$ 2,602	$ 2,214
Working capital components (excluding cash and temporary investments, debt maturing within one year, dividends payable and deferred income taxes)			
(Increase) decrease in net receivables......	**$ 131**	$ 1,123	$ 420
(Increase) decrease in inventories......	**362**	1,027	(139)
(Increase) decrease in other current assets	**(10)**	9	119
Increase (decrease) in accounts payable......	**55**	(309)	(142)
Increase (decrease) in payroll and benefit related liabilities	**(167)**	300	85
Increase (decrease) in other current liabilities	**(444)**	511	(330)
Net (increase) decrease in working capital......	**$ (73)**	$ 2,661	$ 13

The notes on pages 30 through 35 are an integral part of the financial statements.

Notes to Consolidated Financial Statements
Dollars in millions (except per share amounts)

(A) Summary of Significant Accounting Policies

Consolidation

The consolidated financial statements include the accounts of AT&T and all its significant majority-owned subsidiaries other than AT&T Credit Corporation, which is accounted for under the equity method. Investments in 20 to 50 percent-owned companies and joint ventures also are accounted for under the equity method. Other investments are recorded at cost.

Industry Segmentation

AT&T operates predominantly in a single industry segment, the information movement and management industry. This segment constitutes more than 90% of AT&T's total operating revenues, operating income, and identifiable assets. AT&T also is engaged in other activities that in the aggregate are not material and, as such, are not separately reported. These activities include the furnishing of shareholder services and the distribution of computer equipment through retail outlets.

Access Charges

Local telephone companies charge for access to their local telephone networks. These access charges are collected from customers by AT&T and paid to the local telephone companies. Since these charges are collected on behalf of the local telephone companies, access charges are not included in AT&T's reported operating revenues. Access charges amounted to $17,611, $19,593, and $21,521 for 1987, 1986, and 1985, respectively.

Research and Development

Research and development expenditures are charged to expense as incurred. Development costs of software to be marketed are charged to research and development expense until technological feasibility is established after which remaining software production costs are capitalized as other assets. These costs are amortized to product costs over the estimated period of sales, and such amortization amounted to $110, $93, and $42 during 1987, 1986, and 1985, respectively. Unamortized software production costs were $287 and $206 at December 31, 1987 and 1986, respectively.

Investment Tax Credits

For financial reporting purposes, AT&T amortizes the investment tax credit (ITC) as a reduction of income tax expense over the useful life of the property that produced the credit. See also Note (D).

Inventories

Inventories are stated at the lower of cost or market. Cost is determined principally on a first-in, first-out basis for raw materials and work in process and on an average cost basis for completed goods.

At December 31	1987	1986
Completed goods	$1,607	$1,728
In process	1,087	1,300
Raw materials and supplies	463	491
Total	$3,157	$3,519

Plant and Equipment

Commencing in 1984, investment in plant and equipment is stated at cost excluding intercompany profits. Rate regulated plant assets acquired prior to 1984 are recorded at cost, including reasonable intercompany profits in accordance with regulated accounting practices. At divestiture, the carrying value of these assets was significantly reduced to economic value in a competitive environment. These reductions were recorded primarily as increases in the depreciation reserve. Beginning in 1986, the gain or loss on sale of factory machinery and laboratory equipment in the normal course of AT&T's business is reflected in operating results. When other depreciable plant is retired, the amount at which such plant has been carried in plant in service is credited to plant and generally charged to accumulated depreciation. See also Note (E).

Depreciation

Depreciation is calculated using either the group method or, commencing in 1986 for factory machinery and laboratory equipment, the unit method. Factory facilities placed in service subsequent to December 31, 1979 are depreciated on an accelerated basis. All other plant and equipment is depreciated on a straight line basis. See also Note (B).

(B) Business Restructuring, Accounting Change and Other Charges

In 1986, pretax income was reduced by $2,489 ($1,295 after taxes or $1.21 per share) for force reductions and facility consolidations expected to occur over a several year period, as well as for a change in accounting for depreciation, as described below:

— $2,157 ($1,120 after taxes or $1.05 per share) provision for business restructuring, consisting of $1,125 for force termination costs and $1,032 for consolidation of factories, warehouses, and other facilities.

− $332 ($175 net of taxes or $.16 per share) cumulative prior years' effect (to December 31, 1985) of a change from group to unit method of depreciation for factory machinery and laboratory equipment. This change was implemented to provide improved assignment of costs to products and better identification of service lives. The effect of this change on depreciation for any of the years presented is not material.

In addition, $761 ($409 after taxes or $.38 per share) was charged to operations in the fourth quarter of 1986 for inventory writedowns, primarily for communications and office automation products, and for increased depreciation primarily related to rental equipment and other assets.

The Company believes the business restructuring reserve established in 1986 remains adequate for the completion of its force downsizing and facility consolidation activities. At December 31, 1987, the business restructuring reserve totaled $1,175.

(C) Other Income−Net

	1987	1986	1985
Interest, royalties and dividends ..	$266	$267	$260
Equity earnings from			
unconsolidated entities..:....	59	58	44
Miscellaneous-net	9	77	(52)
Total........................	$334	$402	$252

Miscellaneous-net for 1986 includes $73 for an award for damages paid by the Republic of Iran, representing net amounts due AT&T, plus interest, which were written off as uncollectible in prior years. Also included is a gain of $40 reflecting AT&T's portion of the premium above book value paid by third parties for newly issued shares of Ing. C. Olivetti & C., S.p.A..

(D) Income Taxes

The provision for income taxes consists of the following components:

	1987	1986	1985
Current			
Federal	$ 432	$ 269	$ 103
State and local	127	118	117
Foreign	12	7	22
	571	394	242
Deferred			
Federal	533	(410)	743
State and local	109	18	109
Foreign	1	1	3
	643	(391)	855
Deferred investment tax			
credits-net*...............	(82)	(196)	(108)
Provision for income taxes	$1,132	$(193)	$ 989

*Net of amortization of $330 in 1987, $333 in 1986, $300 in 1985.

The provision for income taxes in 1986 was negative because it reflected future tax benefits associated with the restructuring charges described in Note (B) and amortization of investment tax credits. In the absence of the provision for business restructuring, the provision for income taxes would have been $844 in 1986.

Deferred taxes, resulting from timing differences in the recognition of revenue and expense items for tax and financial statement purposes, were as follows:

	1987	1986	1985
Property, plant and equipment ...	$ 39	$ 403	$ 638
Business restructuring, force			
and facility consolidation	502	(851)	234
Pensions and other benefits	174	279	—
Investment credits utilized	94	320	2
Inventory valuation............	96	(230)	(26)
Reversal of a reserve for refunds ..	—	—	161
Other timing differences	(262)	(312)	(154)
Total......................	$ 643	$(391)	$ 855

Principal causes for the differences between federal income tax expense computed at the federal statutory rate and AT&T's provision for income taxes are explained below:

	1987	1986	1985
Statutory federal income tax rate..	40%	46%	46%
Federal income tax at			
statutory rate...............	$1,270	$ 56	$1,171
Amortization of investment			
tax credits	(330)	(333)	(300)
State and local income taxes, net			
of federal income tax effect	142	73	122
Research credits..............	(20)	(42)	(37)
Other differences..............	70	53	33
Provision for income taxes	$1,132	$(193)	$ 989

The recently issued Statement of Financial Accounting Standards No. 96 (FAS 96), "Accounting for Income Taxes," which must be adopted no later than 1989, requires deferred income taxes to be determined based on the enacted income tax rates for the years in which these taxes will be payable or refundable. While the impact of FAS 96 will significantly increase net income in the year of adoption, the amount is not reasonably estimable at this time.

(E) Property, Plant and Equipment

At December 31	1987	1986
Land and improvements	$ 512	$ 499
Buildings and improvements.....	6,502	6,199
Machinery, electronic and other		
equipment.................	32,532	33,190
Total property, plant and		
equipment.................	39,546	39,888
Less: Accumulated depreciation ..	18,865	18,810
Property, plant and		
equipment−net	$20,681	$21,078

(F) Leases

As Lessor: The Company leases equipment to others on an operating lease basis; the majority of operating leases are cancelable. AT&T's net investment in leased equipment was as follows:

At December 31	1987	1986
Machinery and equipment.......	$3,402	$4,060
Less: Accumulated depreciation ..	1,550	1,521
Net investment................	$1,852	$2,539

AT&T also leases its products to others under sales-type leases. The receivables that arise under the long-term agreements are sold to AT&T Credit Corporation. Also see Note (G).

As Lessee: AT&T leases land, buildings and equipment through contracts that expire in various years. Future minimum lease payments at December 31, 1987 are as follows:

	Capital Leases	Operating Leases
1988........................	$150	$ 517
1989........................	93	395
1990........................	77	288
1991........................	56	222
1992........................	46	200
Later years	180	906
Total minimum lease payments ...	602	$2,528
Less: Estimated executory cost ...	4	
Imputed interest	201	
Present value of net minimum lease payments	$397	

Rental expense for operating leases was $906 in 1987, $987 in 1986, and $1,041 in 1985.

(G) Investments

Investment in Finance Subsidiary

The Company's investment in its wholly-owned unconsolidated finance subsidiary, AT&T Credit Corporation (AT&T-Credit), amounted to $309 and $254 at December 31, 1987 and 1986, respectively. AT&T-Credit, which is accounted for under the equity method, is engaged in offering financing arising primarily from product sales by AT&T to customers. During 1987, 1986, and 1985, the Company sold to AT&T-Credit $201, $380, and $921, respectively, of sales-type lease receivables–net of unearned interest income. AT&T-Credit has full recourse against AT&T for $544 of its net investment in finance assets at December 31, 1987. AT&T-Credit's earnings of $19, $14, and $14 in 1987, 1986, and 1985, respectively, are included in other income in AT&T's consolidated statements of income. In 1988, the accounts of AT&T-Credit will be included in AT&T's consolidated financial statements due to the adoption of the Statement of Financial Accounting Standards No. 94 (FAS 94), "Consolidation of All Majority-owned Subsidiaries." This accounting change will increase consolidated debt, but will not affect net income. If FAS 94 had been adopted in 1987, consolidated debt would have increased by approximately $1 billion.

AT&T-Credit Corporation	1987	1986	1985
Revenue, principally finance income	$ 175	$ 125	$ 83
Interest and other expenses......	147	96	54
Net income..................	19	14	14

At December 31	1987	1986
Net investment in finance assets ..	$1,462	$1,013
Other assets	181	81
Total assets...................	$1,643	$1,094
Debt maturing within one year ...	$ 332	$ 267
Other liabilities	332	219
Long-term debt*	799	482
Shareowner's equity	180	126
Total liabilities and shareowner's equity	$1,643	$1,094

*Includes $125 due AT&T.

Other Significant Investments

As of December 31, 1987, additional significant investments at equity included:

Ing. C. Olivetti & C., S.p.A. (Olivetti)–22% of voting shares owned. The market value of AT&T's investment in Olivetti, as measured by the closing price on the Milan, Italy stock exchange at December 31, 1987 and 1986 was $644 and $1,016, respectively.

Joint Venture with N. V. Philips–50% of voting shares owned which increased to 60% in January, 1988.

Joint Venture with Lucky Gold Star Group–44% of voting shares owned.

AT&T's investments at equity (excluding AT&T-Credit) were $702 and $678 at December 31, 1987 and 1986, respectively. AT&T's cumulative equity investment in undistributed earnings of investees (excluding AT&T-Credit) was $73 at December 31, 1987. Dividends received from equity investment entities (excluding AT&T-Credit) were $26 in 1987 and $24 in 1986.

(H) Debt Obligations

Long-term obligations outstanding consisted of the following:

Interest Rates	Maturities	At December 31, 1987	1986
Debentures:			
2⅞% to 4¾%	.....1987–1999......	$1,550	$1,850
5⅛% to 7⅛%	.....1995–2003......	1,850	1,850
7½% to 9%	.......1987–2026......	2,523	2,552
Notes:			
5½% to 7¾%	....1987–2003......	595	607
9% to 12⅞%	......1987–1997......	507	510
		7,025	7,369
Long-term lease obligations..........		397	440
Other.............................		33	16
Less: Unamortized discount–net......		35	36
		7,420	7,789
Less: Current portion			
Long-term debt.............		57	325
Long-term lease obligations ...		120	155
Total long-term obligations		$7,243	$7,309

Long-term debt maturities for the five years subsequent to December 31, 1987 are $57 in 1988, $57 in 1989, $388 in 1990, $142 in 1991, $317 in 1992, and $6,064 in years thereafter.

None of the long-term debt is collateralized by mortgage or pledge of AT&T's assets, nor can it be converted to common or preferred shares. The trust indentures covering the long-term debt do not place any restrictions on payment of dividends.

The remaining portion of debt maturing within one year consisted principally of commercial paper, which amounted to $414 and $251 at December 31, 1987 and 1986, respectively.

(I) Common Shareowners' Equity

	Common Stock	Additional Paid-in Capital	Retained Earnings
Balance at December 31, 1984	$1,038	$7,843	$4,882
Net income 1985	—	—	1,557
Dividends declared			
On $77.50 Preferred	—	—	(40)
On $ 3.64 Preferred	—	—	(34)
On $ 3.74 Preferred	—	—	(36)
On Common shares $1.20 per share	—	—	(1,273)
Shares issued under shareowner plans	12	234	—
Shares issued under employee plans	19	406	—
Other changes	—	—	25
Balance at December 31, 1985	$1,069	$8,483	$5,081
Net income 1986	—	—	139
Dividends declared			
On $77.50 Preferred	—	—	(20)
On $ 3.64 Preferred	—	—	(32)
On $ 3.74 Preferred	—	—	(34)
On Common shares $1.20 per share	—	—	(1,285)
Shares issued under employee plans	3	61	—
Redemption of preferred shares . .	—	—	(22)
Other changes*	—	—	107
Balance at December 31, 1986	$1,072	$8,544	$3,934
Net income 1987	—	—	2,044
Dividends declared			
On $ 3.64 Preferred	—	—	(9)
On $ 3.74 Preferred	—	—	(9)
On Common shares $1.20 per share	—	—	(1,287)
Shares issued under employee plans	2	61	—
Redemption of preferred shares . .	—	—	(34)
Other changes*	—	—	137
Balance at December 31, 1987	**$1,074**	**$8,605**	**$4,776**

*Principally foreign currency translation adjustments.

(J) Redeemable Preferred Shares

The Company has 100,000,000 authorized shares of preferred stock at $1 par value. The outstanding issues are as follows:

Shares Outstanding At December 31	$77.50 Issue, Stated Value $1,000	$3.64 Issue, Stated Value $50	$3.74 Issue, Stated Value $50
1985	512,500	9,100,000	9,400,000
1986	25,000	8,500,000	8,800,000
1987	**—**	**600,000**	**600,000**

During 1987 shares of each of the above issues were redeemed under both mandatory and optional redemption provisions, and such redemptions amounted to $830.

On February 1, 1988, the remaining 600,000 shares of the $3.74 issue were redeemed at stated value.

$3.64 preferred shares may be redeemed at a premium of $2.18 per share on or before April 30, 1988 and at a diminishing premium thereafter. The $3.64 issue contains a sinking fund requirement for the redemption each year of 300,000 shares without a premium; an additional 300,000 shares may be redeemed at the Company's option. The total sinking fund requirement for the $3.64 series is $15 for each of the years 1988 and 1989, at which time all shares will have been redeemed.

(K) Other Information

–Interest expense is net of capitalized amounts of $73, $109, and $97 for 1987, 1986, and 1985, respectively.

–Receivables at December 31, 1987 and 1986 have been reduced by allowances for doubtful accounts of $484 and $317, respectively.

–Additions to property, plant and equipment–net were increased by $520 in 1985 due to the reclassification of reserves previously accrued for restructuring the corporation and adjusting the carrying value of assets.

(L) Employee Benefit Plans

Pension Plans

The Company sponsors non-contributory defined benefit plans covering substantially all management and non-management employees. Benefits for management employees are based on a career average pay plan while the benefits for non-management employees are based on a non-pay-related plan.

The Company's pension contributions are made to trust funds, which are held for the sole benefit of pension plan participants. Contributions are determined in accordance with the aggregate cost method, an acceptable funding method under the Employee Retirement Income Security Act of 1974, and with appropriate Internal Revenue Service regulations. For purposes of determining contributions, rates of investment return are assumed and the weighted average of such rates was 7.6% , 7.8% , and 6.7% for 1987, 1986, and 1985, respectively.

Effective January 1, 1986, AT&T adopted the Statement of Financial Accounting Standards No. 87 (FAS 87), "Employers' Accounting for Pensions." Adoption of FAS 87 required AT&T to change from the aggregate cost method to the projected unit credit method for determining pension cost for financial reporting purposes. Additionally, FAS 87 required that the effects of retroactively applying the new method be amortized over the average remaining service period of active employees, which is estimated to be 15.9 years. Pension cost computed in accordance with FAS 87 was negative and amounted to $316 and $258 for 1987 and 1986, respectively, resulting in a pension credit (i.e., pension income). Pension cost for 1985 using the aggregate cost method was $657. If FAS 87 had not been adopted in 1986, pension cost computed using the aggregate cost method would have been $88 and $327 in 1987 and 1986, respectively.

Pension cost includes the following components:

	1987	1986
Service cost-benefits earned during the period	$ 446	$ 419
Interest cost on projected benefit obligation	1,351	1,296
Amortization of unrecognized prior service costs*	22	13
Less: Return on plan assets		
Actual $1,412	$3,917	
Deferred portion 239	(2,415)	
Expected return	1,651	1,502
Amortization of transition asset	484	484
Pension credit	$ 316	$ 258

*These costs pertain to plan amendments in 1987 and prior years and are amortized on a straight line basis over the average remaining service period of active employees.

The funded status of the plan was as follows:

At December 31	1987	1986
Actuarial present value of accumulated benefit obligation, including vested benefits of $14,623 and $14,222, respectively	$16,484	$16,169
Plan assets at market value........	$26,590	$26,379
Less: Actuarial present value of projected benefit obligation...	17,696	17,481
Excess of assets over projected benefit obligation.............	8,894	8,898
Unrecognized prior service costs ...	467	333
Less: Unrecognized transition asset	6,728	7,211
Unrecognized net gain.......	1,607	1,359
Prepaid pension cost	$ 1,026	$ 661

The projected benefit obligation was determined using discount rates of 8.25% and 8.0% at December 31, 1987 and 1986, respectively, and an assumed long-term rate of compensation increase of 5.0%. The expected long-term rate of return on plan assets used in determining pension cost was 8.0% for 1987 and 1986. Plan assets consist primarily of listed stocks, corporate and governmental debt, and real estate investment.

Savings Plans

The Company sponsors savings plans for substantially all employees. The plans allow employees to contribute a portion of their pretax or after tax income, in accordance with specified guidelines. AT&T matches a percentage of these contributions up to certain limitations. During 1987, 1986, and 1985, such costs amounted to $263, $231, and $228, respectively.

(M) Postretirement Benefits

The Company's benefit plan for retirees includes health care benefits and life insurance coverage.

The health care benefits are provided through insurance company contracts. The annual cost of such benefits is the claims paid for retirees. This cost was $234 and $192 for approximately 91,400 and 87,000 retired employees in 1987 and 1986, respectively. This cost for 1985, which is not separable between active and retired employees, was $868 and included approximately 338,000 active and 76,000 retired employees. In addition, under the terms of the Divestiture Plan of Reorganization, AT&T pays a portion of the health care benefit costs of the divested Bell System operating telephone companies' predivestiture retirees. These costs are expensed as incurred and were $85, $84, and $59 for 1987, 1986, and 1985, respectively.

The cost of providing postretirement life insurance benefits to employees who meet certain age and service requirements is determined and funded under the aggregate cost method. This cost was $23 for 1987, and $27 for each of the years, 1986 and 1985.

(N) Stock Options

The AT&T 1987 Long-Term Incentive Program (Plan), which became effective on July 15, 1987, provides for the granting of stock options, stock appreciation rights (SARs) in tandem with stock options or free-standing, and other awards. Under the Plan, 0.6% of the outstanding shares of the Company's common stock as of the first day of each calendar year is available for grant in such year. All shares available in any year that are not granted under the Plan are available for grant in subsequent years. The exercise price of any stock option or award shall not be less than 100% of the fair market value of the stock on the date of a grant of such option. Under the Plan, exercise of either a related option or a related SAR cancels the other to the extent of such exercise.

Prior to July 15, 1987, stock options were granted under the AT&T 1984 Stock Option Plan. No new options can be granted under the 1984 plan. Under this plan, a maximum of 20,000,000 shares of the Company's common stock were available for grant at fair market value on the date of grant.

Option transactions during 1987, 1986, and 1985 are shown below:

Number of Shares	1987	1986	1985
Balance at January 1	4,910,201	3,295,536	1,508,372
Options granted	2,125,105	1,947,400	2,036,350
Options and SARs exercised	(352,171)	(182,090)	(80,670)
Average price	$19.47	$18.28	$17.90
Options forfeited ...	(232,903)	(150,645)	(168,516)
At December 31:			
Options outstanding	6,450,232	4,910,201	3,295,536
Average price	$22.35	$20.95	$18.80
Options exercisable	4,529,087	3,088,076	1,415,122
Shares available for grant........	6,328,878	14,827,039	16,623,794

During 1987, SARs were granted for 262,000 shares for an average exercise price of $25.28, and 16,890 SARs were exercised. As of December 31, 1987, 797,940 SARs remained unexercised, of which 546,237 SARs were exercisable as of December 31, 1987.

(O) Contingencies

AT&T is a defendant in a number of lawsuits and party to a number of other proceedings that have arisen in the normal course of its business, including certain regulatory proceedings in which revenues are being collected by AT&T subject to possible refund. In the opinion of the Company's legal counsel, any monetary liability or financial impact of such lawsuits and proceedings to which AT&T might be subject after final adjudication would not be material to the consolidated financial position of the Company.

(P) AT&T Technologies, Inc.

AT&T Technologies, Inc. is a wholly-owned subsidiary of the Company and is included in the AT&T consolidated financial statements. The following table provides summarized consolidated financial information for AT&T Technologies, Inc., which includes sales of $3,860, $3,718, $4,369 for 1987, 1986, and 1985, respectively, to AT&T and its affiliates; such sales are eliminated in the AT&T consolidated financial statements. During 1987, the Company reallocated business restructuring reserves of $273 to AT&T Technologies from other AT&T business units. This transfer had no impact on AT&T's consolidated net income.

AT&T Technologies, Inc.	1987*	1986*	1985
Sales......................	$11,044	$10,830	$12,180
Gross profit on sales	3,878	3,361	3,969
Cumulative prior years' effect (to December 31, 1985) of a change in depreciation method (B)....	—	90	—
Net income (loss).............	290	(357)	553

At December 31	1987	1986
Current assets	$ 4,770	$ 4,687
Net property, plant and equipment, long-term investments, and other noncurrent assets ...	3,074	2,962
Total assets	$ 7,844	$ 7,649
Current liabilities.............	$ 2,299	$ 2,674
Long-term debt and other noncurrent liabilities	1,756	1,487
Equity capital	3,789	3,488
Total liabilities and equity capital	$ 7,844	$ 7,649

*Includes $273 and $866 for provision for business restructuring in 1987 and 1986, respectively. See Note (B).

(Q) Quarterly Information (unaudited)

Quarters	First	Second	Third	Fourth	Total
1987					
Operating revenues............................	$ 8,121	$ 8,401	$ 8,474	$ 8,602	$33,598
Operating costs and expenses......................	7,339	7,278	7,611	7,894	30,122
Net income	445	596	505	498	2,044
Earnings per common share	.40	.55	.47	.46	1.88
1986					
Operating revenues............................	$ 8,710	$ 8,421	$ 8,427	$ 8,529	$34,087
Operating costs and expenses......................	7,674	7,628	7,602	10,851	33,755
Income (loss) before cumulative effect of a change in depreciation method...........................	529	422	533	(1,170)	314
Cumulative prior years' effect (to December 31, 1985) of a change in depreciation method	(175)	—	—	—	(175)
Net income (loss).............................	354	422	533	(1,170)	139
Per common share:					
Earnings (loss) before cumulative effect of a change in depreciation method	.47	.37	.48	(1.11)	.21
Earnings (loss)	.31	.37	.48	(1.11)	.05

1986

Fourth Quarter: Includes decrease in net income of $1,504 due to charges for business restructuring activities and other actions. See Note (B).

Third Quarter: Includes increase in net income of $39 for an award for damages paid by the Republic of Iran and $29 attrib-utable to the change in AT&T's ownership interest in Olivetti. See Note (C). Also includes a reduction in net income of $25 due to charges for business restructuring activities. See Note (B).

First Quarter: Includes a decrease in net income of $175 due to the cumulative effect of a change in depreciation method. See Note (B).

Four Year Summary of Selected Financial Data (unaudited)

On January 1, 1984, AT&T was required by Court order to divest those parts of the Bell System operating telephone companies that provided local exchange and exchange access services and printed directory advertising. As a consequence of the divestiture, the financial results of the pre-divestiture years are not comparable to those of 1987, 1986, 1985 and 1984 and are not included below.

Dollars in millions (except per share amounts)	1987	1986*	1985	1984
Results of Operations:				
Total operating revenues	**$33,598**	$34,087	$34,417	$33,187
Total operating costs and expenses	**30,122**	33,755	31,431	30,893
Net income	**2,044**	139	1,557	1,370
Dividends on preferred shares	**23**	86	110	112
Income applicable to common shares	**2,021**	53	1,447	1,258
Earnings per common share	**1.88**	.05	1.37	1.25
Dividends declared per common share	**1.20**	1.20	1.20	1.20
Assets and Capital:				
Property, plant and equipment–net	**$20,681**	$21,078	$22,261	$21,343
Total assets	**38,426**	38,883	40,397	39,773
Long-term debt including capital leases	**7,243**	7,309	7,684	8,718
Preferred shares subject to mandatory redemption	**82**	912	1,457	1,494
Common shareowners' equity	**14,455**	13,550	14,633	13,763
Capital investments	**3,588**	3,598	4,580	3,538
Other Information:				
Operating income as a percent of operating revenues	**10.3%**	1.0%	8.7%	6.9%
Net income as a percent of operating revenues	**6.1%**	0.4%	4.5%	4.1%
Return on average common equity	**14.4%**	0.3%	10.1%	9.5%
Market price per common share at year-end	**$27.00**	$25.00	$25.00	$19.50
Book value per common share at year-end	**$13.46**	$12.64	$13.68	$13.26
Debt ratio at year-end	**35.2%**	35.8%	36.2%	38.5%
Employees at year-end	**303,000**	316,900	337,600	365,200

*1986 data were significantly affected by major charges for business restructuring, an accounting change and other charges. See Note (B) to the financial statements.

Market and Dividend Data (unaudited)

AT&T common stock is traded on the New York, Philadelphia, Boston, Midwest, and Pacific stock exchanges. It also trades on the London, Tokyo, and other foreign stock exchanges. The prices shown in the accompanying table were obtained from the Composite Tape encompassing the trading on all the above U.S. exchanges and trades reported by the National Association of Securities Dealers and Instinet. Common shareowners of record totaled 2,701,876 as of December 31, 1987. AT&T also has preferred shares outstanding that rank prior to common shares as to dividend. The payment of common dividends will depend upon the Company's earnings and financial requirements and other factors. Details of the preferred shares and common shareowners' equity are in Notes (J) and (I), respectively, to the financial statements.

Calendar Quarter		Market Price High	Market Price Low	Dividends Declared
1987	**1st**	**$27 3/8**	**$22 1/4**	**$.30**
	2nd	**29 1/4**	**23 1/4**	**.30**
	3rd	**35 7/8**	**27 1/8**	**.30**
	4th	**34 3/4**	**20**	**.30**
1986	1st	$25 5/8	$20 7/8	$.30
	2nd	26	21 5/8	.30
	3rd	25 1/2	22 3/8	.30
	4rd	27 7/8	22 1/8	.30

Index to Financial Section

Report of Management

Xerox management is responsible for the integrity and objectivity of the financial data presented in this annual report. The consolidated financial statements were prepared in conformity with generally accepted accounting principles and include amounts based on management's best estimates and judgements.

The Company maintains a system of internal accounting controls designed to provide reasonable assurance that assets are safeguarded against loss or unauthorized use and that financial records are adequate and can be relied upon to produce financial statements in accordance with generally accepted accounting principles. This system includes the hiring and training of qualified people, written accounting and control policies and procedures, clearly drawn lines of accountability and delegations of authority. In a business ethics policy that is communicated annually to all employees, the Company has established its intent to adhere to the highest standards of ethical conduct in all of our business activities.

The Company monitors its system of internal accounting controls with direct management reviews and a comprehensive program of internal audits. In addition, Peat Marwick Main & Co., independent certified public accountants, have examined the financial statements and have reviewed the system of internal accounting controls to the extent they considered necessary to support their report which appears below.

The Audit Committee of the Board of Directors, which is composed solely of outside directors, meets regularly with the independent accountants, representatives of management, and the internal auditors to review audits, financial reporting and internal control matters as well as the nature and extent of the audit effort. The Audit Committee also recommends the engagement of independent accountants, subject to shareholder approval. The independent accountants and internal auditors have free access to the Audit Committee.

David T. Kearns
Chairman and
Chief Executive Officer

Stuart B. Ross
Vice President Finance and
Chief Financial Officer

Report of Independent Certified Public Accountants

To the Board of Directors and Shareholders of Xerox Corporation

We have examined the consolidated balance sheets of Xerox Corporation and consolidated subsidiaries and of Xerox Financial Services, Inc. and subsidiaries as of December 31, 1987 and 1986, and their related consolidated statements of income and cash flows for each of the years in the three-year period ended December 31, 1987. Our examinations were made in accordance with generally accepted auditing standards and, accordingly, included such tests of the accounting records and such other auditing procedures as we considered necessary in the circumstances.

In our opinion, the aforementioned consolidated financial statements appearing on pages 34, 36, 39, 40, 42 and 44-61 present fairly the financial position of Xerox Corporation and consolidated subsidiaries and of Xerox Financial Services, Inc. and subsidiaries at December 31, 1987 and 1986, and the results of their operations and their cash flows for each of the years in the three-year period ended December 31, 1987, in conformity with generally accepted accounting principles consistently applied during the period except for the change in 1986, with which we concur, in the method of accounting for pensions as described in the notes to the financial statements.

Peat Marwick Main & Co.
Stamford, Connecticut
January 25, 1988 except as
to Note 16 on page 52 and
Note 6 on page 58, which
are as of March 3, 1988

KPMG Peat Marwick

Peat Marwick Main & Co.

Consolidated Statements of Income

(In millions, except per share data) Year ended December 31	1987	1986	1985
Income			
Sales	$ 5,702	$4,822	$4,318
Service	2,753	2,292	1,763
Rentals	1,865	2,241	2,595
Equity in income from continuing operations of unconsolidated companies:			
Xerox Financial Services, Inc.	342	278	76
Other	78	48	40
Other Income	126	100	106
Total	10,866	9,781	8,898
Costs and Other Deductions			
Cost of sales	2,940	2,412	2,081
Cost of service	1,274	1,040	871
Cost of rentals	1,168	1,362	1,459
Research and development expenses	722	650	597
Selling, administrative and general expenses	3,571	3,370	3,011
Interest expense	226	212	230
Other, net	44	60	39
Income taxes	262	112	166
Outside shareholders' interests	81	75	63
Total	10,288	9,293	8,517
Income from Continuing Operations	578	488	381
Discontinued Operations	—	(65)	94
Cumulative Effect on Prior Years of Change in Accounting Principles for Pension Costs	—	42	—
Net Income	$ 578	$ 465	$ 475
Income (Loss) per Common Share			
Continuing operations	$ 5.35	$ 4.52	$ 3.47
Discontinued operations	—	(.67)	.97
Cumulative effect on prior years of change in accounting principles for pension costs	—	.43	—
Net Income per Common Share	$ 5.35	$ 4.28	$ 4.44
Average Common Shares Outstanding	99.0	97.3	96.2
Dividends on Preferred Stock	$ 48	$ 48	$ 48

The accompanying notes are an integral part of the consolidated financial statements.

Financial Review

The following discussion summarizes the results as reported in the Company's consolidated financial statements.

Income Improved

A combination of good revenue growth and close attention to basic business factors such as cost control programs produced income gains for both of the Company's principal businesses in 1987. Total income from continuing operations increased 19 percent over the prior year to $578 million. This growth corresponds with $5.35 income per common share from continuing operations in 1987, up from $4.52 in 1986 and $3.47 in 1985.

On a total Company basis, net income in 1986 and 1985 was impacted by operations which were discontinued (see Xerox Corporation Note 15 on page 52), and by the effect of a pension accounting change in 1986 (see Xerox Financial Services, Inc. Note 12 on page 61).

Results of Operations

The financial summary on this page presents the overall organizational contribution to the Company's operating results from the continuing Business Products and Systems (BP&S) business and Xerox Financial Services, Inc. (XFSI). In 1987, BP&S achieved profitability improvement and XFSI continued the profitable expansion of its business. A detailed definition and discussion of industry segments are found below and on pages 37 and 38.

New Accounting Pronouncements

There are several recently issued Statements of the Financial Accounting Standards Board (FASB) which have not yet been adopted by the Company or its subsidiaries. The Standards and their effects on the business are discussed further in Xerox Corporation Notes 1 and 8 and XFSI Note 1, which are found on pages 44, 48 and 56.

Financial Summary

(In millions)	1987	1986	1985
Revenues			
Business Products and Systems			
Business Equipment	$10,320	$ 9,355	$ 8,676
Financing	230	127	81
Total Business Products and Systems	10,550	9,482	8,757
Xerox Financial Services, Inc.			
Insurance	4,072	3,163	2,591
Financing	384	297	313
Investment Banking	119	104	100
Total Xerox Financial Services, Inc.	4,575	3,564	3,004
Total Revenues	$15,125	$13,046	$11,761
Income from Continuing Operations			
Business Products and Systems			
Business Equipment	$ 270	$ 240	$ 335
Financing	28	20	16
Total Business Products and Systems	298	260	351
Xerox Financial Services, Inc.			
Insurance	269	189	(16)
Financing	83	84	67
Investment Banking	15	25	26
Other	(87)	(70)	(47)
Total Xerox Financial Services, Inc.	280	228	30
Total Income from Continuing Operations	$ 578	$ 488	$ 381

This Financial Summary describes the revenue and income contributions from each of the industry segments within BP&S and XFSI. The BP&S revenue and income from Financing includes the results of its financing activities. Most of the financing for domestic sales of Xerox equipment is carried out by Xerox Credit Corporation, whose financing revenue and income are reported within XFSI. Included in the XFSI Income from Continuing Operations as Other, are XFSI holding company interest and other expenses, and allocated interest expense related to the acquisitions of financial services subsidiaries and capital contributions.

Definition of Industry Segments

In 1987 the Company expanded its reporting of industry segments, as defined below.

The Business Equipment segment consists of the development, manufacture, marketing and maintenance of the Company's equipment and related supplies. The Company's products include xerographic copiers and duplicators, electronic and electrostatic printers, workstations, information processing products and systems, electronic typewriters, plotters, facsimile transceivers, networks, computer related services and software.

The Xerox Equipment Financing segment includes the Company's financing activities, either directly or through unconsolidated financing subsidiaries, associated with the sale of Xerox products worldwide.

The Third Party Financing segment consists of the non-Xerox financing activities conducted through unconsolidated financing subsidiaries.

The Insurance segment consists of the Company's unconsolidated insurance subsidiary, Crum and Forster, Inc. (C&F), which is primarily a property and casualty insurer. C&F also provides life insurance products through a wholly-owned subsidiary.

The Investment Banking segment consists of the activities of the Company's unconsolidated subsidiaries, Van Kampen Merritt Inc. and Furman Selz Holding Corporation.

Due to allocation methodologies and other operating conditions, the following information may not be representative of operating profits or assets if the segments were independent companies.

Industry Segment Data

(In millions)	Business Equipment	Xerox Equipment Financing	Total	Third Party Financing	Insurance	Investment Banking	Total
	Document Processing						
1987 Revenue from unaffiliated customers	$10,320	$ 396	$10,716	$ 218	$ 4,072	$ 119	$15,125
Operating profit	749	152	901	41	103	25	1,070
General expenses, net	(101)	—	(101)	—	(120)	(24)	(245)
Income (taxes) benefits — Consolidated	(308)	(3)	(311)	—	40	9	(262)
— Other	—	(56)	(56)	(12)	40	(8)	(36)
Outside shareholders' interests	(70)	(10)	(80)	(1)	—	—	(81)
Realized capital gains of C&F, net of taxes	—	—	—	—	132	—	132
Income from operations	$ 270	$ 83	$ 353	$ 28	195	2	$ 578
Allocated interest and other, net of taxes					74	13	
Legal entity profits					$ 269	$ 15	
Assets	$ 8,171	$ 2,997	$11,168	$ 2,082	$ 9,781	$ 431	$23,462
Capital Expenditures	$ 937	—	$ 937	$ 61	$ 46	$ 3	$ 1,047
Depreciation and Amortization	$ 731	—	$ 731	$ 25	$ 42	$ 8	$ 806
1986 Revenue from unaffiliated customers	$ 9,355	$ 324	$ 9,679	$ 100	$ 3,163	$ 104	$13,046
Operating profit (loss)	605	128	733	(19)	(25)	46	735
General expenses, net	(139)	—	(139)	—	(119)	(17)	(275)
Income (taxes) benefits — Consolidated	(157)	(4)	(161)	—	41	8	(112)
— Other	—	(42)	(42)	47	108	(21)	92
Outside shareholders' interests	(69)	(6)	(75)	—	—	—	(75)
Realized capital gains of C&F, net of taxes	—	—	—	—	123	—	123
Income from continuing operations	$ 240	$ 76	$ 316	$ 28	128	16	$ 488
Allocated interest and other, net of taxes					61	9	
Legal entity profits					$ 189	$ 25	
Assets	$ 7,517	$ 2,102	$ 9,619	$ 1,329	$ 8,473	$ 490	$19,911
Capital Expenditures	$ 1,032	—	$ 1,032	$ 19	$ 17	$ 7	$ 1,075
Depreciation and Amortization	$ 806	—	$ 806	$ 21	$ 40	$ 6	$ 873
1985 Revenue from unaffiliated customers	$ 8,676	$ 299	$ 8,975	$ 95	$ 2,591	$ 100	$11,761
Operating profit (loss)	735	130	865	10	(344)	48	579
General expenses, net	(139)	—	(139)	—	(77)	(17)	(233)
Income (taxes) benefits — Consolidated	(201)	(10)	(211)	—	37	8	(166)
— Other	—	(42)	(42)	(2)	234	(22)	168
Outside shareholders' interests	(60)	(3)	(63)	—	—	—	(63)
Realized capital gains of C&F, net of taxes	—	—	—	—	96	—	96
Income (loss) from continuing operations	$ 335	$ 75	$ 410	$ 8	(54)	17	$ 381
Allocated interest and other, net of taxes					38	9	
Legal entity profits (loss)					$ (16)	$ 26	
Assets	$ 7,247	$ 1,788	$ 9,035	$ 947	$ 6,924	$ 467	$17,373
Capital Expenditures	$ 951	—	$ 951	$ 47	$ 17	$ 2	$ 1,017
Depreciation and Amortization	$ 849	—	$ 849	$ 16	$ 40	$ 5	$ 910

Industry segment data for 1986 and 1985 have been restated to reflect 1987 classifications.

Industry Segment Discussion

Document Processing

The Company's total operations in support of its document processing strategy are focused on providing a wide range of quality business products and services on both a sale and rental basis. The Company also offers its document processing customers financing of their purchases of Xerox equipment through its financing operations. Together, the business equipment segment and the Xerox equipment financing segment comprise the Company's total document processing operations which are discussed below. Following an industry trend over the last decade to more outright sale of its products, the financing of customers' purchases of Xerox equipment has become an increasingly important component of the Company's document processing operations.

Marketplace Activity Was Strong
Worldwide market activity across the breadth of the Company's document processing products and services line showed good growth in 1987. There was excellent customer acceptance of the newer Xerox copier models 1012, 1050, 1065 and the new high-end copier, the Xerox model 1090. Electronic printing placements continued to show excellent improvement as the Company maintained a leadership position in this marketplace. The Company's electronic typewriters achieved good year-over-year growth, and placements of office systems and facsimile products recorded solid year-over-year increases.

Revenue Growth Improved
Reflecting the strong marketplace activity, total document processing revenue grew at a rate of 11 percent in 1987, reaching $10.7 billion from 1986 which in turn had increased 8 percent over 1985. Within this total, 1987 revenue from business equipment grew 10 percent to $10.3 billion and Xerox equipment financing revenue grew 22 percent to $396 million. The Company achieved particularly good growth in its international operations. Excluding the impact of currency on business equipment revenues from international operations, management estimates that business equipment revenues would have grown approximately 6 percent in 1987 and 2 percent in 1986.

Sales revenues increased 18 percent in 1987, driven by continued gains in new business placements. Service revenues, which are derived from the maintenance of the Company's sold base of installed equipment, continued to show excellent growth at 20 percent in 1987 and reflected the growing level of sold equipment over the past several years and the increase in the number of copies produced by this population. Following a worldwide industry trend to a higher customer demand for sold equipment, and the continuing conversion of existing rental equipment to sales, rental revenues declined 17 percent in 1987.

Profits Grew Strongly
Total document processing income grew 12 percent to $353 million in 1987 from $316 million in 1986, which had experienced a decline from $410 million in 1985. Within this total, business equipment income increased 13 percent in 1987 to $270 million compared with $240 million in 1986, and equipment financing income grew 9 percent reaching $83 million compared with a 1 percent growth in 1986. The higher growth rate in 1987 primarily reflects the expansion of equipment financing activities of the Company's international operations. Document processing income in 1987 represented over 60 percent of total Company income from operations.

While 1987 operating profit from business equipment showed solid growth over the prior year, income from continuing operations was impacted by a higher effective tax rate. This higher rate was the result of increased taxable earnings, higher effective international tax rates where profits were up strongly, and the impact from a $19 million write-off related to the sale of Rank Xerox South Africa (which was not deductible for income tax purposes).

The increase in 1987 business equipment operating profit primarily reflected the growth in marketplace activity combined with ongoing cost controls with particular emphasis on lowering overhead expenses. Within this operating profit improvement, the 1987 gross profit growth rate was slightly less than the revenue growth rate due primarily to product and distribution mix, investments in customer service, and currency impacts on the cost of products imported into the United States. It is also important to note that the strengthening of the yen versus the U.S. dollar has helped to stabilize industry price levels. At the same time, selling, administrative and general expenses declined to 34.6 percent of revenue in 1987, a 1.4 percentage point improvement over 1986. Finally, the Company continued to invest in research and development which grew slightly faster than revenue but remained at about 7 percent of revenue.

Employees Redeployed
Total employment in the operations of business equipment at the end of the year 1987, excluding employees of discontinued operations and unconsolidated subsidiaries, was somewhat lower at 99,032 people, in the face of strong business growth. The decline in employment levels since year-end 1986 included a reduction of approximately 1,300 people in connection with an early retirement plan. However these reductions, which were primarily in the indirect category, were partially reinvested in the direct service, manufacturing and customer administration functions in line with the Company's objective of increasing its marketing focus and improving service levels in support of customer satisfaction.

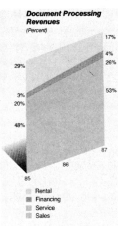

Document Processing Revenues
(Percent)

17%
4%
26%
53%
29%
3%
20%
48%
87
86
85

Rental
Financing
Service
Sales

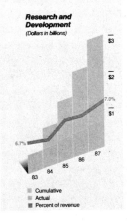

Research and Development
(Dollars in billions)

$3
$2
7.0%
$1
6.7%
83 84 85 86 87

Cumulative
Actual
Percent of revenue

Third Party Financing Segment
Financing Revenue and Income Improved
In recognition of the increasing profit opportunities from third party financing activities, which have evolved as a complement of the Company's strategy of financing the sale of its own equipment, Xerox' third party financing operations have been expanding over the past several years. Revenues from the third party financing segment grew 118 percent to $218 million in 1987. Income from this segment in 1987 totalled $28 million, which was equal to 1986 income but up substantially over the 1985 level of $8 million. It is important to note, however, that the 1986 income of $28 million included a non-recurring $21 million gain related to federal tax-rate changes applicable to the Xerox Credit Corporation (XCC) leveraged lease portfolio.

Insurance Segment
Solid Revenue and Profit Growth Achieved
During 1987, revenues from insurance operations grew 29 percent to $4.1 billion following a 22 percent increase in 1986. This growth primarily reflects the premium increases at Crum & Forster, Inc. (C&F), including the financial impact of past pricing actions combined with some volume increases at C&F's property/casualty operations, and strong gains in the developing business of Xerox Financial Services Life Insurance Company (see New Accounting Pronouncements on page 35). C&F's 1987 income grew 42 percent to $269 million from 1986 income of $189 million, following significant improvement from a $16 million loss in 1985.

Operating Efficiency Improved
The profit growth was primarily driven by higher prices, tighter underwriting standards, better expense control, and increased investment income due to continued strong cash flow.

The improvement in underwriting results is reflected in C&F's 1987 full-year combined ratio of 108.2 percent which decreased 3.2 percentage points from 111.4 percent in 1986 which in turn had declined from 121.6 percent in 1985. The combined ratio is an approximate index of underwriting results, which includes losses and expenses compared with premiums.

C&F's results included capital gains of $132 million in 1987, which compared with $123 million in 1986 and $96 million in 1985.

Investment Banking Segment
Income Impacted by Financial Markets
The operating results of the investment banking segment include those of Van Kampen Merritt Inc. (VKM) and Furman Selz Holding Corporation, which was acquired during the third quarter of 1987.

Driven entirely by Furman Selz' revenue of $27 million in the second half of 1987, the combined revenues

of this business segment increased 14 percent in 1987 to $119 million, compared with $104 million in 1986 and $100 million in 1985. However, income for 1987 declined to $15 million from $25 million in 1986, which compared with $26 million in 1985. The year-over-year declines were the result of lower revenues and profits at VKM due to a general instability in interest rates which have lowered the demand for its fixed-income products.

Capital Resources

Financial Condition Remains Strong
The Xerox balance sheet remains strong as the Company continues to place emphasis on the improved utilization of its assets and maintenance of a conservative capital structure. Shareholders' equity benefited principally from earnings retained in the business, the net proceeds from the sale of common stock (primarily from the Company's Automatic Dividend Reinvestment and Stock Purchase Plan), and the favorable effect of balance sheet currency translation. As a result, the book value per common share of Xerox increased from $48.04 at year-end 1986 to $51.03 at the end of 1987.

During 1987, the Company's total consolidated debt increased $108 million, including a net increase of $299 million in short-term debt and a net decrease of $191 million in long-term debt. The total increase in consolidated debt was due to currency translation impacts as a result of the weaker U.S. dollar.

At December 31, 1987, total consolidated short- and long-term debt of the Company was 25.7 percent of total capitalization compared with 26.3 percent at year-end 1986 and 27.1 percent at the end of 1985.

Although the current ratio (current assets divided by current liabilities) declined to 1.56 at December 31, 1987, the Company's working capital remains at a strong $1.6 billion. The lower ratio was primarily driven by an increase in the current portion of long-term debt.

Return On Assets Rebounded
Return on Assets (ROA) for its Business Products and Systems business remains a major priority for the Company. The Company's internal measurement for return on BP&S assets increased to 10.8 percent in 1987, following a decline to 7.8 percent in 1986, after a steady improvement over the prior three years. The higher 1987 ROA was the result of improved profitability combined with continued emphasis on asset management at BP&S in 1987. The Company's internal measurement for return on BP&S assets is defined as BP&S pre-tax profits, including equipment financing (which includes income from notes transferred to XCC), divided by BP&S average assets of continuing operations.

Higher Total Return On Equity Achieved
As a result of strong profit growth, the Company's return on equity (ROE) for continuing operations continued to improve and reached 10.8 percent in 1987 from 9.7 percent in 1986.

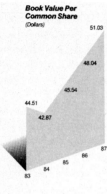

Book Value Per Common Share
(Dollars)

51.03
48.04
45.54
44.51
42.87

83 84 85 86 87

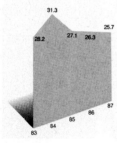

Debt to Capitalization Ratio
(Percent)

31.3
28.2 27.1 26.3 25.7

83 84 85 86 87

Consolidated Balance Sheets

(In millions) December 31	1987	1986
Assets		
Current Assets		
Cash	$ **309**	$ 402
Accounts receivable, net	**2,104**	1,867
Inventories	**1,408**	1,389
Other current assets	**638**	315
Total current assets	**4,459**	3,973
Finance Receivables Due after One Year, net	**300**	341
Rental Equipment, net	**878**	1,070
Land, Buildings and Equipment, net	**1,639**	1,491
Investment in Xerox Financial Services, Inc., at equity	**2,667**	2,530
Other Investments, at equity	**850**	561
Deferred Income Taxes	**302**	258
Other Assets	**503**	384
Total Assets	**$11,598**	$10,608
Liabilities and Common Shareholders' Equity		
Current Liabilities		
Notes payable and current portion of long-term debt	$ **605**	$ 306
Accounts payable	**470**	426
Salaries, profit sharing and other accruals	**1,164**	1,013
Income taxes	**124**	89
Unearned income	**258**	241
Other current liabilities	**229**	131
Total current liabilities	**2,850**	2,206
Long-Term Debt	**1,539**	1,730
Due to Xerox Financial Services, Inc.	**418**	488
Other Noncurrent Liabilities	**592**	490
Outside Shareholders' Interests in Equity of Subsidiaries	**652**	565
$5.45 Cumulative Preferred Stock	**442**	442
Common Shareholders' Equity	**5,105**	4,687
Total Liabilities and Common Shareholders' Equity	**$11,598**	$10,608

The accompanying notes are an integral part of the consolidated financial statements.

Consolidated Statements of Cash Flows

(In millions) Year ended December 31	1987	1986	1985
Net Cash Flows From Operating Activities:			
Net income from continuing operations	$ 578	$ 488	$ 381
Items not requiring (providing) cash included in income:			
Depreciation	731	806	849
Outside shareholders' interests in income	81	75	63
Net book value of rental equipment sold	350	355	355
Equity in income from continuing operations of			
unconsolidated companies, net of dividends	(286)	(197)	(15)
Cash provided by operating activities	1,454	1,527	1,633
Additions to rental equipment	(590)	(704)	(658)
Net (increase) decrease in other working capital	(212)	154	(236)
(Increase) decrease in finance receivables due after one year	41	(131)	57
Other, net	(126)	(137)	(2)
Cash used by operating activities	(887)	(818)	(839)
Total	567	709	794
Cash Flows from Investing Activities:			
Net income (loss) from discontinued operations	—	(65)	94
Items not requiring cash	—	63	400
Subtotal	—	(2)	494
Additions to land, buildings and equipment	(347)	(328)	(293)
Investments in and advances to unconsolidated companies	(162)	14	(348)
Other, net	(24)	(18)	33
Total	(533)	(334)	(114)
Cash Flows from Financing Activities:			
Increase (decrease) in short-term debt, net	299	(97)	(252)
Increase in long-term debt	167	411	252
Reduction of long-term debt	(358)	(264)	(282)
Subtotal	108	50	(282)
Dividends on common and preferred stock	(346)	(340)	(337)
Net proceeds from sales of Xerox common stock and			
stock of Xerox Canada Inc.	154	77	23
Other, net	(43)	(27)	(44)
Total	(127)	(240)	(640)
Cash Increased (Decreased) During the Year	(93)	135	40
Cash at Beginning of Year	402	267	227
Cash at End of Year	$ 309	$ 402	$ 267

The accompanying notes are an integral part of the consolidated financial statements.

Liquidity

Cash Flow Remains Strong

The Company's primary source of liquidity continues to be cash flows from operations. Cash provided by parent company operating activities during 1987 totalled $1,454 million, down from $1,527 million in 1986 due primarily to lower depreciation which results from the Company's declining base of rental equipment.

During 1987, cash of $887 million was used for operating activities, compared with $818 million in 1986. The year-over-year increase in cash used is attributed to an increase in working capital, primarily accounts receivable associated with the Company's higher revenue. As a result, the Company had net cash flows from operating activities of $567 million during 1987, a decline of $142 million from 1986.

During 1987, the Company used $533 million in its investing activities. This usage compares with investments of $334 million in 1986. The year-over-year increase results primarily from additional investments in the Company's expanding unconsolidated subsidiaries.

The net cash usage of financing activities was $127 million in 1987, down from $240 million a year ago. This lower cash usage was caused by an increase in net borrowings combined with higher 1987 proceeds from the sale of Xerox common stock, primarily through the Company's Automatic Dividend Reinvestment and Stock Purchase Plan. Dividends declared to shareholders in 1987 remained at about the same level as the prior year.

As a result of the net cash flows of $567 million from operating activities, the cash usage of $533 million from investing activities and the $127 million net cash usage from financing activities, the Company's cash balance decreased $93 million during the year to $309 million at December 31, 1987.

Capital Expenditures Were Down

Total capital expenditures in 1987 were $937 million, somewhat lower than the $1 billion spent in 1986. This decrease was due to lower spending for rental equipment due to the continuing shift away from rental to sold copier/duplicator placements, offset in part by higher spending for land, buildings, and equipment combined with the impact of currency.

For 1988, capital expenditures to support the continuing demand for business equipment products are expected to remain at about the 1987 level. However, actual expenditures will depend on the lease/sales mix of copier/duplicator placements.

Funding Plans For 1988

Management anticipates that substantial funds will continue to be provided by operations to fund the investments required to support the Company's ongoing document processing strategies. Management believes that no incremental financing will be required at the parent company level in 1988. However, to take advantage of the relatively attractive long-term interest rates which are available, up to $600 million of fixed-rate preferred stock and debt financing may be completed to finance the redemption of Xerox' $5.45 Cumulative Preferred stock, and to refinance maturing term debt. Of the $600 million, approximately $400 million has been completed, as described below.

During January 1988, the Company filed a shelf registration statement with the Securities and Exchange Commission which enabled the sale of up to $300 million of debt securities. Following a $200 million debt financing in February 1988, $100 million remains available from the shelf registration.

In February 1988, the Company offered 2.5 million shares of $3.6875 Ten-Year Sinking Fund Preferred stock at $50 per share and 1.5 million shares of $4.125 Twenty-Year Sinking Fund Preferred stock at $50 per share. The net proceeds from the sale of preferred stock will be used for general corporate purposes, which includes the redemption of the Company's $5.45 Cumulative Preferred stock. The Company also offered holders of currently outstanding $5.45 Cumulative Preferred stock the opportunity to exchange their shares for the $4.125 preferred shares on a one-for-one share basis, up to a maximum of 2 million shares.

During 1987, net long-term borrowings by the Company's unconsolidated subsidiaries totalled approximately $1 billion, the proceeds of which were primarily used to provide funds for expanding business activities.

Borrowings by the Company's unconsolidated financing subsidiaries will continue to be directly related to the levels of financing required to support business products and systems marketing activities and such external investment opportunities as may arise. Management believes that sufficient capital is available to support C&F's 1988 growth in premiums.

Credit Lines Available

At December 31, 1987, the Company had unused short-term domestic lines of credit with banks totalling $150 million, a decrease from $200 million at year-end 1986. These lines of credit are also available to XCC.

The Company also has revolving credit agreements totalling $2 billion, including a $1 billion agreement effective as of February 2, 1988. The agreements expire in 1990 and 1993. Under these arrangements XCC can borrow up to $1.5 billion and XFSI can borrow up to $250 million. Foreign subsidiaries had unutilized lines of credit aggregating $523 million.

The Company has not borrowed from its U.S. banks in several years.

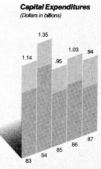

Capital Expenditures
(Dollars in billions)

1.35
1.14
1.03
.95 .94

83 84 85 86 87

■ Land, Buildings and Equipment
▒ Rental Equipment

Geographic Area Data

Information about the Company's operations in different geographic areas follows:

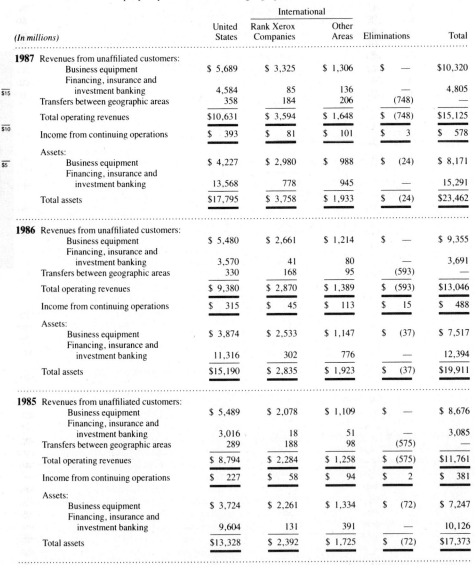

Domestic/International Revenues
(Dollars in billions)
15.1
13.0
11.8
85 86 87

■ Rank Xerox
▨ Other International
▨ United States

	United States	International — Rank Xerox Companies	Other Areas	Eliminations	Total
(In millions)					
1987 Revenues from unaffiliated customers:					
Business equipment	$ 5,689	$ 3,325	$ 1,306	$ —	$10,320
Financing, insurance and investment banking	4,584	85	136	—	4,805
Transfers between geographic areas	358	184	206	(748)	—
Total operating revenues	$10,631	$ 3,594	$ 1,648	$ (748)	$15,125
Income from continuing operations	$ 393	$ 81	$ 101	$ 3	$ 578
Assets:					
Business equipment	$ 4,227	$ 2,980	$ 988	$ (24)	$ 8,171
Financing, insurance and investment banking	13,568	778	945	—	15,291
Total assets	$17,795	$ 3,758	$ 1,933	$ (24)	$23,462
1986 Revenues from unaffiliated customers:					
Business equipment	$ 5,480	$ 2,661	$ 1,214	$ —	$ 9,355
Financing, insurance and investment banking	3,570	41	80	—	3,691
Transfers between geographic areas	330	168	95	(593)	—
Total operating revenues	$ 9,380	$ 2,870	$ 1,389	$ (593)	$13,046
Income from continuing operations	$ 315	$ 45	$ 113	$ 15	$ 488
Assets:					
Business equipment	$ 3,874	$ 2,533	$ 1,147	$ (37)	$ 7,517
Financing, insurance and investment banking	11,316	302	776	—	12,394
Total assets	$15,190	$ 2,835	$ 1,923	$ (37)	$19,911
1985 Revenues from unaffiliated customers:					
Business equipment	$ 5,489	$ 2,078	$ 1,109	$ —	$ 8,676
Financing, insurance and investment banking	3,016	18	51	—	3,085
Transfers between geographic areas	289	188	98	(575)	—
Total operating revenues	$ 8,794	$ 2,284	$ 1,258	$ (575)	$11,761
Income from continuing operations	$ 227	$ 58	$ 94	$ 2	$ 381
Assets:					
Business equipment	$ 3,724	$ 2,261	$ 1,334	$ (72)	$ 7,247
Financing, insurance and investment banking	9,604	131	391	—	10,126
Total assets	$13,328	$ 2,392	$ 1,725	$ (72)	$17,373

Revenues, net income and assets of the Rank Xerox Companies are substantially attributable to European operations; their operations in Africa, Asia, Australia, the South Pacific and the Middle East together comprise less than 3% of the Company's 1987 consolidated amounts. The Other Areas classification includes operations principally in Latin America and Canada.

Liabilities, outside shareholders' interests and the Company's equity in international operations were (in millions) $3,150, $652, and $1,889, respectively in 1987 and $2,485, $565, and $1,708, respectively in 1986. Dividends declared to outside shareholders were (in millions) $67 in 1987, $106 in 1986 and $38 in 1985.

Transfers between geographic areas are generally based on manufacturing cost plus a markup to cover other operating costs and to provide a margin of profit to the selling company.

Quarterly Results of Operations (Unaudited)

Interim financial information follows: *(In millions, except per share data)*	First Quarter	Second Quarter	Third Quarter	Fourth Quarter
1987 Income				
Sales, service and rentals	$2,318	$2,591	$2,579	$2,832
Equity in income of unconsolidated companies and other income	142	143	133	128
Total	2,460	2,734	2,712	2,960
Costs and other deductions				
Cost of sales, service and rentals	1,190	1,345	1,340	1,507
Expenses and other, net	1,067	1,138	1,168	1,190
Income taxes	58	68	45	91
Outside shareholders' interests	10	29	25	17
Total	2,325	2,580	2,578	2,805
Net income	$ 135	$ 154	$ 134	$ 155
Net income per common share	$ 1.25	$ 1.44	$ 1.23	$ 1.43
1986 Income				
Sales, service and rentals	$2,016	$2,300	$2,316	$2,723
Equity in income from continuing operations of unconsolidated companies and other income	108	112	102	104
Total	2,124	2,412	2,418	2,827
Costs and other deductions				
Cost of sales, service and rentals	1,034	1,154	1,200	1,426
Expenses and other, net	971	1,055	1,061	1,205
Income taxes	6	47	27	32
Outside shareholders' interests	10	21	18	26
Total	2,021	2,277	2,306	2,689
Income from continuing operations	103	135	112	138
Discontinued operations	(1)	(13)	—	(51)
Cumulative effect on prior years of change in accounting principles for pension costs	42	—	—	—
Net income	$ 144	$ 122	$ 112	$ 87
Income (loss) per common share				
Continuing operations	$ .93	$ 1.27	$ 1.03	$ 1.29
Discontinued operations	(.01)	(.14)	—	(.52)
Cumulative effect on prior years of change in accounting principles for pension costs	.43	—	—	—
Net income per common share	$ 1.35	$ 1.13	$ 1.03	$ .77

Notes to Consolidated Financial Statements

1. Summary of Significant Accounting Policies

Basis of Consolidation. The accounts of all subsidiaries are consolidated, except for the Company's financial services and real estate subsidiaries which are accounted for by the equity method. Investments in corporate joint ventures, and other companies in which the Company has a 20% to 50% ownership, are accounted for by the equity method. The accounts of Latin American subsidiaries are included for their fiscal years which generally end on November 30.

Rank Xerox Limited, Rank Xerox Holding B.V. and their respective subsidiaries and the other subsidiaries jointly-owned by the Company and The Rank Organisation Plc are referred to as Rank Xerox Companies. The accounts of the Rank Xerox Companies are included for their fiscal years ended October 31.

Consolidated financial statements of Xerox Financial Services, Inc. (XFSI), the Company's domestic financial services subsidiary, are presented, beginning on page 53, in support of the carrying value of the Company's investment in, and equity in the earnings of, XFSI.

Income Recognition. Revenues from the sale of equipment under installment contracts and from sales-type leases are recognized at the time of sale or at the inception of the lease, respectively. Revenues from equipment under other leases are accounted for by the operating lease method and are recognized over the lease term. Operating lease plans include maintenance and parts, but generally do not include supplies such as toner and paper which are sold separately. Service revenues are derived primarily from maintenance contracts on the Company's equipment sold to customers. Rental and service revenues from reprographic products vary each month based on the number of copies produced. Sales to third-party lease finance companies of equipment subject to the Company's operating leases are recorded as sales at the time the equipment is accepted by the third party. The Company has agreed to service these units, to perform non-preferential remarketing services and to administer the leases on a compensatory basis.

Inventories. Inventories are carried at the lower of average cost or market.

Rental Equipment, Buildings and Equipment. Rental equipment, buildings and equipment are depreciated over their estimated useful lives. Assets recorded under capital leases are amortized over their lease terms or, if title to the property will ultimately pass to the Company, over their estimated useful lives. Depreciation is computed using principally the straight-line method. Significant improvements are capitalized; maintenance and repairs are expensed. The cost and accumulated depreciation of assets retired or otherwise disposed of are eliminated from the accounts and any resulting gain or loss is credited or charged to income, as appropriate.

Foreign Currency Translation. The Company's subsidiaries in Latin America operate primarily in hyper-inflationary economies and transact a significant amount of business in

U.S. dollars. Accordingly, the U.S. dollar is deemed to be the functional currency of these subsidiaries and all translation gains and losses are taken into income. The financial position and results of operations of the Company's other foreign subsidiaries are measured using local currency as the functional currency. Revenues and expenses of such subsidiaries have been translated at average exchange rates. Assets and liabilities have been translated at current exchange rates, and the related translation adjustments, together with net gains and losses from hedging exposed net asset positions less related tax effects, are being deferred as a separate component of Shareholders' Equity, until there is a sale or liquidation of the underlying foreign investments. The Company has no present plans for the sale or liquidation of significant investments to which these deferrals relate. Aggregate foreign currency exchange gains and losses are included in determining net income. Net aggregate foreign currency exchange gains (losses) were $52 million, $(5) million and $(35) million in 1987, 1986 and 1985, respectively, and are included in Other, net in the consolidated statements of income.

New Accounting Pronouncements. There are several recently issued Statements of the Financial Accounting Standards Board which have not yet been adopted by the Company and its subsidiaries as of December 31, 1987. Of these new Statements the following have particular relevance to the Company:

Statement No. 94 – This Statement will require the Company to consolidate, beginning in 1988, all majority-owned subsidiaries. At the present time the Company does not consolidate XFSI or its real estate and international finance subsidiaries. Statement No. 94 will not affect the Company's net income or shareholders' equity, although the presentation and display of substantially all other financial data will materially change. The industry segment data on page 36 summarize the Company's total revenues, total assets and certain other data on a fully consolidated basis. Short and long-term debt will significantly increase under Statement No. 94 primarily as a result of consolidating Xerox Credit Corporation and the international finance subsidiaries. These subsidiaries are, by nature, highly leveraged relative to the Company and their borrowing capabilities are essentially determined on an independent basis. The Company does not anticipate any changes in its, or its subsidiaries', borrowing capabilities or practices as a result of applying Statement No. 94. Statement No. 94 is required to be retroactively applied.

Statement No. 96 – This Statement – "Accounting for Income Taxes" – will affect the recognition and measurement of income tax expense and deferred tax assets and liabilities and is more fully discussed in the Company's income tax footnote appearing on page 48 and in the accompanying financial statements of XFSI.

Statement No. 97 – This Statement is applicable to the insurance subsidiaries of XFSI and affects the presentation of realized capital gains and losses and the recognition of earned premiums and related expenses of XFSI's life insurance operations. Statement No. 97, which will have no affect on net income, is more fully discussed in the accompanying financial statements of XFSI.

2. Accounts Receivable

Current and long-term receivables consist of the following:

(In millions)	1987	1986
Accounts receivable	$1,475	$1,346
Accrued revenues	542	499
Investment in sales-type leases	653	614
Total	2,670	2,459
Less: Allowance for doubtful accounts	(84)	(75)
Unearned income and other	(182)	(176)
Total receivables, net	2,404	2,208
Less: Net finance receivables due after one year	(300)	(341)
Total current accounts receivable, net	$2,104	$1,867

The components of the Company's net investment in sales-type leases included in the consolidated balance sheets at December 31, 1987 and 1986 were as follows:

(In millions)	1987	1986
Total minimum lease payments receivable	$ 653	$ 614
Less: Unearned income and other	(182)	(176)
Allowance for doubtful receivables	(18)	(15)
Net investment in sales-type leases	$ 453	$ 423

Total minimum lease payments receivable are collectible as follows (in millions): 1988-$253; 1989-$193; 1990-$106; 1991-$58; and 1992-$43.

3. Rental Equipment, net

Rental equipment is depreciated over estimated useful lives, generally two to seven years. Changes in rental equipment for the three years ended December 31, 1987 are as follows:

(In millions)	1987	1986	1985
Cost			
Balance at January 1	$2,951	$3,401	$3,799
Additions	590	704	658
Dispositions	(1,077)	(1,291)	(1,138)
Translation and other changes	133	137	82
Balance at December 31	2,597	2,951	3,401
Accumulated Depreciation			
Balance at January 1	1,881	2,164	2,279
Depreciation	411	523	577
Dispositions	(727)	(936)	(783)
Translation and other changes	154	130	91
Balance at December 31	1,719	1,881	2,164
Rental equipment, net	$ 878	$1,070	$1,237

The Company's equipment operating lease terms vary, generally from one to thirty-six months. Minimum future rental revenues on the remaining noncancelable operating leases with original terms of one year or longer are (in millions): 1988-$516; 1989-$205; 1990-$76 and in the aggregate-$797. Total contingent rentals, principally usage charges in excess of minimum rentals for operating leases, amounted to (in millions): 1987-$534; 1986-$582; 1985-$627.

4. Land, Buildings and Equipment, net

The components of land, buildings and equipment follow:

(In millions)	Estimated Useful Lives (years)	1987	1986	1985
Land		$ 89	$ 62	$ 66
Buildings and building equipment	20 to 40	692	621	593
Leasehold improvements	Lease Term	271	249	221
Plant machinery	4 to 12	1,155	1,021	948
Office furniture and equipment	3 to 10	1,122	971	868
Other	3 to 20	133	113	129
Construction in progress		89	122	105
Total		$3,551	$3,159	$2,930

Changes in land, buildings and equipment for the three years ending December 31, 1987 are as follows:

(In millions)	1987	1986	1985
Cost			
Balance at January 1	$3,159	$2,930	$2,779
Additions	347	328	293
Dispositions	(147)	(183)	(241)
Translation and other changes	192	84	99
Balance at December 31	3,551	3,159	2,930
Accumulated Depreciation			
Balance at January 1	1,668	1,507	1,387
Depreciation	320	283	272
Dispositions	(112)	(128)	(159)
Translation and other changes	36	6	7
Balance at December 31	1,912	1,668	1,507
Land, buildings and equipment, net	$1,639	$1,491	$1,423

The Company leases certain land, buildings and equipment under capital leases and operating leases which expire through 2018. Total rent expense under operating leases amounted to (in millions): 1987-$372; 1986-$348; 1985-$309. Future minimum lease payments required under capital leases and operating leases that have initial or remaining noncancelable lease terms in excess of one year at December 31, 1987 are summarized below:

(In millions)	Capital Leases	Operating Leases
1988	$ 33	$ 247
1989	31	202
1990	21	155
1991	15	127
1992	11	107
Later years	67	436
Total minimum lease payments	178	$1,274
Less amount representing interest and executory costs	65	
Present value of net minimum lease payments	$113	

Future minimum sublease income under operating leases with noncancelable lease terms in excess of one year amounted to $41 million at December 31, 1987.

5. Investment in Xerox Financial Services, Inc., at equity

Xerox Financial Services, Inc. (XFSI), is the holding company for the Company's wholly owned domestic financial services subsidiaries, primarily Crum and Forster, Inc., Xerox Credit Corporation, Van Kampen Merritt Inc. and Furman Selz Holding Corporation which was acquired during the third quarter of 1987.

The income (loss) of the XFSI companies included in equity in income from continuing operations of unconsolidated companies in the Company's consolidated statements of income for the years ended December 31, 1987, 1986 and 1985 follows:

(In millions)	1987	1986	1985
Crum and Forster, Inc.	$269	$189	$(16)
Xerox Credit Corporation	83	84	68
Van Kampen Merritt Inc.	14	25	26
Furman Selz Holding Corporation	1	—	—
Xerox Financial Services, Inc.	(25)	(20)	(2)
Total	$342	$278	$ 76

The consolidated financial statements of XFSI are included herein on pages 53 to 61.

6. Other Investments, at equity

Other investments, at equity consist of the following at December 31, 1987 and 1986.

(In millions)	1987	1986
Fuji Xerox Co., Ltd.	$473	$397
Xerox Canada Finance, Inc.	146	60
Rank Xerox Leasing International Companies	138	46
Xerox Real Estate Companies	43	35
Other	50	23
Total	$850	$561

Rank Xerox Limited (RXL) owns 50% of the outstanding stock of Fuji Xerox Co., Ltd. (Fuji Xerox), a corporate joint venture. Fuji Xerox is located in the Far East and operates principally in the Business Equipment business. Condensed financial data for Fuji Xerox for its last three fiscal years are as follows:

(In millions)	1987	1986	1985
Summary of Operations			
Total operating revenues	$2,866	$2,060	$1,419
Costs and expenses	2,627	1,890	1,285
Income before income taxes	239	170	134
Income taxes	139	101	77
Net income	$ 100	$ 69	$ 57
Xerox' equity in net income	$ 50	$ 34	$ 28

Balance Sheets	1987	1986	1985
Assets			
Current assets	$1,504	$1,126	$ 747
Noncurrent assets	964	921	669
Total assets	$2,468	$2,047	$1,416
Liabilities and Shareholders' Equity			
Current liabilities	$1,195	$ 973	$ 704
Long-term debt	63	65	29
Other noncurrent liabilities	257	213	142
Shareholders' equity	953	796	541
Total liabilities and shareholders' equity	$2,468	$2,047	$1,416

Xerox Canada Finance Inc. (XCFI) is wholly owned by Xerox Canada Inc. (XCI), a consolidated subsidiary of the Company. XCFI is engaged in financing accounts receivable arising out of equipment sales by XCI and is in the business of financing leases for third parties. Trade receivables and sales-type leases amounting to $341 million and $300 million were sold or transferred to XCFI from XCI during 1987 and 1986, respectively. During 1987 the Company's equity in XCFI increased primarily due to XCI's investment of $67 million in a new series of XCFI's preferred stock.

As of December 31, 1987 the Company, through RXL, organized fourteen international finance companies which are referred to as the Rank Xerox Leasing International Companies (RXLI) whose purpose is to finance the Rank Xerox Companies' sales of Xerox equipment in a manner similar to the financing activities of XCFI. During 1987 the Company's equity in RXLI increased primarily due to RXL's aggregate investment of $59 million in the various RXLI companies.

Condensed financial data for the Company's unconsolidated real estate and international finance companies included in Other Investments, at equity are set forth below and have been combined based on each entity's respective fiscal year:

(In millions)	1987	1986	1985
Summary of Operations			
Total income	$ 189	$ 81	$ 52
Costs and expenses	130	57	17
Income before income taxes	59	24	35
Income taxes	27	11	17
Net income	$ 32	$ 13	$ 18

Balance Sheets	1987	1986	1985
Assets			
Current assets	$ 451	$205	$223
Noncurrent assets	1,194	625	521
Total assets	$1,645	$830	$744
Liabilities and Shareholders' Equity			
Current liabilities	$ 358	$290	$163
Advances from Xerox	—	2	190
Long-term debt	760	306	105
Other noncurrent liabilities	200	97	82
Shareholders' equity	327	135	204
Total liabilities and shareholders' equity	$1,645	$830	$744

7. Retirement Plans

In 1986 the Company adopted, for its U.S. retirement plans, Statements of Financial Accounting Standards (SFAS) No's. 87 and 88 which respectively establish standards for the determination of pension cost and for the settlement of pension plan obligations. During 1987 these Standards were adopted for the Company's major foreign plans. The Company's policy is to immediately recognize gains and losses resulting from the settlement of pension obligations. The accompanying financial statements of XFSI describe the effect of the new pension standards on the Company's unconsolidated subsidiaries.

U.S. Plans. The Company's major plans are noncontributory, trusteed profit sharing retirement plans to which a defined minimum annual contribution is made; any contributions in excess of such minimum contribution are made based upon a formula related to return on assets. These plans are supplemented by trusteed retirement income guarantee plans which assure a defined monthly income to substantially all U.S. employees at retirement to the extent that such defined benefits are not funded under the related profit sharing plans.

Foreign Plans. Pension coverage for employees of the Company's non-U.S. subsidiaries is provided, to the extent deemed appropriate or as legally required, through separate plans. Obligations under such plans are systematically provided for by depositing funds with trustees, under insurance policies or through the Company's established accrued liabilities. Foreign plans for which SFAS 87 was not adopted in 1987 were, in the aggregate, not material. The market value of foreign pension plans' assets generally exceeds the accumulated benefits of such plans.

The funded status of the Company's retirement plans at December 31, 1987 and 1986 is as follows:

(In millions)	1987	1986*
Actuarial present value of:		
Accumulated benefit obligations		
(substantially all of which are vested)	$2,395	$2,339
Projected benefit obligation	$2,535	$2,498
Plan assets at fair market value	2,860	2,503
Excess of plan assets over projected benefit obligations	325	5
Items not yet reflected in the financial statements:		
Remaining unrecognized net transition asset at date of initial application of SFAS 87	(313)	(318)
Unrecognized prior service cost	89	95
Unrecognized net (gain) loss	(300)	3
Accrued pension costs at December 31	$ (199)	$ (215)

*Restated to include data for non-U.S. Plans.

Included in the funded status are two unfunded plans which have projected benefit obligations of $140 million and $118 million at December 31, 1987 and 1986, respectively.

For its U.S. plans, the Company's policy is to fund the annual profit sharing contribution, which amounted to $93 million and $91 million for 1987 and 1986, respectively, early in the succeeding year. The 1987 contribution, which increases plan assets, will be made on or about March 31, 1988.

The components of pension cost for the Company's retirement plans for the years ended December 31, 1987 and 1986 are as follows:

	1987		
(In millions)	Foreign Plans	U.S. Plans	1986
Defined benefit plans subject to SFAS 87:			
Service cost – benefits earned during the period	$ 25	$105	$ 103
Interest on projected benefit obligation	42	84	275
Actual return on plan assets	(282)	(77)	(297)
Net amortization and deferrals	214	(8)	6
Settlement gains	—	(21)	—
Subtotal	(1)	83	87
Pension cost for defined contribution and foreign plans not subject to SFAS 87	30	2	43
Total	$ 29	$ 85	$ 130

Pension cost for 1985, as determined under the previous accounting methods, was $136 million.

SFAS 87 specifies the use of the projected unit credit actuarial method and requires an annual determination of plan assumptions. Plan benefits for the major U.S. plans are principally determined based upon total years of service and the highest five years of compensation. The projected benefit obligation was determined using assumed discount rates of 9.25% and 8.5% at December 31, 1987 and 1986, respectively. Assumed long-term rates of compensation increases vary from 5.5% to 8.25% and the assumed long-term rates of return on plan assets is 9.5%. Unrecognized net transition assets and prior service costs are being amortized over the average remaining working lives of the plans' participants which is approximately 15 years. Plan assets are primarily invested in marketable equity securities. For the company's major foreign plans the assumed discount rate and long-term rate of return on plan assets was 9.75% at both December 31, 1987 and 1986. Assumed long-term rate of compensation increases vary from 7.0% to 9.0%.

During 1986 the Company announced several amendments to the retirement income guarantee plan for salaried U.S. employees. The principal amendment enhanced the early retirement benefits available to eligible members of the plan by providing five additional years of age and service credits to eligible employees' age and years of service as of December 31, 1986 for purposes of calculating each eligible employee's retirement benefit. For the eligible group the amendment has had the effect of reducing the plan's early retirement age by five years to age 50. The actuarial present value of the cost of this amendment is approximately $75 million. Through December 31, 1987 approximately 1,300 individuals have elected to retire under this amendment.

Postretirement Benefit Plans. The Company provides certain health care and life insurance benefits for retired employees. Substantially all of the Company's U.S. employees and employees in certain foreign countries may become eligible for these benefits if they reach retirement age, with defined minimum periods of service, while still working for the Company. The cost of such benefits is recorded as claims or premiums are paid and amounted to $10 million in 1987, $8 million in 1986 and $7 million in 1985.

8. Income Taxes

The parent Company and its domestic subsidiaries including the unconsolidated financial services and real estate subsidiaries file consolidated U.S. income tax returns. Pursuant to tax allocation agreements, each financial services' subsidiary records its tax provision and makes payments to the Company for taxes due or receives payments from the Company for tax benefits utilized. The following data include income from continuing operations of the Company and its consolidated subsidiaries.

Income from continuing operations before income taxes and outside shareholders' interests consists of the following:

(In millions)	1987	1986	1985
Domestic income	$383	$254	$241
Foreign income	538	421	369
Total	$921	$675	$610

Income tax expense of continuing operations consists of the following:

(In millions)	1987	1986	1985
Federal income taxes			
Current	$ —	$ 63	$ 227
Deferred	(6)	(85)	(204)
Investment tax credits			
Received and deferred, net of recapture and amortization	—	(38)	(18)
Foreign income taxes			
Current	121	122	161
Deferred	141	52	(9)
State income taxes			
Current	7	7	38
Deferred	(1)	(9)	(29)
Total income taxes	$262	$112	$ 166

The Company will have a tax liability of approximately $33 million on its consolidated U.S. income tax return. This liability arises from the income of XFSI.

Deferred income tax expense on income from continuing operations arises from the following items:

(In millions)	1987	1986	1985
Installment sales	$201	$ 51	(174)
Intercompany profits	19	11	34
Depreciation	(36)	(112)	(104)
Other	(50)	8	2
Total	$134	$ (42)	$(242)

A reconciliation of the effective tax rate of continuing operations from the U.S. Federal statutory rate follows:

	1987	1986	1985
U.S. Federal statutory rate	40.0%	46.0%	46.0%
Foreign tax rate differential	8.7	0.7	0.5
Investment tax credits	—	(3.6)	(5.3)
Research and development credits	(1.5)	(1.9)	(2.5)
Equity in income of unconsolidated companies on an after-tax basis	(18.2)	(22.2)	(8.8)
Other	(0.6)	(2.4)	(2.7)
Effective tax rate	28.4%	16.6%	27.2%

On a combined basis, the parent Company and its domestic subsidiaries, including the unconsolidated financial services and real estate subsidiaries, provide U.S. income taxes under the Alternative Minimum Tax. As a result of the allocation agreements, the parent Company and its domestic consolidated subsidiaries, as indicated above, provide taxes using the regular tax system.

Investment tax credits are deferred and amortized as a reduction of the provision for income taxes over the periods during which they are earned. Deferred investment tax credits were fully utilized at the end of 1986 through amortization and recapture. For book purposes, the Company and its unconsolidated financial services subsidiaries have tax credit carryforwards of $30 million, $14 million of which expire in 2002, the remainder have an unlimited carryforward period. These carryforwards are not available for alternative minimum tax purposes. For tax return purposes, the Company has tax credits approximating $102 million which expire in varying amounts from 1998 through 2002. The Tax Reform Act of 1986 may reduce the benefit derived from utilizing these credits.

Total current deferred tax charges included in other current assets at December 31, 1987 and 1986 were $146 million and $99 million, respectively. Deferred income taxes have not been provided on the undistributed earnings of foreign subsidiaries and other foreign investments carried at equity. The amount of such earnings included in consolidated retained earnings at December 31, 1987 was approximately $2.0 billion. These earnings have been substantially reinvested and the Company does not plan to initiate any action which would precipitate the payment of income taxes thereon.

In December of 1987, the Financial Accounting Standards Board issued an accounting pronouncement that significantly changes the accounting rules relating to income taxes. Under the new accounting standard, deferred taxes will be adjusted for the cumulative effect of enacted changes in tax laws or rates. Additionally, net deferred tax assets will only be recognized to the extent that they could be realized by carryback to recover taxes already paid. The Company will be required to adopt the new accounting standard in 1989. When the Company adopts this accounting standard there will be charges to prior years' earnings as a result of the accounting change to value deferred taxes in accordance with the new rules. Restatement of prior years' results is permitted under the new rules, and the Company expects to elect this option.

9. Long-Term Debt

A summary of long-term debt follows:

(In millions)	1987	1986
Consolidated U.S. Operations		
8⅝% sinking fund debentures due 1999(a)	$ 108	$ 108
6% subordinated debentures due 1995 – convertible to common at $92 per share(b)	99	108
5% subordinated debentures due 1988 – convertible to common at $148 per share	74	74
13¼% sinking fund debentures due 2014	100	100
10½% notes due 1988	100	100
10⅜% notes due 1993	100	100
8⅛% notes due 1996	100	100
8⅜% notes due 1996	100	100
Extendible notes due 1998(c)	62	62
Notes payable in Swiss francs due 1989-1991 (6.1% average interest rate at December 31, 1987)	241	187
Capital lease obligations	42	44
Other debt, due 1988-2014 (7.2% average interest rate at December 31, 1987)	144	134
Subtotal	1,270	1,217
Consolidated International Operations		
Various obligations, payable in: (Average interest rate at December 31, 1987 in parentheses)		
Canadian dollars, due 1988 (12%)	31	29
Dutch guilders, due 1988-1990 (8.4%)	106	93
European Currency Units, due 1988 (11⅜%)	59	51
German marks, due 1988-1993 (7.5%)	46	38
Pounds sterling, due 1989-1996 (11.0%)	79	75
Swiss francs, due 1993 (5.5%)	79	62
U.S. dollars, due 1988-1995 (7.3%)	125	241
Capital lease obligations	71	64
Other currencies, due 1988-2011 (12.7%)	35	37
Subtotal	631	690
Total	1,901	1,907
Less current portion	362	177
Total long-term debt	$1,539	$1,730

Payments due on long-term debt for the next five years are (in millions): 1988-$362; 1989-$241; 1990-$201; 1991-$265 and 1992-$114. Substantially all long-term debt of the Company is fixed rate debt.

(a) The 8⅝% sinking fund debentures are redeemable by the Company through October 31, 1988 at 102.9% and at reducing percentages thereafter. The Company must redeem a minimum of $12 million annually. At December 31, 1987 a total of $44 million of repurchased debentures was available for sinking fund requirements.

(b) The 6% convertible subordinated debentures are redeemable by the Company, through October 31, 1988, at 100.9% and at reducing percentages thereafter. The Company must redeem a minimum of $8 million annually.

(c) The extendible notes will mature on September 1, 1998 unless the holder elects repayment on September 1, 1989 or on any September 1 thereafter immediately following the end of a specified interest period. The notes are redeemable, at the election of the Company, at not less than 100% during specified redemption periods. The interest rate through August 31, 1989 is 7.45% and thereafter is adjustable for each specified interest period to a rate not less than 102% of the effective rate on comparable maturity U.S. Treasury obligations.

Certain of the Company's other long-term debt agreements contain various sinking fund requirements, premium payments for early redemption, conversion options, etc. None of these are material to an understanding of the consolidated financial statements of the Company.

10. Notes Payable and Lines of Credit

Short-term borrowings of the Company are as follows:

(In millions)	Balance at End of Year	Weighted Average Interest Rates	
		End of Year	Monthly Average During Year
1987			
Bank notes payable	$128	11.8%	11.2%
Commercial paper	115	7.7%	7.1%
Total	$243	9.8%	9.1%
1986			
Bank notes payable	$ 79	10.4%	11.6%
Commercial paper	50	5.9%	7.2%
Total	$129	8.7%	8.7%
1985			
Bank notes payable	$115	12.9%	12.7%
Commercial paper	219	8.2%	8.9%
Total	$334	9.8%	10.3%

Bank notes payable generally represent foreign currency denominated borrowings of non-U.S. subsidiaries.

The maximum aggregate short-term debt outstanding at any month end was (in millions) $468, $544 and $652 during 1987, 1986 and 1985, respectively. Average short-term borrowings during these years were (in millions) $305, $416 and $504, respectively.

At December 31, 1987, the Company and XCC had unused short-term lines of credit aggregating $150 million with U.S. banks at prime interest rates. The Company maintains compensating balances of not more than 5% of these lines of credit. The Company and XCC also have three revolving credit agreements totaling $1 billion with various banks, generally at prime interest rates, which expire in 1990. Commitment fees vary from ¹⁄₁₆ to ⅛ of 1% per annum on the unused average daily balance. No amounts were outstanding at December 31, 1987 under these agreements. Foreign subsidiaries had unused lines of credit aggregating $523 million in various currencies at prevailing interest rates. Information about the Company's new revolving credit agreement, which was entered into in February of 1988, is included in Note 16 on page 52.

11. Selected Financial Statement Information

(In millions)	1987	1986	1985
Marketable securities included			
in cash	$ 9	$ 33	$ 45
Inventories			
Finished products	$1,112	$1,086	$1,093
Work in process	127	130	146
Raw materials and supplies	169	173	231
Total inventories	$1,408	$1,389	$1,470
Supplementary expense data			
Advertising	$ 184	$ 194	$ 176
Maintenance and repairs	137	121	105
Taxes, other than payroll and income			
Personal property	19	26	22
Other	58	58	52

(In millions)	1987	1986	1985
Net (increase) decrease in other			
working capital			
Accounts receivable, net	$(237)	$ (4)	$ 10
Inventories	(19)	62	(203)
Other current assets	(321)	24	(119)
Accounts payable	44	37	94
Salaries, profit sharing and			
other accruals	171	104	26
Income taxes	35	(40)	(5)
Unearned income	17	35	(6)
Other current liabilities	98	(64)	(33)
Net (increase) decrease in other			
working capital	$(212)	$154	$(236)
Investment income included in			
other income	$ 54	$ 54	$ 65

12. Common Shareholders' Equity

The components of common shareholders' equity and the changes therein for the three years ended December 31, 1987 follow:

(Dollars in millions, except per share amounts. Shares in thousands.)	Common Stock Shares	Common Stock Amount	Additional Paid-In Capital	Retained Earnings	Net Unrealized Appreciation of Equity Investments	Translation Adjustments	Total
Balance at December 31, 1984	95,884	$96	$765	$3,760	$17	$(537)	$4,101
Stock option and incentive plans	572		25				25
Net income ($4.44 per share)				475			475
Cash dividends declared —							
Common Stock ($3.00 per share)				(289)			(289)
Preferred stock ($5.45 per share)				(48)			(48)
Net unrealized appreciation of equity investments					61		61
Translation adjustments — net of outside							
shareholders' interests of $48						61	61
Balance at December 31, 1985	96,456	96	790	3,898	78	(476)	4,386
Stock option and incentive plans	955	2	36				38
Stock purchase and dividend reinvestment plan	240		14				14
Sale of stock by Canadian subsidiary			17				17
Net income ($4.28 per share)				465			465
Cash dividends declared —							
Common Stock ($3.00 per share)				(292)			(292)
Preferred Stock ($5.45 per share)				(48)			(48)
Net unrealized appreciation of equity investments					12		12
Translation adjustments — net of outside							
shareholders' interests of $67						95	95
Balance at December 31, 1986	97,651	98	857	4,023	90	(381)	4,687
Stock option and incentive plans	510		24				24
Stock purchase and dividend reinvestment plan	1,935	2	131				133
Net income ($5.35 per share)				578			578
Cash dividends declared —							
Common stock ($3.00 per share)				(298)			(298)
Preferred stock ($5.45 per share)				(48)			(48)
Net unrealized depreciation of equity investments					(84)		(84)
Translation adjustments — net of outside							
shareholders' interests of $97						113	113
Balance at December 31, 1987	100,096	$100	$1,012	$4,255	$ 6	$(268)	$5,105

Common Stock. During 1987 the Company's shareholders approved an increase in the number of authorized shares of $1 par value common stock to 350,000,000 shares from 150,000,000 shares which had been the authorized number since 1982. At December 31, 1987 and 1986, 4.7 million shares and 5.3 million shares, respectively, of an original authorization of 7.9 million shares were reserved for issuance of common stock under the Company's incentive compensation plan and 2.5 million shares were reserved for the conversion of convertible debt. In addition, at December 31, 1987 there were 2.8 million common shares reserved for issuance under the Company's Automatic Dividend Reinvestment and Stock Purchase Plan.

Stock Option and Long-Term Incentive Plans. The Company has a long-term incentive plan (1976 plan) under which eligible employees may be granted incentive stock options, non-qualified stock options, stock appreciation rights (SAR's), performance unit rights and incentive stock rights. These compensation plans are described in the Company's 1988 Proxy Statement. At December 31, 1987 and 1986 1.5 million and 2.2 million shares, respectively, were available for grant of options or rights. Additional data for the stock options and stock rights plans are summarized below:

(In thousands)	Incentive Stock Rights	Stock Options	Average Option Price
Outstanding at January 1, 1987	616	2,434	$48
Granted	21	1,052	68
Cancelled	(38)	(110)	57
Exercised	(55)	(484)	43
Options surrendered for SAR's	—	(238)	40
Outstanding at December 31, 1987	544	2,654	57
Exercisable at December 31, 1987		1,104	
Becoming exercisable in 1988		1,040	

The average unit value when granted of outstanding incentive stock rights was $44. On January 1, 1988 substantially all of these rights became vested.

During 1987, the Company received $21 million from the exercise of stock options.

Net Income Per Common Share. Net income per common share is computed by dividing consolidated net income less dividends on preferred stock by the average number of shares of common stock outstanding during each year. The effect of common stock equivalents (stock options, incentive stock rights and certain convertible debt) and other convertible debt securities are excluded as the potential dilution upon assumed exercise, vesting or conversion thereof is less than 3%.

Retained Earnings. Among the provisions of the several loan agreements are restrictions related to the payment of cash dividends by the Company on common stock. At December 31, 1987 approximately $3.8 billion of consolidated retained earnings was unrestricted.

Preferred Stock Purchase Rights. In April 1987 the Company adopted a shareholder rights plan designed to deter coercive or unfair takeover tactics and to prevent a person or group of persons from gaining control of the Company without offering a fair price to all shareholders.

Under the terms of the plan each common shareholder received a dividend of one preferred stock purchase Right for each outstanding share of the Company's common stock. Each Right entitles the registered holder, under certain circumstances, to purchase from the Company one one-hundredth of a new series of preferred stock at an exercise price of $225.

The Rights may not be exercised until ten days following the earliest of an announcement that a person or affiliated persons has acquired, has commenced or has announced the intention to commence a tender offer to acquire 20% or more of the Company's common shares. If, after the Rights become exercisable, the Company is acquired in a business combination, or alternatively if, in certain circumstances, the Company acquires such person or affiliated persons the Rights entitle the holder to purchase the common stock of the surviving company having a market value two times the exercise price. The Company is entitled to redeem the Rights at $.05 per Right prior to the earlier of the expiration of the Rights in April 1997 or the close of business ten days after the announcement that a 20% position has been acquired. The right to redeem the Rights is reinstated in certain circumstances.

The Rights are non-voting and until they become exercisable, they have no dilutive effect on the earnings per share or book value per share of the Company's common stock.

13. Cumulative Preferred Stock

The Company has 25,000,000 authorized shares of cumulative preferred stock, $1 par value. At December 31, 1987 and 1986, 8,840,205 shares of $5.45 Cumulative Preferred stock were issued and outstanding. These shares have a stated value of $50 per share, are non-voting, have liquidation preference over common stock and are subject to redemption at the stated value through a sinking fund in which the Company must retire 8.18% of the issue cumulatively each year from 1993 through 2002 and the remaining portion in 2003. As discussed in Note 16 on page 52, in early 1988 the Company called for redemption all outstanding shares of the $5.45 Cumulative Preferred stock at a price of $52.725 per share which is equal to the stated value plus a premium of 50% of the annual dividend.

14. Litigation

In 1983, an action was brought against the Company in the United States District Court for the District of New Jersey which alleges age discrimination in violation of the Federal Age Discrimination in Employment Act on behalf of named plaintiffs and a purported class of all persons between the ages of forty and seventy who, since May 1, 1980 had unsuccessfully applied for employment in a salaried position with the Company, or who were employees of the Company in such a position and were denied promotion or were terminated. Pursuant to court notice, approximately 1,300 individuals have indicated they wish to join in the suit. The judge has reserved decision with respect to whether job applicants should be permitted to join in the suit. The named plaintiffs seek reinstatement for themselves, and they seek for themselves and for members of the class injunctive relief, as well as compensatory and liquidated damages doubling the amount of compensatory damages.

The District Court has granted Xerox' motion to de-certify the class and denied as moot plaintiffs' motion for summary judgment or a presumption of class-wide liability. In an effort to overturn the District Court's decision, plaintiffs have filed an appeal and a petition for a writ of mandamus in the Court of Appeals.

An action has been brought against the Company in the Supreme Court of the State of New York on behalf of the members of a family, claiming personal injuries and property damage allegedly resulting from contamination of the drinking water and of the air at their residence caused by the Company's adjacent manufacturing operations. The complaint seeks recovery of $13 million in compensatory damages and $100 million in punitive damages. A similar lawsuit by another family has been settled. The terms of the settlement were not material.

The Company denies any wrongdoing and intends to vigorously defend the foregoing proceedings.

Rank Xerox Limited, a subsidiary of the Company responsible for marketing of its products in the countries which form the European Economic Community (EEC), has been informed by the EEC Commission of the Commission's intention to investigate whether Rank Xerox has engaged in activities which may constitute an abuse of a dominant position. The investigation is based on a complaint made to the Commission by a competitor of Rank Xerox. The Company denies both that it holds a dominant position in the EEC and that it has engaged in any prohibited activities. Rank Xerox is cooperating with the Commission in its investigation.

15. Discontinued Operations

During 1985 the Company announced plans to discontinue the operations of Industrial Indemnity Financial Corporation (IIFC), a unit of Crum and Forster, Inc. The accompanying financial statements of Xerox Financial Services, Inc. provide additional information on, and describe the financial effects of, discontinuing IIFC.

In 1986 the Company sold its Century Data Systems, Inc. (CDS) subsidiary for cash, notes and stock. The Company

incurred after-tax charges of $14 million in connection with the 1986 operating losses and the loss on disposition of CDS.

In 1985 the Company sold its six publishing units for an aggregate cash sales price of $531 million resulting in a pre-tax gain of $348 million and a gain after taxes and outside shareholders' interests of $200 million.

A summary of information, net of income tax charges or benefits, relating to the discontinued operations for the years ended December 31, 1986 and 1985 follows:

(In millions)	1986	1985
Industrial Indemnity Financial Corporation		
Loss from operations	$ —	$(25)
Estimated net losses during phase-out period	(51)	(86)
Net loss	(51)	(111)
Century Data Systems		
Loss from operations	(2)	(1)
Loss on disposition, net	(12)	—
Net loss	(14)	(1)
Publishing		
Income from operations	—	6
Gain on sale of companies, net	—	200
Net income	—	206
Income (loss) from discontinued operations	$(65)	$ 94

16. Subsequent Events

In February 1988, the Company, XFSI and Xerox Credit Corporation (XCC) entered into a $1 billion revolving credit agreement with various banks which expires in 1993. Borrowings, if any, under the agreement will be based upon prevailing interest rates. Under the terms of the agreement the Company or XCC individually may borrow up to $1 billion and XFSI may borrow up to $250 million subject to the condition that total borrowings under the agreement do not exceed $1 billion. The annual facility fee is $1/16$ of 1% of the total amount of the commitment.

In February 1988 the Company sold $200 million of 9¼% debentures which mature on February 15, 2000. The Company also issued two series of sinking fund preferred stock. Shares sold under both series have a stated value of $50 per share. One series is subject to retirement pursuant to a sinking fund in ten years and has a cumulative annual dividend rate of $3.6875. The 2,500,000 shares in this series were sold for $125 million. The second series is subject to retirement pursuant to a sinking fund in twenty years and has a cumulative annual dividend rate of $4.125. The 1,500,000 shares in this series were sold for $75 million.

Also in February the Company made an offer for up to 2,000,000 shares of its outstanding $5.45 Cumulative Preferred Stock to exchange each one of such shares for one share of the twenty-year preferred stock referred to above. The exchange offer expired on March 2, 1988. Subsequent to the expiration of the exchange offer, the Company called for redemption all remaining outstanding shares of the $5.45 Cumulative Preferred Stock. The redemption will be effective on April 2, 1988 at a redemption price of $52.725 per share.

Consolidated Statements of Income

(In millions) Year ended December 31	1987	1986	1985
Income			
Insurance premiums earned	**$3,543**	$2,685	$2,169
Investment income	**505**	440	373
Finance and investment banking income	**419**	355	379
Other income	**108**	84	83
Total income	**4,575**	3,564	3,004
Losses and Expenses			
Insurance losses and loss expenses	**2,942**	2,315	2,160
Insurance acquisition costs and other			
insurance operating expenses	**965**	818	690
Interest expense	**211**	188	171
Administrative and general expenses	**239**	195	180
Total losses and expenses	**4,357**	3,516	3,201
Operating Income (Loss) from			
Continuing Operations Before Income Taxes	**218**	48	(197)
Income (Taxes) Benefits	**(8)**	107	177
Operating Income (Loss) from Continuing Operations	**210**	155	(20)
Realized Capital Gains of C&F, Net of Income Taxes	**132**	123	96
Income from Continuing Operations	**342**	278	76
Discontinued Operations	**—**	(51)	(111)
Cumulative Effect on Prior Years of Change			
in Accounting Principles for Pension Costs	**—**	42	—
Net Income (Loss)	**$ 342**	$ 269	$ (35)

The accompanying notes are an integral part of the consolidated financial statements.

Consolidated Balance Sheets

(In millions) December 31	1987	1986
Assets		
Investments	$ 6,497	$ 5,489
Cash	57	47
Finance receivables, net	2,941	2,181
Premiums receivable, net	750	751
Other receivables, net	775	510
Due from Xerox Corporation, net	241	528
Other assets	926	707
Excess of cost over fair value of net assets acquired	1,069	1,008
Total Assets	**$13,256**	$11,221
Liabilities and Shareholder's Equity		
Liabilities		
Unearned premiums	$ 1,304	$ 1,130
Unpaid losses and loss expenses	5,398	4,268
Notes payable	2,561	1,781
Accounts payable and accrued liabilities	987	1,170
Deferred income taxes	339	342
Total Liabilities	**10,589**	8,691
Shareholder's Equity	**2,667**	2,530
Total Liabilities and Shareholder's Equity	**$13,256**	$11,221

The accompanying notes are an integral part of the consolidated financial statements.

Consolidated Statements of Cash Flows

(In millions) Year ended December 31	1987	1986	1985
Net Cash Flows From Operating Activities:			
Net income from continuing operations	$ 342	$ 278	$ 76
Non cash items included in income:			
Increase in unpaid losses and loss expenses	1,151	682	645
Increase in unearned premiums	174	310	120
Depreciation and amortization	75	67	61
Increase (decrease) in deferred income taxes	(3)	(18)	58
Proceeds from pension plan termination	—	97	—
Cash provided by operating activities	1,739	1,416	960
Increase in premiums and other receivables	(264)	(53)	(291)
Increase (decrease) in accounts payable and			
accrued liabilities	(174)	—	357
Due from Xerox Corporation	287	19	(175)
Other, net	(283)	(264)	(216)
Cash used by operating activities	(434)	(298)	(325)
Total	1,305	1,118	635
Cash Flows from Investing Activities:			
Cash used by discontinued operations	(21)	(124)	(46)
Increase in finance receivables	(760)	(195)	(233)
Purchase of investments	(3,598)	(3,680)	(2,283)
Cost of investments sold	2,593	2,675	1,826
Other investments, net	101	(5)	(9)
Investments/advances to unconsolidated affiliates	(200)	—	—
Net equity of businesses acquired	122	35	—
Excess of cost over fair value of net assets			
acquired	(79)	(31)	—
Total	(1,842)	(1,325)	(745)
Cash Flows from Financing Activities:			
Increase in long-term debt	901	600	295
Reduction of long-term debt	(318)	(189)	(91)
Increase (decrease) in short-term debt, net	197	(13)	(53)
Subtotal	780	398	151
Dividends paid to Xerox Corporation	(121)	(108)	(80)
Increase (decrease) in note payable to Xerox			
Corporation	—	(200)	200
Capital contributed by Xerox Corporation	—	200	—
Total	659	290	271
Cash and Short-Term Investments Increased	122	83	161
Cash and Short-Term Investments at Beginning of Year	800	717	556
Cash and Short-Term Investments at End of Year	$ 922	$ 800	$ 717

The accompanying notes are an integral part of the consolidated financial statements.

Notes to Consolidated Financial Statements

1. Summary of Significant Accounting Policies

Basis of Consolidation. The consolidated financial statements include Xerox Financial Services, Inc. ("XFSI") and the consolidated accounts of XFSI's subsidiaries engaged in property and casualty, and life insurance (Crum and Forster, Inc.), financing activities (Xerox Credit Corporation) and investment banking (Van Kampen Merritt Inc. and Furman Selz Holding Corporation). Investments in corporate joint ventures, and other companies in which XFSI or its subsidiaries have a 20% to 50% ownership, are accounted for by the equity method.

XFSI is a wholly-owned subsidiary of Xerox Corporation. XFSI, its subsidiaries and Xerox participate in a number of transactions including tax allocation agreements, employee benefit plans, equipment sales, service and leasing arrangements and financing arrangements. In addition, Xerox has an earnings support agreement with Xerox Credit Corporation (XCC). These transactions have been recorded on the basis of the terms agreed to by XFSI, its subsidiaries and Xerox.

All significant intercompany transactions among XFSI and its subsidiaries have been eliminated.

Income Recognition. Insurance premiums are generally earned pro-rata over the period the coverage is provided. Unearned premiums represent the portion of premiums written which is applicable to the unexpired terms of policies in force. Insurance acquisition costs, primarily commissions, brokerage and salary costs which are directly associated with the acquisition of new insurance business are deferred and recognized over the periods the related premiums are earned.

Income associated with finance leases and contracts receivable is earned on an accrual basis under an effective annual yield method. At the time of purchase, a portion of the finance charge is recognized as earned income to offset the provision for losses and other acquisition costs on certain finance leases and contracts receivable (see "New Accounting Pronouncements" below).

Allowance for Losses on Finance Receivables. The amount of the allowance for losses is determined principally on the basis of past collection experience. In connection with contracts receivable purchased from Xerox, XCC retains an allowance for losses at the time of purchase which is intended to protect against future losses and Xerox will fund any additional allowance required.

Investments. Bonds and sinking fund preferred stocks are valued at amortized cost. Other stocks are valued at market and short-term investments are carried at cost which approximates market. Realized gains and losses on the sale of investments are determined on the basis of specific costs of investments and are credited or charged to income, net of applicable income taxes. Unrealized gains and losses from revaluation of equity investments, net of applicable deferred income taxes, are credited or charged to shareholder's equity and accordingly have no effect on operating results. Investment income is recorded when earned.

Trading Inventory. Marketable securities and UIT units of the investment banking businesses are included in other assets.

Securities transactions and related commission revenues and expenses are recorded on a settlement-date basis. Securities owned are valued at market value and unrealized gains and losses are reflected in earnings currently.

Insurance Losses and Loss Expenses. Losses and loss expenses are charged to income as incurred. The provisions for unpaid losses and loss expenses are determined on the basis of claim adjusters' evaluations and other estimates including those for incurred but not reported losses and salvage and subrogation recoveries. The methods of determining such estimates and for establishing the resulting reserves are continually reviewed and updated. Any adjustments resulting therefrom are reflected in earnings currently.

Income Taxes. The U.S. operations of each company are included in Xerox' federal income tax return. Financial statement income (taxes) benefits and the tax liabilities or benefits for the respective companies are calculated in accordance with individual tax allocation agreements with Xerox. The amounts due from Xerox primarily relate to the tax benefits that have been or are expected to be included in Xerox' consolidated U.S. tax returns.

Investment Tax Credits. Investment tax credits for assets placed in service prior to January 1, 1986, which result from lease transactions, are deferred and recognized as earned income over the terms of the respective leases.

Excess of Cost Over Fair Value of Net Assets Acquired. The excess of cost over fair value of net assets acquired is amortized on a straight-line basis generally over forty years.

New Accounting Pronouncements – There are several recently issued Statements of the Financial Accounting Standards Board which have not yet been adopted by XFSI and its subsidiaries as of December 31, 1987. Of these new Statements the following have particular relevance to XFSI:

Statement No. 91 – This Statement is applicable to XCC and modifies the timing of the recognition of fees and related costs of lease origination. The Statement also eliminates XCC's existing practice of recognizing as earned income, at the time of purchase, a portion of the finance charge to offset the provision for losses on certain finance leases and contracts receivable. XCC will adopt this Statement on a prospective basis in the first quarter of 1988. The provisions of this Statement will not materially affect net income.

Statement No. 96 – This Statement significantly changes the accounting rules relating to income taxes. Under the Statement deferred taxes will be adjusted for the cumulative effect of an enacted change in tax laws or rates. Additionally, net deferred tax assets will only be recognized to the extent that they could be realized by carryback to recover taxes already paid. XFSI will be required to adopt the new accounting standard in 1989. When XFSI adopts Statement No. 96 there will be a one time charge to prior year's earnings as a result of the accounting change to value deferred taxes in accordance with the new rules. Restatement of prior years' results is permitted under the Statement and is the expected manner of adoption.

Statement No. 97 – This Statement will amend certain of the insurance accounting practices of C&F particularly with regard to the income statement presentation of realized capital gains and losses and the recognition of earned premiums and related expenses of C&F's life insurance operations. When adopted, Statement No. 97 will require realized capital gains and losses to be reported on a pretax basis as a component of income from continuing operations. The Statement also requires C&F to exclude from revenues any earned premiums on life insurance policies that do not subject C&F to significant mortality or morbidity risks but rather in substance represent an investment by the policyholders, however, there will be an offsetting decrease in related operating expenses. For 1987 and 1986 insurance premiums earned and related operating expenses will be reduced by approximately $300 million and $25 million respectively when Statement 97 is adopted. Statement No. 97, which will have no affect on net income, is presently planned to be adopted, as required, on a retroactive basis in 1989.

2. Businesses Acquired

Furman Selz Holding Corporation. During the third quarter of 1987, XFSI acquired all of the outstanding common stock of Furman Selz Holding Corporation, a research, brokerage and investment banking firm which operates in the equity investments markets.

The acquisition was accounted for as a purchase. The purchase price of approximately $110 million exceeded the fair value of the net assets acquired by approximately $79 million and this excess has been recorded on the accompanying consolidated balance sheets.

VMS Realty Partners. Effective January 1, 1987 XCC acquired a 25% interest in VMS Realty Partners and certain affiliated companies (VMS). XCC invested $80 million in VMS and provided loans of $120 million to VMS. VMS, a privately held partnership, is a full service real estate investment firm which is involved in acquiring, financing, and developing real estate throughout the U.S.

3. Discontinued Operations

In 1985 Xerox discontinued the operations of Industrial Indemnity Financial Corporation (IIFC), a unit of C&F that was primarily in the financial guarantee and contract surety businesses. At December 31, 1987, under the terms of the outstanding financial guarantee contracts, IIFC was contingently liable for approximately $2.7 billion, which represents the aggregate par value net of reinsurance, of the guarantee contracts in force. These contingent liabilities will expire as follows (in billions): $.9-1988-1992; $1.2-1993-1997; $.1-1998-2002; and $.5 thereafter. IIFC will not underwrite any new business during the phase-out period. IIFC and C&F will fully honor all contracts in force. IIFC results for the nine months of 1985, prior to discontinuance, resulted in a loss from operations of $25 million. During 1985, C&F provided $86 million, net of an income tax benefit of $74 million, for expected operating losses during the phase-out period which will be lengthy due to the long-term nature of IIFC's outstanding financial guarantees. An additional provision of $51 million, net of an income tax benefit of $44 million, was made in 1986 to the reserve for discontinuance of IIFC. The

additional provision was taken following a management review of both known impaired credits and an assessment of the economic and environmental conditions affecting the remaining contract surety business and outstanding financial guarantees.

Reserves for IIFC's losses, loss expenses and other costs of disposition were $184 million and $218 million at December 31, 1987, and 1986, respectively.

4. Investments and Investment Income

Investments include:

(In millions)	1987	1986
Fixed maturities		
Bonds, at amortized cost		
(market $5,025 and $4,471, respectively)	$4,948	$3,952
Preferred stocks, at amortized cost		
(market $39 and $54, respectively)	31	43
Equity securities		
Preferred stocks, at market		
(cost $38 and $38, respectively)	42	50
Common stocks, at market		
(cost $589 and $572, respectively)	611	691
Short-term investments		
at cost which approximates market	865	753
Total	$6,497	$5,489

The components of investment income follow:

(In millions)	1987	1986	1985
Income on fixed maturities	$424	$360	$294
Income on equity securities	31	31	30
Income on short-term investments	51	50	48
Other, net of investment			
expenses of C&F	(1)	(1)	1
Investment income	$505	$440	$373

Realized gains were as follows:

(In millions)	1987	1986	1985
Realized gains:			
Fixed maturities	$ 84	$132	$ 75
Equity securities	82	66	66
	166	198	141
Provision for income taxes	(34)	(75)	(45)
Total	$132	$123	$ 96

Changes in unrealized appreciation of fixed maturities for the years ended December 31, 1987, 1986 and 1985 were $(445) million, $222 million and $318 million, respectively.

Changes in unrealized appreciation of equity securities of C&F for the years ended December 31, 1987, 1986 and 1985 were $(105) million, $14 million and $81 million. Net unrealized appreciation of equity securities of C&F at December 31, 1987 include gross unrealized gains of $87 million and gross unrealized losses of $61 million.

Securities carried at $683 million, $616 million and $537 million at December 31, 1987, 1986 and 1985, respectively, were deposited by C&F with governmental authorities as required by laws affecting insurers.

5. Finance Receivables, Net

The components of finance receivables, net follow:

(In millions)	1987	1986
Contracts receivable:		
Gross receivable	$2,884	$2,094
Unearned income	(519)	(359)
Allowance for losses	(77)	(76)
Net contracts	2,288	1,659
Investment in finance leases	567	474
Equipment on operating leases, net:		
Xerox Corporation	61	48
Other	25	—
	86	48
Total	$2,941	$2,181

Contracts receivable generally represent purchases of long-term trade accounts receivable from Xerox. XCC purchased $998 million, $629 million, and $699 million of receivables from Xerox in 1987, 1986 and 1985, respectively. At December 31, 1987 and 1986, the percentage of total finance receivables, net that was associated with Xerox' sold equipment was 54% and 55%, respectively. The scheduled maturities of payments to be received under contracts receivable outstanding as of December 31, 1987 are as follows: $1,051 million in 1988, $741 million in 1989, $527 million in 1990, $290 million in 1991, $142 million in 1992 and $133 million thereafter.

Finance leases consist primarily of investments in third party capital assets. The majority of leveraged leases have lease terms of fifteen to eighteen years with a maximum term of thirty-two years. Finance leases also consist of direct finance or non-leveraged leases which generally have lease terms of three to fifteen years. The rentals receivable for leveraged leases are net of principal and interest on third party debt participation. As XCC has no general liability for third party debt participation, the principal and interest on such instruments have not been included in liabilities, but have been offset against the related receivable. XCC's share of rentals receivable is subordinate to the share of the debt participants who also have a security interest in the equipment leased.

The net contractual maturities of rentals receivable relating to finance leases as of December 31, 1987 are as follows (in millions): 1988-$86; 1989-$68; 1990-$56; 1991-$45; 1992-$32; and 1993 and thereafter-$332.

A summary of investment in finance leases follows:

(In millions)	Leveraged Leases		Direct Finance Leases		Total Finance Leases	
	1987	1986	1987	1986	1987	1986
Rentals receivable	$359	$361	$260	$170	$619	$531
Unguaranteed residual values	104	104	12	11	116	115
Unearned income	(94)	(103)	(36)	(27)	(130)	(130)
Deferred investment tax credits	(33)	(35)	(1)	(2)	(34)	(37)
Allowance for losses	—	—	(4)	(5)	(4)	(5)
Investment in finance leases	336	327	231	147	567	474
Less deferred taxes associated with finance leases	(298)	(295)	(8)	(7)	(306)	(302)
Net investment in finance leases	$ 38	$ 32	$223	$140	$261	$172

6. Lines of Credit

At December 31, 1987, XFSI had unused short-term lines of credit aggregating $17 million with a U.S. bank at competitive interest rates. XFSI pays a fee equal to ¼% per annum of the aggregate credit line in lieu of maintaining compensating balances in support of these borrowing arrangements.

Xerox and XCC also have three revolving credit agreements totaling $1 billion with various banks, generally at prime interest rates, which expire in 1990. Under this arrangement, XCC can borrow up to $500 million. These agreements provide for the payment of a commitment fee equal to ⅛% and ¹⁄₁₆% of the unused credit lines of $400 million and $100 million, respectively. In addition, XCC has joint access with Xerox to short-term lines of credit aggregating $150 million with U.S. banks at prime interest rates. No amounts were outstanding at December 31, 1987 under these arrangements.

In February 1988, Xerox, XFSI and XCC entered into a $1 billion revolving credit agreement with various banks which expires in 1993. Borrowings, if any, under the agreement will be based upon prevailing interest rates. Under the terms of the agreement Xerox and/or XCC individually may borrow up to $1 billion and XFSI may borrow up to $250 million subject to the condition that total borrowings under the agreement do not exceed $1 billion. The annual facility fee is ¹⁄₁₆ of 1% of the total amount of the commitment.

7. Leases

XFSI, through its subsidiaries, leases certain land, buildings and equipment under operating leases which expire through 2002. The total rent expense under operating leases for the years ended December 31, 1987, 1986 and 1985 amount to $76 million, $64 million and $53 million, respectively. Future minimum lease payments required under operating leases that have initial or remaining noncancelable lease terms in excess of one year at December 31, 1987 are as follows (in millions): $77 in 1988, $75 in 1989, $68 in 1990, $57 in 1991, $45 in 1992 and $251 thereafter.

8. Notes Payable

The components of notes payable follow:

(In millions)	1987	1986
Commercial paper	$ 353	$ 230
Short-term notes payable	122	123
Current portion of notes payable after one year	94	19
Notes payable after one year	1,992	1,409
Total	$2,561	$1,781

A summary of notes payable after one year follows:

(In millions)	Weighted average interest rates at December 31, 1987	1987	1986
1988 (a)		$ —	$ 240
1989	8.33%	450	450
1990	8.56	399	100
1991 (a)	11.77	452	350
1992	9.20	199	—
1993	9.58	17	—
1994	9.52	167	—
1999	8.00	100	—
Extendible Notes		35	42
Extendible Notes due 1999 (b)		29	100
Zero Coupon Notes due 1992 (c)		250	250
		2,098	1,532
Less unamortized discount (d)		(106)	(123)
Total		$1,992	$1,409

(a) Certain debt issues contain provisions which allow XCC to redeem, generally at par value plus accrued interest, the obligation prior to maturity. Included in notes due in 1991 are $200 million of 15¼%-16% notes which may be redeemed in 1988 or thereafter. During 1987, XCC redeemed at par, its $100 million 12⅞% notes which had a final maturity date in August 1988.

(b) The extendible notes will mature on March 15, 1999 unless the holder elected repayment on March 16, 1987 at which time holders of $71 million of the notes elected repayment. The remaining notes are redeemable by XCC at not less than 100% during specified redemption periods. The interest rate through March 15, 1990 is 7% and thereafter is adjustable for each specified interest period to a rate not less than 102% of the effective rate on comparable maturity U.S. Treasury obligations.

(c) Discounted to yield 14.64% to maturity. The net proceeds of the notes to XCC were $61 million.

(d) The original issue discount and other expenses associated with the debt offerings are amortized over the term of the related issue.

Principal payments on notes payable after one year are: $94 million in 1988; $450 million in 1989; $399 million in 1990; $452 million in 1991; $449 million in 1992 and $348 million thereafter.

9. Insurance Operations

In the ordinary course of business, C&F reinsures certain risks with other insurance companies. Such arrangements serve to limit C&F's maximum loss on catastrophes, large risks and unusually hazardous risks. To the extent that any reinsuring company might be unable to meet its obligations, C&F would be liable for such defaulted amounts. Following are the approximate amounts deducted for reinsurance ceded to other companies:

(In millions)	1987	1986	1985
Insurance premiums written	$1,597	$1,757	$1,454
Insurance premiums earned	1,765	1,676	1,291
Unearned insurance premiums	404	572	490
Unpaid insurance loss and loss expense reserve	3,340	2,378	1,876

In 1984, C&F entered into a quota share reinsurance agreement with Prudential Reinsurance Company ending in September of 1987. Included in the preceding data are premiums written of $231 million, $272 million and $213 million for the years ended December 31, 1987, 1986 and 1985, respectively, premiums earned of $218 million, $248 million and $199 million for the years ended December 31, 1987, 1986 and 1985, respectively, and unearned premiums of $109 million and $86 million at December 31, 1986 and 1985, respectively, relating to this reinsurance agreement. Because of the termination of the agreement, C&F assumed premiums written of $122 million as of September 30, 1987.

Catastrophe reinsurance is maintained on all lines of property and casualty insurance. For the years ended December 31, 1987, 1986 and 1985, the premiums and recoveries under catastrophe reinsurance, which are deducted from premiums earned and losses incurred, respectively, were not material to the consolidated results of operations.

C&F also assumes property and casualty insurance premiums from other companies. Reinsurance premiums assumed that are included in insurance premiums earned were $759 million, $622 million and $512 million for the years ended December 31, 1987, 1986 and 1985, respectively.

Estimates of salvage and subrogation recoveries on unpaid insurance losses have been recorded as a reduction of unpaid insurance losses amounting to $103 million, $87 million and $91 million at December 31, 1987, 1986 and 1985, respectively.

Other insurance operating expenses include $560 million, $467 million and $433 million of acquisition costs amortized during 1987, 1986 and 1985, respectively. Total acquisition costs included in other insurance operating expenses in the consolidated statements of income were $840 million, $685 million and $619 million during 1987, 1986 and 1985, respectively.

10. Income Taxes

Income (taxes) benefits attributable to the continuing operations of the individual companies follow:

(In millions)	1987	1986	1985
C&F	$ 34	$ 91	$232
XCC	(40)	19	(34)
VKM	(9)	(21)	(22)
Furman Selz	(1)	—	—
XFSI	8	18	1
Total	$ (8)	$107	$177

Income (taxes) benefits consist of:

(In millions)	1987	1986	1985
Income (taxes) benefits:			
Federal:			
Current	$(19)	$ (6)	$ 5
Deferred	(16)	29	(52)
Subtotal	(35)	23	(47)
Net Federal benefits of C&F	34	91	232
	(1)	114	185
State:			
Current	(4)	(4)	(1)
Deferred	(3)	(3)	(7)
	(7)	(7)	(8)
Total	$ (8)	$107	$177

On a combined basis Xerox is an Alternative Minimum Tax (AMT) federal taxpayer for financial reporting purposes, as the AMT tax system resulted in a higher overall tax expense than the regular tax system. Income tax expense is allocated among Xerox Corporation and the XFSI subsidiaries based on tax allocation agreements.

At December 31, 1987, deferred income taxes which have been recorded result primarily from differences between financial and tax reporting in the timing of the recognition of lease income and related expenses. Deferred income taxes are also provided on unrealized appreciation (depreciation) of equity investments and cumulative translation adjustments. Deferred U.S. Federal income taxes applicable to operations have not been recorded by C&F. Net timing differences between C&F's financial and tax reporting are reflected in C&F's tax loss carryforwards, which have been made available to Xerox under the tax allocation agreement. Such timing differences consist principally of insurance acquisition costs applicable to unearned premiums, discount on unpaid losses, recognition of unpaid premiums, provision for uncollectible accounts, salvage and subrogation recoveries, the deferred gain on the sale of office properties and undeclared policyholders' dividends.

For financial statement purposes XFSI has unused tax credit carryforwards of $30 million, $14 million of which expire in 2002 with the remainder having an unlimited carryforward period. No carryforward benefits are available for AMT purposes.

On October 22, 1986, the Tax Reform Act of 1986 was signed into law. The effect of the Act on the 1986 operating results relates to the Federal tax rate changes applicable to XCC's leveraged lease portfolio. The cumulative effect of these rate changes increased XCC's net income by $21 million in 1986. The $21 million net income increase is comprised of a decrease to lease income and amortization of investment tax credits of $18 million and $9 million, respectively and a decrease to deferred income tax expense of $48 million.

A reconciliation of the effective tax rate from the U.S. Federal statutory tax rate follows:

	1987	1986	1985
U.S. Federal statutory rate	(40.0)%	(46.0)%	46.0%
Tax exempt interest income	32.8	188.8	43.3
Loss reserve fresh start benefit	33.2	—	—
Dividends received deduction	5.0	28.6	7.1
Amortization of intangibles	(4.5)	(25.9)	(6.2)
State income taxes, net of Federal income tax effect	(2.1)	(7.5)	(2.1)
Amortization of ITC	0.5	3.5	1.3
Effect of 1986 Tax Act on Leveraged Leases	—	74.3	—
Alternative minimum tax	(31.9)	—	—
Other	3.3	7.1	.4
Effective tax rate	(3.7)%	222.9%	89.8%

11. Industry Segment Data

XFSI has grouped its operations into three principal industry segments: insurance, finance and investment banking. Segment data follows:

(In millions)	1987	1986	1985
Income			
Insurance	$ 4,072	$ 3,163	$2,591
Finance	384	297	313
Investment banking	119	104	100
Total income	$ 4,575	$ 3,564	$3,004
Operating Income (Loss)			
Insurance	$ 103	$ (25)	$ (344)
Finance	124	66	102
Investment banking	25	46	48
XFSI	(34)	(39)	(3)
Total	$ 218	$ 48	$ (197)
Assets			
Insurance	$ 9,741	$ 8,436	$7,111
Finance	3,044	2,264	2,097
Investment banking	431	492	471
Reclassifications, eliminations and other	40	29	(212)
Total	$13,256	$11,221	$9,467
Depreciation and Amortization			
Insurance	$ 42	$ 40	$ 40
Finance	25	21	16
Investment banking	8	6	5
Total	$ 75	$ 67	$ 61
Capital Expenditures			
Insurance	$ 46	$ 17	$ 17
Finance	61	19	47
Investment banking	3	7	2
Total	$ 110	$ 43	$ 66

12. Retirement Plans

C&F has one principal defined benefit Pension Plan ("Plan") that covers substantially all employees. The Plan provides benefits that are based on total years of service and compensation during an employee's last five years of employment. C&F annually contributes to the Plan an amount which will enable the Plan to meet future benefit payment requirements. Employees of XCC and XFSI participate in Xerox' profit sharing, retirement, and other postretirement benefit plans which include health care and life insurance benefits. VKM has a profit sharing plan covering all eligible employees.

C&F terminated its former defined benefit pension plan as of December 31, 1985 and established the existing Plan effective January 1, 1986. In connection with the termination, C&F purchased annuity contracts which provide for the payment of accumulated benefits to all participants. The excess of plan assets and balance sheet accruals over the accumulated benefit resulted in a termination gain of $108 million, of which $10 million was amortized to income in 1985.

In 1986, Xerox adopted Statements of Financial Accounting Standards No's. 87 and 88 which respectively establish standards for the determination of pension cost and for the settlement of pension plan obligations. In accordance with these standards, C&F recognized a gain of $42 million ($79

million before related income taxes) related to the terminated plan. The benefits formula of the existing Plan and the adoption of the projected unit credit cost method resulted in a reduction to 1986 pension expense of approximately $7 million. Total pension expense, excluding amortization of termination gain, for the years ended December 31, 1987, 1986 and 1985, was $4 million, $4 million and $12 million, respectively. At December 31, 1987, C&F's Plan had projected benefit obligations of $29 million and trusteed Plan assets (primarily listed stocks and government securities) having a fair market value of $10 million.

The discount rate and rate of increase in future compensation levels used in determining the projected benefit obligation were 8.0% and 7.2%, respectively. The expected long-term rate of return on Plan assets was 8%.

C&F provides certain contributory health care and life insurance benefits for retired employees. Substantially all employees may become eligible for those benefits if they reach retirement age while working for C&F. The cost of these benefits approximated $2 million in 1987 and 1986 and $3 million in 1985. The cost of retiree health care is recognized as an expense as claims are paid. The estimated cost of life insurance benefits is accrued over the working lives of those employees expected to qualify for such benefits.

13. Shareholder's Equity

The components of shareholder's equity and the changes therein for the three years ended December 31, 1987 are as follows:

(In millions)	Common Stock and Additional Paid-In Capital	Retained Earnings	Net Unrealized Appreciation of Equity Investments	Translation Adjustments	Total
Balance at December 31, 1984	$ 989	$1,172	$17	$(3)	$2,175
Net loss		(35)			(35)
Dividends		(80)			(80)
Net unrealized appreciation of equity investments			61		61
Balance at December 31, 1985	989	1,057	78	(3)	2,121
Van Kampen Merritt Inc. acquisition	35				35
Capital contribution from Xerox Corporation	200				200
Net income		269			269
Dividends		(108)			(108)
Net unrealized appreciation of equity investments			12		12
Translation adjustments, net				1	1
Balance at December 31, 1986	1,224	1,218	90	(2)	2,530
Net income		342			342
Dividends		(121)			(121)
Net unrealized depreciation of equity investments			(84)		(84)
Balance at December 31, 1987	$1,224	$1,439	$ 6	$(2)	$2,667

C&F's insurance subsidiaries are restricted by insurance laws as to the amount of dividends they may pay without the approval of regulatory authorities. There are additional restrictions with regard to the amount of loans and advances that these subsidiaries may make to C&F. These restrictions indirectly limit the payment of dividends and the making of loans and advances by C&F. The amount of restricted net assets of C&F's insurance subsidiaries at December 31, 1987 approximated $1,663 million.

Generally accepted accounting principles differ in certain respects from the accounting practices prescribed or permitted by insurance regulatory authorities (statutory basis) for C&F's insurance subsidiaries. The statutory net income (loss) for the years ended December 31, 1987, 1986 and 1985 amounted to $364 million, $173 million and $(291) million, respectively. Statutory policyholders' surplus amounted to $1,198 million and $1,152 million at December 31, 1987 and 1986 respectively.

Six Years in Review

(Dollars in millions, except per share data)	1987	1986	1985
Per Share Data			
Income (Loss) per Common Share			
Continuing Operations	$ 5.35	$ 4.52	$ 3.47
Discontinued Operations	—	(.67)	.97
Accounting Change for Pension Costs	—	.43	—
Net Income per Common Share	5.35	4.28	4.44
Dividends Declared per Common Share	3.00	3.00	3.00
Operations			
Revenues — Business Equipment	$ 10,320	$ 9,355	$ 8,676
Revenues — Xerox Financial Services, Inc.[1]	4,575	3,564	3,004
Revenues — Other	230	127	81
Total Revenues	15,125	13,046	11,761
Research and Development Expenses	722	650	597
Income from Continuing Operations	578	488	381
Net Income	578	465	475
Net Income Applicable to Common Stock	530	417	427
Financial Position			
Working Capital	$ 1,609	$ 1,767	$ 1,686
Rental Equipment, net	878	1,070	1,237
Land, Buildings and Equipment, net	1,639	1,491	1,423
Investment in Xerox Financial Services, Inc., at equity[1]	2,667	2,530	2,121
Total Assets	11,598	10,608	9,817
Long-Term Debt	1,539	1,730	1,583
Outside Shareholders' Interests in Equity of Subsidiaries	652	565	505
$5.45 Cumulative Preferred Stock	442	442	442
Common Shareholders' Equity	5,105	4,687	4,386
Additions to Rental Equipment	590	704	658
Additions to Land, Buildings and Equipment	347	328	293
Selected Data and Ratios			
Average Common Shares Outstanding (in thousands)	98,978	97,260	96,159
Common Shareholders of Record at Year-End	86,388	90,437	92,179
Employees at Year-End[2]	99,032	100,367	101,636
Book Value per Common Share	$ 51.03	$ 48.04	$ 45.54
Year-End Common Share Market Value	$ 56.63	$ 60.00	$ 59.75
Return on Equity[3]	10.8%	9.7%	7.9%
Total Debt[4] to Total Capitalization[5]	25.7%	26.3%	27.1%
Total Debt and Preferred Stock to Total Capitalization	31.0%	32.1%	33.2%

[1] Includes XFSI's predecessor organizations.
[2] Excludes employees of discontinued operations and unconsolidated subsidiaries.
[3] Return on equity is calculated by dividing income from continuing operations less preferred stock dividends by average common shareholders equity.
[4] Total Debt is defined as the sum of notes payable, current portion of long-term debt and long-term debt.
[5] Total capitalization is defined as the sum of total debt, outside shareholders' interests in equity of subsidiaries, $5.45 Cumulative Preferred stock, and common shareholders' equity.

Dividends and Stock Prices

1984	1983	1982
$ 3.28	$ 4.50	$ 4.06
(.75)	(.08)	.94
—	—	—
2.53	4.42	5.00
3.00	3.00	3.00
$ 8,374	$ 7,895	$ 7,895
2,794	2,379	178
74	—	—
11,242	10,274	8,073
555	529	541
362	474	344
291	466	424
243	420	424
$ 1,288	$ 1,349	$ 1,639
1,520	1,529	1,641
1,392	1,470	1,440
2,175	2,017	225
9,537	9,297	7,668
1,614	1,461	850
441	438	445
442	442	—
4,101	4,222	3,724
1,038	810	876
311	325	329
95,691	94,897	84,697
104,045	107,180	109,136
100,146	97,778	103,275
$ 42.87	$ 44.51	$ 44.12
$ 37.88	$ 49.50	$ 37.38
7.5%	10.7%	9.2%
31.3%	28.2%	25.2%
37.4%	34.4%	25.2%

Consecutive Dividends Paid To Shareholders

During 1987, dividends paid to the Company's common stock shareholders totalled $3.00 per share, unchanged from 1986 and 1985. Xerox has declared dividends to its shareholders for 58 consecutive years and has paid consecutive quarterly dividends since 1948.

The Company's Board of Directors, at its February 1, 1988 meeting, declared a quarterly dividend of $0.75 per common share and the regular quarterly dividend of $1.3625 per share on the $5.45 Cumulative Preferred stock. Both of these dividends are payable on April 1, 1988, to shareholders of record March 4, 1988.

The Board of Directors has also declared a pro-rated quarterly dividend of $0.5167 per share on the recently issued $3.6875 Ten-Year Sinking Fund Preferred stock and a pro-rated quarterly dividend of $0.5780 per share on the recently issued $4.125 Twenty-Year Sinking Fund Preferred stock, both to be paid on April 1, 1988, to shareholders of record March 4, 1988.

Xerox Common Stock

		1st Q	2nd Q	3rd Q	4th Q
1987	New York Stock Exchange Composite Prices				
	High	$77¾	$81¼	$85	$79⅛
	Low	59⅜	70½	71½	50
	Dividends Paid	.75	.75	.75	.75
1986	New York Stock Exchange Composite Prices				
	High	$72¼	$67¼	$58⅞	$63¼
	Low	57⅜	53½	48⅝	51⅜
	Dividends Paid	.75	.75	.75	.75

Xerox $5.45 Cumulative Preferred Stock

		1st Q	2nd Q	3rd Q	4th Q
1987	New York Stock Exchange Composite Prices				
	High	$58¼	$56	$56⅛	$56⅜
	Low	55	54¼	53⅜	52½
	Dividends Paid	1.3625	1.3625	1.3625	1.3625
1986	New York Stock Exchange Composite Prices				
	High	$57⅞	$58¼	$57¾	$58
	Low	54	55	53½	55
	Dividends Paid	1.3625	1.3625	1.3625	1.3625

B

Determining
Present Value
and
PV Tables

Present Value Defined

The present value of something is simply today's equivalent cash cost excluding any related interest costs or benefits. An asset acquired today, costing $10,000 cash plus a five year 12 percent interest bearing note for $50,000, has a present value of $60,000 (assuming that 12 percent is the prevailing interest rate and therefore that no interest is capitalized into the face value of the note). The $30,000 of additional interest payments over the next five years are not related to today's cost of the item. They are rental costs on the $50,000 used to purchase the item and will be treated as an expense over the five years. It could have been acquired today with a single cash payment of $60,000, its present value.

Similarly, the present value (cost) of a future liability is simply the amount of cash required today to fully settle the obligation (assuming no prepayment penalty). Future executory interest is excluded from present value. If you have a current liability of $5,000 plus 12 percent interest due in one year with no early payment penalty, its present value to you is $5,000. You could settle the obligation with a cash outlay today of $5,000. What would be the present value (cost) of this same $5,000 liability due in one year (future value of $5,000) if it were not interest bearing; that is, $5,000 cash is all that would have to be paid one year from today? Assume you personally could safely invest cash for a year (perhaps in a bank or savings and loan association) and earn 12 percent interest. The cash cost today of "settling" this $5,000 (future value) obligation due in one year its present value (cost) would be only $4,464 (rounded):

$$PV \$ + 0.12(PV \$) = \$5,000 \text{ FV}$$

You could deposit $4,464 cash today, earn 12 percent interest, and have the necessary $5,000 of future value accumulated at the end of the year to pay off the debt. Assuming a 12 percent interest or discount rate, $4,464 would be to day's cash cost to you to settle this note its present value.[1] What would be the present value (benefit) to you of a $10,000 payment to be received one year from today if your opportunity interest rate (amount you could earn on money) was 10 percent? You are correct if you determined the present value (benefit) of the forthcoming $10,000 as only $9,091 (rounded) today:

$$PV \$ + 0.10(PV \$) = \$10,000$$

You would be as well-off receiving $9,091 in cash today as you would be receiving $10,000 a year from now (assuming a 10 percent opportunity rate is appropriate). You could invest the $9,091 today and have the $10,000 of future value (principal plus inter-

---

[1] Although GAAP require present value measurement of all assets and liabilities as they are initially recorded (see Chapters 11 and 12), it does not mandate discounting the interest component of current items unless explicitly stated, or material in amount. Discounting of small current items is used herein as an introduction to present value measurement.

est) in one year. Do you see where money has a time value because of interest? A specific cash amount to be paid in the future effectively costs you less than if paid today. A specific amount of cash in the future would effectively be worth less than if received today. You would lose the interest you could have earned had the cash arrived today. Present value merely takes into account the time value of money, the opportunity cost of interest saved or lost. As normally used, PV does not attempt to allow for the effects of future inflation; only the effect of interest is included.[2]

Compound Interest

The effects of present value become more significant and dramatic as the time period involved extends beyond one year. The present value of a future value of $1,000 to be received in fifty years at a 12 percent discount is only $3.50. Over the 50 years, $3.50 would only earn $21.00 of simple interest at 12 percent. The remaining $975.50 is accumulated as a result of compound interest, or interest earned on accumulating interest.[3]

At 12 percent, the present value or cost of a $2,000 payment to be made by your in three years is only $1,424 (rounded). If you deposited $1,424 at 12 percent interest compounded for three years, you would accumulate the necessary $2,000 to make the payment. Your cash equivalent cost today would be only $1,424.

Interest calculation (rounded to the nearest $)

First year:	0.12 x $1,424	$171
Second year:	0.12 x ($1,424 + $171)	191
Third year:	0.12 x ($1,424 + $171 + $191)	214
Total Accumulated Interest		$576

Present value is always determined in terms of the present opportunity costs of interest (prevailing rate of interest) applicable to the individual or firm measuring the present value. The present value of any particular future cash flow (discounted at the applicable interest or discount rate) is simply the principal equivalent today that could be invested at the same rate of compound interest and accumulate a future value (principal plus compound interest) equal to the particular future cash flow.

Present (principal) value today + compound interest = future value

Note that a "discount" and a "discount rate" are two different things. The noun discount refers to a dollar amount. A discount may be shown in a valuation contra account

---

[2] PV may also be used outside of the financial accounting system to forecast the effects of inflation, where a reasonable constant inflation rate can be assumed.

[3] The formula taking into account compound interest to arrive at the future value (FV = principal plus accumulating compound interest) of an investment P today is:

$FV = P(1 + i)^n$ Where i = the interest rate per period and n = the number of periods involved.

to offset executory interest, or it may refer to the amount of cost reduction given for prompt payment of an invoice. A discount rate is a percentage. A discount rate (as a percentage of total cost) may refer to an incentive offered for prompt payment. In the context of present value, the term refers to the percentage of compound interest factored out of a future value to determine a present (principal) value. Again in the context of PV, discount as a verb refers to the process of factoring out interest.

Calculating Present Value of a Single Future Payment/Receipt

The calculations to determine present value may be computed using a formula, present value tables, or by using a calculator with present value (business) functions built into it. The present value formula to calculate the present value of a single payment/receipt of $1 is shown below.

Using a Calculator Programmed for PV

Calculating the present value of a single payment/receipt FV in n years (periods) discounted at i percent per period on a calculator programmed for business functions is relatively simple. It is only necessary to appropriately enter (for the particular calculator) the values for:

Number of periods	= n	= 7 years
Interest per period	= i	= 9 percent (per year)
Future value of payment/receipt	= FV	= $11,000

and then to instruct the calculator to compute the present value (PV) which will turn out to be $6,017 (rounded).

Using Present Value Table A for Single Payments/Receipts

Calculating present value can be tedious without a computer or a properly programmed calculator. The formula for the present value of $1 is:

$$PV = \frac{1}{(1 + i)^n}$$

where i = interest or discount rate per period, and n = number of periods involved. You can, of course, determine the present value of any specific number of dollars once you have the appropriate PV of $1 for the particular i and n. Table A provides precalculated PV's of $1 for interest rates (i) from 0.5 percent to 15 percent, and periods from 1 to 50.

What would be the present value of $10,000 discounted at nine percent? Use Table A to determine your answer before reading further.

Table A indicates $0.5470 as the PV of $1 when i = nine percent and n = seven periods. The present value of the payments is determined as follows:

Future value x Present Value Factor = Present Value

$11,000   x   0.5470   = $ 6,017

Calculating Present Value of a Stream of Future Payments/Receipts

As with calculating the present value of a single payment/receipt, there are three methods to calculate the present value of a stream of payments/receipts: formula, present value tables, and business programmed calculators. The formula to calculate the present values of a stream of payments/receipts is at the beginning of Table B. Table B requires that the payment amount be equal each period, that the interest rate is constant, that the payments/ receipts are equally spaced, and that the payment/receipt be made at the end of each period.

Using a Calculator Programmed for PV

Often a particular obligation will involve a stream of payments/receipts over several periods. The PV of each may be separately determined and then all the PV's summed. However, this approach may be unnecessarily time consuming. Using a calculator programmed for business functions, you could enter the values for:

Number of periods	= n	= 4 years
Interest rate per period	= i	= 11% (per year)
Payment/Receipt per period	= PMT	= $10,000

and then instruct the calculator to compute the present value (PV) which will turn out to be $31,024 (rounded).

Using Present Value Table B for Stream of Payments/Receipts

The formula for the present value of $1 paid/received at the end of each period for n periods discounted at i percent interest per period is:

$$PV = \frac{1 - \frac{1}{(1 + i)^n}}{i}$$

i = interest rate per period
n = number of periods

Suppose you desired to determine the present value, of a stream of payments of $10,000 at the end of each year for four years, discounted at 11 percent. You could look up all four separate PV factors in Table A, and perform four separate calculations, plus summarization. An easier way is to use Table B. Table B assumes a flow of $1 each year and provides the cumulative PV for the same discount rate and number of periods as Table A. Using Tables A and B, attempt a solution before proceeding.

Only one calculation is necessary, if you take advantage of Table B, but five calculations must be made using Table A (four present value calculations plus summing).

Table A		PV factor		PV
$10,000	x	.9009	=	$9,009
10,000	x	.8116	=	8,116
10,000	x	.7312	=	7,312
10,000	x	.6587	=	6,587
		3.1024		$31,024

Table B				
$10,000	x	3.1025	=	$31,025

The difference between the answer using Table A and Table B is due to rounding within the present value tables. If you had calculated your answer using tables with five digits to the right of the decimal point your answer using Table A would have been 31,024.40, while Table B would have produced an answer of $31,024.50. The difference between the two tables will always be due to rounding. Since the rounding difference is not material, Table B is preferable for a stream of payments, because it is easier to use.

Determining the Present Value of a Debt Instrument (Note or Bond)

It is essential to identify and distinguish the stated rate of interest for the debt instrument from the prevailing rate (or discount rate unique to the individual or firm), when determining present value for debt instruments (promissory notes or bonds). Only in the rare situation where the stated rate and the discount rate are identical, will the PV be the same as the face/par value of the debt instrument.

In determining the present value of the debt instrument you must determine the actual cash flows involved for each period regardless of whether these flows have been labeled face value, maturity value, par value, stated interest or whatever. These cash flows are then discounted to factor out the prevailing or desired rate of interest to arrive at the present or principal value. Five examples of determining the present value of debt instruments follow.

Capitalized Interest

Find the appropriate initial note receivable discount for a five year noninterest bearing promissory note with a face value of $20,000 when the prevailing interest rate for similar notes is 12 percent.

$$\text{FV x PV factor (Table A)} = \text{PV}$$

Since there is a single cash inflow of $20,000 at the end of five years, Table A is used. The PV of $1 received in five years discounted at 12 percent per year from Table A is $0.5674. The PV of the $20,000 receipt is therefore $11,348 ($20,000 x 0.5674). $8,652 represents executory interest at the time of signing, and therefore should initially be recorded as the discount on this note.

Imputed Interest

Find the appropriate initial note receivable discount for a 10 year promissory note with a face value of $50,000 and with stated interest of three percent. The prevailing rate of interest or notes of this type is 15 percent, and therefore it may be inferred that 12 percent is capitalized into the face value.

The cash flows involved are an inflow of $1,500 per year for 10 years and an additional $50,000 inflow at the end of 10 years. From Table B the stream factor for $1 for 10 years discounted at 15 percent is 5.0188. From Table A the single receipt factor for $1 at the end of 10 years discounted at 15 percent is 0.2472.

PV of interest	$1500	x	5.0188	=	$ 7,528 (rounded)
PV of note	$50,000	x	0.2472	=	$12,360
			PV	=	$19,888

Therefore $30,112 of the face value represents capitalized interest, and should be initially reported as the discount on notes receivable. Observe that the 12 percent apparent interest differential can not be used in the calculation since the three percent is based upon the future value (principal plus interest) of $50,000 and not upon the true principal of $19,888.

Payments Under Fully Amortized Mortgage

An individual is planning to acquire an automobile costing $10,000 by paying $2,000 down and signing a fully amortized 4 year loan (equal monthly payments covering both interest on the outstanding loan balance and a gradual reduction of principal to zero over the life of the loan) for the balance. If the effective interest cost is 12 percent, and if payments are to be made monthly, what are the amounts of the monthly payments?

The cash flows are $2,000 on signing and "X" per month for 48 months. The PV factor for a stream of 48 payments of $1 discounted at one percent per period (12 percent per year is one percent per month) is 37.9740.

$$
\begin{array}{rcll}
\$2,000 & \text{x} & 1.0000 & = \quad \$2,000 \\
\text{X} & \text{x} & 37.9740 & = \underline{37.9740\text{X}} \\
& & \text{PV} & = \quad \underline{\$10,000}
\end{array}
$$

$$
\begin{array}{rcl}
\$2,000 \quad + \quad 37.9740\text{X} & = & \$10,000 \\
\text{X} & = & \$210.67 \quad \text{(Rounded) Payment per month}
\end{array}
$$

Bond Discount

Find the discount at which a 30 year 10 percent bond, with interest payable annually, will sell to yield (prevailing market interest rate) 12 percent.

The cash inflows to the lender will be $100 (10 percent of $1,000 par value) per year for 30 years plus $1,000 at maturity. From Table B the PV factor for a stream of $1 payments for 30 years discounted at 12 percent is 8.0552. From Table A the PV factor for a single receipt of $1 at the end of 30 years discounted at 12 percent is 0.0334.

PV of Interest Payments	$ 100	x	8.0552	=	$805.52
PV of Payment at Maturity	1000	x	0.0334	=	33.40
PV of Bond					$838.92

The bond will initially sell for $838.92 or at a discount of $161.08 ($1,000 – 838.92).

Bond Premium

Find the premium at which a 20 year, 12 percent bond will sell to yield (the prevailing interest rate) 10 percent if the bond interest is paid semiannually.

The cash flows to the lender will be $60 each six month period for 40 periods; and $1,000 received at the end of 40 periods. From Table B the PV factor for a stream of $1 receipts for 40 periods discounted at five percent (interest rate per 6 month period) is 17.1591. From Table A the PV factor for $1 received at the end of 40 periods discounted at five percent is 0.1420.

PV Interest Payments	$ 60	x	17.1591	=	$1,029.55 (rounded)
PV of Payment at Maturity	1,000	x	0.0420	=	142.00
			PV	=	$1,171.55

The bond will initially sell at a premium of $171.55 ($1,000 – 1,171.55).

Determining the Present Value of a Capital Lease

The initial valuation for the lessee of an item under a capital lease with a payment on signing of $10,000 and 20 year-end payments of $15,000 each, when the lessee's borrowing rate for a similar long term mortgage is 14 percent, would be $109,347.

The cash outflows involved are $10,000 on signing (now) and $15,000 per year for 20 years. The PV factor for year zero (now) is 1.0000 (no interest involved). The PV factor for a stream of $1 payments for 20 years discounted at 14 percent from Table B is 6.6231.

PV of Down Payment	$10,000	x	1.000	= $ 10,000
PV of Annual Payments	15,000	x	6.62312	= 99,347 (rounded)
PV of Capital Lease				$109,347

Now calculate the initial valuation for an item under capital lease providing for the following payments, when the lessee's borrowing rate for similar long term debt is 13 percent.

$10,000	on signing
$30,000	each year for the next three years
$20,000	each year for the next seven years

The cash outflows can be viewed as a payment of $10,000 now, a payment of $10,000 per year for three years, and a payment of $20,000 per year for 10 years. From Table B the PV factor for a stream of $1 payments for three years discounted at 13 percent is 2.3612; and a $1 payment for 10 years is 5.4262.

$10,000	x	1.000	=	$ 10,000
10,000	x	2.3612	=	23,612
20,000	x	5.4262	=	108,524
		PV	=	$142,136

The item under capital lease would be initially valued at $142,136.

An alternative method for determining present value would be to calculate the present value of the $30,000 stream of payments for three years. The present value factor for three years was already found to be 2.3612. The second step would be to find the present value of the second stream of $20,000 payments for seven years. The PV factor is 4.226. However, a third calculation must be made using Table A to discount the stream from year 3 back to the present. This PV factor is .6931.

$$
\begin{array}{rclcr}
\$10{,}000 & \times & 1.0000 & = & \$10{,}000 \\
30{,}000 & \times & 2.3612 & = & 70{,}836 \\
.6931(20{,}000 & \times & 4.2260) & = & \underline{61{,}306} \\
& & & & \$142{,}142
\end{array}
$$

The difference is due to rounding in the tables. It is not material and can be ignored.

A third method for calculating the $20,000 stream of payments would be to find the PV factor for a stream of 10 payments less the PV factor for a stream of three payments (5.4262 – 2.3612).

$$
\begin{array}{rclcr}
\$10{,}000 & \times & 1.0000 & = & \$\ 10{,}000 \\
30{,}000 & \times & 2.3612 & = & 70{,}836 \\
20{,}000(5.462 & - & 2.3612) & = & \underline{61{,}300} \\
& & & & \$142{,}136
\end{array}
$$

Note that this method does not create a rounding difference, since all calculations are made from Table B.

Present Value Problems

1. Determine the present value of the following items:
    a) A $3,000 payment to be made next week, discount rate nine percent.
    b) A $4,000 payment to be made in two years, discount rate eight percent.
    c) A $5,000 payment to be made in five years, discount rate seven percent.
    d) A $6,000 payment to be made in fifteen years, discount rate six percent.
    e) A $6,000 receivable due next week, discount rate five percent.
    f) A $7,000 receivable due in three years, discount rate six percent.
    g) An $8,000 receivable due in seven years, discount rate seven percent.
    h) A $9,000 receivable due in thirteen years, discount rate eight percent.

2. Determine the present value of the following items:
    a) A stream of $500 annual interest payments over five years, discount rate five percent annually.
    b) A stream of $1,500 annual interest payments over twelve years, discount rate seven percent annually.
    c) A stream of $400 monthly rental payments over three years, discount rate 12 percent annually.
    d) $500 to be received monthly starting next month for the next four years, discount rate 18 percent annually.

e) $4,000 to be received annually starting at year end for the next four years, discount rate nine percent annually.

f) $500 annual interest to be received over the next twenty years, discount rate ten percent annually.

3. Determine the present value of, and the initial discount or premium on, the following notes receivable:

   a) $5,000 five year note plus interest at eight percent, discount rate eight percent.

   b) $6,000 eight year note, no stated interest, discount rate nine percent.

   c) $7,000 fourteen year note plus interest at six percent, discount rate eight percent.

   d) $8,000 twenty year note plus interest at nine percent, discount rate six percent.

4. Determine the present value of and the initial discount or premium on the following bonds payable:

   a) $10,000 twenty year bond paying nine percent interest, discount rate nine percent.

   b) $10,000 twenty year bond paying nine percent interest, discount rate seven percent.

   c) $20,000 fifteen year bond paying six percent interest, discount rate eight percent.

   d) $50,000 thirty year bond paying eight percent annual interest semi annually when prevailing interest rate for similar bonds is ten percent.

5. Determine the initial asset value of property acquired for:

   a) A $20,000 down payment and a 15 year interest only note (face value payable at maturity) for $400,000 with stated annual interest of 14 percent when the firm's incremental borrowing rate is 14 percent.

   b) A $50,000 down payment and a 20 year interest only note for $500,000 with stated annual interest of three percent when the firm's incremental borrowing rate is 14 percent.

   c) A $40,000 down payment and a 15 year interest only note for $600,000 with stated annual interest of four percent payable semi annually when the firm's incremental borrowing rate is 12 percent.

   d) A $100,000 down payment and a 20 year interest only note for $900,000 with a stated annual interest of six percent payable semi-annually when the firm's borrowing rate is 14 percent.

6. Determine the initial asset value of a capital lease requiring:

a) $5,000 on signing and 10 annual payments of $20,000 each when the firm's incremental borrowing rate is 15 percent.

b) $10,000 on signing and 20 annual payments of $30,000 each when the firm's incremental borrowing rate is 13 percent.

c) $4,000 on signing and 20 semi annual payments of $10,000 each when the firm's incremental borrowing annual rate is 14 percent.

d) $8,000 on signing and 39 semi annual payments of $9,000 each when the firm's incremental borrowing annual rate is 14 percent.

e) $20,000 on signing and five annual payments of $30,000 each followed by 15 annual payments of $10,000 each when the firm's incremental borrowing rate is 12 percent.

f) $10,000 on signing and four annual payments of $40,000 each followed by six annual payments of $20,000 each when the firm's incremental borrowing rate is 15 percent.

7. Determine the amount of the equal payments required on a fully amortized mortgage when:

a) The face value of a 20 year mortgage is $100,000 requiring annual payments and the effective interest rate is 12 percent.

b) The face value of a 30 year mortgage is $200,000 requiring annual payments and the effective interest rate is 13 percent.

c) The face value of a 25 year mortgage is $150,000 and semi annual interest payments are required. The effective annual interest rate is 14 percent.

d) The face value of a four year mortgage is $8,000. It requires monthly payments and the effective annual interest rate is 12 percent.

$i = 01$ to 06; $N = 01$ to 50

N	1%	1.25%	1.5%	2%	3%	4%	5%	6%
0	1.0000	1.0000	1.0000	1.0000	1.0000	1.0000	1.0000	1.0000
1	0.9901	0.9877	0.9852	0.9804	0.9709	0.9615	0.9524	0.9434
2	0.9803	0.9755	0.9707	0.9612	0.9426	0.9246	0.9070	0.8900
3.	0.9706	0.9634	0.9563	0.9423	0.9151	0.8890	0.8638	0.8396
4	0.9610	0.9515	0.9422	0.9238	0.8885	0.8548	0.8227	0.7921
5	0.9515	0.9398	0.9283	0.9057	0.8626	0.8219	0.7835	0.7473
6	0.9420	0.9282	0.9145	0.8880	0.8375	0.7903	0.7462	0.7050
7	0.9327	0.9167	0.9010	0.8706	0.8131	0.7599	0.7107	0.6651
8	0.9235	0.9054	0.8877	0.8535	0.7894	0.7307	0.6768	0.6274
9	0.9143	0.8942	0.8746	0.8368	0.7664	0.7026	0.6446	0.5919
10	0.9053	0.8832	0.8617	0.8203	0.7441	0.6756	0.6139	0.5584
11	0.8963	0.8723	0.8489	0.8043	0.7224	0.6496	0.5847	0.5268
12	0.8874	0.8615	0.8364	0.7885	0.7014	0.6246	0.5568	0.4970
13	0.8787	0.8509	0.8240	0.7730	0.6810	0.6006	0.5303	0.4688
14	0.8700	0.8404	0.8119	0.7579	0.6611	0.5775	0.5051	0.4423
15	0.8614	0.8300	0.7999	0.7430	0.6419	0.5553	0.4810	0.4173
16	0.8528	0.8197	0.7880	0.7284	0.6232	0.5339	0.4581	0.3936
17	0.8444	0.8096	0.7764	0.7142	0.6050	0.5134	0.4363	0.3714
18	0.8360	0.7996	0.7649	0.7002	0.5874	0.4936	0.4155	0.3503
19	0.8277	0.7898	0.7536	0.6864	0.5703	0.4746	0.3957	0.3305
20	0.8195	0.7800	0.7425	0.6730	0.5537	0.4564	0.3769	0.3118
21	0.8114	0.7704	0.7315	0.6598	0.5375	0.4388	0.3589	0.2942
22	0.8034	0.7609	0.7207	0.6468	0.5219	0.4220	0.3419	0.2775
23	0.7954	0.7515	0.7100	0.6342	0.5067	0.4057	0.3256	0.2618
24	0.7876	0.7422	0.6995	0.6217	0.4919	0.3901	0.3101	0.2470
25	0.7798	0.7330	0.6892	0.6095	0.4776	0.3751	0.2953	0.2330
26	0.7720	0.7240	0.6790	0.5976	0.4637	0.3607	0.2812	0.2198
27	0.7644	0.7150	0.6690	0.5859	0.4502	0.3468	0.2678	0.2074
28	0.7568	0.7062	0.6591	0.5744	0.4371	0.3335	0.2551	0.1956
29	0.7493	0.6975	0.6494	0.5631	0.4243	0.3207	0.2429	0.1846
30	0.7419	0.6889	0.6398	0.5521	0.4120	0.3083	0.2314	0.1741
31	0.7346	0.6804	0.6303	0.5412	0.4000	0.2965	0.2204	0.1643
32	0.7273	0.6720	0.6210	0.5306	0.3883	0.2851	0.2099	0.1550
33	0.7201	0.6637	0.6118	0.5202	0.3770	0.2741	0.1999	0.1462
34	0.7130	0.6555	0.6028	0.5100	0.3660	0.2636	0.1904	0.1379
35	0.7059	0.6474	0.5939	0.5000	0.3554	0.2534	0.1813	0.1301
36	0.6989	0.6394	0.5851	0.4902	0.3450	0.2437	0.1727	0.1227
37	0.6920	0.6315	0.5764	0.4806	0.3350	0.2343	0.1644	0.1158
38	0.6852	0.6237	0.5679	0.4712	0.3252	0.2253	0.1566	0.1092
39	0.6784	0.6160	0.5595	0.4619	0.3158	0.2166	0.1491	0.1031
40	0.6717	0.6084	0.5513	0.4529	0.3066	0.2083	0.1420	0.0972
41	0.6650	0.6009	0.5431	0.4440	0.2976	0.2003	0.1353	0.0917
42	0.6584	0.5935	0.5351	0.4353	0.2890	0.1926	0.1288	0.0865
43	0.6519	0.5862	0.5272	0.4268	0.2805	0.1852	0.1227	0.0816
44	0.6454	0.5789	0.5194	0.4184	0.2724	0.1780	0.1169	0.0770
45	0.6391	0.5718	0.5117	0.4102	0.2644	0.1712	0.1113	0.0727
46	0.6327	0.5647	0.5042	0.4022	0.2567	0.1646	0.1060	0.0685
47	0.6265	0.5577	0.4967	0.3943	0.2493	0.1583	0.1010	0.0647
48	0.6203	0.5509	0.4894	0.3865	0.2420	0.1522	0.0961	0.0610
49	0.6141	0.5441	0.4821	0.3790	0.2350	0.1463	0.0916	0.0575
50	0.6080	0.5373	0.4750	0.3715	0.2281	0.1407	0.0872	0.0543

$i = 07$ to 14; $N = 01$ to 50

N	7%	8%	9%	10%	11%	12%	13%	14%
0	1.0000	1.0000	1.0000	1.0000	1.0000	1.0000	1.0000	1.0000
1	0.9346	0.9259	0.9174	0.9091	0.9009	0.8929	0.8850	0.8772
2	0.8734	0.8573	0.8417	0.8264	0.8116	0.7972	0.7831	0.7695
3	0.8163	0.7938	0.7722	0.7513	0.7312	0.7118	0.6931	0.6750
4	0.7629	0.7350	0.7084	0.6830	0.6587	0.6355	0.6133	0.5921
5	0.7130	0.6806	0.6499	0.6209	0.5935	0.5674	0.5428	0.5194
6	0.6663	0.6302	0.5963	0.5645	0.5346	0.5066	0.4803	0.4556
7	0.6228	0.5835	0.5470	0.5132	0.4817	0.4523	0.4251	0.3996
8	0.5820	0.5403	0.5019	0.4665	0.4339	0.4039	0.3762	0.3506
9	0.5439	0.5002	0.4604	0.4241	0.3909	0.3606	0.3329	0.3075
10	0.5083	0.4632	0.4224	0.3855	0.3522	0.3220	0.2946	0.2697
11	0.4751	0.4289	0.3875	0.3505	0.3173	0.2875	0.2607	0.2366
12	0.4440	0.3971	0.3555	0.3186	0.2858	0.2567	0.2307	0.2076
13	0.4150	0.3677	0.3262	0.2897	0.2575	0.2292	0.2042	0.1821
14	0.3878	0.3405	0.2992	0.2633	0.2320	0.2046	0.1807	0.1597
15	0.3624	0.3152	0.2745	0.2394	0.2090	0.1827	0.1599	0.1401
16	0.3387	0.2919	0.2519	0.2176	0.1883	0.1631	0.1415	0.1229
17	0.3166	0.2703	0.2311	0.1978	0.1696	0.1456	0.1252	0.1078
18	0.2959	0.2502	0.2120	0.1799	0.1528	0.1300	0.1108	0.0946
19	0.2765	0.2317	0.1945	0.1635	0.1377	0.1161	0.0981	0.0829
20	0.2584	0.2145	0.1784	0.1486	0.1240	0.1037	0.0868	0.0728
21	0.2415	0.1987	0.1637	0.1351	0.1117	0.0926	0.0768	0.0638
22	0.2257	0.1839	0.1502	0.1228	0.1007	0.0826	0.0680	0.0560
23	0.2109	0.1703	0.1378	0.1117	0.0907	0.0738	0.0601	0.0491
24	0.1971	0.1577	0.1264	0.1015	0.0817	0.0659	0.0532	0.0431
25	0.1842	0.1460	0.1160	0.0923	0.0736	0.0588	0.0471	0.0378
26	0.1722	0.1352	0.1064	0.0839	0.0663	0.0525	0.0417	0.0331
27	0.1609	0.1252	0.0976	0.0763	0.0597	0.0469	0.0369	0.0291
28	0.1504	0.1159	0.0895	0.0693	0.0538	0.0419	0.0326	0.0255
29	0.1406	0.1073	0.0822	0.0630	0.0485	0.0374	0.0289	0.0224
30	0.1314	0.0994	0.0754	0.0573	0.0437	0.0334	0.0256	0.0196
31	0.1228	0.0920	0.0691	0.0521	0.0394	0.0298	0.0226	0.0172
32	0.1147	0.0852	0.0634	0.0474	0.0355	0.0266	0.0200	0.0151
33	0.1072	0.0789	0.0582	0.0431	0.0319	0.0238	0.0177	0.0132
34	0.1002	0.0730	0.0534	0.0391	0.0288	0.0212	0.0157	0.0116
35	0.0937	0.0676	0.0490	0.0356	0.0259	0.0189	0.0139	0.0102
36	0.0875	0.0626	0.0449	0.0323	0.0234	0.0169	0.0123	0.0089
37	0.0818	0.0580	0.0412	0.0294	0.0210	0.0151	0.0109	0.0078
38	0.0765	0.0537	0.0378	0.0267	0.0190	0.0135	0.0096	0.0069
39	0.0715	0.0497	0.0347	0.0243	0.0171	0.0120	0.0085	0.0060
40	0.0668	0.0460	0.0318	0.0221	0.0154	0.0107	0.0075	0.0053
41	0.0624	0.0426	0.0292	0.0201	0.0139	0.0096	0.0067	0.0046
42	0.0583	0.0395	0.0268	0.0183	0.0125	0.0086	0.0059	0.0041
43	0.0545	0.0365	0.0246	0.0166	0.0112	0.0076	0.0052	0.0036
44	0.0509	0.0338	0.0226	0.0151	0.0101	0.0068	0.0046	0.0031
45	0.0476	0.0313	0.0207	0.0137	0.0091	0.0061	0.0041	0.0027
46	0.0445	0.0290	0.0190	0.0125	0.0082	0.0054	0.0036	0.0024
47	0.0416	0.0269	0.0174	0.0113	0.0074	0.0049	0.0032	0.0021
48	0.0389	0.0249	0.0160	0.0103	0.0067	0.0043	0.0028	0.0019
49	0.0363	0.0230	0.0147	0.0094	0.0060	0.0039	0.0025	0.0016
50	0.0339	0.0213	0.0134	0.0085	0.0054	0.0035	0.0022	0.0014

$i = 15$ to 50; $N = 01$ to 50

N	15%	20%	25%	30%	35%	40%	45%	50%
0	1.0000	1.0000	1.0000	1.0000	1.0000	1.0000	1.0000	1.0000
1	0.8696	0.8333	0.8000	0.7692	0.7407	0.7143	0.6897	0.6667
2	0.7561	0.6944	0.6400	0.5917	0.5487	0.5102	0.4756	0.4444
3	0.6575	0.5787	0.5120	0.4552	0.4064	0.3644	0.3280	0.2963
4	0.5718	0.4823	0.4096	0.3501	0.3011	0.2603	0.2262	0.1975
5	0.4972	0.4019	0.3277	0.2693	0.2230	0.1859	0.1560	0.1317
6	0.4323	0.3349	0.2621	0.2072	0.1652	0.1328	0.1076	0.0878
7	0.3759	0.2791	0.2097	0.1594	0.1224	0.0949	0.0742	0.0585
8	0.3269	0.2326	0.1678	0.1226	0.0906	0.0678	0.0512	0.0390
9	0.2843	0.1938	0.1342	0.0943	0.0671	0.0484	0.0353	0.0260
10	0.2472	0.1615	0.1074	0.0725	0.0497	0.0346	0.0243	0.0173
11	0.2149	0.1346	0.0859	0.0558	0.0368	0.0247	0.0168	0.0116
12	0.1869	0.1122	0.0687	0.0429	0.0273	0.0176	0.0116	0.0077
13	0.1625	0.0935	0.0550	0.0330	0.0202	0.0126	0.0080	0.0051
14	0.1413	0.0779	0.0440	0.0254	0.0150	0.0090	0.0055	0.0034
15	0.1229	0.0649	0.0352	0.0195	0.0111	0.0064	0.0038	0.0023
16	0.1069	0.0541	0.0281	0.0150	0.0082	0.0046	0.0026	0.0015
17	0.0929	0.0451	0.0225	0.0116	0.0061	0.0033	0.0018	0.0010
18	0.0808	0.0376	0.0180	0.0089	0.0045	0.0023	0.0012	0.0007
19	0.0703	0.0313	0.0144	0.0068	0.0033	0.0017	0.0009	0.0005
20	0.0611	0.0261	0.0115	0.0053	0.0025	0.0012	0.0006	0.0003
21	0.0531	0.0217	0.0092	0.0040	0.0018	0.0009	0.0004	0.0002
22	0.0462	0.0181	0.0074	0.0031	0.0014	0.0006	0.0003	0.0001
23	0.0402	0.0151	0.0059	0.0024	0.0010	0.0004	0.0002	0.0001
24	0.0349	0.0126	0.0047	0.0018	0.0007	0.0003	0.0001	0.0001
25	0.0304	0.0105	0.0038	0.0014	0.0006	0.0002	0.0001	0.0000
26	0.0264	0.0087	0.0030	0.0011	0.0004	0.0002	0.0001	0.0000
27	0.0230	0.0073	0.0024	0.0008	0.0003	0.0001	0.0000	0.0000
28	0.0200	0.0061	0.0019	0.0006	0.0002	0.0001	0.0000	0.0000
29	0.0174	0.0051	0.0015	0.0005	0.0002	0 0001	0.0000	0.0000
30	0.0151	0.0042	0.0012	0.0004	0.0001	0.0000	0.0000	0.0000
31	0.0131	0.0035	0.0010	0.0003	0.0001	0.0000	0.0000	0.0000
32	0.0114	0.0029	0.0008	0.0002	0.0001	0.0000	0.0000	0.0000
33	0.0099	0.0024	0.0006	0.0002	0.0001	0.0000	0.0000	0.0000
34	0.0086	0.0020	0.0005	0.0001	0.0000	0.0000	0.0000	0.0000
35	0.0075	0.0017	0.0004	0.0001	0.0000	0.0000	0.0000	0.0000
36	0.0065	0.0014	0.0003	0.0001	0.0000	0.0000	0.0000	0.0000
37	0.0057	0.0012	0.0003	0.0001	0.0000	0.0000	0.0000	0.0000
38	0.0049	0.0010	0.0002	0.0000	0.0000	0.0000	0.0000	0.0000
39	0.0043	0.0008	0.0002	0.0000	0.0000	0.0000	0.0000	0.0000
40	0.0037	0.0007	0.0001	0.0000	0.0000	0.0000	0.0000	0.0000
41	0.0032	0.0006	0.0001	0.0000	0.0000	0.0000	0.0000	0.0000
42	0.0028	0.0005	0.0001	0.0000	0.0000	0.0000	0.0000	0.0000
43	0.0025	0.0004	0.0001	0.0000	0.0000	0.0000	0.0000	0.0000
44	0.0021	0.0003	0.0001	0.0000	0.0000	0.0000	0.0000	0.0000
45	0.0019	0.0003	0.0000	0.0000	0.0000	0.0000	0.0000	0.0000
46	0.0016	0.0002	0.0000	0.0000	0.0000	0.0000	0.0000	0.0000
47	0.0014	0.0002	0.0000	0.0000	0.0000	0.0000	0.0000	0.0000
48	0.0012	0.0002	0.0000	0.0000	0.0000	0.0000	0.0000	0.0000
49	0.0011	0.0001	0.0000	0.0000	0.0000	0.0000	0.0000	0.0000
50	0.0009	0.0001	0.0000	0.0000	0.0000	0.0000	0.0000	0.0000

$i = 01$ to 06; $N = 01$ to 50

N	1%	1.25%	1.5%	2%	3%	4%	5%	6%
0	1.0000	1.0000	1.0000	1.0000	1.0000	1.0000	1.0000	1.0000
1	0.9901	0.9877	0.9852	0.9804	0.9709	0.9615	0.9524	0.9434
2	1.9704	1.9631	1.9559	1.9416	1.9135	1.8861	1.8594	1.8334
3	2.9410	2.9266	2.9122	2.8839	2.8286	2.7751	2.7233	2.6730
4	3.9020	3.8781	3.8544	3.8077	3.7171	3.6299	3.5460	3.4651
5	4.8534	4.8179	4.7826	4.7135	4.5797	4.4518	4.3295	4.2124
6	5.7955	5.7460	5.6972	5.6014	5.4172	5.2421	5.0757	4.9173
7	6.7282	6.6628	6.5982	6.4720	6.2303	6.0021	5.7864	5.5824
8	7.6517	7.5682	7.4859	7.3255	7.0197	6.7327	6.4632	6.2098
9	8.5660	8.4624	8.3605	8.1622	7.7861	7.4353	7.1078	6.8017
10	9.4713	9.3456	9.2222	8.9826	8.5302	8.1109	7.7217	7.3601
11	10.3676	10.2179	10.0711	9.7868	9.2526	8.7605	8.3064	7.8869
12	11.2551	11.0794	10.9075	10.5753	9.9540	9.3851	8.8632	8.3838
13	12.1337	11.9302	11.7315	11.3484	10.6350	9.9856	9.3936	8.8527
14	13.0037	12.7706	12.5433	12.1062	11.2961	10.5631	9.8986	9.2950
15	13.8650	13.6006	13.3432	12.8492	11.9379	11.1184	10.3796	9.7122
16	14.7179	14.4204	14.1312	13.5777	12.5611	11.6523	10.8378	10.1059
17	15.5622	15.2300	14.9076	14.2918	13.1661	12.1657	11.2741	10.4773
18	16.3983	16.0296	15.6725	14.9920	13.7535	12.6593	11.6896	10.8276
19	17.2260	16.8194	16.4261	15.6784	14.3238	13.1339	12.0853	11.1581
20	18.0455	17.5994	17.1686	16.3514	14.8775	13.5903	12.4622	11.4699
21	18.8570	18.3698	17.9001	17.0112	15.4150	14.0292	12.8211	11.7641
22	19.6604	19.1307	18.6208	17.6580	15.9369	14.4511	13.1630	12.0416
23	20.4558	19.8821	19.3308	18.2922	16.4436	14.8568	13.4886	12.3034
24	21.2434	20.6243	20.0304	18.9139	16.9355	15.2470	13.7986	12.5504
25	22.0232	21.3574	20.7196	19.5234	17.4131	15.6221	14.0939	12.7834
26	22.7952	22.0814	21.3986	20.1210	17.8768	15.9828	14.3752	13.0032
27	23.5596	22.7964	22.0676	20.7069	18.3270	16.3296	14.6430	13.2105
28	24.3164	23.5026	22.7267	21.2812	18.7641	16.6631	14.8981	13.4062
29	25.0658	24.2001	23.3760	21.8443	19.1885	16.9837	15.1411	13.5907
30	25.8077	24.8890	24.0158	22.3964	19.6004	17.2920	15.3724	13.7648
31	26.5423	25.5694	24.6461	22.9377	20.0004	17.5885	15.5928	13.9291
32	27.2696	26.2415	25.2671	23.4683	20.3888	17.8735	15.8027	14.0840
33	27.9897	26.9052	25.8789	23.9886	20.7658	18.1476	16.0025	14.2302
34	28.7027	27.5606	26.4817	24.4986	21.1318	18.4112	16.1929	14.3681
35	29.4086	28.2080	27.0756	24.9986	21.4872	18.6646	16.3742	14.4982
36	30.1075	28.8475	27.6607	25.4888	21.8322	18.9083	16.5468	14.6210
37	30.7995	29.4790	28.2371	25.9695	22.1672	19.1426	16.7113	14.7368
38	31.4847	30.1027	28.8050	26.4406	22.4925	19.3679	16.8679	14.8460
39	32.1631	30.7187	29.3645	26.9026	22.8082	19.5845	17.0170	14.9491
40	32.8347	31.3271	29.9158	27.3555	23.1148	19.7928	17.1591	15.0463
41	33.4997	31.9280	30.4589	27.7995	23.4124	19.9930	17.2944	15.1380
42	34.1581	32.5215	30.9940	28.2348	23.7014	20.1856	17.4232	15.2245
43	34.8100	33.1077	31.5212	28.6616	23.9819	20.3708	17.5459	15.3062
44	35.4555	33.6866	32.0406	29.0800	24.2543	20.5488	17.6628	15.3832
45	36.0945	34.2584	32.5523	29.4902	24.5187	20.7200	17.7741	15.4558
46	36.7273	34.8231	33.0565	29.8923	24.7754	20.8847	17.8801	15.5244
47	37.3537	35.3808	33.5532	30.2866	25.0247	21.0429	17.9810	15.5890
48	37.9740	35.9317	34.0425	30.6731	25.2667	21.1951	18.0772	15.6500
49	38.5881	36.4758	34.5246	31.0521	25.5017	21.3415	18.1687	15.7076
50	39.1962	37.0131	34.9997	31.4236	25.7298	21.4822	18.2559	15.7619

$i = 07$ to 14; $N = 01$ to 50

N	7%	8%	9%	10%	11%	12%	13%	14%
0	1.0000	1.0000	1.0000	1.0000	1.0000	1.0000	1.0000	1.0000
1	0.9346	0.9259	0.9174	0.9091	0.9009	0.8929	0.8850	0.8772
2	1.8080	1.7833	1.7591	1.7355	1.7125	1.6901	1.6681	1.6467
3	2.6243	2.5771	2.5313	2.4869	2.4437	2.4018	2.3612	2.3216
4	3.3872	3.3121	3.2397	3.1699	3.1025	3.0374	2.9745	2.9137
5	4.1002	3.9927	3.8897	3.7908	3.6959	3.6048	3.5172	3.4331
6	4.7665	4.6229	4.4859	4.3553	4.2305	4.1114	3.9976	3.8887
7	5.3893	5.2064	5.0330	4.8684	4.7122	4.5638	4.4226	4.2883
8	5.9713	5.7466	5.5348	5.3349	5.1461	4.9676	4.7988	4.6389
9	6.5152	6.2469	5.9953	5.7590	5.5371	5.3283	5.1317	4.9464
10	7.0236	6.7101	6.4177	6.1446	5.8892	5.6502	5.4262	5.2161
11	7.4987	7.1390	6.8052	6.4951	6.2065	5.9377	5.6869	5.4527
12	7.9427	7.5361	7.1607	6.8137	6.4924	6.1944	5.9177	5.6603
13	8.3577	7.9038	7.4869	7.1034	6.7499	6.4236	6.1218	5.8424
14	8.7455	8.2442	7.7862	7.3667	6.9819	6.6282	6.3025	6.0021
15	9.1079	8.5595	8.0607	7.6061	7.1909	6.8109	6.4624	6.1422
16	9.4467	8.8514	8.3126	7.8237	7.3792	6.9740	6.6039	6.2651
17	9.7632	9.1216	8.5436	8.0216	7.5488	7.1196	6.7291	6.3729
18	10.0591	9.3719	8.7556	8.2014	7.7016	7.2497	6.8399	6.4674
19	10.3356	9.6036	8.9501	8.3649	7.8393	7.3658	6.9380	6.5504
20	10.5940	9.8182	9.1286	8.5136	7.9633	7.4694	7.0248	6.6231
21	10.8355	10.0168	9.2923	8.6487	8.0751	7.5620	7.1016	6.6870
22	11.0612	10.2007	9.4424	8.7715	8.1757	7.6447	7.1695	6.7429
23	11.2722	10.3711	9.5802	8.8832	8.2664	7.7184	7.2297	6.7921
24	11.4693	10.5288	9.7066	8.9847	8.3481	7.7843	7.2829	6.8351
25	11.6536	10.6748	9.8226	9.0770	8.4218	7.8431	7.3300	6.8729
26	11.8258	10.8100	9.9290	9.1610	8.4881	7.8957	7.3717	6.9061
27	11.9867	10.9352	10.0266	9.2372	8.5478	7.9426	7.4086	6.9352
28	12.1371	11.0511	10.1161	9.3066	8.6016	7.9844	7.4412	6.9607
29	12.2777	11.1584	10.1983	9.3696	8.6501	8.0218	7.4701	6.9830
30	12.4090	11.2578	10.2737	9.4269	8.6938	8.0552	7.4957	7.0027
31	12.5318	11.3498	10.3428	9.4790	8.7332	8.0850	7.5183	7.0199
32	12.6466	11.4350	10.4062	9.5264	8.7686	8.1116	7.5383	7.0350
33	12.7538	11.5139	10.4644	9.5694	8.8005	8.1354	7.5560	7.0482
34	12.8540	11.5869	10.5178	9.6086	8.8293	8.1566	7.5717	7.0599
35	12.9477	11.6546	10.5668	9.6442	8.8552	8.1755	7.5856	7.0701
36	13.0352	11.7172	10.6118	9.6765	8.8786	8.1924	7.5979	7.0790
37	13.1170	11.7752	10.6530	9.7059	8.8996	8.2075	7.6087	7.0868
38	13.1935	11.8289	10.6908	9.7327	8.9186	8.2210	7.6183	7.0937
39	13.2649	11.8786	10.7255	9.7570	8.9357	8.2330	7.6269	7.0998
40	13.3317	11.9246	10.7574	9.7791	8.9511	8.2438	7.6344	7.1050
41	13.3941	11.9672	10.7866	9.7991	8.9649	8.2534	7.6410	7.1097
42	13.4525	12.0067	10.8134	9.8174	8.9774	8.2619	7.6469	7.1138
43	13.5070	12.0432	10.8380	9.8340	8.9887	8.2696	7.6522	7.1173
44	13.5579	12.0771	10.8605	9.8491	8.9988	8.2764	7.6568	7.1205
45	13.6055	12.1084	10.8812	9.8628	9.0079	8.2825	7.6609	7.1232
46	13.6500	12.1374	10.9002	9.8753	9.0161	8.2880	7.6645	7.1256
47	13.6916	12.1643	10.9176	9.8866	9.0236	8.2928	7.6677	7.1277
48	13.7305	12.1891	10.9336	9.8969	9.0302	8.2972	7.6705	7.1296
49	13.7668	12.2122	10.9482	9.9063	9.0362	8.3010	7.6730	7.1312
50	13.8007	12.2335	10.9617	9.9148	9.0417	8.3045	7.6752	7.1327

$i = 15$ to 50; $N = 01$ to 50

N	15%	20%	25%	30%	35%	40%	45%	50%
0	1.0000	1.0000	1.0000	1.0000	1.0000	1.0000	1.0000	1.0000
1	0.8696	0.8333	0.8000	0.7692	0.7407	0.7143	0.6897	0.6667
2	1.6257	1.5278	1.4400	1.3610	1.2894	1.2245	1.1653	1.1111
3	2.2832	2.1065	1.9520	1.8161	1.6959	1.5889	1.4933	1.4074
4	2.8550	2.5887	2.3616	2.1662	1.9970	1.8492	1.7195	1.6049
5	3.3522	2.9906	2.6893	2.4356	2.2200	2.0352	1.8755	1.7366
6	3.7845	3.3255	2.9514	2.6428	2.3852	2.1680	1.9831	1.8244
7	4.1604	3.6046	3.1611	2.8021	2.5075	2.2628	2.0573	1.8829
8	4.4873	3.8372	3.3289	2.9247	2.5982	2.3306	2.1085	1.9220
9	4.7716	4.0310	3.4631	3.0190	2.6653	2.3790	2.1438	1.9480
10	5.0188	4.1925	3.5705	3.0915	2.7150	2.4136	2.1681	1.9653
11	5.2337	4.3271	3.6564	3.1473	2.7519	2.4383	2.1849	1.9769
12	5.4206	4.4392	3.7251	3.1903	2.7792	2.4559	2.1965	1.9846
13	5.5832	4.5327	3.7801	3.2233	2.7994	2.4685	2.2045	1.9897
14	5.7245	4.6106	3.8241	3.2487	2.8144	2.4775	2.2100	1.9932
15	5.8474	4.6755	3.8593	3.2682	2.8255	2.4839	2.2138	1.9954
16	5.9542	4.7296	3.8874	3.2832	2.8337	2.4885	2.2164	1.9970
17	6.0472	4.7746	3.9099	3.2948	2.8398	2.4918	2.2182	1.9980
18	6.1280	4.8122	3.9279	3.3037	2.8443	2.4941	2.2195	1.9987
19	6.1982	4.8435	3.9424	3.3105	2.8476	2.4958	2.2203	1.9991
20	6.2593	4.8696	3.9539	3.3158	2.8501	2.4970	2.2209	1.9994
21	6.3125	4.8913	3.9631	3.3198	2.8519	2.4979	2.2213	1.9996
22	6.3587	4.9094	3.9705	3.3230	2.8533	2.4985	2.2216	1.9997
23	6.3988	4.9245	3.9764	3.3254	2.8543	2.4989	2.2218	1.9998
24	6.4338	4.9371	3.9811	3.3272	2.8550	2.4992	2.2219	1.9999
25	6.4642	4.9476	3.9849	3.3286	2.8556	2.4994	2.2220	1.9999
26	6.4906	4.9563	3.9879	3.3297	2.8560	2.4996	2.2221	2.0000
27	6.5135	4.9636	3.9903	3.3305	2.8563	2.4997	2.2221	2.0000
28	6.5335	4.9697	3.9923	3.3312	2.8565	2.4998	2.2222	2.0000
29	6.5509	4.9747	3.9938	3.3317	2.8567	2.4999	2.2222	2.0000
30	6.5660	4.9789	3.9951	3.3321	2.8568	2.4999	2.2222	2.0000
31	6.5791	4.9825	3.9960	3.3324	2.8569	2.4999	2.2222	2.0000
32	6.5905	4.9854	3.9968	3.3326	2.8570	2.5000	2.2222	2.0000
33	6.6006	4.9878	3.9975	3.3328	2.8570	2.5000	2.2222	2.0000
34	6.6091	4.9898	3.9980	3.3329	2.8570	2.5000	2.2222	2.0000
35	6.6166	4.9915	3.9984	3.3330	2.8571	2.5000	2.2222	2.0000
36	6.6231	4.9930	3.9987	3.3331	2.8571	2.5000	2.2222	2.0000
37	6.6288	4.9941	3.9990	3.3331	2.8571	2.5000	2.2222	2.0000
38	6.6338	4.9951	3.9992	3.3332	2.8571	2.5000	2.2222	2.0000
39	6.6381	4.9959	3.9993	3.3332	2.8571	2.5000	2.2222	2.0000
40	6.6418	4.9966	3.9995	3.3332	2.8571	2.5000	2.2222	2.0000
41	6.6450	4.9972	3.9996	3.3333	2.8571	2.5000	2.2222	2.0000
42	6.6479	4.9976	3.9997	3.3333	2.8571	2.5000	2.2222	2.0000
43	6.6503	4.9980	3.9997	3.3333	2.8571	2.5000	2.2222	2.0000
44	6.6524	4.9984	3.9998	3.3333	2.8571	2.5000	2.2222	2.0000
45	6.6543	4.9986	3.9998	3.3333	2.8571	2.5000	2.2222	2.0000
46	6.6559	4.9989	3.9999	3.3333	2.8571	2.5000	2.2222	2.0000
47	6.6573	4.9991	3.9999	3.3333	2.8571	2.5000	2.2222	2.0000
48	6.6585	4.9992	3.9999	3.3333	2.8571	2.5000	2.2222	2.0000
49	6.6596	4.9993	3.9999	3.3333	2.8571	2.5000	2.2222	2.0000
50	6.6605	4.9995	3.9999	3.3333	2.8571	2.5000	2.2222	2.0000

C

**Glossary of
Business and
Accounting Terms**

Note: For those terms discussed in greater depth in the text, the number of the chapter in which the term is introduced is shown in parentheses. Since a term may be discussed further in subsequent chapters, you may wish to consult the index for additional page references.

AAA (1) American Accounting Association.

Accelerated depreciation (9) Any method of calculating depreciation where the charges become progressively smaller. See Double declining balance and Year's digits methods.

Account (4) A file for the accumulation of data on an item or group of similar items.

Accounting changes (6) Changes in accounting method, accounting estimate, or the accounting entity.

Accounting cycle (4) The sequence of steps followed by accountants throughout the year (period).

Accounting entity See **Entity.**

Accounting estimate (9) An estimate incorporated in a particular accounting measurement such as the period of useful life and the salvage value for a long-lived asset.

Accounting method (8) A procedure for measuring and reporting financial information in conformance with GAAP.

Account number (5) A code used to identify a particular account.

Accounts payable (2) A current liability representing obligation to creditors for goods and services purchased on account.

Accounts receivable (2) A current asset representing claims against customers for goods or services sold on account.

Accrual (4) An amount recorded by an adjusting entry in recognition of a claim earned or obligation owed as of the adjustment date for which formal invoicing or payment has not yet occurred.

Accrual basis income (4) Income measured on the basis of revenues earned less expenses (currently incurred or representing asset expiration) related to such revenues, independent of the timing of cash receipts and payments.

Accumulated depreciation (2) A contra-asset reporting the sum of all depreciation charges since an asset was put in use.

Acid test ratio See Quick ratio.

Acquisition (of a firm) (14) See Business combination.

ACRS For income tax determination, the Accelerated Cost Recovery System under the 1981 tax code for depreciable assets put in service after 12/31/80, but before 1/1/87. Under ACRS, recovery deductions are allowed for the full cost of recovery property, over specified recovery periods (depending upon the type of asset) at specified recovery percentages each year.

Additional paid-in capital (10) That portion of capital contributed by owners excess of amounts shown as par or stated value of stock issued. May also include donations (rare) received from outsiders.

Adjusted original cost (2) A description the current GAAP basis for measuring and reporting nonmonetary assets. These assets are originally recorded at cost and subsequently adjusted downwards to reflect expiration of usefulness or loss of recoverable value.

Adjusted trial balance (5) The trial balance taken after completion of adjustments and before closing.

Adjusting entry (4) An entry usually made at the end of an accounting period to update the books and record events not previously recorded. Examples include accruals, asset expirations, loss of recoverable values, discount or premium amortizations, revenue deferrals, and so forth.

Adjustment (4) The change in account balances resulting from an adjusting entry.

Affirmatively misleading (3) Reporting amounts with such detail that an impression of accuracy (which is not realistic) is given to the reader. An example would be depreciation calculated and reported to the nearest cent.

Aging accounts receivable The classification of accounts on the basis of the time passed since the date of sale.

AICPA (1) American Institute of Certified Public Accountants.

Allowance for bad debts (2) A contra-asset in indicating the amount of still active/open receivables that are expected to prove uncollectible.

Allowance for depreciation See Accumulated depreciation.

Amortization (2) The general process of systematically reducing an account balance to reflect asset expiration or the allocation of premiums and discounts to time periods. Known as depletion for wasting assets, and as depreciation for tangible long-lived assets owned other than land.

Amount to be depreciated See Depreciable base.

Annual report (1) A report prepared once a year by a corporation for its stockholders and other interested parties. It contains the year's financial statements, footnotes, auditor's opinions, and such other non-audited information as management desires to disseminate.

Applications of funds Five possible uses of net working capital (NWC) other than funds lost in operations may be considered applications. They include NWC lost as an extraordinary loss, NWC used to a quire noncurrent assets, NWC used to retire noncurrent debt, dividends declared, and, finally, NWC generated elsewhere and used to increase the year-end balance of net working capital on hand.

Appropriation (10) In financial accounting, the segregation of a portion of retained earnings by action of the Board of Directors, to reflect a legal restriction of retained earnings available for dividends or to reflect an intention to withhold future dividends. In governmental accounting, the authorization for a specific expenditure.

Arm's length Refers to transactions between unrelated parties that may be used as evidence of fair market value.

Arrears (10) The total of dividends in arrears (not declared) on only cumulative preferred stock. Arrearage does not exist for noncumulative preferred or for common stock. It is disclosed by statement footnote and must be paid along with the current preferred dividend before any common dividend may be paid. Arrearage adds to preferred claim in liquidation. However, until dividend covering arrearage are declared, arrearage is not a liability.

Asset (2) A property, right, or claim with future objectively measurable value that is either owned or else effectively controlled (via a capital lease) by the firm.

Asset composition (3) A term used in financial analysis refer ring to the mix of more liquid net working capital as compared with less liquid long-lived assets.

Asset composition ratio (3) A measure of relative liquidity. Net working capital divided by the sum of NWC and total long-lived assets.

Asset expiration (4) The decline in future service potential of an asset as a result of deterioration and obsolescence, or management decision.

Asset turnover (13) A measure of sales performance with respect to assets employed. Net sales for the period divided by the average total assets in use during that period. Can be interpreted as the number of sales dollars generated per dollar of average assets employed.

Audit (1) An examination of accounting records, procedures, and internal controls to ensure their adequacy in conformance with GAAP and company objectives.

Audit trail (5) A system of cross referencing information throughout accounting records, from original source document to final account posting.

Auditor's opinion (1) The auditor's statement accompanying the financial statements indicating the extent of the audit and giving an evaluation of the adequacy and fairness of the financial statements in conformance with GAAP.

Authorized stock (10) The maximum number of shares of stock that a corporation may issue without obtaining further authorization from the state in which it is incorporated.

Average In financial accounting, unless identified as "weighted average," refers to the simple average. The sum of beginning and ending balances divided by two.

Average Cost See Weighted average cost inventory.

Average days' receivables (13) A measure of the average time necessary to collect accounts receivable. Calculated by dividing receivables turnover into 365.

Average day's (sales in) inventory (13) A measure of inventory on hand in terms of daily sales. Calculated by dividing inventory turnover into 365.

Bad debt A receivable that is not deemed collectible.

Bad debts expense (11) The sum of all individual accounts receivable determined to have become uncollectible during the year, plus an estimate of those year-end receivables that are expected to subsequently prove uncollectible.

Balance sheet (1) The financial statement reporting assets and equities as of a specific date. Also known as a **Statement of Financial Position.**

Balance sheet diagram (3) A diagram used in this text to illustrate the ultimate balance sheet effect of transactions and adjustments upon assets, liabilities, and owners' equity.

Balance sheet effect worksheet (4) An extension of the balance sheet diagram used in this text to record the ultimate effects on the firm's balance sheet of all (or age some portion of) transactions and adjustments during a period.

Balance sheet equality (2) The fundamental equality underlying the entire financial accounting system. Total Assets = Total Equities, or Total Assets = Total Liabilities + Owners' Equity, or Total Assets − Total Liabilities = Owners' Equity.

Base year cost (8) The cost of inventory in terms of base year prices. Used in calculating dollar value LIFO. The base year is the year in which the firm adopted the dollar value LIFO method.

Basket purchase (9) The acquisition of a group of assets for a single price where the cost must be allocated to different members of the group for accounting purposes.

Beginning inventory The amount of inventory on hand at the start of an accounting period.

Betterment (9) An improvement to a long-lived asset that is capitalized as an increase in the asset's book value.

Board of directors (10) A group of individuals elected by the voting stockholders of a corporation to govern the company.

Bond (11) A negotiable certificate as evidence of debt.

Bond conversion See Debt Conversion.

Bond discount (11) A contra account representing the amount of interest capitalized into the face value of bonds and not yet earned/owed.

Bond premium (11) An account representing the amount of cash given by the bond buyer in excess of face value of the bonds acquired for the privilege of receiving greater than "normal" future interest payments.

Bond sinking fund (11) See Sinking fund.

Bonds payable (12) A liability, usually noncurrent, reporting the face value of outstanding bond indebtedness.

Book value (2) The amount recorded in the firm's accounts. For particular assets and liabilities, refers to the item net of valuation accounts. For common stock, refers to share of total assets not claimed by creditors and preferred stockholders. For the firm as a whole, equals net asset (total assets minus total liabilities).

Book value of common stock (10) The amount of assets not claimed by creditors or preferred stockholders. Also known as common shareholders' equity. See Book value per share.

Book value per share (of common stock) (10) Total stockholders' equity less preferred claims, divided by number of common shares outstanding at end of period.

Booked (2) Slang for "recorded in the firm's accounts."

Bottom line (6) Commonly used term referring to reported net income, the bottom line of the income statement.

Budget In business, refers to a plan of activity expressed in terms of expected revenues and expenses or of expected cash flows. In governments, represents a legal ceiling on types and amounts of expenditure.

Business combination (14) The joining of two previously separate firms into a single accounting entity, whether by consolidation or statutory merger. Accounted for by following either the pooling or the purchase method.

Business entities (2) See Entity.

Call premium (12) The amount of excess over face or maturity value that a firm must pay if it elects to retire debt before maturity.

Callable bonds (12) Bonds that may be called (or retired) in advance of maturity.

Capacity assets (3) See Long-lived assets.

Capital assets For income tax determination, generally any asset in business use other than cash, receivables, inventory, and depreciable assets eventually sold for less than original cost. See Capital gains/losses.

Capital budgeting (7) Refers to the process of evaluating, selecting, and scheduling acquisition of long-lived assets, and of planning the financing of such acquisitions.

Capital gains/losses For income tax determination, the difference between original cost and sale proceeds of assets qualifying as capital assets. See Capital assets.

Capital invested Refers to resources (assets) invested in a firm by creditors and owners.

Capitalize (6) To record the effect of an expenditure as an asset rather than as an expense.

Capital lease (9) A lease that, in substance, is effectively a purchase financed by a 100 percent fully amortized loan. Leases that qualify as capital leases under specific FASB criteria are capitalized and shown as long-lived assets and as debt.

Capital lease obligations (12) A liability. The present value of remaining obligations under leases qualifying as capital leases. Capital lease obligations may be both current and noncurrent.

Capital markets Various markets to which a firm may turn to raise additional invested capital. Examples would be the bond markets and the stock markets.

Capital stock The ownership shares of a corporation.

Capital structure (3) The composition of a firm's noncurrent equities. The mix of long-term debt, and owner's equity.

Capital surplus An inferior term for additional paid-in capital.

Capitalized interest (11) Interest incorporated into the face value of a debt instrument (note or bond). Also, interest included as part of the cost of an asset.

Capitalized retained earnings (10) That portion of retained earnings reclassified to contributed capital (common stock and additional paid-in capital on common) as a result of a common stock dividend.

Cash (2) On hand and on deposit in banks.

Cash basis (income) (4) In come measured on the basis of cash revenues received less cash expenditures occurring in the same period.

Cash budgets/budgeting See Cash management.

Cash discount (6) A reduction in sales or purchase price as invoiced given for prompt payment.

Cash from operating activities (7) The amount of cash generated from ordinary business revenues, less expenses for the period, and including any changes within certain current assets and liabilities.

Cash flow statement See Statement of cash flow.

Cash generated in operations See Cash from operating activities.

Cash management The planning and control of cash receipts and disbursements within the firm. The objective is to avoid cash shortage and to temporarily invest excess cash.

Cash sales (4) Sales to customers for cash. Customer pays cash at time of purchase.

Catch-up depreciation A term used in this text referring to inadequate accumulated depreciation for current cost replacement resulting from prior years' depreciation expense being based on lower than current costs.

Certain liabilities (12) Liabilities that exist as a result of past transactions and where the amount and date of payment are specifically known.

Certified financial statements (1) Statements that are accompanied by an independent auditor's (CPA's) certificate, opinion, or report.

Change in accounting method See Accounting method.

Change of accounting estimate See Accounting estimate.

Charge/charging (5) Generally used to mean purchase on account. In bookkeeping, also used synonymously with debit.

Chart of accounts (5) A listing, usually by type and in useful account number sequence, of all specific accounts authorized for use in a given firm.

Close/closing (accounts) (5) In bookkeeping, the process at year-end of transferring the balances in all nominal or temporary accounts to the real or permanent balance sheet accounts. For example, all revenue, gain, expense, and loss accounts at year-end are closed to retained earnings (owner's capital) through a temporary income summary account.

CMA (1) Certificate in Management Accounting awarded by the National association of Accountants.

Collection of receivable (4) The receipt of cash in partial or full settlement of a claim that has previously been recorded as a receivable.

Common book value (stock) (10) See Book value of common stock.

Common stock (10) Shares in a corporation, usually voting shares, and representing a residual claim against assets after settlement of creditors' and preferred stockholders' prior claims.

Comparative analysis (3) In financial statement analysis, the comparison of one firm's statements with those of other firms or with industry norms. See Trend analysis.

Completed contract method (6) Refers to the timing of revenue and expense recognition, revenues and expenses are normally included in income determination only after the job is finished. Alternative to percentage of completion method.

Composite depreciation See Group depreciation.

Compound entry (5) A journal affecting more than two accounts concurrently.

Compound interest Interest based on principal and accumulated prior period interest.

Comptroller See Controller.

Conglomerate A parent corporation with subsidiaries in different and dissimilar lines of business.

Conservatism (1) A measurement principle under GAAP, wherein expenses and losses are recognized and reported when incurred or expected, but revenues and gains are not recognized and reported until they are realized or earned.

Consignment (8) Refers to inventory transferred from the owner (consignor) to another (consignee) for sale to third parties.

Consistency (3) A measurement principle under GAAP providing for continued use by a firm of the same accounting method or procedure once adopted. Consistency requires that changes in accounting method be infrequent and be justified by changing circumstances.

Consolidated financial statements (14) Financial statements prepared for an economic entity comprised of several legal entities a parent and its subsidiaries.

Constant dollar accounting (15) One alternative for accounting during periods of inflation wherein financial statements are revised to reflect the effects of general inflation by restating nonmonetary items in terms of constant dollars. See Constant dollars.

Constant dollars (15) In financial accounting, defined to mean dollars of equal average general purchasing power during the most recent year (period). In general usage refers to dollars of average general purchasing power as of some prior agreed base year.

Constant purchasing power dollars See Constant dollars.

Consumer price index An index prepared by the federal government indicating the effect of general inflation upon consumer purchasing power. See CPI.

Contingent liability (12) A potential liability, such as a pending lawsuit, which is dependent upon a future event (an adverse judgement being rendered) before becoming definite.

Contra account (2) Any valuation account whose balance is subtracted from another account on the balance sheet. Examples include allowance for bad debts, accumulated depreciation, receivables discount, bond discount, or treasury stock.

Contributed capital (10) The amount of capital permanently invested or contributed by the owners. Normally, indicated by the sum of any stock and additional paid-in capital account balances.

Control account (5) An account in the general ledger that shows the sum of the balances in individual subsidiary accounts kept in a subsidiary ledger.

Controller The title often used for the officer responsible for all accounting and sometimes all information systems activities within a firm.

Conversion index An index constructed from two representative prices, used to adjust groups of assets for changing price levels or replacement costs.

Convertible debenture (12) A debenture that may be exchanged by the bondholder for a given number of shares of capital stock.

Corporation (10) A legal entity authorized by a state to conduct business or perform some other function.

Correcting entry (5) An entry prepared to correct books for a posting error or a previously recorded erroneous entry.

Cost accounting system (1) The system for recording and allocating product costs to inventory and cost of goods sold.

Cost expiration (2) The recognition by accountants of a decline in future use fulness or eventual recoverable value of an asset. See Amortization, Depreciation, and Depletion.

Cost flow assumption (8) With respect to valuation of inventory and cost of goods sold in periods of changing prices (costs), an assumption or arbitrary assignment relating specific purchase costs to items sold regardless of actual physical flows of goods. Necessary when specific identification of each unit with its purchase cost is not economically feasible. Otherwise may still be desirable for financial reporting or tax purposes. See Average cost, FIFO, and LIFO.

Cost method (for investments) (11) The measurement normally applied to all investments except for voting common stock representing more than 25 percent of outstanding shares. The investment is carried at acquisition cost, and revenue is recognized only when received or receivable interest earned or dividends declared. Alternative to equity method.

Cost of goods sold (6) The cost of inventory that has been sold to customers or that has otherwise disappeared. Another term is inventory expense.

Cost of sales See Cost of goods sold.

Cost or market, whichever is lower See LCM.

Cost principle The measurement principle under GAAP that requires assets to be reported at adjusted original cost.

Coupon bonds (12) Bonds with dated coupons attached that are "clipped" by the bondholder and redeemed for interest due.

CPA (1) Certified Public Accountant.

CPI (15) The U.S. Urban Consumer Price Index prepared by the U.S. Department of Labor. Used in calculating constant dollar data. See Constant dollar accounting.

CR (or Cr) Abbreviation for Credit.

Credit (5) In general business usage, refers to the privilege of purchasing or borrowing, with payment or repayment at a later date. In bookkeeping, refers to the right side of an account or to the recording of an amount on the right side of an account.

Creditor (1) Someone who has a legal claim against the firm's assets resulting from supplying the firm with goods or services, lending funds, or some other commitment (customer claim for warranty, government claim for taxes, plaintiff claim for legally awarded judgment, or stockholder claim for dividends previously declared).

Credit sales (4) Sales to customers on account.

Cumulative preferred (10) One variation from simple preferred stock wherein any annual dividends that were passed (undeclared) in prior years must also be retroactively paid before any common dividends may be paid. See Arrears.

Current assets (2) Cash and any other assets that are expected to be converted into cash, sold, or consumed within a year or within the firm's normal operating cycle, whichever is longer. Includes prepaid items/expenses expected to expire within a year from acquisition.

Current capital lease obligations (12) The present value of amounts owed within one year (period) under leases qualifying as capital leases.

Current cost (2) The current costs of existing nonmonetary items in their present condition as distinct from their adjusted original or historical costs.

Current cost accounting (15) One alternative for accounting during periods of inflation wherein financing statements are revised to reflect the effects of specific inflation by restating nonmonetary items in terms of current costs. See Current cost.

Current liabilities (2) Those liabilities that are payable within one year or the firm's normal operating cycle, and which will require current assets in settlement.

Current notes payable (2) Promissory notes both maturing within one year (period) and requiring cash in settlement.

Current notes receivable (2) Promissory notes on which collection is expected within one year (period).

Current ratio (3) A measure of solvency. Total current assets divided by total current liabilities.

Current service costs (12) Necessary contributions to a pension fund to cover employee benefits accruing subsequent to the date of adoption of the pension plan. See Past service costs.

CVD (12) See Convertible debenture.

DDB See Double declining balance method.

Debenture (12) A bond that is not secured by a prior claim against specific assets or income.

Debit (5) In bookkeeping, refers to the left side of an account, or to the recording of an amount on the left side of an account.

Debt Any amount owed that is not executory.

Debt capacity (3) A term used in this text to refer to the amount of additional debt a firm could incur before reaching its debt ceiling (the maximum amount creditors would be willing to make available).

Debt conversion (7) The exchange of a creditor claim for an ownership claim. Usually the result of bondholders exchanging their convertible debentures for stock.

Debt ratio See Long-term debt ratio.

Debt refinancing (12) Arranging for the exchange of new debt for existing debt, with the new debt usually having a later maturity. In the case of bonds, may be called a refunding.

Declining balance method (9) An accelerated method of calculating depreciation or amortization by applying a constant percentage to the declining book value in successive periods. See Double declining balance method.

Deduction For income tax determination, an expense that is subtracted in the calculation of taxable income.

Deferral The carrying forward to a subsequent period for appropriate matching purposes of any item that will ultimately be recognized as revenue or expense.

Deferred charges (2) A long-lived asset. Expenditures capitalized as assets to be amortized over future years. Similar to prepaid items but having a useful life beyond that which would qualify for current classification.

Deferred income tax Usually a liability of indeterminate term (and, possible, amount) representing taxes postponed through timing differences resulting from the use of different income accounting methods in tax returns and financial statements. May be an asset representing taxes prepaid as a result of timing differences or recoverable because of loss carrybacks.

Deferred method One method of accounting for the investment tax credit. Following the deferred method, the amount of tax savings is taken as a reduction of fixed asset cost. Alternatively it may be established as a deferred credit and amortized along with the related asset's depreciation. The tax benefit is thus deferred and picked up in higher income over the asset's useful life through lower net depreciation charges.

Deferred revenue See Unearned revenue.

Deficit (10) Negative retained earnings shown as contra to stockholders' equity.

Depletion (9) The amortization reflecting use of wasting assets natural resources such as oil, minerals, and timber.

Depreciable base (cost) (9) The cost of a tangible long-lived asset to be depreciated over the asset's useful life: the cost less the estimated salvage value.

Depreciate/depreciation (2) The amortization of tangible fixed assets to allocate cost expiration over their useful life.

Discontinued operations (6) Activities or segments of a business that are being phased out. Revenues, gains, expenses, and losses related to discontinued operations are required by GAAP to be classified on the income statement, together with extraordinary items following income from operations.

Discounted present value (11) The value today of a future cash flow, or stream of cash flows, with the assumed interest cost or benefit eliminated.

Discount on notes receivable (11) A contra-asset representing interest capitalized into the face amount of the receivable, but not yet earned.

Discount on payables (12) A contra-liability representing interest capitalized into the face amount of the liability but not yet owed.

Discount on purchases or sales See Cash discount.

Discounting a receivable (11) The practice of borrowing funds in exchange for a receivable or with the receivable essentially serving as collateral for the loan.

Discount rate (11) The interest rate assumed in the calculation of discounted present value.

Discretionary resource exchanges A term used to apply to flows of resources into and out of a firm that occur as a result of management decisions and do not affect cash. Discretionary resource exchanges are reported in a separate schedule on The Statement of Cash flows as noncash investing and financing activities.

Distributable income (6) The amount of current income that, assuming adequate solvency, could be withdrawn by the owner(s) and still maintain the owner invested capital as variously defined.

Dividend (10) A distribution of income to corporate stockholders.

Dividends per share (13) The amount of dividends accruing to the benefit of the holder of a single share of the firm's currently outstanding stock.

Dividend yield (13) A measure of return on investment to the holder of preferred or common stock. The annual cash dividend per share divided by the market price per share and expressed as a percentage.

Dollar value LIFO (8) A method of maintaining inventory records wherein LIFO pools (including all similar items or even all or a firm's products) are layered and costed using composite price indexes instead of individual unit or weighted average unit costs.

Double declining balance method (9) A method of calculating depreciation or amortization using the declining balance approach and using a fixed percentage equivalent to twice the straight line percentage (the percentage that would be used following straight line depreciation).

Double entry (5) Any bookkeeping system where transactions and adjustments are recorded in such a way as to constantly maintain the balance sheet equality.

DR (or Dr) Abbreviations for Debit.

Drawing account (5) A temporary account used in partnerships and proprietorships to record individual owner withdrawals during the year (period).

Drawings (5) Assets withdrawn by an owner during the year.

Dual column statements Financial statements prepared showing two measurements for the same items. For example, statements prepared on an historical cost (GAAP) basis and also on a current cost basis could disclose the two measurements in two adjoining columns. Suggested as a means to facilitate changeover to a new measurement system if and when adopted.

Early debt retirement (12) The repayment or other extinguishment of debt prior to scheduled maturity.

Earned surplus An archaic and now improper term for retained earnings.

Earnings See Net income.

Earnings multiple (13) Stock prices are often expressed as a multiple of earnings per share; for example, "The XYZ Company is selling at ten times earnings."

Earnings per share (common stock) (13) Net income available for common stockholders (net income minus preferred dividend, whether or not declared) divided by the weighted average (by months) number of common shares outstanding.

EBIT (13) Earnings before interest and taxes. Used as the best earnings measure for calculating earnings on average assets employed independent of the method by which such assets are financed. In use, means earnings before Drawing interest, taxes, and any extraordinary or discontinued operation items.

Effective interest cost (11) The discount rate that would result in the net present value of all cash flows related to the investment being zero. The actual, as possibly different from stated, interest cost of the investment expressed as an annual rate.

Effective yield See Effective interest cost.

Eliminations in business combinations (14) Elimination of intercompany ownership, debt, profit, inventory, revenues, and expenses as part of the preparation of financial statements for business combinations. Necessary since such items do not reflect transactions with those outside of the combination.

Eliminations in consolidation See Eliminations in business combinations.

Encumbrance In state and municipal fund accounting, a reduction of otherwise available expenditure to reflect a commitment made.

Ending inventory (4) The amount of inventory on hand at the end of the year (period) which will be carried forward in the balance sheet to the following year.

Entity (2) In financial accounting for business, the economic organization or business unit being reported upon in the financial statement. May correspond to a legal entity in the case of a corporation, or represent an artificial entity in the cases of segments, proprietorships, partnerships, and consolidations. In nonprofit accounting, each separate fund is a distinct entity.

EPS See Earnings per share.

Equities (2) Claims against or sources of assets. The sum of all liabilities and owner's equity on a balance sheet.

Equity method (investments) A measurement principle required under GAAP for common stock investments where the stock held (between 20 and 50 percent) represents significant influence over the other firm. Following the equity method, the investor records, as an increase to investments and as revenue, its proportionate share of the investee's earnings each year. Any dividends are then treated as a collection of "future dividends receivable included in investments." Alternative to cost method.

Equity pickup (investments) (11) A term used in this text referring to the share of the earnings of another firm recognized as revenue and as an addition to the investments account under the equity method.

Estimated liabilities (12) Those liabilities where the precise amount and/or the specific creditor may not be known with certainty, but where the liability

is not contingent. Examples would be accruals of estimated warranty repair or replacement costs.

Estimated warranty costs (2) The statistically estimated liability for repair service or replacement of products already sold and still under warranty.

Exclusion For income tax determination, amounts of revenue that may be excluded in computing taxable income. Examples include interest on state and municipal bonds and portions of long-term capital gains.

Executory (2) Not yet completed or still to be performed.

Executory agreement (4) An agreement where neither party has completed any (or some portion) of intended performance, and therefore no claim arising out of past performance exists.

Exemption For individual income tax determination, a standard amount that may be subtracted in determining taxable income and that varies with the status of the individual.

Exogenous Outside of or resulting from occurrences beyond the control of the firm.

Expendable fund In nonprofit accounting, any fund whose assets, as distinct from revenues, may be wholly or partially expended in the current fiscal year.

Expenditure (6) The disbursement of cash or the commitment to pay cash for goods and services received. Does not include cash disbursed in settlement of previously incurred debt or as a distribution to/withdrawal by owner(s).

Expense (noun) (4) Any reduction in net assets (total assets minus total liabilities) not involving a distribution to owners. The use, expiration, or loss of an asset, or the incurrence of a liability, not matched by a new reportable asset. Unusual expenses are often referred to as losses.

Expense (verb) (6) To write off or record as an ultimate reduction of owners' equity anything other than an owner distribution/withdrawal.

External source (funds) (7) A place or group from which a firm might obtain working capital or other resources. The two possible external sources for any firm are long-term creditors and owners (stockholders).

Extraordinary items (6) An expense (loss) or revenue (gain) that is characterized as being unusual in nature for the particular business, not expected to recur in the foreseeable future, and material in amount. Extraordinary items are classified on the income statement following income from operations.

Face value (11) The stated amount due at maturity on a bond or note. May include all or a portion of required interest, or additional interest may be separately stated.

Fair market value (2) A price or cost arrived at in an arm's length transaction or exchange, where both parties may be assumed to be acting in their rational self interest.

FASB (1) Financial Accounting Standards Board.

FICA (12) Federal Insurance Contributions Act. FICA employee and employer taxes are more commonly known as "Social Security."

Fiduciary fund See Nonexpendable fund.

FIFO (8) First-in, first-out. One of several possible inventory cost flow assumptions. FIFO assumes that earliest costs apply to inventory sold (cost of goods sold) and most recent cost apply to ending inventory on hand.

Financial accounting (1) The accounting system for reporting the firm's financial position, income, cash flow, changes in owner's capital to outside investors and other interested parties using GAAP.

Financial leverage (13) Refers to the degree to which the firm is trading on equity; that is, the degree to which the firm is using "less costly" creditor and preferred stockholder invested capital to generate earnings for the benefit of the common stockholder.

Financial management The management of financial activities as distinguished from operations (operating management) and tax liabilities (tax management).

Financial statements (1) Those accounting reports required by GAAP the balance sheet, the income statement, the statement of cash flows, the statement of retained earnings (owner's capital), and the necessary footnotes thereto.

Financial structure See Capital structure.

Financial transaction (7) Transactions involved with investing and financial activities.

Financing activities (7) Those activities of the firm involved in raising of new capital, owner withdrawals, acquiring new debt, or the repayment of debt principal.

Financing lease See Capital lease.

Finished goods An inventory account for a manufacturer representing the cost of products completed and ready for sale.

First-in, first-out See FIFO.

Fiscal year (2) A 12 month reporting period for a firm. May or may not correspond to the calendar year.

Fixed assets An inferior term for property, plant, and equipment. Land, buildings, equipment, furniture and fixtures, and properties held under capital lease are all fixed assets.

Flow of working capital A change in the balance of net working capital.

Flow through method One method of accounting for the investment tax credit that reported all benefits of the credit in the year such benefits were realized as a reduction of the current year's tax provision.

Foreign operations (14) Operations of a firm or of its subsidiaries conducted outside of the United States. If foreign operations are significant, certain supplementary information concerning same must be disclosed along with the financial statements.

Franchise A legal right or privilege to use a name or to sell certain brand products or services.

Freight-in See Transportation-in.

Full acquisition cost (8) A term used to reflect the GAAP initial measurement basis for assets. All normal costs of acquisition are properly included in the overall cost of an asset.

Full disclosure (2) A GAAP requirement that all material and relevant information to the investor concerning the firm be included in the financial statements or footnotes thereto.

Fully amortized loan (11) A loan requiring periodic payments (usually equal in size) that include both interest on the unpaid principal. Under a fully amortized loan, the final periodic payment covers the remaining loan obligation.

Fully amortized mortgage (11) A fully amortized loan secured by real or personal property. See Fully amortized loan.

Fully depreciated (9) Refers to a depreciable asset whose book value is equal to its estimated salvage value, and for which no further expiration (depreciation) will be recorded.

Fully diluted EPS (13) The smallest possible EPS figure that would have been reported had all possible outstanding potential dilution (convertible securities, warrants, and options) taken place.

Fund (11) In financial accounting, an asset or group of assets set aside for a specific purpose and classified as noncurrent. In nonprofit accounting, a designated accounting entity for a specific purpose.

Fund accounting (1) An accounting system different from financial accounting, used for government, governmental institutions, and many nonprofit organizations.

Fund balance In nonprofit accounting, the amount of assets in a particular fund not claimed by creditors and not otherwise reserved.

Fund equation In fund accounting, different balance sheet equations are applicable to different types of funds since some funds do not have long-lived assets or long-term debt. The general form of the fund equation is: Current Monetary Liabilities + Long-lived Assets = Current Monetary Debt + Long-term Debt + Reserves + Fund Balance.

Funds (3) Usually used synonymously with net working capital. May also refer to cash or cash and cash equivalent.

Funds flow statement An ambiguous term that may refer to The Statement of Changes in Financial Position.

Funds from operations Working capital generated in operations the difference between fund revenue (revenue involving an inflow of working capital) and fund expense (expense involving a reduction of net working capital), less any gains on the sale of long-lived assets and before the effect of extraordinary and discontinued items.

Funds statement See Statement of Changes in Financial Position.

FUTA (12) Federal Unemployment Tax Act. Provides for employer payroll taxes to cover costs of worker unemployment compensation.

GAAFR Governmental Accounting, Auditing, and Financial Reporting. A statement of principles promulgated by the National Council on Governmental Accounting. May be viewed as GAAP applicable to governmental accounting.

GAAP (1) Generally Accepted Accounting Principles.

Gain (6) Excess of proceeds over costs for a specific transaction.

GAO The General Accounting Office of the federal government. The GAO reports to Congress and audits the executive branch.

General fund The fund used in an organization or institution to account for all resources and obligations not specifically assigned to another special purpose fund.

General inflation (15) Refers to the decline in the general or average purchasing power of the monetary unit or to the overall increase in prices, as distinct from the change in price for a specific item. See Specific inflation.

General journal (5) In bookkeeping for very small firms, the only journal in which all transactions, adjustments, and closings are first recorded. In the more common situation, the journal used for the original entry of transactions that are not appropriately recorded in special journals, for adjusting entries, and for closing entries. See Special journals.

General ledger (4) In bookkeeping, refers to the collection or group of all open/active accounts in the firm except for detailed subsidiary (subset) accounts.

General partner (10) An owner in a partnership who has unlimited personal liability for the debts of the partnership.

Going concern assumption (2) The measurement assumption underlying financial statements prepared in accordance with GAAP. It is assumed that the firm will continue in the same business at least as long as the longest of its debt maturities or the remaining useful lives of its existing assets.

Goods in process See Work in process.

Goods available for sale (4) Sum (cost) of beginning inventory and net purchases (gross purchases plus transportation-in minus purchase returns minus purchase discounts) during an accounting period.

Goodwill (2) The excess of the cost over the fair market value of the net assets acquired in a purchase of legal control over another firm.

Gross margin See Gross profit.

Gross profit (6) Net sales minus cost of goods sold.

Gross profit method (8) A method used for estimating ending inventory and cost of goods sold for interim reports and in the event of destruction of accounting records. Cost of goods sold is estimated as a percentage of sales, using the prior period's gross profit percentage. The gross profit method is not acceptable for measuring inventory and cost of goods sold in the annual financial statements.

Gross profit ratio (13) A measure of the overall markup maintained on items sold during the period. Gross profit divided by net sales and expressed as a percentage.

Gross purchases (8) The total of all invoice prices for inventory purchased during the period, not including transportation-in and before recognizing purchase discounts and purchase returns.

Gross sales (6) Total of all sales completed at invoiced prices before deductions for returns, allowances, and discounts.

Group depreciation (9) A method of calculating depreciation charges for assets taken as a group rather than separately.

Historical cost See Original cost.

Holding company (14) A firm whose primary activity consists of holding the controlling stock of other operating companies.

Holding gain (8) Difference between ending and beginning cost of assets held during a period of inflationary prices.

Horizontal analysis (6) An approach to analyzing financial data for successive periods in which the percentage change from the prior period is indicated for each separate item. See Trend analysis.

Imputed interest (11) The amount of interest that may be inferred as capitalized into the face value of an obligation and its present value discounted at an interest rate appropriate for the firm at the date the obligation was incurred.

Income (4) A change in the overall wealth of the firm as measured by total owner's (stockholders') equity other than that resulting from owner investment, donations received, or owner withdrawals (dividends). Revenues minus expenses for a given period. Synonymous with profit and earnings. Negative income is known as a loss. In tax accounting may be used referring only to revenue.

Income from continuing operations (6) All revenues and gains minus all expenses and losses during a particular period except those specifically qualifying as extraordinary, or related to discontinued operations, or the effect of accounting changes.

Income statement (1) The final statement reporting all revenues, gains, expenses, and losses for the period, together with EPS data.

Incremental borrowing rate (12) The interest rate that would need to be paid by the firm for its next material long-term secured loan. Used as the discount rate in the determination of the present value of obligations by a lessee under a capital lease.

Independent auditor (1) The CPA engaged to audit and give a professional opinion on the firm's financial statements and supporting systems.

Insolvent (3) Unable to pay obligations when they are due.

Installment basis (6) See Installment (sales) method.

Installment (sales) method A method of revenue and expense recognition where gross profit is recognized in proportion to collection of the related receivable

Installment sales Credit sales where payments are scheduled in specific amounts over a specific period usually exceeding one year.

Intangibles and other assets (2) A category of long-lived assets including intangible assets, deferred charges, assets involved in discontinued operations, goodwill, and miscellaneous long-lived assets.

Intangible assets Nonphysical long-lived assets, other than properties held under capital lease, which represent rights, claims, or other deferred prior expenditures. Examples include leasehold improvement, patents, trademarks, copy rights, franchises and good will.

Intercompany debt (14) Refers to obligations between a parent and a subsidiary which must be eliminated in consolidation.

Intercompany ownership (14) The controlling interest of a parent (included in the parent's investments account) in the common stock of the subsidiary (included in the subsidiary's stockholders' equity) which must be eliminated in consolidation. Any intercompany ownership of preferred stock or bonds would also be eliminated.

Intercompany transactions (14) Transactions occurring between a parent and a subsidiary which must be eliminated from the consolidated statements.

Interest The cost or rent for the use of money.

Interest bearing note (11) Promissory note with some or all interest explicitly stated separately from the face value of the note.

Interest only loan (12) In contrast to a partially or fully amortized loan, a loan requiring no repayment of principal until maturity. Periodic payments of interest may be required.

Interest payable (2) Interest already earned by creditors and not yet paid as of the statement date. Does not include future (executory) interest covering periods beyond the statement date.

Interim reports (statements) (14) Financial statements, often abbreviated, which are issued covering periods shorter than the firm's fiscal year or normal operating cycle.

Internal auditor (5) As distinct from the independent auditor, an employee of the firm responsible to examine and report on the firm's internal records, procedures, and controls.

Internal controls (5) Policies, procedures, and physical safeguards designed to assure proper financial reporting and conformance with overall company objectives.

Internal source (funds) (7) Assets or activities from which a firm's management may obtain for activities without having to seek additional capital from long-term creditors or owners. Internal sources may be thought of as including cash from operating activities and sale of long-lived assets.

Interperiod tax allocation (12) The apportionment of income tax to two or more periods on the basis of required payment (or benefit) dates. See Deferred income tax and Provision for income taxes.

Inventory (2) A current asset representing goods and materials on hand ready for sale (merchandise inventory or finished goods inventory) or which will be manufactured for sale to customers (raw materials inventory and work-in-process inventory). "To inventory" means to physically count items in stock or to calculate the cost of items on hand.

Inventory flow assumption See Cost flow assumption.

Inventory turnover (13) A measure of the rapidity of movement of average inventory through the operating cycle during the year. The cost of goods sold for a year divided by the average inventory on hand during that year.

Investing activities (7) Those activities of the firm involved in acquisition, investment, collection on the principal of notes receivable, and sale of assets.

Investment tax credit A direct reduction in business income tax liability granted to businesses by the government in the year of acquisition of qualifying long-lived assets to subsidize replacement (modernization) of capacity assets. Expired 12/31/86.

Investments and funds (2) A subclassification of long-lived assets including both noncurrent investments and also various special funds such as sinking funds.

Investors (1) All those who commit goods or services to a firm. Investors include both owners and creditors, specifically including suppliers and employees.

Invoice (4) A document registering a claim for payment as part of a sales transaction a "bill".

IRS Internal Revenue Service.

Issued shares (10) Shares of a corporation's authorized stock that have been distributed to stockholders.

ITC See Investment tax credit.

Item LIFO (8) A term used to identify LIFO systems wherein LIFO pools are not used and separate inventory records are maintained for each product. See LIFO pool.

Journal (4) In bookkeeping, a record in which entries reflecting transactions and adjustments are originally recorded in chronological order.

Journal entry (4) In bookkeeping, an instruction to change balances in certain accounts that is recorded in a journal to reflect the effect of transactions and adjustments.

Journalize (5) In bookkeeping, to record an entry in a journal.

Labor (cost) The cost of direct labor (hours worked in actual production) capitalized as part of product cost by a manufacturer.

Land (2) A long-lived asset recorded at full acquisition cost and usually not depreciated.

Last-in, first-out See LIFO.

Leasehold Property held under operating lease. Shown as intangible asset when prepaid lease is purchased from another.

Leasehold improvement (2) An improvement or betterment to property under operating lease that is attached to the property and reverts to the lessor upon expiration of the lease.

Ledger (4) A group or collection of accounts.

Legal capital (10) The amount of capital that is required by law to be retained in a corporation for the protection of creditors.

Lessee One who leases (uses) property belonging to another.

Lessor One who owns the property (landlord) under lease to another.

Leverage See Financial leverage.

Liability (2) A legal obligation to provide resources to another as the consequence of a past event.

LIFO (8) Last-in, first-out. One of several possible inventory cost flow assumptions LIFO assumes that most recent costs apply to inventory sold (cost of goods sold), and earliest costs apply to ending inventory on hand. Under LIFO, balance sheet inventory amounts may reflect very old, unrealistically low costs while cost of goods sold is reported in current costs.

LIFO index (8) An index number indicating current year inventory cost in relationship to base year cost. Used in calculating dollar value LIFO.

LIFO pool (8) A group of nearly identical products accounted for together under a LIFO system as if the pool was a single item.

Limited liability (10) Refers to the fact that corporate stockholders (owners) are not personally liable for the debts of the company, whereas proprietors and general partners, as owners of their companies, have unlimited personal liability for such obligations.

Limited partner (10) An owner in a partnership who has limited liability; he or she is not personally liable for the debts of the partnership.

Liquid (2) Readily convertible into cash.

Liquidate To sell an asset(s), other than to customers in the normal course of business.

Liquidation The payment of an obligation. Also, in the context of an entire firm, the conversion of all noncash assets into cash, the settlement of all liabilities, and the distribution of any remaining assets (after payment of liquidation costs) to owners.

Liquidation value (2) The expected net cash proceeds from sale, other than in the normal course of business.

Liquidity (3) Refers to the relative ease with which a firm's assets could be converted into cash and the ability to borrow additional cash. A firm with a high proportion of relatively liquid assets is said to have high liquidity.

Liquidity ratio See Quick ratio.

LCM (8) A GAAP requirement for inventory measurement and reporting, under which ending inventory must be written down below acquisition cost, if eventual net recoverable value is lower than original cost.

Long-lived assets (2) A balance sheet classification covering all assets other than those classified as current. Includes subclasses of Investments, Property and Equipment, and Intangible and Other. Synonymous with noncurrent assets.

Long-term debt (2) Obligations that will not require current assets in settlement within one year (period) of the balance sheet date. May include liabilities maturing within one year where arrangements have been completed to refund or refinance beyond a year. Synonymous with noncurrent liabilities.

Long-term debt ratio (3) A measure of the firm's capital structure and debt capacity. Total long-term debt divided by the sum of total long-term debt and owners' equity.

Loss The excess of expense or cost over revenue (proceeds) for a particular transaction; or an expiration, extinction, or disappearance of an asset with no matching revenue; or negative income for a period.

Lower of cost or market See LCM.

Major customer (14) A term designating a single customer (individual, firm, or government agency) responsible for 10 percent or more of a firm's revenue. GAAP require supplementary disclosure in the financial statements of data related to any major customers.

Managerial accounting (1) As distinct from financial accounting, refers to those systems and reports designed to provide accounting information for internal management use within the firm.

Manufacturing cost Factory costs (direct material, direct labor, and manufacturing overhead) included in arriving at full product costs for a manufacturer.

Manufacturing overhead Includes all manufacturing costs except direct labor and direct materials. Included as part of full product cost by a manufacturer.

Markdown (8) The amount of reduction of a retail selling price below that originally established.

Marketable securities (2) A current asset classification for readily salable securities held as temporary investments of excess cash (will normally be sold as cash is needed). Most current marketable securities are in the form of short term government paper and certificates of deposit. The term is also used to apply to stocks and bonds of other firms and governments that are readily salable. In this context, where marketable securities are held with no intention of selling within one year (period), they are classified as long-lived assets under investments.

Market price (of stock) (10) The price per share at which stock of a given firm may be traded or bought/sold.

Market value (of stock) (10) The current sale value of all stock owned by an individual in a particular firm. The product of the number of shares owned times the market price per share.

Markup (8) The difference between cost and the originally established selling price. Usually expressed as a percentage of selling price rather than of cost.

Matching principle (6) The GAAP income measurement principle involving the recognition of expenses on the income statement in the same period as that in which the related revenues are recognized (reported).

Material (cost) The direct cost of raw material included by a manufacturer as part of full product cost.

Materiality (3) The GAAP disclosure principle involving separate identification of only those events or statement effects where the result is significant in terms of total assets or net income.

Maturity The date when the principal of an obligation is due and payable. An obligation is said to mature when it becomes payable.

Meeting the payroll Slang for maintaining solvency.

Merge/merger (14) The joining of two firms into a single economic entity.

Minority See Minority stockholders.

Minority interest (14) An equity account appearing on a consolidated balance sheet representing the share in total assets attributable to stockholders who do not hold stock in the parent corporation. (See Minority stockholders.) Minority interests or claims against combined income are also subtracted on a consolidated income statement so that the bottom line will represent income available to the parent's stockholders.

Minority stockholders (14) Stockholders in a corporation where another individual or firm has controlling interest (more than 50 percent of the voting stock). Usually considered in the context of a subsidiary corporation that is not wholly owned. See Minority interest.

Monetary gain or loss (15) A firm's gain or loss in general purchasing power resulting from holding net monetary debt or net monetary assets during a period of general inflation (deflation). Monetary gain or loss is currently not measured and reported in primary financial statements.

Monetary items (2) Cash and other assets and liabilities where claims (receivable and payables) in terms of dollars and time are fixed.

Mortgage bonds (12) Bonds that are secured by a lien on property.

Multiple-step format (6) An acceptable and preferable approach to classifying revenues and expenses on an income statement, involving subtotals for such items as gross profit and operating profit (as distinct from income from operations).

Municipal accounting As distinct from financial accounting, a form of fund accounting covered by GAAFR and used by local governments.

NAA (1) National Association of Accountants.

Net assets (2) The share of total assets claimed or contributed by owners. Total assets minus total liabilities.

Net current assets Another term for net working capital. Total current assets minus total current liabilities.

Net income (4) The difference between the total of all revenue and gains and the total of all expenses and losses for a period. The "bottom line" of the income statements.

Net loss (6) Negative net income.

Net monetary items (16) The difference between monetary assets and monetary liabilities. A source of gain (net monetary debt) or loss (net monetary assets) in general purchasing power during periods of general inflation.

Net present value (11) The algebraic sum of the discounted present values of all cash inflows (pluses) and all cash outflows (minuses) related to a particular investment. A positive NPV indicates an investment return greater than the discount rate used and vice versa.

Net purchases (6) The net total acquisition cost of all merchandise or material acquired and accepted during the year. Gross purchases plus transportation-in minus purchase returns minus purchase discounts.

Net quick assets (3) Quick assets (cash, marketable securities, and net receivables) minus current liabilities.

Net realizable value (8) The amount of net cash that could result from the disposition and sale of an item. The selling price less costs of completion.

Net sales (6) Gross sales less sales returns, allowances, and sales discounts.

Net working capital (3) The amount of working capital in the firm representing a necessary long-term investment by creditors and owners. Equals total current assets minus total current liabilities. See Working capital.

Net worth (2) A possibly misleading term for a business sometimes used in place of net assets or owners' equity.

Nominal account (5) In bookkeeping, a temporary account opened each year (or period) to accumulate desired detailed information. Nominal accounts are closed at year-end to real or balance sheet accounts.

Nominal capital (15) Total owners' investment or net assets measured in nominal dollars. See Nominal dollars.

Nominal dollars (15) Dollars representing prices/costs at the time of original transactions not adjusted to reflect units of the same general purchasing power. Primary (conventional) financial statements report in nominal dollars.

Noncurrent assets See Long-lived assets.

Noncurrent capital-lease obligations (12) The present or principal value of amounts owed beyond one year (period) under leases qualifying as capital leases.

Noncurrent liabilities See Long-term debt.

Noncurrent notes payable (2) Promissory notes with maturities beyond one year (period) and those maturing within one year where arrangements have been completed to refinance or extend maturities beyond a year.

Nonfund resource pair A term used to identify pairs of discretionary resource flows that do not involve flows of cash. The most common pairs include: a portion of a new long-lived asset obtained in exchange for additional long-term debt; new long-lived asset acquired as a direct owner investment; and conversion of long-term debt to newly issued stock. Any of these pairs are included in the Statement of Cash Flows in Noncash Investing and Financing Activities.

Noninterest bearing note (11) A promissory note with all required interest capitalized in the face or maturity value. A note with no explicitly stated interest separate from the face value.

Nonmonetary item Any asset or equity that is not monetary.

Nonoperating revenue Revenue that is not derived from the firm's principal line(s) of business. Often designated as other revenue.

Note payable (2) An unconditional obligation in writing to pay a specific amount of cash at either a specific time or else on demand.

Note receivable (2) An unconditional obligation in writing by another to pay to the firm a specific amount of cash at either a specific time or else on demand.

NPV See Net present value.

NRV See Net realizable value.

NWC See Net working capital.

Objectivity (1) A GAAP measurement principle, which defers (perhaps indefinitely) recognition and recording of events and items until they can be reasonably measured in monetary terms, and the measurement is capable of independent verification.

Obligation Generally a debt to another. In federal government accounting the equivalent of an encumbrance in state and municipal accounting.

Obligations under capital leases (12) May appear as both a current and a noncurrent liability. The noncurrent portion represents the present value of all payments due beyond one year under capital lease agreements. The current portion represents the present value of the currently maturing payment(s) plus accrued interest charges (incorporated in the payment) which have been earned.

Off-balance-sheet financing (9) The practice of acquiring property under a long-term lease that may be (in substance) a purchase, but which does not qualify as a capital lease and is therefore accounted for as an operating lease.

On account (1) Term referring to a purchase or sale where the privilege of delayed payment is extended and no promissory note as evidence of the debt is required. Synonymous with the term "on credit."

On consignment See Consignment.

Operating Refers to revenues and expenses related to the firm's primary line(s) of business.

Operating cycle (2) The average time period involved for completion of the following series of events: Cash is converted into goods and services; goods and services are converted into receivables. Also known as the earnings cycle.

Operating expenses (6) All expenses and losses for the period except extraordinary items and those related to discontinued operations. Often more narrowly defined to exclude cost of goods sold, interest expense, losses, and provision for income taxes.

Operating income Used interchangeably with income from operations, or may be more narrowly defined to include only revenues and expenses directly related to the firm's primary line(s) of business and specifically excluding other revenue, gains and losses on financial activities, interest expense, and provision for income taxes (income tax expense). See Income from continuing operations.

Operating lease (2) Any lease not meeting FASB criteria for identification as a capital lease. Operating leases are accounted for as executory contracts no asset is recorded and the liability and associated expense are only recognized when earned by the lessor.

Operating management Term used to describe supervision of day-to-day activities related to the firm's primary line(s) of business, as distinct from financial and tax management activities.

Operating profit See Operating income.

Operating ratio (13) A measure of the firm's profitability. Net income (or preferably income from operations) divided by net sales and expressed as a percentage.

Opinion (auditor's) (1) The auditor's report attesting to the financial statements, or disclaiming attestation.

Opportunity costs The income that could have been earned or the cost that could have been saved, by using an asset in its next best alternative use. Opportunity cost is not measured and reported in financial statements.

Original cost (2) The initial or historical cost(s) of an asset.

Other revenue (income) See Nonoperating revenue.

Outstanding stock (10) Number of shares issued less any shares held as treasury stock.

Overhead (cost) See Manufacturing overhead.

Owner (partner) withdrawal The transfer of assets (usually cash) from the firm to the owner(s). In a corporation, referred to as a dividend.

Owner's capital (2) Refers to that portion of total assets in a firm contributed (claimed) by the single owner (proprietor) or one of the partners in a partnership (partner's capital). See Owners' equity.

Owners' equity (2) That share of total assets not claimed by creditors; total assets minus total liabilities. Same as net assets.

Paid-in capital in excess of par See Additional paid-in capital.

Parent (company) (14) A firm owning voting control (more than 50 percent of voting common stock) of another firm which is then known as a subsidiary.

Partnership (10) A firm with two or more owners (general or limited partners) that is not incorporated. A partnership must have at least one general partner.

Partnership agreement (10) The agreement among partners specifying the division of earnings, division of net asset upon dissolution, and procedures to be followed upon death or disability of a partner.

Par value (10) The face value or the face amount of a security (bond, note, or stock).

Past service costs (12) Necessary contributions to a pension fund to cover employee benefits granted retroactively from the date of first employment to the date of adoption of the pension plan. See Current service costs.

Payable (2) A debt owed by the firm to a supplier or creditor.

Percentage-of-completion method (6) An alternative method for reporting revenues and expenses on a specific project under which they are recognized in proportion to the percentage of completion of the project.

Period cost An expenditure, asset expiration, or incurrence of a liability regularly expensed in the period when incurred rather than being included as part of product cost or capitalized as another asset.

Periodic inventory (8) A system wherein inventory shipments to customers are not recorded perpetually throughout the year (period). Instead, cost of goods sold is calculated at year-end by taking a physical inventory to obtain ending inventory, and then subtracting ending inventory from goods available for sale.

Periodic LIFO (8) LIFO determined under the periodic inventory method, wherein all shipments are presumed to have occurred at year-end.

Permanent adjustment (4) A term used in this text to identify those end-of-period adjustments that are not reversed at the start of the next accounting cycle. Normally includes adjustments for asset expiration and amortization of discounts and premiums.

Permanent difference A difference between financial accounting income and taxable income which is permanent, that is does not result from a temporary timing difference in the recognition of revenue and expense.

Permanent holding loss (11) A loss of recoverable value on investments that is deemed permanent and is therefore recognized as a loss in the income statement for the current period.

Permanent investment (3) A term referring to the long-term invested capital in a business, the sum of long-term debt and owners' equity or, equivalently, the sum of net working capital and long-lived assets.

Permanent loss (11) See Permanent holding loss.

Perpetual inventory (system) (8) A system in which inventory accounts are regularly up dated to reflect both purchases and shipments.

Perpetual LIFO (8) LIFO determined under the perpetual inventory method, wherein purchases and shipments are recorded as they occur. Strict perpetual LIFO maintains records of LIFO layers as far back as the last stock-out. Modified perpetual LIFO begins each period with a single opening layer at average cost, and only layers purchases during the year.

Physical inventory Refers to physically counting and determining the cost of inventory on hand.

Placed on C.O.D. A condition wherein a customer is denied credit privileges and is required to pay for purchases "cash on delivery."

Plant assets See Property and equipment.

Point of sale (6) The point in time where a sale is completed and title transferred. Usually the point when revenue is recognized.

Pooling of interests (14) A business combination similar to the formation of a partnership instead of one where one firm purchases control of another. In a pooling, one corporation (parent) acquires substantially all of the voting common stock of the other (subsidiary) from the subsidiary's stockholders in exchange for newly issued stock in the parent. Both groups of stockholders therefore have continuity of ownership in the combination and no new basis for asset valuation is deemed to have occurred. See Purchase and Purchase treatment.

Pooling treatment (method) (14) Accounting for a business combination that qualifies as a pooling by adding together the book values of assets and equities of the separate firms and eliminating intercompany debt, ownership, and transactions. Under the pooling method, there are no asset revaluations or purchased goodwill.

Posting (4) Recording changes in ledger account balances as directed by journal entries.

Preemptive right (10) A stockholder privilege of first refusal on the purchase of any additional stock issued, which guarantees to the stockholder the option to maintain proportionate interest and voting rights within the corporation.

Preferred claim A specified dollar amount per share (established as part of the preferred stock agreement at the time of original authorization and issue) representing the prior claim against residual assets over common stockholders in the event of corporate liquidation. May also be increased by any dividends in arrears, if preferred is cumulative. See Arrears and Cumulative preferred.

Preferred stock (10) Stock with preference over common stock as to dividends and assets in liquidation. Preferred stock is usually nonvoting.

Prepaid items (2) Current assets that represent past expenditures for services to be consumed in the near future (normally within a year). Prepaid items can be thought of as current receivables for services rather than for cash.

Present value See Discounted present value.

Price earnings ratio (13) A relative measure of stock value. The market price per share of a firm's common stock divided by the most recent year's EPS.

Price level adjusted statements See Constant dollar accounting.

Primary EPS (13) Earnings per share calculated under the assumption that the more probable dilutions have occurred. Primary EPS will usually be less than simple EPS, and will always be equal to or greater than fully diluted EPS.

Primary financial statements (15) Those statements conventionally prepared under GAAP on an historical cost/nominal dollar basis. A term used to distinguish conventionally prepared statements from others that might be prepared on a constant dollar or current cost basis.

Principal value (11) That portion of a receivable or payable not representing interest. The face or maturity value of an interest bearing loan where no interest is capitalized into the face value. Alternately, where all or a portion of effective interest is not separately stated, the present value of all cash flows associated with the obligation discounted at an interest rate appropriate in the circumstances. See Imputed interest.

Prior period adjustment Certain balance sheet adjustments for errors in earlier periods made directly to the ending balance sheet and bypassing the income statement. GAAP narrowly restricts items that may qualify for treatment as a prior period adjustment.

Product cost As distinct from period costs that are expensed in the period when incurred, product costs are all costs that are included (capitalized) in inventory and not expensed until sale occurs.

Production basis A method allowed under GAAP for recognizing profit upon completion of production and prior sale. Restricted to items having ready markets such as precious metals and certain commodities.

Profit See Income.

Pro forma statements Hypothetical or projected statements.

Promissory note See Note payable and Note receivable.

Property, Plant, and Equipment (2) A subcategory of long-lived assets on the balance sheet for those that are tangible in nature and intended for use in the business rather than for sale. Includes: land; buildings, equipment, furniture, and fixtures (net of any accumulated depreciation); and properties held under capital lease (net of any depreciation).

Property and equipment turnover (13) A measure of the relative efficiency of capacity asset utilization. Net sales for the period divided by the average net property and equipment in use during that period. Can be interpreted as the number of sales dollars generated per dollar invested in plant and equipment.

Property under capital lease (2) A long-lived asset indicating the present value of all payments required for property effectively controlled under a long-term, noncancellable lease that qualifies as a capital lease.

Proprietary fund In fund accounting, a fund established for an operation to be run as a quasi-business usually intended to either break even or generate some "profit" to cover costs in other funds. Proprietary funds for operations dealing with the public are known as enterprise funds. Those for internal service known as internal service funds.

Proprietorship (2) A one owner business, or the owner's equity of a one owner business.

Provision for income taxes (6) An expense item (income tax expense) appearing on a corporation's income statement. Reported as the amount of tax for the period matched to income from operations. The tax calculation excludes the tax effect on extraordinary or discontinued operations items and assumes no timing differences between reported income and taxable income.

Purchase (14) A business combination where one firm acquires control of a subsidiary through giving the subsidiary stockholders cash or debt instruments in exchange for their voting stock. Proportionate voting interest in the new economic entity is not maintained by the original subsidiary stockholders who have been bought out. See Purchase method.

Purchase allowances (8) As distinct from discounts offered for prompt payment, a reduction of previously invoiced price granted in lieu of return for partially damaged or substandard merchandise or material. See Cash discount.

Purchase discount See Cash discount.

Purchase method (14) Accounting for a business combination that does not qualify as a pooling, by recording the acquired firm's assets at the amounts effectively paid for them, with any payment in excess of the fair market value of the assets acquired being classified as goodwill.

Purchase returns (8) Merchandise or material purchased from a supplier and recorded in the accounts, which are subsequently returned to the supplier for any reason. See Purchase allowances.

Purchased goodwill See Goodwill.

Quick assets (3) Assets that are cash or can quickly become cash. Includes cash, marketable securities, and receivables.

Quick ratio (3) A more rigorous measure of solvency than the current ratio. Total quick assets divided by total current liabilities. Also known as the acid test or liquidity ratio.

Raw material A current asset representing inventory on hand and not yet used by a manufacturer for use in manufacturing its product(s).

Real account (5) In bookkeeping, a permanent or balance sheet account, as distinct from a nominal or temporary account.

Realization principle (6) A measurement principle under GAAP wherein revenue is not recognized and reported as having been earned until all activities related to sale have been substantially completed and the collection of any receivable is reasonably certain. See Conservatism.

Receivables turnover (13) A measure of the rapidity of receivables collections. Net credit sales (or, alternatively, net sales) for a period divided by average net accounts receivable during that period.

Reconcile Explain the difference between two items.

Recovery deduction For income tax determination, the amount of depreciation taken for tax purposes following the ACRS. See ACRS.

Recovery percentage For income tax determination, the percentage of original cost taken in a particular year as a deduction for tax purposes following the ACRS. See ACRS.

Recovery period For income tax determination, the useful for tax depreciation purposes following the ACRS. Generally 3, 5, 10, or 15 years depending upon the type of asset. See ACRS.

Recovery property For income tax determination, property subject to depreciation for tax purposes following the ACRS. See ACRS.

Refunding (12) Refers to refinancing bonds payable with new bonds.

Replacement cost For an asset, the current cost of acquiring an asset of equivalent usefulness or productive capacity and in the same condition.

Reserve (10) As properly used in accounting, refers only to an appropriation of retained earnings. In accounting, a reserve is not a fund, it does not imply that assets have been set aside.

Reserve for depreciation An inferior term for accumulated depreciation.

Restricted retained earnings (10) An amount of retained earnings not legally available for dividends as a result of a contractual agreement with creditors or as a result of treasury stock acquired and not yet resold.

Retail inventory method (8) A method commonly used by retail firms for determining the cost of year-end inventory, and for estimating interim cost of goods sold. Inventory costs are estimated by using a percentage of selling price. The percentage is the weighted moving average percentage of goods available for sale at cost to goods available at selling.

Retained earnings (10) Net income not yet distributed to owners. The sum of net income/net loss since the start of the corporation, less all dividends declared (cash and stock).

Retroactive depreciation See Catch up depreciation.

Return on assets employed (13) A measure of income derived from assets used regardless of how such assets were financed. EBIT divided by average total assets for the period and expressed as a percentage. As a decimal can be interpreted as the number of dollars of EBIT generated per dollar invested in assets for such purpose.

Return on common equity (13) A measure of return on common stockholder investment. Net income (or alternatively income from operations) for the period minus any preferred (whether or not declared) divided by average common equity (total stockholders' equity minus preferred claims) and expressed as a percentage.

Return on investment The net earnings on any investment (rent, interest, dividends) for a period, divided by the average amount invested during the period.

Return on owners' equity (13) A measure of return on overall owner investment. Net income (or income from operations) divided by average total owners' equity for the period.

Revenue (4) An inflow of net assets not donated, or not resulting from additional owner investment. Assets received from the sale of goods or services to customers and from investments, or net assets received from the sale of long-lived assets.

Revenue collected in advance See Unearned revenue.

Reversing entry (5) In bookkeeping, an entry that is the opposite of a previous entry, and which therefore cancels the effect of the previous entry. Commonly used at the start of an accounting cycle to cancel the effect of certain year-end adjustments for the purpose of simplifying the current period's bookkeeping. See Temporary adjustments.

Sale (4) A revenue transaction where in goods or services are supplied to a customer in exchange for cash or a receivable.

Sales discount See Cash discount.

Sales returns and allowances (6) A contra-revenue item including merchandise returned for credit by a customer and reductions of previously invoiced prices made to compensate for damaged, defective, or otherwise undesirable items sold to and retained by the customer.

Salvage value (9) The net recoverable cost (actual or estimated) of tangible long-lived assets.

SEC (1) Securities and Exchange Commission.

Security A document evidencing ownership or indebtedness.

Segment (of a business) (14) A portion of a firm's operations representing a line of business or type of activity distinct from others.

Self liquidating (loan) A loan made for the purpose of acquiring assets such as inventory which, in the normal course of business, will be converted to cash within a year.

Separately reportable segment (14) A segment of sufficient size to require supplementary disclosure of certain summary data as required by GAAP.

Serial bonds (12) An issue of bonds with staggered maturities, part of the issue maturing on one date and other parts on other dates.

Service life See Useful life.

Shareholder (10) One who owns shares of a corporation's common or preferred stock. See Stockholder.

Short-term (Current) Due within one year.

Shrinkage (6) The difference between the balance of inventory shown after all transactions have been recorded and the actual quantity on hand. May result from theft, deterioration, loss, or clerical error.

Significant influence (11) The standard used to determine whether the equity method of accounting is required for investments in another firm's common stock. In the absence of evidence to the contrary, it is presumed that ownership of 20 percent or more of the voting common stock of a corporation represents significant influence over the amount and timing of that corporation's dividend declarations; and, therefore, the equity method or consolidated method (for over 50%) of accounting for such investments is required.

Single-step (format) (6) An alternative for the classification of revenues and expenses on the income statement, wherein all revenues are grouped and totaled, followed by all expenses, in arriving at income from operations before income taxes.

Sinking fund (11) A long-lived asset. A fund like a savings account established to accumulate cash or marketable securities for the retirement of long-term debt or for some other specific purpose.

Solvency (3) The ability to pay current obligations when due.

Sources of funds The places, activities, individuals, or groups from which a firm may obtain working capital for application on the Statement of Changes in Financial Position. Sources include operations, extraordinary gains, sale of long-lived assets, new long-term debt and new owner investment.

Special journals (5) In bookkeeping, a journal designed to simplify the initial recording of high volumes of repetitive transactions of the same type. Common special journals include those for Purchases, Cash Payments, Sales, and Cash Receipts. All transaction entries that are not provided for in special journals, and all adjusting and closing entries, are initially recorded in the general journal.

Specific (cost) identification (8) One of the methods for measuring inventory costs, wherein items are each identified with their acquisition cost and an inventory cost flow assumption becomes unnecessary.

Specific inflation/specific price changes (15) Changes in the prices of certain specific goods or services as distinguished from general price level changes averaged for all goods and services. Specific changes move independently, and can even move in the opposite direction of general inflation.

Stated value (stock) See Par value.

Statement of cash flow (7) A statement indicating cash generated from operating activities during the period, together with cash from investing activities and cash from financing activities during the period. The change in cash balance must be reconciled to beginning and ending cash. Investing and financing activities not involving cash are listed separately in a schedule accompanying the statement.

Statement of changes in financial position The predecessor to the Statement of Cash Flows discloses sources and applications of working capital (or cash), together with other major resource changes ("nonfund resource pairs") occurring during the year.

Statement of financial position Another term for balance sheet.

Statement of owner's capital (4) A supplementary financial statement required for a proprietorship. Reconciles owner's equity at the end of the period to the beginning balance.

Statement of partners' capital (10) A supplementary financial statement required for a partnership. Reconciles partners' equity at the end of the period to the beginning balance. A combined statement of owners' capital for each partner in a partnership.

Statement of retained earnings (10) A supplementary financial statement required for a corporation. Reconciles retained earnings at the end of the period to the beginning balance.

Statutory consolidation (14) Term used to describe a statutory merger wherein the single surviving corporate entity is a new corporation replacing both the merging companies.

Statutory merger (14) A business combination resulting from either a purchase or a pooling, where the resulting economic entity is organized as a single legal entity and a parent subsidiary relationship no longer exist.

Stock dividend (10) A pro-rata issuance and distribution of additional common stock at no cost to existing stockholders. Usually limited to less than 25 percent of the shares previously outstanding. Market value of stock issued is transferred from retained earnings to contributed capital accounts.

Stockholder (10) An owner of the capital stock of a corporation.

Stockholders' equity The owners' equity of a corporation.

Stock option (10) Right to purchase previously unissued shares of stock at a predetermined price. Often granted to executives as incentive compensation.

Stock right (10) A right to purchase previously unissued shares of stock at a predetermined price. Often given to existing shareholders in proportion to their preemptive rights as part of an additional issue/sale of stock.

Stock split (10) An issuance and distribution of additional shares of common stock on a pro-rata basis, to existing stockholders, at no cost to them. Generally limited to distributions in excess of 25 percent of shares previously outstanding and of any par or stated value per share. Has no effect on the dollar amounts shown on the balance sheet.

Stock warrant (10) A certificate granting a stock right. May be included as a "sweetener" along with the sale of other securities bonds or preferred stock.

Straight-line method (depreciation) (2) A method of allocating depreciation or amortization wherein the depreciable base (cost less salvage value) is expensed in equal amounts over the asset's useful life.

Subchapter S corporation For income tax determination, a corporation that qualifies and elects to be treated as a partnership for tax purposes under Subchapter S of the Tax Code.

Subsidiary (14) A corporation legally owned or controlled by another corporation (parent) which owns more than 50 percent of the subsidiary's voting common stock.

Subsidiary account (5) In bookkeeping, a detail account carried in a subsidiary ledger. The subsidiary account's balance is combined with other like balances in a control (summary) account carried in the general ledger.

Subsidiary ledger (5) In bookkeeping, a ledger combining like subsidiary accounts whose total is carried in a corresponding control (summary) account in the general ledger.

Sum-of-the-Years' digits method (9) One of the common methods of accelerated depreciation or amortization. The digits representing the useful life are summed and divided into the depreciable base to obtain a single portion. The asset is then depreciated each year by an amount equal to the year's digit times one portion, in inverse order the highest digit is used the first year. Also known as years' digits.

Supplies (2) A current asset representing the cost of items acquired for consumption within one year as part of normal business operations.

SYD See Sum-of-the-Years' digits method.

T-account (5) A symbol used as an instructional device to portray an account. Debits and credits are shown on the two sides, and the account title across the top.

Take-home pay (12) Employee earnings less taxes withheld and other payroll deductions. The portion of total wages or salary earned that is actually received in cash by the employee.

Tangible assets Assets that have physical form such as inventory, supplies, land, buildings, equipment, office furniture and fixtures, and properties under capital lease

Taxable entity For income tax determination, the entity subject to tax. The individual is the taxable entity for proprietorships, partnerships, and Subchapter S corporations. The corporation itself is the only business which is a taxable entity.

Taxable income (6) The amount of income used as the basis for computing income-tax liability. Taxable revenue and gains less tax deductions, exemptions, and exclusions. Rarely the same as reported income before taxes because of both permanent differences and timing differences in the measurement of income between the two systems.

Tax accounting (1) The accounting necessary to satisfy the IRS. The maintenance of adequate supporting records and filing of necessary tax returns.

Tax credit For income tax determination, amounts that may be subtracted from actual taxes otherwise payable as distinct from deductions subtracted in the computation of income subject to tax. Examples include the investment tax credit (ITC) and taxes on income paid to certain foreign governments.

Tax deduction An amount specifically allowable as a deduction from taxable revenue and gain in the determination of taxable income. Similar to an expense in accounting; however, something that may logically be an expense may not be allowable under the tax code as a tax deduction.

Tax management (1) The inclusion of "tax-consequence thinking" in the planning and execution of operating and financial decisions; and the preparation of required tax returns in such a manner as the minimize the firm's tax liability within the law.

Tax shield A tax deduction that does not involve a cash outflow in the current period. For example, depreciation serves as a tax shield.

Taxes payable (2) A current liability covering all current and past due obligations to governments for taxes that are unpaid as of the balance sheet date.

Temporary adjustment (4) A term used in this text to identify those end-of-period adjustments that are reversed at the start of the next accounting cycle. Normally includes adjustments for accruals of revenues and expenses. See Reversing entry.

Temporary holding loss (investments) (11) A loss in recoverable (market) value of a noncurrent investment that is deemed temporary; that is, it is expected to be recovered at or before the intended time when the specific investment is to be liquidated.

Temporary loss See Temporary holding loss.

Temporary revaluations of long-term investments (11) When a market loss is considered temporary, the investment is revalued (written down and written up but not above original cost) in the same manner as for current marketable securities. However, the corresponding temporary loss or gain is not intended in the determination of net income. Instead it is reflected in a special valuation contra account included within owners' equity, which may be called "temporary investments revaluation," or a similar title.

Terms of sale Any conditions relating to payment connected with a particular sale transaction. For example, the terms "2/10, N/30" offer a two percent cash discount if payment is made within ten days, and indicate full (net) payment is due within 30 days.

Times interest earned (13) A measure of a firm's potential ability to cover interest payments in the future. EBIT divided by annual interest expense.

Timing differences Differences between the period in which particular revenues and expenses are reported in the financial statements and in the firm's tax returns. The result of differences in requirements and electives between GAAP and the tax code. Usually result in the postponement of tax liability from the period otherwise due had there been no timing differences. See Interperiod tax allocation and Deferred income tax.

Total assets (2) The sum of all assets less all contra-assets appearing on the balance sheet.

Trade discount A reduction from a list price offered or given to customers of a given type, such as a wholesale discount. Note that trade discounts are not recorded in the accounting system. Sales are initially recorded net of trade discounts. See Volume discounts.

Trading on equity (13) An an owner, earning money on the capital invested by others (noncurrent creditors and preferred stockholders). The objective of desirable debt financing. See Financial leverage.

Trading profit The difference between the price obtained upon sale of an item and its current replacement cost—the currently repeatable gross margin.

Transaction (4) Any exchange between the firm and another entity that affects the firm's financial position as reported on its balance sheet.

Transaction entry (4) In bookkeeping, a term used in this text to distinguish between entries recording the effect of outside exchanges (transactions) and those other internal adjusting entries.

Transportation-in (8) The cost of delivering inventory from the supplier to the firm's selling locations (including to consignee's). If this cost is not already included in the invoice price for the inventory items, it is accumulated for inclusion in inventory-acquisition cost as part of net purchases.

Treasury stock (10) The portion of a firm's own stock previously outstanding that has been reacquired (repurchased) and is being held for some purpose. A firm's own treasury stock is not shown as an asset on the balance sheet. Instead it is classified contra within stockholder's equity.

Trend analysis (3) In financial statement analysis, a term referring to the comparison of data for a given period with like data for similar periods for the same firm.

Trial balance (5) In bookkeeping, a summarization of all account balances at a given time with debits and credits separately totaled.

Turnover The average number of times a particular asset, group of assets, or even total assets may be thought of as having been replaced during the year or period.

Unamortized cost The amount of original cost of an intangible asset that has not yet been amortized to reflect expiration.

Unappropriated retained earnings (10) The amount of retained earnings that the directors indicate may serve as a basis for future dividends, subject to any footnoted restrictions, and subject to adequate solvency to allow declaration of a dividend.

Unaudited financial statements (1) Financial statements that have not been subjected to an independent review by a CPA.

Uncollectible account (2) A customer receivable that cannot be collected in cash and is therefore worthless.

Uncollectible accounts expense See Bad debt expense.

Undepreciated cost The current book value of a tangible long-lived asset.

Undercapitalized Refers to a state wherein a firm has insufficient invested assets to support its current or intended level of activity.

Unearned revenue (2) A liability, usually current, for delivery of goods or services to customers or clients who have already paid cash in advance. Synonymous with unearned income.

Unit LIFO (8) A term used in place of specific identification LIFO to refer to all LIFO systems, other than dollar value LIFO, wherein separate cost records are maintained for individual products and/or LIFO pools.

Units-of-production method (9) One method of allocating useful life of a tangible long-lived asset. The useful life is determined in terms of a usage measurement (e.g., a truck may have 200,000 miles of useful life). Annual depreciation is based on the proportion of current year's usage to useful life, times the depreciable base.

Units-of-service method See Units-of-production method.

Unlimited liability (10) The legal status of proprietors and general partners (not true for limited partners or stockholders). Refers to full personal liability for all of the debts of the firm.

Unrealized holding gain (15) An increase in the net recoverable cost of an asset occurring during a period as a result of specific inflation where such increase has not yet been realized (validated) by sale to outsiders.

Unreported assets (9) A term used in this text to identify those self-developed intangible assets of a firm not presently considered capable of objective measurement, and therefore not included it its balance sheet. Examples include human resources or human capital, creditor goodwill, customer goodwill, and supplier goodwill.

Useful life (9) The period of time during which an asset is expected to provide benefit to the firm. The time period between date of acquisition and intended date of disposal.

Uses of funds See Application of funds.

Valuation account See Contra account.

Verifiability (1) A principle of GAAP supporting the goal of objectivity in financial reporting. Verifiability requires that the transactions recognized in the financial statements must be supported by physical evidence such as receipts, cancelled checks, and so forth.

Vertical analysis (6) In financial statement analysis, the translation of all amounts on a statement into percentages of a common base. Commonly used for income statements with net sales for the period and for balance sheets with total assets as the common base.

Volume discount A discount from list price offered for large quantity purchases. Like trade discounts, volume discounts are not recorded in the accounting system. Sales are initially recorded net of any volume discounts.

Voting stock (10) The capital stock of a corporation (usually only the common stock) which entitles the holder to vote for the election of directors and make other ownership decisions.

Voucher (5) In bookkeeping, an internal control document both authorizing and justifying the disbursement of cash (issuance of a check).

Wages payable (2) A current liability to employees for wages (and salaries) earned and unpaid through the statement date excluding all authorized payroll deductions.

Warranty A commitment by a seller to repair or replace products sold that prove defective within some stated time limit following the sale.

Wasting asset (9) A natural resource that is limited in amount and is therefore depleted as used. Examples include oil and gas, minerals, and timber.

Weighted average The result of summing the products of each item times the item's weighting factor, and then dividing this sum by the total number of items to determine the weighted average factor. The weighted average is distinct from the simple unweighted average which can prove misleading. See Weighted Average cost (inventory) and Earnings per share.

Weighted average cost (inventory) (8) One of several possible periodic inventory cost flow assumptions. Weighted average cost assumes that the cost of items shipped represented a proportional sample of the cost of all items available for sale. Ending inventory and cost of goods sold are priced at the same average cost per unit under this method. The average cost per unit is calculated by taking the sum of the products of (quantity times cost) for beginning inventory and net purchases, and then dividing by the quantity of items available for sale.

Wholly owned subsidiary (14) A corporation, 100 percent of whose voting stock is owned by another corporation (parent) where there are no minority stockholders.

Withdrawals Assets transferred from a firm to its owner(s).

Working capital (3) In general business use and in this text, refers only to total current assets. Total current assets less total current liabilities are defined as net working capital. Possibly because accountants are accustomed to using the term current assets, many accounting texts define working capital as current assets minus current liabilities, and therefore discard net working capital as redundant. Unfortunately, both definitions are in use, and you must be careful to identify the meaning of this term in each situation.

Working capital balance sheet (3) An abbreviated balance sheet convenient in financial analysis for focusing attention on the capital structure of the firm. A working capital balance sheet has total current liabilities eliminated from the assets and equities. It therefore consists of net working capital and long-lived assets balanced by long-term debt and owners' equity.

Working capital flow (7) Any transaction ⌐ adjustment that changes the balance of net work⌐ capital.

Working capital funds from operations See Funds from operations.

Work in process A current asset representing, for a manufacturer, inventory on hand at year-end in various states of partial completion. The cost of such items will therefore be greater than their material cost but less than the full cost of a finished product.

Worksheet (5) In bookkeeping, a multi-column working paper for convenient and rapid completion of the process of preparation of financial statements.

Write-off (down) To reduce an asset account balance, and charge either expense or loss.

Write-up To increase an asset account balance not reflecting an actual transaction involving a flow of funds. GAAP currently allow write-ups in only three situations. Investments representing significant influence are written up to recognize proportional share of the other's earnings in advance of dividends. Current marketable securities may be written up, but not above original cost, to reflect market value recovery of a previous write-down. Investments previously written down to reflect a temporary loss may be written up, but not above adjusted cost, to reflect recovery of market value.

Years' digits method See Sum-of-the-Years' digits method.

Yield method A method of amortizing the premium or discount related to bonds or other long-term receivables or payables. Under the yield method the book value of the investment or liability (face value plus unamortized premium or minus unamortized discount) is maintained at present value (discounted at yield rate at time of acquisition or issuance) each year to maturity. The yield method is preferred under GAAP, but straight-line amortization is acceptable where differences are not material. Also known as the interest method.

Zero bracket amount For individual income tax determination, the equivalent of a uniform standard deduction granted to each person and already incorporated in the tax tables. An individual may only claim qualifying deductions in excess of the zero bracket amount.

D

Solutions to
Odd-Numbered
Problems

Chart of Accounts

Current Montetary Assets
001 Cash
002 Current Marketable Securities
003 Current Notes Receivable
004 Accounts Receivable
005 Interest Receivable
006 Rent Receivable
007 Dividends Receivable
008 Subscriptions Receivable

Inventories
010 Inventory
011 Gross Purchases
012 Freight-in

Other Current Assets
020 Supplies
021 Prepaid Items

Investments and Funds
100 Noncurrent Notes Receivable
101 Bond Investments
102 Bond Investments Premium
103 Preferred Stock Investments
104 Common Stock Investments
105 Other Investments
106 Sinking Funds

Property Plant and Equipment
110 Land
111 Buildings
112 Equipment
113 Furniture and Fixtures
114 Properties Held Under Capital Lease

Intangibles and Others
120 Leasehold Improvements
121 Patents
122 Franchises
123 Copyrights
124 Trademarks
125 Deferred Charges
126 Goodwill

Current Contra-Assets
200 Discount on Current Notes Receivable
201 Notes Receivable Discounted
202 Purchase Returns and Allowances
203 Purchase Discounts
205 Allowance for Bad Debts

Noncurrent Contra-Assets
210 Discount on Noncurrent Notes Receivable
211 Discount on Bond Investments
212 Accumulated Depreciation, Buildings
213 Accumulated Depreciation, Equipment
214 Accumulated Depreciation, Office F & F

Current Monetary Liabilities
300 Current Notes Payable
301 Accounts Payable
302 Wages and Salaries Payable
303 Interest Payable
304 Taxes Payable
305 Rent Payable
306 Current Capital Lease Obligations
307 Dividends Payable
308 Other Current Liabilities

Nonmonetary Current Liabilities
310 Estimated Warranty Costs
311 Unearned Revenue
312 Deferred Gross Profit Installment Sales (current)

Long-term Payables
400 Noncurrent Notes Payable
401 Bonds Payable
402 Bond Premium
403 Noncurrent Capital Lease Obligations

Other Noncurrent Liabilities
410 Deferred Income Taxes
411 Deferred Gross Profit Install. Sales (noncurrent)

Proprietorship
500 Proprietor's Capital

Partnership
510 P artner A Capital
511 Partner B Capital
512 Partner C Capital

Contributed Capital (Corporation)
520 Preferred Stock
521 Additional Paid-in Capital, Preferred
522 Common Stock
523 Additional Paid-in Capital, Common
524 Additional Paid-in Capital, Treasury Stock
525 Additional Paid-in Capital, Stock Options
526 Common Stock Subscribed
527 Common Stock Distributable

Retained Earnings (Corporation)
530 Appropriated for Contingencies
531 Appropriated for Self Insurance
532 Appropriated for Treasury Stock
533 Appropriated for Dividend Restrictions
540 Retained Earnings (unappropriated)

Contra-Liabilites
600 Discount on Current Notes Payable
601 Discount on Noncurrent Notes Payable
602 Bond Discount

Contra-Equities
610 Temporary Loss on Investments
611 Treasury Stock
612 Deferred Compensation Expense

Revenues and Gains
700 Gross Sales
711 Interest Revenue
712 Rent Revenue
713 Gain on Current Marketable Securities
714 Gain on Sale of Investments
715 Gain on Disposition of Property and Equipment
717 Miscellaneous Revenue

Extraordinary and Discontinued Gains
720 Extraordinary Gain
721 Revenue Related to Discontinued Operations

Operating Expenses
800 Cost of Goods Sold
801 Wages and Salaries
802 Rent
803 Interest
804 Taxes (other than income)
805 Supplies
806 Insurance
808 Depreciation
809 Amortization
810 Warranty Repairs
811 Maintenance and Repairs
812 Utilities
813 Miscellaneous

Other Expenses and Losses
820 Loss on Current Marketable Securities
821 Discounts Lost
822 Loss on Inventory Revaluation
823 Loss on Investments
824 Loss on Disposition of Prop., Plant and Equip.
825 Loss on Disposition of Intangibles
830 Provision for Income Taxes

Extraordinary and Discontinued Losses
840 Extraordinary Loss
841 Expenses Related to Discontinued Operations

Contra-Revenue
900 Sales Returns and Allowances

Proprietorship Withdrawals
910 Owner Withdrawal

Partnership Withdrawals
920 Partner A Withdrawals
921 Partner B Withdrawals
922 Partner C Withdrawals

Dividends (Corporation)
930 Dividends Declared

Income Summary
950 Income Summary

EP 2.1

MR. SMITH'S PERSONAL NET
WORTH STATEMENT

Possessions:	Dollar Amount
Balance in personal bank account	$1,500
Personal possessions	500
Personal automobile	2,000
($4,000 cost, less $2,000 depreciation)	
Balance of cash on hand in business	100
Business accounts receivable	200
Cost of merchandise on hand for sale	800
Total possessions	$5,100

Debts:	
Amount owed on personal bills	$ 300
Amount owed by business to suppliers	400
Total debts	$ 700
Mr. Smith's net worth ($5,100 - 700)	$4,400

EP 2.3

JONES COMPANY ABBREVIATED
BALANCE SHEET
As of 12/31/XX

ASSETS

Current assets	$400
Long-lived assets	500
Total Assets	$900

EQUITIES

Current liabilities	$200
Long-term debt	300
Total Liabilities	$500
Owner's Capital*	**400**
Total Equities	$900

*Total Assets - Total Liabilities = Owner's Capital
$900 – ($200 + 300) = $400

EP 2.5 Cash
Marketable Securities
Receivables (Notes and Accounts)
Inventory
Supplies
Prepaid Items

EP 2.7 Current Assets:

Cash		$ 100
Accounts receivable	$ 400	
Less **allowance for doubtful accounts**	(50)*	350
Inventory		600
Prepaid items		200
Total Current Assets		$1,250

*$1,250 - ($100 + 600 + 200 + 400) = $(50)

EP 2.9

JOHNSON COMPANY BALANCE SHEET
CURRENT LIABILITY PORTION
As of 12/31/X2

Current notes payable	$ 600
Accounts payable	7,000
Wages and salaries payable	1,600
Interest payable	1,200
Taxes payable	800
Current capital lease obligations	1,500
Unearned revenue	2,400
Total Current Liabilities	**$15,100**

EP 2.11

SMITH COMPANY BALANCE SHEET
As of 12/31 X5

ASSETS

Cash		$ 100
Marketable securities		200
Accounts receivable	$ 340	
Less allowance for doubtful accounts	40	300
Inventory		400
Supplies		25
Prepaid items		**75**
Total Current Assets		$1,100
Investments		150
Land		250
Buildings	$ 425	
Accumulated depreciation, Bldg.	(75)	350
Equipment	$ 570	
Accumulated depreciation, Equip.	(120)	450
Intangibles		50
TOTAL ASSETS		$2,350

(SP 2.11 continued)

EQUITIES

Accounts payable	$ 125
Interest payable	35
Wages payable	**175**
Taxes payable	165
Total Current Liabilities	$ 500
Noncurrent note payable	400
Total Liabilities	$ 900
Owner's capital	**1,450**
TOTAL EQUITIES	$2,350

SP 2.13

MARY'S BOOKSTORE BALANCE SHEET
As of 12/31/X4

ASSETS

Cash		$2,835 [a]
Accounts receivable	$4,000 [b]	
Uncollectibles allowance	(80) [c]	3,920
Inventory		11,820 [d]
Total Current Assets		$18,575
Equipment	$5,000	
Accum. depr.	(3,200) [e]	1,800
Deferred charges		1,200 [f]
TOTAL ASSETS		$21,575

EQUITIES

Accounts payable	$ 3,905 [g]
Current notes payable	1,000 [h]
Total Current Liabilities	$ 4,000
Noncurrent notes payable	3,000 [i]
Total Liabilities	$ 7,905
Mary Chin, capital	13,670 [j]
TOTAL EQUITIES	$21,575

Notes:
- (a) $3,000 less uncleared checks ($270) plus cash on hand ($105).
- (b) Personal receivable ($2,000) excluded from firm's balance sheet.
- (c) 2% of $4,000.
- (d) $12,000 less cost of items withdrawn for personal use ($180).
- (e) Reflects expiration of four out of six years of useful life.
- (f) Classified as noncurrent since covers December 19X6 rent.
- (g) $4,000 less personal liability ($210) plus $115 previously unrecorded
- (h) $1,000 of notes identified as current.
- (i) Excludes $2,000 personal loon.
- (j) To balance.

EP 3.1 (a) Pamela was more solvent at the end of 19X3, as revealed by higher current and quick ratios.

(b) At the end of 19X3, Paul appeared to have a solvency problem with a quick ratio of only 0.54 and a current ratio of only 1.22.

(c) At the end of 19X3, Paul appeared to have more available debt capacity — a long-term debt ratio of 0.154 compared to Pamela's 0.360. At the some time both firms appeared to be equally liquid, each having an asset composition ratio of about 0.3.

EP 3.3 (a) Current ratio $\dfrac{\$70,000}{\$40,000} = 1.75$

(b) Quick ratio $= \dfrac{\$15,000 + 20,000 + 12,000}{40,000} = 1.18$

(c) Long-term debt ratio $= \dfrac{\$10,000}{\$95,000} = .105$

(d) Asset composition ratio $= \dfrac{\$30,000}{\$95,000} = .316$

(e) Yes, since Dowd's LTD ratio is only .105

(f) Let X = potential additional long-term debt at capacity:

$$\dfrac{\$10,000 + X}{\$95,000 + X} = .25$$

X = $18,000 (rounded)

EP 3.5 Betty Company: Yes.

Current ratio $= \dfrac{84,600}{47,000} = 1.8 > 1.7$

Quick ratio $= \dfrac{51,700}{47,000} = 1.1 > 1.0$

Mary Company: No.

Current ratio $= \dfrac{70,400}{32,000} = 2.2 > 1.7$

Quick ratio $= \dfrac{28,800}{32,000} = 0.9 < 1.0$

Mary Company's quick ratio is insufficient.

SP 3.7

PBFF COMPANY ABBREVIATED
BALANCE SHEET
As of 12/31/XO (000 omitted)

ASSETS

Current Assets:

Cash	$ 93
Marketable securities	27
Accounts receivable (net)	30
Inventory	56
Supplies	14
Prepaid items	12
Total Current Assets	$232
Long-lived assets (net)	495
TOTAL ASSETS	$727

EQUITIES

Current Liabilities:

Current notes payable	$ 20
Accounts payable	70
Other current liabilities	25
Total Current Liabilities	$115
Long-Term Debt:	
Noncurrent notes payable	177
Total Liabilities	$292
Owners' equity	**4 3 5**
TOTAL EQUITIES	$727

a) $435,000   b) $117,000   c) 2.02
d) 1.30   e) .289   f) .191

SP 3.9   a) $4,355 million   b) 1.39   c) 0.93
             d) .477   e) .157

SP 3.11 a) $1,767 million   b) 1.80   c) 1.03
             d) .322*   e) .210

* Long-term debt numerator includes all items
reported as noncurrent liabilities except outside
shareholders' interests that are included as part of
owners' equity.

EP 4.1

(1) NC	(10) IA and DA
(2) IA and IO	(11) IA, DA, and IL
(3) IA and DA	(12) DA, DL, and EXP
(4) IA and IL	(13) IA, DA, and IL
(5) NC	(14) IA and DA
(6) IA and REV	(15) IA and REV
(7) IA and REV	(16) DA and EXP
(8) IA and IL	(17) DA and DL
(9) IA and IL	(18) DA and DO

EP 4.3   (a) *See page AP 107*

(b) $7,200 as the income before adjustments.

(c)   ALBERTSON COMPANY BALANCE SHEET
BEFORE ADJUSTMENTS
As of 12/13/X1

ASSETS

Current Assets:

Cash	$6,800
Current notes receivable	4,000
Accounts receivable	500
Inventory	2,700
Supplies	600
Prepaid items	900
Total Current Assets	$15,500
Long-Lived Assets:	
Equipment	20,000
Leasehold improvement	6,000
TOTAL ASSETS	$41,500

EQUITIES

Current Liabilities:

Current notes payable	$ 4,500
Accounts payable	2,300
Total Current Liabilities	$ 6,800
Long-Term Debt:	
Noncurrent note payable	8,000
Total Liabilities	$14,500
Mike Albertson, capital	26,700
TOTAL EQUITIES	$41,500

EP 4.5   (A) NC
             (B) IA and REV
             (C) NC
             (D) DA and EXP
             (E) DA and EXP
             (F) DA and EXP
             (G) DA and EXP
             (H) DA and EXP
             (I) IL and EXP
             (J) IL and EXP

EP 4.7   (a) *See page AP 108*

(b) Income decreased as a result of adjustments by
$5,265.

EP4.3 (a)   BALANCE SHEET EFFECTS OF TRANSACTIONS FOR ALBERTSON COMPANY
For the year 19X1

Cash	$ +	20,000	(2)		Current Notes Payable	$ +	10,000	(4)	
	-	900	(3)			+	4,500	(11)	
	+	10,000	(4)			-	10,000	(12)	$ 4,500
	+	2,000	(6)						
	+	2,500	(10)		Accounts Payable	+	2,700	(8)	
	-	1,500	(11)			+	60	(9)	
	-	10,700	(12)			-	1,000	(17)	2,300
	-	12,000	(13)						
	-	4,000	(14)		Noncurrent Note Payable	+	8,000	(13)	6,800
	+	3,200	(15)						
	-	300	(16)						
	-	1,000	(17)						
	-	500	(18)	$ 6,800					
Current Notes Receivable	+	4,000	(14)	4,000	Mike Albertson, Capital				
Accounts Receivable	+	3,000	(7)						
	-	2,500	(10)	500					
Inventory	+	2,700	(8)	2,700					
Supplies	+	600	(9)	600					
Prepaid Items	+	900	(3)						
Equipment	+	20,000	(13)						
Leasehold Improvement	+	6,000	(11)						
TOTAL ASSETS				$41,500	TOTAL EQUITIES				$41,500

Income box (under Mike Albertson, Capital):

+	2,000	(6)
+	3,000	(7)
-	700	(12)
+	3,200	(15)
-	300	(16)	7,200

+	20,000	(2)	
-	500	(18)	19,500

EP4.7 (a)   BALANCE SHEET EFFECTS OF ADJUSTMENTS FOR ALBERTSON COMPANY
For the year 19X1

Current Assets:				**Current Liabilities:**			
Interest receivable	$ +	320	(B)	Accounts payable	$+	35	(J)
Inventory	-	1,850	(D)	Interest payable	+	650	(I)
Supplies	-	450	(E)	**Long-term Debt:**			
Prepaid items	-	900	(F)				
Long-Lived Assets:				**Owner's Equity:**			
Accumulated depreciated	-	1,200	(G)				
Leasehold improvement	-	500	(H)				

Income box (under Owner's Equity):

+	320	(B)
-	1,850	(D)
-	450	(E)
-	900	(F)
-	1,200	(G)
-	500	(H)
-	650	(I)
-	35	(J)	- 5,265

TOTAL CHANGE		$-4,580	TOTAL CHANGE			$-4,580

EP 4.9 (a)

BALANCE SHEET EFFECT WORKSHEET FOR ALBERTSON COMPANY
For the year 19X1
(π = net income, e = ending balance)

Cash					Current Notes Payable				
	$ +	20,000	(2)			$ +	10,000	(4)	
	−	900	(3)			+	4,500	(11)	
	+	10,000	(4)			−	10,000	(12)	$ 4,500 (e)
	+	2,000	(6)						
	+	2,500	(10)		Accounts Payable				
	−	1,500	(11)			+	2,700	(8)	
	−	10,700	(12)			+	600	(9)	
	−	12,000	(13)			−	1,000	(17)	
	−	4,000	(14)			+	35	(J)	2,335 (e)
	+	3,200	(15)						
	−	300	(16)		Interest Payable	+	650	(I)	650 (e)
	−	1,000	(17)						
	−	500	(18)	$6,800 (e)	Noncurrent Note Payable	+	8,000	(13)	8,000 (e)

Current Notes Receivable	+	4,000	(14)	4,000 (e)

Mike Albertson, capital

Accounts Receivable	+	3,000	(7)	
	−	2,500	(10)	500 (e)

	Income		
	+	2,000	(6)
	+	3,000	(7)
	−	700	(12)
	+	3,200	(15)
	−	300	(16)
	+	320	(B)
	−	1,850	(D)
	−	450	(E)
	−	900	(F)
	−	1,200	(G)
	−	500	(H)
	−	650	(I)
	−	35	(J)
	+	1,935	(π)

Interest Receivable	+	320	(B)	320 (e)

Inventory	+	2,700	(8)	
	−	1,850	(D)	850 (e)

Supplies	+	600	(9)	
	−	450	(E)	150 (e)

Prepaid Items	+	900	(3)	
	−	900	(F)	0 (e)

	+	20,000	(2)	
	−	500	(18)	
	+	1,935	(π)	21,435 (e)

Equipment	+	20,000	(13)	20,000 (e)

Accum. Depr. Equipment	−	1,200	(G)	(1,200) (e)

Leasehold Improvement	+	6,000	(11)	
	−	500	(H)	5,500 (e)

TOTAL ASSETS	$	36,920	TOTAL EQUITIES	$	36,920

EP 4.9 (b) Albertson's 19X1 income was $1,935.

(c) ALBERTSON COMPANY BALANCE SHEET
As of 12/31/X1
ASSETS

Current Assets:

Cash		$6,800
Current notes receivable		4,000
Accounts receivable		500
Interest receivable		320
Inventory		850
Supplies		150
Total Current Assets		$12,620

Long-Lived Assets:

Equipment	$20,000		
Less accum. depr.	(1,200)	18,800	
Leasehold improvement		5,500	
TOTAL ASSETS		$36,920	

EQUITIES

Current Liabilities:

Current notes payable		$ 4,500
Accounts payable		2,335
Interest payable		650
Total Current Liabilities		$ 7,485
Noncurrent notes payable		8,000
Total Liabilities		$15,485
Mike Albertson, capital		21,435
TOTAL EQUITIES		$36,920

EP 4.11

	Total Current Assets	Total Assets	Total Current Liabilities	Total Liabilities	Owner's Capital
(a)	$14,800	$25,800	$ 9,000	$ 13,500	$ 12,300
(b)	13,500	24,500	9,000	13,500	11,000
(c)	16,000	24,200	9,000	13,500	10,700
(d)	16,000	26,000	9,000	13,500	12,500
(e)	16,000	27,000	10,500	16,500	10,500

EP 4.13 (a) $500,000 total assets equal to the capital invested;

(b) $100,000 provided by short-term creditors;

(c) $ 25,000 provided by long-term creditors;

(d) $375,000 provided by owner;

(e) $215,000 shore of total assets represents profits accumulated and not yet withdrawn ($375,000 Owner's present share, less $160,000 capital originally contributed by owner).

SP 4.15 WADE COMPANY BALANCE SHEET
As of end of 19X3
ASSETS

Cash	$ 15,450
Marketable securities	35,000
Accounts receivable (net)	85,000
Inventory	110,000
Supplies	13,000
Prepaid items	5,000
Total Current Assets	$263,450
Investments	110,000
Land	60,000
Buildings and equipment	510,000
Less accumulated depreciation	(130,000)
Intangibles	28,000
TOTAL ASSETS	$841,450

EQUITIES

Accounts payable	$ 55,000
Wages and salaries payable	5,000
Taxes payable	10,000
Miscellaneous payables	3,000
Total Current Liabilities	$ 73,000
Noncurrent notes payable	175,000
Total Liabilities	$248,000
Owner's equity	593,450
TOTAL EQUITIES	$841,450

See page AP-110 for Balance Sheet Effect Worksheet

SP 4.17 (b) LUIGI'S AUTO PARTS
INCOME STATEMENT FOR PERIOD 2*

Net sales (7 and 8)		$40,000
Cost of goods sold (A)		24,000
Gross Profit		$16,000
Operating expenses:		
Wages and salaries (15 + I)	$ 8,000	
Rent and insurance (C and D)	4,800	
Utilities (16 and G)	300	
Supplies (B)	90	
Depreciation (E)	75	
Amortization of leasehold improvement (E)	250	13,515
Income from Operations		$2,485
Other expense: Interest (13, 14, and H)		1,116
NET INCOME		$1,369

The numbers and letters in parenthesis following account titles identify transactions and adjustments during the period that affected the account balance. Note that such references are for your clarification and do not appear on ncome statements in good form.

SP 4.15

BALANCE SHEET EFFECT WORKSHEET
Wade Company for 19X3
(b = beginning balance; e = ending balance; π = net income)

Cash	$ 10,000	(b)		Current Note Payable	$ 15,000	(b)	
	+ 50,000	(1)			− 15,000	(8)	0
	+ 540,000	(2)					
	− 10,000	(3)		Accounts Payable	90,000	(b)	
	+ 5,450	(4)			+ 400,000	(5)	
	− 5,000	(6)			+ 3,000	(7)	
	− 125,000	(8)			− 90,000	(8)	
	− 350,000	(9)			− 350,000	(9)	
	− 75,000	(10)			+ 2,000	(F)	55,000 (e)
	− 20,000	(11)					
	− 5,000	(12)	15,450 (e)	Taxes Payable	14,000	(b)	
					− 14,000	(8)	
Marketable Securities	25,000	(b)			+ 10,000	(H)	10,000 (e)
	+ 10,000	(3)	35,000 (e)				
				Wages and Salaries Payable	0	(b)	
Current Notes Receivable	5,000	(b)			+ 5,000	(G)	5,000 (e)
	− 5,000	(4)	0				
				Other Current Liabilities	6,000	(b)	
Accounts Receivable (Net)	75,000	(b)			− 6,000	(8)	
	+ 550,000	(1)			+ 3,000	(I)	3,000 (e)
	− 540,000	(2)	85,000 (e)				
				Noncurrent Notes Payable	175,000	(b)	175,000 (e)
Inventory	100,000	(b)					
	+ 400,000	(5)		Owner's Capital	600,000	(b)	
	− 390,000	(A)	110,000 (e)		− 6,550	(π)	593,450 (e)
Supplies	28,000	(b)					
	+ 5,000	(6)					
	− 20,000	(B)	13,000 (e)				

Income		
+ 600,000	(1)	
+ 450	(4)	
− 75,000	(10)	
− 20,000	(11)	
− 5,000	(12)	
− 390,000	(A)	
− 20,000	(B)	
− 5,000	(C)	
− 60,000	(D)	
− 12,000	(E)	
− 2,000	(F)	
− 5,000	(G)	
− 10,000	(H)	
− 3,000	(I)	
− 6,550	(π)	

Prepaid Items	7,000	(b)	
	+ 3,000	(7)	
	− 5,000	(C)	5,000 (e)
Investments	110,000	(b)	110,000 (e)
Land	60,000	(b)	60,000 (e)
Buildings and Equipment	510,000	(b)	510,000 (e)
Accum. Depreciation	(70,000)	(b)	
	− 60,000	(D)	(130,000)(e)
Leasehold Improvement	40,000	(b)	
	− 12,000	(E)	28,000 (e)
TOTAL ASSETS			$841,450

TOTAL EQUITIES $841,450

SP 4.17 (a)

BALANCE SHEET EFFECT WORKSHEET
Luigi's Auto Parts – Period 2
(b = beginning balance; e = ending balance; π = net income)

Cash	$	3,450	(b)		Current Notes Payable	$ 0 (b)	
	+	2,000	(1)			+ 3,000 (10)	
	−	6,000	(3)			− 3,000 (13)	$ 0 (e)
	−	50	(4)				
	−	1,900	(6)		Accounts Payable	13,000 (b)	
	+	11,000	(7)			+ 900 (2)	
	+	27,000	(9)			+ 25,000 (5)	
	+	3,000	(10)			+ 260 (16)	
	+	6,000	(11)			− 25,200 (17)	
	−	300	(12)			+ 40 (G)	14,000 (e)
	−	3,120	(13)				
	−	240	(14)		Wages and Salaries	600 (b)	
	−	7,850	(15)			− 600 (15)	
	−	25,200	(17)			+ 750 (I)	750 (e)
	−	1,500	(18)	$ 6,290 (e)			
					Interest Payable	0 (b)	
Accounts Receivable		40,000	(b)			+ 756 (H)	756 (e)
	+	29,000	(8)				
	−	27,000	(9)	42,000 (e)	Noncurrent Notes Payable	24,000 (b)	
						+ 6,000 (11)	
Inventory		35,000	(b)			+ 900 (12)	30,900 (e)
	+	25,000	(5)				
	−	24,000	(A)	36,000 (e)	Luigi Cavelli, Capital		

Income box:

	Income	
+	11,000	(7)
+	29,000	(8)
−	120	(13)
−	240	(14)
−	7,250	(15)
−	260	(16)
−	24,000	(A)
−	90	(B)
−	300	(C)
−	4,500	(D)
−	75	(E)
−	250	(F)
−	40	(G)
−	756	(H)
−	750	(I)
+	1,369	(π)

Supplies		50	(b)				
	+	50	(4)				
	−	90	(B)	10 (e)			
Prepaid Items		0	(b)			43,750 (b)	
	+	900	(2)			+ 2,000 (1)	
	+	6,000	(3)			− 1,500 (18)	
	−	3000	(C)			+ 1,369 (π)	45,619 (e)
	−	4,500	(D)	2,100 (e)			
Equipment		0	(b)				
	+	1,200	(12)	1,200 (e)			
Accum. Depr.—Equip.		0	(b)				
	−	75	(E)	(75) (e)			
Leasehold Improvement		2,850	(b)				
	+	1,900	(6)				
	−	250	(F)	4,500 (e)			
TOTAL ASSETS				**$92,025**	TOTAL EQUITIES		**$92,025**

(c) LUIGI'S AUTO PARTS - STATEMENT
OF OWNER'S CAPITAL FOR PERIOD 2

Luigi Cavelli, capitol, end of period I	$43,750
Additional investment	2,000
Net income	1,369
	$47,119
Less owner withdrawal	1,500
Luigi Cavelli, capital, end of Period 2	$45,619

(d) LUIGI'S AUTO PARTS - BALANCE
SHEET AS OF END OF PERIOD 2

ASSETS

Cash	$ 6,290
Accounts receivable	42,000
Inventory	36,000
Supplies	100
Prepaid items	2,100
Total Current Assets	$ 86,400
Equipment	1,200
Leasehold improvement	4,500
TOTAL ASSETS	$ 92,025

EQUITIES

Accounts payable	$ 14,000
Wages and salaries payable	750
Interest payable	756
Total Current Liabilities	$ 15,506
Noncurrent notes payable	30,990
Total Liabilities	$ 46,406
Luigi Covelli, capital	45,619
TOTAL EQUITIES	$ 92,025

(e)	Net working capitol	= $70,894
	Current ratio	= 5.57 to I
	Quick ratio	= 3.11 to I
	Long-term debt ratio	= .404
	Asset composition ratio	= .926

PP 5.1

		DR	CR
1)	No entry		
2)	Cash	20,000	
	Proprietor's Capital		20,000
3)	Prepaid Items	900	
	Cash		900
4)	Cash	10,000	
	Current Notes Payable		10,000
5)	no entry		

PP 5.1 (continued)

		DR	CR
6)	Cash	2,000	
	Sales		2,000
7)	Accounts Receivable	3,000	
	Sales		3,000
8)	Inventory	2,700	
	Accounts Payable		2,700
9)	Supplies	600	
	Accounts Payable		600
10)	Cash	2,500	
	Accounts Receivable		2,500
11)	Leasehold Improvements	6,000	
	Cash		1,500
	Current Notes Payable		4,500
12)	Current Notes Payable	10,000	
	Interest Expense	700	
	Cash		10,700
13)	Equipment	20,000	
	Cash		12,000
	Noncurrent Notes Payable		8,000
14)	Current Notes Receivable	4,000	
	Cash		4,000
15)	Cash	3,200	
	Sales		3,200
16)	Utilities Expense	300	
	Cash		300
17)	Accounts Payable	1,000	
	Cash		1,000
18)	Proprietor's Capital	500	
	Cash		500

PP 5.3

A)	No entry		
B)	Interest Receivable	320	
	Interest Revenue		320
C)	No entry		
D)	Cost of Goods Sold	1,850	
	Inventory		1,850
E)	Supplies Expense	450	
	Supplies		450
F)	Insurance Expense	900	
	Prepaid Items		900
G)	Depreciation Expense	1,200	
	Accum. Depr.—Equipment		1,200
H)	Amortization Expense	500	
	Leasehold Improvement		500
I)	Interest Expense	650	
	Interest Payable		650
J)	Utilities Expense	35	
	Accounts Payable		35

PP 5.5a

		DR	CR
1)	Cash	50,000	
	Accounts Receivable	550,000	
	Sales		600,000
2)	Cash	540,000	
	Accounts Receivable		540,000
3)	Current Marketable Securities	10,000	
	Cash		10,000
4)	Cash	5,450	
	Interest Revenue		450
	Current Notes Receivable		5,000
5)	Inventory	400,000	
	Accounts Payable		400,000
6)	Supplies	5,000	
	Cash		5,000
7)	Prepaid Items	3,000	
	Accounts Payable		3,000
8)	Current Notes Payable	15,000	
	Accounts Payable	90,000	
	Taxes Payable	14,000	
	Other Current Liabilities	6,000	
	Cash		125,000
9)	Accounts Payable	350,000	
	Cash		350,000
10)	Wages and Salaries Expense	75,000	
	Interest Expense	20,000	
	Maintenance and Repairs Expense	5,000	
	Cash		100,000

PP 5.5b

A)	Cost of Goods Sold	390,000	
	Inventory		390,000
B)	Supplies Expense	20,000	
	Supplies		20,000
C)	Insurance Expense	5,000	
	Prepaid Items		5,000
D)	Depreciation Expense	60,000	
	Accum. Depr.— Equip.		60,000
E)	Amortization Expense	12,000	
	Leasehold Improvements		12,000
F)	Utilities Expense	2,000	
	Wages and Salaries Expense	5,000	
	Taxes Expense	10,000	
	Miscellaneous Expense	3,000	
	Accounts Payable		2,000
	Taxes Payable		10,000
	Other Current Liabilities		3,000
	Wages and Salaries Payable		5,000

PP 5.7a

		DR	CR
1)	Cash	2,000	
	Proprietor's Capital		2,000
2)	Prepaid Items	900	
	Accounts Payable		900
3)	Prepaid Items	6,000	
	Cash		6,000
4)	Supplies	50	
	Cash		50
5)	Inventory	25,000	
	Accounts Payable		25,000
6)	Leasehold Improvements	1,900	
	Cash		1,900
7)	Cash	11,000	
	Sales		11,000
8)	Accounts Receivable	29,000	
	Sales		29,000
9)	Cash	27,000	
	Accounts Receivable		27,000
10)	Cash	3,000	
	Current Notes Payable		3,000
11)	Cash	6,000	
	Noncurrent Notes Payable		6,000
12)	Equipment	1,200	
	Cash		300
	Noncurrent Notes Payable		900
13)	Current Notes Payable	3,000	
	Interest Expense	120	
	Cash		3,120
14)	Interest Expense	240	
	Cash		240
15)	Wages and Salaries Expense	7,250	
	Wages and Salaries Payable	600	
	Cash		7,850
16)	Utilities Expense	260	
	Accounts Payable		260
17)	Accounts Payable	25,200	
	Cash		25,200
18)	Luigi Cavelli, Capital	1,500	
	Cash		1,500

PP 5.7b & c *Note: b = beginning or opening balance.*

001			Cash
b	3,450	3	6,000
1	2,000	4	50
7	11,000	6	1,900
9	27,000	12	300
10	3,000	13	3,120
11	6,000	14	240
		15	7,850
		17	25,200
		18	15,000
	6,290		

004			Accounts Receivable
b	40,000	9	27,000
8	29,000		
	42,000		

010			Inventory
b	35,000		
5	25,000		
	60,000		

020			Supplies
b	50		
4	50		
	100		

021			Prepaid Items
2	900		
3	6,000		
	6,900		

112			Equipment
12	1,200		

120			Leasehold Improvement
b	2,850		
6	1,900		
	4,750		

300			Currents Notes Payable
13	3,000	10	3,000

301			Accounts Payable
17	25,200	b	13,000
		2	900
		5	25,000
		16	260
			13,960

302			Wages and Salaries Payable
15	600	b	600

400			Noncurrent Notes Payable
		b	24,000
		11	6,000
		12	900
			30,900

500			Proprietor's Capital
18	1,500	b	43,750
		1	2,000
			44,250

700			Sales
		7	11,000
		8	29,000
			40,000

801			Wages and Salaries Expense
15	7,250		

803			Interest Expense
13	120		
14	240		
	360		

812			Utilities Expense
16	260		

PP 5.7d & e Luigi's Auto Parts Worksheet

Accounts	Before adjusting Debit	Before adjusting Credit	Adjustments Debit	Adjustments Credit	Adjusted Debit	Adjusted Credit	Income statement Debit	Income statement Credit	Balance sheet Debit	Balance sheet Credit
Cash	$ 6,290	$	$	$	$ 6,290					
Accounts receivable	42,000				42,000					
Inventory	60,000			(A) 24,000	36,000					
Supplies	100			(B) 90	10					
Prepaid Items	6,900			(C) 4,800	2,100					
Equipment	1,200				1,200					
Leasehold Improvements	4,750			(F) 250	4,500					
Accounts payable		13,960		(E) 40		14,000				
Noncurrent notes payable		30,900				30,900				
Owner's capital		44,250				44,250				
Gross sales		40,000				40,000				
Wages and Salaries Expense	7,250		750 (I)		8,000					
Interest Expense	360		756 (H)		1,116					
Utilities Expense	260		40 (G)		300					
Cost of goods sold			24,000 (A)		24,000					
Supplies expense			90 (B)		90					
Insurance expense			300 (C)		300					
Rent expense			4,500 (C)		4,500					
Depreciation expense			75 (E)		75					
Accumulated depreciation			(E)	75		75				
Amortization expense			250 (F)		250					
Interest payable			(H)	756		756				
Wages and salaries payable			(I)	750		750				
Total	129,110	129,110	30,761	30,761	130,731	130,731				

PP 5.7i & j

	ADJUSTING ENTRIES	PR	DR	CR
A)	Cost of Goods Sold	800	24,000	
	Inventory	010		24,000
B)	Supplies Expense	805	90	
	Supplies	020		90
C)	Insurance Expense	806	300	
	Prepaid Items	021		300
D)	Rent Expense	802	4,500	
	Prepaid Items	021		4,500
E)	Depreciation Expense	808	75	
	Accum. Depr.—Equipment	213		75
F)	Amortization Expense	809	250	
	Leasehold Improvements	120		250
G)	Utilities Expense	812	40	
	Accounts Payable	301		40
H)	Interest Expense	803	756	
	Interest Payable	303		756
I)	Wages and Salaries Expense	801	750	
	Wages and Salaries Payable	302		750

PP 5.7f & g   Luigi's Auto Parts Worksheet

Accounts	Before adjusting Debit	Before adjusting Credit	Adjustments Debit	Adjustments Credit	Adjusted Debit	Adjusted Credit	Income statement Debit	Income statement Credit	Balance sheet Debit	Balance sheet Credit
Cash	$ 6,290	$	$	$	$ 6,290				6,290	
Accounts receivable	42,000				42,000				42,000	
Inventory	60,000			(A) 24,000	36,000				36,000	
Supplies	100			(B) 90	10				10	
Prepaid Items	6,900			(C) 4,800	2,100				2,100	
Equipment	1,200				1,200				1,200	
Leasehold Improvements	4,750			(F) 250	4,500				4,500	
Accounts payable		13,960		(E) 40		14,000				14,000
Noncurrent notes payable		30,900				30,900				30,900
Owner's capital		44,250				44,250				44,250
Gross sales		40,000				40,000		40,000		
Wages and Salaries Expense	7,250			(I) 750	8,000		8,000			
Interest Expense	360			(H) 756	1,116		1,116			
Utilities Expense	260			(G) 40	300		300			
Cost of goods sold			24,000 (A)		24,000		24,000			
Supplies expense			90 (B)		90		90			
Insurance expense			300 (C)		300		300			
Rent expense			4,500 (C)		4,500		4,500			
Depreciation expense			75 (E)		75		75			
Accumulated depreciation				(E) 75		75				75
Amortization expense			250 (F)		250		250			
Interest payable				(H) 756		756				756
Wages and salaries payable				(I) 750		750				750
Net Income							1,369			1,369
Total	129,110	129,100	30,761	30,761	130,231	130,231	40,000	40,000	92,100	92,100

PP 5.7i & j

	CLOSING ENTRIES	PR	DR	CR
C1)	Sales	700	40,000	
	Wages and Salaries Expense	801		8,000
	Interest Expense	803		1,116
	Utilities Expense	812		300
	Cost of Goods Sold	800		24,000
	Supplies Expense	805		90
	Insurance Expense	806		300
	Rent Expense	802		4,500
	Depreciation Expense	808		75
	Amortization Expense	809		250
	Income Summary	950		1,369
C2)	Income Summary	950	1,369	
	Proprietor's Capital	500		1,369

PP 5.7i & j *Note: b = beginning or opening balance and* ✔✔ *indicates ending balance.*

001				Cash
b	3,450	3	6,000	
1	2,000	4	50	
7	11,000	6	1,900	
9	27,000	12	300	
10	3,000	13	3,120	
11	6,000	14	240	
		15	7,850	
		17	25,200	
		18	15,000	
✔✔	6,290			

004				Accounts Receivable
b	40,000	9	27,000	
8	29,000			
✔✔	42,000			

010				Inventory
b	35,000			
5	25,000			
	60,000	(A)	24,000	
✔✔	36,000			

020				Supplies
b	50			
4	50	(B)	90	
	100			
✔✔	10			

021				Prepaid Items
2	900			
3	6,000			
	6,900	(C)	300	
		(D)	4,500	
✔✔	2,100			

112				Equipment
12	1,200			
✔✔	1,200			

120				Leasehold Improvement
b	2,850			
6	1,900			
	4,750	(F)	250	
✔✔	4,500			

213				Accum. Depr.—Equipment
		(E)	75	
		✔✔	75	

300				Currents Notes Payable
13	3,000	10	3,000	

301				Accounts Payable
17	25,200	b	13,000	
		2	900	
		5	25,000	
		16	260	
			13,960	
		(G)	40	
		✔✔	14,000	

302				Wages and Salaries Payable
15	600	b	600	
		(I)	750	
		✔✔	750	

400				Noncurrent Notes Payable
		b	24,000	
		11	6,000	
		12	900	
		✔✔	30,900	

500				Proprietor's Capital
18	1,500	b	43,750	
		1	2,000	
			44,250	
		C2	1,369	
		✔✔	45,619	

700				Sales
		7	11,000	
		8	29,000	
C1	40,000		40,000	

800				Cost of Goods Sold
(A)	24,000	C1	24,000	

801				Wages and Salaries Expense
15	7,250			
(I)	750	C1	8,000	

PP 5.7I & j *(continued)*

803		Interest Expense	
13	120		
14	240		
	360		
(H)	756	C1	1,116

805		Supplies Expense	
(B)	90	C1	90

806		Insurance Expense	
(C)	300	C1	300

808		Depreciation Expense	
(E)	75	C1	75

809		Amortization Expense	
(F)	250	C1	250

812		Utilities Expense	
16	260		
(G)	40	C1	300

950		Income Summary	
C2	1,369	C1	1,369

PP 5.9   CASH RECEIPTS JOURNAL   Page No.

Date	Account Creditied	Post Ref.	Other Accounts CR	Accounts Receivable CR	Sales CR	Sales Discounts DR	Cash DR
1	Gross Sales				4,000		4,000
3	Mike Smith			3,000			3,000
4	Note Receivable		5,000				5,000
4	Interest on Note		400				400
6	Gross Sales				1,500		1,500
7	John Smith			1,000			1,000

PP 5.9   SALES JOURNAL   Page No.

Date	Invoice No.	Account Debited	Post Ref	Accounts Rec. DR and Sales CR
2		Leonard Schwarz		2,000
5		Sally White		2,500

PP 5.11   CASH DISBURSEMENTS JOURNAL   Page No.

Date	Check No.	Account Debited	Post Ref.	Sundry Accounts DR	Accounts Payable DR	Purchase Discount CR	Cash CR
1	747	Purchases		2,000			2,000
3	748	Equipment		6,000			6,000
5	749	Jones Manufacturing			2,000		2,000
6	750	Miscellaneous Expenses			440		440

PP 5.11   PURCHASES JOURNAL   Page No.

Date	Account Credited	Post Ref.	Accounts Payable CR	Purchases DR	Supplies DR	Sundry Accounts DR Account	Post Ref.	Account DR
2	Jones Manufacturing		8,000	8,000				
4	Smith Supply Company		4,500		4,500			
6	Clark Company		7,000			Equipment		7,000

EP 6.1   SNOW COMPANY INCOME STATEMENT
For the year 19X7 ($ in thousands)

Net sales		$400
Cost of goods sold		(220)
Gross profit		$180
Operating expenses:		
Wages and salaries	$100	
Insurance	4	
Interest	7	
Property taxes	6	
Depreciation	20	(137)
Operating Profit		$ 43
Other revenue:		
Rent		2
Income from operations before taxes		$ 45
Less provision for income taxes		(18)
NET INCOME		$ 27

EP 6.3   SNOW COMPANY INCOME STATEMENT
For the year 19X7 ($ in thousands)

Net sales		$400
Rent revenue		2
Total revenue		$402
Expenses:		
Cost of goods sold	$220	
Wages and salaries	100	
Insurance	4	
Interest	7	
Property taxes	6	
Depreciation	20	(357)
Income from operations before taxes		$ 45
Less provision for income taxes		18
NET INCOME		$ 27

EP 6.5

SNOW COMPANY BALANCE SHEET
As of 12/31/X7 ($ in thousands)

ASSETS

Current Assets:

Cash		$ 15
Accounts receivable		50
Inventory		36
Supplies		5
Prepaid items		8
Total Current Assets		$114

Long-Lived Assets:

Land		$30
Building	$140	
Accum. depr.—Bldg.	(60)	80
Equipment	$ 90	
Accum. depr.—Equip.	(45)	45
TOTAL ASSETS		$269

EQUITIES

Current Liabilities:

Accounts payable	$ 25
Wages and salaries payable	3
Total Current Liabilities	$ 28

Long-Term Debt:

Noncurrent notes payable	72
Total Liabilities	$ 100
John Snow, capital	169
TOTAL EQUITIES	$269

EP 6.7

(1) Neither	(8) Neither
(2) Neither	(9) Neither
(3) E, decrease	(10) Neither
(4) R, increase	(A) E, decrease
(5) R, increase	(B) E, decrease
(6) E, decrease	(C) E, decrease
(7) E, decrease	

E P 6.9

	Account	Statement	Effect on the account
(a)	Bad debt expense	E	Increase
	Accounts receivable	B/S	Decrease
(b)	Supplies expense	E	Increase
	Supplies	B/S	Decrease
(c)	Interest receivable	B/S	Increase
	Interest revenue	R	Increase
(d)	Rent receivable	B/S	Increase
	Rent revenue	R	Increase
(e)	Wages and salaries expense	E	Increase
	Wages and salaries payable	B/S	Increase
(f)	Telephone expense	E	Increase
	Accounts payable	B/S	Increase

EP 6.11 (a) SPRINGFIELD COMPANY SCHEDULE OF COST
OF GOODS SOLD
For the year 19X8 ($ in thousands)

Beginning inventory	$75
Net purchases	305
Goods available for Sale	$380
Less ending inventory	(80)
Cost of Goods Sold	$300

(b) SPRINGFIELD COMPANY INCOME STATEMENT
For the year ended 12/31/X8 ($ in thousands)

Net Sales		$ 710
Cost of Goods Sold		(420)
Gross Profit		$ 290
Less Operating Expenses:		
Wages	$202	
Rent	22	
Utilities	12	
Supplies	25	(261)
Net Income		$ 29

SPRINGFIELD COMPANY BALANCE SHEET
As of 12/31/X8 ($ in thousands)

Assets

Cash	144
Accounts Receivable	90
Inventory	80
Supplies	8
TOTAL ASSETS	$322

Equities

Accounts Payable	$128
Wages Payable	2
Unearned Revenue	50
Total Liabilities	$180
Owners' Capital	142
TOTAL EQUITIES	$322

SPRINGFIELD COMPANY STATEMENT OF
OWNERS' CAPITAL
for the yeear-ended 12/31/X8 ($ in thousands)

Owners's Capital 12/31/X7	$125
Net income for 19X7	29
	$154
less Owner Withdrawal	(12)
Owner's Capital 12/31/X8	$142

EP6.11 (a) BALANCE SHEET EFFECTS OF TRANSACTIONS FORSPRINGFIELD COMPANY
For the year 19X8

Cash	$ +	100	(b)		Accounts Payable		122	(b)
	+	200	(1)			+	425	(5)
	+	150	(2)			+	23	(6)
	+	390	(4)			−	450	(8)
	−	5	(7)			−	2	(11)
	−	450	(8)			+	4	(C)
	−	203	(9)			+	6	(E) 128
	−	16	(10)		Wages Payable		3	(b)
	−	10	(11)			−	3	(0)
	−	12	(12) 144			+	2	(D) 2
Accounts Receivable		70	(b)		Unearned Revenue	+	200	(1)
	+	450	(3)			−	150	(14) 50
	−	390	(4)					
	−	40	(13) 90		Owners' Capital		125	(b)
Inventory		75	(b)			−	12	(12)
	+	425	(5)			+	29	(π) 142
	−	420	(A) 80					
Supplies		5	(b)					
	+	23	(6)					
	+	5	(7)					
	−	25	(8) 8					

Income		
+	150	(2)
+	450	(4)
−	200	(9)
−	16	(10)
−	8	(11)
−	40	(13)
+	150	(14)
−	420	(A)
−	25	(B)
−	4	(C)
−	2	(D)
−	6	(E)
+	29	(π)

TOTAL ASSETS $322   TOTAL EQUITIES $322

EP 6.13   BAUER COMPANY

	Amount	Percent of Sales
Sales	$500,000	100.0
Cost of goods sold	$300,000	60.0
Wages and salaries	112,000	22.4
Rentals	20,000	4.0
Utilities	4,000	0.8
Insurance	6,000	1.2
Supplies	9,000	1.8
Depreciation on equipment	18,000	3.6
Amortization of leasehold improvement	22,000	4.4
Total Expenses	$491,000	98.2
Income from operations	9,000	1.8
Extraordinary loss on LLA	18,000	3.6
Extraordingary loss on inventory	27,000	5.4
Net loss	$(36,000)	7.2

SP 6.15   Bauer   60%
            Mason   55%

SP 6.17   ALBERT COMPANY BALANCE SHEET
              As of 12/31/X6 ($ in thousands)

ASSETS

Cash	$126
Accounts receivable	150
Inventory	85
Supplies	10
Prepaid insurance	4
Total Current Assets	$375
Land	40
Buildings	200
Accum. depr. on bldgs.	(140)
Equipment	175
Accum. depr. on equip.	(145)
Patents	9
Deferred charges	6
TOTAL ASSETS	$520

ALBERT COMPANY STATEMENT OF
OWNER'S CAPITAL
For the year ending - 12/31/X6 ($ in thousands)

Owner's capital 12/31/X5	$284
Add net income	27
Less withdrawals	(21)
Owner's capital 12/31/X6	$290

SP 6.17   ALBERT COMPANY BALANCE SHEET
(continued)   As of 12/31/X6 ($ in thousands)

EQUITIES

Accounts payable	$ 85
Taxes payable	14
interest payable	3
Wages payable	8
Total Current Liabilities	$ 110
Noncurrent notes payable	120
Total Liabilities	$ 230
Owner's Equity	290
TOTAL EQUITIES	$ 520

ALBERT COMPANY INCOME STATEMENT
For the year ending 12/31/X6 ($ in thousands)

Sales		$900
Cost of goods sold		(590)
Gross profit		$310
Operating expenses:		
Wages and salaries	$128	
Utilities	6	
Supplies	25	
Insurance	4	
Depreciation	24	
Amortization	2	
Interest	12	(201)
Operating Profit		$109
Loss on inventory		20
Loss on patent		(5)
Gain on sale of equipment*		2
Income from Operations Before Taxes		$ 86
Less provision for income taxes		34
Income From Operations		$ 52
Extraordinary earthquake loss		25
NET INCOME		$ 27

* Equipment cost $15,000 book value $5,000; thereforeaccumulated depreciation 10,000. Sale of equipment recorded by:

Increasing cash	$ 7,000
Decreasing accumulated depreciation	10,000
Decreasing equipment	15,000
Increasing gain on sale of equipment	2,000

SP 6.19 (a)

BALANCE SHEET EFFECT WORKSHEET
Luigi's Auto Parts – Period 4
(b = beginning balance; e = ending balance; π = net income)

Cash	$ 13,144	(b)		**Current Notes Payable**	$ 0 (b)	
	+ 15,000	(1)			+ 30,000 (K)	
	– 1,500	(3)			– 5,000 (L)	35,000 (e)
	+ 6,000	(5)		**Accounts Payable**	13,030 (b)	
	+ 34,500	(9)			+ 36,000 (6)	
	– 4,500	(11)			+ 200 (8)	
	– 12,000	(12)			+ 400 (14)	
	– 1,032	(13)			– 34,580 (16)	
	+ 110	(15)			+ 50 (E)	15,000 (e)
	– 34,580	(16)		**Wages and Salaries**	600 (b)	
	– 4,000	(16)	11,142 (e)		– 600 (12)	
					+ 900 (D)	900 (e)
Current Notes Receivable	0	(b)		**Interest Payable**	36 (b)	
	+ 2,000	(10)	2,000 (e)		– 36 (13)	0 (e)
				Taxes Payable	0 (b)	
Accounts Receivable	36,000	(b)			+ 700 (J)	700 (e)
	+ 50,000	(1)		**Unearned Revenue**	0 (b)	
	– 3,000	(2)			+ 6,000 (5)	
	– 500	(4)			– 4,000 (7)	
	– 34,500	(9)			+ 110 (15)	
	– 2,000	(10)	46,000 (e)		+ 110 (H)	2,000 (e)
Interest Receivable	0	(b)		**Noncurrent Notes Payable**	30,900 (b)	
	+ 100	(I)	100 (e)		– 30,000 (K)	900 (e)
Rent Receivable	0	(b)		**Luigi Cavelli, Capital**		
	+ 220	(H)	220 (e)			

Income box (Luigi Cavelli, Capital):

	Income	
+	65,000	(1)
–	3,000	(2)
–	1,500	(3)
–	500	(4)
–	4,000	(7)
–	11,400	(12)
–	996	(13)
–	300	(14)
–	4,000	(17)
–	38,000	(A)
–	190	(B)
–	4,800	(C)
–	900	(D)
–	50	(E)
–	250	(F)
–	75	(G)
+	330	(H)
+	100	(I)
–	700	(J)
–	5,000	(L)
+	1,769	(π)

Inventory	37,000 (b)	
	+ 36,000 (6)	
	– 38,000 (A)	35,000 (e)
Supplies	50 (b)	
	+ 200 (8)	
	– 190 (B)	60 (e)
Prepaid Items	300 (b)	
	+ 4,500 (11)	
	– 4,800 (C)	0 (e)
Equipment	1,200 (b)	1,200 (e)
Accum. Depr.—Equip.	(150) (b)	
	– 75 (G)	(225) (e)
Leasehold Improvement	4,250 (b)	
	– 250 (F)	4,000 (e)

Capital ending section:

	47,228	(b)
–	4,000	(17)
+	1,769	(π) 44,997 (e)

TOTAL ASSETS		**$99,497**	**TOTAL EQUITIES**	**$99,497**

LUIGI'S AUTO PARTS—INCOME STATEMENT FOR PERIOD 4*

Gross sales (1 and 7)		$69,000
Less sales returns and allowances		
(2, 3, and 4)		(5,000)
Net Sales		$ 64,000
Cost of goods sold (A)		(38,000)
Gross Profit		$ 26,000
Operating expenses:		
Wages and salaries (12 and D)	$12,300	
Rent and insurance (C)	4,800	
Interest (13)	996	
Utilities (14 and E)	350	
Amortization of leasehold		
improvement (F)	250	
Supplies (B)	190	
Depreciation (G)	75	
Property taxes (J)	700	(19,661)
Income from operations		$ 6,339
Other revenue		
Interest (I)	$ 100	
Rent (H)	330	430
Income before extraordinary item		$ 6,769
Extraordinary loss from lawsuit (L)		(5,000)
NET INCOME		$ 1,769

* The numbers and letters in parenthesis immediately following account titles identify all transactions and adjustments during the period that affected the account balance reported. Note that such references are for your clarification and would never appear on a final income statement in good form.

LUIGI'S AUTO PARTS - STATEMENT OF OWNER'S CAPITAL FOR PERIOD 4

Luigi Cavelli, capitol, end of Period 3	$47,228
Net income	1,769
	$48,997
Less owner withdrawal	4,000
Luigi Cavelli, capital, end of Period 4	$44,997

LUIGI'S AUTO PARTS - BALANCE SHEET AS OF END OF PERIOD 4

ASSETS

Cash	$11,142
Current notes receivable	2,000
Accounts receivable	46,000
Interest receivable	100
Rent receivable	220
Inventory	35,000
Supplies	60
Total Current Assets	$94,522
Equipment	1,200
Accum. depr. equip.	(225)
Leasehold improvement	4,000
TOTAL ASSETS	$99,497

EQUITIES

Current notes payable	$35,000
Accounts payable	15,000
Wages and salaries	900
Taxes payable	700
Unearned revenue	2,000
Total Current Liabilities	$53,600
Noncurrent note payable	900
Total Liabilities	$54,500
Luigi Cavelli, capital	44,997
TOTAL EQUITIES	$99,497

(c)	Net working capital	$40,922
	Current ratio	1.76
	Quick ratio	1.11
	Long-term debt ratio	.020
	Asset composition ratio	.892
	Gross profit ratio	.594

AP 6.21 20 percent completion:

Actual costs incurred	$ 25,000,000
Revised estimate of total costs	
($25,000,000 ÷.2)	$125,000,000
(a) Revenue recognized in 19X4	$ 28,000,000
(b) Expenses recognized in 19X4	25,000,000
(c) 19X4 gross profit	3,000,000

AP 6.23

	Year	Cash Collected	Percent Sales	Gross Profit Recognized*
(a)	19X2	200,000	10%	$80,000
(b)	19X3	500,000	25%	200,000
(c)	19X4	400,000	20%	160,000
(d)	19X5	300,000	15%	120,000
	TOTALS	1,400,000	70%	560,000

* Total potential gross profit $800,000.

PP 6.1a

		DR	CR
1)	Cash	300,000	
	Sales		300,000
2)	Accounts Receivable	900,000	
	Sales		900,000
3)	Sales Returns and Allowances	120,000	
	Cash		36,000
	Accounts Receivable		84,000
4)	Cash	75,000	
	Unearned Revenue		75,000
5)	Unearned Revenue	60,000	
	Sales		60,000
6)	Cash	20,000	
	Proprietors Capital		20,000
7)	Inventory	650,000	
	Accounts Payable		650,000
8)	Supplies	3,000	
	Cash		1,000
	Accounts Payable		2,000
9)	Prepaid items	4,500	
	Cash		4,500
10)	Equipment	15,000	
	Cash		4,000
	Noncurrent Notes Payable		11,000
11)	Leasehold Improvements	13,600	
	Cash		13,600
12)	Prepaid Items	37,500	
	Cash		37,500
13)	Inventory	30,000	
	Prepaid items		30,000
14)	Cash	15,000	
	Current Notes Payable		15,000
15)	Cash	766,000	
	Accounts Receivable		766,000

		DR	CR
16)	Marketable Securities	30,000	
	Cash		30,000
17)	Cash	25,000	
	Marketable Securities		20,000
	Gain on Marketable Securities		5,000
18)	Current Notes Receivable	40,000	
	Accounts Receivable		40,000
19)	Cash	38,150	
	Current Notes Receivable		35,000
	Interest Revenue		3,150
20)	Utilities Expense	20,000	
	Accounts Payable		20,000
21)	Accounts Payable	662,000	
	Cash		662,000
22)	Current Notes Payable	15,000	
	Interest Expense	700	
	Cash		15,700
23)	Wages and Salaries Payable	2,200	
	Wages and Salaries Expense	217,000	
	Cash		219,200
24)	Interest Expense	7,800	
	Cash		7,800
25)	Taxes Payable	1,000	
	Taxes Expense	1,400	
	Cash		2,400
26)	Taxes Payable	39,800	
	Cash		39,900
27)	Rent Expense	18,000	
	Cash		18,000
28)	Cash	1,300	
	Interest Revenue		1,300
29)	Owner Withdrawals	90,000	
	Cash		90,000

PP 6.1b

		DR	CR
A)	Cost of Goods Sold	675,000	
	Inventory		675,000
B)	Supplies Expense	4,000	
	Supplies		4,000
C)	Insurance Expense	1,500	
	Prepaid Items		1,500
D)	Depreciation Expense	32,000	
	Accum. Depr. Bldg		20,000
	Accum. Depr. Equip.		12,000
E)	Utilities Expense	800	
	Accounts Payable		800
F)	Wages and Salaries Expense	3,000	
	Wages and Salaries Payable		3,000
G)	Interest Expense	8,500	
	Interest Payable		8,500
H)	Taxes Expense	1,000	
	Taxes Payable		1,000
I)	Provision for Income Taxes	63,660	
	Taxes Payable		63,660
J)	Interest Receivable	2,100	
	Interest Revenue		2,100
K)	Amortization Expense	1,700	
	Leasehold Improvement		1,700
L)	Noncurrent Notes Payable	20,000	
	Current Notes Payble		20,000

PP 6.1k

		DR	CR
c1	Sales	1,260,000	
	Interest Revenue	6,550	
	Gain on Marketable Securities	5,000	
	Cost of Goods Sold		675,000
	Wages and Salaries Expense		220,000
	Rent Expense		18,000
	Interest Expense		17,000
	Taxes Expense		2,400
	Supplies Expense		4,000
	Insurance Expense		1,500
	Depreciation Expense		32,000
	Amortization Expense		1,700
	Utilities Expense		20,800
	Provision for Income Taxes		63,660
	Sales Returns & Allowances		120,000
	Income Summary		95,490
c2)	Income Summary	95,490	
	Properietor's Capital		95,490
c3)	Proprietor's Capital	90,000	
	Owner's Withdrawal		90,000

PP 6.3

		DR	CR
1)	Cash	100,000	
	Proprietor's Capital		100,000
2)	Inventory	50,000	
	Accounts Payable		50,000
3)	Rent Expense	400	
	Cash		400
4)	Cash	40,000	
	Sales		40,000
5)	Accounts Receivable	30,000	
	Sales		30,000
6)	Utilities Expense	200	
	Accounts Payable		200
7)	Wages and Salaries Expense	20,000	
	Cash		20,000
8)	Cash	25,000	
	Accounts Receivable		25,000
9)	Accounts Payable	30,000	
	Cash		30,000
10)	Supplies	5,000	
	Accounts Payable		5,000
ll)	Supplies Expense	2,000	
	Supplies		2,000
12)	Interest Expense	300	
	Interest Payable		300

PP 6.5

		DR	CR
*1)	Cash	15,000	
	Accounts Receivable	50,000	
	Sales		65,000
2)	Sales Returns and Allowances	3,000	
	Accounts Receivable		3,000
3)	Sales Returns and Allowances	1,500	
	Cash		1,500
4)	Sales Returns and Allowances	500	
	Accounts Receivable		500
5)	Cash	6,000	
	Unearned Revenue		6,000
*6)	Inventory	36,000	
	Accounts Payable		36,000
7)	Unearned Revenue	4,000	
	Sales		4,000
*8)	Supplies	200	
	Accounts Payable		200
*9)	Cash	34,500	
	Accounts Receivable		34,500
10)	Current Note Receivable	2,000	
	Accounts Receivable		2,000
*11)	Prepaid Items	4,500	
	Cash		4,500
*12)	Wages and Salaries Expense	11,400	
	Wages and Salaries Payable	600	
	Cash		12,000
*13)	Interest Expense	996	
	Interest Payable	36	
	Cash		1,032
14)	Utilities Expense	300	
	Accounts Payable		300
15)	Cash	110	
	Unearned Revenue		110
*16)	Accounts Payable	34,580	
	Cash		34,580

		DR	CR
* 17)	Owner Withdrawals	4,000	
	Cash		4,000
	ADJUSTING ENTRIES		
*A)	Cost of Goods Sold	38,000	
	Inventory		38,000
*B)	Supplies Expense	190	
	Supplies		190
*C)	Rent Expense	4,500	
	Insurance Expense	300	
	Prepaid Items		4,800
*D)	Wages and Salaries Expense	900	
	Wages and Salaries Payable		900
*E)	Utilities Expense	50	
	Accounts Payable		50
*F)	Amortization Expense	250	
	Leasehold Improvement		250
*G)	Depreciation Expense	75	
	Accum. Depr. Equipment		75
H)	Rent Receivable	220	
	Unearned Revenue	110	
	Rent Revenue		330
I)	Interest Receivable	100	
	Interest Revenue		100
J)	Taxes Expense	700	
	Taxes Payable		700
K)	Noncurrent Notes Payable	30,000	
	Current Notes Payable		30,000
L)	Extraordinary Loss	5,000	
	Current Notes Payable		5,000

EP 7.1 Wellmat Company

a) operating inflow
b) operating inflow
c) financing outflow
d) investing inflow
e) *
f) investing outlfow

g) financing outflow
h) investing inflow
i) operating outflow
j) *
k) operating outflow

* included in cash income

EP 7.3 Molina Company Schedule of Operating Activities (Direct Method) for the year-ended 12/31/X7

Cash Flow from operating activities:

Cash received from customers	$145
Cash paid for inventory	(80)
Cash paid for other operating costs	(11)
Cash paid for interest	(2)
Cash paid for taxes	(16)
Net cash provided by operating activities	$36

EP 7.5 Wahoo Company Statement of Cash Flows for the year ended 12/31/X1

Cash from operating activites:

Cash collected from customers	$1,150	
Cash paid for operating expenses	(1,055)	
Cash paid for interest	(7)	
Cash paid for taxes	(15)	
Net cash provided by operating activities		$73
Cash from investing activities:		
Payments for investments	(2)	
Proceeds from sale of land	25	
Proceeds from sale of equipment	7	
Payments for purchase of equip.	(27)	
Payments for leasehold improve.	(7)	
Net cash used in investing activities		(4)
Cash from financing activities:		
Proceeds from issue noncurr. note	3	
owner withdrawal	(3)	
Net cash from financing activities		0
Increase in cash		$69
cash balance 12/31/X0		40
cash balance 12/31/X1		$109

Schedule of operating activites:

Net income	$68
Depreciation	45
Amortization	15
Loss on sale of equipment	5
Increase in Accounts Receivable	(50)
Increase in Inventory	(20)
Increase in Accounts Payable	5
Increase in Taxes Payable	5
Net Cash from operating activities	$73

EP 7.7 Waterstreet Company Statement of Cash Flows for the year-ended 12/31/X9

Cash from operating activities:

Net income	$50	
Depreciation	25	
Amortization	26	
Increase in Accounts Receivable	(10)	
Increase in Inventory	(10)	
Increase in Other Current Assets	(10)	
Increase in Accounts Payable	20	
Decrease in Interest Payable	(16)	
Increase in Taxes Payable	6	
Net cash from operating activities		$81
Cash from investing activities:		
Payment to issue Note receivable	(10)	
Payment to purchase Investments	(3)	
Proceeds from sale of equipment	5	
Payment for purchase of equipment	(120)	
Net cash used in investing activities		(128)
Cash from financing activities:		
Proceeds from issuing Note Payable	65	
Proceeds from Owner investment	25	
Owner withdrawal	(5)	
Net cash provided by financing activities		85
Increase in cash		$38
Cash balance 12/31/X8		30
Cash balance 12/31/X9		$68

SP 7.9 Luigi's Auto Parts Statement of Cash Flows for Period 2

Cash from operating activities:

Net Income	$1,369	
Depreciation	75	
Amortization	250	
Increase in Accounts Receivable	(2,000)	
Increase in Inventory	(1,000)	
decrease in Supplies	40	
Increase in Prepaid Items	(2,100)	
Increase in Accounts Payable	1,000	
Increase in Wages Payable	150	
Increase in Interest Payable	756	
Net cash used in operating activities		($1,460)
Cash from investing activities:		
Payment for equipment purchase	(300)	
Payment for leasehold improve.	(1,900)	
Net cash used in investing activities		(2,200)
Cash from financing activities:		
Proceeds from issuing Note Payble	6,000	
Proceeds from owner investment	2,000	
Owner withdrawal	(1,500)	
Net cash from financing activities		6,500
Increase in cash		$2,840
cash balance Period 1		3,450
cash balance Period 2		$6,290

Noncash investing and financing activities:
Equipment was acquired in by issuing a noncurrent note payable for $900.

SP 7.11   Luigi's Auto Parts Statement of Cash Flows
for Period 4

Cash from operating activities:

Net Income	$1,769
Extraordinary loss	5,000
Depreciation	75
Amortization	250
Increase Notes Receivable*	(2,000)
Increase Accounts Receivable	(10,000)
Increase Rent Receivable	(220)
Decrease in Inventory	2,000
Increase in Supplies	(10)
Decrease in Prepaid Items	300
Increase in Accounts Payable	1,970
Increase in Wages Payable	300
Decrease in Interest Payable	(36)
Increase in Taxes Payable	700
Increase in Unearned Revenue	2,000
Net cash provided by operating activities	$1,998

Cash from financing activities:

Owner withdrawal	(4,000)	
Net cash used in financing activites		(4,000)
Decrease in cash		$(2,002)
Cash balance Period 3		13,144
Cash balance Period 4		$11,142

Noncash investing and financing activities:
A current note payable was issued for $5,000 in settlement of a lawsuit.

* The note receivable is an operating activity because it was accepted in settlement of a customer account

SP 7.13   Albert Company Statement of Cash Flows
for the year-ended 12/31/X6

Cash from operating activities:

Net Income	$27	
Extraordinary earthquake loss	25	
Depreciation	24	
Amortization	2	
Loss on Patent	5	
Gain on sale of Equipment	(2)	
Increase in Accounts Receivable	(18)	
Decrease in Inventory	25	
Decrease in Supplies	25	
Decrease in Prepaid Items	4	
Increase in Accounts Payable	10	
Increase in Interest Payable	3	
Increase in Wages Payable	8	
Decrease in Other Current Liabilities	(27)	
Net cash provided by operating activities		$85

Cash from investing activities:

Payment on repair of building	(25)	
Proceeds on Sale of Equipment	7	
Net cash used in investing activities		(18)

Cash from financing activities:

Owner withdrawal	(21)	
Net cash used in financing activities		(21)
Increase in cash		$46
Cash balance 12/31/X5		80
Cash balance 12/31/X6		$126

Noncash investing and financing activities:
A loss on patents of $5 was taken during the year.

PP 7.1 *(see next page)*

PP 7.3		**DR**	**CR**
a)	Operating activity: net income	68	
	Owner's capital		68
b)	Operating activity: Depreciation expense	45	
	Accumulated Depreciation, Bldg.		20
	Accumulated Depreciation, Equip.		25
c)	Operating activity: Amortization expense	15	
	Leasehold Improvement		15
d)	Operating activity: loss on equipment	5	
	Accumulated depreciation, Equip.	5	
	Investing activity: Proceeds Sale of Equip.	7	
	Equipment		17
e)	Operating activity: increase Accts Rec.	50	
	Accounts Receivable		50
f)	Operating activity: increase Inventory	20	
	Inventory		20
g)	Operating activity: increase Accts Payable	5	
	Accounts Payable		5
h)	Operating activity: increase Taxes Payable	5	
	Taxes Payable		5
i)	Investments	2	
	Investing activity: Payment on Invest.		2
j)	Investing activity: Proceeds sale of land	25	
	Land		25

(continued after PP 7.1)

PP 7.1
Wahoo Company Cash Flow Worksheet
for the year-ended 12/31/X1

	12/31/X0	12/31/X1	change	Debit		Credit	
Debits:							
Cash	40	109	69	(o)	69		
Accounts Receivable	200	250	50	(e)	50		
Inventory	20	40	20	(f)	20		
Investments	90	92	2	(i)	2		
Land	105	80	(25)			(j)	25
Buildings	200	200	—				
Equipment	150	160	10	(k)	27	(d)	17
Leasehold improvement	80	72	(8)	(l)	7	(c)	15
totals	885	1,003	118				
Credits:							
Accum. depr. building	120	140	20			(b)	20
Accum. depr. equipment	50	70	20	(d)	5	(b)	25
Accounts Payable	95	100	5			(g)	5
Wages Payable	5	5	—				
Taxes Payable	30	35	5			(h)	5
noncurrent Note Payable	160	163	3			(m)	3
Owner's capital	425	490	65	(n)	3	(a)	68
totals	885	1,003	118				
Cash flow from operating activities:							
Net Income				(a)	68		
Depreciation				(b)	45		
Amortization				(c)	15		
loss on equipment				(d)	5		
increase in accounts receivable						(e)	50
increase in inventory						(f)	20
increase in accounts payable				(g)	5		
increase in taxes payable				(h)	5		
Cash flow from investing activities:							
payment on investment						(i)	2
proceeds sale of land				(j)	25		
payment for purchase of equipment						(k)	27
payment for leasehold improvement						(l)	7
Cash flow from financing activities:							
proceeds issue noncurrent note payable				(m)	3		
owner withdrawal						(n)	3
Net increase in cash						(o)	69
totals					361		361

(PP7.3 *continued***)**

k) Equipment   27
   Investing activity: Payment for equip.   27

l) Leasehold improvement   7
   Investing activity: payment for
     leasehold improv.   7

m) Financing activity: Proceeds issue
     note payable   3
   Noncurrent Note Payable   3

n) Owner's capital   3
   Financing activity: owner withdrawal   3

o) Cash   69
   Net increase in cash   69

EP 8.1

Gross purchases	$473,000
Transportation-in	27,000
Purchase returns	(32,000)
Purchase discounts and allowances	(8,000)
Net purchases	$460.000

EP 8.3

Beginning inventory		$125,000
Net Purchases:		
Gross Purchases	$590,00	
Purchase Returns	(40,000)	
Purchase Discounts		
and Allowances	(10,000)	
Transportation-in	**35,000**	575,000
Goods Available for Sale		**$700,000**
Ending Inventory		(140,000)
Cost of Goods Sold		$560,000

EP 8.5

	Units	Cost	Total
Beginning inventory	200	30	$ 6,000
Purchases: July	300	35	10,500
November	150	40	6,000
January	200	50	10,000
Goods available	850		$32,500
Ending inventory	(300)		(11,472)
Cost of goods sold	550		$21,028

EP 8.7

	Units	Unit cost	Value
Beginning inventory	200	$30	$ 6,000
July purchase	300	35	10,500
Available	500		16,500 ÷ 500 = $33.00
September shipment	(250)		
October shipment	(100)		
Inventory remaining	150	33	$4,950
November purchase	150	40	6,000
Available	300	$36.50	10,950 ÷ 300 = $36.50
December shipment	(200)		
Ending Inventory	100	36.50	3,650
Goods Available for Sale	650		22,500
Ending Inventory	(100)		(3,650)
Cost of Goods Sold	550		$18,850

EP 8.9

B's cost of goods sold (FIFO)	$160,000
B's cost of goods sold (LIFO)	205,000
Increase in expense under LIFO	45,000
B's income under FIFO	$ 70,000
Less increased LIFO expense	45,000
B's income under LIFO	$ 25,000

EP 8.11   (a) $95,000 is less than M
            (b) $87,000 since M less than cost

SP 8.13   LUIGI'S AUTO PARTS—SCHEDULE OF
            COST OF GOODS SOLD FOR PERIOD 6

Beginning Inventory	$ 39,000
Net Purchases	63,000 *
Goods Available for Sale	102,000
Less Ending Inventory	42,000 **
Cost of Goods Sold	$60,000

* Gross Purchases	$65,250
Plus Freight In	3,300
Less: Purchase Returns	(4,350)
Purchase Discounts	(1,200)
Net Purchases	$63,000

**Under Periodic LIFO:
Start with 39,000 average units costing $1.00 each
Add layer of 42,000 average units costing $1.50 each
Ending inventory of 41,000 units assumed to consist of:

39,000 x $1.00	=	$39,000
2,000 x $1.50	=	3,000
		$42,000

SP 8.13 (a)

BALANCE SHEET EFFECT WORKSHEET
Luigi's Auto Parts – Period 6
(p = preliminary balance; e = ending balance; π = net income)

Cash	$	67,860	(b)		Current Notes Payable	$	0	(p)	0 (e)
	+	2,200	(1)						
	–	62,250	(14)	$ 7,810 (e)	Accounts Payable		17,250	(p)	
						+	65,250	(10)	
Current Notes Receivable		2,000	(p)			–	4,350	(11)	
	–	2,000	(1)	0 (e)		+	3,300	(12)	
						–	63,450	(14)	18,000 (e)
Accounts Receivable		60,000	(b)	60,000 (e)					
					Wages and Salaries		1,200	(p)	1,200 (e)
Inventory		39,000	(p)						
	–	39,000	(F)		Interest Payable		800	(p)	800 (e)
	–	42,000	(G)	42,000 (e)					
					Taxes Payable		0	(p)	0 (e)
Gross Purchases		0	(p)						
	+	65,250	(10)		Noncurrent Notes Payable		20,000	(p)	20,000 (e)
	–	65,250	(F)	0 (e)					
Freight-in		0	(p)						
	+	3,300	(12)						
	–	3,300	(F)	0 (e)					
Purchase Returns		0	(p)						
	–	4,350	(11)						
	+	4,350	(F)	0 (e)					
Purchase Discounts		0	(p)						
	–	1,200	(14)		Luigi Cavelli, Capital				
	+	1,200	(F)	0 (e)					
Supplies		1,010	(b)						
	–	635	(H)	375 (e)					
Prepaid Items		800	(p)	800 (e)					
Equipment		1,200	(p)	1,200 (e)					
Accum. Depr.—Equip.		(375)	(p)	(375) (e)					
Leasehold Improvement		3,500	(p)	3,500 (e)					

Income	
72,539	(p))
– 102,000	(F)
+ 42,000	(G)
– 635	(H)
+ 11,904	(π)

	43,750	(p)	
+	11,904	(π)	75,310 (e)

TOTAL ASSETS	$115,310	TOTAL EQUITIES	$115,310

SP 8.13 (c) LUIGI'S AUTO PARTS - INCOME STATEMENT
FOR PERIOD 6

Net sales		$100,000
Cost of goods sold		(60,000)
Gross Profit		$ 40,000
Operating expenses:		
Wages and salaries	$ 20,900	
Rent	4,500	
Supplies	635	
Utilities and services	500	
Insurance	400	
Depreciation - equipment	75	
Amortization - leasehold improvement	250	(27,260)
Income from operations		$ 12,740
Less interest		(836)
NET INCOME		$ 11,904

SP 8.13 (d) AUTO PARTS - STATEMENT OF OWNER'S
CAPITAL FOR PERIOD 6

Luigi Cavelli, capital, end of Period 5	$63,406
Net Income	11,904
Luigi Cavelli, capital, end of Period 6	$75,310

SP 8.13(e) LUIGI'S AUTO PARTS--- BALANCE SHEET
AS-OF END OF PERIOD 6

ASSETS

Cash	$ 7,810
Accounts receivable	60,000
Inventory	42,000
Supplies	375
Prepaid items	800
Total Current Assets	110,985
Equipment	1,200
Accum. depr. equip.	(375)
Leasehold improvement	3,500
TOTAL ASSETS	$ 115,316

EQUITIES

Accounts payable	$ 18,000
Wages and salaries	1,200
Interest payable	800
Total Current Liabilities	$ 20,000
Noncurrent notes payable	20,000
Total Liabilities	$40,000
Luigi Cavelli, capital	75,310
TOTAL EQUITIES	$115,310

SP 8.13(f) LUIGI'S AUTO PARTS - STATEMENT OF CASH
FLOWS FOR PERIOD 6

Cash Flows from Operating Activities:		
Net income		$11,904
Adjustments to reconcile net income:		
Depreciation	75	
Amortization	250	
increase in Accts. Receivable	(10,000)	
decrease in Int. Receivable	200	
increase in Inventory	(3,000)	
increase in Supplies	(115)	
decrease in Prepaid Items	400	
increase in Accounts Payable	1,500	
increase in Wages and Salaries	900	
decrease in Interest Payable	(36)	
decrease in Taxes Payable	(800)	(10,626)
Net Cash Provided by Operating Activities		$ 1,278
Cash Flows from Investing Activities:		
Payment received on Notes Receivable		2,000
Cash Flows from Financing Activities:		
Payment made on Notes Payable		(900)
Net Increase in cash		$ 2,378
Cash balance Period 5		5,432
Cash balance Period 6		$ 7,810

SP 8.13(g)

Net working capital	$90,985
Current ratio	5.55
Quick ratio	3.39
Long-term debt ratio	.210
Asset composition ratio	.955

Sp 8.15

- Gross profit percentage

previous fiscal year	60%
Sales during first quarter	$160,000
Estimated gross profit first quarter	96,000

- Cost of goods sold percentage

previous fiscal year	40%
Sales during first quarter	$160,000
Est. cost of goods sold 1st quarter	$ 64,000

Beginning inventory	$ 100,000
Net purchases during 1st quarter	70,000
Merchandise available for sale	$170,000
Estimated cost of goods sold during quarter	64,000
Estimated inventory at end of first quarter	$106,000

SP 8.17(a)

	Cost	Cost Selling	Percentage
Beginning inventory	$ 22,000	$ 34,000	NA
Net purchases	140,000	226,000	NA
Markdowns	NA	(15,000)	
Goods available	$162,000	$245,000	66%

Ending inventory at selling	40,000
Ending inventory at cost (.66 x 40,000)	26,400

(b) Ignoring markdowns, goods available cost percentage
    (162,000 + 260,000) = 62%

    Ending inventory at cost (.62 x 40,000) $24,800

SP 8.19(a)   LIFO Indexes:

19X4	19X5
$\frac{11,500}{10,000} = 115$	$\frac{12,550}{10,000} = 126$ (rounded)

(b) Determination of 19X4 ending inventory of dollar-value
    LIFO cost:

(1) 19X3 ending inventory at base-year cost
    = $ 100,000

    19X4 ending inventory at base-year cost
    $80.000 = (\$92,000 \times \frac{100}{115})$

    Inventory quantity decrease at base-year cost
    $ 20,000 = $100,000

(2) 19X4 beginning dollar-value LIFO inventory
    = $ 100,000

    Less reduction of costs of recent layers
    $20,000 = (\$20,000 \times \frac{100}{100})$

    19X4 ending dollar-value LIFO inventory
    $ 80,000 = $100,000 - 20,000

(c) Determination of 19X5 ending inventory at dollar-value
    LIFO cost:

(1) 19X4 ending inventory at base-year cost
    $ 80,000 = (\$92,000 \times \frac{100}{115})$

    19X5 ending inventory at base-year cost
    $128.968 = (\$162,500 \times \frac{100}{126})$

Inventory quantity increase of base-year cost
    $ 48,968 = $128,968 - 80,000

(2) 19X5 beginning dollar-value LIFO inventory
    = $ 80,000

    Add increase at current cost
    $61,700 = (\$48,968 \times \frac{126}{100})$

    19X5 ending dollar-value LIFO inventory
    $141,700 = $80,000 + 61,700

EP 9.1 Cost to be in equipment account:

Basic machine cost	$260,000
Freight-in	4,000
Insurance covering freight-in	400
Cost of machine base	500
Cost of supplying power	1,600
Installation	1,300
Cost of materials used during installation	300
TOTAL	$268,100

EP 9.3

	A Straight-line	B Years' Digits	C Double-declining balance
cost	$50,000	50,000	$50,000
Salvage	5,000	5,000	N.A.
Depreciable base	$45,000	$45,000	$50,000
Estimated life	5 yrs	5 yrs	5 yrs
First year's deprec.	$ 9,000	$15,000	$20,000

Notes: a) Sum of digits = 15; 5/15 x $45,000 = $15,000.
       b) 40 percent of $50,000 = $20,000.

EP 9.5 Value of assets at time of sale $28,000
           Gain (over book value) on sale   2,000
           Sale proceeds $30,000

EP 9.7 Let X = Original cost on 1/1/X3.
           Depreciation expense for 19X3 = 0.4X.
           Book value as of 1/1/X4 = 0.6X.
           Depreciation expense for 19X4 = 0.4(0.6X).
           Accumulated depreciation as of
               12/31/X4 = 0.4X + 0.4(0.6X) = $30,600.
           X = $47,813 (rounded).

EP 9.9

12/31/X9 Book value	$28,125
12/31/X9 Accumulated depreciation	21,875
Original cost	$50,000
First-year depreciation (25 percent)	12,500
Book value, end of first year	$37,500
Second-year depreciation (25 percent)	9,375
Book value, end of second year	$28,125
Therefore, asset was acquired	1/1/X8

EP 9.11

a)

Equipment original cost	$200,000	
Less salvage value	60,000	
Amount to be depreciated	$ 140,000	
Original straight line rate	$20,000	per year
Original total useful life	7 years	
Machine use to date	4 years	
Remaining useful life	3 years	
Depreciation on original cost	$20,000	per year
Depreciation on betterment	10,000	per year
Annual deprec. starting in 19X8	$30,000	per year

b) As of 12/31/X8:

Equipment	$230,000
Accumulated depreciation	110,000
Net book value	$120,000

SP 9.13

a)

Book value of old asset	$6,000
plus Cash price	18,500
New asset Valuation	$24,500

b)

Fair market value old	$ 7,500
plus Cash paid	18,500
New asset valuation	$26,000

Note: The problem should have stated that the book value of the old asset was $6,000

SP 9.15

Depreciable base	$48,000
Third-year straight-line depreciation	12,000
Third-year SYD depreciation (2/10)	9,600
Higher under straight-line	$ 2,400

Therefore, for comparison, Hatch should mentally increase his reported operating income by $2,400.

9.17(a)

	BUILDING	
Period	Period's DDB Depreciation*	Remaining Book Value
Acquisition	0	$ 125,000
8	$6,300	118,700
9	5,900	112,800
10	5,600	107,200
11	5,400	101,800
12	5,100	96,700
13	4,800	91,900
14	4,600	87,300
15	4,400	82,900
16	4,100	78,800
17	3,900	74,900
18	3,700	71,200
19	3,600	67,600
20	3,400	64,200

* Based on 40-period estimated life, 5 percent per period (rounded to nearest $100).

	EQUIPMENT	
Period	Period's SYD Depreciation*	Remaining Book Value
Acquisition	0	$20,000
8	$1,500	18,500
9	1,400	17,100
10	1,300	15,800
11	1,200	14,600
12	1,100	13,500
13	1,000	12,500
14	900	11,600
15	800	10,800
16	700	10,100
17	600	9,500
18	500	9,000
19	400	8,600
20	300	8,300

**SYD = $n(n+1)/2 = 120$; where n = number of years of useful life
Amount to be depreciated = $12,000
Increment to be multiplied by years' digit = $100

SP 9.17   (b)

BALANCE SHEET EFFECT WORKSHEET
Luigi's Auto Parts – Period 8
(p = preliminary balance; e = ending balance; π = net income)

Cash	$ 58,085 (p)		Accounts Payable	6,100 (p)	
	− 21,200 (2)			+ 4,000 (5) 10,100 (e)	
	− 10,000 (3)				
	+ 1,000 (4)		Wages and Salaries	1,300 (p) 1,300 (e)	
	− 4,000 (14)				
	− 5,000 (15) 18,885 (e)		Interest Payable	3,575 (p) 3,575 (e)	
Accounts Receivable	65,000 (p) 65,000 (e)		Noncurrent Notes Payable	20,000 (p)	
				− 20,000 (2)	
Inventory	42,000 (p) 42,000 (e)			+ 135,000 (3)	
				+ 16,000 (5) 151,000 (e)	
Supplies	300 (p) 300 (e)				
Prepaid Items	0 (p) 0 (e)				
Land	0 (p)				
	+ 25,000 (3) 25,000 (e)				
Buildings	0 (p)		Luigi Cavelli, Capital		
	+ 120,000 (3)				
	+ 5,000 (15) 125,000 (e)				

Income	
− 3,425 (p)	
− 1,200 (2)	
+ 250 (4)	
− 4,000 (14)	
− 3,250 (G)	
− 6,300 (H)	
− 1,500 (I)	
− 19,425 (π)	

Accum. Depr. Buildings	0 (p)	
	− 6,300 (H) (6,300) (e)	
Equipment	1,200 (p)	
	− 1,200 (4)	
	+ 20,000 (5) 20,000 (e)	
Accum. Depr.—Equip.	(450) (p)	
	+ 450 (4)	
	− 1,500 (I) (1,500) (e)	
Leasehold Improvement	3,250 (p)	
	− 3,250 (G) 0 (e)	

141,835 (p)
− 19,425 (π) 122,410

TOTAL ASSETS	$288,385	TOTAL EQUITIES	$288,385

SP 9.17(c)   LUIGI'S AUTO PARTS - INCOME STATEMENT
FOR PERIOD 8*

Net sales		$90,000
Cost of goods sold		54,000
Gross Profit		$36,000
Operating expenses:		
Wages and salaries	$26,900	
Rent	4,500	
Utilities	650	
Supplies	625	
Insurance	400	
Depreciation	7,800	40,875
Loss from operations		$(4,875)
Other revenues and (expenses):		
Gain on asset disposition (4)	$ 250	
Leasehold amortization	(3,250)**	
Miscellaneous - moving (14)	(4,000)**	
interest (2, 4, D, and F)	(7,550)	(14,550)
NET INCOME (LOSS)		$(19,425)

*Where shown, the numbers and letters in parenthesis immediately following account titles identify all transactions and adjustments during the period that affected the account balance reported. Note that such references are for your clarification and would never appear on a final income statement in good form.

**Classified as nonoperating since, even though not qualifying as extraordinary, clearly not part of ordinary operations.

SP 9.17(d)   LUIGI'S AUTO PARTS - STATEMENT OF
OWNER'S CAPITAL FOR PERIOD 8

Luigi Cavelli, capital, end of Period 7	$ 91,835
Owner investment	50,000
	$141,835
Net loss for the period	(19,425)
Luigi Cavelli, capital, end of Period 8	$122,410

SP 9.17(e)   LUIGI'S AUTO PARTS - BALANCE SHEET
AS OF END OF PERIOD 8

ASSETS

Cash	$ 18,885
Accounts receivable	65,000
Inventory	42,000
Supplies	300
Total Current Assets	$126,185
Land	25,000
Buildings	125,000
Accum. depr. bldgs.	(6,300)
Equipment	20,000
Accum. depr. equip.	(1,500)
TOTAL ASSETS	$288,385

EQUITIES

Accounts payable	$ 10,100
Wages and salaries	1,300
Interest payable	3,575
Total Current Liabilities	$ 14,975
Noncurrent notes payable	151,000
Total Liabilities	$165,975
Luigi Cavelli, capital	122,410
TOTAL EQUITIES	$288,385

PP9.1

	DR	CR
Land	30,000	
Building	260,000	
Cash		20,000
Noncurrent Notes Payable		270,000

PP9.3

Depreciation Expense	39,600	
Accum. Depr. Building		39,600

PP9.5

Depreciation Expense	4,000	
Accum. Depr.-Equip.		4,000
Cash	40,000	
Accum. Depr.-Equipment	194,000	
Equipment		230,000
Gain on Disposition of Equipment		4,000

PP9.7	DR	CR
Depreciation Expense	1,500	
Accum. Depr. - Equip.		1,500
Equipment	17,500	
Accum. Depr.-Equipment	8,500	
Equipment		15,000
Cash		6,000
Noncurrent Notes Payable		5,000

PP9.9

2)	Noncurrent Note Payable	20,000	
	Interest Expense	1,200	
	Cash		21,200
3)	Land	25,000	
	Building	125,000	
	Cash		15,000
	Noncurrent Notes Payable		135,000
4)	Cash	1,000	
	Accum. Depr.--Equip.	450	
	Equipment		1,200
	Gain on Disposition of Equipment		250
5)	Equipment	20,000	
	Accounts Payable		4,000
	Noncur. Notes Payable		16,000
14)	Miscellaneous Expense	4,000	
	Cash		4,000

ADJUSTING ENTRIES

F)	Interest Expense	1,280	
	Interest Payable		1,280
G)	Amortization Expense	3,250	
	Leasehold Improvement		3,250
H)	Depreciation Expense	6,250	
	Accum. Depr. Bldg.		6,250
I)	Depreciation Expense	1,500	
	Accum. Depr. Equip.		1,500

EP 10.1 (a)

	Profit balance to be allocated	Pat	Mike	Remaining amount to be allocated
Step 1	$120,000	$ 9,000 *	$ 6,000	$ 105,000
Step 2	105,000	56,000**	24,000	25,000
Step 3	25,000	12,500	12,500	zero
Total allocation		$77,500	$42,500	
Capitol account balance before allocation		57,000	40,000	
Year-end capital account balance		$ 134,500	$82,500	

* .15 ($63,000 - $57,000) / 2
** .7($80,000)

b) Because the partnership agreement did not specify how to share losses, the loss would be divided equally.

EP 10.3   FERRERA CORPORATION BALANCE SHEET
STOCKHOLDERS' EQUITY
As of 12/31/X9

Contributed capital:		
Preferred stock	$ 75,000	
Additional paid-in capital - preferred	15,000	
Common stock	150,000	
Additional paid-in capital - common	60,000	
Total Contributed Capital		$300,000[b]
Retained earnings:		
Appropriated	$20,000	
Unappropriated	80,000	
Total Retained Earnings		100,000
Total Stockholders' Equity		400,000[a]

STATEMENT OF RETAINED EARNINGS

Unappropriated retained earnings 12/31/X8	$20,000
Add 19X9 net income	100,000
	$120,000
Less 19X9 dividends	(40,000)
Unappropriated retained earnings 12/31/X9	$80,000

Notes: (a) Total assets minus total liabilities
(b) Total stockholders' equity minus retained earnings

EP 10.5

(a)
Preferred stock ($100 par, 14%)	$1,000,000
Additional paid-in capital - preferred	150,000
Common stock*	2,000,000
Additional paid-in capital - common	300,000
Total Contributed Capital	$3,450,000

*$10 par, 1,000,000 shares authorized, 200,000 shares issued and outstanding

(b)
Preferred stock ($100 par, 14%)	$ 1,000,000
Additional paid-in capital - preferred	150,000
Common stock*	3,000,000
Additional paid-in capital - common	2,700,000
Total Contributed Capital	$6,850,000

*$10 par, 1,000,000 shares authorized, 300,000 shares issued and outstanding

(c)
Preferred stock ($100 par, 14%)	$ 1,000,000
Additional paid-in capital - preferred	150,000
Common stock*	3,000,000
Additional paid-in capital - common	2,700,000
Retained earnings**	1,150,000
Total Stockholders' Equity	$8,000,000

* $10 par, 1,000,000 shares authorized, 300,000 shares issued and outstanding
** beginning retained earnings plus income less dividends

(d) 12/31/X3 book value per share
$3,000,000 ÷ 200,000 shares = <u>$15.00</u>

(e) 12/31/X4 book value per share
(a) Total stockholders' equity less preferred liquidation claim divided by 300,000 shares = <u>$23.33</u>

EP 10.7)   STOCKHOLDERS' EQUITY SECTION
OF ARNOLD CORPORATION'S BALANCE SHEET
As of 2/1/X4

(a) Assuming no January 19X4 net income:
Common stock*	$2,200,000
Additional paid-in capital - common	460,000
Retained earnings	340,000
Total Stockholders' Equity	$3,000,000

* $ 10 par, 1,000,000 shares authorized, 220,000 shares issued and outstanding.

(b) Same as above except retained earnings would be $415,000 and total stock-holders' equity would be $3,075,000 reflecting $75,000 of additional net income.

EP 10.9   STOCKHOLDERS' EQUITY SECTION
ARNOLD CORPORATION'S BALANCE SHEETS
(in thousands) As of:

(a)	3/31/X4	6/30/X4	9/30/X4
Common stock*	$2,000	$2,000	$2,000
Additional paid-in capital	300	300	304
Retained earnings:			
Approp. for conting.	-0-	200	200
Unappropriated**	700	500	500
Treasury Stock	(54)	(54)	(18)
Total Stockholders' Equity	$2,946	$2,946	$2,986
(b)			
Common stock*	$2,000	$2,000	$2,000
Additional paid-in capital - common	300	300	304
Approp. for conting.	-0-	200,000	200,000
Appropriated for treasury stock restriction	54	54	18
Unappropriated	846	871	1,157
Treasury stock	(54)	(54)	(18)
Total Stockholders' Equity	$3,146	$3,371	$3,661

*3/31/X4: $10 par, 1,000,000 shares authorized, 200,000 shares issued, 197,000 shares outstanding

*6/30/X4: $10 par, 1,000,000 shares authorized, 200,000 shares issued, 197,000 shares outstanding

*9/30X4: $10 par, 1,000,000 shares authorized, 200,000 shores issued, 199,000 shares outstanding

**3/31/X4:   restricted by $54,000 for treasury stock
**6/30/X4:   restricted by $54,000 for treasury stock
**9/30/X4:   restricted by $18,000 for treasury stock

SP 10.11   ABLE CORPORATION BALANCE SHEET
As of 12/31/X1
ASSETS

Cash	$	250,000
Other assets		840,000
TOTAL ASSETS	$1,090,000	

EQUITIES

Total Liabilities	$	220,000
Common stock*		440,000
Additional paid-in capital		190,000
Retained earnings		240,000
TOTAL EQUITIES	$1,090,000	

* $5 par; 88,000 shares issued and outstanding.

SP 10.13

Unappropriated retained earnings, 12/31/XO		$1,670,000
Add: 19X1 net income	$400,000	
Reduction of appropriation	400,000	800,000
		$2,470,000
Deduct: Preferred dividend	$ 60,000	
Common cash dividend	300,000	
Common stock dividend	400,000	760,000
Unappropriated retained earnings, 12/31/Xl		$1,710,000

SP 10.15   DAWE CORPORATION BALANCE SHEET
OWNERS' EQUITY SECTION
As of 12/31/Xl

Common stock*	$200,000
Additional paid-in capital	62,000
Appropriated for treasury stock restriction	28,500
Unappropriated retained earnings	321,500
Treasury stock (500 shares)	(28,500)
Total Stockholders' Equity	$583,500

*$5 par 40,000 shores issued, 39,500 share outstanding

SP 10.17 (a) *(see next page)*

SP 10.17(b)   LUIGI AND TONY'S AUTO PARTS
INCOME STATEMENT FOR PERIOD 10

Net soles		$125,000
Cost of goods sold		73,000
Gross Profit		$ 52,000
Operating expenses:		
Wages and salaries	$ 27,000	
Utilities	680	
Supplies	670	
Insurance	500	
Depreciation	6,900	35,750
Income from operations		$16,250
Other expenses:		
Interest		3,200
NET INCOME		$ 13,050

SP 10.17(c)   LUIGI AND TONY'S AUTO PARTS
STATEMENT OF PARTNER'S CAPITAL FOR
PERIOD 10

	Luigi	Tony	Total
Partner's capital beginning Period 10	$112,010	$ 0	$112,010
Add: Additional invest- ments	0	75,000	75,000
Subtract: Withdrawals	4,083	0	4,083
Basis Step 1 Allocation	$107,927	$ 75,000	$182,927
Step 1 Allocation of $5,488 (3% of $182,927)*	3,238	2,250	5,488
Step 2 Allocation of $7,562	5,671	1,891	7,562
Partner's Capital End of Period 10	$116,836	$ 79,141	$195,977

* Step 1 allocation is 59% Luigi and 41% Tony. Step 2 is 75% Luigi and 25% Tony.

SP 10.17(d)   LUIGI AND TONY'S AUTO PARTS
BALANCE SHEET AS OF END OF PERIOD 10
ASSETS

Cash	$ 20,397
Accounts receivable	75,000
Inventory	46,000
Supplies	380
Prepaid items	1,000
Total Current Assets	$142,777
Land	25,000
Buildings	125,000
Accum. depr. bldgs.	(17,800)
Equipment	20,000
Accum. depr. equip.	(4,200)
TOTAL ASSETS	$290,770

EQUITIES

Accounts payable	$15,000
Wages and salaries	600
Interest payable	3,200
Total Current Liabilities	18,800
Noncurrent notes payable	76,000
Total Liabilities	9,800
Tony Sorbo, capital	79,141
TOTAL EQUITIES	290,777

SP 10.17 (a)   BALANCE SHEET EFFECT WORKSHEET
                                  Luigi and Tony's Auto Parts – Period 10
                          (b = beginning balance; e = ending balance; π = net income)

Cash	$	9,960	(b)		Accounts Payable		20,000	(b)	
	+	30,000	(1)			+	72,000	(3)	
	+	90,000	(2)			+	600	(4)	
	−	27,200	(5)			+	680	(6)	
	−	78,280	(7)			−	78,280	(7)	15,000 (e)
	−	4,083	(9)	20,397 (e)					
					Wages and Salaries		800	(b)	
Accounts Receivable		70,000	(b)			−	800	(5)	
	+	95,000	(1)			+	600	(D)	600 (e)
	−	90,000	(2)	42,000 (e)					
					Interest Payable		0	(b)	
Inventory		47,000	(b)			+	3,200	(F)	3,200 (e)
	+	72,000	(3)						
	−	73,000	(A)	46,000 (e)	Noncurrent Notes Payable		151,000	(b)	
						−	75,000	(8)	76,000 (e)
Supplies		450	(b)						
	+	600	(4)						
	−	670	(B)	380 (e)	Luigi Cavelli, Capital		112,010	(b)	
						−	4,083	(9)	
Prepaid Items		1,500	(b)			+	8,909	(π)	116,836 (e)
	−	500	(C)	1,000 (e)					
					Tony Sorbo, Capital		0	(b)	
Land		25,000	(b)	25,000 (e)		+	75,000	(8)	
						+	4,141	(π)	79,141 (e)
Buildings		125,000	(b)	125,000 (e)					

Income		
+	125,000	(1)
−	26,400	(5)
−	680	(6)
−	73,000	(A)
−	670	(B)
−	500	(C)
−	600	(D)
−	6,900	(E)
−	3,200	(F)
+	13,050	(π)

Accum. Depr. Buildings	(12,200)	(b)		
	−	5,600	(E)	(17,800) (e)
Equipment	20,000	(b)	20,000 (e)	
Accum. Depr.—Equip.	(2,900)	(b)		
	−	1,300	(E)	(4,200) (e)

TOTAL ASSETS		$ 290,777	TOTAL EQUITIES	$290,777

SP 10.17(e)   LUIGI AND TONY'S AUTO PARTS
STATEMENT OF CASH FLOWS FOR PERIOD 10

Cash Flows from Operating Activities:

Net Income		$13,050
Adjustments to reconcile net income:		
Depreciation	$6,900	
increase in Accts Receivable	(5,000)	
decrease in Inventory	1,000	
decrease in Supplies	70	
decrease in Prepaid Items	500	
decrease in Accounts Payable	(5,000)	
decrease in Wages and Salaries	(200)	
increase in Interest Payable	3,200	1,470
Net cash provided by operating activities		$14,520

Cash Flows from Financing Activities:

Partner withdrawal	(4,083)
Net increase in Cash	$10,437
Cash Balance Period 9	9,960
Cash Balance Period 10	$20,397

Investing and Financing Activities not involving cash included a partner assuming a note payable of $75,000.

Net working capital	$ 123,977
Current ratio	7.59
Quick ratio	5.07
Long-term debt ratio	.279
Asset composition ratio	.456

SP 10.19(b)   LUTON CORPORATION - INCOME
STATEMENT FOR PERIOD 12

Net sales		$150,000
Cost of goods sold		90,000
Gross Profit		$ 60,000
Operating expenses:		
Wages and salaries	$ 30,000	
Supplies	800	
Utilities	850	
Insurance	500	
Depreciation	6,200	38,350
Operating profit		21,650
Less other expenses:		
Interest	$ 3,200	
Miscellaneous*	1,200	4,400
Income From Operations Before Taxes		$17,250
Less provision for income taxes		2,900
NET INCOME		$ 14,350

*Costs of incorporation classified as nonoperating since, even though not qualifying as extraordinary, clearly not part of ordinary operations.

SP 10.19(c)   LUTON CORPORATION
STATEMENT OF RETAINED EARNINGS FOR
PERIOD 12

Retained earnings end Period 11		$ 0
Net Income– Period 12		14,350
		14,350
Less: Preferred dividend	$ 2,500	
Common cash dividend	1,890	
Stock dividend	9,000	13,390
Retained earnings– end Period 12		$ 960

SP 10.19(d) LUTON CORPORATION - BALANCE SHEET AS
OF END OF PERIOD 12

ASSETS

Cash	$ 150,200
Accounts receivable	75,000
Inventory	46,000
Supplies	600
Total Current Assets	$271,800
Land	25,000
Buildings	125,000
Accum. depr. bldgs.	(28,300)
Equipment	20,000
Accum. depr. equip.	(6,500)
TOTAL ASSETS	$407,000

EQUITIES

Accounts payable	$ 17,000
Wages and salaries	900
Interest payable	1,600
Taxes payable	2,900
Dividends payable	1, 890
Total Current Liabilities	$ 24,290
Noncurrent notes payable	76,000
Total Liabilities	$100,290
Preferred stock*	100,000
Addtl. paid in capital - Pfd.	10,000
Common stock**	189,000
Addtl. paid in capital - Common	6,750
Retained earnings	960
TOTAL EQUITIES	$407,000

* $100 par; 20,000 shares authorized;1,000 shares issued and outstanding.

** $5 par; 200,000 shares authorized; 37,800 shares issued and outstanding.

SP 10.19   (a)

BALANCE SHEET EFFECT WORKSHEET
LUTON Corporation – Period 12
(p = preliminary balance; e = ending balance; π = net income)

Cash	$ 43,900 (p)			Accounts Payable	17,000 (p)	17,000 (e)
	− 1,200 (9)			Wages and Salaries	900 (p)	900 (e)
	+ 110,000 (11)					
	− 2,500 (12)	150,200 (e)		nterest Payable	1,600 (p)	1,600 (e)
Accounts Receivable	75,000 (p)	75,000 (e)		Taxes Payable	0 (p)	
					+ 2,900 (H)	2,900 (e)
Inventory	46,000 (p)	76,000 (e)		Dividends Payable	0 (p)	
Supplies	600 (p)	600 (e)			+ 1,890 (14)	1,890 (e)
Land	25,000 (p)	25,000 (e)		Noncurrent Notes Payable	75,000 (p)	76,000 (e)
Buildings	125,000 (p)	125,000 (e)		Luigi Cavelli, Capital	113,025 (p)	
					− 113,025 (10)	0 (e)
Accum. Depr. Buildings	(28,300) (p)	(28,300) (e)		Tony Sorbo, Capital	73,725 (p)	
					− 73,725 (10)	0 (e)
Equipment	20,000 (p)	20,000 (e)		Preferred Stock	0 (p)	
Accum. Depr. Equipment	(6,500) (p)	(6,500) (e)			+ 100,000 (11)	100,000 (e)

Addtl. Paid-in Capital
Preferred   0 (p)
+ 10,000 (11)   10,000 (e)

Common Stock   0 (p)
+ 180,000 (10)
+ 9,000 (13)   189,000 (e)

Addtl. Paid-in Capital
Common   0 (p)
+ 6,750 (10)   6,750 (e)

Retained Earnings   0 (p)
+ 14,350 (π)
− 2,500 (12)
− 9,000 (13)
− 1,890 (14)   960 (e)

Income	
+ 18,450	(p)
− 1,200	(9)
− 2,900	(H)
+ 14,350	(π)

TOTAL ASSETS $ 407,000	TOTAL EQUITIES $407,000

SP10.19(e)   LUTON CORPORATION - STATEMENT OF
CASH FLOWS FOR PERIOD 12

Cash Flow from Operating Activities:

Net Income		$14,350
Adjustments to reconcile net income:		
Depreciation	$ 6,200	
decrease in Accounts Rec.	5,000	
decrease in Inventory	2,000	
increase in Supplies	(200)	
decrease in Prepaid Items	500	
increase in Accounts Payable	1,000	
decrease in Wages and Salaries	(600)	
increase in Interest Payable	1,600	
increase in Taxes Payable	2,900	18,400
Net cash provided by operating activities		$32,750

Cash Flows from Financing Activities:

Proceeds of Preferred Stock	110,000	
Payment of dividends	(2,500)	
Cash provided from financing activities		107,500
Net Increase in Cash		$140,250
Cash Balance Period 11		9,950
Cash Balance Period 12		$150,200

Investing and Financing activities not involving cash included declaration of cash dividends to common stockholders for $1,890.

Net working capital	$247,510
Current ratio	11.19
Quick ratio	9.27
Long-term debt ratio	.199
Asset composition ratio	.647
Book value per share*	$4.81

* Total stockholders' equity ($306,710) less pre-ferred claim in liquidation ($120,000) divided by 37,800 outstanding common shares.

PP 10.1

	DR	CR
Cash	1,150,000	
Preferred Stock		1,000,000
Addtl. PIC-Preferred		150,000
Cash	3,400,000	
Common Stock		1,000,000
Addtl. PIC-Common		2,400,000
Income Summary	900,000	
Retained Earnings		900,000

	DR	CR
Dividends Declared	140,000	
Dividends Payable		140,000
Dividends Declared	310,000	
Dividends Payable		310,000
Retained Earnings	450,000	
Dividends Declared		450,000

PP 10.3

Retained Earnings	360,000	
Common Stock		200,000
Addtl. PIC-Common		160,000

PP 10.5

Treasury Stock	54,000	
Cash		54,000
Unappropriated Ret. Earnings	200,000	
Appropriated Retained Earnings		200,000
Cash	40,000	
Treasury Stock		36,000
Addtl. PIC-Common		4,000

PP 10.7

*1)	Cash	30,000	
	Accounts Receivable	95,000	
	Sales		125,000
*2)	Cash	90,000	
	Accounts Receivable		90,000
*3)	Inventory	72,000	
	Accounts Payable		72,000
*4)	Supplies	600	
	Accounts Payable		600
*5)	Wages and Salaries Expense	26,400	
	Wages and Salaries Payable	800	
	Cash		27,200
*6)	Utilities Expense	680	
	Accounts Payable		680
*7)	Accounts Payable	78,280	
	Cash		78,280

ADJUSTING ENTRIES

		DR	CR
*A)	Cost of Goods Sold	73,000	
	Inventory		73,000
*B)	Supplies Expense	670	
	Supplies		670
*C)	Insurance Expense	500	
	Prepaid Items		500
*D)	Wages and Salaries Expense	600	
	Wages and Salaries Payable		600
*E)	Depreciation Expense	6,900	
	Accum. Depr. - Bldg.		5,600
	Accum. Depr.-Equip.		1,300
*F)	Interest Expense	3,200	
	Interest Payable		3,200

Pp 10.9

		DR	CR
*1)	Cash	40,000	
	Accounts Receivable	110,000	
	Sales		150,000
*2)	Cash	115,000	
	Accounts Receivable		115,000
*3)	Inventory	88,000	
	Accounts Payable		88,000
*4)	Supplies	1,000	
	Accounts Payable		1,000
*5)	Wages and Salaries Payable	1,500	
	Wages and Salaries Expense	29,100	
	Cash		30,600
*6)	Utilities Expense	800	
	Accounts Payable		800
*7)	Interest Expense	1,600	
	Cash		1,600
*8)	Accounts Payable	88,850	
	Cash		88,850

ADJUSTING ENTRIES

		DR	CR
*A)	Cost of Goods Sold	90,000	
	Inventory		90,000

		DR	CR
*B)	Supplies Expense	800	
	Supplies		800
*C)	Insurance Expense	500	
	Prepaid Items		500
*D)	Wages and Salaries Expense	900	
	Wages and Salaries Payable		900
*E)	Depreciation Expense	6,200	
	Accum. Depr. - Bldg.		5,100
	Accum. Depr.-Equip.		1,100
*F)	Utilities Expense	50	
	Accounts Payable		50
*G)	Interest Expense	1,600	
	Interest Payable		1,600

EP 11.1 (a) As of 12/31/X2:

Accounts receivable			$425,000*
Less allowance for bad debt			(17,000)
beginning accounts receivable			$400,000
19X2 sales on account			2,500,000
			2,900,000
Less: collections (old)	$383,000		
	$2,900,000		
collections (new)	2,000,000		
write-off (old)	17,000		
write-off (new)	75,000	2,475,000	
Ending accounts receivable			$ 425,000

* beginning accounts receivable

(b) 12/31/X2 allowance for bad debts	$17,000
12/31/X1 allowance for bad debts	16,000
19X2 addition to allowance	1,000
19X2 write-offs	92,000
19X2 bad debt expense	$93,000

EP 11.3

(a)	Notes receivable	$8,400	
	Less discount	(400)	$8,000
(b)	Notes receivable	$8,400	
	Less discount	(200)	$8,200
(c)	Interest revenue for first three months = $200		

EP 11.5

at 12/31:	Cost	Market	LCM	Income Statement
12/31/X1	$90	$93	$90	0
12/31/X2	90	80	80	10 loss
12/31/X3	90	88	88	8 gain

EP 11.7

at 12/31:	19X2	19X3	19X4	19X5
(a) Investments:				
Cost basis	$ 100	$ 100	$94*	$94*
Current market	105	90	98	100
Balance sheet				
amount	$ 100	$90	$94	$94

(b) On income statement:

Gain (loss	none	none	$(6)	none
(c) Temporary loss on				
investments	none	$10	none	none

*reflects $6,000 permanent loss reducing cost ceiling

EP 11.13

	(o)	$74,694
	(b)	$70,959

EP 11.9

(a)	Balance 12/31/XO	$412,000
	Share of 19X1 Nice Corporation	
	earnings	60,000
		472,000
	Less dividends received during 19X1	20,000
	Balance 12/31/Xl	$452,000

(b) Reported investments revenue for 19X1
$60,000

(c) In determining funds from operations, $40,000 of
included investments revenue
not involving inflow of NWC must be subtracted.

EP 11.15

Payments under mortgage note	15% Discount Factor	PV
$20,000 down	1.0000	$20,000
$ 8,000 per year for 20 years	6.2593	50,074
$400,000 at maturity	0.0611	24,400
Net present value of mortgage		
and down payment		$94,574
Less appraised value of land		25,000
Initial valuation (cost) of building		$69,514

EP 11.11

Date	Beginning Book Value	Interest Revenue	Interest Payment	Amortization	Ending Book Value
X Bonds:					
6/30/X0	$54,648*	$3,279	$3,500	$241	$54,427
12/31/X0	54,427	3,266	3,500	234	54,193
6/30/X1	54,193	3,252	3,500	248	53,945
12/31/X0	53,945	3,237	3,500	263	53,682
Y Bonds:					
6/30/X0	66,397**	3,984	3,750	234	66,631
12/31/X0	66,631	3,998	3,750	248	66,879
6/30/X1	66,879	4,013	3,750	263	67,142
12/31/X1	67,142	4,029	3,750	279	67,421

  * ($3,500 x 9.2950) + ($50,000 x .4423) = $54,648
** ($3,750 x 11.4699) + ($75,000 x .3118) = $66,397

12/31/X1 Balance Sheet:		19X1 Interest Revenue:	
X Bonds	$50,000	X Bonds	$6,489
Premium	3,682	Y Bonds	8,042
Y Bonds	75,000	Total	$14,531
Discount	(7,579)		

SP 11.17 (a)   BALANCE SHEET EFFECT WORKSHEET
                                    LUTON Corporation – Period 14
                   (p = preliminary balance; e = ending balance; π = net income)

Cash	$ 17,480	(p)		Accounts Payable	45,000	(p)	45,000 (e)
	+ 115,000	(12)		Wages and Salaries	3,000	(p)	3,000 (e)
	− 80,000	(15)		Interest Payable	1,600	(p)	1,600 (e)
	− 32,000	(16)					
	+ 800	(17)		Taxes Payable	7,000	(p)	7,000 (E)
	− 10,0009180		11,280 (e)	Current Capital Lease	0	(p)	
Marketable Securities	140,000	(p)		Obligations	+ 10,000	(18)	
	− 100,000	(12)			− 10,000	(18)	0 (e)
	− 5,000	(H)	35,000 (e)				
Notes Receivable	0	(p)		Noncurrent Notes Payable	75,000	(p)	76,000 (e)
	+ 10,600	(13)	10,600 (e)				
Notes Receivable Discount	0	(p)					
	− 600	(13)					
	+ 300	(I)	(300) (e)	Preferred Stock	100,000	(p)	100,000 (e)
Accounts Receivable	100,000	(p)		Addtl. Paid-in Capital			
	− 10,000	(13)		Preferred	10,000	p)	10,000 (e)
	− 2,800	(14)	87,200 (e)				
Allowance for bad debt	0	(p)		Common Stock	189,000	(p)	189,000 (e)
	+ 2,800	(14)		Addtl. Paid-in Capital			
	− 4,600	(J)	(1,800) (e)	Common	6,750	(p)	6,750 (e)
Inventory	66,000	(p)	66,000 (e)				
Supplies	900	(p)	900 (e)	Retained Earnings	11,600	(b)	
Prepaid Items	1,400	(p)	1,400 (e)		− 15,730	(10)	
Investments	0	(p)			+ 30,360	(π)	26,290 (e)
	+ 80,000	(15)					
	+ 40,000	(16)					
	+ 10,000	(K)	130,000 (e)				

Income	
+ 17,000	(p)
+ 15,000	(12)
+ 800	(17)
− 5,000	(H)
+ 300	(I)
− 4,600	(J)
+ 10,000	(K)
+ 400	(L)
− 3,540	(M)
+ 30,360	(π)

Bond Investments Discount	0	(p)	
	− 8,000	(16)	
	+ 400	(L)	(7,600) (e)
Land	25,000	(p)	25,000 (e)
Buildings	125,000	(p)	125,000 (e)
Accum. Depr. Buildings	(37,700)	(p)	(37,700) (e)
Equipment	20,000	(p)	20,000 (e)
Accum. Depr. Equipment	(8,400)	(p)	(8,400) (e)
Property Capital Lease	0	(p)	
	+ 70,862	(18)	70,862 (e)
Accum. Depr. Lease	0	(p)	
	− 3,540	(M)	(3,540) (e)

TOTAL ASSETS	$	523,902
TOTAL EQUITIES	$	523,902

LUTON CORPORATION - INCOME STATEMENT
FOR PERIOD 14*

Net sales		$200,000
Cost of goods sold		120,000
Gross Profit		$ 80,000
Operating expenses:		
Wages and salaries	$ 45,000	
Supplies	1,500	
Insurance	700	
Utilities	1,100	
Bad debt accounts (J)	4,600	
Depreciation	5,500	
Capital lease depreciation (M)	3,540	61,940
Income from operations		$ 18,060
Other revenues and (expenses):		
Investments and interest revenue		
(11, 17, I, K, and L)	$ 12,500	
Net gain on marketable		
securities (12 and H)	10,000	
Interest expense (7)	(3,200)	19,300
Income From Operations Before Taxes		$ 37,360
Less provision for income taxes		7,000
NET INCOME		$ 30,360

* Where shown, the numbers and letters in parenthesis immediately following account titles identify
all transactions and adjustments during the period
that affected the account balance reported. Note
that such references are for your clarification and
would never appear on a final income statement in
good form.

SP 11.17(c)   LUTON CORPORATION STATEMENT OF
RETAINED EARNINGS FOR PERIOD 14

Retained earnings - end Period 13		$ 11,660
Net income - Period 14		30,360
		$ 42,020
Less: Preferred dividend	$ 2,500	
Common cash dividend	13,230	15,730
Retained Earnings - end Period 14		$26,290

SP 11.17(d)   LUTON CORPORATION - BALANCE SHEET AS
OF END OF PERIOD 14

ASSETS

Cash		$ 11,280
Marketable securities		35,000
Notes receivable	$ 10,600	
Less: Discount	(300)	10,300
Accounts receivable	$ 87,200	
Less: Allowance bad debts	(1,800)	85,400
Inventory		66,000
Supplies		900
Prepaid items		1,400
Total Current Assets		$210,280
Investments	$130,000	
Less: Discount	(7,600)	122,400
Land		25,000
Buildings	$ 125,000	
Accum. depr.—Bldg.	(37,700)	87,300
Equipment	$ 20,000	
Accum. depr.—Equip.	(8,400)	11,600
Properties under capital lease	70862	
Accum. Depr.—Lease	(3,540)	67,322
TOTAL ASSETS		$523,902

EQUITIES

Accounts payable		$ 45,000
Wages and salaries		3,000
Taxes payable		7,000
Total Current Liabilities		$ 55,000
Noncurrent notes payable		76,000
Noncurrent cap. lse. oblig.		60,000
Total Liabilities		$191,862
Preferred stock*		100,000
Addtl. paid in capital - pfd.		10,000
Common stock**		189,000
Addtl. paid in capital - com.		6,750
Retained earnings		26,290
TOTAL EQUITIES		$523,902

Net Working Capital	$155,280
Current ratio	3.82
Quick ratio	2.58
Long-term debt ratio	.292
Asset composition ratio	.331
Book value per shore	$5.48

PP 11.1		DR	CR
1)	Cash	383,000	
	Bad Debt Allowance	17,000	
	Accounts Receivable		400,000
2)	Accounts Receivable	2,500,000	
	Sales		2,500,000
3)	Cash	2,000,000	
	Accounts Receivable		2,000,000
4)	Bad Debt Allowance	75,000	
	Accounts Receivable		75,000
5)	Bad Debt Expense	76,000	
	Bad Debt Allowance		76,000

PP 11.3			
a)	Current Notes Receivable	8,400	
	Discount on Current		
	Notes Receivable		400
	Accounts Receivable		8,000
b)	Discount on Current		
	Notes Receivable	200	
	Interest Revenue		200

PP 11.5			
19X2	Loss on Current Marketable		
	Securities	10,000	
	Current Marketable Securities		10,000
19X3	Current Marketable Securities	8,000	
	Gain on Current Marketable Sec.		8,000

PP 11.7			
	Cash	20,000	
	Common Stock Investments		20,000
	Common Stock Investments	60,000	
	Investments Revenue		60,000

PP 11.9			
	Cash	7,000	
	Premium on X Corp. Bonds		300
	Interest Revenue		6,700
	Cash	7,000	
	Discount on Y Corpora-tion Bonds		225
	Interest Revenue		7,225

PP 11.11			
	Land	25,000	
	Building	69,515	
	Cash		20,000
	Noncurrent Notes Payable		74,515

PP 11.13			
12)	Cash	115,000	
	Current Marketable Securities		100,000
	Gain on Current Marketable Sec.		15,000
13)	Current Notes Receivable	10,600	
	Accounts Receivable		10,000
	Discount on Current		
	Notes Receivable		600
14)	Bad Debt Allowance	2,800	
	Accounts Receivable		2,800
15)	Common Stock Investments	80,000	
	Cash		80,000
16)	Bond Investments	40,000	
	Investments		8,000
	Cash		32,000
17)	Cash	800	
	Interest Revenue		800
18)	Properties Held Under		
	Capital Lease	70,862	
	Noncurrent Capital		
	Lease Obligations		60,862
	Cash		10,000

ADJUSTING ENTRIES

H)	Loss on Current Marketable		
	Securities	5,000	
	Current Marketable Securities		5,000
I)	Discount on Current Notes		
	Receivable	300	
	Interest Revenue		300
J)	Uncollectibles Exp.	4,600	
	Uncollectibles Allow.		4,600
K)	Common Stock Investments	10,000	
	Investments Revenue		10,000
L)	Discount on Bond Investments	400	
	Interest Revenue		400
M)	Depreciation Expense	3,540	
	Properties Held Under		
	Capital Lease		3,540

AP11.15(a)

Bank reconciliation
From Bank Statement

Balance per statement	$15,050
Add:	
Deposits in transit	1,000
Cash on hand	600
Deduct:	
Outstanding checks	2,000
Correct cash balance	$14,650

From Firm's Account

Balance per books	$16,000
Add:	
Interest credited	60
Deduct:	
NSF deposit	1,400
Service charges	10
Correct Cash balance	$14,650

(b)

	DR	CR
• Accounts Receivable	1,400	
• Cash		1,400
• Miscellaneous Expense	10	
Cash		10
• Cash	60	
Interest Revenue		60

EP 12.1(a)

	First Quarter	Second Qaarter	Third Quarter	Fourth Quarter
Current note	116,000	116.000	116.000	0
Discount	(12,000)	(8,000)	(4,000)	0
Interest Payable	15,220*	5,440	20,660	0
Noncurrent Note	272,000	272,000	272,000	272,000
Discount	(66,000)	(60,000)	(54,000)	(48,000)
Bonds Payable	500,000	500,000	500,000	500,000
Bond Discount	(59,000)	(58,000)	(57,000)	(56,000)
Total	766,220	767,440	793,660	668,000

* Interest on noncurrent note of $2,720 per quarter plus bond interest of $12,500 per quarter.

(b)
discount amort:

Current Note	4,000	4,000	4,000	4,000
Noncurrent Note	6,000	6,000	6,000	6,000
Bond:	1,000	1,000	1,000	1,000
Stated interest:				
Noncurrent Note	2,720	2,720	2,720	2,720
Bonds	12,500	12,500	12,500	12,500
Reported Interest	26,220	26,220	26,220	26,220

(c) In determinng 19X4 cash from operating activities, discount amortizations included as part of reported interest expense should be added to net income since they did not involve an outflow of cash.

EP 12.3(a) As of 12/31/X8:

Bonds payable	$800,000
Bond premium	76,000

(b)

19X8 stated interest paid or accrued	$112,000
Less 19X8 premium amortization	4,000
19X8 reported interest expense	$108,000

(c) In determining funds from operations, the $4,000 bond premium amortization must be subtracted from reported income since this expense reduction did not represent a reduction in the actual interest NWC outflow.

EP 12.5 Partial (First-Half-Year) Loan Repayment Schedule for 19X1

Monthly Payment	Amount	Interest Portion	Principal Portion	Remaining Loan Balance
January	$100	$41.49*	$58.51	$2,707.49
February	100	40.61	59.39	2,6 48. 10
March	100	39.72	60.28	2,587.82
April	100	38.82	61.18	2,526.64
May	100	37.90	62.10	2,464.54
June	100	36.97	63.03	2,401.51

* 1.5 percent monthly interest rate times initial loan balance of $2,766

EP 12.7

	(a) As of 1/1/X2	(b) As of 12/31/X2
Properties under capital lease	$240,000^x	$210,0003
Current lease obligation	31,980^y	18,797^z
Noncurrent lease obligation	208,020	189,223^y
Interest expense for 19X2	-0-	33,655
Amortization expense for 19X2	-0-	30,000

(x) Present value of all payments under lease.
(y) Interest portion of first year's $50,000 payment equals $33,655 ($224,365 "loan balance" times 15% and rounded). Principal portion is therefore $16,345. $16,345 plus down payment of $15,635 equals present value of first year's payments.
(z) Interest portion of second year's payment is $31,203 ($208,020 x .15); and therefore maturing principal portion is $18,797.

EP 12.9 (u) $300,000*
      (b) $ 40,000
      (c) 1,275,000 (300 bonds x 25 shares x $10 par
          added)
      (d) 585,000

      * $300,000 less $40,000 discount = $260,000
         book value of CVD's converted. $260,000 less
         $75,000 par value of shares exhanged equals
         $185,000.

EP 12.11

(a)
Face value of 320 debentures retired	$320,000
Call premium on 320 debentures retired	12,800
Interest to 6/30 on entire issue	36,000
Total cash disbursed	$368,800

(b) Balances in bond-related accounts at time of
    conversion/retirement:

Bonds payable	$800,000
Bond premium	52,500*
Deferred charges	(15,000)*
	$837,500

*Reflects 6 months amortization.

Book value of debt retired	$335,000
Book value of debt converted	502,500
Total	$837,500

Book value of debt converted	$502,500
Par value of stock exchanged (480x80x10)	384,000
Add. paid-in capital from conversation	$118,500
After conversion:	
Common stock	$1,584,000
Additional paid-in capital	568,500

(c)
Net book value of debt retired	$335,000
Costs of retirement (excludes interest)	332,800
Extraordinary gain on debt retirement*	$ 2,200

*Might be classified as non-extraordinary
"otherrevenue" since relatively immaterial.

(d)
Gross interest savings last 6 months 19X2	$ 36,000
Less additional income taxes on interest savings	12,600
Net increase in income from operations	$23,400*

*Could be $25,600 if gain on retirement not
classified as extraordinary.

SP12.13

(a) Incremental refunding costs (ignoring interest):

Face value of bonds retired	$900,000
Call premium on bonds retired	45,000
Issue costs of new bonds	35,000
Cash to be obtained from new issue	$980,000
Net proceeds per new bond	$980
Number new bonds sold	1,000 bonds

(b) Balances in accounts (other than interest)
    related to old issue at retirement:

Bonds payable	$900,000
Bond discount	(5 1,000)*
Deferred charges (asset)	(8.500)*
	$840,500

*Reflects 9 months amortization.

Book value of old bonds retired	$840,500
Costs of retirement (old issue other than interest)	945.000
Extraordinary loss on debt extinguishment reported on the 19X5 income statement	$104,500

(c) On 12/31/X5 balance sheet:

Bonds payable	$ 1,000,000
Bond discount	19,500*
Deferred charges (asset)	34,125**

*$20,000 discount to amortize over 20
years. Assuming straight-line amortization,
equals $1,000 per year or $500 for six
months.
**$35,000 of deferred charges to amortize
over 20 years. Assuming straight-line
amortization, equals $1,750 per year or
$875 for six months.

(d)
Interest on old issue through 6/30/X5	$ 45,000
Interest on old issue 6/30 - 9/30	22,500
Interest on new issue 7/1 - 12/31	40,000
Total	$107,500

(e)
Interest paid accrued (per above)	$ 107,500
Amort. old issue deferred charges to 9/30	1,500
Amortization old issue discount to 9/30	9,000
Amortization new issued deferred charges 7/1 - 12/31	875
Amortization new issue discount 7/1 - 12/31	500
Total 19X5 reported interest expense	$119,375

SP 12.15(a) Calculation of selling price per bond:

Year(s)	Cash Outflow[1]	PV Factor [2]	Present Value
1-20	$ 60	13.3317[3]	$799.90
20	$1,000	.0728	72.80
			$872.70

Notes: (1) Based on stated or coupon rate.
(2) Discounted at 14% market rate.
(3) For 40 periods at 7% per period.

Balance sheet effects on 1/1/X1:

Cash net increase ($872.70 x 2,000 less $40,000)	$1,705,400
Deferred charges increase	40,000
Bonds payable	2,000,000
Bond discount	254,600

(b) 12/31/X1:

Bonds payable	$2,000,000
Bond discount	(241,870)*
Deferred charges (asset)	38,000 **

 * Reflects $12,730 annual straight-line amortization.
 ** Reflects $2,000 annual straight-line amortization.

(c)

Interest paid or accrued	$240,000
Discount amortization	12,730
Deferred charg amortization	2.000
Total reported 19X1 interest expense	$254,730

SP 12.17

(a)

Present value of payment on signing	$ 10,000
Present value of annual payments discounted at 14%	208,644
Initial value of capital lease	$218,644
Interest portion of first annual payment	$ 29,210*
Principal portion of first annual payment	10,790
Interest portion of second annual payment	27,700**
Principal portion of second annual payment	12,300

 * 14 percent of "loan balance" of $208,644.
 ** 14 percent of "loan balance" of $197,854.
As of 1/1/X4:

Properties under capital lease	$218,644
Current capital lease obligation	20,790
Noncurrent capital lease obligation	197,854

SP12.17 (*continued*)

(b) As of 12/31/X4:

Properties under capital lease	$ 196,780*
Current capital lease obligation	40,000**
Noncurrent capital lease obligation	197,854

 * Reflects straight-line amortization of $21,864.
 ** $40,000 first annual payment (principal portion of second annual payment not due within one year).

SP 12.19 *is on the next page*

PP 12.1

• Interest Expense	4,000	
Discount on NotesPayable		4,000
• Interest Expense	2,720	
Interest Payable		2,720
• Interest Expense	6,000	
Bond Discount		6,000
• Interest Expense	12,500	
Interest Payable		12,500
• Interest Expense	1,000	
Bond Discount		1,000

PP 12.3

a)	Property Capital Lease	240,000	
	Current Cap. Lse. Oblg.		31,980
	Noncurrent Cap. Lse. Oblg.		208,020
b)	Current Cap. Lse. Oblg.	15,635	
	Cash		15,635
c)	Depreciation Expense	30,000	
	Accum. Depr., Lease		30,000
	Noncurent Cap. Lse. Oblg.	18,797	
	Current Cap. Lse. Oblg.		18,797

PP 12.5

•	7% CVD's Payable	300,000	
	Discount on Debentures		40,000
	Common Stock		75,000
	Additional PIC, Common		185,000

SP 12.19

BALANCE SHEET EFFECT WORKSHEET
LUTON Corporation – Period 16
(p = preliminary balance; e = ending balance; π = net income)

Assets		
Cash	$ 42,780 (p)	
	+ 33,000 (12)	
	− 5,000 (13)	
	− 20,000 (15)	
	+ 2,500 (16)	
	+ 57,500 (17)	
	− 6,000 (18)	
	− 63,000 (19)	
	− 1,676 (20)	23,304 (e)
Marketable Securities	35,000 (p)	
	− 35,000 (12)	0 (e)
Accounts Receivable	95,820 (p)	95,820 (e)
Allowance for bad debt	(1,820) (p)	(1,820) (e)
Inventory	78,000 (p)	78,000 (e)
Supplies	1,350 (p)	1,350 (e)
Investments	151,000 (p)	
	+ 20,000 (15)	171,000 (e)
Bond Investments Discount	(6,800) (p)	(6,800) (e)
Land	25,000 (p)	25,000 (e)
Buildings	125,000 (p)	125,000 (e)
Accum. Depr. Buildings	(46,200) (p)	(46,200) (e)
Equipment	20,000 (p)	
	+ 10,000 (20)	30,000 (e)
Accum. Depr. Equipment	(9,900) (p)	
	− 400 (M)	(10,300) (e)
Property Capital Lease	70,862 (p)	70,862 (e)
Accum. Depr. Lease	(10,620) (p)	(10,620) (e)
Deferred Charges	0 (p)	
	+ 6,000 (18)	
	− 200 (L)	5,800 (e)
TOTAL ASSETS		**$ 550,396**

Equities		
Current Notes Payable	16,000 (p)	
	− 16,000 (13)	0 (e)
Accounts Payable	60,000 (p)	60,000 (e)
Wages and Salaries	1,000 (p)	1,000 (e)
Interest Payable	0 (p)	
	+ 2,000 (J)	
	+ 110 (N)	2,110 (e)
Taxes Payable	0 (p)	
	+ 5,300 (R)	5,300 (e)
Current Capital Lease Obligations	5,000 (p)	
	− 5,000 (14)	
	− 2,668 (P)	
	− 2,332 (Q)	5,000 (e)
Noncurrent Notes Payable	60,000 (p)	
	− 60,000 (19)	
	+ 11,000 (20)	11,000 (e)
Notes Payable Discount	0 (p)	
	− 2,676 (20)	
	+ 270 (O)	(2,406) (e)
Noncurrent Capital Lease Obligation	58,296 (p)	
	− 2,668 (P)	55,628 (e)
Bonds Payable	0 (p)	
	+ 50,000 (17)	50,000 (e)
Bond Premium	0 (p)	
	− 250 (K)	7,250 (e)
Deferred Income Tax	0 (p)	
	+ 1,200 (R)	1,200 (e)
Preferred Stock	100,000 (p)	100,000 (e)
Addtl. PIC Preferred	10,000 (p)	10,000 (e)
Common Stock	189,000 (p)	189,000 (e)
Addtl. PIC Common	6,750 (p)	6,750 (e)
Retained Earnings	24,316 (p)	
	+ 24,248 (π)	48,564 (e)

Income			
+ 39,110	(p)	− 200	(L)
− 2,000	(12)	− 400	(M)
− 800	(13)	− 110	(N)
+ 2,500	(16)	− 270	(O)
− 3,000	(19)	− 2,332	(Q)
− 2,000	(J)	− 6,500	(R)
+ 250	(K)	+ 24,248	(π)

TOTAL EQUITIES   **$ 550,396**

PP 12.7

• Wages and Salaries Expense	60,000	
Employee Taxes Payable		12,000
FICA Employee Taxes Payable		3,600
Union Dues Payable		300
Cash		44,100
• Payroll Tax Expense	6,000	
Health Plan Expense	4,800	
FICA Taxes Payable		3,600
FUTA Taxes Payable		2,400
Health Plan Payable		4,800

EP 13.1
- (a) Current ratio — 3.13
- (b) Quick ratio — 1.60
- (c) Long-term debt ratio — .105
- (d) Times interest earned — 17.6 times

EP 13.3
- (a) Asset turnover — 1.87 times
- (b) Receivables turnover — 9.0 times
- (c) Avg days' receivables — 40.6 days
- (d) Inventory turnover — 4.0 times
- (e) Average days, sales in inventory — 91.3 days
- (f) Property and equip turnover — 6.69 times
- (9) Return on investment — 23.8%

EP 13.5
- (a) Return on average total stockholders' equity — 18.0%
- (b) Return on avg common equity — 19.2%

EP 13.7
- (a) Simple EPS — $3.87
- (b) Dividends per share — $1.27
- (c) Earnings yield — 6.5%
- (d) Dividend yield — 2.1%

EP 13.9
- (a) No, it has been decreasing:
  19X0 = 58%
  19X1 = 56%
  19X2 = 54%
- (b) Yes, using EBIT/Sales as the preferred method of calculating operating ratio, the ratio has definitely improved:
  19X0 = 21%
  19X1 = 22%
  19X2 = 25%
- (c) An owner/manager might wish to investigate further both the significantly declining gross profit ratio and also the rapidly declining expenditure for maintenance. All other expenses appear reasonably in control in comparison to other years.

SP 13.13
- (a) Return on investment data is not provided. Independent of assets invested, Sugarman appears to be doing a slightly better job. Both hove the same EBIT/SALES of 21% for 19X0. However, Sugarman's gross profit and bottom line are significantly better.
- (b) Sugarman is significantly better than Tilamook with respect to gross profit. Assuming both firms follow the same inventory flow assumption, Sugarman might be purchasing more advantageously than Tilamook and/or Tilamook might be discounting more prices. Other items are either not significant or not controllable (taxes).
- (c) If Sugarman were using FIFO, and Tilomook LIFO, then Tilamook could be 1 doing o better job, depending upon the rate of inflation.

SP13.13
- (a)

1) Naomi	5) Naomi	9) Naomi
2) Naomi	6) Francine	10) Francine
3) Francine	7) Francine	11) Naomi
4) Naomi	8) Same	12) Naomi

- (b) Naomi is better. Earnings yield 6.7% compared with Francines's 6.5% and the dividend yield 3.6% compared to 2,1%.
- (c) Naomi is taking more advantage of debt leverage.

SP 13.15(a) *(see next page)*

SP 13.15 (a)   BALANCE SHEET EFFECT WORKSHEET
                                          LUTON Corporation – Period 18
                          (p = preliminary balance; e = ending balance; π = net income)

Cash	$ 3,384 (p)		Accounts Payable	198,000 (p)	198,000 (e)
	+ 42,000 (15)		Wages and Salaries	5,000 (p)	5,000 (e)
	+ 2,500 (16)		Interest Payable	0 (p)	
	+ 4,000 (21)	49,384 (e)		+ 110 (17)	
				− 110 (19)	0 (e)
Marketable Securities	0 (p)		Taxes Payable	0 (p)	
	+ 20,000 (20)	20,000 (e)		+ 21,900 (M)	21,900 (e)
Accounts Receivable	200,000 (p)	200,000 (e)	Current Capital Lease	5,000 (p)	5,000 (e)
			Obligations		
Allowance for bad debt	(4,000) (p)	(4,000) (e)	Dividends Payable	28,350 (p)	28,350 (e)
Inventory	220,000 (p)	220,000 (e)	Noncurrent Notes Payable	11,000 (p)	
				− 11,000 (19)	0 (e)
Supplies	2,050 (p)	2,050 (e)	Notes Payable Discount	(2,136) (p)	
				+ 270 (18)	
Prepaid Items	1,600 (p)	1,600 (e)		+ 1,866 (19)	0 (e)
Investments	166,000 (p)		Noncurrent Capital Lease	49,967 (p)	49,967 (e)
	− 40,000 (16)		Obligation		
	− 20,000 (20)	106,000 (e)	Bonds Payable	50,000 (p)	50,000 (e)
			Bond Premium	6,750 (p)	6,750 (e)
Bond Investments Discount	(6,400) (p)		Deferred Income Tax	2,200 (p)	
	+ 6,400 (16)	0 (e)		− 900 (M)	1,300 (e)
Land	25,000 (p)	25,000 (e)	Preferred Stock	100,000 (p)	100,000 (e)
			Addtl. PIC Preferred	10,000 p)	10,000 (e)
Buildings	125,000 (p)	125,000 (e)	Common Stock	189,000 (p)	
				+ 9,000 (190	198,000 (e)
Accum. Depr. Buildings	(53,800) (p)	(53,800) (e)	Addtl. PIC Common	6,750 (p)	
				+ 244 (19)	6,994 (e)
Equipment	30,000 (p)	30,000 (e)			
			Retained Earnings	35,719 (p)	
Accum. Depr. Equipment	(12,200) (p)	(12,200) (e)		+ 50,616 (π)	86,335 (e)
Property Capital Lease	70,862 (p)	70,862 (e)			
Accum. Depr. Lease	(17,700) (p)	(17,700) (e)			
Deferred Charges	5,400 (p)	5,400 (e)			

```
                                                    Income
                                               +  59,596  (p)
                                               +   8,400 (16)
                                               −     110 (17)
                                               −     270 (18)
                                               +   4,000 (21)
                                               −  21,000 (M)
                                               +  50,616  (π)
```

TOTAL ASSETS $ 550,396   TOTAL EQUITIES $ 550,396

SP 13.15(b) LUTON CORPORATION INCOME STATEMENT FOR PERIOD

Net sales	$275,000
Cost of goods sold	165,000
Gross Profit	110,000

Operating expenses:

Wages and salaries	$55,000	
Supplies	1,700	
Insurance	800	
Utilities	1,500	
Bad debt accounts	4,200	
Depreciation	4,600	
Lease depreciation	3,540	71,340
Operating Profit		$38,660

Other revenue and (expense):

Investments revenue (21 and G)	$ 29,000	
Gain on securities sale	8,400	
interest expense (13, 17, 18, I, K and L)	(4,444)	32,956
Income from Operations Before Tax		$71,616
Less provision for income before Taxes		21,000
NET INCOME		$50,616

* Where shown, the numbers and letters in Parenthesis immediately following account titles identify all transactions and adjustments during the period that affected the account balance reported. Note that such references are for your clarification and would never appear on a final income statement in good form.

SP 13.15(c) LUTON CORPORATION STATEMENT OF RETAINED EARNINGS FOR PERIOD 18

Retained earnings - end Period 17		$ 66,569
Net income - Period 18		50,616
		$117,185
Less: Preferred dividend	$ 2,500	
Common dividend	28,350	30,850
Retained earnings - end Period		$86,335

(e) LUTON CORPORATION - STATEMENT OF CASH FLOWS FOR PERIOD 18

Cash Flows from Operating Activities:

Net Income		$50,616

Adjustments to reconcile net income:

Depreciation	$ 4,600	
Lease Amortization	3,540	
Deferred Charge Amort.	200	
Note Payable discount Amort.	270	
Equity Dividends	5,000	
Bond Payable Prem. Amort.	(250)	
Maturing Deferred Taxes	(900)	
Gain on Sale of Investments	(8,400)	
Int. Exp. converted to equity	(110)	
Increase in Accounts Rec.	(10,900)	
increase in Inventory	(60,000)	
increase in Supplies	(300)	
decrease in Prepaid Items	800	
decrease in Accounts Payable	(2,000)	
increase in Wages and Salaries	2,000	
increase in Taxes Payable	17,900	
decrease int. portion cap lease	(111)	(48,441)
Net cash provided by operating activities		$ 2,175

Cash Flows from Investing Activities:

Proceeds Sale of Investments	42,000	
Payment on lease principle	(2,775)	
Net Cash provided from investing activities		39,225

Cash Flows from Financing Activities:

Paid dividends		(5,000)
Increase in Cash		$36,400
Cash Balance Period 17		12,984
Cash Balance Period 18		$49,384

Investing and Financing Activities not involving cash flow include: declaration of dividends for $28,350, conversion of note payable into common stock at $9,244, and reclassification of investments to marketable securities at a cost of $20,000.

SP 13.15(d)   LUTON Corporation Balance Sheet as
of end of Period 18

Assets

Cash	$ 49,384
Marketable Securities	20,000
Accounts Receivable	200,000
Allowance for bad debts	(4,000)
Inventory	220,000
Supplies	2,050
Prepaid Items	1,600
Total Current Assets	$489,034
Investments	106,000
Land	25,000
Buildings	125,000
Accum. depr.—Bldg.	(53,800)
Equipment	30,000
Accum. depr.—Equip.	(12,200)
Properties under capital lease	53,162
Deferred charges	5,400
TOTAL ASSETS	$767,596

EQUITIES

Accounts payable	$198,000
Wages and salaries	5,000
Taxes payable	21,900
Current cap. lse. obligations	5,000
Dividends payable	28,350
Total Current Liabilities	$258,250
Noncurrent cap. lse. oblig.	49,967
Bonds payable	50,000
Bond premium	6,750
Deferred income taxes	1,300
Total Liabilities	$366,267
Preferred stock*	100,000
Addtl. paid-in capital—Pfd.	10,000
Common stock**	198,000
Addtl. paid-in capital—Com.	6,994
Retained earnings	86,335
TOTAL EQUITIES	$767,596

* $100 par; 20,000 shares authorized; 1,000 shares
issued and outstanding.

** $5 par; 200,000 shares authorized; 39,600 shares
issued and outstanding.

SP 13.15	(f)	(g)	(h)
1)	$ 1 47,734	$230,784	Improved
2)	1.69	1.89	Improved
3)	.92	1.03	Improved
4)	.245	.212	Improved
5)	.300	.453	Improved
6)	$6.5	$6.98	Improved
7)	$.47	$1.26	Improved
8)	$30,060	$76,060	Improved
9)	7 times	17 times	Improved
10)	.40 times	.37 times	Worse
11)	1.33 times	1.00 times	Worse
12)	68 days	91 days	Worse
13)	1.26 times	87 times	Worse
14)	72 days	105 days	Worse
15)	1.39 times	1.61 times	Improved
16)	4.8%	10.3%	Improved
17)	7.5%	18.4%	Improved

(i) 1) Yes. Solvency, liquidity, and the long-term debt
ratio were all improved through selling investments, reclassifying investment securities to current, conversion of long-term debt, and retention of
39 percent of earnings.

2) Yes. Operating profit as a percent of soles was up
from 1 1.5 percent to 14.1 percent but receivables
and inventory turnovers were down substantially.

3) Yes. However, all but approximately $10,000 of the
increase was attributable to investments revenue.

4) Receivables collections appear alarmingly out of
control. One might expect average days' receivables
to be in the range of 45 to 60 days. For customers
on average to be paying receivables 91 days after
sale is causing an unnecessarily high proportion of
LUTON's funds to be tied up in receivables.

INDEX

Index

Index

Index